GO!
with Microsoft®

Office 2016
Integrated Projects

**Shelley Gaskin and
Nancy Graviett**

Boston   Columbus   Indianapolis   New York   San Francisco   Hoboken
Amsterdam   Cape Town   Dubai   London   Madrid   Milan   Munich   Paris   Montréal   Toronto
Delhi   Mexico City   São Paulo   Sydney   Hong Kong   Seoul   Singapore   Taipei   Tokyo

Vice President, Career Skills: Andrew Gilfillan
Executive Editor: Jenifer Niles
Team Lead, Project Management: Laura Burgess
Project Manager: Holly Haydash
Program Manager: Emily Biberger
Development Editor: Shannon LeMay-Finn
Editorial Assistant: Michael Campbell
Director of Product Marketing: Maggie Waples
Director of Field Marketing: Leigh Ann Sims
Field Marketing Managers: Molly Schmidt and Joanna Conley
Marketing Coordinator: Susan Osterlitz
Operations Specialist: Maura Zaldivar-Garcia
Manager, Rights & Permissions: Gina Cheselka

Senior Art Director: Diane Ernsberger
Cover Photos: GaudiLab, Rawpixel.com, Pressmaster, Eugenio Marongiu, Boggy, Gajus, Rocketclips, Inc
Associate Director of Design: Blair Brown
Director of Media Development: Blaine Christine
Media Project Manager, Production: John Cassar
Full-Service Project Management: iEnergizer Aptara®, Ltd.
Composition: iEnergizer Aptara®, Ltd.
Printer/Binder: LSC Communications
Cover Credits and Designer: Carie Keller/Cenveo
Cover Printer: LSC Communications
Text Font: Times LT Pro

Credits and acknowledgments borrowed from other sources and reproduced, with permission, in this textbook appear on the appropriate page within text. Microsoft and/or its respective suppliers make no representations about the suitability of the information contained in the documents and related graphics published as part of the services for any purpose. All such documents and related graphics are provided "as is" without warranty of any kind.

Microsoft and/or its respective suppliers hereby disclaim all warranties and conditions with regard to this information, including all warranties and conditions of merchantability, whether express, implied or statutory, fitness for a particular purpose, title and non-infringement. In no event shall Microsoft and/or its respective suppliers be liable for any special, indirect or consequential damages or any damages whatsoever resulting from loss of use, data or profits, whether in an action of contract, negligence or other tortious action, arising out of or in connection with the use or performance of information available from the services.

The documents and related graphics contained herein could include technical inaccuracies or typographical errors. Changes are periodically added to the information herein. Microsoft and/or its respective suppliers may make improvements and/or changes in the product(s) and/or the program(s) described herein at any time. Partial screen shots may be viewed in full within the software version specified.

Microsoft® and Windows® are registered trademarks of the Microsoft Corporation in the U.S.A. and other countries. This book is not sponsored or endorsed by or affiliated with the Microsoft Corporation.

Many of the designations by manufacturers and sellers to distinguish their products are claimed as trademarks. Where those designations appear in this book, and the publisher was aware of a trademark claim, the designations have been printed in initial caps or all caps.

Library of Congress Cataloging-in-Publication Data

Names: Gaskin, Shelley, author. | Graviett, Nancy, author.
Title: Go! with Microsoft Office 2016 integrated projects/Shelley Gaskin
  and Nancy Graviett.
Description: Boston : Pearson, 2016. | Includes index.
Identifiers: LCCN 2016010709| ISBN 9780134444925 (pbk.) | ISBN 0134444922
  (pbk.)
Subjects: LCSH: Microsoft Office. | Business—Computer programs.
Classification: LCC HF5548.4.M525 G36734 2016 | DDC 005.5—dc23 LC
  record available at http://lccn.loc.gov/2016010709

9 2020

ISBN 10:   0-13-444492-2
ISBN 13: 978-0-13-444492-5

Brief Contents

Contents

About the Authors

Shelley Gaskin, Series Editor, is a professor in the Business and Computer Technology Division at Pasadena City College in Pasadena, California. She holds a bachelor's degree in Business Administration from Robert Morris College (Pennsylvania), a master's degree in Business from Northern Illinois University, and a doctorate in Adult and Community Education from Ball State University. Before joining Pasadena City College, she spent 12 years in the computer industry where she was a systems analyst, sales representative, and Director of Customer Education with Unisys Corporation. She also worked for Ernst & Young on the development of large systems applications for their clients. She has written and developed training materials for custom systems applications in both the public and private sector, and has written and edited numerous computer application textbooks.

This book is dedicated to my students, who inspire me every day.

Nancy Graviett is a professor and department chair in Business Technology at St. Charles Community College in Cottleville, Missouri. She holds a bachelor's degree in marketing and a master's degree in business education from the University of Missouri and has completed a certificate in online education. Nancy has authored textbooks on WordPerfect, Google, Microsoft Outlook, and Microsoft Access.

This book is dedicated to my husband, Dave, and my children, Matthew and Andrea.
I cannot thank my family enough for the love and support they share everyday.

Teach the Course You Want in Less Time

A Microsoft® Office textbook designed for student success!

- **Project-based** – students learn by creating projects that they will use in the real world.
- **Microsoft Procedural Syntax** – steps are written to put students in the right place at the right time.

- **Teachable Moment** – expository text is woven into the steps—at the moment students need to know it—not chunked together in a block of text that will go unread.
- **Sequential pagination** – students have actual page numbers instead of confusing letters and abbreviations.

Student Outcomes and Learning Objectives – Objectives are clustered around projects that result in student outcomes.

Project Activities – A project summary stated clearly and quickly.

Project Files – Clearly shows students which files are needed for the project and the names they will use to save their documents.

Scenario – Each chapter opens with a story that sets the stage for the projects the student will create.

Project Results – Shows students how their final outcome will appear.

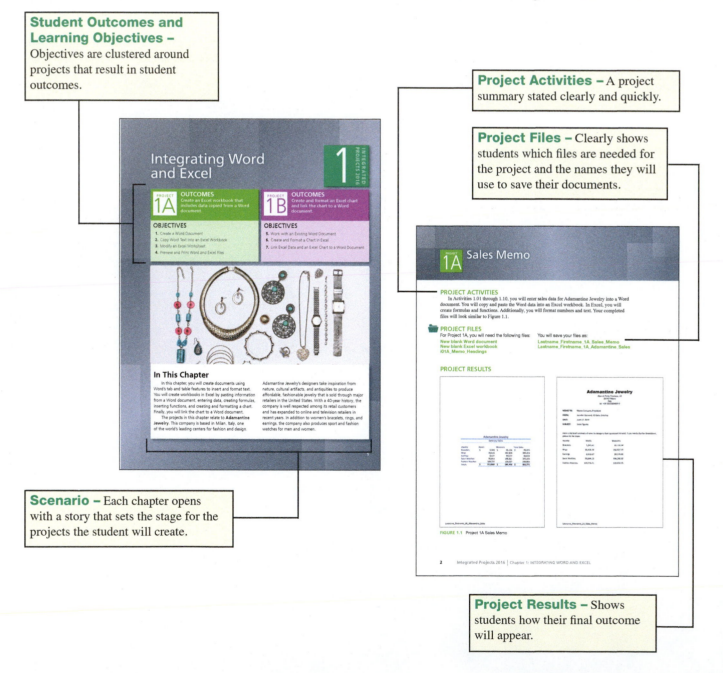

Microsoft Procedural Syntax – Steps are written to put the student in the right place at the right time.

Key Feature

Color Coding – Color variations between the two projects in each chapter make it easy to identify which project students are working on.

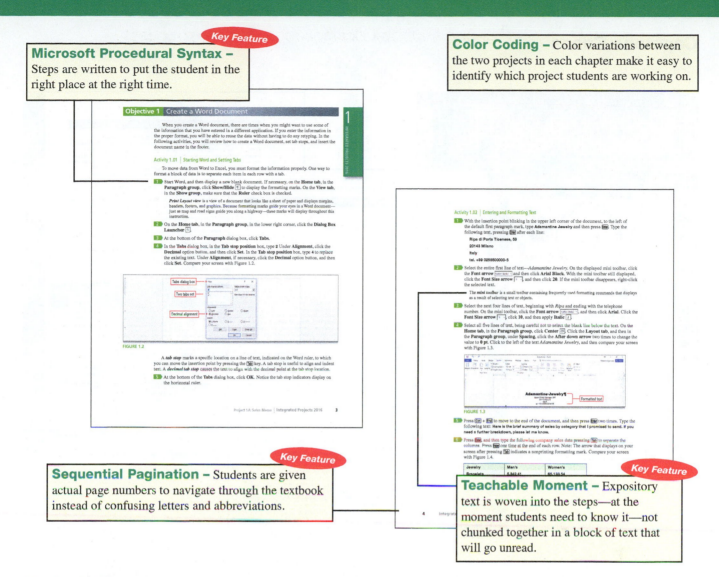

Sequential Pagination – Students are given actual page numbers to navigate through the textbook instead of confusing letters and abbreviations.

Key Feature

Teachable Moment – Expository text is woven into the steps—at the moment students need to know it—not chunked together in a block of text that will go unread.

Key Feature

End-of-Chapter
Content-Based Assessments – Assessments with defined solutions.

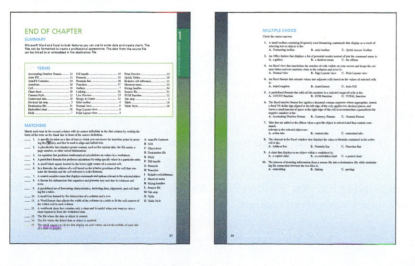

Capstone Cases

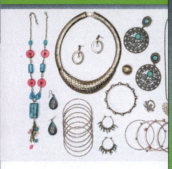

All student data files are available on **pearsonhighered.com/go.**

Instructor Materials

Scorecards – Can be used either by students to check their work or by you as a quick check-off for the items that need to be corrected.

Other Resources – PowerPoints, Scoring Rubrics, Solution Files, Answer Keys, and Student Data Files are all at the Instructor Resource site, **pearsonhighered.com/go.**

Integrating Word and Excel

PROJECT 1A

OUTCOMES
Create an Excel workbook that includes data copied from a Word document.

OBJECTIVES
1. Create a Word Document
2. Copy Word Text into an Excel Workbook
3. Modify an Excel Worksheet
4. Preview and Print Word and Excel Files

PROJECT 1B

OUTCOMES
Create and format an Excel chart and link the chart to a Word document.

OBJECTIVES
5. Work with an Existing Word Document
6. Create and Format a Chart in Excel
7. Link Excel Data and an Excel Chart to a Word Document

NAR studio/Shutterstock

In This Chapter

In this chapter, you will create documents using Word's tab and table features to insert and format text. You will create workbooks in Excel by pasting information from a Word document, entering data, creating formulas, inserting functions, and creating and formatting a chart. Finally, you will link the chart to a Word document.

The projects in this chapter relate to **Adamantine Jewelry**. This company is based in Milan, Italy, one of the world's leading centers for fashion and design.

Adamantine Jewelry's designers take inspiration from nature, cultural artifacts, and antiquities to produce affordable, fashionable jewelry that is sold through major retailers in the United States. With a 40-year history, the company is well respected among its retail customers and has expanded to online and television retailers in recent years. In addition to women's bracelets, rings, and earrings, the company also produces sport and fashion watches for men and women.

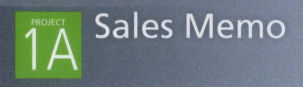
PROJECT ACTIVITIES

In Activities 1.01 through 1.10, you will enter sales data for Adamantine Jewelry into a Word document. You will copy and paste the Word data into an Excel workbook. In Excel, you will create formulas and functions. Additionally, you will format numbers and text. Your completed files will look similar to Figure 1.1.

PROJECT FILES

For Project 1A, you will need the following files:

New blank Word document
New blank Excel workbook
i01A_Memo_Headings

You will save your files as:

Lastname_Firstname_1A_Sales_Memo
Lastname_Firstname_1A_Adamantine_Sales

PROJECT RESULTS

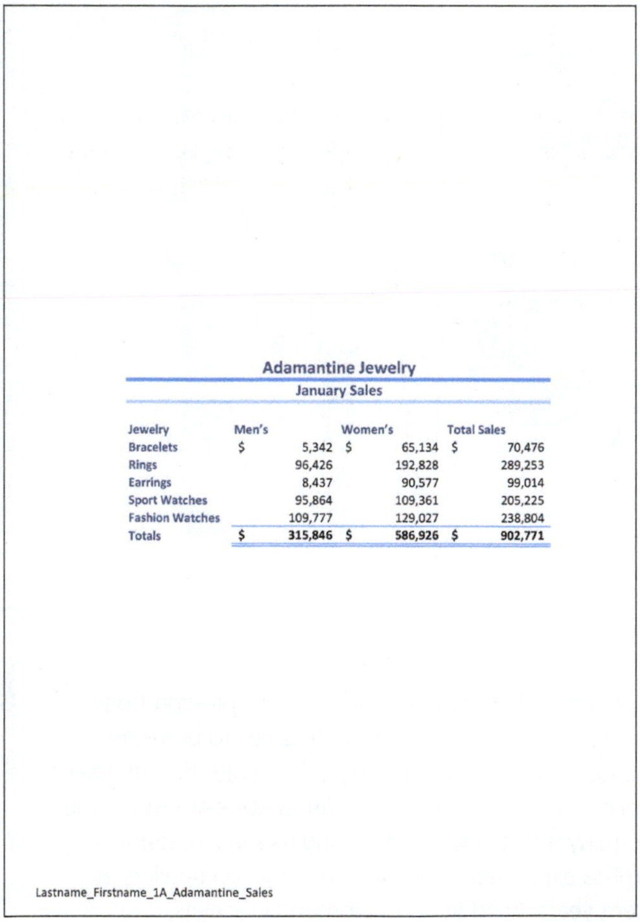

Adamantine Jewelry

January Sales

Jewelry	Men's		Women's		Total Sales
Bracelets	$	5,342	$	65,134	$ 70,476
Rings		96,426		192,828	289,253
Earrings		8,437		90,577	99,014
Sport Watches		95,864		109,361	205,225
Fashion Watches		109,777		129,027	238,804
Totals	$	315,846	$	586,926	$ 902,771

Lastname_Firstname_1A_Adamantine_Sales

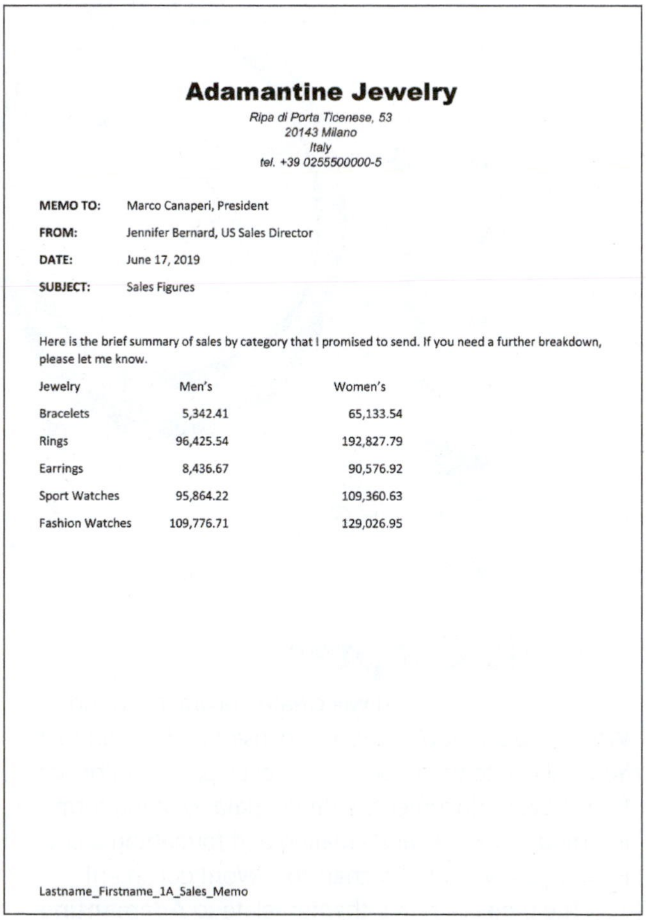

Adamantine Jewelry

Ripa di Porta Ticenese, 53
20143 Milano
Italy
tel. +39 0255500000-5

MEMO TO:	Marco Canaperi, President
FROM:	Jennifer Bernard, US Sales Director
DATE:	June 17, 2019
SUBJECT:	Sales Figures

Here is the brief summary of sales by category that I promised to send. If you need a further breakdown, please let me know.

Jewelry	Men's	Women's
Bracelets	5,342.41	65,133.54
Rings	96,425.54	192,827.79
Earrings	8,436.67	90,576.92
Sport Watches	95,864.22	109,360.63
Fashion Watches	109,776.71	129,026.95

Lastname_Firstname_1A_Sales_Memo

FIGURE 1.1 Project 1A Sales Memo

When you create a Word document, there are times when you might want to use some of the information that you have entered in a different application. If you enter the information in the proper format, you will be able to reuse the data without having to do any retyping. In the following activities, you will review how to create a Word document, set tab stops, and insert the document name in the footer.

Activity 1.01 | Starting Word and Setting Tabs

To move data from Word to Excel, you must format the information properly. One way to format a block of data is to separate each item in each row with a tab.

1 ▶ Start Word, and then display a new blank document. If necessary, on the **Home tab**, in the **Paragraph group**, click **Show/Hide** ¶ to display the formatting marks. On the **View tab**, in the **Show group**, make sure that the **Ruler** check box is checked.

> *Print Layout view* is a view of a document that looks like a sheet of paper and displays margins, headers, footers, and graphics. Because formatting marks guide your eyes in a Word document— just as map and road signs guide you along a highway—these marks will display throughout this instruction.

2 ▶ On the **Home tab**, in the **Paragraph group**, in the lower right corner, click the **Dialog Box Launcher** ⌐.

3 ▶ At the bottom of the **Paragraph** dialog box, click **Tabs**.

4 ▶ In the **Tabs** dialog box, in the **Tab stop position** box, type **2** Under **Alignment**, click the **Decimal** option button, and then click **Set**. In the **Tab stop position** box, type **4** to replace the existing text. Under **Alignment,** if necessary, click the **Decimal** option button, and then click **Set**. Compare your screen with Figure 1.2.

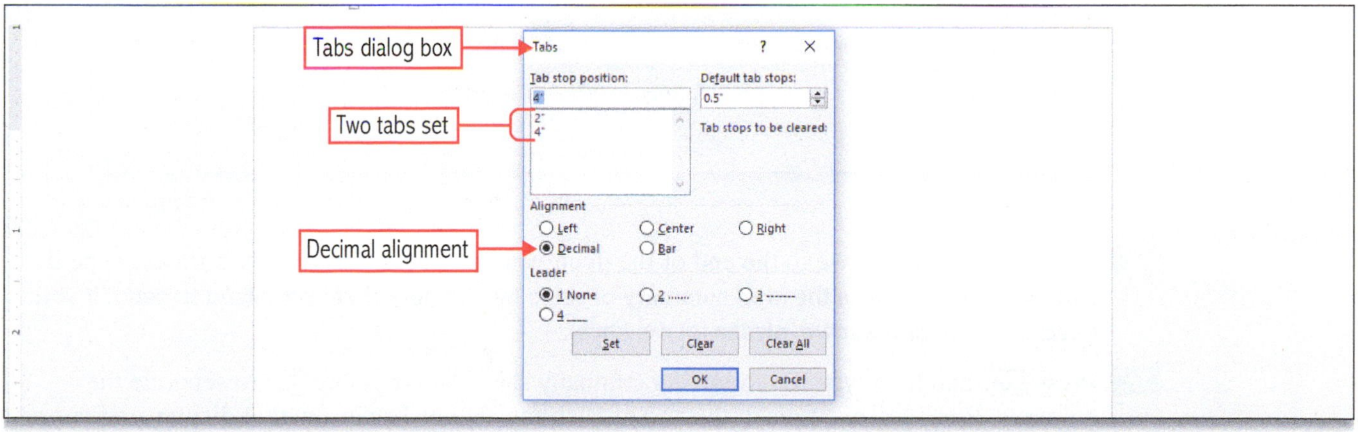

FIGURE 1.2   Word 2016, Windows 10, Microsoft Corporation

A *tab stop* marks a specific location on a line of text, indicated on the Word ruler, to which you can move the insertion point by pressing the Tab key. A tab stop is useful to align and indent text. A *decimal tab stop* causes the text to align with the decimal point at the tab stop location.

5 ▶ At the bottom of the **Tabs** dialog box, click **OK**. Notice the tab stop indicators display on the horizontal ruler.

Activity 1.02 | Entering and Formatting Text

1 With the insertion point blinking in the upper left corner of the document, to the left of the default first paragraph mark, type **Adamantine Jewelry** and then press Enter. Type the following text, pressing Enter after each line:

> **Ripa di Porta Ticenese, 53**
>
> **20143 Milano**
>
> **Italy**
>
> **tel. +39 0255500000-5**

2 Select the entire first line of text—*Adamantine Jewelry*. On the displayed mini toolbar, click the **Font arrow** Calibri (Body) ▾ and then click **Arial Black**. With the mini toolbar still displayed, click the **Font Size arrow** 11 ▾, and then click **20**. If the mini toolbar disappears, right-click the selected text.

> The *mini toolbar* is a small toolbar containing frequently used formatting commands that displays as a result of selecting text or objects.

3 Select the next four lines of text, beginning with *Ripa* and ending with the telephone number. On the mini toolbar, click the **Font arrow** Calibri (Body) ▾, and then click **Arial**. Click the **Font Size arrow** 11 ▾, click **10**, and then apply **Italic** *I*.

4 Select all five lines of text, being careful not to select the blank line below the text. On the **Home tab**, in the **Paragraph group**, click **Center** ≣. Click the **Layout tab**, and then in the **Paragraph group**, under **Spacing**, click the **After down arrow** two times to change the value to **0 pt**. Click to the left of the text *Adamantine Jewelry*, and then compare your screen with Figure 1.3.

FIGURE 1.3   Word 2016, Windows 10, Microsoft Corporation

5 Press Ctrl + End to move to the end of the document, and then press Enter two times. Type the following text: **Here is the brief summary of sales by category that I promised to send. If you need a further breakdown, please let me know.**

6 Press Enter, and then type the following company sales data pressing Tab to separate the columns. Press Enter one time at the end of each row. Note: The arrow that displays on your screen after pressing Tab indicates a nonprinting formatting mark. Compare your screen with Figure 1.4.

Jewelry	Men's	Women's
Bracelets	5,342.41	65,133.54
Rings	96,425.54	192,827.79
Earrings	8,436.67	90,576.92
Sport Watches	95,864.22	109,360.63
Fashion Watches	109,776.71	129,026.95

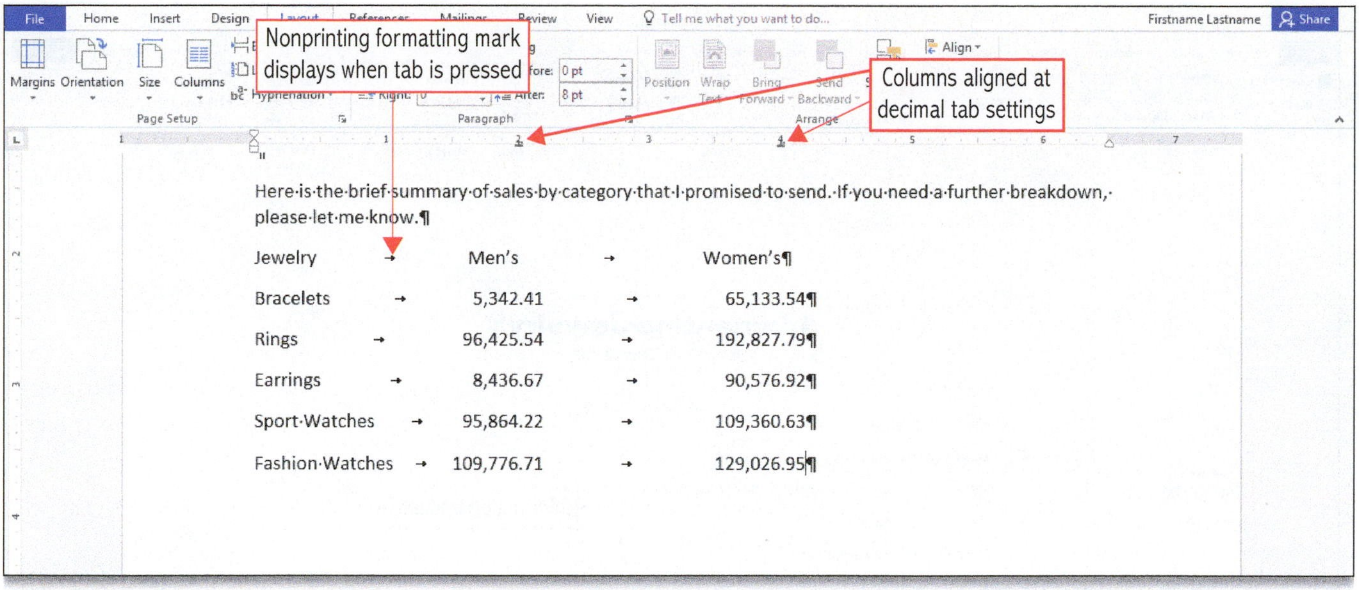

The following text appears within the screenshot figure:

Nonprinting formatting mark displays when tab is pressed

Columns aligned at decimal tab settings

Here·is·the·brief·summary·of·sales·by·category·that·I·promised·to·send.·If·you·need·a·further·breakdown,· please·let·me·know.¶

Jewelry	→	Men's	→	Women's¶
Bracelets	→	5,342.41	→	65,133.54¶
Rings	→	96,425.54	→	192,827.79¶
Earrings	→	8,436.67	→	90,576.92¶
Sport·Watches	→	95,864.22	→	109,360.63¶
Fashion·Watches	→	109,776.71	→	129,026.95¶

FIGURE 1.4

Word 2016, Windows 10, Microsoft Corporation

Activity 1.03 | Inserting Text from Another Word Document

1 In the second blank line below the centered text, click to position the insertion point.

2 Click the **Insert tab**, and then in the **Text group**, click the **Object arrow**, and then click **Text from File**.

3 In the **Insert File** dialog box, navigate to the location where the student data files for this chapter are stored. Locate the file **i01A_Memo_Headings**, click the file name to select it, and then click **Insert**.

Text from the Word document *i01A_Memo_Headings* is inserted in the current Word document.

4 In the *MEMO TO* line, select **[Name, Title]**, and then type **Marco Canaperi, President**

5 Use the same procedure to replace the data after the three memo headings with the following:

FROM	Jennifer Bernard, US Sales Director
DATE	June 17, 2019
SUBJECT	Sales Figures

6 Compare your screen with Figure 1.5.

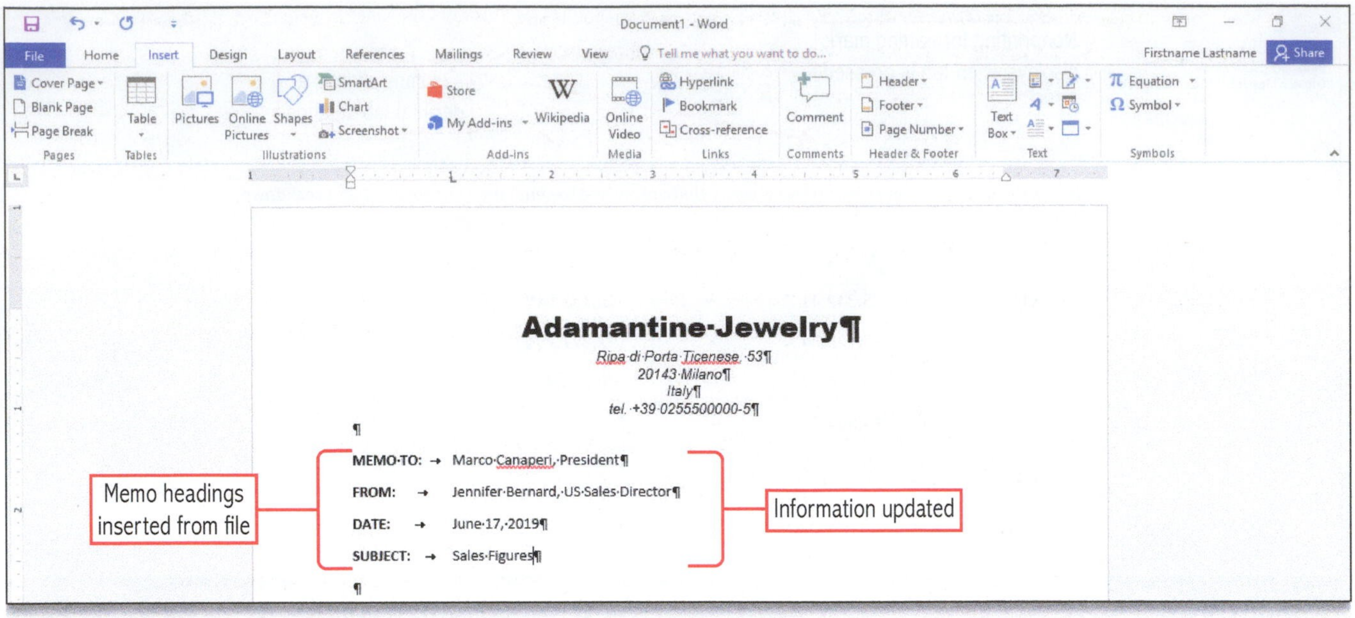

FIGURE 1.5

Activity 1.04 | Saving a Document, Creating a Footer, and Inserting Document Info

1 On the **Quick Access Toolbar**, click **Save** 🖫, and then click **Browse**. In the **Save As** dialog box, navigate to the location where you are storing your projects for this chapter, and then on the toolbar, click **New folder**.

In the file list, a new folder is created, and the text *New folder* is selected.

2 Type **Integrated Projects Chapter 1** to replace the selected text, and then press Enter.

In Windows-based programs, the Enter key confirms an action.

3 With the **Integrated Projects Chapter 1** folder selected, at the lower right of the **Save As** dialog box, click **Open**. Compare your screen with Figure 1.6.

The name of your folder displays in the address bar. In the File name box, Word inserts the text at the beginning of the document as a suggested file name.

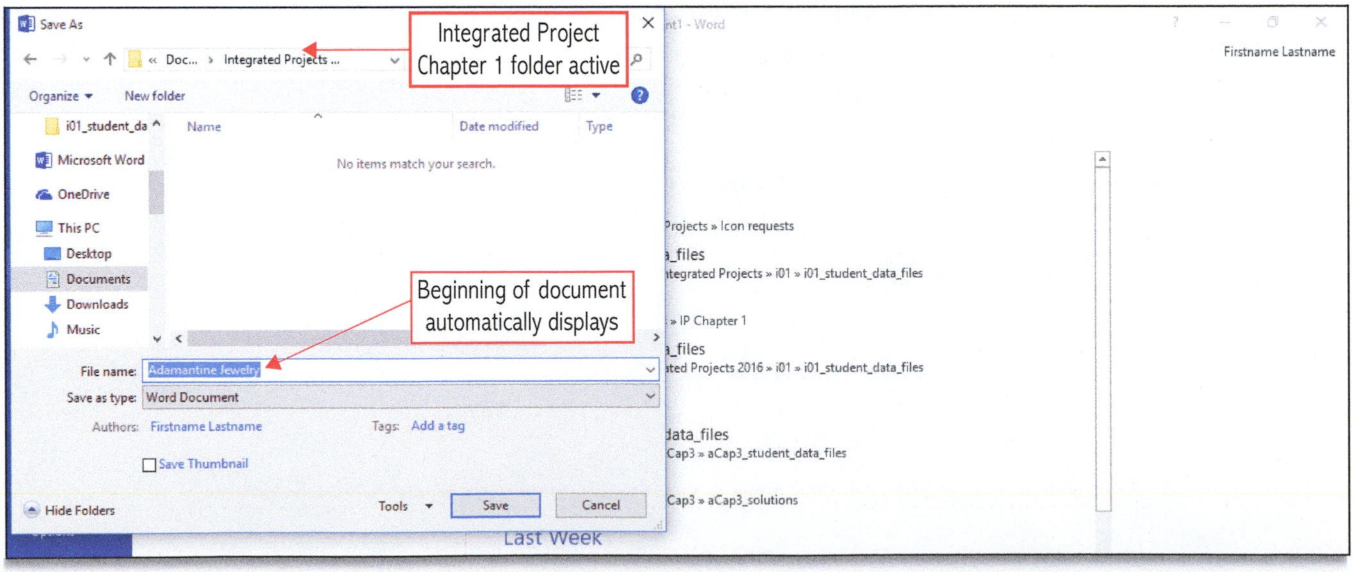

FIGURE 1.6

4 With the text in the **File name** box selected, using your own first and last name, type **Lastname_Firstname_1A_Sales_Memo** being sure to include the underscore—[Shift] + [-]—instead of spaces between words.

> The Microsoft Windows operating system recognizes file names with spaces; however, some Internet file transfer programs do not. In this instruction, underscores are used instead of spaces in file names.

5 In the lower right corner, click **Save**, or press [Enter].

> Your new file name displays in the title bar, indicating that the file has been saved to the location that you have specified. The file extension .docx may or may not display, depending on your Windows settings.

6 On the **Insert tab**, in the **Header & Footer group**, click **Footer** to display the **Footer** gallery. At the bottom of the **Footer** gallery, click **Edit Footer**. Notice that the document text displays as light gray when the footer is active.

> A *gallery* displays a list of potential results instead of just the command name.

🔄 **ANOTHER WAY**   Right-click near the bottom edge of the page, and then from the shortcut menu, click Edit Footer.

7 Under **Header & Footer Tools**, on the **Design tab**, in the **Insert group**, click **Document Info**, and then click **File Name** to place the file name in your footer as a field. Compare your screen with Figure 1.7.

> A *field* is a placeholder that displays preset content, such as the current date, the file name, a page number, or other stored information.

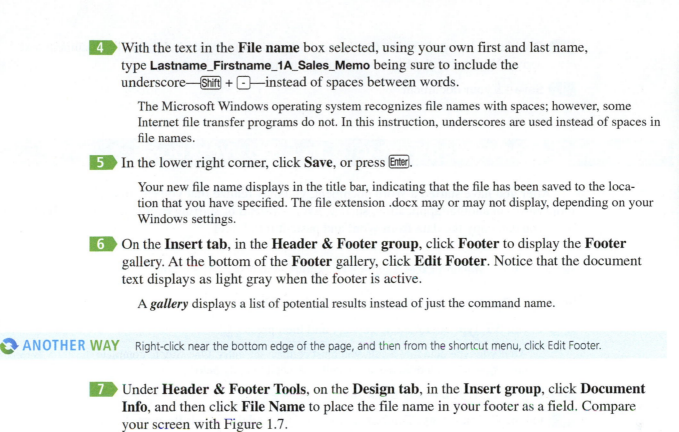

FIGURE 1.7

8 ▸ Double-click anywhere in your document to close the footer and make the document text active. Notice that the file name displays in the footer as light gray.

9 ▸ **Save** 🖫 your document.

Objective 2 | **Copy Word Text into an Excel Workbook**

After you have started a Word document, you may realize that you can manipulate the data more easily in another application, such as Excel. Instead of starting over and retyping all of your data, you can copy the data from Word and paste it into Excel.

Activity 1.05 | Starting Excel, Saving a Workbook, and Inserting a Footer

1 ▸ Start Excel, and then display a new blank workbook.

2 ▸ In cell **A1**, type **Adamantine Jewelry** and then press [Enter].

After you type data into a cell, you must confirm the entry. One way to complete the entry is to press [Enter], which moves the active cell to the cell directly below.

3 ▸ In cell **A2**, type **January Sales** and then press [Enter].

4 ▸ On the **Quick Access Toolbar**, click **Save** 🖫, and then click **Browse**. In the **Save As** dialog box, navigate to your **Integrated Projects Chapter 1** folder.

5 ▸ In the **File name** box, using your own first and last name, type **Lastname_Firstname_1A_ Adamantine_Sales** and then click **Save** or press [Enter]. Compare your screen with Figure 1.8.

The new file name displays in the title bar. The file extension .xlsx may or may not display, depending on your Windows settings.

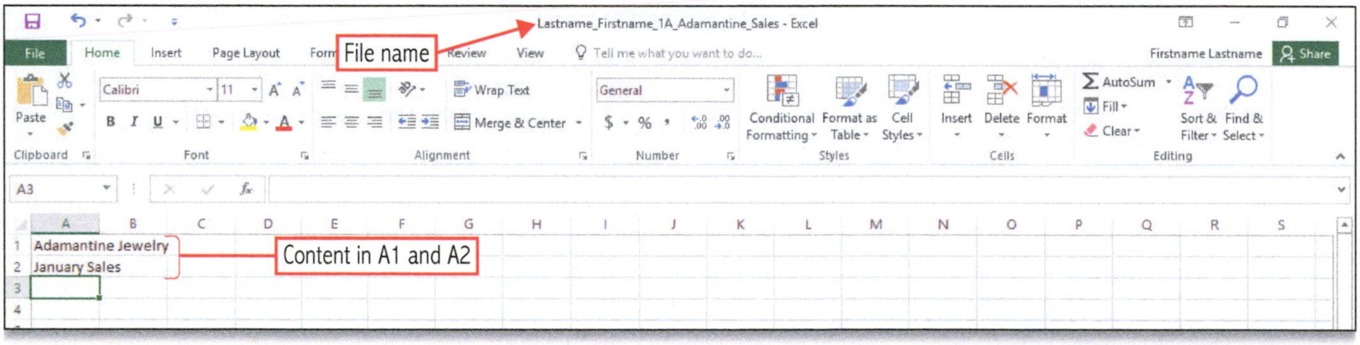

FIGURE 1.8

Excel 2016, Windows 10, Microsoft Corporation

6 ▸ Click the **Insert tab**, and then in the **Text group**, click **Header & Footer** to switch to Page Layout view.

Page Layout view is a screen view in which you can use the rulers to measure the width and height of data, set margins for printing, hide or display the numbered row headings and lettered column headings, and change the page orientation. This view is useful in preparing your worksheet for printing.

7 ▸ Under **Header & Footer Tools**, on the **Design tab**, in the **Navigation group**, click **Go to Footer**.

The insertion point displays in the center section of the footer area.

8 ▸ In the **Footer** area, click just above the word *Footer*, and then in the **Header & Footer Elements group**, click **File Name**. Compare your screen with Figure 1.9.

Notice the file name field displays on the left side of the footer area.

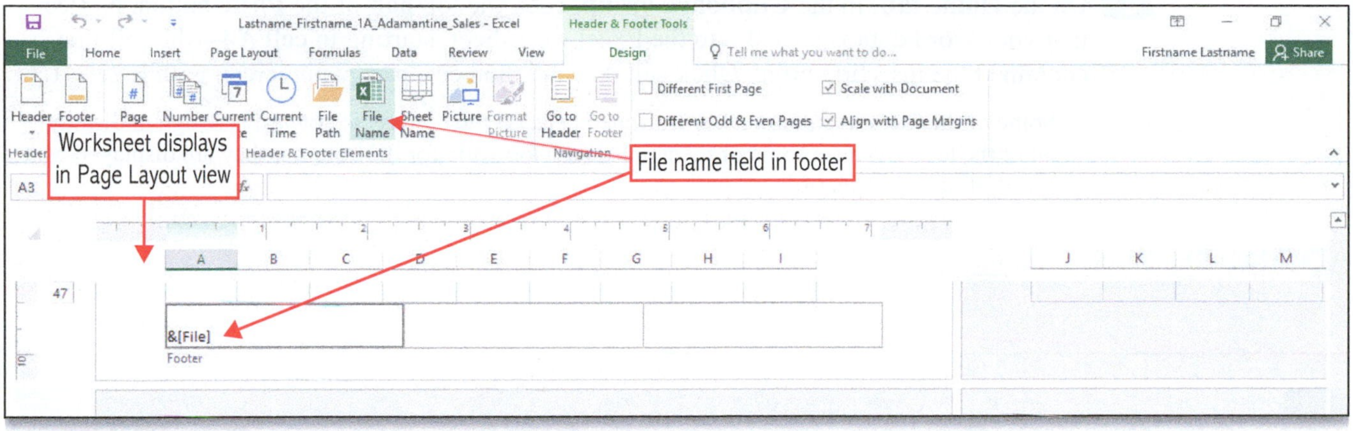

FIGURE 1.9

Excel 2016, Windows 10, Microsoft Corporation

9 ▸ Click the cell above the footer to exit the footer.

The file name field in the footer area is replaced with the file name.

10 ▸ Near the right side of the status bar, click **Normal** ⊞ to return to Normal view.

Normal view maximizes the number of cells visible on your screen and keeps the column letters and row numbers close to the columns and rows.

11 ▸ Press Ctrl + Home to display the top of your worksheet and to make cell **A1** the active cell.

Activity 1.06 | Copying and Pasting Word Text into an Excel File

1 ▸ On the taskbar, click the **Word icon** to display your **Lastname_Firstname_1A_Sales_Memo**.

2 ▸ In the first tabbed paragraph, point to the left of the word *Jewelry* to display the pointer. Drag down to select the six rows of tabbed text, as shown in Figure 1.10.

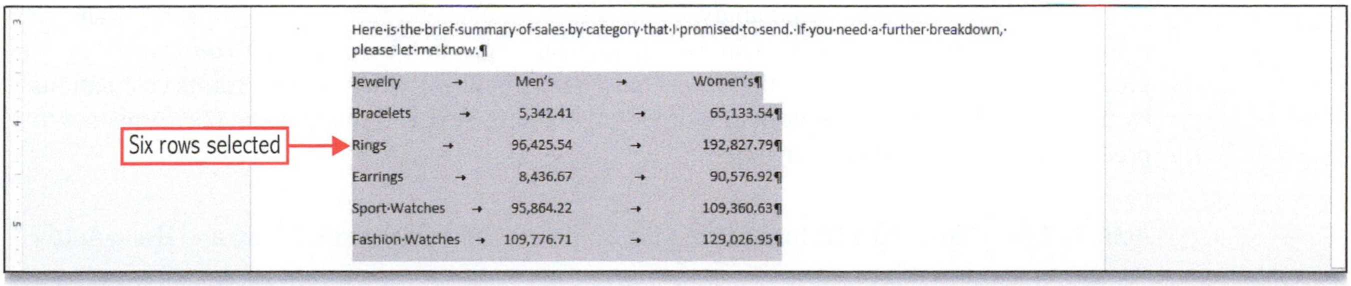

FIGURE 1.10

Word 2016, Windows 10, Microsoft Corporation

3 ▸ On the **Home tab**, in the **Clipboard group**, click **Copy**.

🔁 **ANOTHER WAY**   Press Ctrl + C.

4 ▶ On the taskbar, click the **Excel icon** [x] to display your **Lastname_Firstname_1A_ Adamantine_Sales** workbook.

5 ▶ Click cell **A4** to make it the active cell.

6 ▶ On the **Home tab**, in the **Clipboard group**, click the top half of the **Paste** button. Notice that your Word data is pasted into the Excel worksheet, starting in cell **A4**—the cell that contained the insertion point. Click cell **A1**, and then compare your screen with Figure 1.11.

Some of the titles in column A are truncated because the column is not wide enough to display all of the text. Because some of the numbers are too wide for the column, they are displayed as a series of pound signs (#).

↻ ANOTHER WAY   Press [Ctrl] + [V].

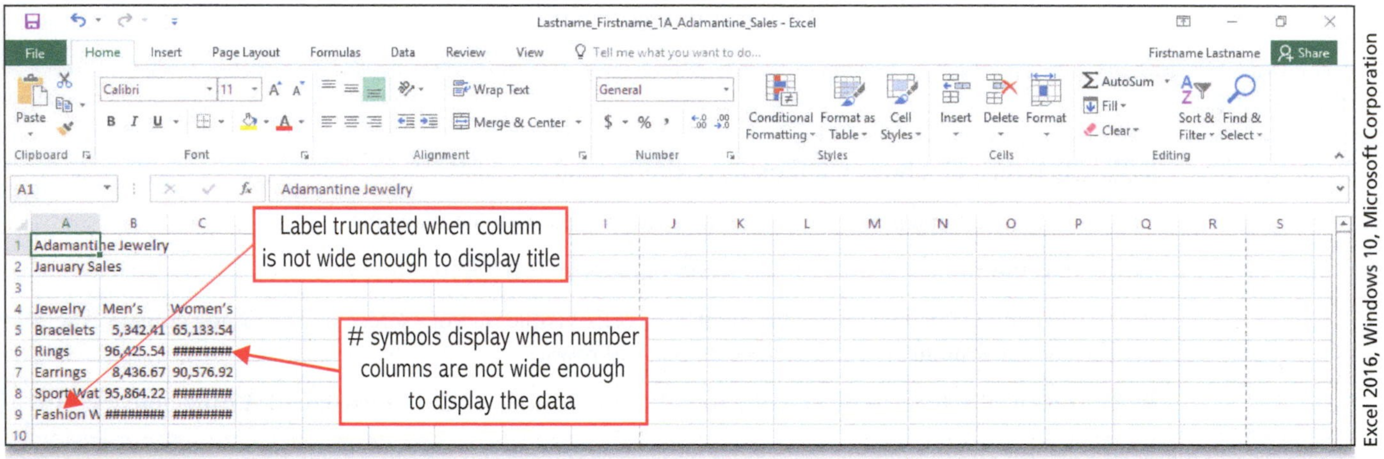

FIGURE 1.11

7 ▶ **Save** [💾] your workbook.

Objective 3   Modify an Excel Worksheet

In Excel, you can create and analyze data with formulas and functions. A *formula* is an equation that performs mathematical calculations on values in a worksheet. A *function* is a predefined formula—a formula that Excel has already built for you—that performs calculations by using specific values in a particular order or structure. Text and numbers can be formatted to present data in a professional manner.

Activity 1.07   Creating a Formula, Using the SUM Function to Calculate Totals, and Using Auto Fill

1 ▶ Click cell **D4** to make it the active cell. Type **Total Sales** and then press [Enter].

2 ▶ In cell **D5**, type **=b5+c5** and then press [Enter].

The result of the formula calculation displays in cell D5.

3 ▶ Click cell **D5** to make it the active cell.

The *fill handle*—a small square in the lower right corner of a selected cell—displays.

4 ▶ Point to the fill handle to display the ⊞ pointer. Hold down the left mouse button, and then drag down to cell **D9**. Release the mouse button, and then compare your screen with Figure 1.12.

Excel copies the formula from cell D5 into cells D6 through D9 using a *relative cell reference*, which, in a formula, is the address of a cell based on the relative positions of the cell that contains the formula and the cell referred to in the formula. *Auto Fill* is an Excel feature that generates and extends values into adjacent cells based on the values of selected cells. Because some of the numbers are too wide for the column, they are displayed as a series of pound signs (#).

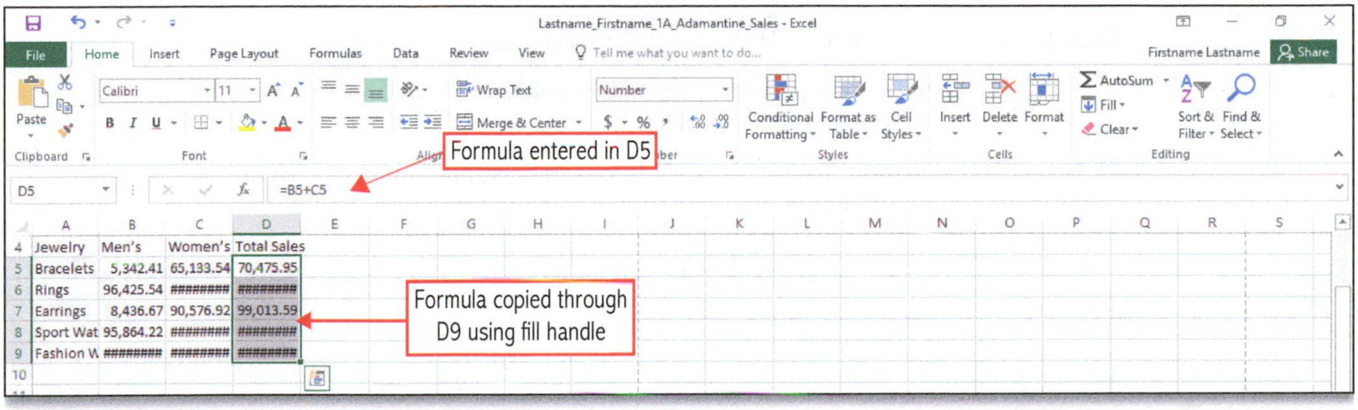

FIGURE 1.12

Excel 2016, Windows 10, Microsoft Corporation

5 ▶ Click cell **B10**. On the **Home tab**, in the **Editing group**, click **AutoSum**, and then press Enter.

This button is also referred to as the Sum button. The *SUM function* is a predefined formula that adds all the numbers in a selected range of cells.

6 ▶ Click cell **B10**. Point to the fill handle to display the ⊞ pointer, hold down the left mouse button, and then drag right to cell **D10**. Release the mouse button.

The SUM function from cell B10 is copied into cells C10 and D10.

7 ▶ Click cell **A10**, type **Totals** and then press Enter. Compare your screen with Figure 1.13.

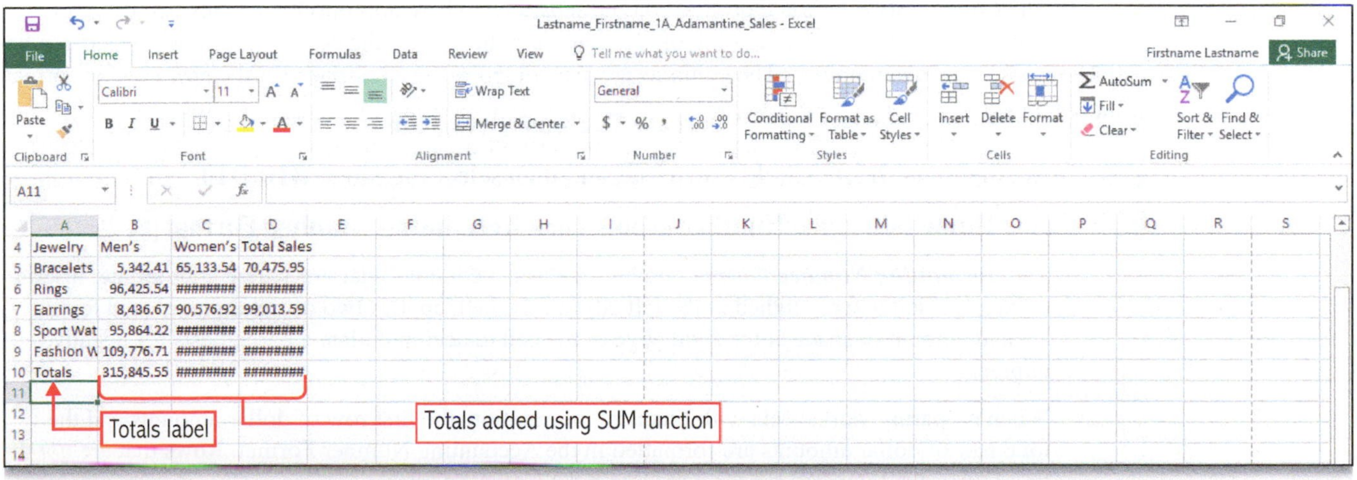

FIGURE 1.13

Excel 2016, Windows 10, Microsoft Corporation

8 ▶ **Save** 🖫 your workbook.

Activity 1.08 | Formatting Numbers and Text

1 Select the range **A1:D1**. On the **Home tab**, in the **Alignment group**, click **Merge & Center**.

The *Merge & Center* command joins selected cells into one large cell and then centers the contents in the merged cell.

2 In the **Styles group**, click **Cell Styles**, and then under **Titles and Headings**, click **Heading 1**.

3 Select the range **A2:D2**. In the **Alignment group**, click **Merge & Center**. In the **Styles group**, display the **Cell Styles** gallery, and then under **Titles and Headings**, click **Heading 2**.

4 Select the range **A4:A10**. Hold down Ctrl, and then select the range **B4:D4**.

This action selects both the row titles and the column titles. By holding down Ctrl while selecting cells, you can select nonadjacent cells.

5 In the **Styles group**, display the **Cell Styles** gallery, and then click **Heading 4**. Compare your screen with Figure 1.14.

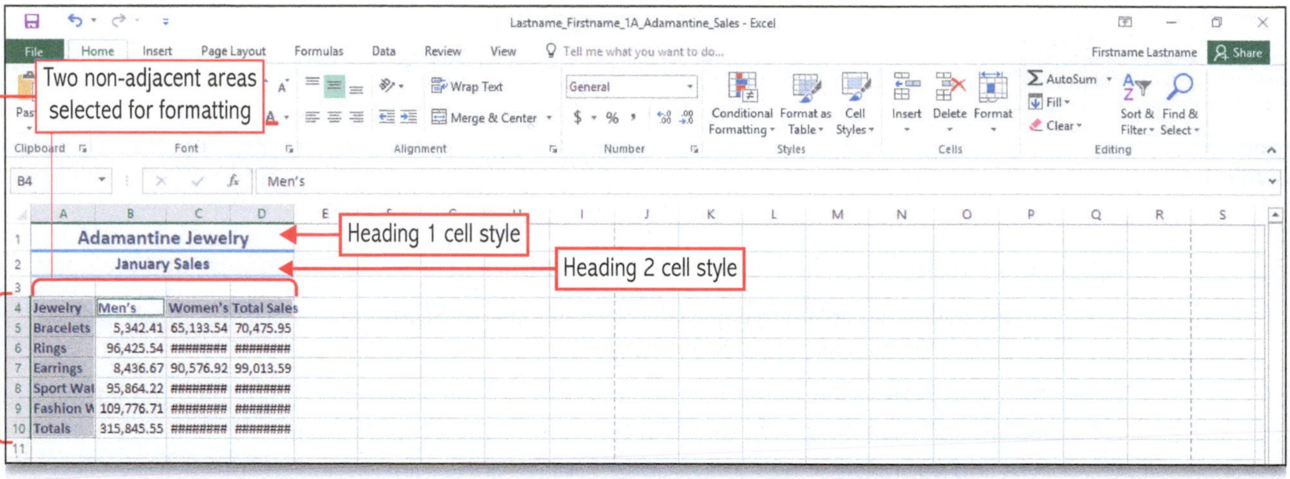

FIGURE 1.14

6 Select the range **B6:D9**. On the **Home tab**, in the **Number group**, click **Comma Style**.

The *Comma Style* inserts thousand comma separators where appropriate, applies two decimal places, and leaves a small amount of space at the right edge of the cell to accommodate a parenthesis for negative numbers. The columns are also widened to make space for the new number format.

7 In the **Number group**, click **Decrease Decimal** two times.

8 Select the range **B5:D5**, hold down Ctrl, and then select the range **B10:D10**.

9 On the **Home tab**, in the **Number group**, click **Accounting Number Format**.

The *Accounting Number Format* applies a thousand comma separator where appropriate, inserts a fixed US dollar sign aligned at the left edge of the cell, applies two decimal places, and leaves a small amount of space at the right edge of the cell to accommodate a parenthesis for negative numbers.

When preparing worksheets with financial information, the first row of dollar amounts and the total row of dollar amounts are formatted in the Accounting Number Format. Rows that are *not* the first row or the total row are formatted with the Comma Style.

10 Point to either of the selected ranges, and then right-click to display a shortcut menu and the mini toolbar. On the mini toolbar, click **Decrease Decimal** two times.

A *shortcut menu* is a context-sensitive menu that displays commands and options relevant to the selected object.

11 ▶ Select the range **B10:D10**. In the **Styles group**, display the **Cell Styles** gallery, and then under **Titles and Headings**, click **Total**.

12 ▶ Select columns **A:D**. On the **Home tab**, in the **Cells group**, click **Format**. Under **Cell Size**, click **Column Width**, and then in the **Column Width** dialog box, type **15** and click **OK**. Compare your screen with Figure 1.15.

Columns A through D are widened. The column width number represents the number of characters that can be displayed across the width of a cell.

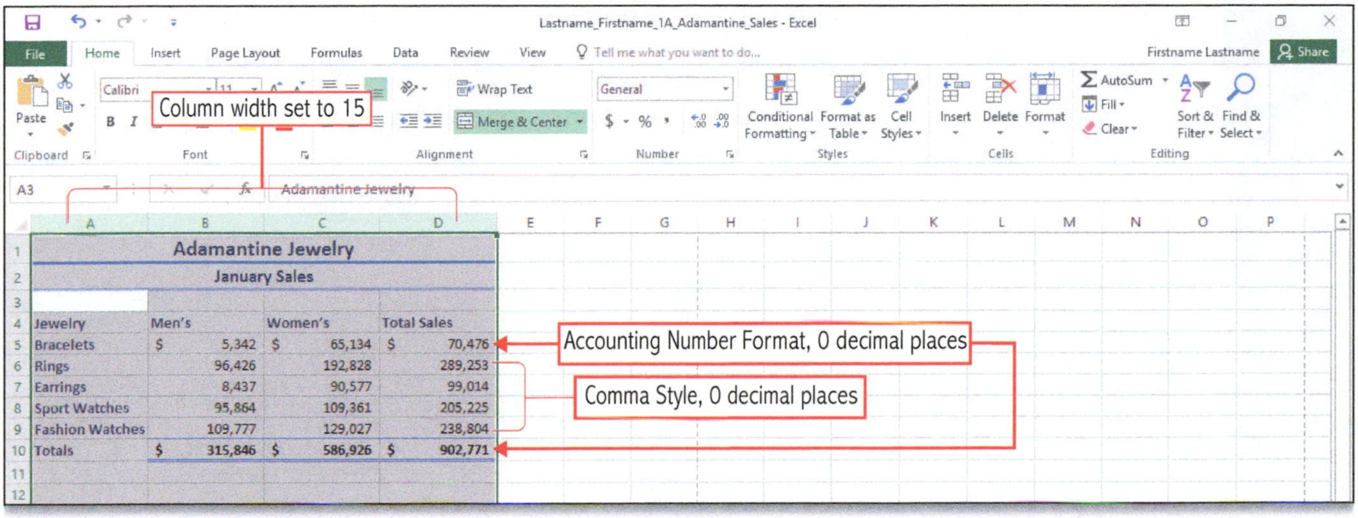

FIGURE 1.15

13 ▶ Hold down Ctrl and press Home to make cell **A1** the active cell.

14 ▶ **Save** 🖫 your workbook.

Objective 4 | Preview and Print Word and Excel Files

Excel and Word enable you to preview the printed page before you actually print the file. You will preview your files, center the worksheet on the page, and then print the files.

Activity 1.09 | Previewing and Printing an Excel Workbook

1 ▶ With the Excel workbook still active, click the **Page Layout tab**, and then in the **Page Setup group**, click the **Dialog Box Launcher** 🔲.

2 ▶ In the **Page Setup** dialog box, click the **Margins tab**. Under **Center on page**, select both the **Horizontally** check box and the **Vertically** check box, and then click **OK**.

3 ▶ Click the **File tab** to display **Backstage** view. With the **Info tab** selected, in the lower right corner, click **Show All Properties**. Under **Related People**, be sure your name displays as the **Author**—change it if necessary. Click to the right of **Subject**, and then type your course name and section number. Click to the right of **Tags**, and then type **sales worksheet**

4 ▶ On the left, click **Save** to return to your workbook.

5 ▶ In the upper left corner, click the **File tab** again to display **Backstage** view, and then click the **Print tab** to display the **Print Preview**. Compare your screen with Figure 1.16.

Print Preview displays information exactly as it will print based on the options that are selected. Your data is centered horizontally and vertically on the page, and the file name displays on the left edge of the footer area.

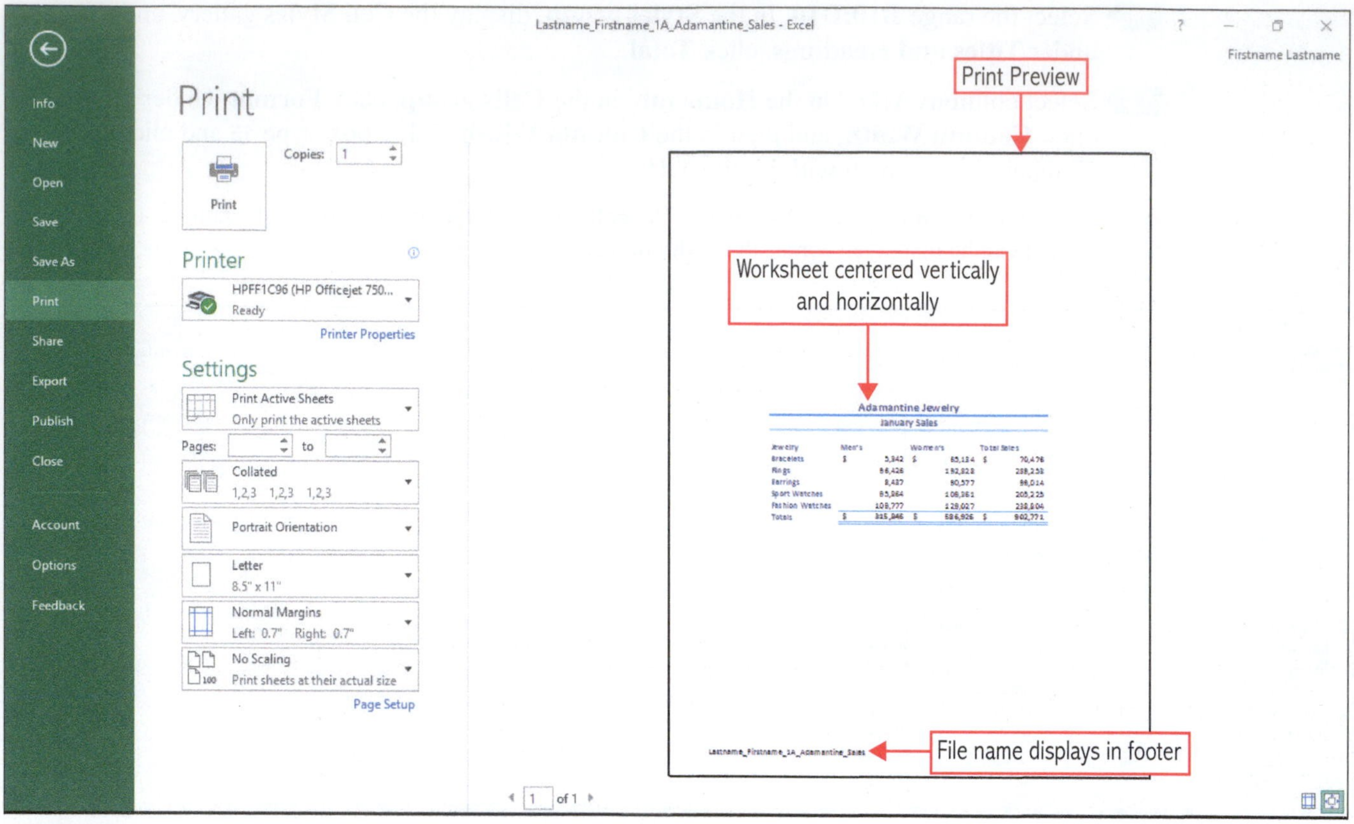

FIGURE 1.16

6 ▸ If your instructor directs you to submit your files electronically, go to Step 8.

7 ▸ To print your worksheet, under **Print**, click **Print**.

8 ▸ Click **Back** ⊙, and then click the **Formulas tab**. In the **Formula Auditing group**, click **Show Formulas**.

> Your formulas display on the worksheet. When viewing formulas, the Show Formulas button doubles the width of every column.

9 ▸ Click the **File tab** to display **Backstage** view, and then click the **Print tab** to display the **Print Preview**. Below the Print Preview, notice a navigation bar that indicates you are viewing page 1 of 2.

> If printed with the current settings, your worksheet will print on two pages.

10 ▸ At the bottom of the screen, to the left of the **Print Preview**, under **Settings**, click **Page Setup** to display the **Page Setup** dialog box.

11 ▸ In the **Page Setup** dialog box, on the **Page tab**, under **Orientation**, click the **Landscape** option button. Under **Scaling**, click the **Fit to** option button. Verify the options are *1 page(s) wide by 1 tall*, and then click **OK**. Compare your screen with Figure 1.17.

> Your worksheet will print on one page.

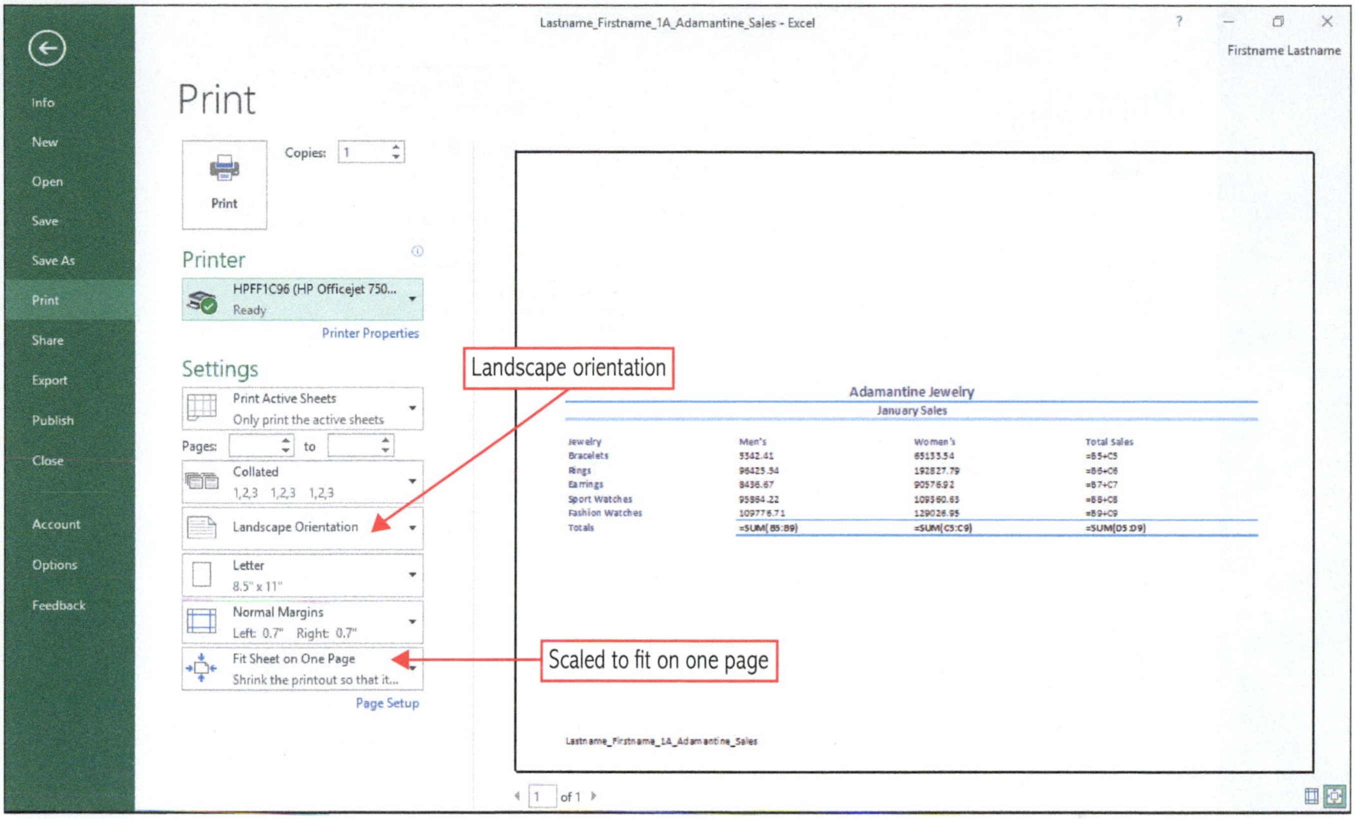

FIGURE 1.17

Excel 2016, Windows 10, Microsoft Corporation

12 ▶ If your instructor directs you to submit your files electronically, click **Back** ⟵, and then go to Step 14.

13 ▶ To print your worksheet, under **Print**, click **Print**.

14 ▶ In the upper right corner of the Excel window, **Close** ☒ Excel. When asked *Do you want to save the changes you made?*, click **Don't Save**.

Saving your worksheet now would save the view displaying your formulas.

Activity 1.10 | Previewing and Printing a Word Document

1 ▶ If necessary, on the taskbar, click the **Word** 🔲 button to make your Word document active. Press Ctrl + Home.

2 ▶ Click the **File tab** to display **Backstage** view, and then on the left, click the **Print tab** to display the **Print Preview**. Notice that the file name displays in the footer. Compare your screen with Figure 1.18.

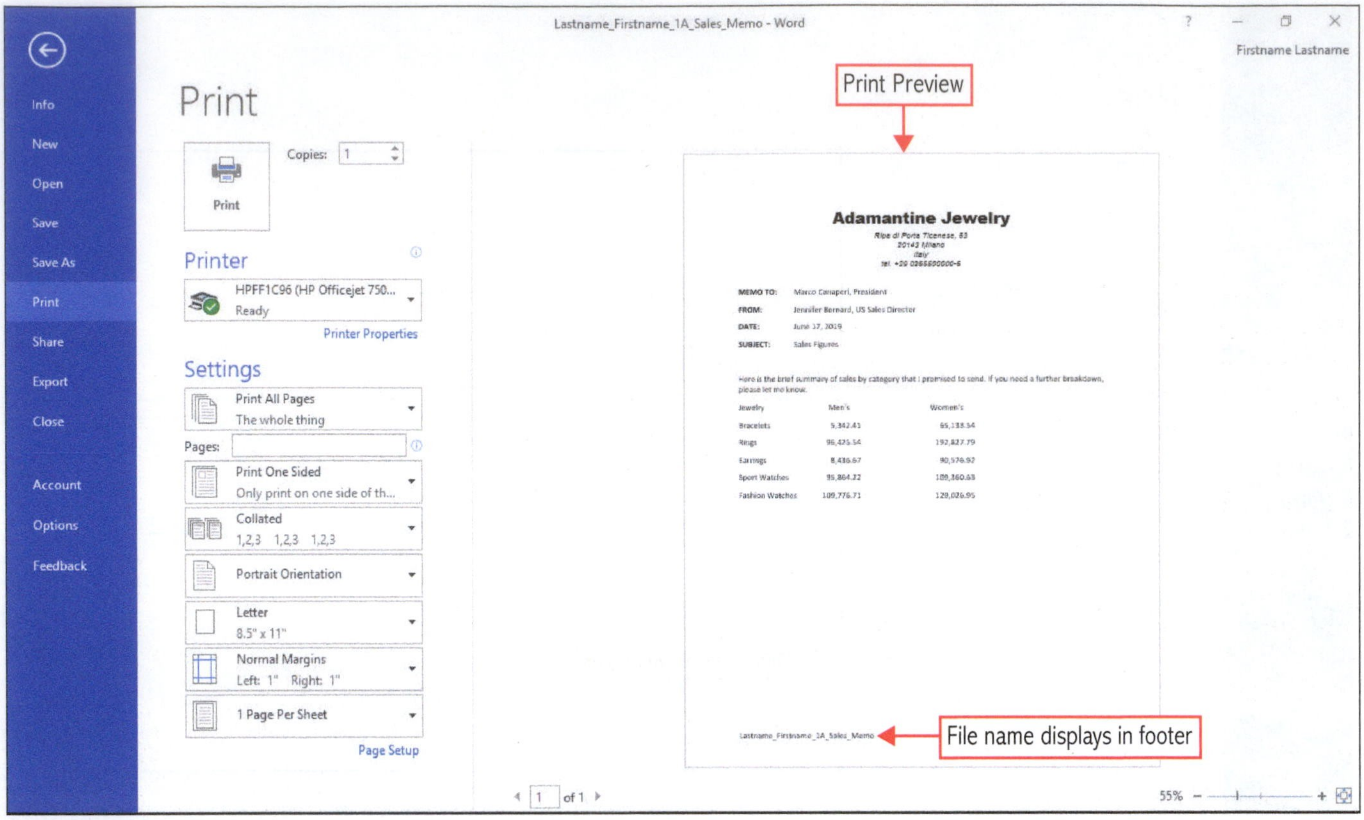

Word 2016, Windows 10, Microsoft Corporation

FIGURE 1.18

3 If your instructor directs you to submit your files electronically, go to Step 5.

4 If your instructor directs you to print your document, under **Print**, click **Print**.

5 In **Backstage** view, click the **Info tab**. In the lower right corner, click **Show All Properties**. Under **Related People**, be sure your name displays as the **Author**—change it if necessary. Click to the right of **Subject**, and then type your course name and section number. Click to the right of **Tags**, and then type **sales memo**

6 On the left, click **Save**, and then **Close** [×] Word.

7 Submit your printed or electronic files as directed by your instructor.

END | You have completed Project 1A

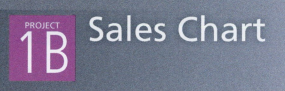

Sales Chart

PROJECT 1B

PROJECT ACTIVITIES

In Activities 1.11 through 1.21, you will create a table in a Word document that lists the different designers who create the fashionable jewelry sold by Adamantine Jewelry. You will create and format a chart in Excel, and then link the Excel data and chart into the Word document. Claudio Lenti, the Creative Director of Adamantine Jewelry, will provide you with new sales data. You will update the Excel data to reflect the new information. You will review the Word document to see that the changes made in Excel are updated in both files. Your completed files will look similar to Figure 1.19.

PROJECT FILES

For Project 1B, you will need the following files:

i01B_US_Sales
i01B_Sales_Chart

You will save your files as:

Lastname_Firstname_1B_US_Sales
Lastname_Firstname_1B_Sales_Chart

PROJECT RESULTS

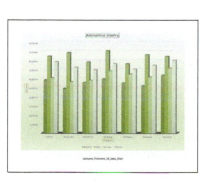

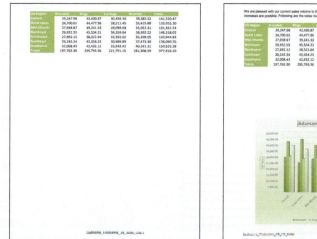

FIGURE 1.19 Project 1B Sales Chart

A *table* is a format for information that organizes and presents text and data in columns and rows. You can insert a table by choosing from a selection of preformatted tables or by selecting the number of rows and columns that you want. After you create a table, you can format the table using a *Table Style*—a predefined set of formatting characteristics, including font, alignment, and cell shading—or you can apply your own custom formatting.

Activity 1.11 | Creating a Table in Word

1 Start Word. Click **File**, and then click **Open**. Click **Browse**, and then navigate to the location where the student data files for this chapter are stored. Locate and open the file **i01B_US_Sales**. If necessary, display formatting marks, and be sure your screen displays in Print Layout view. Display the **Save As** dialog box, navigate to your **Integrated Projects Chapter 1** folder, and then save the document as **Lastname_Firstname_1B_US_Sales**

2 Click the **Insert tab**, and then in the **Header & Footer group**, click **Footer**. At the bottom of the **Footer** gallery, click **Edit Footer**. Under **Header & Footer Tools**, on the **Design tab**, in the **Insert group**, click **Document Info**, and then click **File Name**. Double-click in your document to close the footer. Compare your screen with Figure 1.20.

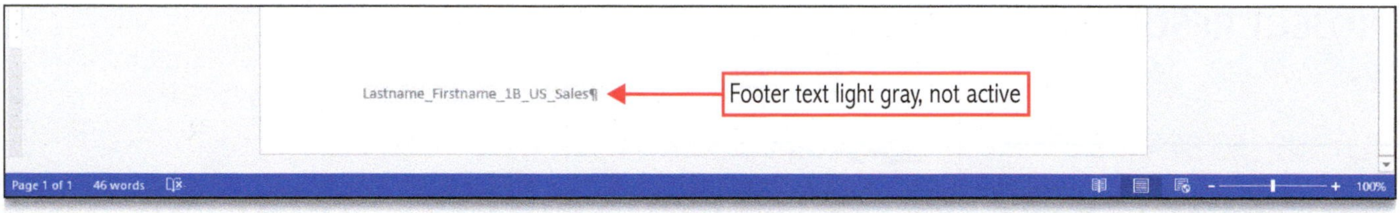

Lastname_Firstname_1B_US_Sales¶ ← Footer text light gray, not active

FIGURE 1.20   Word 2016, Windows 10, Microsoft Corporation

3 Press Ctrl + End to place the insertion point at the end of the document, and then press Enter two times.

4 Click the **Insert tab**, and then in the **Tables group**, click **Table**. In the **Table** grid, move the pointer down to the cell in the eighth row and the fourth column. Compare your screen with Figure 1.21.

The cells are selected, and the table size—4×8 Table—displays at the top of the menu.

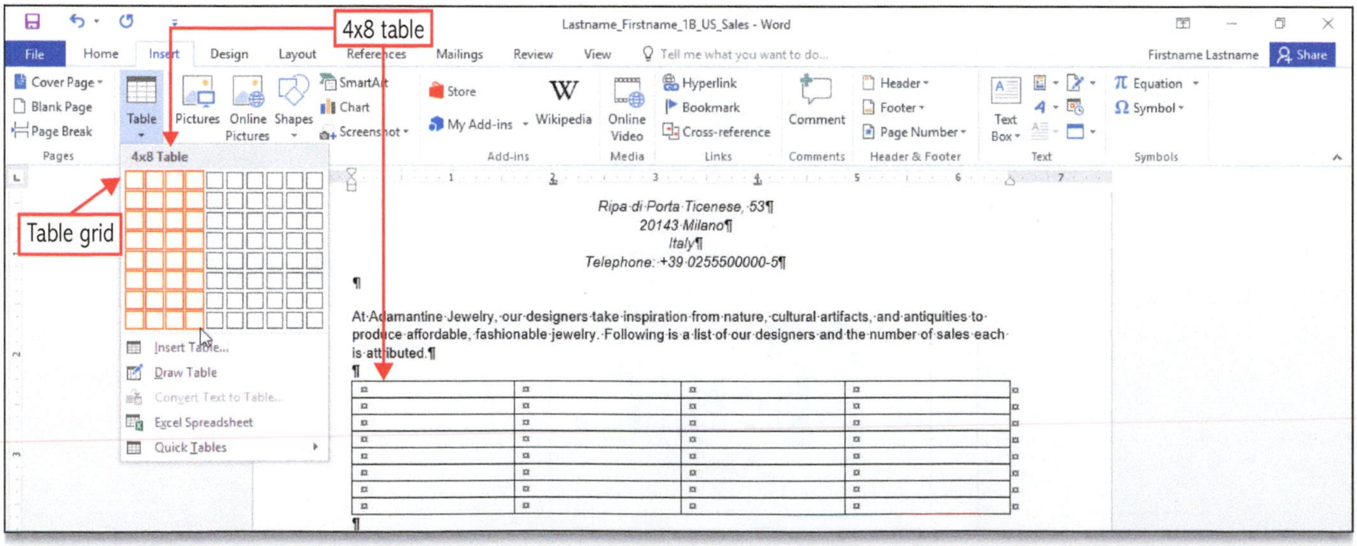

FIGURE 1.21

5 Click the last outlined cell to insert a table with eight rows and four columns.

A *cell* is the small box formed by the intersection of a column and a row. The insertion point is positioned in the upper left cell of the table. On the ribbon, the *contextual tabs* for Table Tools display. Contextual tabs are added to the ribbon when a specific object, such as a table, is selected and contain commands relevant to the selected object.

6 With the insertion point in the first cell, type **Designer Name** and then press Tab to move to the second column in the first row of the table.

You can use the Tab key to move from cell to cell in a Word table. You can press Enter to create another line in the same cell.

7 Type the following data in your table:

Designer Name	Bracelets	Earrings	Watches
Logan Garron	9,634.08	12,942.32	13,492.89
Mano Gauthier	7,452.23	9,994.13	18,448.01
Cameron Mathers	10,863.77	9,356.44	5,793.15
Kim Ngan	6,210.89	13,301.02	6,493.22
Sammie Tate	4,700.76	7,535.50	25,985.39
Miguel Torres	10,745.34	12,994.36	19,091.07
Hayden Vaught	7,311.12	4,929.68	29,783.23

8 Press Ctrl + End, and then press Enter.

Ctrl + End places the insertion point at the end of the document and below the table.

9 Type the following paragraph, including any misspelled words or grammatical errors:

We believe watches are an upcoming fashion trend. Adamantine Jewelry will be focusing on all the special watch lines during the next six months and selected designers will introduce a number of new watch styles in both the sport and fashion areas for men and women. The following designers will apply there unique emphasis on these watch styles:

10 Press Enter two times. Click the **Insert tab**. In the **Tables group**, click **Table**, and then at the bottom of the list, point to **Quick Tables**. In the **Quick Tables** gallery, under **Built-In**, scroll down and locate **Tabular List**. Compare your screen with Figure 1.22.

Quick Tables enables you to choose from a selection of preformatted tables.

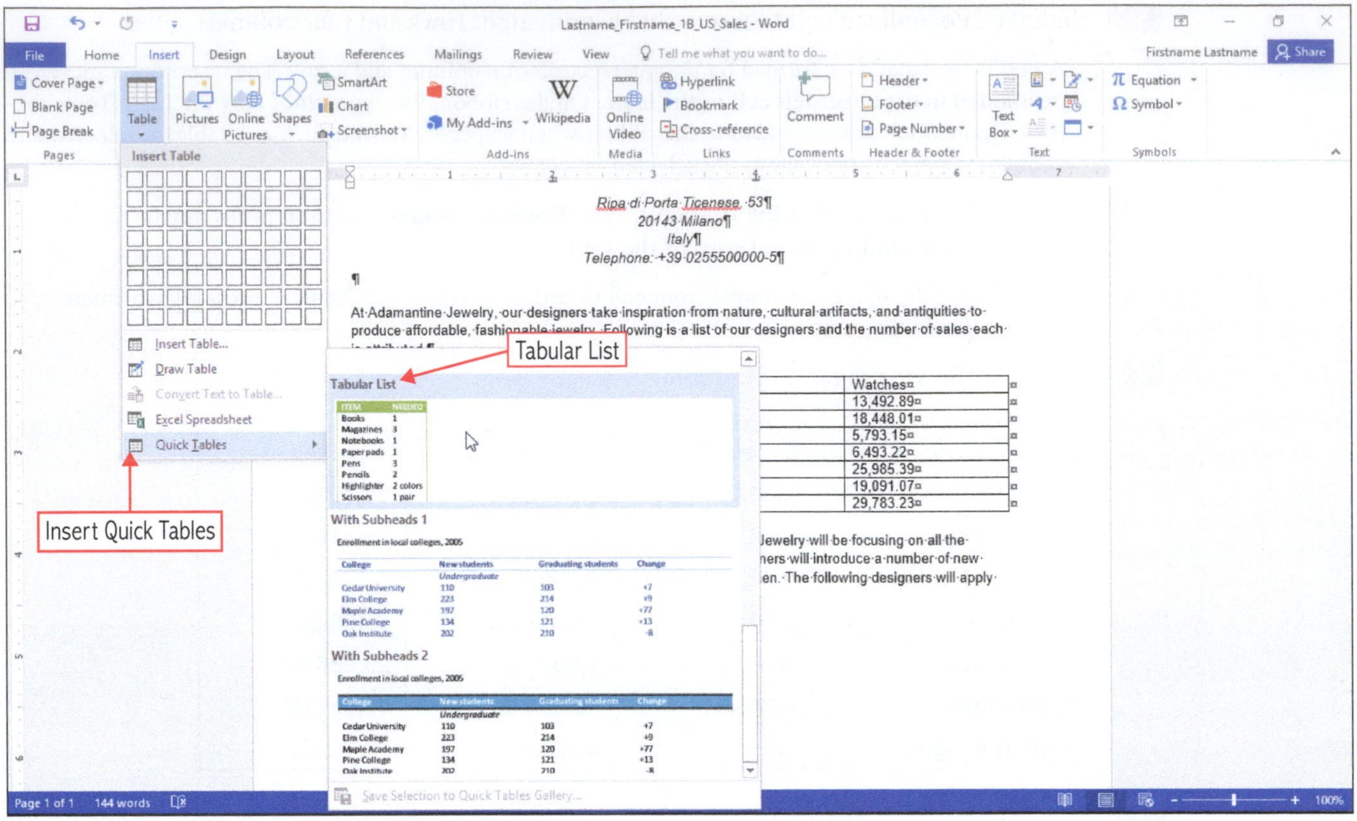

FIGURE 1.22

11 ▸ Click **Tabular List**. In the first cell of the inserted table, delete the word *ITEM*. Type **Watch Styles** press `Tab`, and then type **Designer**

Pressing `Tab` moves the insertion point to the next cell and selects the contents of the cell. Because the cell contents are selected, the content in those cells will be deleted when you begin to type. You do not have to delete the contents before you begin to type your data.

12 ▸ Type the following information in the table using `Tab` to move between the cells.

Men's Sport	Lydia Barnes
Men's Fashion	Trent Gaston
Women's Sport	Sammie Tate
Women's Fashion	Hayden Vaught

13 ▸ **Save** 🖫 your Word document.

More Knowledge | **Navigating in a Table**

You can move to a previous cell in a table by pressing `Shift` + `Tab`. This action selects the contents of the previous cell. The selection moves back one cell at a time each time you press `Tab` while holding down `Shift`. You can also use the up or down arrow keys to move up or down a column. The left and right arrow keys, however, move the insertion point one character at a time within a cell.

Activity 1.12 | **Inserting and Deleting Table Rows and Table Columns**

To change the size of a table, you can add or delete rows or columns at the beginning, middle, or end of a table.

1 ▸ In the first table you created, in the fourth row, click the first cell containing the text *Cameron Mathers* to position the insertion point in that cell.

2 Under **Table Tools**, click the **Layout tab**, and then in the **Rows & Columns group**, click **Insert Above**. Compare your screen with Figure 1.23.

A blank row is inserted above the *Cameron Mathers* row.

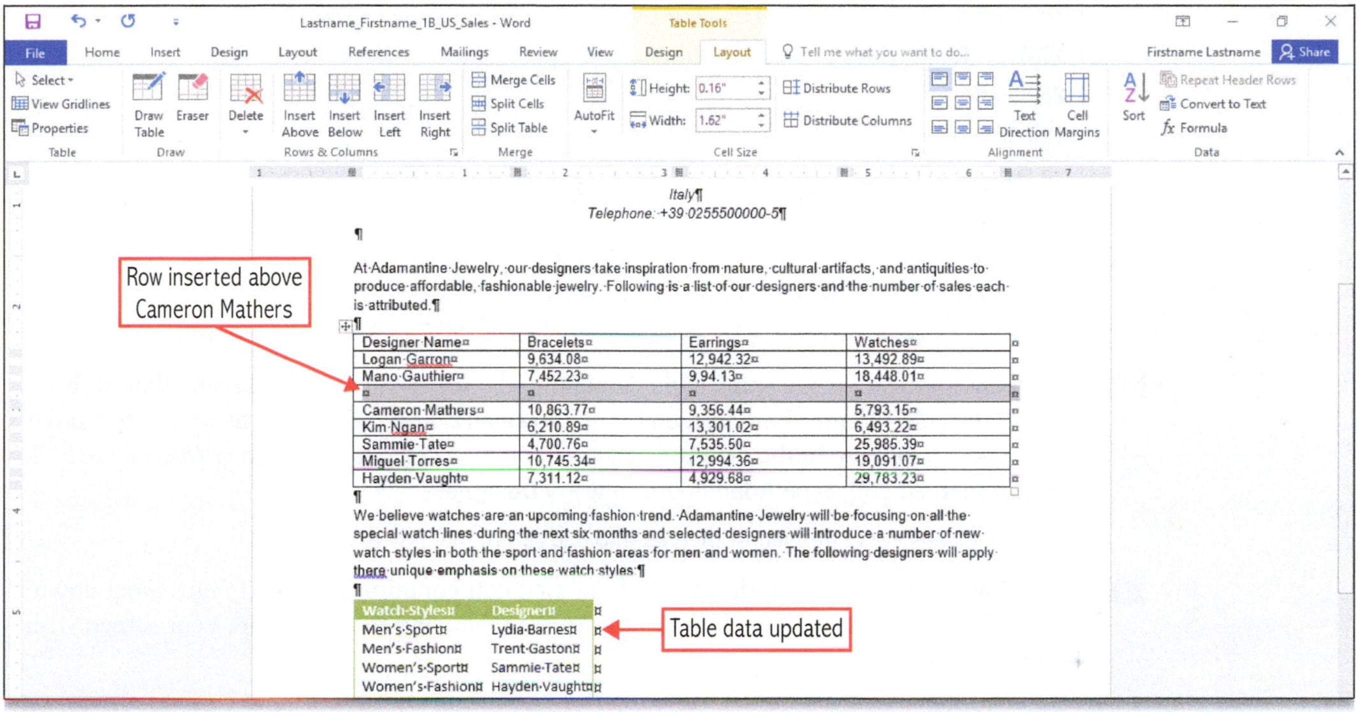

FIGURE 1.23

Word 2016, Windows 10, Microsoft Corporation

3 Type the following information in the new blank row:

Noel Jamison	**5,012.53**	**8,900.03**	**3,221.43**

4 In the same table, in the second column, right-click in the first cell containing the text *Bracelets*. On the shortcut menu, point to **Insert**, and then click **Insert Columns to the Right**. Compare your screen with Figure 1.24.

A blank column is inserted to the right of the *Bracelets* column.

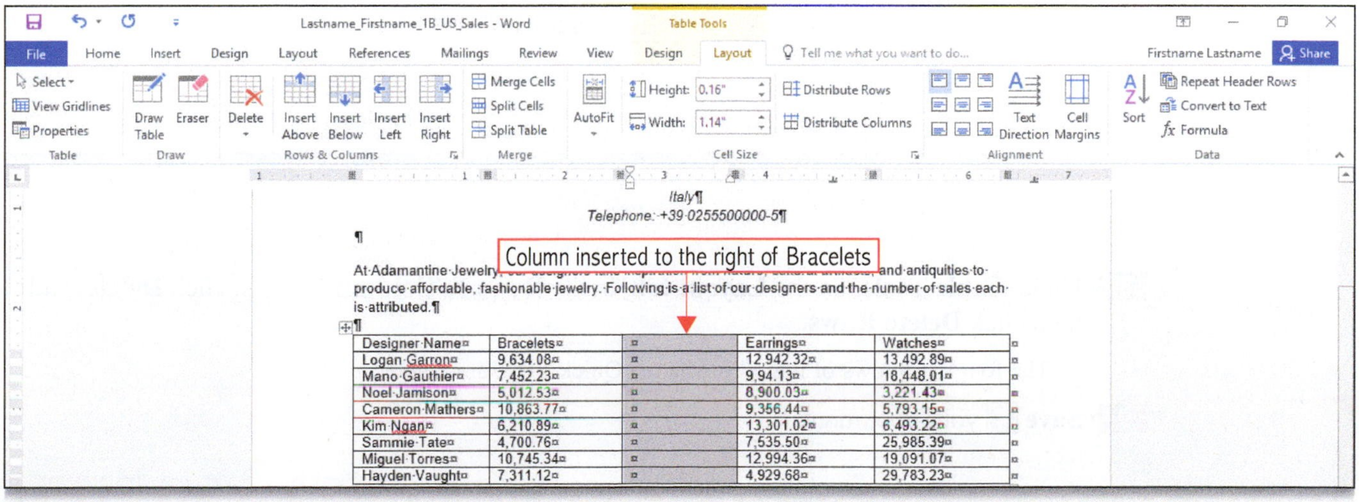

Word 2016, Windows 10, Microsoft Corporation

FIGURE 1.24

5 Click in the first cell of the new column. Type the following information in the new blank column, using the ↓ key to move down to the next cell.

Rings
18,654.67
20,312.11
25,569.54
12,690.03
10,240.56
20,978.60
17,967.88
27,643.45

6 Locate the first cell of the same table containing the text *Designer Name*, and then right-click in the cell. On the shortcut menu, point to **Insert**, and then click **Insert Rows Above**. Right-click anywhere in the new row, and then on the shortcut menu, click **Merge Cells**. In the new merged cell, type **Adamantine Jewelry Designers**

The five cells are combined or merged into one cell in the new row.

7 In the lower table, in the sixth row, click the first cell containing the text *Pens*. Drag down and to the right to select the last four rows of the table, and then compare your screen with Figure 1.25.

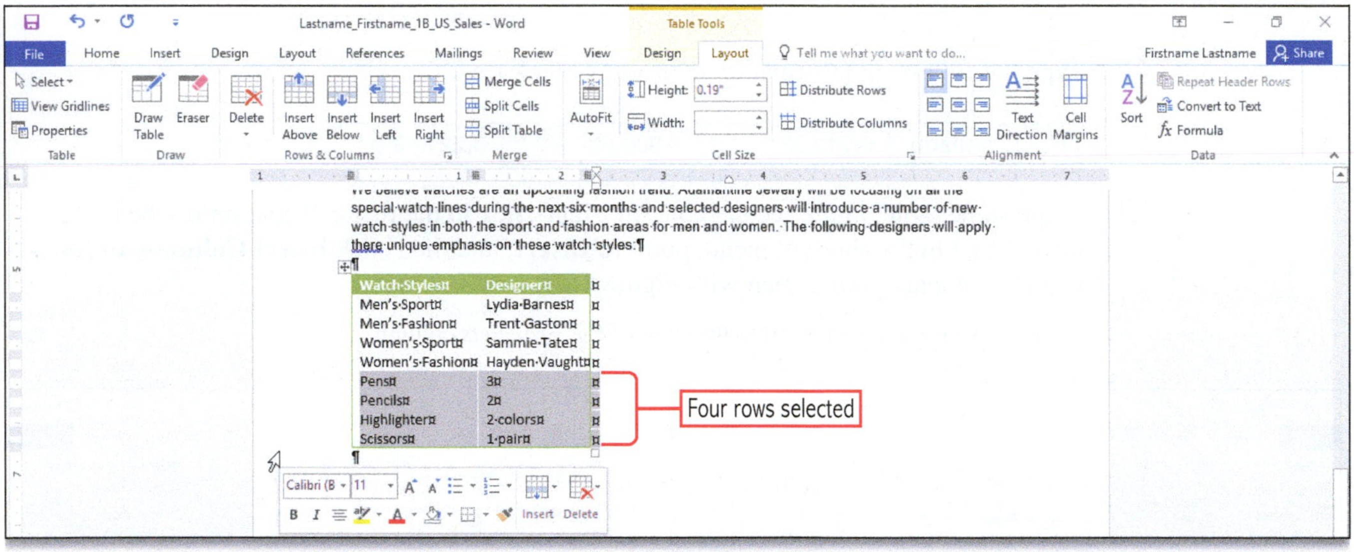

Word 2016, Windows 10, Microsoft Corporation

FIGURE 1.25

8 Under **Table Tools**, on the **Layout tab**, in the **Rows & Columns group**, click **Delete**, and then click **Delete Rows**.

The four extra rows of the preformatted Quick Table are deleted.

9 **Save** your document.

Activity 1.13 | Formatting a Table

Formatting a table will make the information easier to read. You can select the text, rows, columns, or the entire table that you want to format, and then choose the formats you want to apply.

1 ▸ Click in any cell in the upper table. Under **Table Tools**, click the **Design tab**, and then in the **Table Styles group**, in the **Table Style** gallery, click **More**. Scroll down as necessary, and then under **List Tables**, in the first row, point to the third style—**List Table 1 Light - Accent 2**. Notice that the Live Preview previews the change to your table. Compare your screen with Figure 1.26.

Live Preview is a technology that shows the result of applying an editing or formatting change as you point to possible results—*before* you actually apply the change.

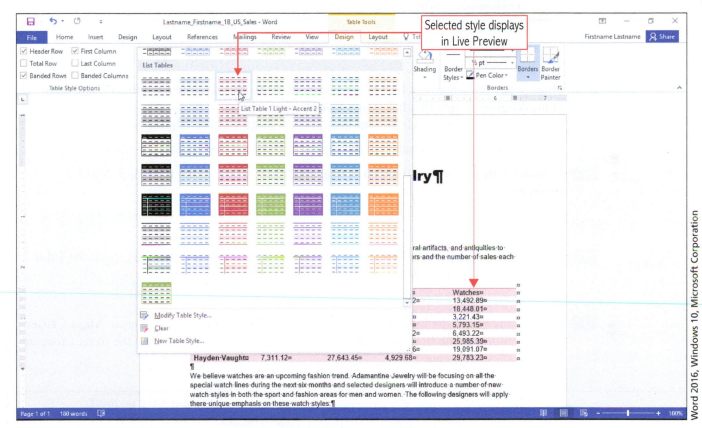

FIGURE 1.26

Word 2016, Windows 10, Microsoft Corporation

2 ▸ Click **List Table 1 - Accent 2** to apply the style to the entire table.

3 ▸ In the same table, position the insertion point to the left of the second row to display the pointer. Click one time to select all the cells in the second row. In the **Table Styles group**, click the **Shading button arrow**, and then in the seventh column, click the first color—**Olive Green, Accent 3**. With the second row still selected, click the **Home tab**, and then in the **Font group**, click **Bold** two times.

4 ▸ With the second row still selected, in the **Font group**, click the **Font Color arrow**, and then under **Theme Colors**, in the first column, click the first color—**White, Background 1**. Compare your screen with Figure 1.27.

Adamantine Jewelry¶

Ripa di Porta Ticenese, 53¶
20143 Milano¶
Italy¶
Telephone: +39 0255500000-5¶

¶

At Adamantine Jewelry, our designers take inspiration from nature, cultural artifacts, and antiquities to produce affordable, fashionable jewelry. Following is a list of our designers and the number of sales each is attributed.¶

Adamantine Jewelry Designers¤

> **Shading applied, font formatted**

Designer Name¤	Bracelets¤	Rings¤	Earrings¤	Watches¤	¤
Logan Garron¤	9,634.08¤	18,654.67¤	12,942.32¤	13,492.89¤	¤
Mano Gauthier¤	7,452.23¤	20,312.11¤	9,94.13¤	18,448.01¤	¤
Noel Jamison¤	5,012.53¤	25,569.54¤	8,900.03¤	3,221.43¤	¤
Cameron Mathers¤	10,863.77¤	12,690.03¤	9,356.44¤	5,793.15¤	¤
Kim Ngan¤	6,210.89¤	10,240.56¤	13,301.02¤	6,493.22¤	¤
Sammie Tate¤	4,700.76¤	20,978.60¤	7,535.50¤	25,985.39¤	¤
Miguel Torres¤	10,745.34¤	17,967.88¤	12,994.36¤	19,091.07¤	¤
Hayden Vaught¤	7,311.12¤	27,643.45¤	4,929.68¤	29,783.23¤	¤

FIGURE 1.27

5 In the table, select the first two rows. Under **Table Tools**, click the **Layout tab**, and then in the **Alignment group**, click **Align Center** 🔲. In the same table, select all the cells that contain numbers. In the **Alignment group**, click **Align Center Right** 🔲.

Each column heading is centered in the columns, and the numbers are right-aligned.

6 With the cells selected, in the **Cell Size group**, click **AutoFit**, and then click **AutoFit Contents**.

AutoFit Contents adjusts the width of the columns in a table to fit the cell content of the widest cell in each column.

7 In the **Tables group**, click **Properties**. In the **Table Properties** dialog box, click the **Table tab**, if necessary. Under **Alignment**, click **Center**, and then click **OK**.

The Designer table is centered horizontally on the page.

8 Click in any cell in the lower table. Using the techniques you practiced, apply **Align Center** to the headings in the first row, and then **Center** the table horizontally on the page. Compare your screen with Figure 1.28.

is attributed.¶
¶

Adamantine Jewelry Designers¤

> **Titles in first two rows are centered in the cells**

Designer Name¤	Bracelets¤	Rings¤	Earrings¤	Watches¤	
Logan Garron¤	9,634.08¤	18,654.67¤	12,942.32¤	13,492.89¤	¤
Mano Gauthier¤	7,452.23¤	20,312.11¤	9,94.13¤	18,448.01¤	
Noel Jamison¤	5,012.53¤	25,569.54¤	8,900.03¤	3,221.43¤	
Cameron Mathers¤	10,863.77¤	12,690.03¤	9,356.44¤	5,793.15¤	
Kim Ngan¤	6,210.89¤	10,240.56¤	13,301.02¤	6,493.22¤	
Sammie Tate¤	4,700.76¤	20,978.60¤	7,535.50¤	25,985.39¤	
Miguel Torres¤	10,745.34¤	17,967.88¤	12,994.36¤	19,091.07¤	
Hayden Vaught¤	7,311.12¤	27,643.45¤	4,929.68¤	29,783.23¤	

> **Tables Autofit to Contents and centered between the margins**

We believe watches are an upcoming fashion trend. Adamantine Jewelry will be focusing on all the special watch lines during the next six months and selected designers will introduce a number of new watch styles in both the sport and fashion areas for men and women. The following designers will apply there unique emphasis on these watch styles.¶
¶

Watch Styles¤	Designer¤	
Men's Sport¤	Lydia Barnes¤	¤
Men's Fashion¤	Trent Gaston¤	¤
Women's Sport¤	Sammie Tate¤	¤
Women's Fashion¤	Hayden Vaught¤	¤

¶

FIGURE 1.28

9 **Save** 🔲 your document.

Activity 1.14 | Correcting Spelling Errors

When you check the spelling of a document, Word compares your words to those in the Word dictionary and compares your phrases and punctuation to a list of grammar rules. Words that are not in the Word dictionary are marked with a wavy red underline. Phrases and punctuation that differ from the grammar rules are marked with a wavy blue underline.

1 ▸ Press [Ctrl] + [Home]. Click the **Review tab**, and then in the **Proofing group**, click **Spelling & Grammar**. Compare your screen with Figure 1.29.

The first identified word—*Ripa*—is highlighted in the Spelling pane on the right. This word is a proper noun, and it is spelled correctly. You can add this word to your dictionary or choose to ignore it. If a word is added to the dictionary, in the future, Microsoft Word will consider it to be spelled correctly and will no longer flag the word.

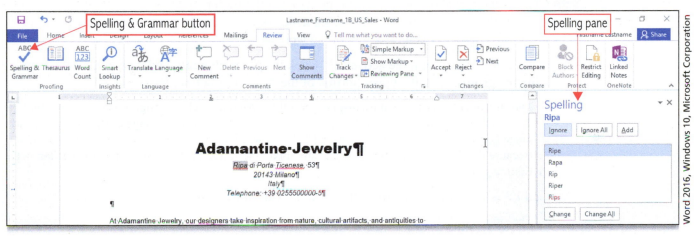

FIGURE 1.29

2 ▸ Click **Ignore All**.

3 ▸ The next two identified words—*Porta* and *Ticenese*—are both proper nouns. As each displays in the **Spelling** pane, click **Ignore All**. For each designer name that is identified, check the spelling, and if the name is spelled correctly, click **Ignore All**. Correct the spelling if the name is not correct.

4 ▸ The next identified word—*there*—is a grammar error. In the **Grammar** pane, with *their* selected, click **Change**. In the message box indicating that the spelling and grammar check is complete, click **OK**.

5 ▸ **Save** 🖫 your document.

Objective 6 | Create and Format a Chart in Excel

When looking at numbers in an Excel worksheet, analyzing the data may be difficult. A chart is a visual way to illustrate your Excel data in an understandable manner. You will create a chart from existing Excel data, and then copy the data and the chart to your Word document.

Activity 1.15 | Inserting an AutoSum Formula

Before creating the chart, you will add totals to the worksheet.

1 Start Excel, on the left click **Open Other Workbooks**, and then navigate to the location where the student data files for this chapter are stored. Locate and open the workbook **i01B_Sales_Chart**. Display the **Save As** dialog box, navigate to your **Integrated Projects Chapter 1** folder, and then save the workbook as **Lastname_Firstname_1B_Sales_Chart**

2 Click the **Insert tab**, and then in the **Text group**, click **Header & Footer**. Under **Header & Footer Tools**, on the **Design tab**, in the **Navigation group**, click the **Go to Footer** button. In the **Footer** area, click just above the word *Footer*, and then in the **Header & Footer Elements group**, click **File Name**.

The file name field displays on the left side of the footer area.

3 Click in the cell above the file name field to exit the footer, and then notice that the file name replaces the file name field. Near the right side of the status bar, click **Normal** ▦, and then press Ctrl + Home to display the top of the worksheet.

4 Click cell **F2** to make it the active cell. Click the **Formulas tab**, and then in the **Function Library group**, click the upper portion of the **AutoSum** button. Press Enter.

The sum of cells B2 through E2 displays in cell F2. AutoSum adds contiguous cells in a column or a row. The AutoSum function will first look above the active cell for a range of cells to sum. If no range is above the active cell, such as in F2, Excel will look to the left for a range of cells to sum. Because the AutoSum function is frequently used, it also has its own button on the Home tab in the Editing group.

5 Cell **F3** is currently the active cell. Click the **AutoSum** button and then press Enter.

The sum of cells B3:E3 is displayed in cell F3.

6 With cell **F4** as the active cell, click the upper portion of the **AutoSum** button again, and then compare your screen with Figure 1.30.

The *AutoSum* function automatically looks above the active cell to add a range of numbers. The AutoSum function sees numbers *above* cell F4 and will add the numbers in cells F2 and F3. This would be an incorrect answer because the sum of row 4 should display in cell F4. The incorrect formula displays in cell F4 and in the *Formula Bar*. The Formula Bar displays the value or formula contained in the active cell and permits you to enter or edit the values or formulas.

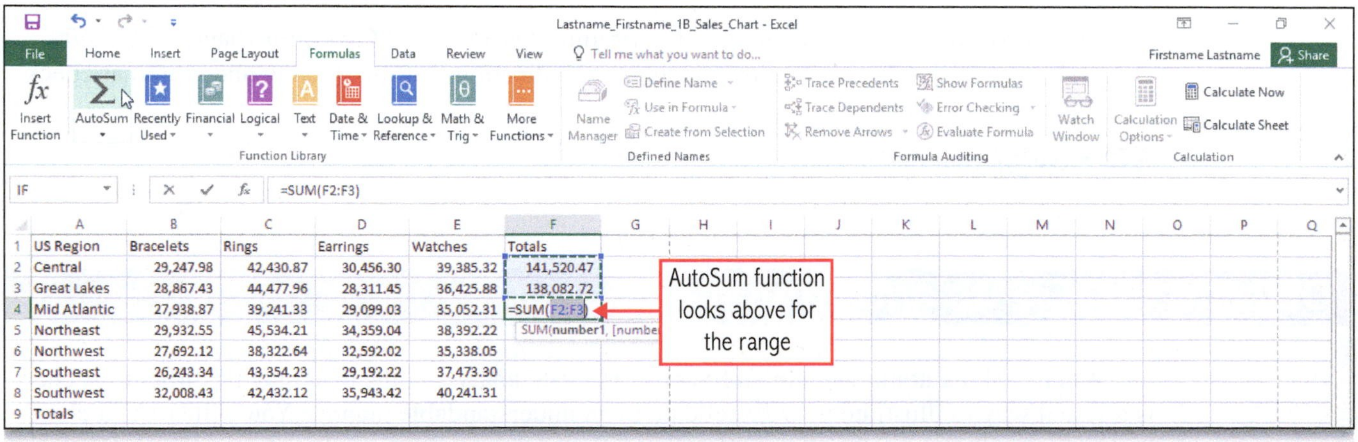

FIGURE 1.30

7 Press Esc to cancel the function.

8 ▸ Click cell **F3** to make it the active cell. Point to the fill handle to display the ⊞ pointer. Hold down the left mouse button, drag down to cell **F8**, and then release the mouse button. Compare your screen with Figure 1.31.

The formula in cell F3 is copied with a relative cell reference to cells F4 through F8.

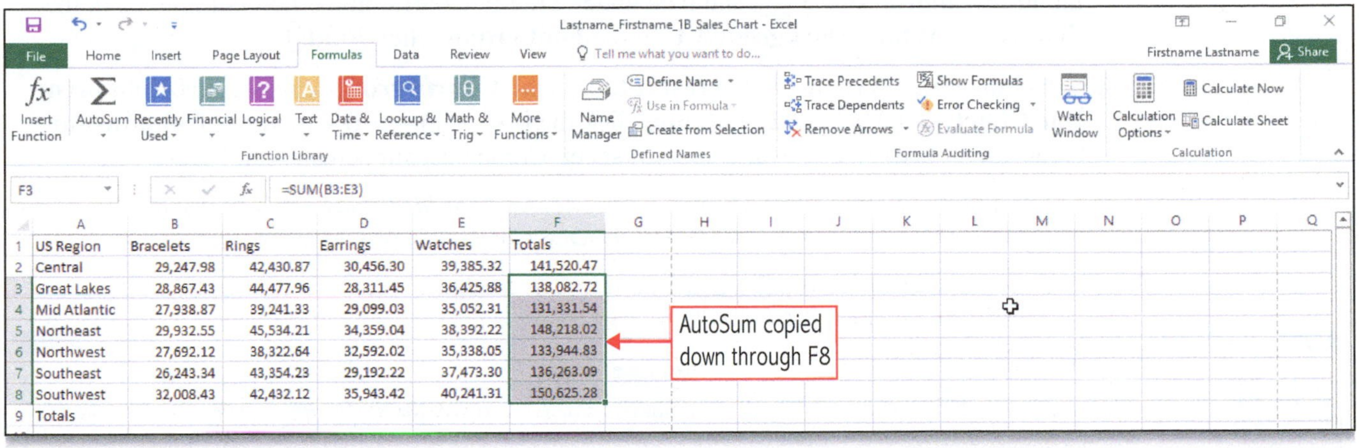

	A	B	C	D	E	F
1	US Region	Bracelets	Rings	Earrings	Watches	Totals
2	Central	29,247.98	42,430.87	30,456.30	39,385.32	141,520.47
3	Great Lakes	28,867.43	44,477.96	28,311.45	36,425.88	138,082.72
4	Mid Atlantic	27,938.87	39,241.33	29,099.03	35,052.31	131,331.54
5	Northeast	29,932.55	45,534.21	34,359.04	38,392.22	148,218.02
6	Northwest	27,692.12	38,322.64	32,592.02	35,338.05	133,944.83
7	Southeast	26,243.34	43,354.23	29,192.22	37,473.30	136,263.09
8	Southwest	32,008.43	42,432.12	35,943.42	40,241.31	150,625.28
9	Totals					

AutoSum copied down through F8

FIGURE 1.31

Excel 2016, Windows 10, Microsoft Corporation

9 ▸ Click cell **B9** to make it the active cell. On the **Formulas tab**, in the **Function Library group**, click the upper portion of the **AutoSum** button, and then in the **Formula Bar**, click **Enter** ✓.

Clicking the Formula Bar Enter button will accept the change and leave the current cell as the active cell.

10 ▸ In cell **B9**, point to the fill handle to display the ⊞ pointer, drag to the right to cell **F9**, and then release the mouse button. Compare your screen with Figure 1.32.

The formula in cell B9 is copied with a relative cell reference to cells C9 through F9.

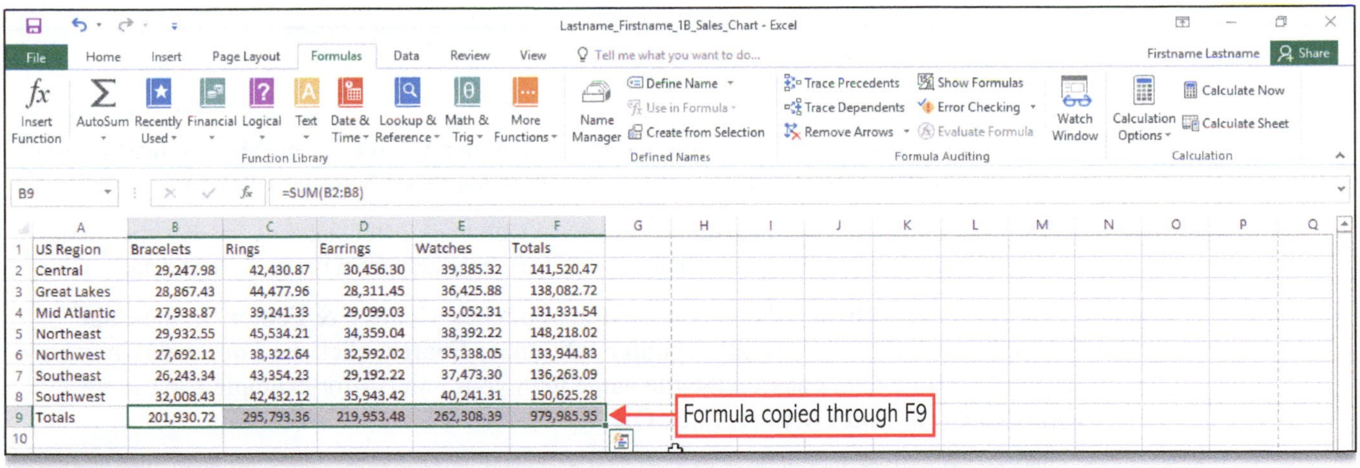

	A	B	C	D	E	F
1	US Region	Bracelets	Rings	Earrings	Watches	Totals
2	Central	29,247.98	42,430.87	30,456.30	39,385.32	141,520.47
3	Great Lakes	28,867.43	44,477.96	28,311.45	36,425.88	138,082.72
4	Mid Atlantic	27,938.87	39,241.33	29,099.03	35,052.31	131,331.54
5	Northeast	29,932.55	45,534.21	34,359.04	38,392.22	148,218.02
6	Northwest	27,692.12	38,322.64	32,592.02	35,338.05	133,944.83
7	Southeast	26,243.34	43,354.23	29,192.22	37,473.30	136,263.09
8	Southwest	32,008.43	42,432.12	35,943.42	40,241.31	150,625.28
9	Totals	201,930.72	295,793.36	219,953.48	262,308.39	979,985.95
10						

Formula copied through F9

FIGURE 1.32

11 ▸ **Save** 🖫 your workbook.

1 ▶ Select the range **A1:F1**. Hold down Ctrl, and then select the range **A2:A9**. Click the **Home tab**, and then in the **Font group**, click the **Fill Color arrow** [A ▾]. Under **Theme Colors**, in the seventh column, click the first color—**Olive Green, Accent 3**. In the **Font group**, click the **Font Color arrow** [A ▾], and then under **Theme Colors**, in the first column, click the first color—**White, Background 1**. In the **Font group**, click **Bold** [B].

2 ▶ Select the range **A1:E8**. On the **Insert tab**, in the **Charts group**, click **Insert Column or Bar Chart** [📊 ▾]. Under **3-D Column**, click the first chart—**3-D Clustered Column**—to create an embedded chart on your worksheet. Compare your screen with Figure 1.33.

Excel inserts the chart, and the chart is selected. An ***embedded chart*** is a chart that displays as an object within a worksheet. The CHART TOOLS tabs display on the ribbon.

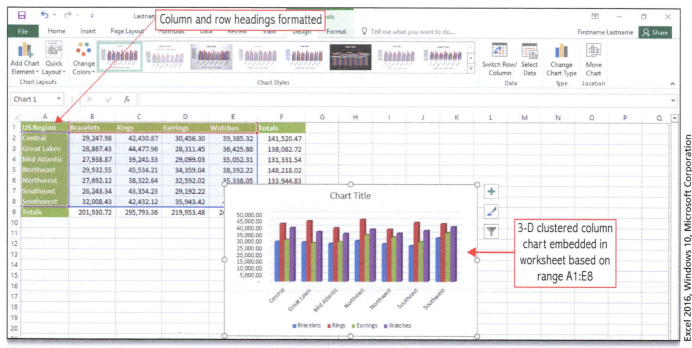

FIGURE 1.33

3 ▶ On the **Design tab**, in the **Location group**, click **Move Chart**. In the **Move Chart** dialog box, click the **New sheet** option button, type **US Sales Chart** and then click **OK**.

The chart moves to a new ***chart sheet***, which is a workbook sheet that contains only the chart. A chart sheet is useful when you want to view a chart separately from the worksheet data.

4 ▶ Click the **Insert tab**, and then in the **Text group**, click **Header & Footer**. In the **Page Setup** dialog box, on the **Header/Footer tab**, under **Footer**, click the **Footer down arrow**, scroll down, and then click on the file name with your name—for example **Lastname_Firstname_1B_Sales_Chart**. Click **OK**.

The footer will display in Print Preview and will print, but the footer does not display on the Excel chart sheet.

5 ▶ Under **Chart Tools**, click the **Design tab**, and then in the **Chart Styles group**, click **More** [▾]. By pointing to the styles, locate and click **Style 11**. In the **Chart Styles group**, click **Change Colors**, and then under **Monochromatic**, locate and click **Color 7**—the green columns.

6 In the upper right corner of the chart, click **Chart Elements** ⊞. On the displayed menu, point to Chart Title, click the **arrow**, and then click **More Options**. In the **Format Chart Title** pane, if necessary, click **Fill**, and then click **Gradient fill** to display fill options. Click the **Preset gradients arrow**, and then in the gallery, in the first row, locate and click the third color—**Light Gradient - Accent 3**. Compare your screen with Figure 1.34.

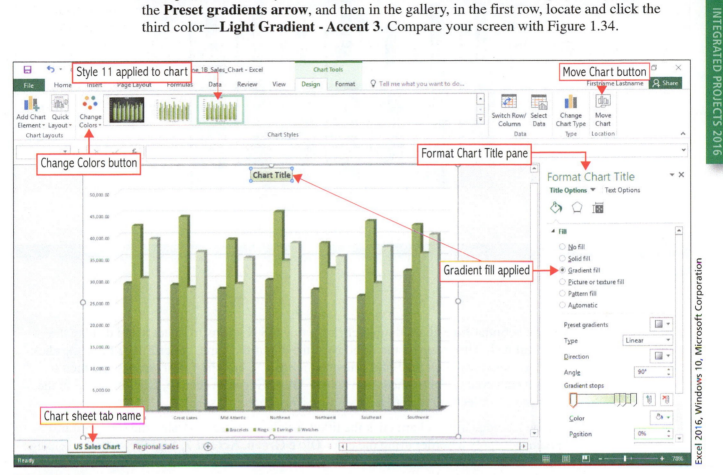

FIGURE 1.34

7 In the **Format Chart Title** pane, click **Effects** ⬠, and then click **3-D Format**. Click the **Top bevel arrow**, and then under **Bevel**, locate and click **Soft Round**.

8 At the top of the chart, notice that the **Chart Title** is selected. Type **Adamantine Jewelry** and press **Enter** to create the title for the chart. On the right, in the upper right corner of the **Format Chart Title** pane, click **Close** ☒.

9 In the upper right corner of the chart, click **Chart Elements** ⊞, click the **Axis Titles arrow**, and then select the **Primary Horizontal** check box. At the bottom of the chart, with **Axis Title** selected, type **US Regions** and then press **Enter**.

10 By using the steps you just practiced, select the **Primary Vertical** axis, and then as the axis name type **US Sales** and press **Enter**. Compare your screen with Figure 1.35.

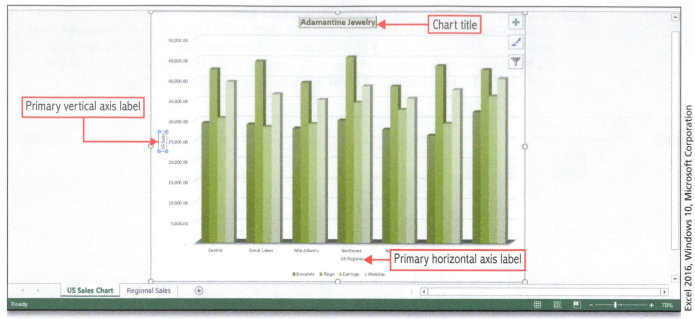

FIGURE 1.35

11 ▶ At the bottom of the chart, double-click the title **US Regions** to select it and display the **Format Axis Title** pane on the right. Near the top of the pane, under **Fill & Line** ⬙, click **Border**, and then click the **Solid line** option button. Click the **Color arrow**, and then in the seventh column, click the fourth color—**Olive Green, Accent 3, Lighter 40%**. In the **Width** box, select the current number, type **3** and then press Enter.

12 ▶ At the left edge of the chart, click the title **US Sales** to select it. Using the steps you just practiced, apply a border using the color **Olive Green, Accent 3, Lighter 40%**, and change the **Width** of the border to **3 pt**.

13 ▶ In the chart, point to the white area to the right of the chart title until the ScreenTip *Chart Area* displays, and then double-click to display the **Format Chart Area** pane on the right. Click **Fill & Line** ⬙, and then under **Fill**, click the **Gradient fill** option button. Click the **Preset gradients arrow**, and then click the first green gradient—**Light Gradient - Accent 3**. **Close** ☒ the **Format Chart Area** pane, click outside of the chart to deselect it, and then compare your screen with Figure 1.36.

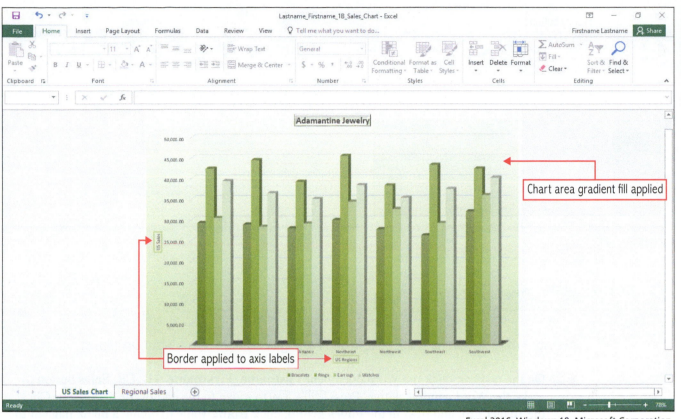

FIGURE 1.36

Excel 2016, Windows 10, Microsoft Corporation

14 **Save** 🖫 your workbook.

Objective 7 | Link Excel Data and an Excel Chart to a Word Document

You can connect the contents of one file to another file by linking the files. *Linking* is the process of inserting information from a source file into a destination file while maintaining a connection between the two files. The *source file* is the file where the data or object is created. The *destination file* is the file where the linked data or object is inserted. When linked, any changes that you make in the source file are reflected in the destination file.

Activity 1.17 | Copying Excel Data

1 At the bottom of the screen, right-click the **US Sales Chart sheet tab**, and then on the shortcut menu, point to **Tab Color**. Under **Theme Colors**, in the fifth column, click the first color—**Blue, Accent 1**.

2 Right-click the **Regional Sales sheet tab**, point to **Tab Color**, and then under **Theme Colors**, in the seventh column, click the first color—**Olive Green, Accent 3**.

3 On the **Regional Sales** worksheet, select the range **A1:F9**. On the **Home tab**, in the **Clipboard group**, click **Copy** 🗐. Compare your screen with Figure 1.37.

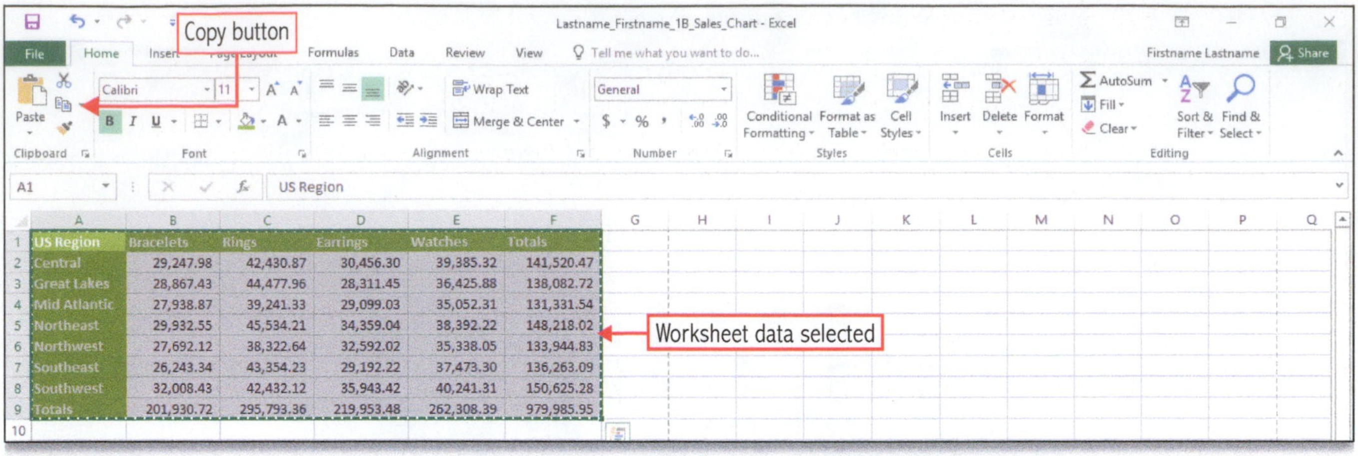

FIGURE 1.37

Excel 2016, Windows 10, Microsoft Corporation

ANOTHER WAY Press Ctrl + C.

Activity 1.18 | Accessing Paste Special and Pasting Excel Data into a Word Document

1. On the taskbar, click the Word document **Lastname_Firstname_1B_US_Sales** button to make the Word window active. Press Ctrl + End to move to the end of the document. Click the **Insert tab**, and then in the **Pages group**, click **Blank Page** to create a blank page at the insertion point.

2. Type the following paragraph in your Word document:

    We are pleased with our current sales volume in the United States, but as always, we believe sales increases are possible. Following are the sales numbers broken down by US region.

3. Press Enter two times. Click the **Home tab**. In the **Clipboard group**, click the **Paste arrow**, and then click **Paste Special**. In the **Paste Special** dialog box, click the **Paste link** option button, and then under **As**, click **Microsoft Excel Worksheet Object**. Compare your screen with Figure 1.38.

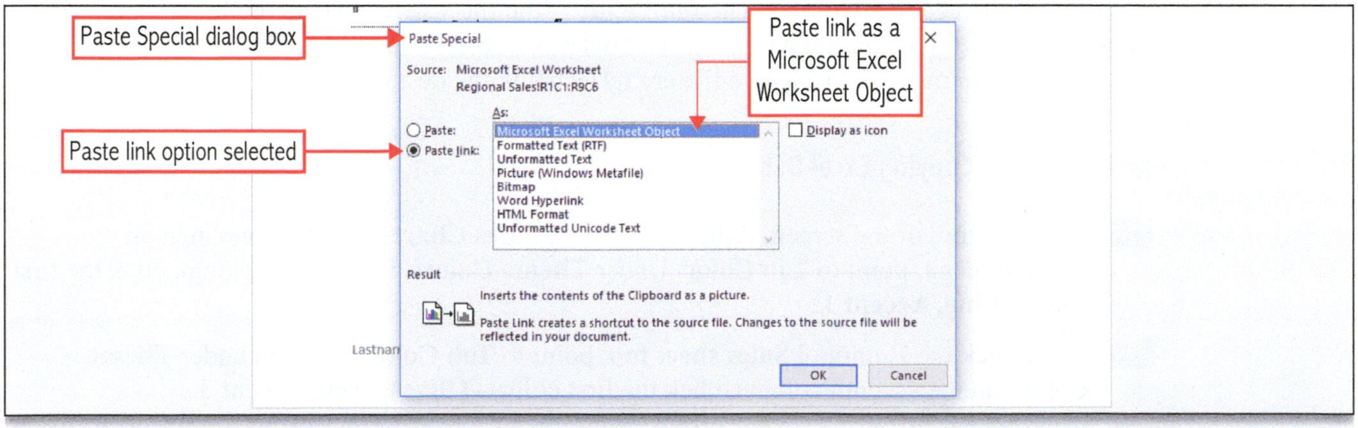

FIGURE 1.38

Word 2016, Windows 10, Microsoft Corporation

4. Click **OK**, and then press Enter two times.

    This action pastes the linked data from Excel into the Word document.

5 **Save** 🖫 your Word document.

6 Point anywhere in the pasted data in your Word document and double-click to access the Excel source file. Notice that Excel becomes the active window.

7 Press [Esc] to cancel the moving border around the copied Excel cells. If necessary, maximize the Excel workbook window.

Activity 1.19 | Copying and Linking an Excel Chart into a Word Document

1 Click the **US Sales Chart sheet tab** to make it the active Excel worksheet.

2 Click the edge of the chart to select it, and then on the **Home tab**, in the **Clipboard group**, click **Copy** 🖹.

3 On the taskbar, click the Word document **Lastname_Firstname_1B_US_Sales** button to make the Word window active. Press [Ctrl] + [End] to move to the end of the document, and then press [Enter] two times.

4 On the **Home tab**, in the **Clipboard group**, click the **Paste arrow**. Under **Paste Options**, point to the third option—*Use Destination Theme & Link Data (L)*. Compare your screen with Figure 1.39.

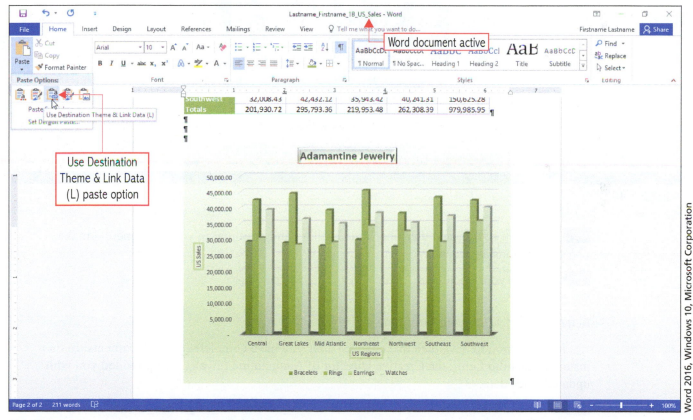

FIGURE 1.39

5 Under **Paste Options**, click the third option—**Use Destination Theme & Link Data (L)**.

6 In the Word document, click the edge of the chart to make it the active object. Under **Chart Tools**, click the **Format tab**, and then in the **Arrange group**, click **Position**. Under **With Text Wrapping**, in the third row, click the second option—**Position in Bottom Center with Square Text Wrapping**.

The chart moves independently of the surrounding text.

7 With the chart still selected, under **Chart Tools**, on the **Format tab**, in the **Size group**, set the **Shape Height** to **4.5** and press Enter. Set the **Shape Width** to **5.5** and press Enter. Compare your screen with Figure 1.40.

Sizing handles are the small squares or circles that display on each corner and in the middle of each side of a chart or graphic. Sizing handles are used to increase or decrease the size of the chart or graphic.

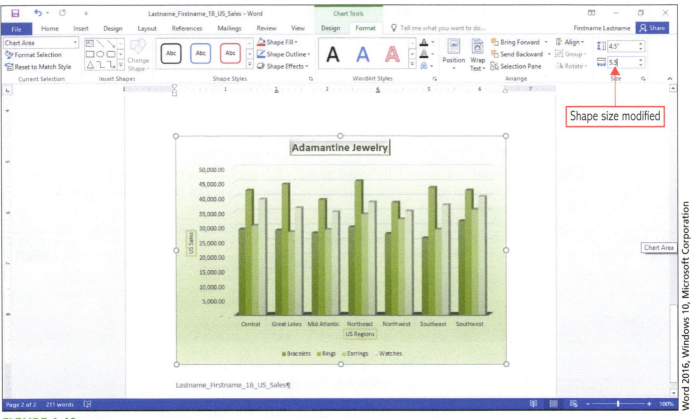

FIGURE 1.40

8 Press Ctrl + Home, and then check the spelling and grammar in your document—make corrections as necessary.

9 **Save** your document.

Activity 1.20 | Modifying Excel Data

It is common to have data that changes after you have completed your documents. In this instance, Claudio Lenti, the Creative Director of Adamantine Jewelry, has provided you with updated sales data.

1 On the taskbar, click the Excel file **Lastname_Firstname_1B_Sales_Chart** button to make the Excel window active. Click on the **Regional Sales sheet tab**.

2 Click cell **B3** to make it the active cell, type **24,700.01** and then press Enter. Click cell **D7** to make it the active cell, type **30,989.89** and then press Enter.

New data displays for *Bracelets* in the *Great Lakes* region and for *Earrings* in the *Southeast* region.

3 Click the **US Sales Chart sheet tab** to make it the active worksheet—the columns representing the updated data have been automatically updated to reflect the new data. Compare your screen with Figure 1.41.

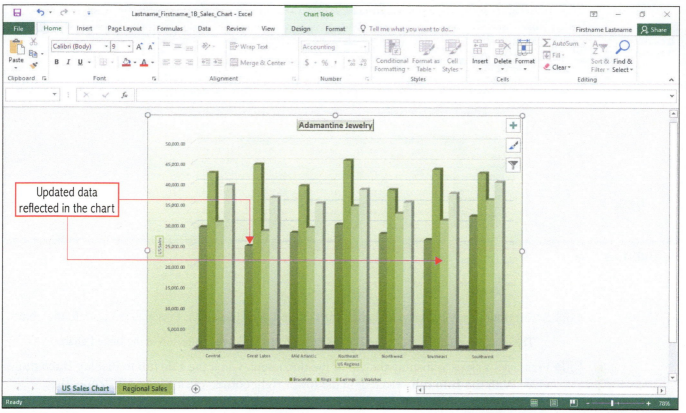

FIGURE 1.41

Excel 2016, Windows 10, Microsoft Corporation

4 Click the **File tab** to display **Backstage** view. With the **Info tab** selected, in the lower right corner, click **Show All Properties**. Under **Related People**, be sure your name displays as the **Author**—change it if necessary. Click to the right of **Subject**, and then type your course name and section number. Click to the right of **Tags**, and then type **sales worksheet**

5 On the left, click **Save**. As directed by your instructor, print or submit your workbook electronically. To print your entire workbook, click the **File tab** to display **Backstage** view. On the left, click the **Print tab**, under **Settings**, click the **Print Active Sheets** button, and then click **Print Entire Workbook**. Click the **Print** button.

6 **Close** ✕ Excel.

Activity 1.21 | Viewing Data and Chart Changes in a Word Document

1 If necessary, on the taskbar, click the Word document **Lastname_Firstname_1B_US_Sales** button to make the Word window active.

2 Click the edge of the table on page 2 to select it. Press F9. (On a laptop, you might have to hold down your fn key and then press F9.) Notice that the changes made to the regional sales numbers in Excel are reflected in the linked table. Compare your screen with Figure 1.42.

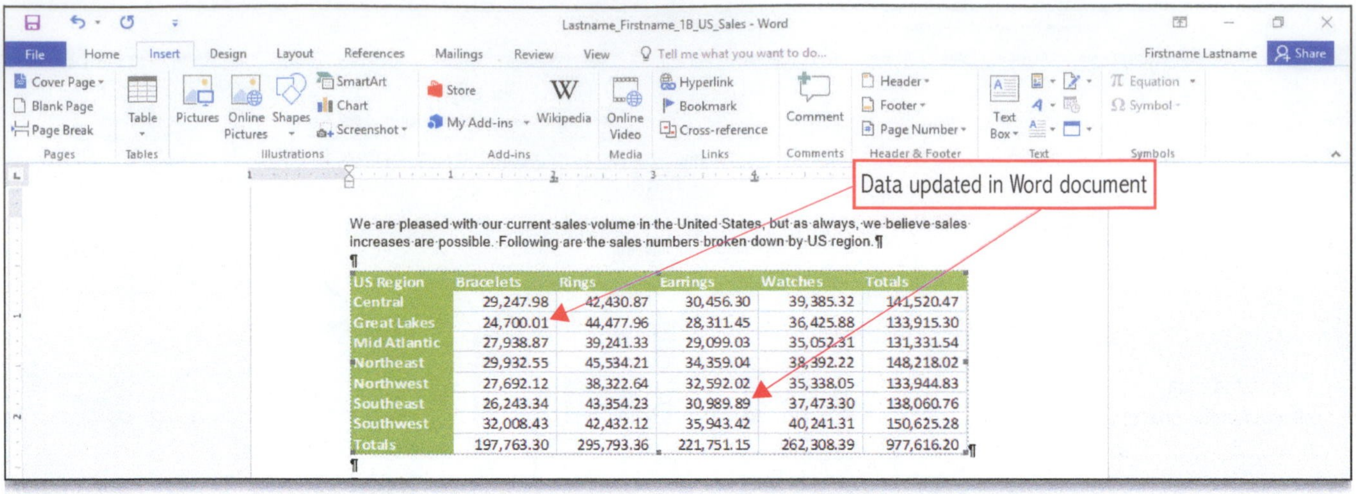

FIGURE 1.42

3 ▶ Scroll down as necessary, and click the right edge of the chart. Press F9 to update the chart.

The changes made to the regional sales numbers in Excel are reflected in the linked chart.

4 ▶ Press Ctrl + Home to display the top of the document. Click the **File tab** to display **Backstage** view. With the **Info tab** selected, in the lower right corner, click **Show All Properties**. Under **Related People**, be sure your name displays as the **Author**—change it if necessary. Click to the right of **Subject**, and then type your course name and section number. Click to the right of **Tags**, and then type **designers, jewelry, linked**

5 ▶ On the left, click **Save**. As directed by your instructor, print or submit your Word document electronically. To print your document, click the **File tab** to display **Backstage** view. Click the **Print tab**, and then click **Print**.

6 ▶ **Close** ☒ Word.

END | You have completed Project 1B

END OF CHAPTER

SUMMARY

Microsoft Word and Excel include features you can use to enter data and create charts. The files can be formatted to create a professional appearance. The data from the source file can be linked to or embedded in the destination file.

MATCHING

Match each term in the second column with its correct definition in the first column by writing the letter of the term on the blank line in front of the correct definition.

_____ 1. A specific location on a line of text to which you can move the insertion point by pressing the [Tab] key, and that is used to align and indent text.

_____ 2. A placeholder that displays preset content, such as the current date, the file name, a page number, or other stored information.

_____ 3. An equation that performs mathematical calculations on values in a worksheet.

_____ 4. A predefined formula that performs calculations by using specific values in a particular order.

_____ 5. A small black square located in the lower right corner of a selected cell.

_____ 6. In a formula, the address of a cell based on the relative positions of the cell that contains the formula and the cell referred to in the formula.

_____ 7. A context-sensitive menu that displays commands and options relevant to the selected object.

_____ 8. A format for information that organizes and presents text and data in columns and rows.

_____ 9. A predefined set of formatting characteristics, including font, alignment, and cell shading for a table.

_____ 10. A small box formed by the intersection of a column and a row.

_____ 11. A Word feature that adjusts the width of the columns in a table to fit the cell content of the widest cell in each column.

_____ 12. A workbook sheet that contains only a chart and is useful when you want to view a chart separately from the worksheet data.

_____ 13. The file where the data or object is created.

_____ 14. The file where the linked data or object is inserted.

_____ 15. The small squares or circles that display on each corner and in the middle of each side of a chart or graphic.

A AutoFit Contents

B Cell

C Chart sheet

D Destination file

E Field

F Fill handle

G Formula

H Function

I Relative cell reference

J Shortcut menu

K Sizing handles

L Source file

M Tab stop

N Table

O Table Style

MULTIPLE CHOICE

Circle the correct answer.

1. A small toolbar containing frequently used formatting commands that display as a result of selecting text or objects is the:
   A. Formatting toolbar   **B.** mini toolbar   **C.** Quick Access Toolbar

2. An Office feature that displays a list of potential results instead of just the command name is:
   A. a gallery   **B.** a shortcut menu   **C.** the ribbon

3. An Excel view that maximizes the number of cells visible on your screen and keeps the column letters and row numbers close to the columns and rows is:
   A. Normal view   **B.** Page Layout view   **C.** Print Layout view

4. An Excel feature that extends values into adjacent cells based on the values of selected cells is:
   A. AutoComplete   **B.** AutoCorrect   **C.** Auto Fill

5. A predefined formula that adds all the numbers in a selected range of cells is the:
   A. COUNT function   **B.** SUM function   **C.** TOTAL function

6. The Excel number format that applies a thousand comma separator where appropriate, inserts a fixed US dollar sign aligned at the left edge of the cell, applies two decimal places, and leaves a small amount of space at the right edge of the cell to accommodate a parenthesis for negative numbers is the:
   A. Accounting Number Format   **B.** Currency Format   **C.** General Format

7. Tabs that are added to the ribbon when a specific object is selected and that contain commands
   relevant to the selected object are:
   A. action tabs   **B.** content tabs   **C.** contextual tabs

8. The element in the Excel window that displays the value or formula contained in the active cell is the:
   A. Address Bar   **B.** Formula Bar   **C.** Function Bar

9. A chart that displays as an object within a worksheet is:
   A. a copied chart   **B.** an embedded chart   **C.** a pasted chart

10. The process of inserting information from a source file into a destination file while maintaining the connection between the two files is:
    A. embedding   **B.** linking   **C.** pasting

Mastering Integration Project 1C China Expansion

Apply 1A skills from these Objectives:

1 Create a Word Document

2 Copy Word Text into an Excel Workbook

3 Modify an Excel Worksheet

4 Preview and Print Word and Excel Files

In the following Mastering Integration project, you will prepare a proposal for Adamantine Jewelry to expand into China. Your completed files will look similar to Figure 1.43.

PROJECT FILES

For Project 1C, you will need the following files:

New blank Word document

New blank Excel workbook

i01C_Company_Headings

You will save your files as:

Lastname_Firstname_1C_Chinese_Expansion

Lastname_Firstname_1C_Chinese_Expenses

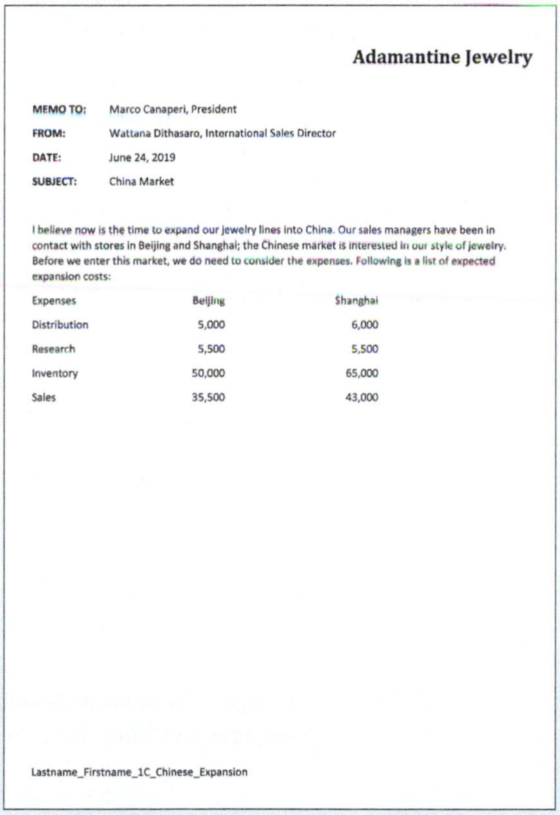

PROJECT RESULTS

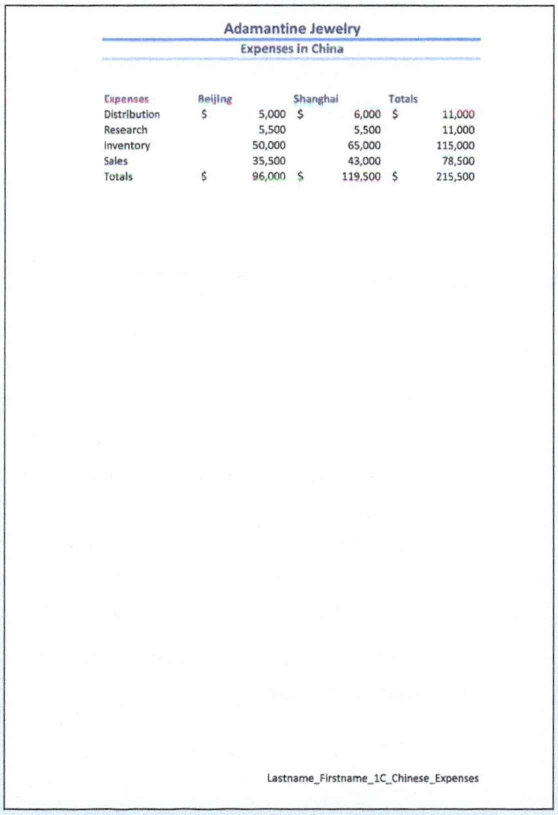

FIGURE 1.43

Word 2016, Windows 10, Microsoft Corporation

(Project 1C China Expansion continues on the next page)

1 Start Word. If necessary, display formatting marks. Insert **Decimal Tab stops** at **2.5** inches and **4.5** inches. At the top of the document, type **Adamantine Jewelry** and then press Enter three times. Select the first paragraph, change the **Font** to **Cambria**, change the **Font Size** to **18**, apply **Bold**, and then **Align Text Right**.

2 Press Ctrl + End. Type **I believe now is the time to expand our jewelry lines into China. Our sales managers have been in contact with stores in Beijing and Shanghai; the Chinese market is interested in our styles of jewelry. Before we enter this market, we do need to consider the expenses. Following is a list of expected expansion costs:** Press Enter, and then type the following in tabbed columns:

Expenses	Beijing	Shanghai
Distribution	5,000	6,000
Research	5,500	5,500
Inventory	50,000	65,000
Sales	35,500	43,000

3 Near the top of the document, in the second blank line, click to position the insertion point. Insert **Text from File**, using the data file **i01C_Company_Headings**. To the right of each heading, replace the existing text with the following:

MEMO TO	Marco Canaperi, President
FROM	Wattana Dithasaro, International Sales Director
DATE	June 24, 2019
SUBJECT	China Markets

4 Save the document in your **Integrated Projects Chapter 1** folder as **Lastname_Firstname_1C_Chinese_Expansion** Insert the file name in the footer.

5 Start Excel. In cell **A1**, type **Adamantine Jewelry** and then in cell **A2**, type **Expenses in China Save** the

workbook in your **Integrated Projects Chapter 1** folder as **Lastname_Firstname_1C_Chinese_Expenses** Make your Word document window active. Select and copy the five lines of tabbed text. Make the Excel workbook window active, move the insertion point to cell **A5**, and then **Paste** the Word data. Insert the file name in the footer, and then return to **Normal** view.

6 In cells **D5** and **A10**, type **Totals** and then **Sum** all of the rows in the range **D6:D9**. **Sum** all of the columns in the range **B10:D10**. Apply the **Accounting Number Format** to the ranges **B6:D6** and **B10:D10**, and then **Decrease Decimal** to zero decimals. Apply the **Comma Style** to the range **B7:D9**, and then **Decrease Decimal** to zero decimals.

7 **Merge & Center** the first worksheet title over columns **A:D**, and then format the title by changing the **Cell Style** to **Heading 1**. **Merge & Center** the second worksheet title over columns **A:D**, and then format the title by changing the **Cell Style** to **Heading 2**. Select the ranges **A5:D5** and **A6:A10**, and then change the **Cell Style** to **Heading 4**. Change the **Column Width** of columns **A:D** to **15**.

8 Rename the **Sheet1 tab** as **China Expenses** Press Ctrl + Home. In **Backstage** view, click **Show All Properties**. In the **Author** box, type your first name and last name; in the **Subject** box, type your course name and section number; and then in the **Tags** box, type **expense totals Save** your workbook, and then **Close** Excel.

9 In your Word document, press Ctrl + Home. In **Backstage** view, click **Show All Properties**. In the **Author** box, type your first name and last name; in the **Subject** box, type your course name and section number; and then in the **Tags** box, type **China expenses totals Save** your document, and then **Close** Word.

10 Submit your printed or electronic files as directed by your instructor.

END | You have completed Project 1C

Mastering Integration | Project 1D Brazil Proposal

Apply 1B skills from these Objectives:

5 Work with an Existing Word Document

6 Create and Format a Chart in Excel

7 Link Excel Data and an Excel Chart to a Word Document

In the following Mastering Integration project, you will prepare a proposal for Adamantine Jewelry to hire Brazilian designers. Your completed files will look similar to Figure 1.44.

PROJECT FILES

For Project 1D, you will need the following files:

i01D_Brazil_Proposal
i01D_Brazil_Chart

You will save your files as:

Lastname_Firstname_1D_Brazil_Proposal
Lastname_Firstname_1D_Brazil_Chart

PROJECT RESULTS

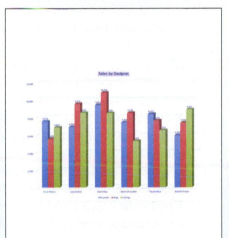
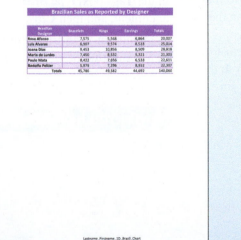

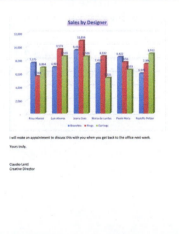

FIGURE 1.44

(Project 1D Brazil Proposal continues on the next page)

Mastering Integration | Project 1D Brazil Proposal (continued)

1 Start Word. Open the document **i01D_Brazil_Proposal**. Display formatting marks. **Save** the document in your **Integrated Projects Chapter 1** folder as **Lastname_Firstname_1D_Brazil_Proposal** Insert the file name in the footer.

2 Click to position the insertion point in the second blank paragraph immediately below the paragraph that begins *Following is a list*. Insert a table that is **4 columns** by **6 rows**, and then type the following data:

Brazilian Designer	Bracelets	Rings	Earrings
Rosa Afonso	No	Yes	Yes
Luis Alvares	Yes	Yes	Yes
Joana Dias	Yes	No	No
Maria de Lurdes	No	Yes	No
Rodolfo Peltier	No	No	Yes

3 Click in the last row of the table, if necessary, and then insert a new row above. Type the following data in the new row:

Paulo Mata	Yes	Yes	Yes

4 Apply the Table Style **Grid Table 5 Dark – Accent 4. AutoFit Contents** to adjust column width, and then **Center** the table between the left and right margins.

5 Start Excel. Open the workbook **i01D_Brazil_Chart. Save** the workbook in your **Integrated Projects Chapter 1** folder as **Lastname_Firstname_1D_Brazil_Chart** Insert the file name in the footer, return to Normal view, and then click cell **A1. Sum** all of the rows in the range **E6:E11. Sum** all of the columns in the range **B12:E12. Merge & Center** the range **A2:E2**. Format the title by changing the **Fill Color** to **Purple, Accent 4**; the

Font Color to **White, Background 1**; the **Font Size** to **18**; and applying **Bold** emphasis.

6 Select the range **A5:D11**. Insert a **3-D Clustered Column** chart on a new sheet, and then insert the file name on the footer of the new sheet named **Designer Sales Chart** Apply **Chart Style 5**. In the chart title, type **Sales by Designer** To the chart title, apply the **Gradient fill, Preset color** format **Light Gradient – Accent 4. Save** your changes.

7 On the **Brazilian Sales** sheet, copy cells **A5:E12**; and then in the Word document, below the Brazilian Designer table, in the blank paragraph, press Enter. **Paste link** the cells. Press Enter three times. In Excel, copy the **Designer Sales Chart** sheet; and then in the Word document, at the top of **page 2**, in the first blank paragraph, paste the chart with the option **Use Destination Theme & Link Data (L)**. Press Enter. **Save** your changes.

8 In Excel, change the *Earrings* sales for *Joana Dias* to **8,509** and then change the *Rings* sales for *Paulo Mata* to **7,656** In your workbook, press Ctrl + Home. In **Backstage** view, click **Show All Properties**. In the **Author** box, type your first name and last name; in the **Subject** box, type your course name and section number; and then in the **Tags** box, type **Brazil, sales Save** your changes, and then **Close** Excel. In your Word document, **Update** the linked Excel data and chart. Press Ctrl + Home. In **Backstage** view, click **Show All Properties**. In the **Author** box, type your first name and last; in the **Subject** box, type your course name and section number; and then in the **Tags** box, type **Brazil, designers Save** your document, and then **Close** Word.

9 Submit your printed or electronic files as directed by your instructor.

END | You have completed Project 1D

Apply a combination of the 1A and 1B skills.

GO! Solve It   Project 1E Website Expansion

PROJECT FILES

For Project 1E, you will need the following files:

i01E_Web_Proposal
i01E_Web_Chart

You will save your files as:

Lastname_Firstname_1E_Web_Proposal
Lastname_Firstname_1E_Web_Chart

Adamantine Jewelry is considering an expansion of the company website to sell more merchandise. Jennifer Bernard, US Sales Director, has asked you to complete the proposal.

From the student files that accompany this chapter, open the **i01E_Web_Chart** file, and then save the Excel workbook in your **Integrated Projects Chapter 1** folder as **Lastname_Firstname_1E_Web_Chart** Complete the Excel worksheet by inserting totals in row 10, merging and centering the titles, and formatting data. Create a 3-D clustered column chart to display the quarterly low end sales, expected sales, and high end sales on a separate sheet with an appropriate sheet name. Modify the chart style and format appropriate chart elements. Insert the file name in the footer, and add appropriate document properties.

(Project 1E Website Expansion continues on the next page)

GO! Solve It | **Project 1E Website Expansion** (continued)

From the student files that accompany this chapter, open the **i01E_Web_Proposal** file, and then save the Word document in your **Integrated Projects Chapter 1** folder as **Lastname_Firstname_1E_Web_Proposal** In the Word document include the linked Excel data and chart. Insert the file name in the footer, and add appropriate document properties. Submit your printed or electronic files as directed by your instructor.

Performance Level

Performance Criteria	Exemplary: You consistently applied the relevant skills.	Proficient: You sometimes, but not always, applied the relevant skills.	Developing: You rarely or never applied the relevant skills.
Complete Excel workbook	Worksheet includes totals, and merged and centered titles, appropriately formatted	Worksheet includes totals, and merged and centered titles, but some elements are incorrect	Worksheet missing totals, merged and centered titles, and formatting
Create column chart	Column chart created on a separate sheet with an appropriate chart style and formatted chart elements	Column chart created, but not formatted correctly	Column chart not created
Excel data and chart linked to Word document	Excel data and chart correctly linked to the Word document	Excel data and chart incorrectly incorporated in the Word document	The data and chart not included in the Word document

END | You have completed Project 1E

OUTCOMES-BASED ASSESSMENTS (CRITICAL THINKING)

RUBRIC

The following outcomes-based assessments are open-ended assessments. That is, there is no specific correct result; your result will depend on your approach to the information provided. Make Professional Quality your goal. Use the following scoring rubric to guide you in how to approach the problem and then to evaluate how well your approach solves the problem.

The *criteria*—Software Mastery, Content, Format and Layout, and Process—represent the knowledge and skills you have gained that you can apply to solving the problem. The *levels of performance*—Professional Quality, Approaching Professional Quality, or Needs Quality Improvements—help you and your instructor evaluate your result.

	Your completed project is of Professional Quality if you:	Your completed project is approaching Professional Quality if you:	Your completed project needs Quality Improvements if you:
1-Software Mastery	Choose and apply the most appropriate skills, tools, and features and identify efficient methods to solve the problem.	Choose and apply some appropriate skills, tools, and features, but not in the most efficient manner.	Choose inappropriate skills, tools, or features, or are inefficient in solving the problem.
2-Content	Construct a solution that is clear and well organized, contains content that is accurate, appropriate to the audience and purpose, and is complete. Provide a solution that contains no errors of spelling, grammar, or style.	Construct a solution in which some components are unclear, poorly organized, inconsistent, or incomplete. Misjudge the needs of the audience. Have some errors in spelling, grammar, or style, but the errors do not detract from comprehension.	Construct a solution that is unclear, incomplete, or poorly organized, contains some inaccurate or inappropriate content, and contains many errors of spelling, grammar, or style. Do not solve the problem.
3-Format and Layout	Format and arrange all elements to communicate information and ideas, clarify function, illustrate relationships, and indicate relative importance.	Apply appropriate format and layout features to some elements, but not others. Overuse features, causing minor distraction.	Apply format and layout that does not communicate information or ideas clearly. Do not use format and layout features to clarify function, illustrate relationships, or indicate relative importance. Use available features excessively, causing distraction.
4-Process	Use an organized approach that integrates planning, development, self-assessment, revision, and reflection.	Demonstrate an organized approach in some areas, but not others; or, use an insufficient process of organization throughout.	Do not use an organized approach to solve the problem.

Apply a combination of the 1A and 1B skills.

GO! Think Project 1F Watch Sales

PROJECT FILES

For Project 1F, you will need the following files:

i01F_Watches_Memo
i01F_Watch_Sales

You will save your files as:

Lastname_Firstname_1F_Watches_Memo
Lastname_Firstname_1F_Watch_Sales

Adamantine Jewelry wants to introduce its fashion watches lines into the Miami, New York City, and San Francisco markets. You have been asked to create a memo that includes charts with sales forecasts, low-end sales, expected sales, and high-end sales that will be sent to all sales representatives from Jennifer Bernard, US Sales Director.

From the student data files that accompany this chapter, open the **i01F_Watches_ Memo** file, and then save the Word document as **Lastname_Firstname_1F_Watches_Memo** In the memo heading, next to FROM:, add your first name and last name as the memo sender. On the blank line below the heading, include a paragraph explaining that the new watch lines have sold well in Europe and will be introduced in the three new markets over the next year. Insert a table, and format the data displayed here:

Introduction Time Line			
Watch Lines	Miami	New York City	San Francisco
Men's Sport	3rd Quarter	1st Quarter	1st Quarter
Men's Fashion	2nd Quarter	3rd Quarter	2nd Quarter
Women's Sport	2nd Quarter	2nd Quarter	1st Quarter
Women's Fashion	2nd Quarter	3rd Quarter	2nd Quarter
Children's Sport	4th Quarter	2nd Quarter	1st Quarter

From the student data files that accompany this chapter, open the **i01F_Watch_Sales** Excel workbook, insert appropriate totals, format the worksheet, and create an Excel chart to display on its own sheet. Save the Excel workbook as **Lastname_Firstname_1F_ Watch_Sales** Paste the Excel chart in the Word document. In both files, insert the file name in the footer and add appropriate document properties. Submit your printed or electronic files as directed by your instructor.

END | You have completed Project 1F

Integrating Word and PowerPoint

PROJECT 2A

OUTCOMES
Create a PowerPoint presentation that includes data imported from a Word document.

OBJECTIVES

1. Create an Outline in Word
2. Import a Word Outline into a PowerPoint Presentation
3. Modify a PowerPoint Presentation
4. Create a Footer and Save a PowerPoint Presentation
5. Preview and Print a Presentation, Slide Handouts, and Speaker's Notes

PROJECT 2B

OUTCOMES
Create a PowerPoint presentation from a template and save it as an RTF file to be modified in Word.

OBJECTIVES

6. Create a PowerPoint Presentation from a Template
7. Save a Presentation as an Outline/RTF File
8. Modify a Word Document in Outline View
9. Create a New Presentation from a Modified Word Outline

Viacheslav Nikolaenko/Shutterstock

In This Chapter

In this chapter, you will create an outline in Word. You can promote and demote the outline levels and move levels from one location to another in the outline. When the outline is imported into PowerPoint, slides are created automatically based on the assigned outline levels. In PowerPoint, you can modify the presentation. You can insert and delete slides, change the slide layout and design themes, and add SmartArt graphics and shapes. Notes can be added to the presentation for the speaker to refer to as the presentation is delivered. In PowerPoint, you will use a template to create a presentation. The preformatted presentation contains fonts, bullets, placeholders, background colors, text, pictures, and shapes, all of which can be modified to better suit your needs. When the presentation is complete, you can save it in the Outline/RTF format in Word.

The projects in this chapter refer to **Skyline Bakery & Café**, a chain of casual dining restaurants and bakeries based in Boston. Each restaurant has its own in-house bakery, which produces a wide variety of high-quality specialty breads, breakfast sweets, and desserts. Breads and sweets are sold by counter service along with gourmet teas, fresh juices, and sodas. The full-service restaurant area features a menu of sandwiches, salads, soups, and light entrees. Fresh, high-quality ingredients and a professional and courteous staff are the hallmarks of every Skyline Bakery & Café.

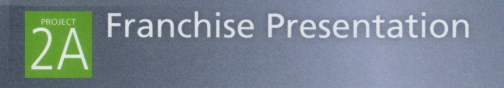
PROJECT ACTIVITIES

In Activities 2.01 through 2.13, you will create a Word outline for Samir Taheri, the CEO of Skyline Bakery & Café. He has decided to expand the company by offering franchise locations to interested chefs and businesspeople. You will open and modify a Word document, and then import the Word document into PowerPoint. You will modify the PowerPoint presentation by inserting slides, changing slide layouts, and changing the design theme. You will also create speaker's notes to accompany the slides. Your completed files will look similar to Figure 2.1.

PROJECT FILES

For Project 2A, you will need the following files:

New blank PowerPoint presentation
i02A_Franchisee_Information

You will save your files as:

Lastname_Firstname_2A_Franchisee_Information
Lastname_Firstname_2A_Franchisee_Presentation

PROJECT RESULTS

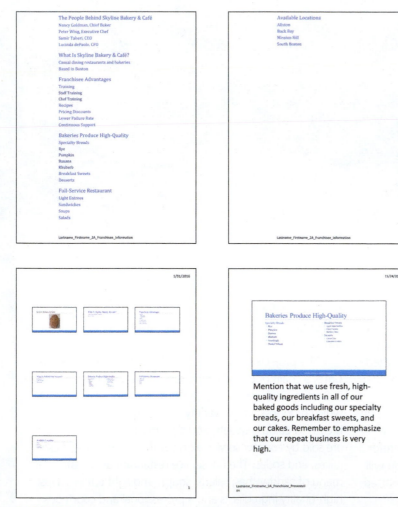

FIGURE 2.1 Project 2A Franchise Presentation

In Word, Outline view shows the headings of a document as a representation of their level in the document structure. The outline can be collapsed to make it easier to view and reorganize the levels, or it can be expanded to view all levels. Many students find Word to be an easy program to learn. Students find that they can create and modify a Word document quickly, and then they can import the Word document into another software application such as PowerPoint. PowerPoint will use the outline levels to set up the slides in a presentation.

Activity 2.01 | Changing to Outline View in Word

1 Start Word, and then navigate to the location of the student files for this chapter. Locate and open the file **i02A_Franchisee_Information**. Display formatting marks and the rulers if they are not visible.

2 Click the **File tab** to display **Backstage** view, and click **Save As**. Navigate to the location where you are saving your files for this chapter, and then on the toolbar, click **New folder**. Type **Integrated Projects Chapter 2** and then press Enter two times. In the **File name** box, select the existing text, type **Lastname_Firstname_2A_Franchisee_Information** and then click **Save**.

3 On the **Insert tab**, in the **Header & Footer group**, click **Footer**, and then click **Edit Footer**. On the **Design tab**, in the **Insert group**, click **Document Info**, and then click **File Name**. Double-click in the document to exit the footer area.

4 Click the **View tab,** and then in the **Views group**, click **Outline** to display the document in Outline view. Compare your screen with Figure 2.2.

Outline view is a document view that shows headings and subheadings, which can be expanded or collapsed. Each paragraph is treated as a separate topic or level in the outline. All paragraphs are preceded by an *outline symbol*—a small gray circle that identifies heading and body text paragraphs in an outline. In Outline view, the Outlining tab displays on the ribbon.

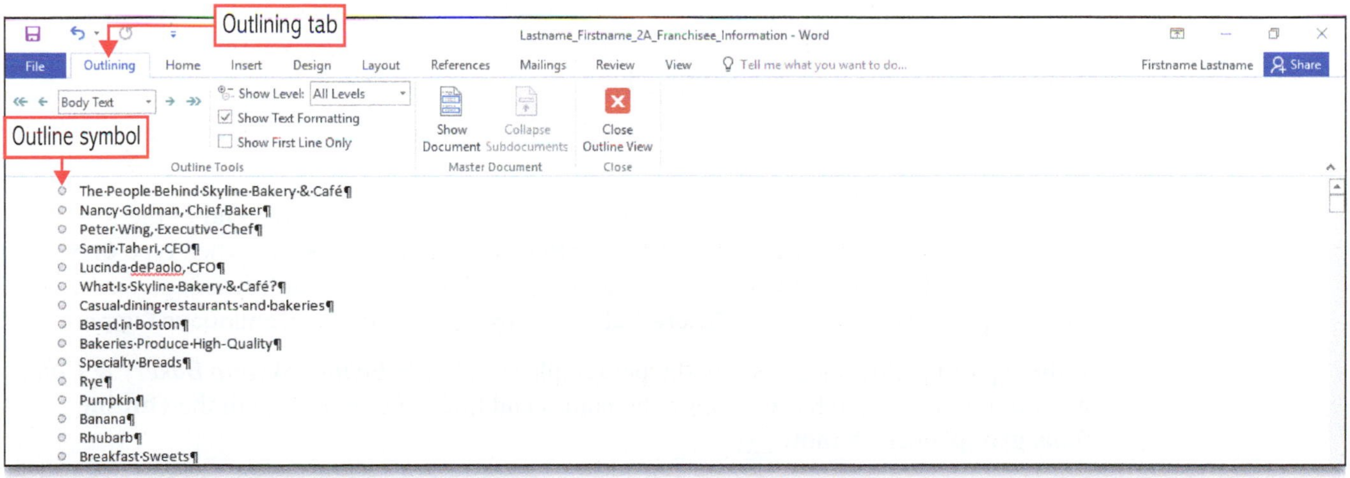

FIGURE 2.2

5 If necessary, on the status bar, use the **Zoom slider** ‖———‖———+ to adjust the zoom level to **100%**.

Zooming is the action of increasing or decreasing the viewing area on the screen.

6 **Save** 🖫 the document.

Activity 2.02 | Promoting and Demoting Levels in an Outline

In Outline view, levels are identified in a document, and you can promote or demote a level by using the Outline tools.

1 At the beginning of the document, move the pointer to the left of the first paragraph, *The People Behind Skyline Bakery & Café*. When the ⇗ pointer displays, click one time to select the paragraph. On the **Outlining tab**, in the **Outline Tools group**, click **Promote to Heading 1** ⏪. Compare your screen with Figure 2.3.

The first paragraph is formatted with the built-in Level 1 style, the highest outline level. A ***plus outline symbol*** displays to the left of the paragraph indicating there are subordinate heading or body text paragraphs.

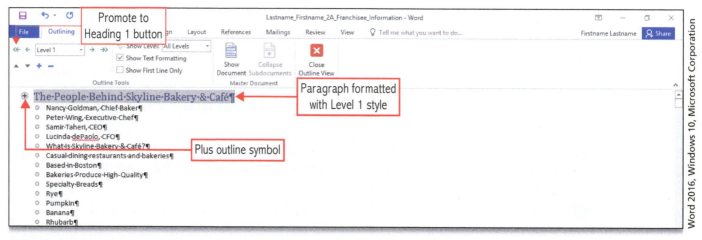

FIGURE 2.3

2 Select the sixth paragraph, *What Is Skyline Bakery & Café?*, and then click **Promote to Heading 1** ⏪.

3 Select the paragraph *Bakeries Produce High-Quality*. Hold down Ctrl, and then select the following paragraphs: *Full-Service Restaurant*, *Franchisee Advantages*, and *Available Locations*. Click **Promote to Heading 1** ⏪.

The four paragraphs are formatted with the Level 1 style. You can hold down Ctrl to select multiple items and then promote or demote them all at once.

4 Near the end of the document, click to position the insertion point to the end of the paragraph *Training*, and then press Enter. Type **Staff Training** press Enter, and then type **Chef Training** Click to position the insertion point to the end of the paragraph *Pricing Discounts*, and then press Enter. Type **Lower Failure Rate** press Enter, and then type **Continuous Support**

5 At the top of the document, below the paragraph *The People Behind Skyline Bakery & Café*, select the four paragraphs containing the names and titles of employees. In the **Outline Tools group**, click **Demote** ➡.

The four paragraphs are demoted to the Level 2 style. A ***minus outline symbol*** displays, indicating there are no subordinate heading or body text paragraphs.

6 Below the paragraph *What Is Skyline Bakery & Café?*, select the next two paragraphs, and then press Tab.

The paragraphs are demoted to the Level 2 style. At the beginning of a paragraph, you can press Tab to demote a paragraph. Pressing Shift + Tab will promote a paragraph.

7 Below the paragraph *Bakeries Produce High-Quality*, select the seven paragraphs listing the baked goods. Hold down Ctrl. Below *Full-Service Restaurant*, select the next four paragraphs; below *Franchisee Advantages*, select the next seven paragraphs; and then below *Available Locations*, select the remaining four paragraphs. Release Ctrl, and then in the **Outline Tools group**, click **Demote** →.

8 Locate the Level 1 heading *Franchisee Advantages*. Below the Level 2 heading *Training*, select the two paragraphs *Staff Training* and *Chef Training*, and then click **Demote** →.

The two paragraphs are demoted to the Level 3 style.

9 Locate the Level 1 heading *Bakeries Produce High-Quality*. Below the Level 2 heading *Specialty Breads*, select the four paragraphs *Rye*, *Pumpkin*, *Banana*, and *Rhubarb*, and then click **Demote** →. Compare your screen with Figure 2.4.

FIGURE 2.4

10 Save 🖫 the document.

Activity 2.03 │ Moving Outline Levels in Word

In Outline view, you can collapse the entire document or parts of a document to see an overview of the document. When parts of the document are collapsed, it is easy to move or delete sections of the document.

1 To the left of the paragraph *Franchisee Advantages*, click the **plus outline symbol**.

This action selects the Level 1 heading and all the subtopics.

2 On the **Outlining tab**, in the **Outline Tools group**, click **Collapse** – two times.

Collapsing an outline level *hides* all subordinate heading and body text paragraphs. In this case, you must click twice to hide both the Level 2 and Level 3 headings.

3 To the left of the paragraph *Franchisee Advantages*, click the **plus outline symbol**. Hold down the left mouse button and drag the paragraph up above the paragraph *Full-Service Restaurant* until a black horizontal line displays, as shown in Figure 2.5, and then release the mouse button.

Dragging a paragraph in Outline view causes a horizontal line to display.

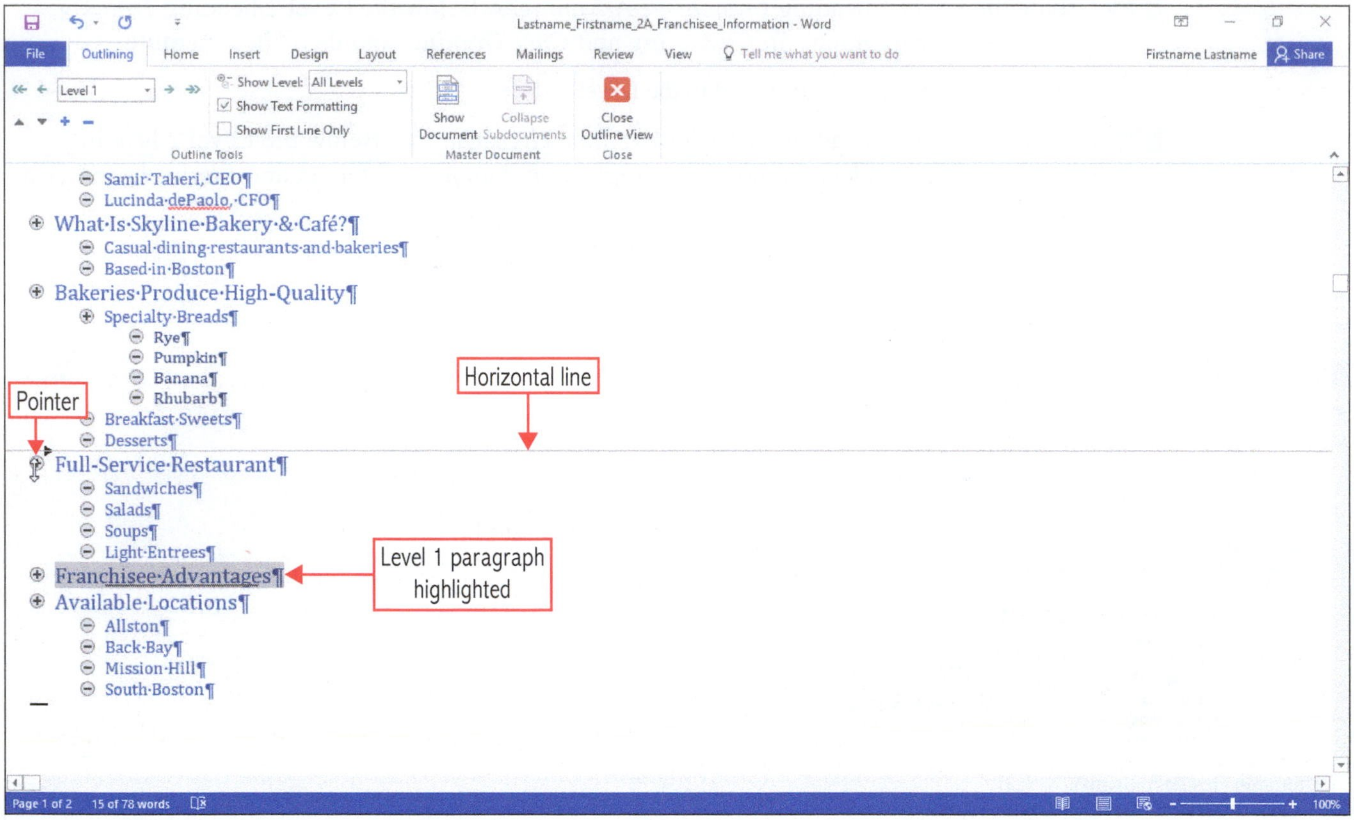

Word 2016, Windows 10, Microsoft Corporation

FIGURE 2.5

4 Using the technique you just practiced, drag *Franchisee Advantages* up until the black horizontal line is above the paragraph *Bakeries Produce High-Quality*, and then release the mouse button.

The selected Level 1 paragraph and all of its subtopics are moved.

5 With the paragraph *Franchisee Advantages* still selected, in the **Outline Tools group**, click **Expand** [+] two times to display the sublevels.

6 Below the Level 1 heading *Full-Service Restaurant*, to the left of the paragraph *Light Entrees*, click the **minus outline symbol**. In the **Outline Tools group**, click **Move Up** [▲] three times.

This action moves the paragraph above the other three Level 2 paragraphs below the Level 1 heading.

7 To the left of the paragraph *Salads*, click the **minus outline symbol**, and then in the **Outline Tools group**, click **Move Down** [▼] one time. Compare your screen with Figure 2.6.

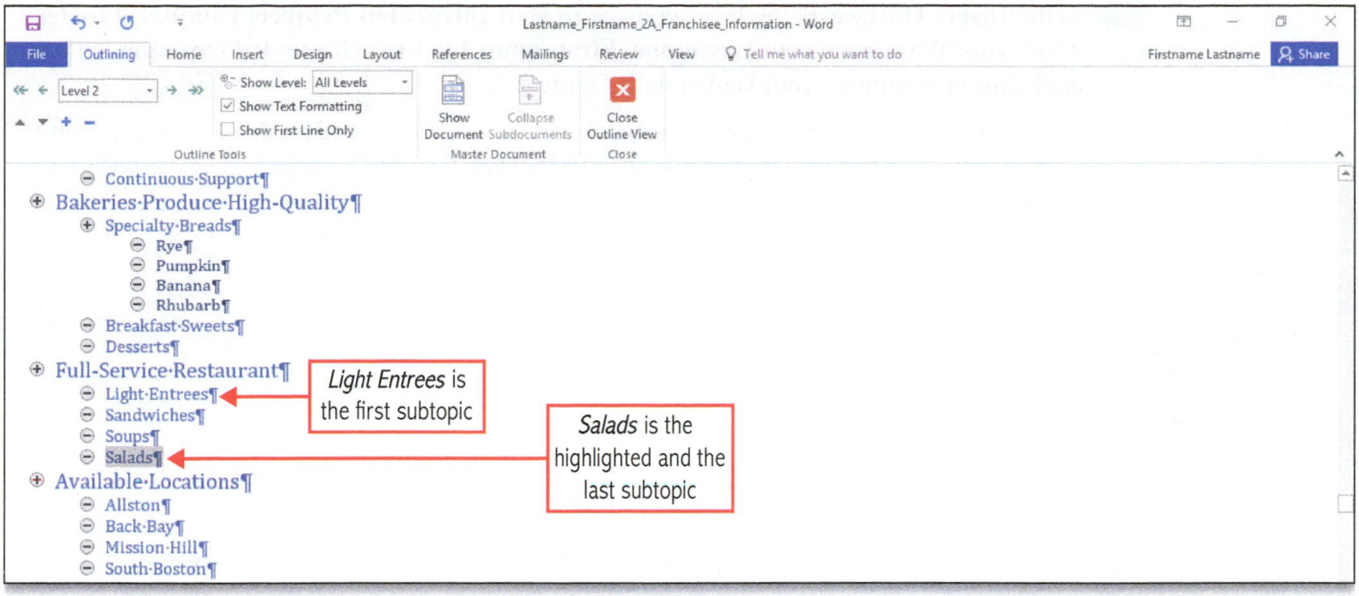

Light Entrees is the first subtopic

Salads is the highlighted and the last subtopic

FIGURE 2.6

8 Click the **File tab** to display **Backstage** view. With the **Info tab** selected, in the lower right corner, click **Show All Properties**. Under **Related People**, be sure your name displays as the **Author**—change it if necessary. Click to the right of **Subject**, and type your course name and section number. Click to the right of **Tags**, and then type **franchisee, outline**

9 **Save** 💾 your document. Print or submit this Word document electronically as directed by your instructor.

10 **Close** ☒ Word.

Objective 2 | Import a Word Outline into a PowerPoint Presentation

You can import a Word outline into PowerPoint to automatically create slides. Each Word paragraph formatted with Level 1 will become the title of a new PowerPoint slide. Each Word paragraph formatted with Level 2 will become a bullet point on a PowerPoint slide.

Activity 2.04 | Importing a Word Outline into a PowerPoint Presentation

1 Start PowerPoint, and then click **Blank Presentation**. If necessary, on the **View tab**, in the **Show group**, select the **Ruler** check box.

2 On the **Home tab**, in the **Slides group**, click the **New Slide button arrow**, and then below the gallery, click **Slides from Outline**.

3 In the **Insert Outline** dialog box, navigate to your **Integrated Projects Chapter 2** folder, select your Word document **Lastname_Firstname_2A_Franchisee_Information**, and then click **Insert**. Compare your screen with Figure 2.7.

PowerPoint creates seven slides based on the outline levels you designated in your Word outline. Heading 1 style paragraphs display as the title for each slide. Subordinate paragraphs display as bulleted items.

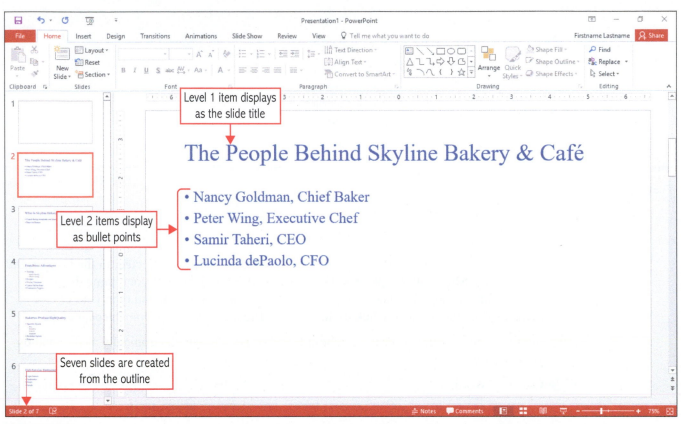

FIGURE 2.7

4 From **Backstage** view, click **Save As**, and then click **Browse** to display the **Save As** dialog box. Navigate to your **Integrated Projects Chapter 2** folder. **Save** the file as **Lastname_Firstname_2A_Franchisee_Presentation**

5 On the **View tab**, in the **Presentation Views group**, click **Outline View** to view your imported Word outline on the left. Compare your screen with Figure 2.8, and then take a moment to study the table in Figure 2.9.

Normal view is the primary editing view in PowerPoint where you write and design your presentation. Outline view is useful to edit and move between your slides in the Outline pane.

FIGURE 2.8

PowerPoint 2016, Windows 10, Microsoft Corporation

MICROSOFT POWERPOINT SCREEN ELEMENTS	
SCREEN ELEMENT	**DESCRIPTION**
Slide pane	Displays a large image of the active slide.
Left pane	Displays either the presentation outline or all of the slides in the presentation in the form of thumbnails.
Notes pane	Displays below the Slide pane and allows you to type notes regarding the active slide.
Status bar	A horizontal bar at the bottom of the presentation window that displays the current slide number, number of slides in a presentation, the applied theme, View buttons, Zoom slider, and Fit slide to current window button.
View buttons	A set of commands that control the look of the presentation window.

FIGURE 2.9

6 ▶ On the **View tab**, in the **Presentation Views group**, click **Normal** to return to the slide thumbnails.

More Knowledge   **Using Body Text in an Outline**

As you create your Word outline for the purpose of creating PowerPoint slides, be sure to apply heading styles to all paragraphs, because regular body text paragraphs will not display in the slides after importing.

In PowerPoint, you start with a basic design, and then you can modify a presentation by inserting and deleting slides, modifying the slide layout, and changing the design theme and color to give the presentation a professional appearance.

Activity 2.05 | Inserting and Deleting Slides

Slide layouts may contain a *placeholder*, which is a slide element that reserves a portion of a slide and serves as a container for text, graphics, and other slide elements.

1 ▶ From the slide thumbnails on the left, click **Slide 1** to make it the active slide. In the **Slide pane**, click in the text *Click to add title*, which forms the title placeholder, and then type **Skyline Bakery & Caf** being careful not to type the final *e*.

2 ▶ Click the **Insert tab**, and then in the **Symbols group**, click **Symbol**. In the **Symbol** dialog box, click the **Font arrow**, scroll to the top of the list, and then click **(normal text)**. Locate and click the symbol **é**. Click **Insert**, and then click **Close**. Compare your screen with Figure 2.10.

The name of the bakery, including the *é*, displays on the first slide. You should insert this symbol any time you type the bakery name in this instruction.

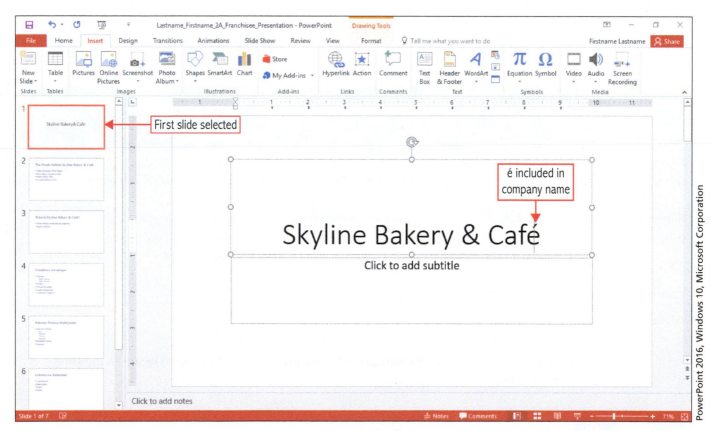

FIGURE 2.10

3 ▶ From the slide thumbnails on the left, click **Slide 2**—*The People Behind Skyline Bakery & Café*—and then press [Delete].

This action deletes Slide 2 so that Slide 3 becomes the new Slide 2, and all subsequent slides are automatically renumbered for a total of six slides in the presentation.

4 ▶ Display **Slide 3**—*Franchisee Advantages*. Click the **Home tab**, and then in the **Slides group**, click the upper portion of the **New Slide** button to insert a new slide using the same layout.

> A new Slide 4 is added below the current slide; all subsequent slides are automatically renumbered.

5 ▶ On **Slide 4**—the new slide—click the title placeholder, and then type **What Is Behind Our Success?** Click in the text *Click to add text*—the content placeholder—and then type **Excellent food** Press ⏎, and then type **Exceptional people** Press ⏎, and then type **Great ambiance**

> The text you typed displays as a bulleted list.

6 ▶ **Save** 💾 the presentation.

Activity 2.06 │ Changing Slide Layouts

1 ▶ Display **Slide 5**—*Bakeries Produce High-Quality*. On the **Home tab**, in the **Slides group**, click **Layout**, and then click **Two Content**. Compare your screen with Figure 2.11.

> A new content placeholder displays to the right of the existing placeholder.

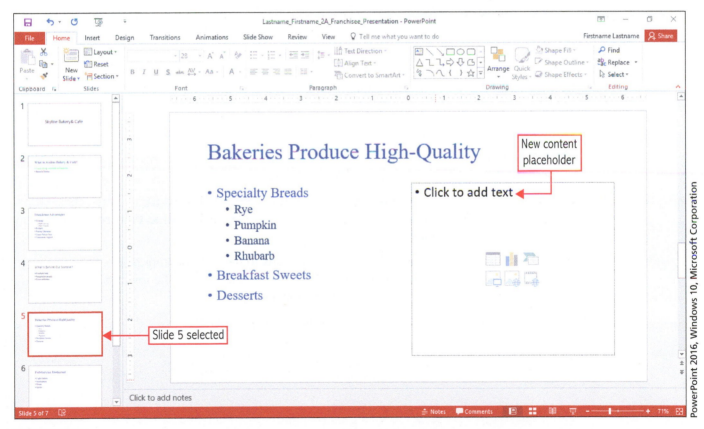

FIGURE 2.11

2 ▶ In the left placeholder, select the last two bullet points, *Breakfast Sweets* and *Desserts*. Point to the selection, hold down the left mouse button, and drag the selection to the top of the right placeholder—*Click to add text*. Release the mouse button.

> The two bullet points are moved to the right placeholder.

3 ▶ Click at the end of the paragraph *Breakfast Sweets*, press [Enter], and then press [Tab]. Type **Apple Spice Muffins** and then press [Enter]. Compare your screen with Figure 2.12.

Pressing [Tab] at the beginning of a bullet point increases the indent.

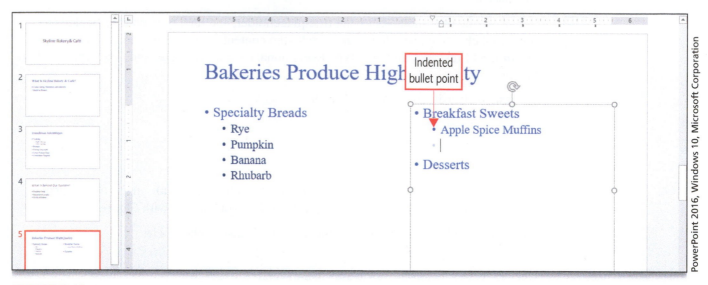

FIGURE 2.12

4 ▶ Type **Cherry Scones** press [Enter], and then type **Blueberry Bars**

5 ▶ Click at the end of the bullet point *Desserts*. Press [Enter], and then press [Tab]. Type **Carrot Cake** press [Enter], and then type **Chocolate Cookies**

6 ▶ In the left placeholder, click at the end of the bullet point *Rhubarb*, and then press [Enter]. Type **Sourdough** press [Enter], and then type **Dusted Wheat**

7 ▶ Display **Slide 1**. On the **Home tab**, in the **Slides group**, click **Layout**, and then click **Title and Content**. In the content placeholder below the title, click **Online Pictures** 🖼 to display the **Insert Pictures** dialog box.

8 ▶ With the insertion point blinking in the search box to the right of *Bing Image Search*, type **bakery** and press [Enter]. Click an image of baked items, and then in the lower right corner, click **Insert**. Compare your screen with Figure 2.13.

The picture displays in the center of the placeholder and is selected.

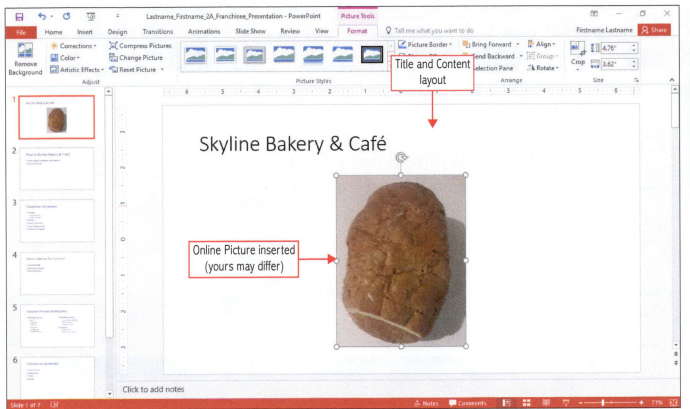

FIGURE 2.13

PowerPoint 2016, Windows 10, Microsoft Corporation

9 ▶ **Save** 🖫 the presentation.

Activity 2.07 | Changing the Design Theme

You can format an entire PowerPoint presentation quickly by applying a document *theme*, which is a predefined set of colors, fonts, lines, and fill effects that are professionally designed.

1 ▶ Click **Slide 1** to deselect the image. Click the **Design tab**, and then in the **Themes group**, click **More** ⊽. In the **Themes** gallery, under **Office**, point to several different themes and use Live Preview to view how the slides will display. Notice that ScreenTips display the name of the theme. Locate and click **Retrospect**.

2 ▶ In the **Variants group**, click **More** ⊽, and then click the variant with a blue band at the bottom. Notice that the presentation color scheme is changed, as shown in Figure 2.14.

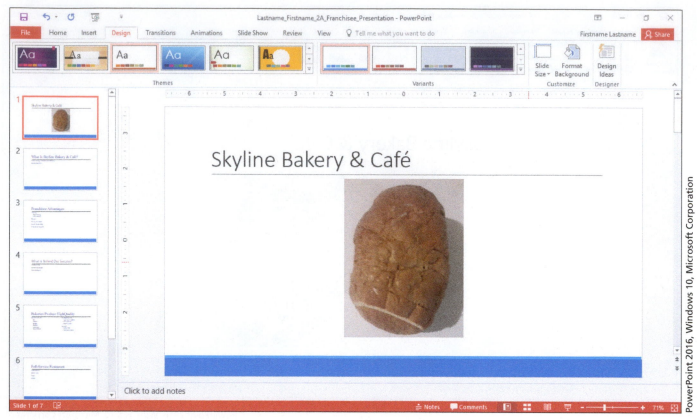

FIGURE 2.14

> **3** **Save** 🖫 the presentation.

Activity 2.08 | Adding Speaker's Notes

On individual slides, you can insert *speaker's notes*—notes that display under a slide to which the speaker can refer as he or she is delivering the presentation. The audience will not view the speaker's notes unless they are printed on the handouts.

> **1** Display **Slide 2**—*What Is Skyline Bakery & Café?*—to make it the active slide. At the lower edge of the screen, on the **Status Bar**, click **Notes** to display the Notes pane below the slide. Click in the **Notes pane**, and then type **Introduce Samir Taheri, our Chief Executive Officer, and Lucinda dePaolo, our Chief Financial Officer.**

> **2** Display **Slide 5**—*Bakeries Produce High-Quality*. Click the **View tab**, and then in the **Presentation Views group**, click **Notes Page**. Below the slide, click in the **Notes pane**, and then type **Mention that we use fresh, high-quality ingredients in all of our baked goods including our specialty breads, our breakfast sweets, and our cakes. Remember to emphasize that our repeat business is very high.**

> In *Notes Page view* you can work with your notes in a full page format. Speaker's notes are printed in this format; that is, with a copy of the slide at the top of the page and the speaker's notes at the bottom of the page.

> **3** In the **Notes pane**, select the text. On the mini toolbar, click the **Font Size button arrow** 🔲, and then click **28**. Click anywhere on the page to deselect the text, and then compare your screen with Figure 2.15.

> The presenter will refer to the notes during the slide show. A large font size makes the notes easier to read, especially in low light conditions.

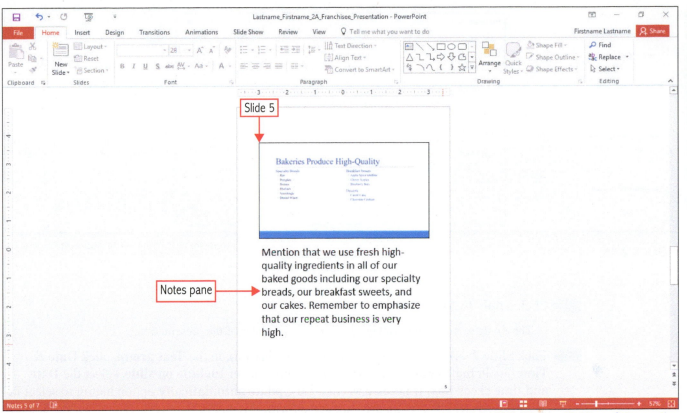

FIGURE 2.15

PowerPoint 2016, Windows 10, Microsoft Corporation

4 Below the vertical scroll bar, locate and then click **Next Slide** ▾ to make **Slide 6—** *Full-Service Restaurant*—the active slide. Click in the **Notes pane**, and then type **Mention that Nancy Goldman, our Chief Baker, trains our chefs. Introduce Nancy to the group.**

5 Using the technique you practiced in Step 3, change the **Font Size** of the note to **28**.

6 On the **View tab**, in the **Presentation Views group**, click **Normal**, and then **Save** 🖫 the presentation.

Objective 4 | Create a Footer and Save a PowerPoint Presentation

You can print your PowerPoint presentation as slides, handouts, notes pages, or in Outline view. Depending on how you are planning to print the presentation, you may want to add footers to these different views. When the footer is created, it can be added to one slide or applied to all the slides in the presentation.

Activity 2.09 | Inserting a Footer in a Presentation

1 Click the **Insert tab**, and then in the **Text group**, click **Header & Footer**. In the **Header and Footer** dialog box, on the **Slide tab**, under **Include on slide**, select the **Slide number** check box. Select the **Footer** check box, and then in the **Footer** box, using your own name, type **Lastname_Firstname_2A_Franchisee_Presentation** Compare your screen with Figure 2.16.

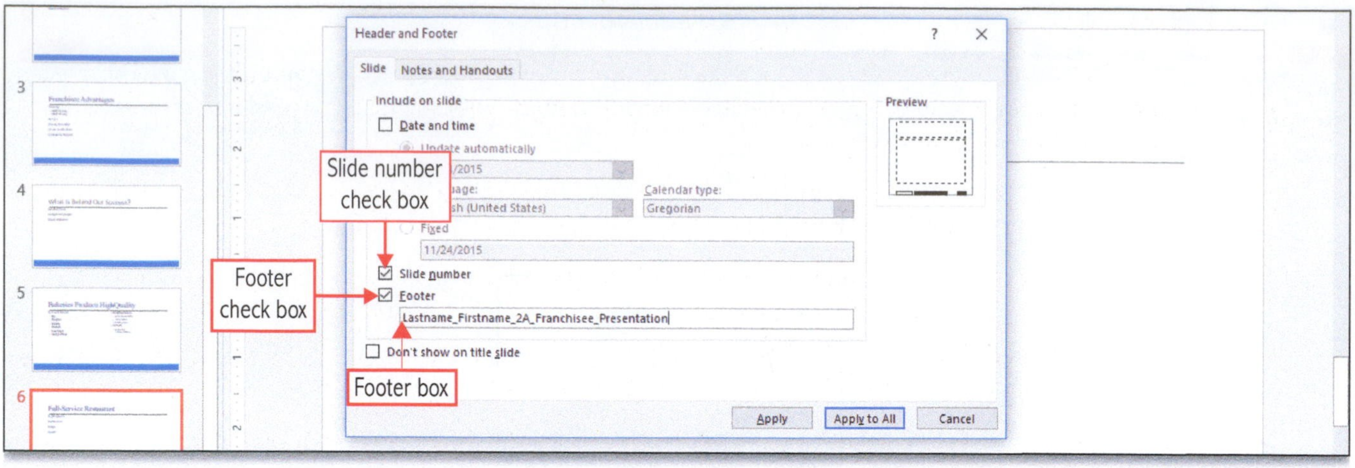

FIGURE 2.16

PowerPoint 2016, Windows 10, Microsoft Corporation

2 Click **Apply to All**.

The *Apply to All* option displays the footer on all slides of the presentation.

3 Click **Slide 7**—*Available Locations*. On the **Insert tab**, in the **Text group**, click **Date & Time**. In the **Header and Footer** dialog box, under **Include on slide**, select the **Date and time** check box. If necessary, click the **Update automatically** option button to select it. Click **Apply**, and then compare your screen with Figure 2.17.

The Apply button displays the date in the footer only on the selected slide. The Update automatically option causes the date to be updated to the current date each time the presentation is opened.

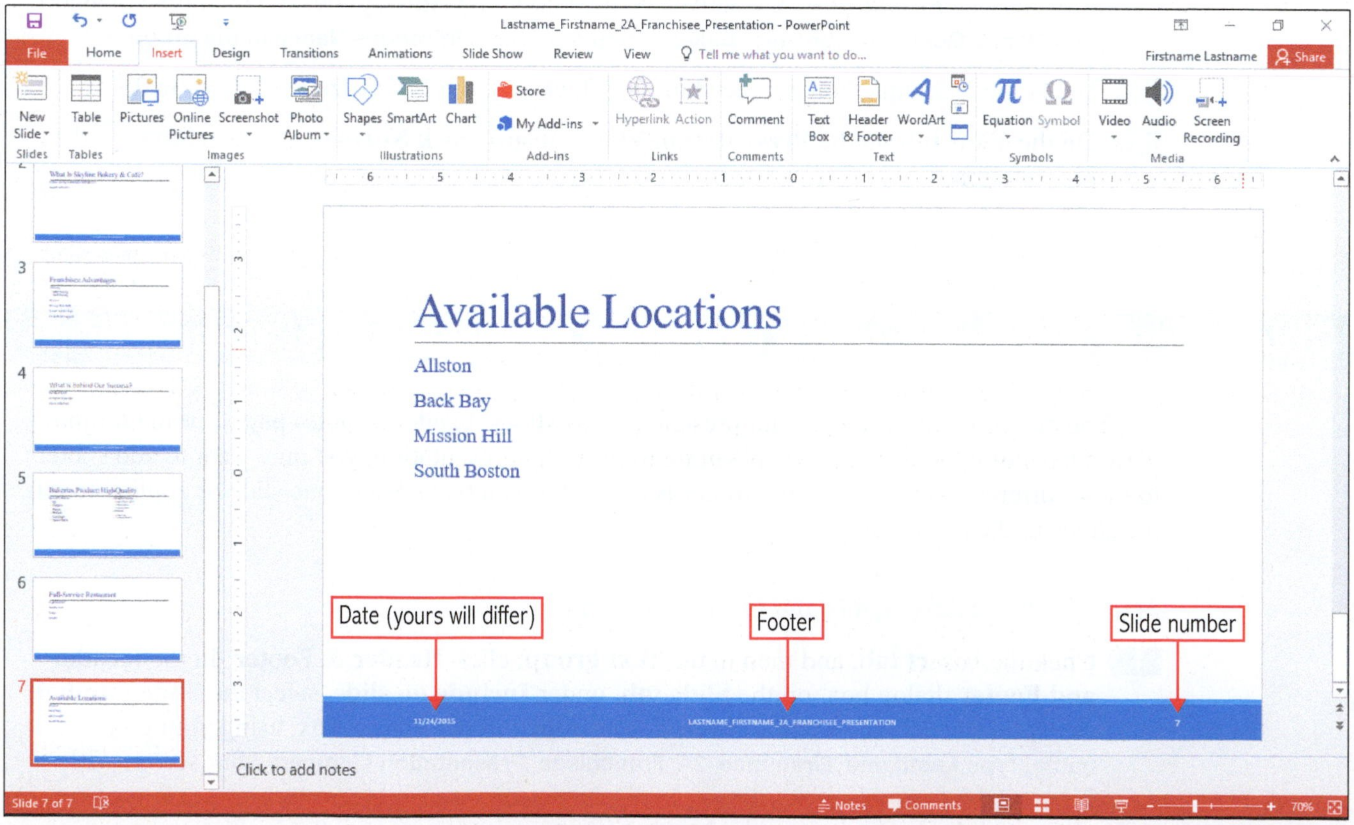

FIGURE 2.17

PowerPoint 2016, Windows 10, Microsoft Corporation

Activity 2.10 | Inserting a Footer in Slide Handouts

Your presentation can be printed as a handout. If you print and distribute copies of the handout, your audience can follow along as you deliver your presentation and can also save the presentation for future reference.

1 On the **Insert tab**, in the **Text group**, click **Header & Footer**. In the **Header and Footer** dialog box, click the **Notes and Handouts tab**.

2 Under **Include on page**, select the **Date and time** check box, and then click the **Fixed** option button. If necessary, insert the current date if it does not display.

> Each time you open the presentation, a fixed date will remain as the date entered in the Fixed box and display on the handout. By default the Page number check box is selected.

3 Select the **Footer** check box, and then in the **Footer** box, using your own name, type **Lastname_Firstname_2A_Franchisee_Presentation** Compare your screen with Figure 2.18.

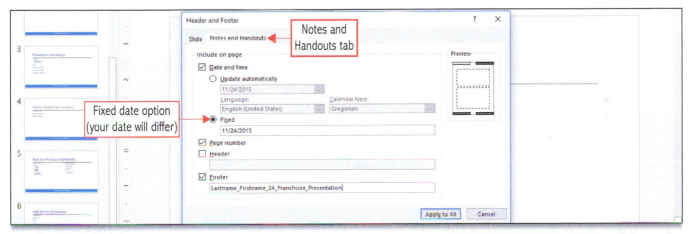

FIGURE 2.18

PowerPoint 2016, Windows 10, Microsoft Corporation

4 Click **Apply to All**, and then **Save** 🖫 the presentation.

Objective 5 | Preview and Print a Presentation, Slide Handouts, and Speaker's Notes

Previewing your presentation as a slide show should always be part of your preparation process so that you can see how your graphics and effects will look during the actual presentation. The PowerPoint presentation, slide handouts, and speaker's notes can all be previewed before printing.

Activity 2.11 | Previewing and Printing a Presentation

1 Display **Slide 3**, select the text *Franchisee Advantages*, and then on the mini toolbar, click **Format Painter** 🖌. In the thumbnails on the left, click **Slide 4**, and then drag to select the text *What Is Behind Our Success?* to copy the format.

2 Display **Slide 3**, select the text *Recipes*, and then on the mini toolbar, double-click **Format Painter** 🖌. In the thumbnails on the left, click **Slide 4**, and then drag to select the first item, and then the second item, and then the third item to copy the format. Press [Esc] to cancel the Format Painter.

3 ▶ Display **Slide 1**. Click the **Slide Show tab**, and then in the **Start Slide Show group**, click **From Beginning** to open Slide Show view.

In *Slide Show view*, the slides fill the screen, which enables you to view your presentation the way your audience will see it.

4 ▶ Click the left mouse button to advance to the second slide.

⟳ **ANOTHER WAY**   Press [Spacebar], [Enter], or [↓] to advance to the next slide.

5 ▶ Continue to click to advance through the slides. When a black slide displays, click one more time to display the presentation in Normal view.

After the last slide in a presentation, a *black slide* displays, indicating that the presentation is over.

6 ▶ Click the **File tab** to display **Backstage** view, and then click the **Print tab**. Under **Settings**, in the **Slides** box, type **3** and then compare your screen with Figure 2.19. Note: If you do not have a color printer connected to your computer, the Print Preview will display in grayscale.

The *Custom Range* option enables you to indicate what slides to print. Because you typed 3, only Slide 3 will print. The default setting—*Full Page Slides*—will print each slide on a separate page. The Print Preview of Slide 3 displays on the right.

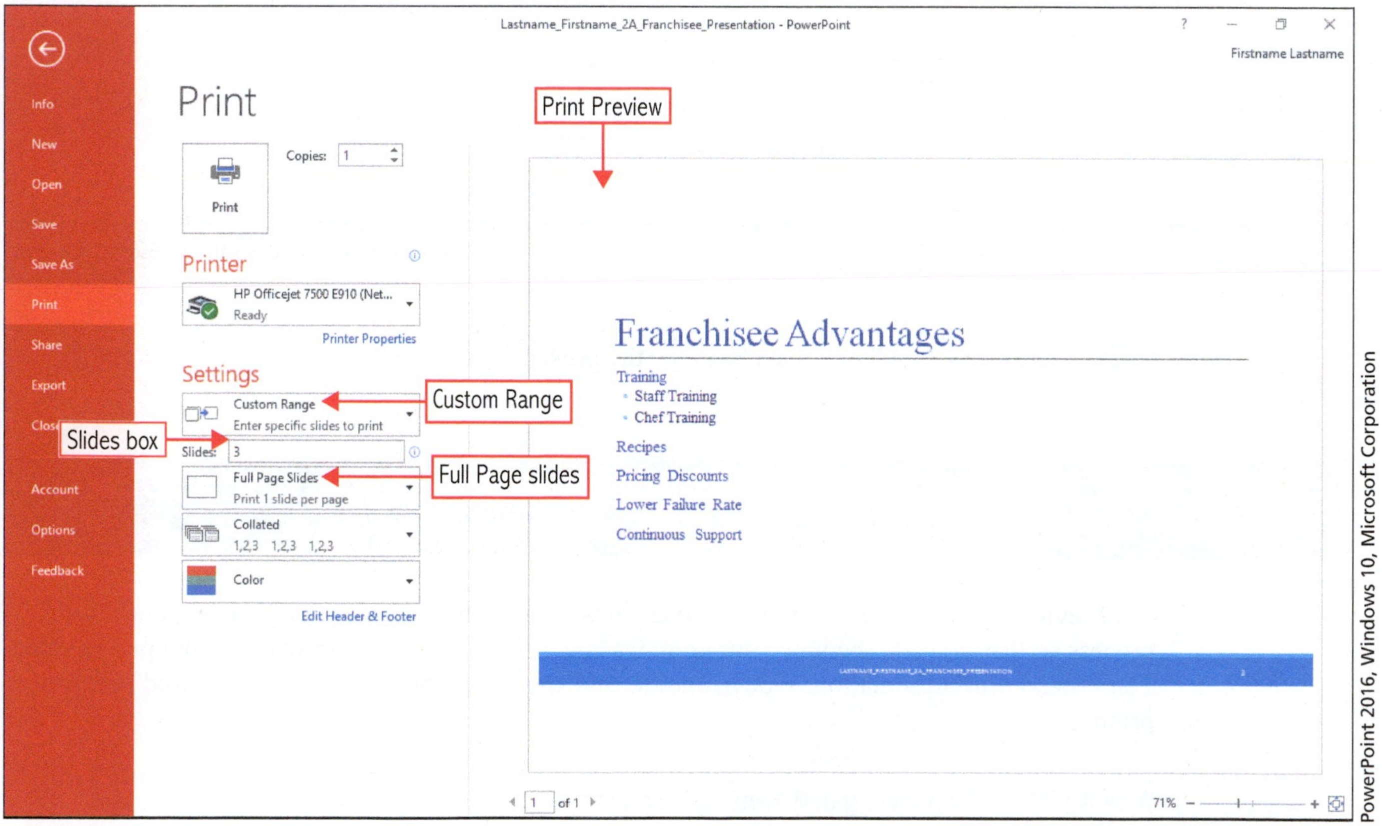

FIGURE 2.19

7 ▶ Under **Print**, in the **Copies** box, verify that **1** displays.

Activity 2.12 | Previewing and Printing Slide Handouts

1 Under **Settings**, click **Custom Range**, and then click **Print All Slides**. Click **Full Page Slides**, and then under **Handouts**, click **9 Slides Horizontal**.

The setting *9 Slides Horizontal* will print nine slides on a single page, with slides 1, 2, and 3 displayed in the first row. Because your presentation only has seven slides, all seven slides will print on one page.

2 Print the single page of handouts, or submit electronically as directed by your instructor.

Activity 2.13 | Previewing and Printing Speaker's Notes

Speaker's notes are referenced by the speaker during a presentation. When you print speaker's notes, the slide prints on the top half of the page, and the notes print on the bottom half of the page.

1 Display **Backstage** view and then click **Print**. Under **Settings**, click **9 Slides Horizontal**, and then under **Print Layout**, click **Notes Pages**.

2 At the bottom of the **Print Preview**, click **Next Page** ▶ four times so that **Page 5** displays.

Indicated below the Notes page are the current slide number and the number of pages that will print when Notes Pages is selected. You can use the Next Page and Previous Page arrows to display each Notes page in the presentation.

3 In the **Slides** box, type **5** and then compare your screen with Figure 2.20.

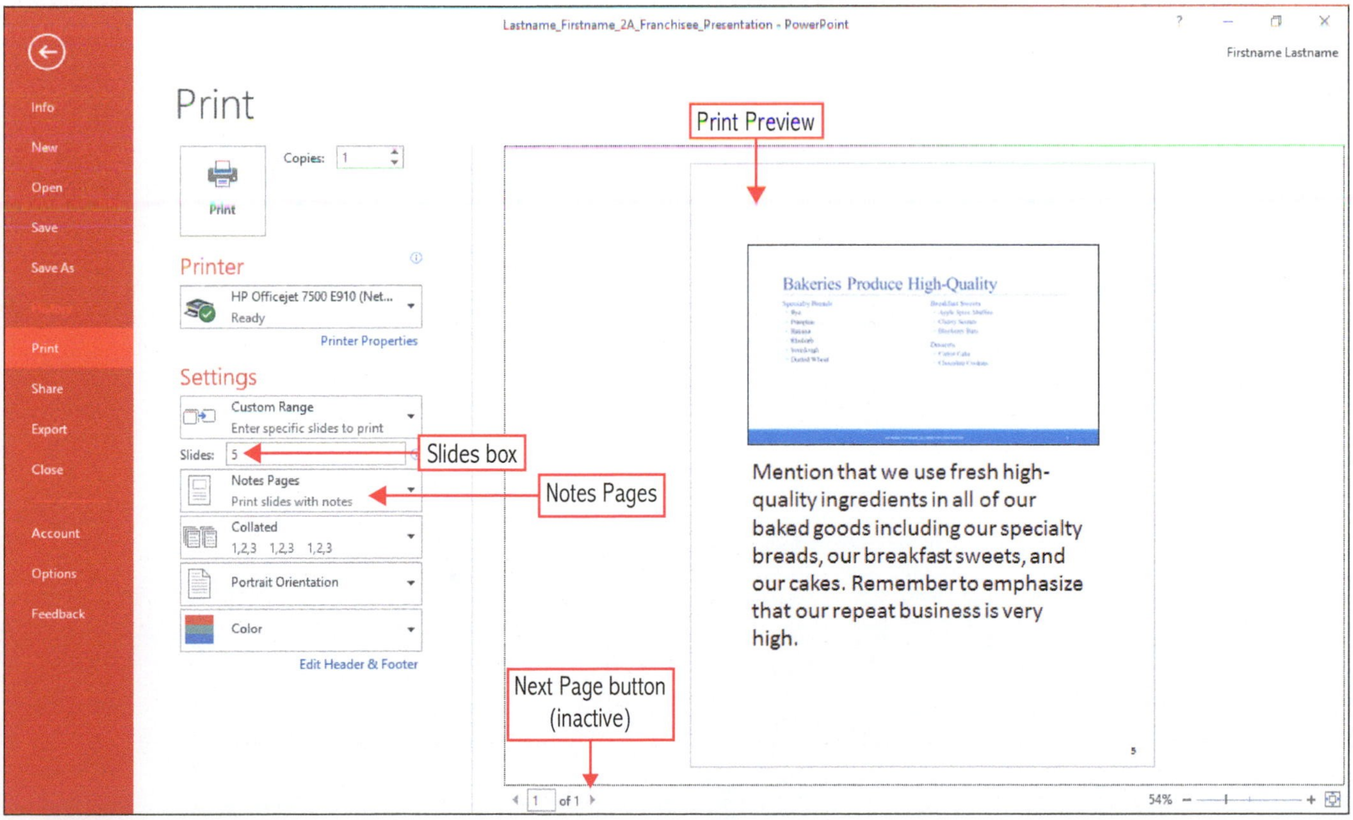

FIGURE 2.20

PowerPoint 2016, Windows 10, Microsoft Corporation

4 If directed by your instructor, print this single slide with its speaker's note.

5 In **Backstage** view, click the **Info tab**. In the lower right corner, click **Show All Properties**. Under **Related People**, be sure your name displays as the **Author**—change it if necessary. Click to the right of **Subject**, and then type your course name and section number. Click to the right of **Tags**, and then type **franchisee, outline**

6 **Save** 💾 the presentation, and then **Close** ☒ PowerPoint. Submit your printed or electronic files as directed by your instructor.

> **END | You have completed Project 2A**

Restaurant Presentation

PROJECT ACTIVITIES

In Activities 2.14 through 2.23, you will create a PowerPoint presentation from a template. You will modify the presentation by changing character spacing, adding a text shadow, and inserting shapes and pictures. You will save the presentation in Rich Text Format, and then open the file in Word. You will modify the Word document in Outline view and then create a new presentation from the modified outline. Your completed Word document and the two PowerPoint presentations will look similar to Figure 2.21.

PROJECT FILES

For Project 2B, you will need the following files:

New blank PowerPoint presentation
i02B_Skyline_Template
i02B_Bakery1
i02B_Bakery2
i02B_Bakery3
i02B_Entree1
i02B_Entree2
i02B_Entree3
i02B_Taheri

You will save your files as:

Lastname_Firstname_2B_Restaurant_Presentation
Lastname_Firstname_2B_Menu_Outline
Lastname_Firstname_2B_Menu_Presentation

PROJECT RESULTS

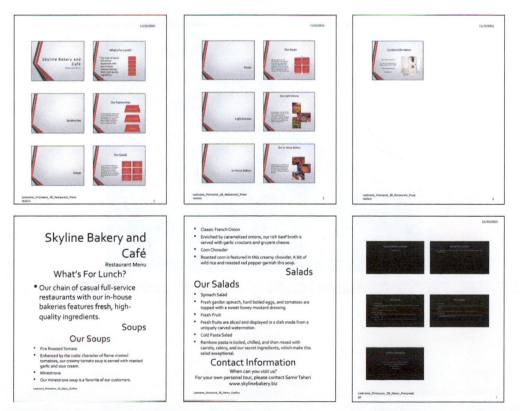

FIGURE 2.21 Project 2B Restaurant Presentation

Objective 6 | Create a PowerPoint Presentation from a Template

A PowerPoint template is a preformatted presentation containing a pre-determined size and type of fonts and bullets, placeholder sizes and position, and background styles and colors. You can preview and change suggested text, pictures, and shapes in the template to fit your content. Various templates are installed on your computer, or you may search online for many additional template options. In this project, you will use a template designed by Jasmine Turner, who is the Marketing Director of Skyline Bakery & Café.

Activity 2.14 | Opening a PowerPoint Template

In this activity, you will open a PowerPoint template to create a new presentation.

1 Navigate to the folder containing the student data files for this chapter. Locate and right-click on the file **i02B_Skyline_Template**, and then click **New**. Compare your screen with Figure 2.22.

PowerPoint opens and displays a new, unsaved, eight-slide presentation based on the Skyline template. Because this presentation was created from a template, the presentation opens unsaved with the name Presentation followed by a number. This ensures that you do not make changes to and then overwrite the template file.

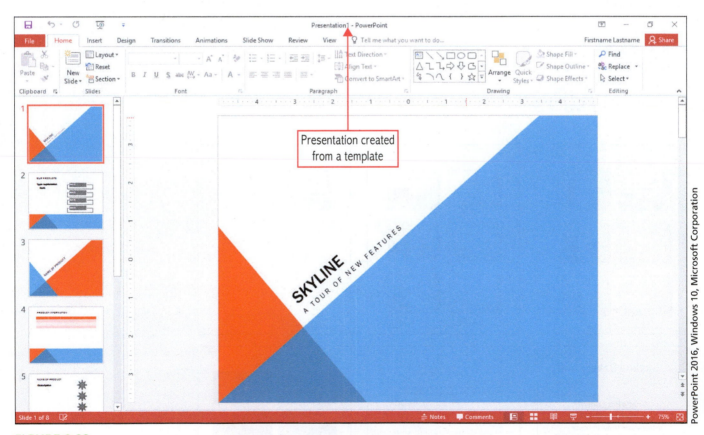

FIGURE 2.22

2 Display **Backstage** view, click the **Save As tab**, and then navigate to your **Integrated Projects Chapter 2** folder. Using your own name, save the PowerPoint presentation as **Lastname_Firstname_2B_Restaurant_Presentation**

3 Click the **Insert tab**, and then in the **Text group**, click **Header & Footer**. In the **Header and Footer** dialog box, click the **Notes and Handouts tab**. Select the **Footer** check box; in the **Footer** box, using your own name, type **Lastname_Firstname_2B_Restaurant_Presentation** and then click **Apply to All**.

The footer will print on the handouts or notes pages but will not display on the slides.

4 Click the **Design tab**, and then in the **Themes group**, click **More** [▾]. In the **Themes** gallery, use the ScreenTips to locate and then click **Parallax**. In the **Variants group**, click the **Red** variant.

This Parallax variant displays with a dark gray and a red bent stripe on the left side.

Activity 2.15 | Changing Character Spacing and Text Shadow

1 With **Slide 1** displayed, in the title placeholder, click to the right of *Skyline*. Press Spacebar and then type **Bakery & Caf** Insert the symbol **é** to complete the name of the bakery. Select the entire title. On the **Home tab**, in the **Font group**, click **Character Spacing** [AV], and then click **Very Loose**. Compare your screen with Figure 2.23.

Character spacing increases or decreases the space between characters. In this instance, the space is increased and the title is spaced across the slide.

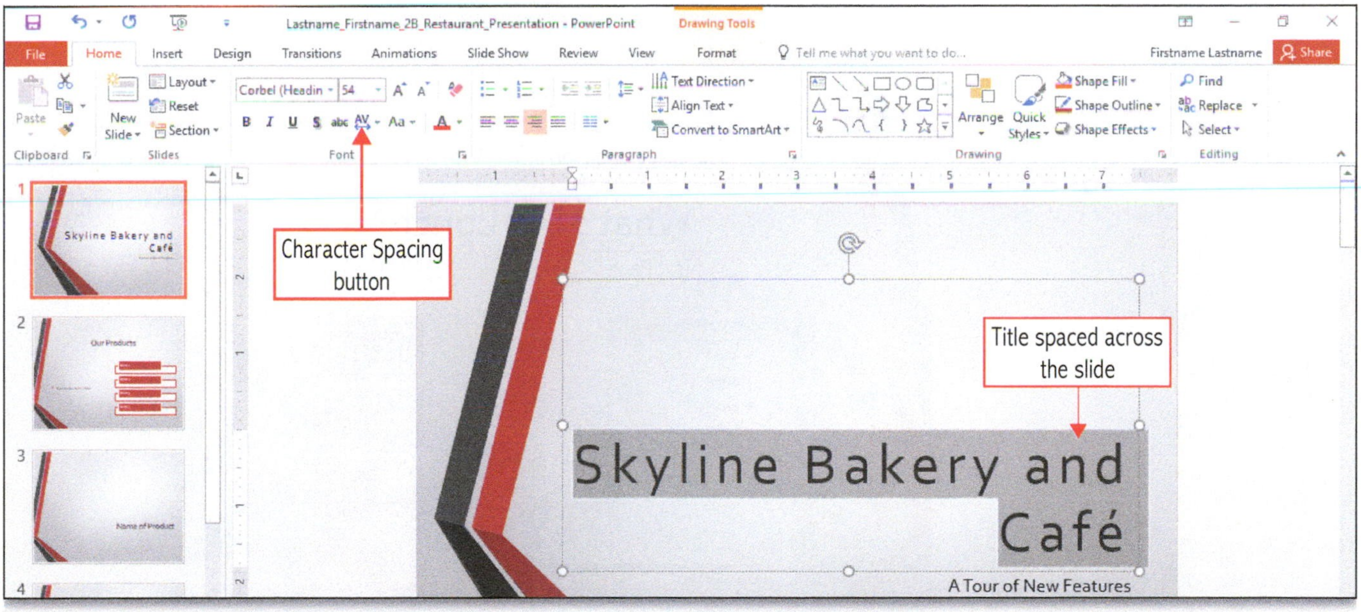

FIGURE 2.23

2 In the bottom subtitle placeholder, delete the existing text, type **Restaurant Menu**, and then select the text. In the **Font group**, click **Character Spacing** [AV], and then click **Loose**. In the **Font group**, click the **Font Size button arrow** [60], and then click **24**.

3 ▶ Display **Slide 2**. Delete the title, and then type **What's For Lunch?** In the left content placeholder, delete the existing text, and then type **Our chain of casual full-service restaurants with our in-house bakeries features fresh, high-quality ingredients.** Select the text you just typed. From the mini toolbar, click the **Font Size button arrow** [60 ▾], and then click **32**. Select the word *fresh*. In the **Font group**, click **Text Shadow** [S].

> Text Shadow adds a shadow behind the selected text to make it stand out from the surrounding text.

4 ▶ In the right content placeholder, click in the first text box of the SmartArt graphic.

> *SmartArt* graphics are designer-quality visual representations of your information that you can create by choosing from the many different layouts to communicate your message or ideas effectively.

5 ▶ On the ribbon, under **SmartArt Tools**, click on the **Design tab**. In the **Layouts group**, click **More** [▾], and then use the ScreenTips to locate and select the **Vertical Block List**. If the text pane does not display, on the Design tab, in the Create Graphic group, click Text Pane. Compare your screen with Figure 2.24.

> The *text pane*—the pane where text that displays in the graphic can be entered and edited—displays to the left of the SmartArt graphic. The description of the selected graphic may not display in the SmartArt task pane.

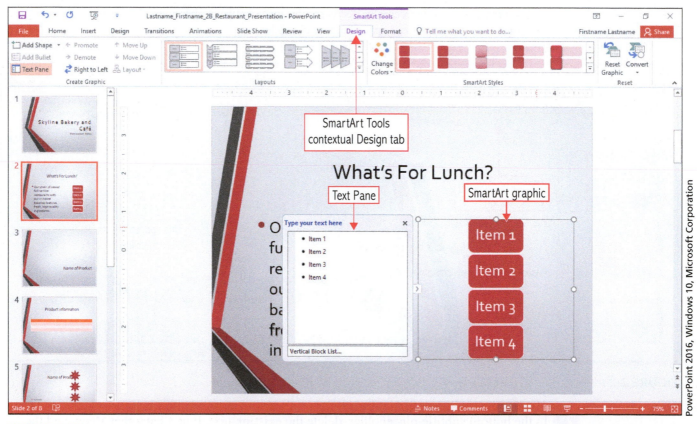

FIGURE 2.24

6 ▶ In the **Text Pane**, under **Type your text here**, select the text *Item 1* and replace it by typing **Sandwiches** Using the same technique, type **Salads** as the second item, type **Soups** as the third item, and type **Light Entrees** as the fourth item. Press [Enter] to add a fifth box to the SmartArt graphic, and then type **Desserts**

7 Under **SmartArt Tools**, click the **Design tab**. In the **Create Graphic group**, click **Text Pane** to close the text pane, and then compare your screen with Figure 2.25.

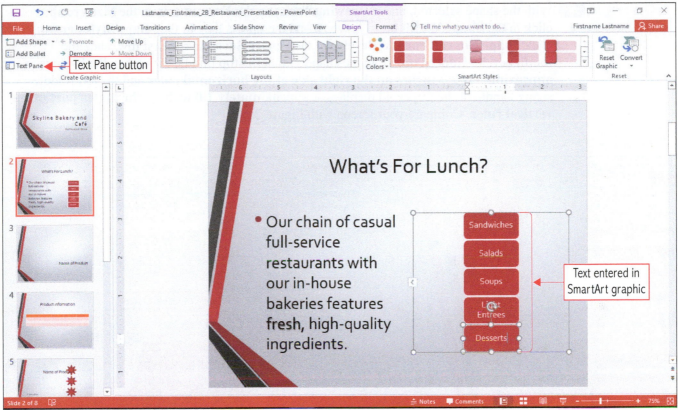

FIGURE 2.25

8 Display **Slide 3**. Click in the title placeholder, delete the existing text, and then type **Sandwiches**

9 On the left, in the thumbnails, point to **Slide 4** and right-click, and then on the shortcut menu, click **Delete Slide**.

> PowerPoint renumbers the slides.

10 **Save** 💾 the presentation.

Activity 2.16 | Inserting and Modifying a Shape

You can modify the appearance of a shape by adjusting the fill or by adding effects, such as shadows, glows, and bevels.

1 With **Slide 4** displayed, click in the title placeholder, delete the existing text, and then type **Our Sandwiches** In the left content placeholder, delete the existing text, and then type **Our sandwiches are prepared with our own specialty breads, which are baked daily in our own bakery. After finishing your meal, we would be pleased to offer you a tour of our bakery next door. Favorite sandwiches include:**

2 On the right side of the slide, click the top shape—*Sun*. Hold down Ctrl, and then click each of the other two shapes. Press Delete to delete the three shapes.

> By holding down Ctrl, you can select more than one shape at a time. When multiple shapes are selected, any formatting changes are applied to all selected shapes.

3 Click the **Insert tab**. In the **Illustrations group**, click **Shapes**, and then under **Basic Shapes**, in the first row, click the sixth shape—**Trapezoid**. On the right side of the slide, below the title placeholder, click one time to insert a trapezoid shape.

4 With the shape selected, under **Drawing Tools,** on the **Format tab**, in the **Size group**, click in the **Shape Width** box 📐, type **3** and then press Enter. In the **Shape Styles group**, click **Shape Effects**. Point to **Bevel**, and then under **Bevel**, in the first row, click the fourth bevel—**Cool Slant**. Drag the shape so that the top middle sizing handle displays at **approximately 2.5 inches on the right side of the horizontal ruler** and the left middle sizing handle of the trapezoid displays at **approximately 1.0 inch on the upper part of the vertical ruler**. Compare your screen with Figure 2.26.

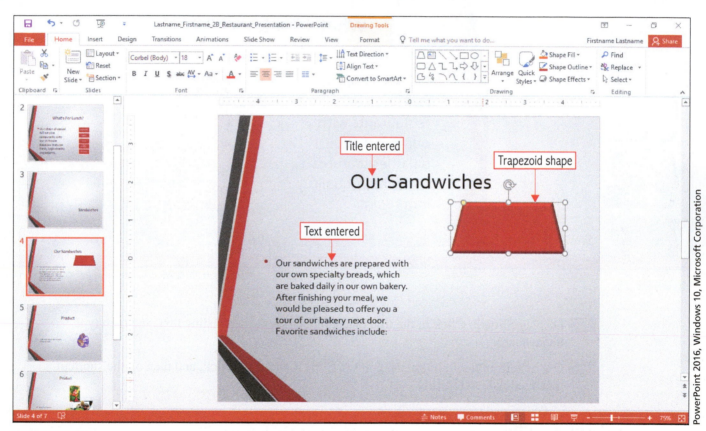

FIGURE 2.26

5 With the shape selected, press Ctrl + D.

The trapezoid shape is copied in the same area as the original shape.

6 Drag the selected shape down until the bottom middle sizing handle displays at **approximately 2.5 inches on the right side of the horizontal ruler** and the bottom displays at **approximately 3.5 inches on the lower portion of the vertical ruler**.

7 Press Ctrl + D. Drag the selected shape up until the top middle sizing handle displays at **approximately 2.5 inches on the right side of the horizontal ruler** and the shape is approximately in the middle of the other two trapezoids—dotted alignment guides will display to assist you.

8 ▸ Click the top trapezoid, hold down Ctrl, and then click the other two shapes. Under **Drawing Tools**, click the **Format tab**. In the **Arrange group**, click **Align**, and then click **Align Left**. Click **Align** again, and then click **Distribute Vertically**. Compare your screen with Figure 2.27.

The left borders of the shapes are aligned and the spaces are equally spaced vertically.

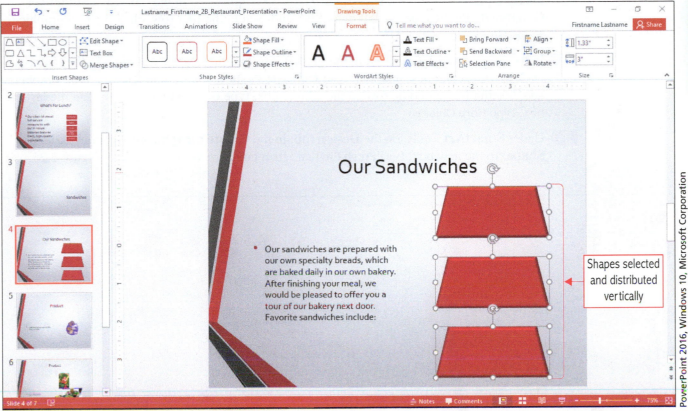

PowerPoint 2016, Windows 10, Microsoft Corporation

FIGURE 2.27

9 ▸ Click in the title placeholder to cancel the selection of the three shapes. Click the top trapezoid shape, and then type **Vegetarian** Click the middle shape, and then type **Cheese Steak** Click the bottom shape, and then type **Turkey** Select all three shapes. Click the **Home tab**. In the **Font group**, click the **Font Size button arrow** 60 ⌄, and then click **28**.

10 ▸ **Save** ⊟ the presentation.

Activity 2.17 | Inserting and Modifying a SmartArt Graphic

SmartArt graphics present your information visually in a professionally designed manner. You can customize the look of SmartArt graphics by changing edges or shadows or by applying a three-dimensional perspective. In this activity, you will insert and modify a SmartArt graphic.

1 ▸ From the thumbnails on the left, display **Slide 3**. On the **Home tab**, in the **Clipboard group**, click **Copy** 🗐. Click **Slide 4** to make it the active slide, and then in the **Clipboard group**, click the upper portion of the **Paste** button.

A copy of Slide 3 is pasted after Slide 4 creating a new Slide 5, for a total of eight slides in your presentation.

2 ▸ With **Slide 5** selected, click in the title placeholder, delete *Sandwiches*, and then type **Salads**

3 Display **Slide 6**. In the title placeholder, select *Product*, and then type **Our Salads**

4 In the left content placeholder, select the existing text, and then type **In our hectic lives, salads are a healthy alternative to fast food. At Skyline Bakery & Café, our chefs use only the freshest ingredients brought in daily by farmers. We are proud to support the growers in the local Boston area.**

5 In the right content placeholder, click the picture, and then press Delete. In the middle of the right placeholder, click **Insert a SmartArt Graphic**. In the **Choose a SmartArt Graphic** dialog box, on the left click **List**, and then in the first row, click the first graphic—**Basic Block List**. Click **OK**.

6 In the SmartArt Graphic, click in the top left box, and then type **Snap Bean** In the top row, click in the second box, and then type **Antipasto Pasta** In the middle left box, type **Cranberry and Walnuts** In the middle row, in the second box, type **Garden Pasta** and then in the last box, type **Herb Chicken**

7 Under **SmartArt Tools**, on the **Design tab**, in the **Create Graphic group**, click **Add Shape**. In the new box, type **Fresh Fruit** and then compare your screen with Figure 2.28.

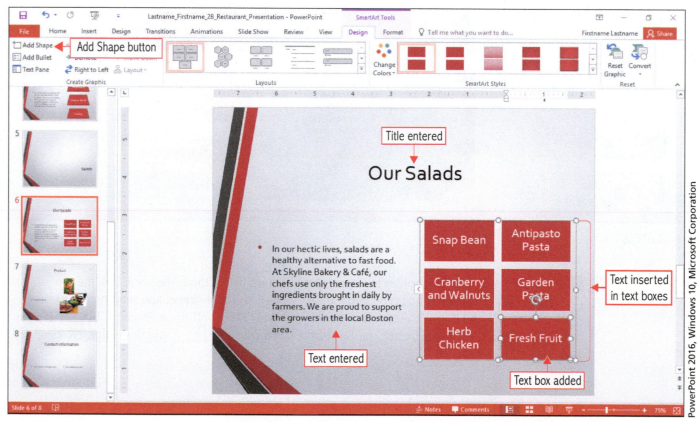

FIGURE 2.28

8 Under **SmartArt Tools**, on the **Design tab**, in the **SmartArt Styles group**, click **More**. Under **3-D**, in the first row, click the first style—**Polished**.

9 On the left, in the slide thumbnails, in the **Slides/Outline pane**, click **Slide 5**, hold down Ctrl, and then click **Slide 6** to select the two slides. On the **Home tab**, in the **Clipboard group**, click **Copy**. Click **Slide 6** to make it the active slide, and then in the **Clipboard group**, click the upper portion of the **Paste** button two times.

Two copies of Slides 5 and 6 are pasted after Slide 6. You now have 12 slides in your presentation.

10 ▶ Click **Slide 7**. Replace the text *Salads* by typing **Soups**

11 ▶ Click **Slide 8**. In the title placeholder, select *Our Salads* and type **Our Soups** In the left content placeholder, delete the existing text, and then type **We are proud to serve our delicious homemade soup with our salads. Our soups change seasonally depending on the availability of fresh ingredients. Our chefs are always combining various ingredients to surprise you with a scrumptious new soup.**

12 ▶ In the right content placeholder, click above the top row of shapes, to display the border that surrounds the SmartArt graphic and to select the graphic. Under **SmartArt Tools**, on the **Design tab**, in the **Layouts group**, click **More** ▼, and then at the bottom click **More Layouts**. In the **Choose a SmartArt Graphic** dialog box, on the left click **Matrix**, and then click the first layout—**Basic Matrix**. Click **OK**.

13 ▶ In the **Text Pane**, replace *Snap Bean* with **Homemade** Replace *Antipasto Pasta* with **Great Chefs** Replace *Cranberry and Walnuts* with **Full Flavored** Replace *Garden Pasta* with **Prepared Daily Close** ☒ the **Text Pane**, and then compare your screen with Figure 2.29.

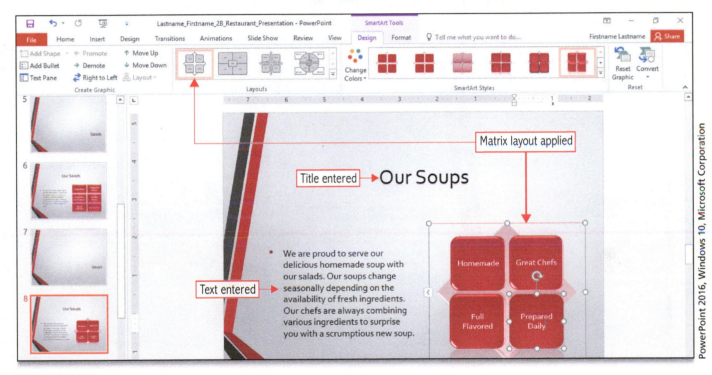

FIGURE 2.29

14 ▶ **Save** 🖫 the presentation.

Activity 2.18 | Replacing and Modifying Pictures

1 ▶ Display **Slide 9**. In the title placeholder, replace *Salads* with **Light Entrees**

2 ▶ Click **Slide 10**, and then press ⌴Delete⌴.

Slide 10 is deleted; 11 slides remain in your presentation.

3 ▶ On **Slide 10**, replace *Product* with **Our Light Entrees** Replace *Type description* with **Immediately as you enter Skyline Bakery & Café, you know you are in for a pleasurable eating experience. The aroma that greets you is warm and welcoming. Our Light Entrees are as delicious to look at as they are to eat.**

4 On the right side of the slide, click the top picture to select it. Under **Picture Tools**, click the **Format tab**, and then in the **Adjust group**, click **Change Picture**. In the **Insert Pictures** box, in the first row, to the right of **From a file**, click **Browse**, and then navigate to the location of the student data files that accompany this chapter. Locate and insert the file **i02B_Entree1**. In the **Size group**, click in the **Shape Height** box, type **2.1** and then press Enter.

5 Click one time on the bottom picture to select it, and then change the picture to **i02B_Entree2**. In the **Size group**, click in the **Shape Height** box, type **2.1** and then press Enter.

6 Click the middle picture to select it, and then change the picture to **i02B_Entree3**. Press ↓ two times, and then press → five times. In the **Arrange group**, click **Bring Forward**. Compare your screen with Figure 2.30.

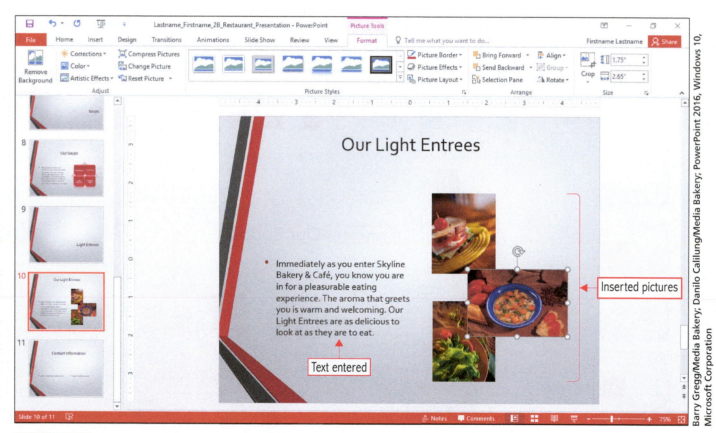

FIGURE 2.30

7 From the slide thumbnails on the left, click **Slide 9**, hold down Ctrl, and then click **Slide 10**. On the **Home tab**, in the **Clipboard group**, click **Copy**. Click to make **Slide 10** the active slide, and then in the **Clipboard group**, click the upper portion of the **Paste** button.

> Slide 9 and Slide 10 are pasted after Slide 10. You now have 13 slides in your presentation.

8 Click **Slide 11**. In the title placeholder, replace *Light Entrees* with **In-House Bakery**

9 ▶ Click **Slide 12**. In the title placeholder, replace *Our Light Entrees* with **Our In-House Bakery** In the left content placeholder, replace the existing text with **A delightful way to conclude your visit to the Skyline Bakery & Café is a stop at our in-house bakery. Our pastry chefs are pleased to serve you a wondrous selection of desserts.**

10 ▶ By using the techniques you have practiced, on the right side of the slide, change the top and bottom pictures using the files **i02B_Bakery1** for the top picture and **i02B_Bakery2** for the bottom picture. With the bottom picture selected, hold down ⌃Ctrl and then click the top picture. With both pictures selected, change the **Shape Height** to **1.6** and then press ⌅Enter. Change the middle picture using the file **i02B_Bakery3**. If necessary, in the **Arrange group**, click **Bring Forward** so that the middle picture overlays the top and bottom pictures. Compare your screen with Figure 2.31. Use the arrow keys to nudge the image as necessary.

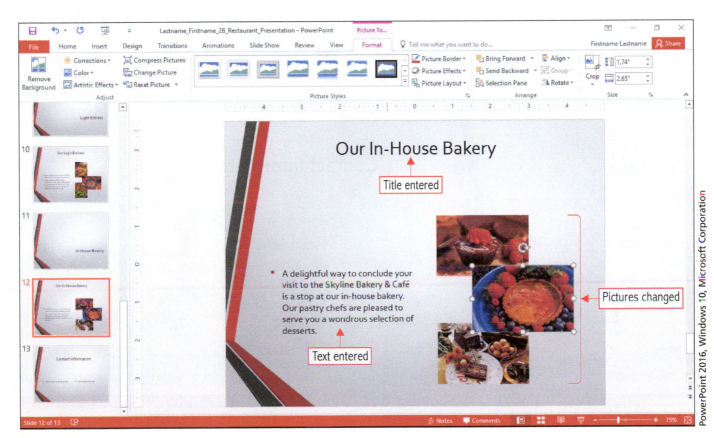

FIGURE 2.31

11 ▶ Display **Slide 13**, which is the last slide in the presentation. In the left content placeholder, replace *Type contact information here* with **When can you visit us?** and then press ⌅Enter. Type **For your own personal tour, please contact Samir Taheri** and then press ⌅Enter. Type **www.skylinebakery.biz** press ⌅Enter, and then type **617-555-0037** Right-click anywhere on the text *www.skylinebakery.biz*, and then on the shortcut menu, click **Remove Hyperlink**.

12 On the left, select all the text in the four bulleted items, and then on the **Home tab**, in the **Font group**, click **Increase Font Size** [A] one time. In the **Paragraph group**, click **Bullets** [≡ ▾] to turn off the bulleted formatting. With the text still selected, in the **Paragraph group**, click **Center** [≡], click **Line Spacing** [↕≡ ▾], and then click **Line Spacing Options**. In the **Paragraph** dialog box, under **Spacing**, click the **Before spin box up arrow** and change to **12 pt**. Click the **After up arrow** and change to **12 pt**, and then click **OK**.

13 In the right content placeholder, delete the existing text, and then in the middle of the placeholder, click **Pictures** [🖼]. In the **Insert Picture** dialog box, navigate to your student files for this chapter, select the file **i02B_Taheri**, and then click **Insert**. Compare your screen with Figure 2.32.

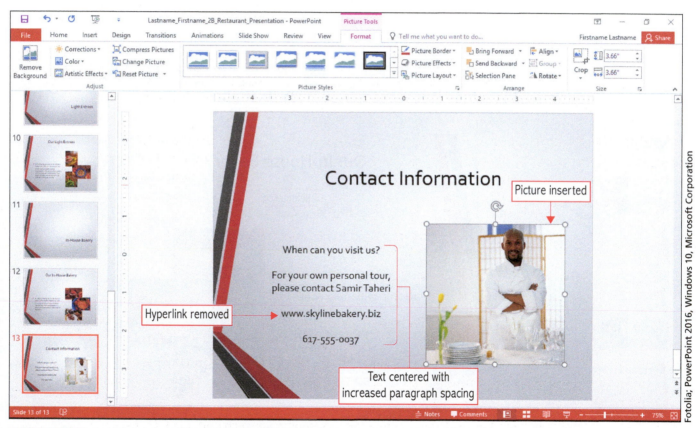

FIGURE 2.32

14 Click the **Review tab**, and then in the **Proofing group**, click **Spelling**. Check the spelling in the presentation and correct any misspelled words.

The spelling tool will check the spelling of the words on the slides and the words in the footer.

15 **Save** [💾] the presentation.

You can save a PowerPoint presentation as a text-only document by saving it in the Outline/RTF format. This is useful if you want to open the file in another software application, such as Word, or in an older version of PowerPoint. When a presentation is saved as an Outline/RTF file, the graphical content of the presentation and any text in the Notes pane will not be saved.

Activity 2.19 | Saving a File as an Outline/RTF File

1 Display **Backstage** view, click the **Save As tab**, and then on the right, click **Browse** to display the **Save As** dialog box. Navigate to your **Integrated Projects Chapter 2** folder, and then using your own name as the file name type **Lastname_Firstname_2B_Menu_Outline** Click the **Save as type arrow**, and then near the bottom of the list, click **Outline/RTF**. Click **Save**.

> *Rich Text Format,* or *RTF*, is a universal document format that can be read by nearly all word pro-cessing programs and retains most text and paragraph formatting. A PowerPoint presentation saved as an RTF file will include only the text of the presentation in an outline format. This enables you to share the information in the presentation with others who may not have the same version of PowerPoint.

2 Click the **File tab** again to display **Backstage** view. With the **Info tab** selected, in the lower right corner, click **Show All Properties**. Under **Related People**, be sure your name displays as the **Author**—change it if necessary. Click to the right of **Subject**, and then type your course name and section number. Click to the right of **Tags**, and then edit as necessary so that the tags are **menu, bakery template**

3 **Save** 🔲 your presentation, and then **Close** ⊠ PowerPoint.

Activity 2.20 | Opening an Outline/RTF in Word

Nancy Goldman, the chief baker, has asked you to modify the PowerPoint presentation to emphasize the soups and salads. You can open an Outline/RTF file in Word, modify the document, and then create a new PowerPoint presentation from the modified Word document.

1 Start Word. Display **Backstage** view. Under **Open**, click **Browse**, and then navigate to your **Integrated Projects Chapter 2** folder. Open the RTF file **Lastname_Firstname_2B_ Menu_Outline**. Insert the file name in the footer.

2 Click the **View tab**, and then in the **Document Views group**, click **Outline**.

3 Click the **Home tab**. In the **Editing group**, click **Select**, and then click **Select All** to select the entire document.

🔁 **ANOTHER WAY**   Press Ctrl + A.

4 In the **Font group**, click the **Font Color button arrow** 🅰 ▾, and then click **Automatic**. Compare your screen with Figure 2.33.

> The text in the document is the same font color as in the presentation. Because some of your pres-entation text was white, by changing the font color to automatic—black—all document text is now visible. The text you typed in the SmartArt and the shapes is not part of the Word document.

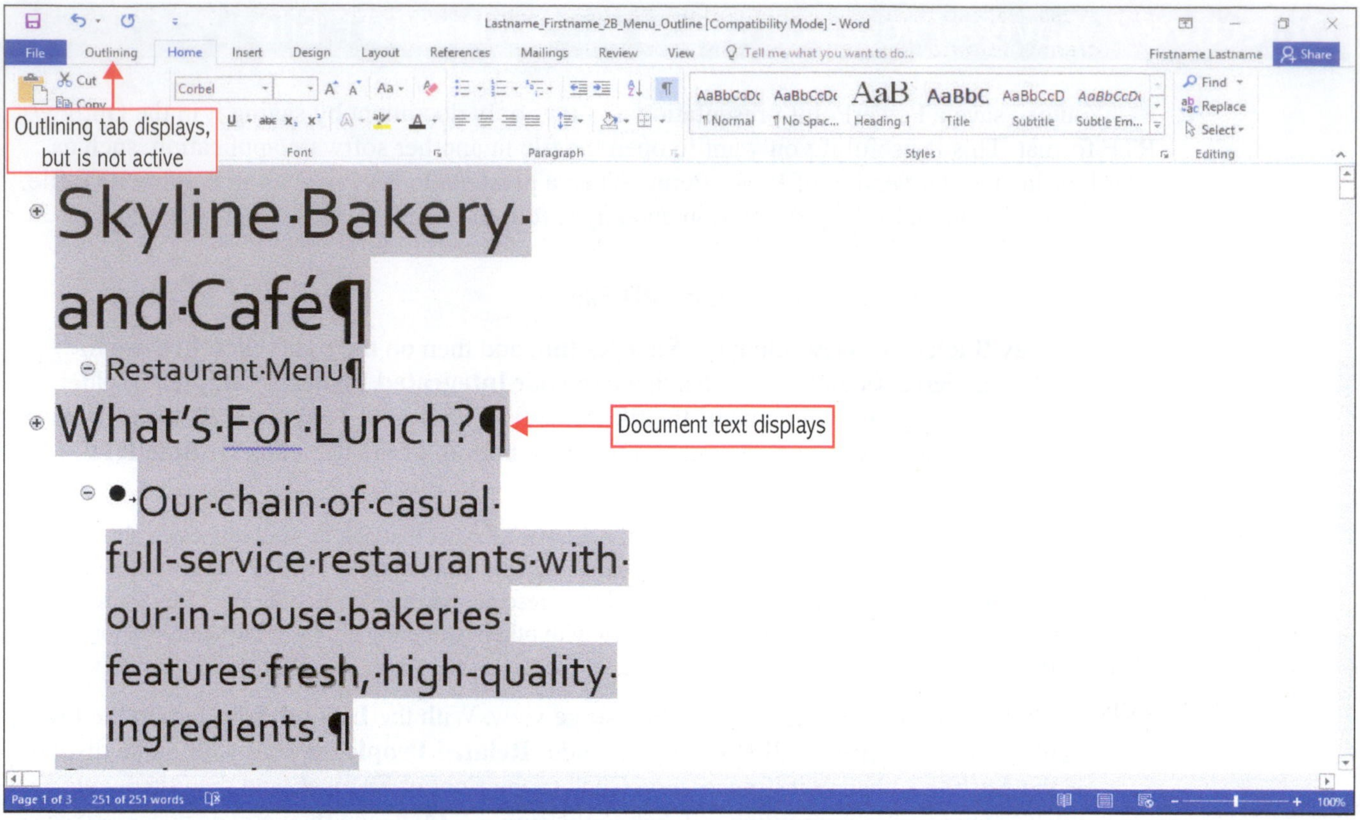

Word 2016, Windows 10, Microsoft Corporation

FIGURE 2.33

5 Display **Backstage** view, and then, under *Info*, click **Convert**. In the message box, click **OK**.

This action changes your document from an RTF file to a Word document. The message box warns you that you are changing your document from .rtf format to .docx format and that the file format change may cause differences in the layout of the document.

Objective 8 Modify a Word Document in Outline View

When you have more than four or five slides, it can be easier to type text and keep track of slides by opening the presentation in Word and making modifications to the Word outline. Doing so enables you to see more text and to make modifications easily.

Activity 2.21 | Collapsing Outline Levels

Recall that in Outline view, parts of a Word document can be collapsed or expanded to view or move sections of the document.

1 Click the **Outlining tab**. In the **Outline Tools group**, click the **Show Level arrow**, and then click **Level 1**.

2 To the left of *Our Salads*, click the **plus outline symbol**, and then in the **Outline Tools group**, click **Expand** [+]. To the left of *Our Soups*, click the **plus outline symbol**, and then click **Expand** [+].

3 To the left of the paragraph that begins *We are proud*, click the **minus outline symbol**, and then type **Fire Roasted Tomato** Press Enter.

Clicking the minus outline symbol selects all the text for that item. When you begin to type, the selected text is automatically deleted.

4 ▶ Press `Tab` and then type **Enhanced by the rustic character of flame roasted tomatoes, our creamy tomato soup is served with roasted garlic and sour cream.** Press `Enter`.

Instead of clicking the Demote and Promote buttons in the Outline Tools group, you can press `Tab` to demote a paragraph and press `Shift` + `Tab` to promote a paragraph. In this instance, the paragraph you typed is demoted.

5 ▶ Press `Shift` + `Tab`, type **Minestrone** and then press `Enter`. Press `Tab`, and then type **Our minestrone soup is a favorite of our customers.** Press `Enter`, and then compare your screen with Figure 2.34.

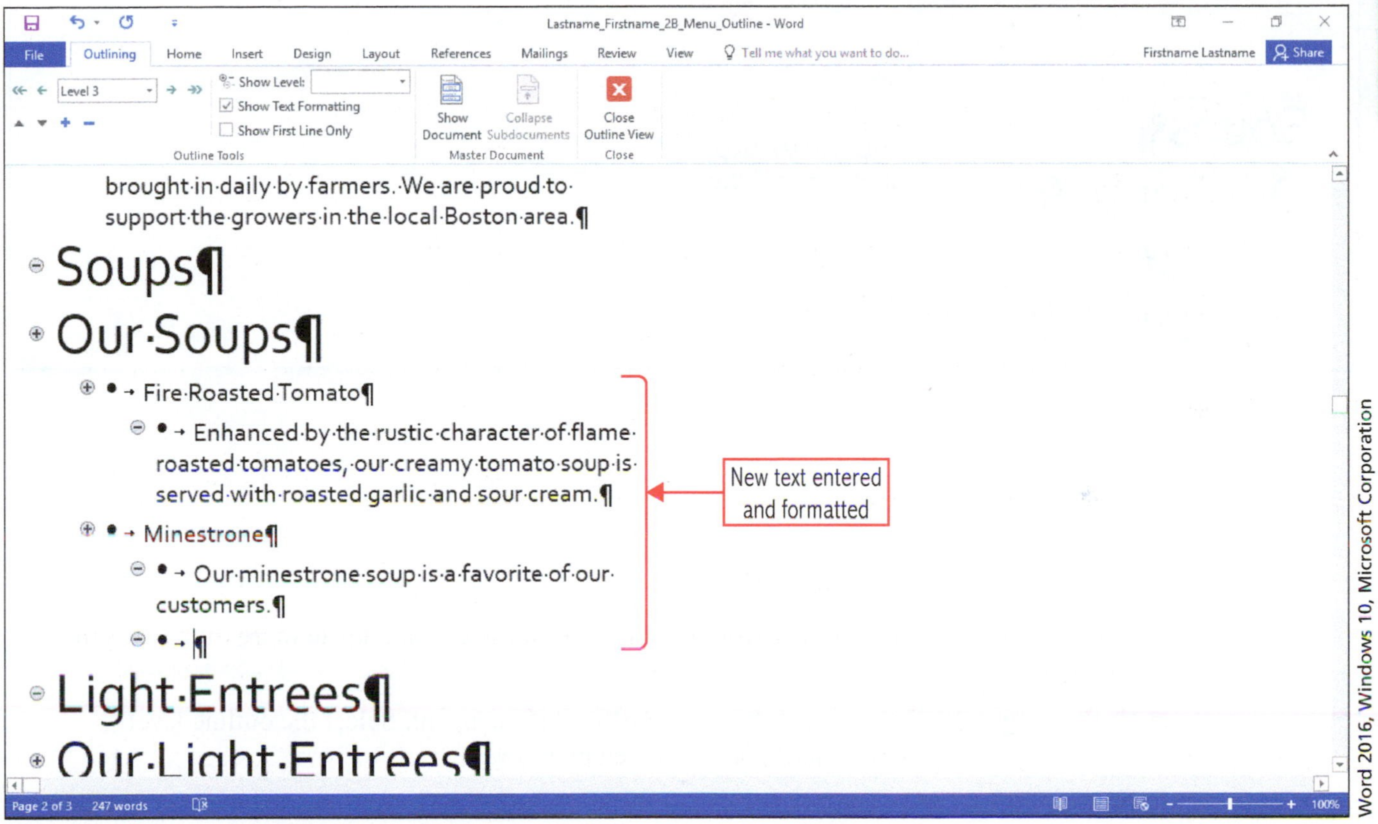

Word 2016, Windows 10, Microsoft Corporation

FIGURE 2.34

6 ▶ Press `Shift` + `Tab`, type **Classic French Onion** and then press `Enter`. Press `Tab`, and then type **Enriched by caramelized onions, our rich beef broth is served with garlic croutons and gruyere cheese.** Press `Enter`.

7 ▶ Press `Shift` + `Tab`, type **Corn Chowder** and then press `Enter`. Press `Tab`, and then type **Roasted corn is featured in this creamy chowder. A bit of wild rice and roasted red pepper garnish this soup.**

8 ▶ To the left of the paragraph that begins *In our hectic lives*, click the **minus outline symbol**. Type **Spinach Salad** and then press `Enter`. Press `Tab`, and then type **Fresh garden spinach, hard boiled eggs, bacon, and tomatoes are topped with a sweet honey mustard dressing.** Press `Enter`.

9 ▶ Press `Shift` + `Tab`, type **Fresh Fruit** and then press `Enter`. Press `Tab`, and then type **Fresh fruits are sliced and displayed in a dish made from a uniquely carved watermelon.** Press `Enter`.

10 ▶ Press `Shift` + `Tab`, type **Cold Pasta Salad** and then press `Enter`. Press `Tab`, and then type **Rainbow pasta is boiled, chilled, and then mixed with carrots, celery, and our secret ingredients, which make this salad exceptional.**

11 ▶ In the **Outline Tools group**, click the **Show Level button arrow**, and then click **Level 1**.

12 To the left of the paragraph *Soups*, click the **minus outline symbol**. Hold down (Shift), and then to the left of the paragraph *Our Soups*, click the **plus outline symbol**. In the **Outline Tools group**, click **Move Up** [▲] two times, and then compare your screen with Figure 2.35.

The *Soup* and *Our Soups* outline levels, and related text, are moved above *Salads*. Holding down (Shift) enables you to select consecutive levels.

FIGURE 2.35

13 Save [⊟] the document.

Activity 2.22 │ Deleting Outline Levels

With the levels collapsed in a Word outline, you can select and delete more of the document at one time.

1 Press (Ctrl) + (Home) to move to the beginning of the document. Select the outline level *Sandwiches* and *Our Sandwiches*, and then press (Delete).

2 Select the outline level *Light Entrees*. Hold down (Shift), and then select the outline level *Our In-House Bakery*. Press (Delete) to delete the four paragraphs in the outline.

3 Save [⊟] the document.

4 Click the **File tab** to display **Backstage** view. With the **Info tab** selected, in the lower right corner, click **Show All Properties**. Under **Related People**, be sure your name displays as the **Author**—change it if necessary. Click to the right of **Subject**, and then type your course name and section number. Click to the right of **Tags**, and then type **menu, soups, salads**

5 On the left click **Save**. Print or submit electronically as directed by your instructor. **Close** [×] Word.

Objective 9 │ Create a New Presentation from a Modified Word Outline

After modifying your outline in Word, you can create a new PowerPoint presentation from the outline.

Activity 2.23 | Creating a Modified PowerPoint Presentation

1 Start PowerPoint, and then click **Blank Presentation**. On the **Home tab**, in the **Slides group**, click the **New Slide button arrow**, and then below the gallery, click **Slides from Outline**. In the **Insert Outline** dialog box, navigate to your **Integrated Projects Chapter 2** folder, click the **Lastname_Firstname_2B_Menu_Outline file**, and then click **Insert**.

2 Display **Backstage** view, and then click the **Save As tab**. Click **Browse**, and then in the **Save As** dialog box, navigate to your **Integrated Project Chapter 2** folder. Using your own name, save the presentation as **Lastname_Firstname_2B_Menu_Presentation**

3 Click the **Insert tab**, and then in the **Text group**, click **Header & Footer**. In the **Header and Footer** dialog box, click the **Notes and Handouts tab**, and then under **Include on page**, select the **Footer** check box. As the footer, using your own name, type **Lastname_Firstname_2B_Menu_Presentation** and then click **Apply to All**.

4 Click the **Design tab**, and then in the **Themes group**, click **More**. In the **Themes** gallery, locate and click the **Slate** theme.

5 Click **Slide 1**, and then press Delete.

There are seven slides in the presentation.

6 Click **Slide 7**. In the bottom content placeholder, replace the text *When can you visit us?* with **For more information about our Soups and Salads** Replace the text for the second bullet with **Contact Nancy Goldman, our Chief Baker**

7 Select all of the text in the four bulleted items, and then click the **Home tab**. In the **Paragraph group**, click **Bullets** to remove the bullet formatting. Click **Center**. Click **Align Text**, and then click **Middle**. Compare your screen with Figure 2.36.

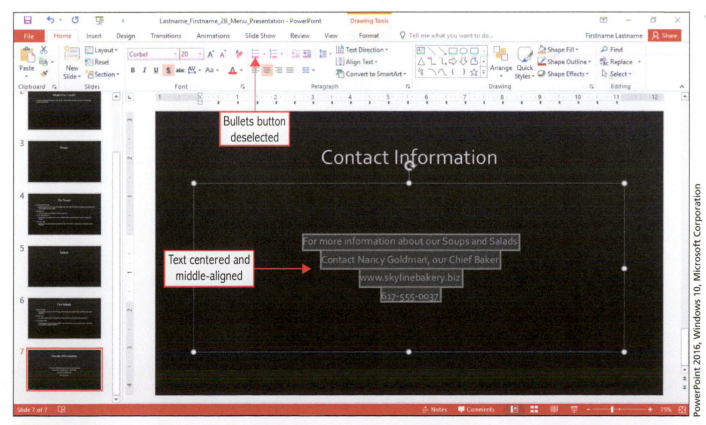

FIGURE 2.36

8 ▶ Click **Slide 1**, and then click anywhere in the bulleted item. On the **Home tab**, in the **Paragraph group**, click **Bullets** ≣▾ to remove bullet formatting, and then click **Center** ≣.

9 ▶ Click **Slide 3**, *Soups*, hold down Ctrl, click **Slide 5**, *Salads*, and then press Delete.

Five slides remain in your presentation.

10 ▶ Click the **Slide Show tab**, and then in the **Start Slide Show group**, click **From Beginning**. View your presentation.

11 ▶ Click the **Review tab**, and then in the **Proofing group**, click **Spelling**. Check the spelling of the presentation and correct any misspelled words.

12 ▶ Save ⊟ the presentation.

13 ▶ Display **Backstage** view. With the **Info tab** selected, in the lower right corner, click **Show All Properties**. Under **Related People**, be sure your name displays as the **Author**—change it if necessary. Click to the right of **Subject**, and then type your course name and section number. Click to the right of **Tags**, and then type **soups, salads, presentation**

14 ▶ Display **Backstage** view, and then click the **Print tab**. Under **Settings**, be sure **Print All Slides** displays. Click **Full Page Slides**, and then under **Handouts**, click **6 Slides Horizontal**. Print or submit electronically.

15 ▶ Save ⊟ the presentation, and then **Close** ✕ PowerPoint.

END | You have completed Project 2B

END OF CHAPTER

SUMMARY

You can create and modify the text in a Word outline, and then import the outline into PowerPoint. You can customize a PowerPoint presentation by inserting and deleting slides, changing text formats, and modifying the theme. Insert SmartArt graphics, pictures, and shapes to add interest to your presentations. You can save a PowerPoint presentation as an outline in Rich Text Format. The RTF outline can be modified in Word.

KEY TERMS

MATCHING

Match each term in the second column with its correct definition in the first column by writing the letter of the term on the blank line in front of the correct definition.

_____ 1. A document view that shows headings and subheadings, which can be expanded or collapsed.

_____ 2. The action of increasing or decreasing the viewing area on the screen.

_____ 3. A formatting mark that indicates there are subordinate heading or body text paragraphs.

_____ 4. A formatting mark that indicates there are no subordinate heading or body text paragraphs.

_____ 5. The primary editing view in PowerPoint where you write and design your presentation.

_____ 6. A PowerPoint screen element that displays a large image of the active slide.

_____ 7. The commands that control the look of the presentation window.

_____ 8. A slide element that reserves a portion of a slide and serves as a container for text, graphics, and other slide elements.

_____ 9. A predefined set of colors, fonts, lines, and fill effects that are professionally designed.

_____ 10. A view where you can work with notes in a full page format.

_____ 11. A view where slides fill the computer screen, which enables you to view the presentation the way your audience will see it.

_____ 12. A slide that displays at the end of a PowerPoint presentation indicating that the slide show is over.

_____ 13. An Office feature that allows you to increase or decrease the space between characters.

_____ 14. A designer-quality representation of your information that you can create by choosing from many different layouts to communicate your message or ideas effectively.

_____ 15. A universal document format that can be read by nearly all word processing programs and that retains most text and paragraph formatting.

A Black slide

B Character spacing

C Minus outline symbol

D Normal view

E Notes Page view

F Outline view

G Placeholder

H Plus outline symbol

I RTF

J Slide pane

K Slide Show view

L SmartArt

M Theme

N View buttons

O Zooming

MULTIPLE CHOICE

Circle the correct answer.

1. A small gray circle that identifies heading and body text paragraphs in an outline is:
    A. a bullet   **B.** a level indicator   **C.** an outline symbol

2. A PowerPoint screen element that displays either the presentation outline or all of the slides in the form of thumbnails is the:
    A. Slide Sorter   **B.** Left pane   **C.** Slide pane

3. A PowerPoint element that displays below the Slide pane and enables you to type notes regarding the active slide is the:
    A. Message pane   **B.** Notes pane   **C.** Notes placeholder

4. A horizontal bar at the bottom of the presentation window that displays the current slide number, number of slides in a presentation, the applied theme, and other elements is the:
    A. Status bar   **B.** Taskbar   **C.** Slide pane

5. In an outline, a paragraph that is assigned Level 1:
    A. has been demoted
    B. is designated as the highest outline level
    C. is a subordinate paragraph

6. In the Themes gallery, built-in themes are arranged:
    A. in alphabetical order   **B.** by color   **C.** in order of use

7. Notes to which the speaker can refer as a presentation is being delivered are referred to as:
    A. a speaker's handout   **B.** presentation notes   **C.** speaker's notes

8. When a shape is selected, you can automatically copy the shape in the same area of a slide by pressing:
    A. Alt + C   **B.** Alt + D   **C.** Ctrl + D

9. A SmartArt element where text that displays in the graphic can be entered and edited is the:
    A. Text pane   **B.** SmartArt dialog box   **C.** SmartArt Design tab

10. RTF is the acronym for:
    A. Real Text Format   **B.** Rich Text Format   **C.** Rich Type Format

CONTENT-BASED ASSESSMENTS (MASTERY AND TRANSFER OF LEARNING)

Apply 2A skills from these Objectives:

1 Create an Outline in Word
2 Import a Word Outline into a PowerPoint Presentation
3 Modify a PowerPoint Presentation
4 Create a Footer and Save a PowerPoint Presentation
5 Preview and Print a Presentation, Slide Handouts, and Speaker's Notes

Mastering Integration Project 2C Advertising Budget

In the following Mastering Integration project, you will create a Word outline for Skyline Bakery & Café promoting an increase in the company advertising budget. You will import the outline into a PowerPoint presentation and make modifications. Your completed files will look similar to Figure 2.37.

PROJECT FILES

For Project 2C, you will need the following files:

New blank PowerPoint presentation
i02C_Advertising_Budget

You will save your files as:

Lastname_Firstname_2C_Advertising_Budget
Lastname_Firstname_2C_Advertising_Presentation

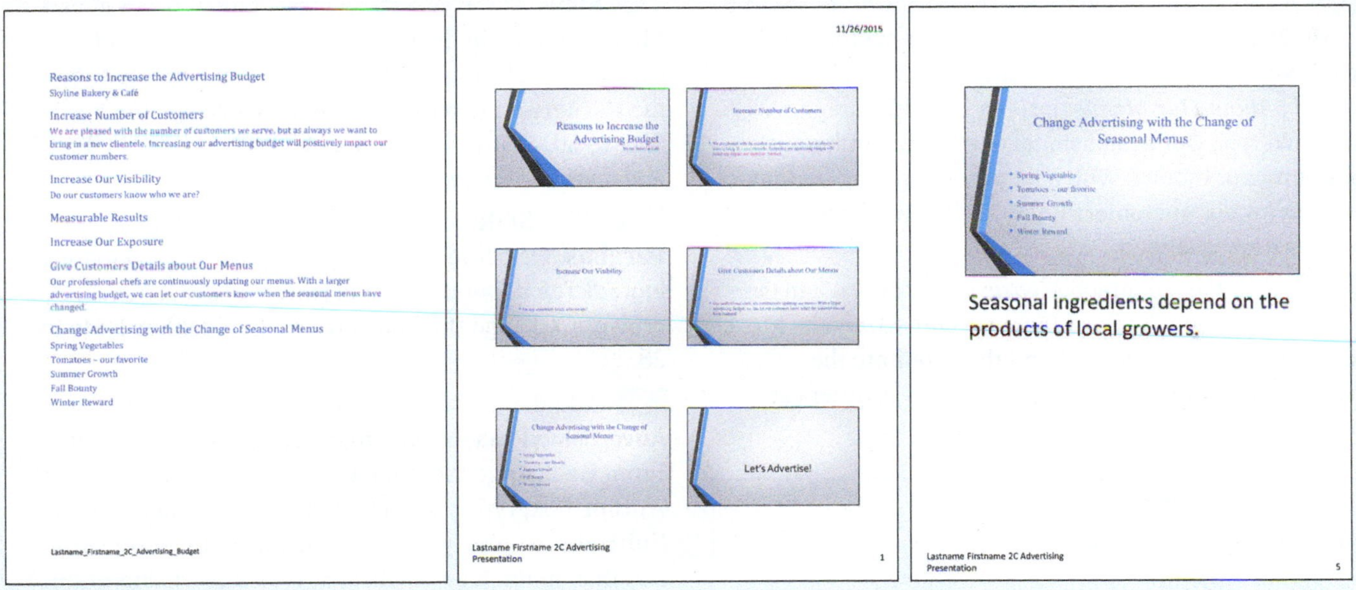

FIGURE 2.37

(Project 2C Advertising Budget continues on the next page)

1 Start Word. Locate and open the document **i02C_Advertising_Budget**. **Save** the document in your **Integrated Projects Chapter 2** folder with the file name **Lastname_Firstname_2C_Advertising_Budget** Insert the file name in the footer, and then change to **Outline View**.

2 Change the style of all seven paragraphs to **Level 1**. At the end of the first paragraph, press Enter, type **Skyline Bakery & Café** and then **Demote** this paragraph to **Level 2**. After the paragraph *Increase Number of Customers*, insert a **Level 2** paragraph, and then type **We are pleased with the number of customers we serve, but as always we want to bring in new clientele. Increasing our advertising budget will positively impact our customer numbers.**

3 After the paragraph *Increase Our Visibility*, insert a **Level 2** paragraph, and then type **Do our customers know who we are?** After the paragraph *Give Customers Details About Our Menus*, insert a **Level 2** paragraph, and then type **Our professional chefs are continuously updating our menus. With a larger advertising budget, we can let our customers know when the seasonal menus have changed.**

4 Select the paragraph *Measurable Results*, and then move the paragraph above *Increase Our Exposure*. Move to the end of the document, and then **Demote** the paragraph. Type the following, pressing Enter after each item except the last:

Spring Vegetables
Tomatoes – our favorite
Summer Growth
Fall Bounty
Winter Reward

5 In the **Close group**, click **Close Outline View**. From **Backstage** view, display the **Document Information Properties**. In the **Author** box, type your first name and last name; in the **Subject** box, type your course name and section number; and then in the **Keywords** box, type **outline, advertising Save** your changes, and then **Close** Word.

6 Start PowerPoint. Using your Word document **Lastname_Firstname_2C_Advertising_Budget**, create **Slides from Outline**. **Save** the presentation in your **Integrated Projects Chapter 2** folder with the file name **Lastname_Firstname_2C_Advertising_Presentation**

7 Delete **Slide 1**, the new **Slide 4**—*Measurable Results*, and then the new **Slide 4**—*Increase Our Exposure*. On the new **Slide 1**, change the **Layout** to **Title Slide**. At the end of the presentation, insert a **New Slide**, and then in the bottom placeholder, type **Let's Advertise!** Select the text, and then on the **Home tab**, in the **Paragraph group**, click **Bullets**. Change the **Font Size** to **60**, change the **Font Color** to **Gray-80%, Text 2**, and then **Center** the text.

8 Click **Slide 1**. Change the design **Theme** to **Parallax**. On **Slide 5**, in the **Notes pane**, type **Seasonal ingredients depend on the products of the local growers.** Change the **Font Size** of the **Speaker Note** to **28**.

9 Add the file name **Lastname Firstname 2C Advertising Presentation** to the footer in all handouts. From **Backstage** view, click **Show All Properties**. In the **Author** box, type your first name and last name; in the **Subject** box, type your course name and section number; and then in the **Keywords** box, type **advertising budget Save** the presentation, and then **Close** PowerPoint. Submit your printed or electronic files as directed by your instructor.

END | You have completed Project 2C

Mastering Integration   Project 2D Equipment Upgrade

Apply 2B skills from these Objectives:

6 Create a PowerPoint Presentation from a Template

7 Save a Presentation as an Outline/RTF File

8 Modify a Word Document in Outline View

9 Create a New Presentation from a Modified Word Outline

In the following Mastering Integration project, you will create a PowerPoint presentation from a template to persuade the management of Skyline Bakery & Café to upgrade the equipment so that the products can be sold in local health food stores. You will create an outline based on the presentation, make modifications in Word, and then import the outline into PowerPoint to create a second version of the presentation. Your completed files will look similar to Figure 2.38.

PROJECT FILES

For Project 2D, you will need the following files:

New blank PowerPoint presentation
i02D_Equipment_Template
i02D_Breads
i02D_Muffins
i02D_Kitchen

You will save your files as:

Lastname_Firstname_2D_Equipment_Presentation
Lastname_Firstname_2D_Equipment_Outline
Lastname_Firstname_2D_Store_Locations_Presentation

FIGURE 2.38

(Project 2D Equipment Upgrade continues on the next page)

2
INTEGRATED PROJECTS 2016

1 Start PowerPoint. Navigate to your student data files for this chapter, and then click the file **i02D_Equipment_ Template** to select it. Right-click, and click **New. Save** the presentation in your **Integrated Projects Chapter 2** folder with the file name **Lastname_Firstname_2D_ Equipment_Presentation** Add the file name to the footer of all the handout pages.

2 On **Slide 1**, delete the text in the left placeholder, type **Skyline Bakery & Café** and then change the **Character Spacing** to **Loose**. In the right placeholder, delete the text, and then type **Let's Grow! Center** the text. On **Slide 2**, change **Layout** to **Two Content**. Change the title to **Local Health Food Stores** In the left placeholder, type **Our customers want the convenience of purchasing our breads and other baked goods in more locations. In** the right placeholder, insert the picture **i02D_Breads.**

3 On **Slide 3**, change the title to **Equipment** In the left placeholder, type **We have the capacity, with our current baking equipment, to operate another shift.** In the right placeholder, click in the first text box of the **SmartArt** graphic. On the **SmartArt Tools Design tab**, in the **Layouts group**, click **More**, and then in the fourth row, click the sixth layout—**Staggered Process**. In the first text box, type **Mixing** In the second text box, type **Proofing** and then in the third text box, type **Baking** Add two more text boxes. In the fourth text box, type **Slicing** and then in the last text box, type **Packaging**

4 On **Slide 5**, change the title to **Baked Goods** In the left placeholder, type **We have a surplus of the fresh, high- quality ingredients for our baked goods. Let's increase our profits by increasing our market.** In the right placeholder, delete the shapes. Display the **Shapes** gallery, and then under **Basic Shapes**, click **Hexagon**. Click one time in the right placeholder. Change the **Shape Width** to **4**, and then change the **Shape Height** to **3.3** Change the **Shape Effect** to **Preset 4** and then move the shape so the left middle sizing handle displays at **approximately 0 inches on the horizontal ruler** and at **0 inches on the vertical ruler**. In the shape, type **Specialty Breads** press Enter; type **Breakfast Sweets** press Enter; and then type **Desserts** Select the three paragraphs, and then change the **Line Spacing** to **1.5.**

5 On **Slide 6**, change the title to **Let's Bake!** In the right placeholder, type **Peter Wing, Executive Chef** Press Enter, and then type **617-555-0037** Select all the text, turn off the **Bullet** formatting, and then **Center** the text. In the left placeholder, change the picture to the data file **i02D_ Kitchen**. Change the **Height** of the picture to **3**. Position the picture so the top left sizing handle displays at **approximately 4.5 inches on the left side of the horizontal ruler** and at **1 inch in the upper portion of the vertical ruler**. Delete **Slide 4**.

6 From **Backstage** view, click **Save As. Save** the presentation as an **Outline/RTF** document in your **Integrated Projects Chapter 2** folder with the file name **Lastname_Firstname_2D_Equipment_Outline** From **Backstage** view, click **Show All Properties**. In the **Author** box, type your first name and last name; in the **Subject** box, type your course name and section number; and then in the **Tags** box, type **equipment, marketing Save** the presentation, and then **Close** PowerPoint.

7 Start Word, open your RTF file **Lastname_ Firstname_2D_Equipment_Outline**, and then **Convert** the file to a Word document. Insert the file name in the footer. In **Outline View**, change the **Font Color** of all document text to **Automatic.**

8 Display the **Level 1** paragraphs. Select the **Level 1** paragraph *Equipment*, and then delete the paragraph as well as any sublevels. Under *Baked Goods*, select the **Level 2** text, and then on separate lines, type the Level 2 paragraphs **Breads** and **Breakfast Sweets** and **Desserts** Move the *Baked Goods* paragraph and its associated sublevels up so that it is the second **Level 1** paragraph. **Expand** the **Level 1** paragraph *Local Health Food Stores*; select the **Level 2** text below; and then on separate lines, type the Level 2 paragraphs **Boston Organic Market** and **Brownstone Mill Organics** and **Health Food Craze** and **Natural Foods**

9 Close Outline View. From **Backstage** view, click **Show All Properties**. In the **Author** box, type your first name and last name; in the **Subject** box, type your course name and section number; and then in the **Tags** box, type **modified outline Save** your document, and then **Close** Word.

(Project 2D Equipment Upgrade continues on the next page)

Mastering Integration Project 2D Equipment Upgrade (continued)

10 Start PowerPoint, and create a **Blank Presentation**. Use **Slides from Outline** to insert the outline **Lastname_Firstname_2D_Equipment_Outline**. **Save** the presentation to your **Integrated Projects Chapter 2** folder with the file name **Lastname_Firstname_2D_Store_Presentation** Add the file name to the footer of all the handout pages.

11 Change the **Theme** to **Quotable**. Delete **Slide 1**. On **Slide 2**, change the **Layout** to **Two Content**. In the right placeholder, insert the picture **i02D_Muffins**, and then change the **Height** of the picture to **4**. Move the picture to the left so the top middle sizing handle displays at **approximately 2 inches on the right side of the horizontal ruler**.

12 On **Slide 3**, insert the shape **Rounded Rectangle**, and then change the **Shape Height** to **2.5** and the **Shape Width** to **4.5**. Move the shape to the bottom right corner

of the slide so the bottom right sizing handle displays at **approximately 4.5 inches on the right side of the horizontal ruler** and **3.0 inches on the lower portion of the vertical ruler**. Click in the shape, and then type **Let's give our customers what they want – more locations to purchase our baked goods.** Select the text you typed, and change the **Font Size** to **24**.

13 On **Slide 1**, change the **Layout** to **Title Slide**. Select the text in the subtitle, and change the **Font Size** to **24**.

14 From **Backstage** view, click **Show All Properties**. In the **Author** box, type your first name and last name; in the **Subject** box, type your course name and section number; and then in the **Tags** box, type **store locations Save** the presentation, and then **Close** PowerPoint. Submit your printed or electronic files as directed by your instructor.

END | You have completed Project 2D

Apply a combination of the 2A and 2B skills.

GO! Solve It | Project 2E Staff Orientation

PROJECT FILES

For Project 2E, you will need the following files:

New blank PowerPoint presentation
i02E_Staff_Orientation

You will save your files as:

Lastname_Firstname_2E_Orientation_Outline
Lastname_Firstname_2E_Orientation_Presentation

Because the company is growing and adding more staff, Lucinda dePaolo—the CFO for Skyline Bakery & Café—wants all staff orientations to be more consistent than they have been in the past. She has started a list of topics to be covered. Ms. dePaolo has asked you to complete the list and create a PowerPoint presentation. She also wants you to include a new employee benefit: Profit Sharing—**Five percent of net profits will be shared with employees**.

Open the Word file **i02E_Staff_Orientation**. Promote, demote, and move items so that the items display in a more logical order. Save the file as **Lastname_Firstname_2E_ Orientation_Outline** Import the Word document into PowerPoint. Modify the presentation by inserting or deleting slides, applying a theme, changing the slide layout, applying character spacing, applying text shadow, and inserting and modifying at least one SmartArt graphic or shape. Add speaker's notes to at least two slides. Save the presentation as **Lastname_Firstname_2E_Orientation_Presentation** In both files, insert the file name in the footer and add appropriate document properties. Submit both files as directed.

Performance Level

Performance Criteria	Exemplary: You consistently applied the relevant skills.	Proficient: You sometimes, but not always, applied the relevant skills.	Developing: You rarely or never applied the relevant skills.
Modify Outline	Outline is modified to display information in a logical order	Outline is modified, but items do not display in a logical order	Outline is not modified
Create PowerPoint presentation	Presentation created using Word Outline, modified to include a theme, varied slide layouts, character spacing, text shadow, and SmartArt	Presentation created, but it is missing two or fewer modifications	Presentation is missing more than two modifications
Speaker notes included in presentation	Speaker notes are added to at least two slides	Speaker notes are added to only one slide	No speaker notes are added to the presentation

END | You have completed Project 2E

RUBRIC

The following outcomes-based assessments are open-ended assessments. That is, there is no specific correct result; your result will depend on your approach to the information provided. Make Professional Quality your goal. Use the following scoring rubric to guide you in how to approach the problem and then to evaluate how well your approach solves the problem.

The *criteria*—Software Mastery, Content, Format and Layout, and Process—represent the knowledge and skills you have gained that you can apply to solving the problem. The *levels of performance*— Professional Quality, Approaching Professional Quality, or Needs Quality Improvements—help you and your instructor evaluate your result.

	Your completed project is of Professional Quality if you:	Your completed project is approaching Professional Quality if you:	Your completed project needs Quality Improvements if you:
1-Software Mastery	Choose and apply the most appropriate skills, tools, and features and identify efficient methods to solve the problem.	Choose and apply some appropriate skills, tools, and features, but not in the most efficient manner.	Choose inappropriate skills, tools, or features, or are inefficient in solving the problem.
2-Content	Construct a solution that is clear and well organized, contains content that is accurate, appropriate to the audience and purpose, and is complete. Provide a solution that contains no errors of spelling, grammar, or style.	Construct a solution in which some components are unclear, poorly organized, inconsistent, or incomplete. Misjudge the needs of the audience. Have some errors in spelling, grammar, or style, but the errors do not detract from comprehension.	Construct a solution that is unclear, incomplete, or poorly organized, contains some inaccurate or inappropriate content, and contains many errors of spelling, grammar, or style. Do not solve the problem.
3-Format and Layout	Format and arrange all elements to communicate information and ideas, clarify function, illustrate relationships, and indicate relative importance.	Apply appropriate format and layout features to some elements, but not others. Overuse features, causing minor distraction.	Apply format and layout that does not communicate information or ideas clearly. Do not use format and layout features to clarify function, illustrate relationships, or indicate relative importance. Use available features excessively, causing distraction.
4-Process	Use an organized approach that integrates planning, development, self-assessment, revision, and reflection.	Demonstrate an organized approach in some areas, but not others; or, use an insufficient process of organization throughout.	Do not use an organized approach to solve the problem.

Apply a combination of the 2A and 2B skills.

GO! Think | Project 2F Bagels Menu

PROJECT FILES

For Project 2F, you will need the following files:

New blank PowerPoint presentation
i02F_Bagels_Menu
i02F_Bagels

You will save your files as:

Lastname_Firstname_2F_Bagels_Menu
Lastname_Firstname_2F_Bagels_Presentation

Nancy Goldman, the Chief Baker for the Skyline Bakery & Café, wants to add bagels to the menu. She has asked you to complete a Word document listing the reasons why bagels would be a good addition to the menu. When the document is completed, she wants you to create a PowerPoint presentation to present to the management team. Ms. Goldman has indicated the bagel varieties would include sesame seed, poppy seed, cinnamon raisin, blueberry, caraway seed, pumpernickel, and cheddar cheese.

Open the Word file **i02F_Bagels_Menu.** Promote or demote paragraphs and move at least one level to a different location so that the items display in a more logical order. Save the file as **Lastname_Firstname_2F_Bagels_Menu** Import the Word document into PowerPoint. Modify the presentation by inserting or deleting slides, applying a different theme, changing the slide layout, adding character spacing, adding text shadow, inserting and modifying at least one SmartArt graphic, and inserting the picture **i02F_Bagels**. Add speaker's notes to at least two slides. Save the presentation as **Lastname_Firstname_2F_Bagels_Presentaton** In both files, insert the file name in the footer and add appropriate information to the Document Properties. Submit both files as directed.

END | You have completed Project 2F

Integrating Word and Access

PROJECT 3A

OUTCOMES
Create an Access database from a template and export Access data to Word.

OBJECTIVES

1. Create an Access Database Using a Template
2. Use an Access Form to Enter and Edit Records
3. Export an Access Table to a Word Document
4. Format a Word Document

PROJECT 3B

OUTCOMES
Use Mail Merge to generate letters and envelopes.

OBJECTIVES

5. Use Mail Merge in Word to Complete Letters Using Access Data
6. Use Mail Merge in Word to Create Envelopes Using Access Data
7. Create and Modify a Query in Access
8. Use Mail Merge in Access

asharkyu/Shutterstock

In This Chapter

In this chapter, you will create an Access database using a template. Access provides a variety of installed templates, or you can go online and download a wide range of templates to suit your needs. In Access, you can enter data in a table or form. You can also create a query or report to display specific data from the table. You can export data to a Word document in a variety of ways. For example, a database may contain contact information—such as names and addresses of customers. Using the mail merge feature in Word, you can create personalized letters and envelopes.

The projects in this chapter relate to **Southwest Gardens**, a television show produced by Media Southwest Productions. The southwest style of gardening is popular in many areas of the country, not just in the yards and gardens of Arizona and New Mexico. The stylish simplicity and use of indigenous, hardy plants that are traditional in the southwestern United States make for beautiful, environmentally friendly gardens in any part of the country. The show, which is broadcast nationwide, and its website provide tips and tricks for beautiful gardens and highlight new tools and techniques. The show's hosts present tours of public and private gardens that showcase the southwest style.

PROJECT ACTIVITIES

In Activities 3.01 through 3.11, you will create a list of gardeners who tend gardens that Southwest Gardens wants to feature on the Garden Walks section of the show. You will enter and update the gardeners' contact information using an Access table and an Access form. You will export the table to a Rich Text Format (RTF) file and then open the file in Word. You will modify the Word document by using the Page Layout features, adding borders, and inserting and modifying a text box. Your completed documents will look similar to Figure 3.1.

PROJECT FILES

For Project 3A, you will need the following files:

New blank Access database
i03A_Garden_Walk

You will save your files as:

Lastname_Firstname_3A_Garden_Contacts
Lastname_Firstname_3A_Gardeners
Lastname_Firstname_3A_Garden_Walk

PROJECT RESULTS

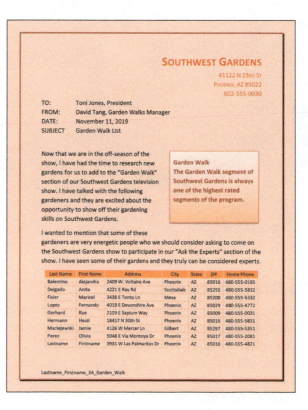

FIGURE 3.1 Project 3A Walks List

A *database* is an organized collection of facts about people, events, things, or ideas related to a particular topic or purpose. You can use a *template* to create a database or begin with a new blank database. An Access template is a preformatted database designed for a specific purpose. A wide variety of templates are provided when Access is installed. Additional templates can be downloaded from the Internet. A template contains the tables, queries, forms, and reports needed to perform a specific task.

Activity 3.01 │ Creating a Database Using a Template

In this Activity, you will create an Access database by using a template.

1 Start Access. Under **Available Templates**, click **Desktop student database**. If necessary, click in the Search for online templates box, and type Contacts. Scroll down, and then select Updated: Students. Compare your screen with Figure 3.2.

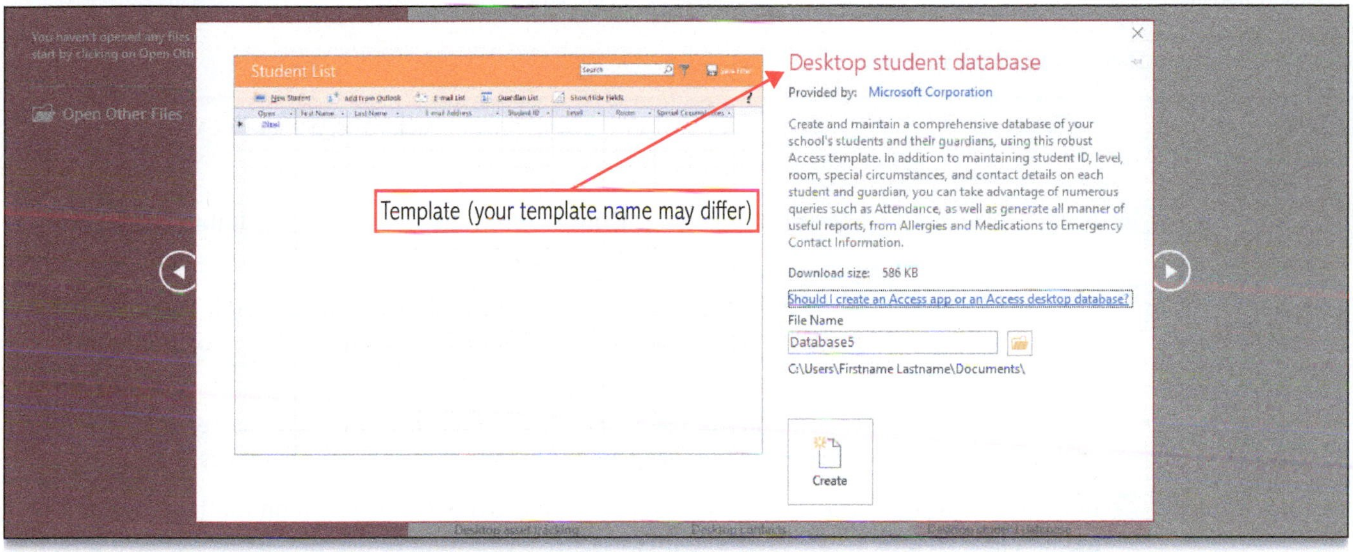

Template (your template name may differ)

Access 2016, Windows 10, Microsoft Corporation

FIGURE 3.2

2 On the right side of the screen, to the right of the **File Name** box, click **Browse**. In the **File New Database** dialog box, navigate to the location where you are saving your files for this chapter, click **New folder**, type Integrated Projects Chapter 3 and then press Enter. Then click **Open** to open the new folder you just created.

3 In the **File name** box, using your own name, replace the existing text with **Lastname_ Firstname_3A_Garden_Contacts** and then click **OK**.

On the right, the name of your database displays in the File Name box, and the drive and folder where the database is stored displays under the File Name box. An Access database has the file extension *.aacdb*.

4 Under the **File Name** box, click **Create** to create the new database.

Access creates a new database and opens a form *object* named Student List. Objects are the basic parts of a database that you create to store your data and to work with your data; for example, *tables*, forms, queries, and reports. A table is the Access object that stores data organized in an arrangement of columns and rows, and which is the foundation of an Access database.

5 ▶ Directly below the ribbon, on the **Message Bar**, check to see if a Security Warning displays. Compare your screen with Figure 3.3.

When you open an Access file, you may see a Security Warning in the *Message Bar*, which is the area directly below the ribbon that displays information—for example, security alerts—when there is potentially unsafe, active content in a document that you open. All databases provided by Microsoft and the student data files that accompany this chapter are safe to use on your computer.

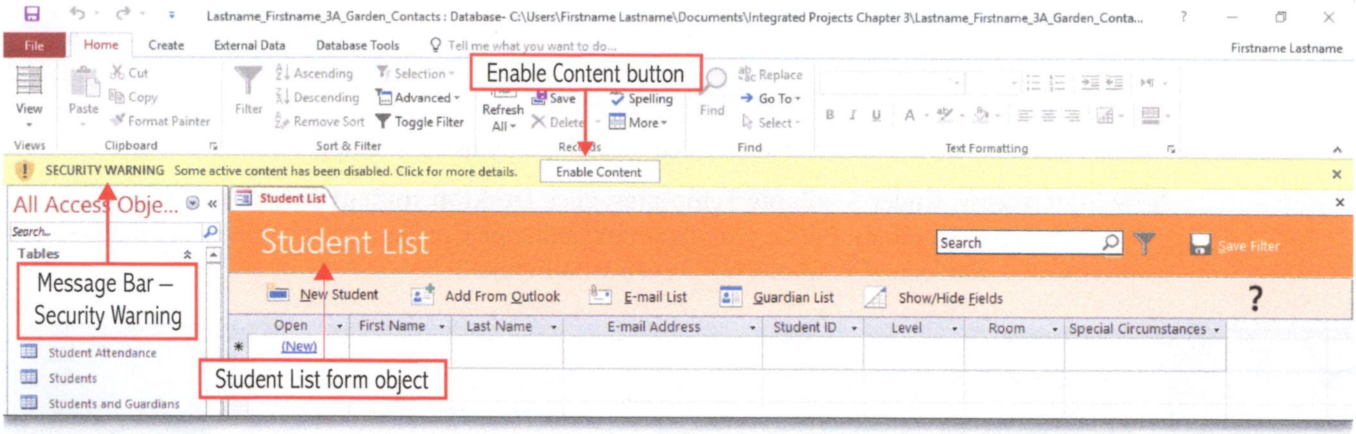

FIGURE 3.3

Access 2016, Windows 10, Microsoft Corporation

6 ▶ If necessary, on the **Message Bar**, click **Enable Content**. If a Welcome dialog box opens, close it.

7 ▶ Right-click the **Student List form tab**, and then on the shortcut menu, click **Close**. If necessary, on the left side of the window, click Shutter Bar Open/Close ⟩⟩ to expand the Navigation Pane.

The *Navigation Pane* is the area of the Access window that displays and organizes the names of the objects in a database. From the Navigation Pane, you can open objects for use.

8 ▶ In the **Navigation Pane**, under **Tables**, right-click **Guardians**, and then on the shortcut menu, click **Delete**. In the **message box** asking if you want to delete the table *Guardians*, click **Yes**. Then delete all other objects in the database other than the Students table.

In this project, you will not use any of the existing objects displayed under Queries, Forms, or Reports.

9 ▶ Under **Tables**, right-click **Students**, and then on the shortcut menu, click **Rename**. Using your own name, type the new table name **Lastname Firstname 3A Gardeners** and then press Enter. Double-click the new table name **Lastname Firstname 3A Gardeners** to open the table, and then compare your screen with Figure 3.4.

Your table displays in *datasheet view*—the Access view that displays data organized in columns and rows similar to an Excel worksheet. In a table object, each row forms a *record*—all of the categories of data pertaining to *one* person, place, thing, event, or idea. Each column forms a *field*—a single piece of information that is stored in every record.

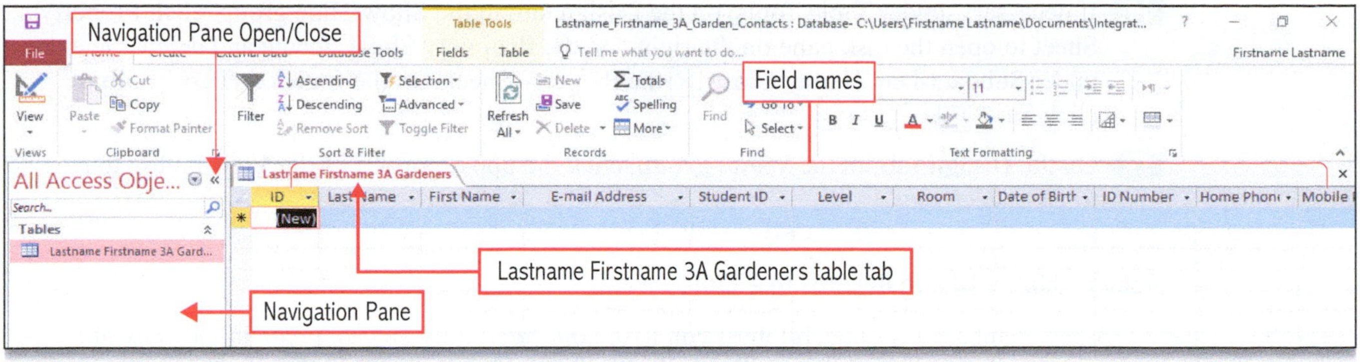

FIGURE 3.4

10 ▷ On the **Home tab**, in the **Views group**, click the **View button arrow**, and then click **Design View**. Compare your screen with Figure 3.5.

The table opens in *Design view*—an Access view that displays the detailed structure of a table, query, form, or report, and the view in which some tasks must be performed. The first field name—ID—is the *primary key* in this table, noted with a key in the row selector box. A primary key is a field that uniquely identifies a record in a table. A *data type* is the characteristic that defines the kind of data that can be entered into a field; for example, numbers, text, or dates. The ID field has the data type *AutoNumber*—an Access feature that creates a unique number for each record.

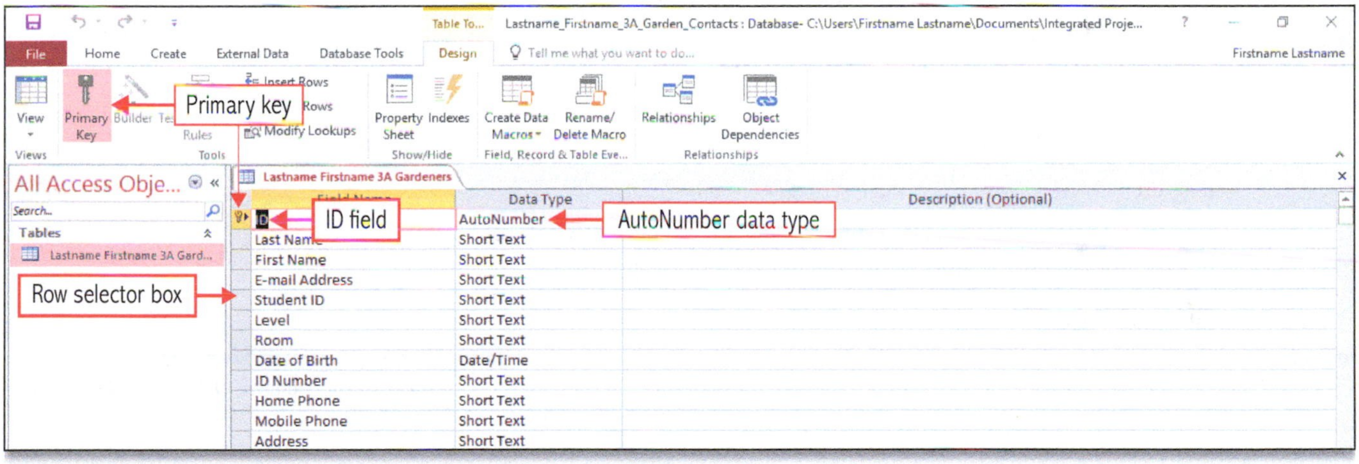

FIGURE 3.5

11 ▷ To the left of the **E-mail Address** field, click the small gray square—the row selector box. Hold down Shift, point to the row selector box until the ➡ pointer displays, hold down the left mouse button, and then drag down to select all the fields beginning with **E-mail Address** and ending with **ID Number**. Release the left mouse button, and then with all six fields selected, under **Table Tools**, on the **Design tab**, in the **Tools group**, click **Delete Rows**. In the displayed message, click **Yes** to delete the rows. By using the technique you just practiced, select and then delete the **Mobile Phone** field. Then, beginning with **Country/Region**, delete the last 11 fields in the table.

Your table should have eight fields beginning with ID and ending with ZIP/Postal Code.

12 ▷ Click the **State/Province** field name, and then delete the text **/Province**. Click the **ZIP/ Postal Code** field name, and then delete **/Postal Code**.

13 ▷ Click the row selector box for the **Home Phone** field. Point to the row selector box, hold down the left mouse button, and then drag the field down below the **ZIP** field name.

14 If necessary, under Table Tools, on the Design tab, in the Show/Hide group, click Property Sheet to open the task pane on the right. On the **Property Sheet**, locate and delete the entry under Subdatasheet Name. **Close** ☒ the Property Sheet. On the **Quick Access Toolbar**, click **Save** 🖫.

15 On the **Design tab**, in the **Views group**, click the upper portion of the **View** button to return to Datasheet view.

Activity 3.02 │ Adding Records to a Table

A new database is not useful until you have **populated** it by entering data in the **cells** of a table. To populate the database means to fill the table with records. Recall that a cell is the intersection of a row and a column in a table.

1 Close ⏪ the **Navigation Pane**.

2 In the first record, below **Last Name**, click in the cell, and then type **Balentine**. Press ⎄. In the **First Name** cell, type **Alejandra** and then press ⎄. In the **Address** cell, type **2409 W Voltaire Ave** and press ⎄; in the **City** cell, type **Phoenix** and then press ⎄. In the **State** cell, type **AZ** and press ⎄; in the **ZIP** cell, type **85016** and press ⎄; and then in the **Home Phone** cell, type **480-555-0185** then press ⎄ two times and compare your screen with Figure 3.6.

Pressing ⎄ two times moves you to the next row—the next record. As soon as you move to the next row, the record for the first gardener is saved in the 3A Gardeners table.

FIGURE 3.6   Access 2016, Windows 10, Microsoft Corporation

🔄 **ANOTHER WAY**   Press ⎆ to move to the next field.

3 Be sure that the cell under *Balentine* is the active cell.

You can skip the ID field because it is an AutoNumber field.

4 Using the technique you just practiced, enter the contact information for two additional gardeners.

Last Name	First Name	Address	City	State	ZIP	Home Phone
Delgado	Anita	4221 E Ray Rd	Scottsdale	AZ	85255	480-555-5832
Fisler	Maricela	3438 E Tonto Ln	Mesa	AZ	85208	480-555-5332

> **NOTE** Correct Typing Errors
>
> Correct typing errors by using the techniques you have practiced in other Office applications. For example, use ⌫ Backspace to remove characters to the left, use ⌦ Delete to remove characters to the right, or select the text you want to replace and type the correct information. Press ⎋ Esc to exit out of a record that has not been completely entered.

5 ▶ Right-click your **Lastname Firstname 3A Gardeners table tab**, and then on the shortcut menu, click **Close** to close the table.

Objective 2 — Use an Access Form to Enter and Edit Records

An Access **form** is a database object you can use to enter data, edit data, or display data from a table or **query**. A query is a database object that retrieves specific data from one or more database objects—either tables or other queries—and then, in a single datasheet, displays only the data you specify. Most forms are **bound**—a term that describes objects and controls that are based on data stored in one or more tables or queries in the database. Although a form is based on a table or query, it does not need to include all of the fields in the underlying objects.

Activity 3.03 | Adding Records Using a Form

Although there are various ways to create a form in Access, the quickest way is to use the Form tool, which creates a form that displays all of the fields from the underlying data source (table) one record at a time. Records that you create or edit in a form are automatically added to or updated in the underlying table.

1 ▶ **Open** 》 the **Navigation Pane**.

2 ▶ In the **Navigation Pane**, with the **Lastname Firstname 3A Gardeners** table selected, click the **Create tab**, and then in the **Forms group**, click **Form**. Compare your screen with Figure 3.7.

Access creates a form based on the selected table—your Lastname Firstname 3A Gardeners table. The form displays in **Form view**—the Access view in which you can view the records, but you cannot change the layout or design of the form. The data from the underlying data source displays. Here, each field displays data for the first record—*Alejandra Balentine*—from the underlying table.

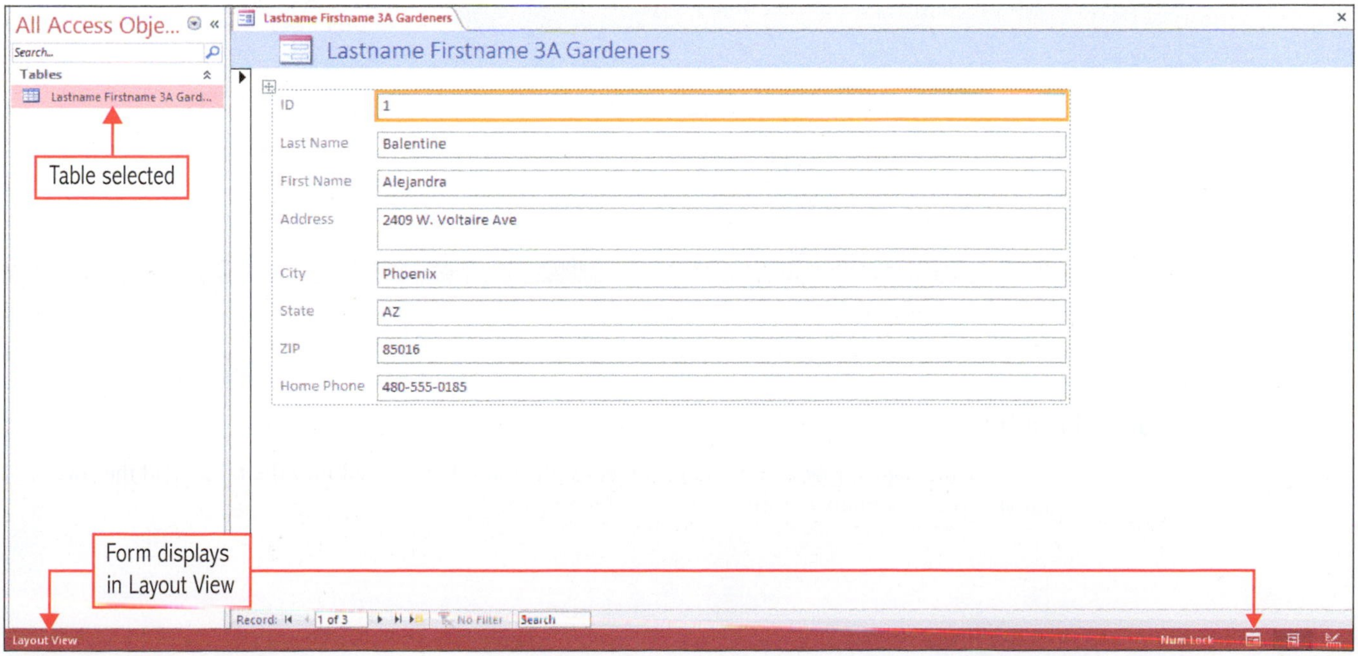

FIGURE 3.7

3 On the **Quick Access Toolbar**, click **Save** 🖫. In the **Save As** dialog box, type **Lastname_ Firstname 3A Gardeners Form** and then click **OK**.

The form is saved, and the new name displays on the form tab.

4 Under **Form Layout Tools**, on the **Design tab**, in the **Views group**, click the upper portion of the **View** button.

The form displays in *Layout view*—the view in which you can view and edit the records but you cannot change the layout or design of the form.

5 At the bottom of the form, in the navigation area, click **New (blank) record** ▶⊞.

A new blank form displays, indicated in the navigation area by *4 of 4*.

6 Press ⎢Tab⎥. In the **Last Name** field, type **Lopez** and then press ⎢Tab⎥.

Use the ⎢Tab⎥ key to move from field to field in a form. This is known as *tab order*—the order in which the insertion point moves from one field to the next in a form when you press ⎢Tab⎥.

7 Type **Fernando** and then press ⎢Tab⎥. Continue to enter the following data, pressing ⎢Tab⎥ to move to the next field. After typing the Home Phone, compare your screen with Figure 3.8.

Address	City	State	ZIP	Home Phone
4019 E Devonshire Ave	**Phoenix**	**AZ**	**85029**	**480-555-4772**

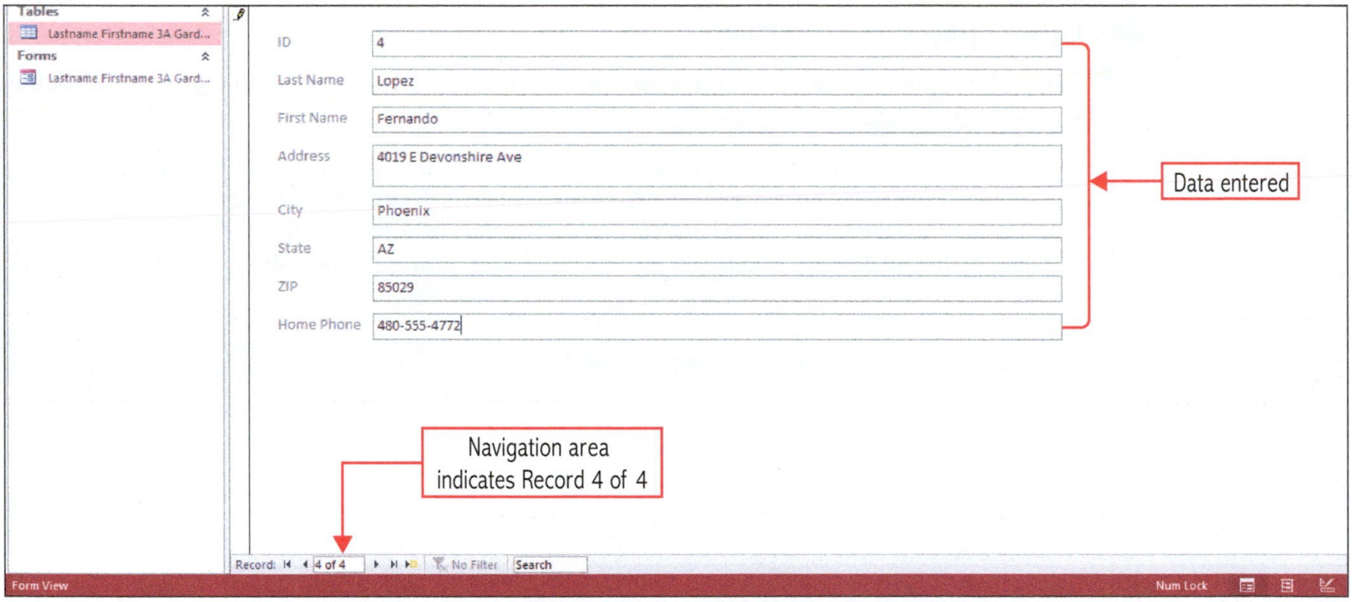

FIGURE 3.8

Access 2016, Windows 10, Microsoft Corporation

8 Press ⎢Tab⎥.

By pressing ⎢Tab⎥ or ⎢Enter⎥ at the end of a record, the record is entered into the table, and the form moves to a new blank record.

9 ▶ Using the technique you just practiced, enter the contact information for five additional gardeners, and then compare your screen with Figure 3.9.

Last Name	First Name	Address	City	State	ZIP	Home Phone
Gerhard	Rae	21062 N 33rd Ave	Phoenix	AZ	85031	480-555-0031
Herrmann	Heidi	18417 N 30th St	Phoenix	AZ	85016	480-555-5831
Levens	Noreen	619 E Briles Rd	Chandler	AZ	85226	480-555-0992
Maciejewski	Jamie	4126 W Mercer Ln	Gilbert	AZ	85297	480-555-5351
Perez	Olivia	5048 E Via Montoya Dr	Phoenix	AZ	85017	480-555-8156

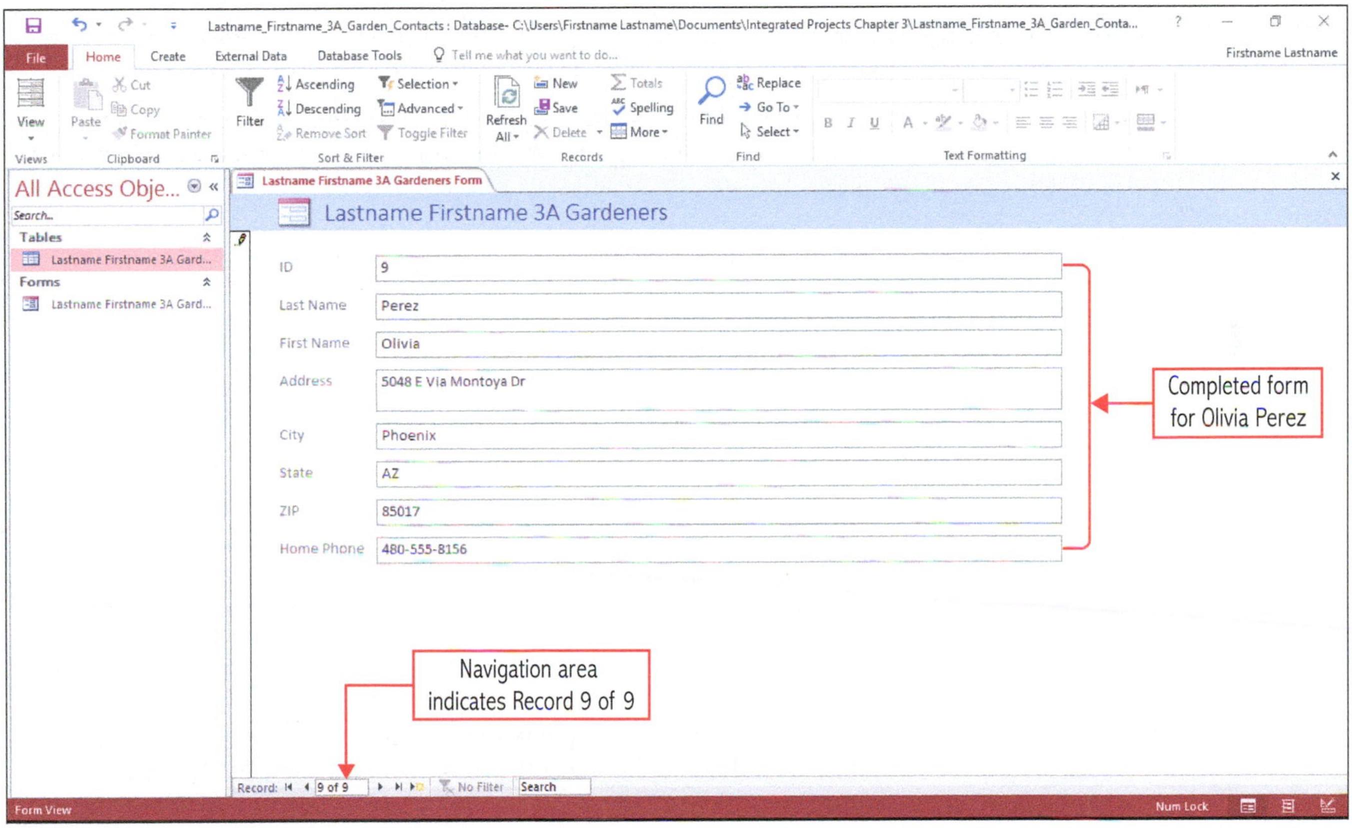

FIGURE 3.9

10 ▶ Press Tab to accept the record for Olivia Perez and to display a new blank form.

11 ▶ Enter the following data using your own **First Name** and **Last Name**, and then press Tab.

Last Name	First Name	Address	City	State	ZIP	Home Phone
Lastname	Firstname	3931 W Las Palmaritas Dr	Phoenix	AZ	85016	480-555-4821

The navigation area, located below the form, indicates Record 11 of 11, which is a blank form.

12 ▶ In the **Navigation Pane**, under **Tables**, double-click the **Lastname Firstname 3A Gardeners** table to display the table. Verify that your record displays as the last record in the table.

13 ▶ At the top of the object window, click the **Lastname Firstname 3A Gardeners Form tab** to display the form. At the bottom of the screen, in the navigation area, click **First record** . To view the records, click **Next record** until your record is visible.

Activity 3.04 | Finding and Editing a Record Using a Form

A form is useful when you want to find specific occurrences of a value in a field, find blank fields, or edit a specific record in the Access database. Using a single-record form to add, delete, or edit records reduces the likelihood of data entry errors.

1 In the **Lastname Firstname 3A Gardeners Form**, click anywhere in the **Address** field. On the **Home tab**, in the **Find group**, click **Find**. In the **Find and Replace** dialog box, in the **Find What** box, type **21062** and then click the **Match arrow**, click **Any Part of Field**, and then click **Find Next**. Compare your screen with Figure 3.10.

The information for Rae Gerhard displays in the form.

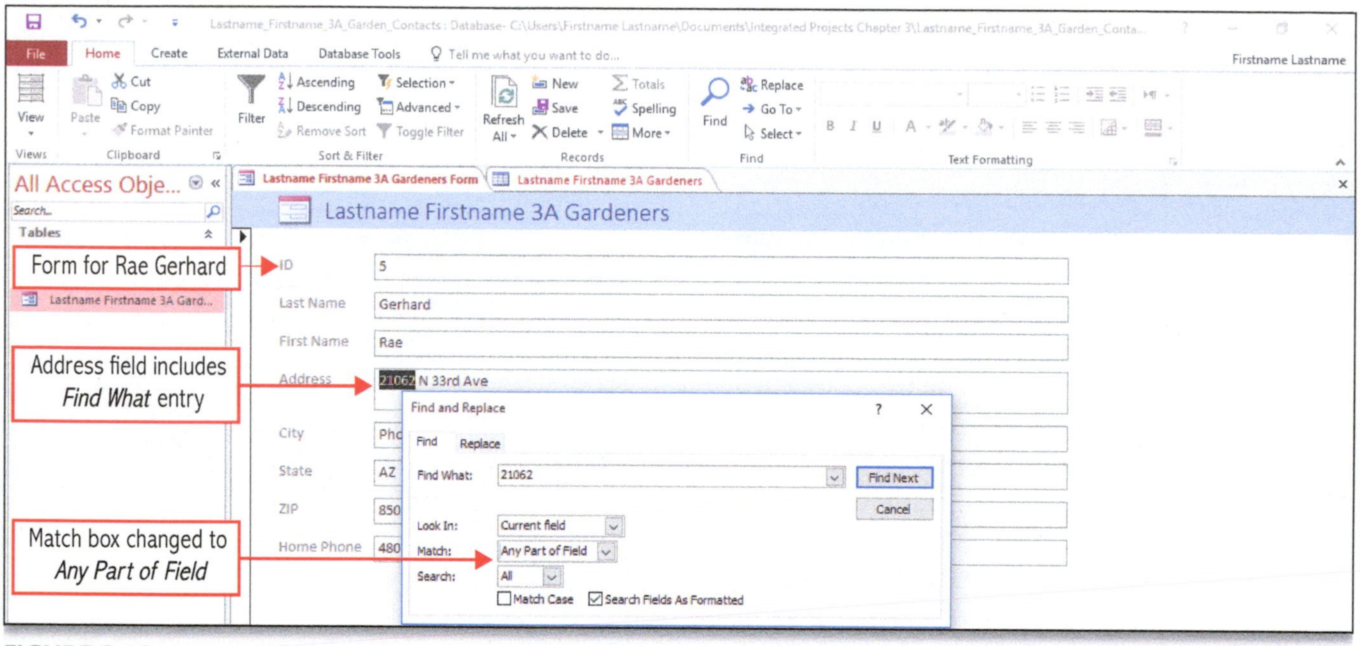

Access 2016, Windows 10, Microsoft Corporation

FIGURE 3.10

2 If necessary, drag the Find and Replace dialog box to the right so that you can view the entire Address field. In the **Address** field, select the entire address, type **2103 E Sapium Way** and then press Tab three times. In the **ZIP** field, type **85009** and then press Tab to update the record in the table.

3 In the displayed record, if necessary, click anywhere in the Home Phone field. Click in the **Find and Replace** dialog box to make it active. In the **Find What** box, type **480-555-8156** and then click **Find Next**. **Delete** the last four digits of the phone number, type **2081** and then press Tab to update the phone number. Keep the Find and Replace dialog box open for the next activity.

Activity 3.05 | Deleting Records Using a Form

After you locate a record by using a form, you can use the form to delete the record from the table.

1 In the displayed record, click anywhere in the **Last Name** field. In the **Find and Replace** dialog box, in the **Find What** box, type **Levens** and then click **Find Next** to display information for Noreen Levens.

2 **Close** ☒ the **Find and Replace** dialog box. On the **Home tab**, in the **Records group**, click the **Delete button arrow**, and then compare your screen with Figure 3.11.

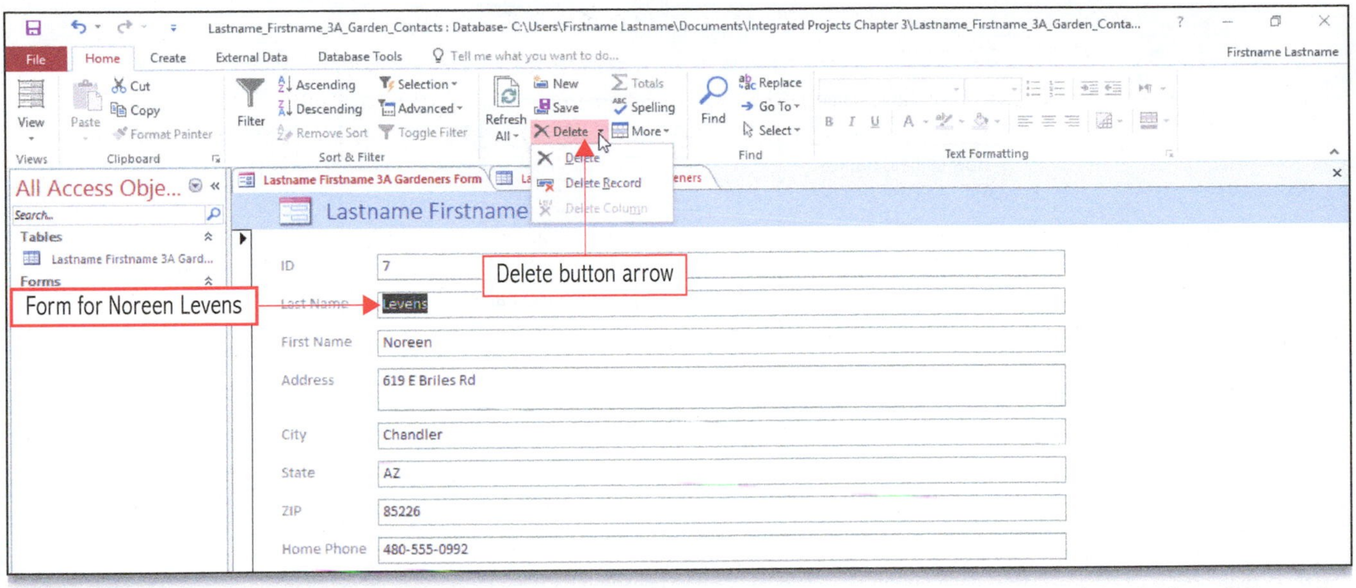

FIGURE 3.11

Access 2016, Windows 10, Microsoft Corporation

3 In the displayed list, click **Delete Record**.

A message displays alerting you that you are about to delete *1 record*. In Access, if you click Yes and delete a record, you cannot use Undo to reverse the action. To undo the action, you would have to re-create the entire record.

4 Click **Yes** to delete the record. Notice the navigation area indicates that there are nine total records.

Because the ID field is an AutoNumber data type, the ID number for each existing record does not change.

5 Right-click the **Lastname Firstname 3A Gardeners Form tab**. On the shortcut menu, click **Close All**.

Activity 3.06 | Printing an Access Table

Although you might choose to print a table for proofreading, you usually create an Access report to display the contents of a table in a professional manner. In this activity, you will print the table for proofreading.

1 In the **Navigation Pane**, click the **Lastname Firstname 3A Gardeners** table to select it. Click the **File tab** to display **Backstage** view. On the left click the **Print tab**, and then, under *Print*, click **Print Preview**. Compare your screen with Figure 3.12. Notice that the Address column is too narrow to display all the information.

The name of the table displays at the top of the page. If a table will print on more than one page, at the bottom of the window, in the navigation area, you can click Next Page to view the subsequent pages.

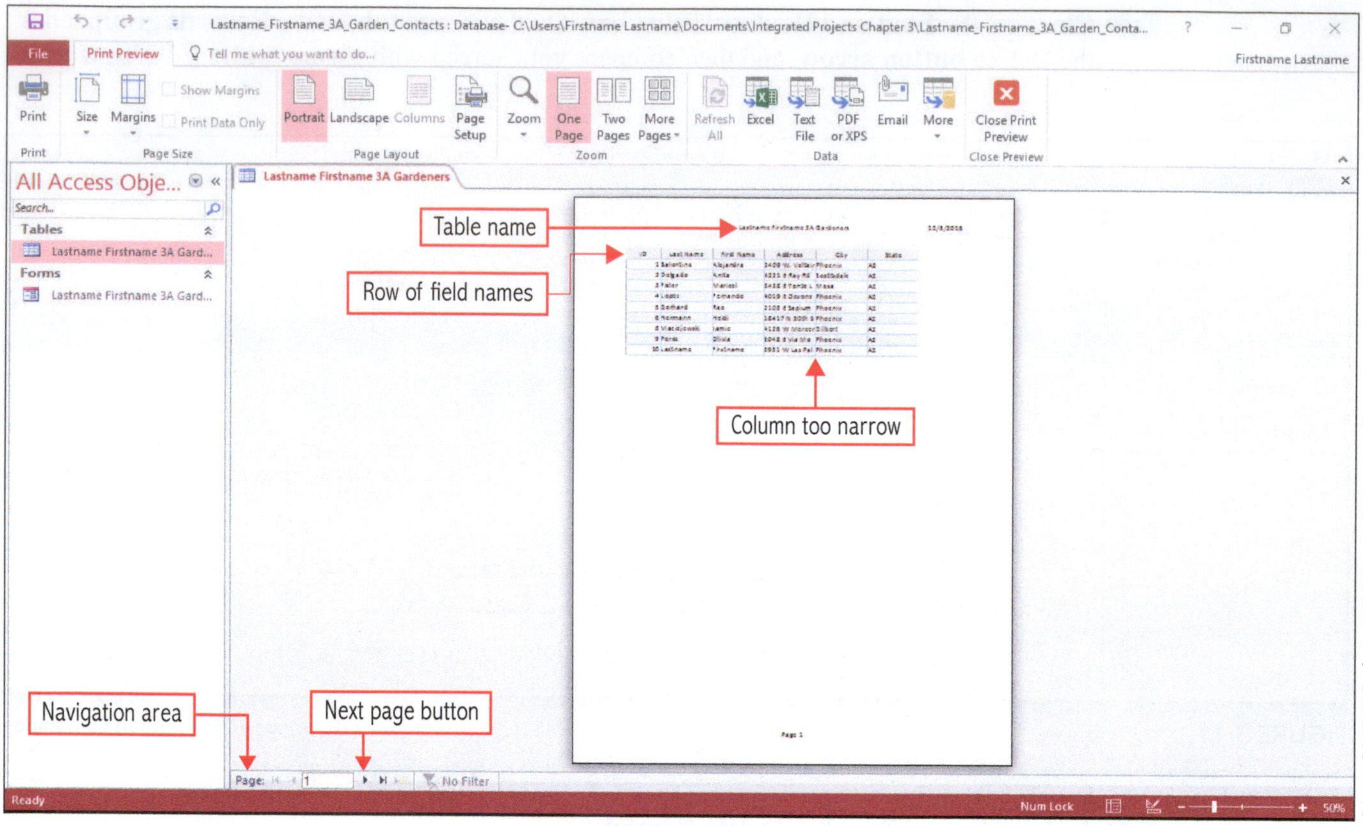

Labels on figure:
- Table name
- Row of field names
- Column too narrow
- Navigation area
- Next page button

FIGURE 3.12

2 ▸ On the **Print Preview tab**, in the **Close Preview group**, click **Close Print Preview**.

3 ▸ In the **Navigation Pane**, under **Tables**, double-click the **Lastname Firstname 3A Gardeners** table to open it.

4 ▸ In the row of field names, point to the right boundary of the **ID** field to display the ⊞ pointer, and then double-click.

Double-clicking the right border of a column changes the column width to fully display the field name and the longest entry in the column.

5 ▸ Click the **Last Name** field, hold down ⇧Shift, point to *Last Name* to display the ⬇ pointer, hold down the left mouse button, and then drag to the right to the **Home Phone** field.

All the fields from *Last Name* through *Home Phone* are selected.

6 ▸ Point to the **Home Phone** field, and then right-click. On the shortcut menu, click **Field Width**, and then in the **Column Width** dialog box, click **Best Fit**. Compare your screen with Figure 3.13.

The column widths of all the selected columns are adjusted to best fit the existing data.

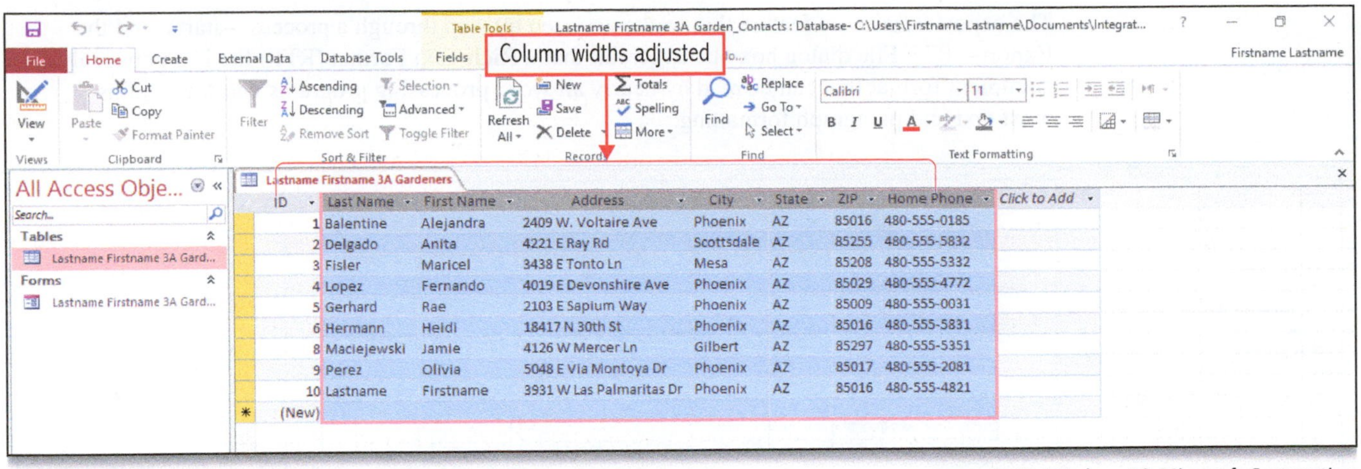

Column widths adjusted

FIGURE 3.13

Access 2016, Windows 10, Microsoft Corporation

7 Display **Backstage** view, click the **Print tab**, and then click **Print Preview**. On the **Print Preview tab**, in the **Page Layout group**, click **Landscape**.

In the navigation area, notice that the Next Page button is dimmed, indicating that this is a one-page document.

8 **Save** 🖫 the changes you have made to the design of the table. As directed by your instructor, print or create an electronic copy of the print results.

9 In the **Close Preview group**, click **Close Print Preview**.

10 Right-click the **Lastname Firstname 3A Gardeners table tab**, and then on the shortcut menu, click **Close**.

11 Point to the right edge of the Navigation Page until the ↔ displays. Hold down the left mouse button and drag to the right until all object names display fully. Release the left mouse button.

12 Display **Backstage** view, and then on the right, click **View and edit database properties**. In the **Properties** dialog box, on the **Summary tab**, in the **Subject** box, type your course name and section number; in the **Author** box, type your first name and last name; and then in the **Keywords** box, type **gardener contacts** Click **OK** to close the dialog box, and then in the upper left corner, click ⬅ to return to the database with the **Home tab** displayed.

Objective 3   Export an Access Table to a Word Document

Exporting, similar to copying and pasting, is a way to output data and database objects to another database, worksheet, or file format to be used in another file or application. For example, you can export an Access table to Word instead of retyping the information. Exporting can save you time and reduce the number of errors.

Activity 3.07 │ Exporting an Access Table to an RTF File

1 With the **Navigation Pane** open, under **Tables**, be sure your **Lastname Firstname 3A Gardeners** table is selected—but do not open the table. Click the **External Data tab**. In the **Export group**, click **More**, and then click **Word**. Compare your screen to Figure 3.14.

The export *wizard*—a feature that walks you step by step through a process—starts, and the Export—RTF File dialog box opens. Recall that a Rich Text Format (RTF) file is a universal document format that can be read by nearly all word processing programs and that retains most text and paragraph formatting.

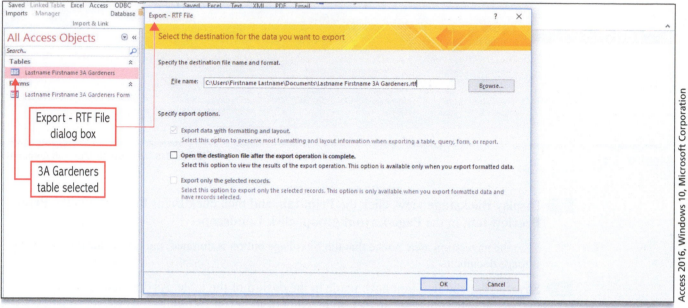

FIGURE 3.14

> **2** In the **Export - RTF File** dialog box, click **Browse**, and then navigate to your **Integrated Projects Chapter 3** folder. In the **File Save** dialog box, in the **File name** box, select the existing text, type **Lastname_Firstname_3A_Gardeners** and then click **Save**.

> **3** In the **Export - RTF File** dialog box, click **OK**. In the **Export - RTF File** dialog box, when asked *Do you want to save these export steps?*, be sure the **Save export steps** check box is *not* selected. Click **Close**.

> The Access table has been saved as *Lastname_Firstname_3A_Gardeners.rtf.* If you plan to repeat an export operation, you can save the settings used in an Import or Export wizard.

> **4** Close ⊠ Access.

Activity 3.08 | Inserting Access Data in a Word Document

David Tang is the manager of the Garden Walks segment of the show. He has been in contact with local gardeners whom he would like to feature on his segment. Mr. Tang has started a memo to Toni Jones, President of Southwest Gardens. He has asked you to complete the memo by including the list of gardeners.

> **1** Start Word, and then navigate to the student data files that accompany this chapter. Locate and open the document **i03A_Garden_Walk**.

> **2** Display **Backstage** view, on the left click **Save As**, and then click **Browse** to display the **Save As** dialog box. Navigate to your **Integrated Projects Chapter 3** folder. In the **File name** box, select the existing text, and then using your own name, type **Lastname_Firstname_3A_Garden_Walk** and then click **Save**.

> **3** On the **Insert tab**, in the **Header & Footer group**, click **Footer**, and then click **Edit Footer**. Under **Header & Footer**, on the **Design tab**, in the **Insert group**, click **Document Info**, and then click **File Name**. Double-click in the document to close the footer area. If necessary, click Show/Hide ¶ to display formatting marks.

4 Press Ctrl + End to move to the end of the document. Click the **Insert tab**. In the **Text group**, click the **Object button arrow**, and then click **Text from File**. In the **Insert File** dialog box, verify that your **Integrated Projects Chapter 3** folder displays, click your Rich Text File **Lastname_Firstname_3A_Gardeners.rtf**, and then click **Insert**. Compare your screen with Figure 3.15.

Your exported Access table displays in the Word document.

> **ALERT** **What if the .rtf extension does not display?**
>
> The file extension may or may not display on your system, depending on the computer settings.

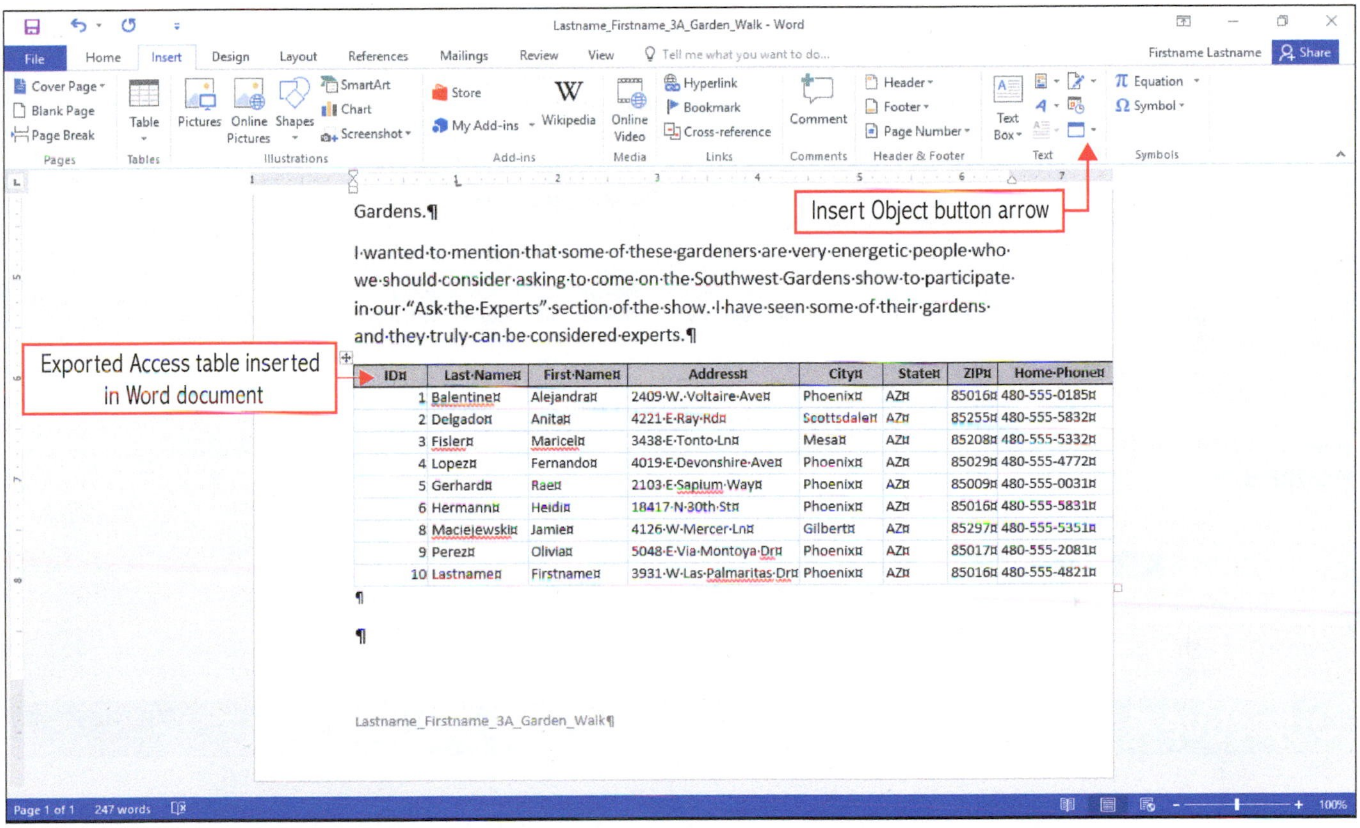

Word 2016, Windows 10, Microsoft Corporation

FIGURE 3.15

5 In the first row of the new table, click in the first cell **ID** to make the cell active. Under **Table Tools**, click the **Layout tab**, in the **Rows & Columns group**, click **Delete**, and then click **Delete Columns** to delete the ID column from the table.

6 Under **Table Tools**, click the **Design tab**, and then in the **Table Styles group**, click **More**. In the **Table Styles** gallery, scroll down as necessary to view the **List Tables**. Use the ScreenTips to locate and select the orange **List Table 4–Accent 6**.

7 Under **Table Tools**, on the **Design tab**, in the **Borders group**, click the **Borders button arrow**, and then click **Borders and Shading**. In the **Borders and Shading** dialog box, on the **Borders tab**, click the **Width arrow**, click **1½ pt**. In the left column, under *Setting:* click **All**, and then click **OK**.

8 In the **Table Style Options group**, click to select the **Header Row** check box. *Clear* (uncheck) the **Banded Rows** check box and the **Banded Columns** check box.

9 ▶ Under **Table Tools**, click the **Layout tab**. In the **Cell Size group**, click **AutoFit**, and then click **AutoFit Contents**. In the **Table group**, click **Properties**. In the **Table Properties** dialog box, on the **Table tab**, under **Alignment**, click **Center**, and then click **OK**. Compare your screen with Figure 3.16.

The columns are automatically resized to fit the contents of the cells, and the table is centered in the document.

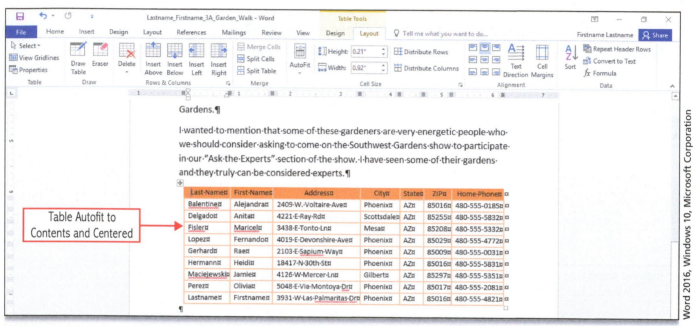

Table Autofit to Contents and Centered

FIGURE 3.16

10 ▶ **Save** 🖫 the document.

Word galleries display predefined style and graphics that you can use to create a more polished document. You can add text boxes, page color, and page borders. Recall that modifying a document theme changes the appearance of text, tables, and graphics throughout the document.

Activity 3.09 | Formatting a Word Document Using Page Layout

1 ▶ Press [Ctrl] + [Home] to move to the top of the document. Select the first paragraph—*Southwest Gardens*. On the **Home tab**, in the **Styles group**, click **More** ⊡. In the **Quick Styles** gallery, click **Intense Reference**. In the **Font group**, click the **Font Size button arrow** ⌷, and then click **26**.

2 ▶ Select the second, third, and fourth paragraphs beginning with *41122 N 23rd St*. In the **Styles group**, click **More** ⊡, and then click **Subtle Reference**. In the **Font group**, click the **Font Size button arrow** ⌷, and then click **14**.

3 Select the first four paragraphs, and then in the **Paragraph group**, click **Align Right**. Click **Line and Paragraph Spacing**, and then click **Remove Space After Paragraph**. In the **Font group**, click the **Font Color button arrow**, and then in the last column, click the fifth color—**Orange, Accent 6, Darker 25%**. Compare your screen with Figure 3.17.

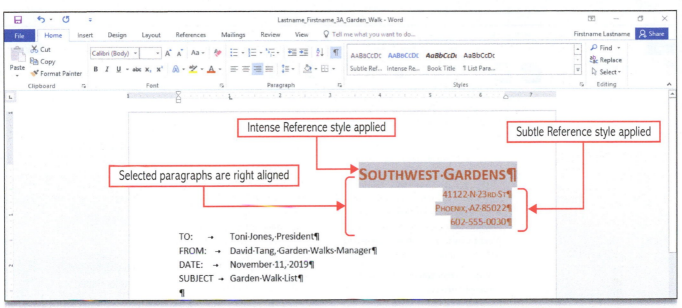

Intense Reference style applied

Subtle Reference style applied

Selected paragraphs are right aligned

SOUTHWEST·GARDENS¶
41122·N·23RD·ST¶
PHOENIX,·AZ·85022¶
602-555-0030¶

TO: →   Toni·Jones,·President¶
FROM: →   David·Tang,·Garden·Walks·Manager¶
DATE: →   November·11,·2019¶
SUBJECT →   Garden·Walk·List¶
¶

FIGURE 3.17

Word 2016, Windows 10, Microsoft Corporation

4 Click anywhere in your document to deselect the text, and then **Save** your document.

Activity 3.10 | Inserting and Modifying a Text Box

A **text box** is a movable, resizable container for text or graphics. You can use text boxes to position several blocks of text on a page or to give text a different orientation from other text in the document.

1 Click the **Insert tab**, in the **Text group**, click **Text Box**, scroll down, and then click **Retrospect Quote**.

The text box displays on the right side of your document.

2 Under **Drawing Tools**, on the **Format tab**, in the **Size group**, if necessary, click **Size**. Use the spin box arrows to change the **Shape Height** 0.29" to **2.1** and the **Shape Width** 1.07" to **2.6**. In the **Shape Styles group**, click **More**. Under **Theme Styles**, in the fourth row, click the seventh style—**Subtle Effect – Orange, Accent 6**. Click the **Shape Outline** button, and then in the last column, click the fifth color—**Orange, Accent 6, Darker 25%**.

3 Type **Garden Walk** and then press Enter. Type **The Garden Walk segment of Southwest Gardens is always one of the highest rated segments of the program.**

4 Select all of the text in the text box. On the mini toolbar, click **Increase Font Size** one time. Click the **Font Color button arrow**, and then in the last column, click the sixth color—**Orange, Accent 6, Darker 50%**. Select the first paragraph *Garden Walk*, and then on the mini toolbar, click **Bold**.

5 ▸ Point to any border on the text box until the ⬚ pointer displays. Hold down the left mouse button, and then drag the text box to the right of the paragraph that begins *Now that we are*. Use the green dotted guides that display to position the text box in line with the top of the paragraph and in line with the right margin. If necessary, use the guides to place the text box. Compare your screen with Figure 3.18.

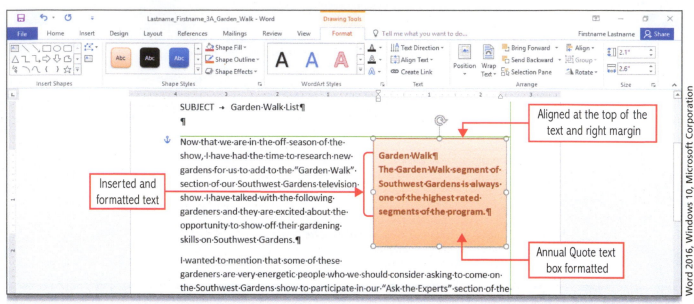

FIGURE 3.18

6 ▸ Release the mouse button, and then **Save** 🖫 your changes.

Activity 3.11 | Adding Page Borders and Page Color

Page borders add interest and emphasis to your document pages. You can add page borders to all pages, only specific pages, sides of pages, or sections. Page borders include many line styles and colors and a variety of graphical borders.

1 ▸ Press Ctrl + Home. Click the **Design tab**, and then in the **Page Background group**, click **Page Borders**. In the **Borders and Shading** dialog box, on the **Page Border tab**, under **Setting**, click **Shadow**. Click the **Color arrow**, and then in the last column, click the fifth color—**Orange, Accent 6, Darker 25%**. Click the **Width arrow**, and then click **2¼ pt**. Under **Apply to**, be sure **Whole document** displays, and then click **OK**.

2 ▸ In the **Page Background group**, click **Page Color**. Under **Theme Colors**, in the last column, click the third color—**Orange, Accent 6, Lighter 60%**. Compare your screen with Figure 3.19.

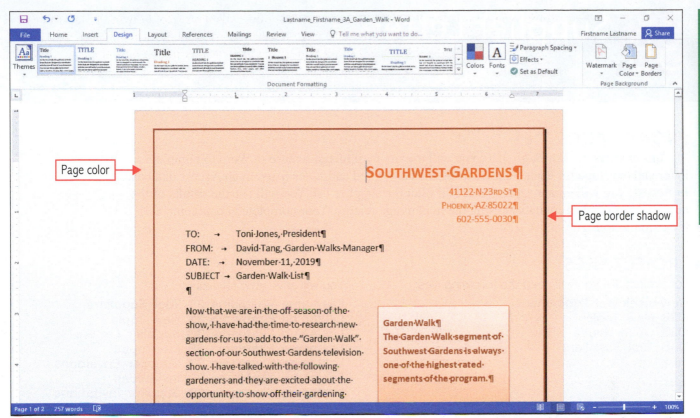

FIGURE 3.19

Word 2016, Windows 10, Microsoft Corporation

---

3 ▶ Display **Backstage** view. With the **Info tab** selected, in the lower right corner, click **Show All Properties**. Under **Related People**, be sure your name displays as the **Author**—change it if necessary. Click to the right of **Subject**, and then type your course name and section number. Click to the right of **Tags**, and then type **gardener memo, contacts** Click ⊙ to return to the document.

4 ▶ Press Ctrl + End. If your document displays a second page, press Backspace to delete the paragraph mark.

5 ▶ Press Ctrl + Home. **Save** 🔖 your document.

6 ▶ If your instructor directs you to submit your files electronically, go to Step 7. To print your document, display **Backstage** view, click the **Print tab**, and then click **Print**.

7 ▶ **Close** ✕ Word, saving as necessary.

END | You have completed Project 3A

Supplier Letter

PROJECT ACTIVITIES

In Activities 3.12 through 3.20, you will use the mail merge feature in Word to complete a letter and envelope for each supplier using the names and addresses listed in an Access database. In Access, you will create a query that will filter the supplier list. You will use the results of the query to complete an invitation using the mail merge feature. Your completed documents will look similar to Figure 3.20.

PROJECT FILES

For Project 3B, you will need the following files:

New blank Word document
i03B_New_Tools
i03B_Open_House
i03B_Tool_Suppliers

You will save your files as:

Lastname_Firstname_3B_Tool_Suppliers
Lastname_Firstname_3B_New_Tools
Lastname_Firstname_3B_Supplier_Letters
Lastname_Firstname_3B_Envelopes
Lastname_Firstname_3B_Supplier_Envelopes
Lastname_Firstname_3B_Invitations
Lastname_Firstname_3B_Supplier_Invitations

PROJECT RESULTS

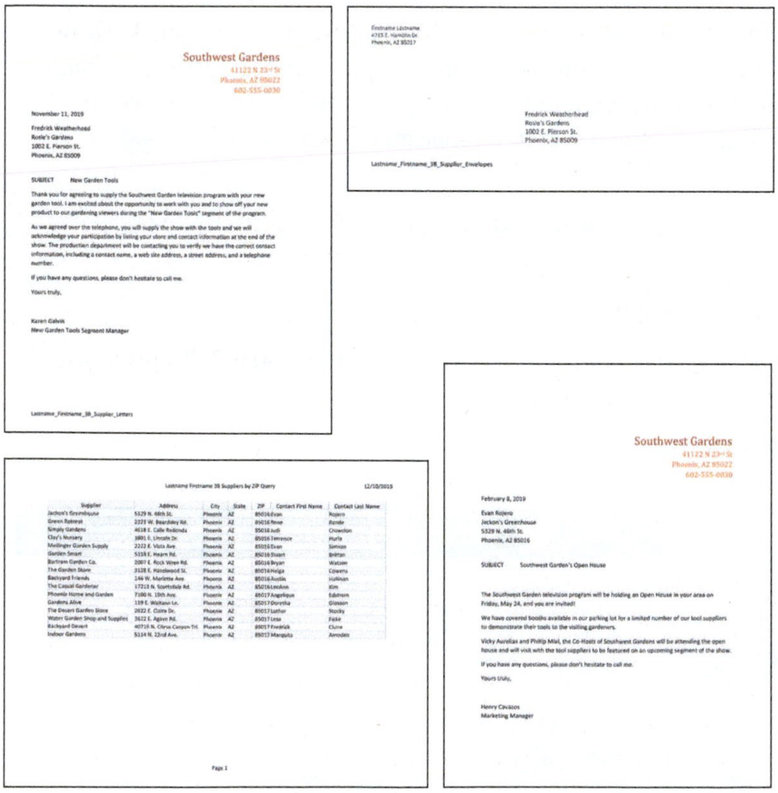

FIGURE 3.20 Project 3B Supplier Letter

Objective 5 | Use Mail Merge in Word to Complete Letters Using Access Data

It is common for a business to send out identical letters to its contacts. In order to personalize the letters, the business may use *mail merge*, a Microsoft Word feature that joins a main document and a data source to create customized letters, envelopes, or labels. Mail merge enables you to select data from various sources, such as an Access database. You can sort or filter the data before it is merged into the document.

Activity 3.12 | Starting Mail Merge in Word

You can start the mail merge feature in either Word or Access. Karen Galvin has created a letter that you will use for the *main document* in your mail merge. In a mail merge, the main document contains the text and formatting that remain constant. Karen knows the contact information for tool suppliers is located in an Access database. For this activity, you will use a table in the database as the *data source*—a list of variable information, such as names and addresses of tool suppliers—that is merged with a main document to create customized form letters, envelopes, or labels.

1 From the **Start** menu, navigate to the student data files that accompany this chapter, and then click one time to select the Access file **i03B_Tool_Suppliers**. Right-click the file, and then on the shortcut menu, click **Copy**.

2 Navigate to and then open your **Integrated Projects Chapter 3** folder. In an open area, right-click, and then on the shortcut menu, click **Paste** to copy the database to your folder.

3 Right-click the selected file name, and then on the shortcut menu, click **Rename**. Using your own first and last name, type **Lastname_Firstname_3B_Tool_Suppliers** Press Enter to save the file with the new name. **Close** ⊠ the window.

ALERT | **Does a Confirm File Rename message display?**

If the file you have copied has a Read-only property applied, a message box will display to alert you when you attempt to rename a file. In the message box, click Yes to rename the file. Right-click the file name, and then on the shortcut menu, click Property. In the Properties dialog box, on the General tab, under Attributes, click to clear the Read-only check mark, click OK to accept the change, and then close the dialog box.

---

4 Start Word. From your student data files, locate and open the document **i03B_New_Tools**.

5 From **Backstage** view, click **Save As**, and then click **Browse** to display the **Save As** dialog box. Navigate to your **Integrated Projects Chapter 3** folder. In the **File name** box, select the existing text, type **Lastname_Firstname_3B_New_Tools** and then click **Save**. If necessary, display formatting marks.

6 Click the **Mailings tab**. In the **Start Mail Merge group**, click **Start Mail Merge**, and then click **Step-by-Step Mail Merge Wizard**. On the right, in the **Mail Merge** pane, under **Select document type**, verify that the **Letters** option button is selected.

7 At the bottom of the **Mail Merge** pane, click **Next: Starting document** to display **Step 2 of 6**. Under **Select starting document**, verify that the **Use the current document** option button is selected, and then at the bottom, click **Next: Select recipients** to display **Step 3 of 6**.

8 Under **Select recipients**, confirm that the **Use an existing list** option button is selected. Under **Use an existing list**, click **Browse**. Navigate to your **Integrated Projects Chapter 3** folder, select your **Lastname_Firstname_3B_Tool_Suppliers** Access database, and then click **Open**. Compare your screen with Figure 3.21.

The Select Table dialog box displays. Here you can select the table or query that contains the names and addresses of the recipients for this letter. This database contains more than one object—both tables and queries.

FIGURE 3.21

9 ▶ In the **Select Table** dialog box, be sure **Supplier Contacts** is selected, and then click **OK**.

The Mail Merge Recipients dialog box displays. Here you can add or edit data in a table—in this instance, the names and addresses.

10 ▶ In the **Mail Merge Recipients** dialog box, scroll to the right to view the **Contact Last Name** field. Click the **Contact Last Name** field column heading. Compare your screen with Figure 3.22.

You can sort any of the fields by clicking the field column heading. *Sorting* is the process of arranging data in a specific order based on the value in each field. Here, the records are sorted in ascending order by last name.

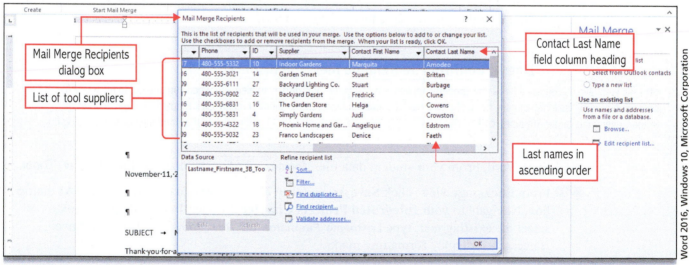

FIGURE 3.22

11 ▶ At the bottom of the **Mail Merge Recipients** dialog box, click **OK**.

Activity 3.13 | Adding Merge Fields

1 ▶ At the bottom of the **Mail Merge** pane, click **Next: Write your letter** to display **Step 4 of 6**. In the letter, under the date, click to position the insertion point in the first blank paragraph below the date. This is the location in the letter where you will insert the address of the recipient.

2 In the **Mail Merge** pane, under **Write your letter**, click **Address block**. In the **Insert Address Block** dialog box, under **Specify address elements**, verify that the **Joshua Randall Jr.** format is selected. Compare your screen with Figure 3.23.

On the right side of the Insert Address Block dialog box, under Preview, notice that the Supplier business name and the contact name are not listed—only the line with the street address and the line with the city, state, and ZIP code display.

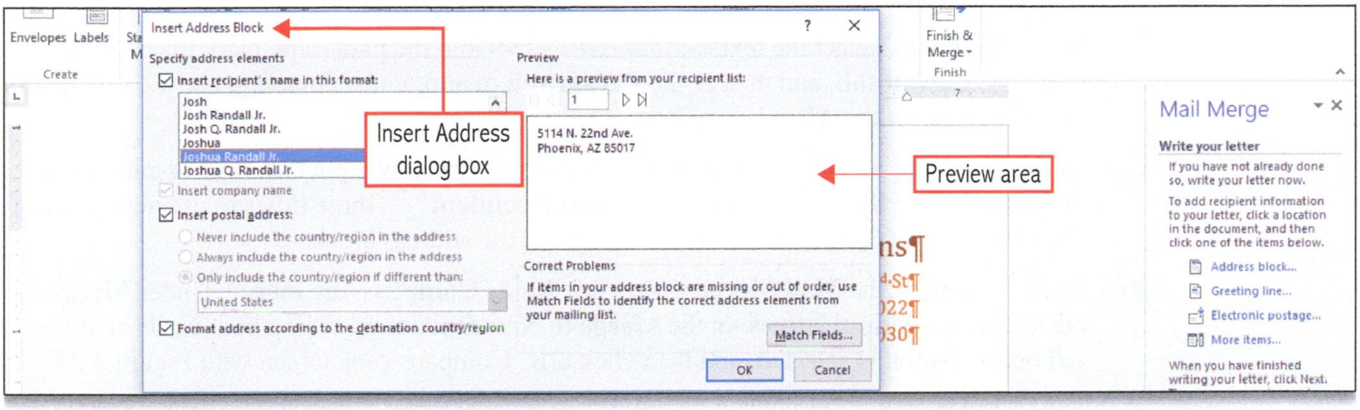

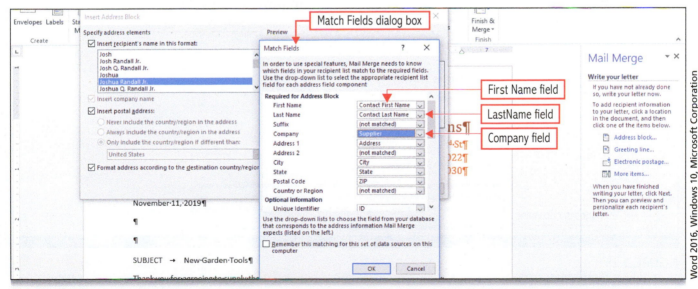

FIGURE 3.23 Word 2016, Windows 10, Microsoft Corporation

3 Near the bottom of the **Insert Address Block** dialog box, click **Match Fields**. In the **Match Fields** dialog box, under **Required for Address Block**, click the **First Name arrow**, and then click **Contact First Name**. Click the **Last Name arrow**, and then click **Contact Last Name**. Click the **Company arrow**, click **Supplier**, and then compare your screen with Figure 3.24.

Because Word did not recognize the Contact First Name, Contact Last Name, and Supplier fields in the table, it was necessary to associate them with the corresponding predefined fields. You can use the Match Fields feature to select the fields you want to include.

FIGURE 3.24 Word 2016, Windows 10, Microsoft Corporation

4 At the bottom of the **Match Fields** dialog box, click **OK**. A message box may display indicating that the data may be read by others. In the message box, click **Yes**. In the **Insert Address Block** dialog box, under **Preview**, confirm that the **Contact First Name**, **Contact Last Name**, and **Supplier** name display in the address, and then click **OK**.

This action inserts a mail merge field—the address block—in your letter. When you insert a mail merge field into the main document, the field name is surrounded by double angle brackets (<< >>). These double angle brackets help distinguish the fields in the main document and will not display in the final document.

5 In the document, select the text <<*AddressBlock*>> and the paragraph mark that follows it. Click the **Layout tab**, and then in the **Paragraph group**, under **Spacing**, use the **down spin box arrow** to set the **After** box to **0 pt**.

6 At the bottom of the **Mail Merge** pane, click **Next: Preview your letters** to display **Step 5 of 6**. Under **Preview your letters**, click **Next Recipient** [>>] three times to preview some of the letters. All the letters are identical except for the address block.

7 At the bottom of the **Mail Merge** pane, click **Next: Complete the merge**. Under **Merge**, click **Edit individual letters**. In the **Merge to New Document** dialog box, verify that the **All** option button is selected, and then click **OK**. Compare your screen with Figure 3.25.

This action creates a new Word document containing 29 letters—one letter for each contact in the Supplier list.

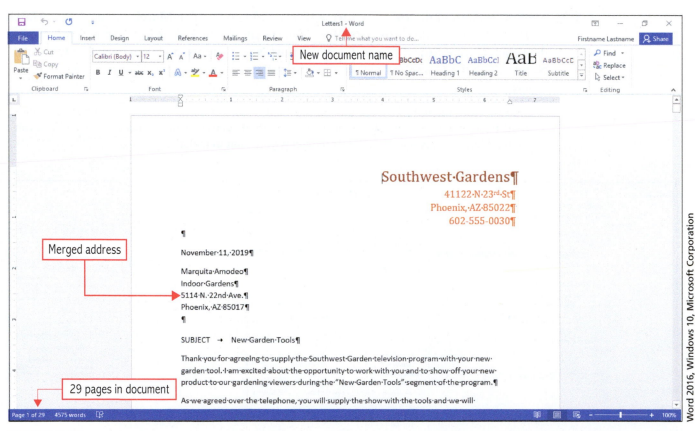

FIGURE 3.25

8 From **Backstage** view, click **Save As**, and then click **Browse** to display the **Save As** dialog box. Navigate to your **Integrated Projects Chapter 3** folder. In the **File name** box, with the existing text selected, and then using your own name, type **Lastname_Firstname_3B_ Supplier_Letters** Click **Save**.

9 In your **Lastname_Firstname_3B_Supplier_Letters** document, display **Backstage** view, and then with the **Info tab** selected, in the lower right corner, click **Show All Properties**. Under **Related People**, be sure your name displays as the **Author**—change it if necessary. Click to the right of **Subject**, and then type your course name and section number. Click to the right of **Tags**, and then type **supplier letter, merged**

10 In the upper left corner, click ⊙ to return to the document. On the **Insert tab**, in the **Header & Footer group**, click **Footer**, and then click **Edit Footer**. On the **Design tab**, in the **Insert group**, click **Document Info**, and then click **File Name**. Double-click in the document to exit the footer area.

Activity 3.14 │ Printing Letters

Your document contains all the customized letters to the suppliers. Because you have saved this merged document, you have the ability to print one, several, or all of the letters.

1 If your instructor directs you to submit your files electronically, go to Step 3.

2 Press Ctrl + End to move to the end of the document. From **Backstage** view, click the **Print tab**. Under *Settings*, click **Print All Pages**, and then click **Print Current Page**. Click **Print**.

Only the last letter of the 29 letters is printed.

3 **Save** 🔲 and then **Close** ✕ the **Lastname_Firstname_3B_Supplier_Letters** Word document.

4 In the **Lastname_Firstname_3B_New_Tools** Word document, display **Backstage** view, and then with the **Info tab** selected, in the lower right corner, click **Show All Properties**. Under **Related People**, be sure your name displays as the **Author**—change it if necessary. Click to the right of **Subject**, and then type your course name and section number. Click to the right of **Tags**, and then type **letter, merge fields**

5 In the upper left corner, click ⊙ to return to the document.

6 **Save** 🔲 your **Lastname_Firstname_3B_New_Tools** document, and then from **Backstage** view, on the left, click **Close** to close the document but leave Word open.

Objective 6 │ Use Mail Merge in Word to Create Envelopes Using Access Data

Another feature of mail merge is the ability to create customized envelopes. Using the same data source that you use for the letters, you can enter or edit the delivery and return addresses, specify the formatting of text, and choose the envelope size. You can either save the completed envelopes for later editing and printing, or you can print the envelopes without saving the document.

Activity 3.15 │ Starting Mail Merge for Envelopes and Inserting a Return Address

1 In Word, press Ctrl + N to display a new document. On the **Quick Access Toolbar**, click **Save** 🔲, in **Backstage** view, click **Browse**, and then navigate to your **Integrated Projects Chapter 3** folder. Using your own name, save the file as **Lastname_Firstname_3B_Envelopes**

2 Click the **Mailings tab**, in the **Start Mail Merge group**, click **Start Mail Merge**, and then click **Envelopes**.

3 In the **Envelope Options** dialog box, under **Envelope size**, verify that **Size 10** is selected, and then click **OK**. Compare your screen with Figure 3.26.

A standard business size envelope displays. A return address may display in the top left corner of the envelope, depending on your computer settings.

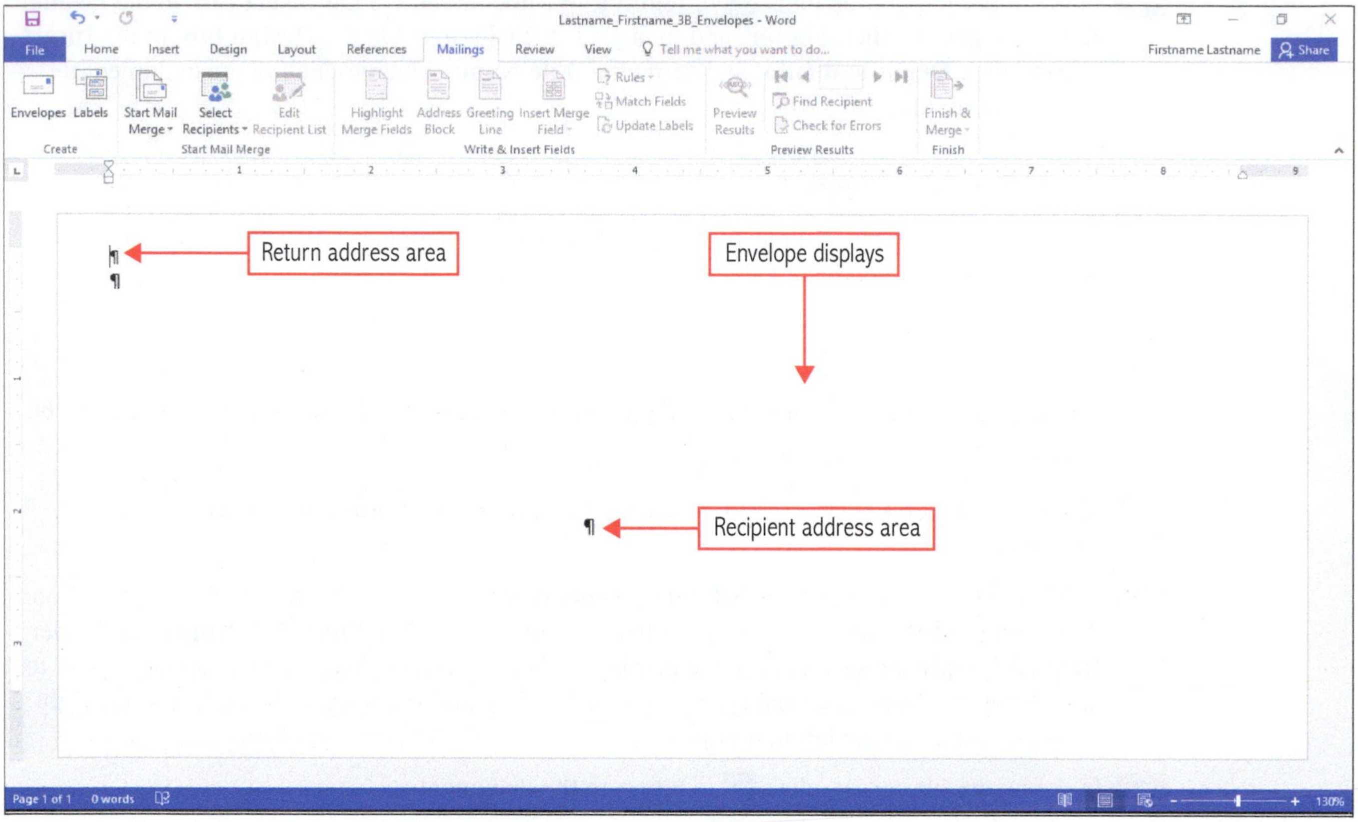

Return address area

Envelope displays

Recipient address area

Word 2016, Windows 10, Microsoft Corporation

FIGURE 3.26

4 On the **Mailings tab**, in the **Start Mail Merge group**, click **Select Recipients**, and then click **use an existing list**. In the **Select Data Source** dialog box, navigate to your **Integrated Projects Chapter 3** folder, select your Access database **Lastname_Firstname_3B_Tool_Suppliers** file, and then click **Open**. In the **Select Table** dialog box, verify that **Supplier Contacts** is selected, and then click **OK**.

5 In the **Start Mail Merge group**, click **Edit Recipient List**. In the **Mail Merge Recipients** dialog box, scroll to the right, and then click the field column heading **Contact Last Name** to sort the records by last name in ascending order. Click **OK**.

6 If necessary, click to position the insertion point at the top left corner of the envelope. Using your own name, type Firstname Lastname and then press Enter. Type **4715 E. Hamblin Dr** press Enter, and then type **Phoenix, AZ 85017** Compare your screen with Figure 3.27.

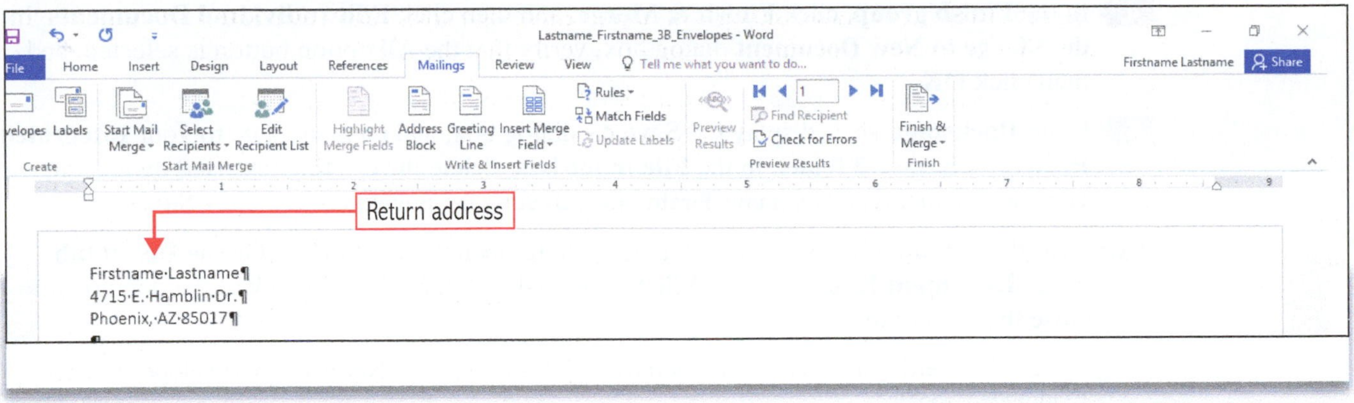

FIGURE 3.27

7 ▸ **Save** 🖫 your changes.

Activity 3.16 │ Completing and Printing Envelopes

1 ▸ In the middle of the envelope, notice the paragraph mark. Click one time on the paragraph mark to display the address placeholder. On the **Mailings tab**, in the **Write & Insert Fields group**, click **Address Block**. In the **Insert Address Block** dialog box, under **Specify address elements**, verify that the **Joshua Randall Jr.** format is selected. In the lower right corner, click **Match Fields**. Under **Required for Address Block**, click the **First Name arrow**, and then click **Contact First Name**. Click the **Last Name arrow**, and then click **Contact Last Name**. Click the **Company arrow**, and then click **Supplier**.

2 ▸ In the **Match Fields** dialog box, click **OK**. If a dialog box displays indicating your data may be read by others, click **Yes**. In the **Insert Address Block** dialog box, under **Preview**, confirm that the **Contact First Name**, **Contact Last Name**, and **Supplier** name display in the address, and then at the bottom of the **Insert Address Block** dialog box, click **OK**.

This action inserts the address block mail merge into your envelope.

3 ▸ On the ribbon, in the **Preview Results group**, click **Preview Results**, and then compare your screen with Figure 3.28.

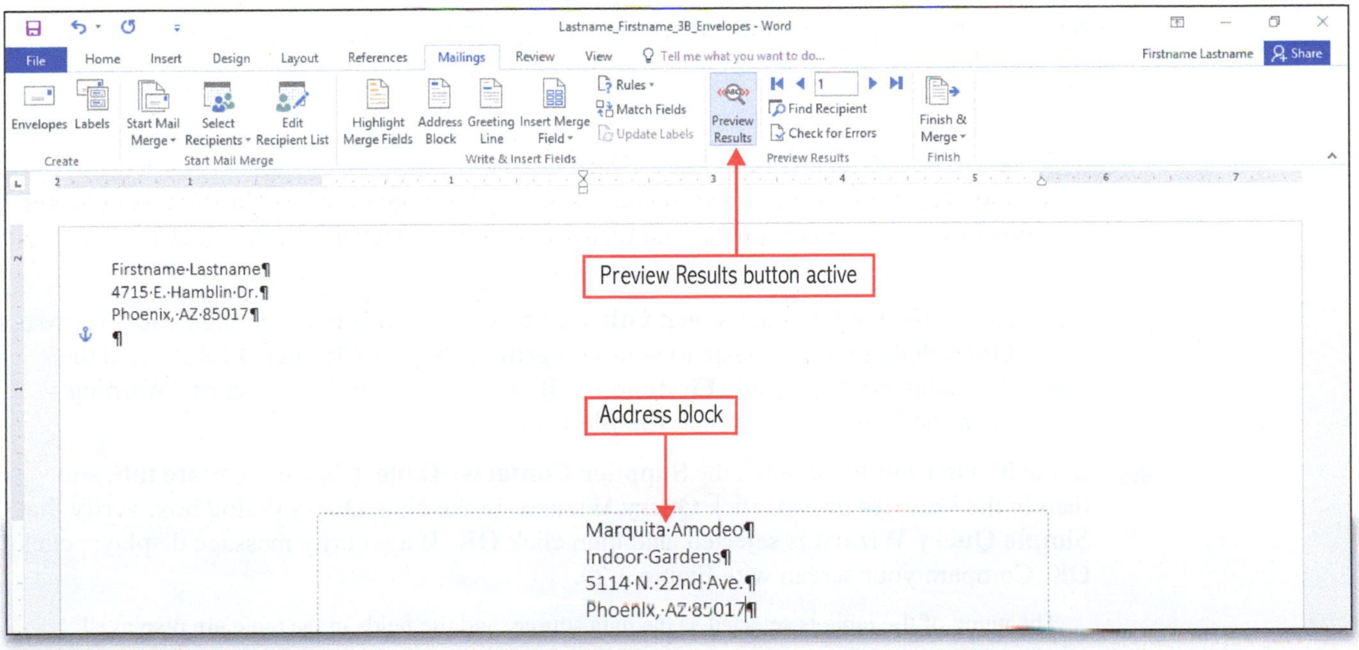

FIGURE 3.28

4 In the **Finish group**, click **Finish & Merge**, and then click **Edit Individual Documents**. In the **Merge to New Document** dialog box, verify that the **All** option button is selected, and then click **OK**.

5 From **Backstage** view, display the **Save As** dialog box, and then navigate to your **Integrated Projects Chapter 3** folder. In the **File name** box, delete the existing text, and then using your own name, type **Lastname_Firstname_3B_Supplier_Envelopes** and click **Save**.

6 Near the bottom of the envelope, double-click to open the footer area. On the **Insert tab**, under **Document Info**, insert the **FileName** field, and then double-click in the document to close the footer area.

> You are inserting a footer only for purposes of this instruction. Normally, an envelope does not include a footer.

7 If your instructor directs you to submit your files electronically, go to Step 9.

8 Press Ctrl + End to move to the end of the document. From **Backstage** view, click the **Print tab**. Under *Settings*, click **Print All Pages**, and then click **Print Current Page**. Click **Print**.

> Only the last envelope of the 29 envelopes is printed.

9 Display **Backstage** view, and then with the **Info tab** selected, in the lower right corner, click **Show All Properties**. Under **Related People**, be sure your name displays as the **Author**—change it if necessary. Click to the right of **Subject**, and then type your course name and section number. Click to the right of **Tags**, and then type **supplier envelopes, merged**

10 Save 🖫 your document that contains the 29 envelopes. **Close** ⊠ your **Lastname_Firstname_3B_Supplier_Envelopes** Word document. **Close** ⊠ your **Lastname_Firstname_3B_Envelopes** Word document, saving changes.

Objective 7 | Create and Modify a Query in Access

Recall that a query is a database object that requests data from a database. A query answers a question such as *Which tool suppliers are located within a specific ZIP code?* Database users rarely need to see all of the records in all of the tables. That is why a query is useful; it creates a *subset* of records—a portion of the total records—according to your specifications and then displays only those records.

Activity 3.17 | Creating a Query Using the Query Wizard

In this Activity, you will create a *select query*, which is a type of query that retrieves specific data from one or more tables or queries and then displays the selected data in a datasheet. You can create a select query in Design view or by using a wizard.

1 Start Access. On the left, click **Open Other Files**, click **Computer**, and then click **Browse**. In the **Open** dialog box, navigate to your **Integrated Project Chapter 3** folder, and then open your database **Lastname_Firstname_3B_Tool_Suppliers**. If a Security Warning displays on the **Message Bar**, click **Enable Content**.

2 In the **Navigation Pane**, click the **Supplier Contacts: Table**. Click the **Create tab**, and then in the **Queries group**, click **Query Wizard**. In the **New Query** dialog box, verify that **Simple Query Wizard** is selected, and then click **OK**. If a security message displays, click OK. Compare your screen with Figure 3.29.

> The name of the table is selected as the data source, and the fields in the table are displayed.

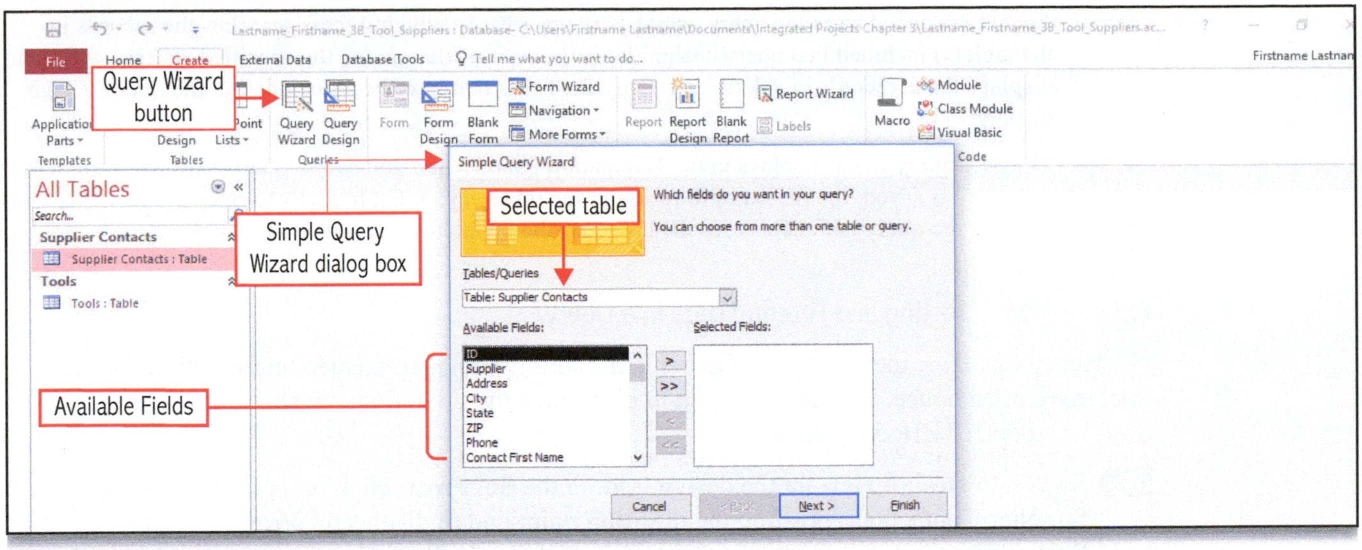

FIGURE 3.29 Access 2016, Windows 10, Microsoft Corporation

3 Under **Available Fields**, click **Supplier**, and then click **Add Field** [>] to move the field to the **Selected Fields** list on the right.

The Available Fields list includes all the fields in the selected table or query. The Selected Fields list contains the fields you want to include in your new query.

ANOTHER WAY Double-click the field name to move it to the Selected Fields list.

4 Using the technique you just practiced, add the following fields to the **Selected Fields** list: **Address**, **City**, **State**, **ZIP**, **Contact First Name**, and **Contact Last Name**. Compare your screen with Figure 3.30.

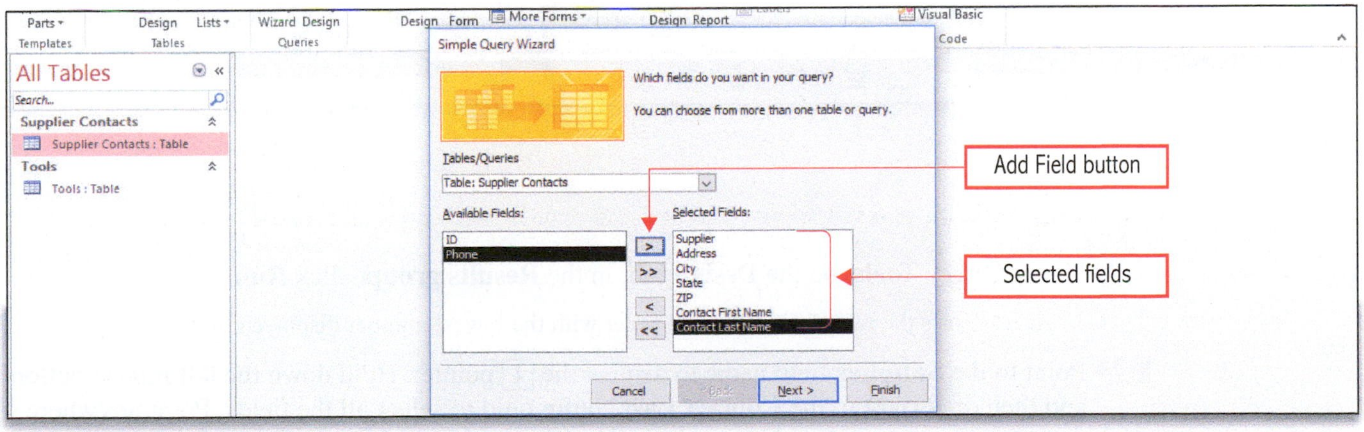

FIGURE 3.30 Access 2016, Windows 10, Microsoft Corporation

5 At the bottom of the **Simple Query Wizard** dialog box, click **Next**. Under **Would you like a detail or summary query?**, verify that the **Detail** option button is selected, and then click **Next**. On the next screen, under **What title do you want for your query?**, using your own name, type **Lastname Firstname 3B Supplier Query** and then click **Finish**.

Access saves and *runs* the query, which is the process in which Access searches the records in the table(s) included in a query design, finds the records that match the specified criteria, and then displays those records in a datasheet. Only the fields that have been included in the query design display.

The new query name displays in the Navigation Pane. When you save a query, only the design of the query is saved; the records still reside in the table object. Each time you open a query, Access will run the query and display results based on the updated data stored in the table.

Activity 3.18 │ Sorting and Filtering Data in a Query

Henry Cavazos, the Southwest Gardens Marketing Manager, created an invitation for the upcoming open house. He has asked you to customize the invitations for the suppliers in the 85016 and 85017 ZIP code areas.

1 ▶ Switch to **Design** view. In the design grid, in the **Sort row**, click in the **ZIP** field (below Supplier Contacts) to position the insertion point and to display an arrow. Click the **Sort arrow**, and then in the displayed list, click **Ascending**. Compare your screen with Figure 3.31.

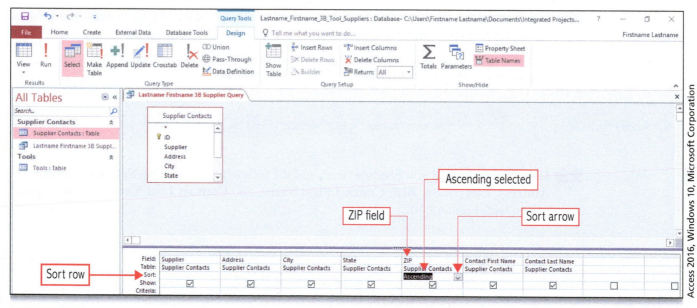

FIGURE 3.31

2 ▶ Under **Query Tools**, on the **Design tab**, in the **Results group**, click **Run**.

Access sorts the records in ZIP code order with the lowest number displayed first.

3 ▶ Point to the **Supplier** field name to display the ↓ pointer. Hold down the left mouse button, and then drag right to the **Contact Last Name** field to select all the fields. Point anywhere over the selected area, and then right-click. On the shortcut menu, click **Field Width**, and then in the **Column Width** dialog box, click **Best Fit**.

4 On the **Home tab**, in the **Views group**, click **View** to switch to Design view. In the design grid, click in the **Criteria row** under **ZIP** field, type **85016** and then press ↓ to move to the next row—with the row heading **or**. Type **85017** and then compare your screen with Figure 3.32.

By typing specific ZIP codes as the *criteria*, the data will be filtered. Criteria are the conditions in a query that identify the specific records for which you are looking. *Filtering* is the process of displaying only a portion of the data based on matching a specific value to show only the data that meets the criteria you specify. In this case, when you run the query, only records containing the 85016 and 85017 ZIP codes will display.

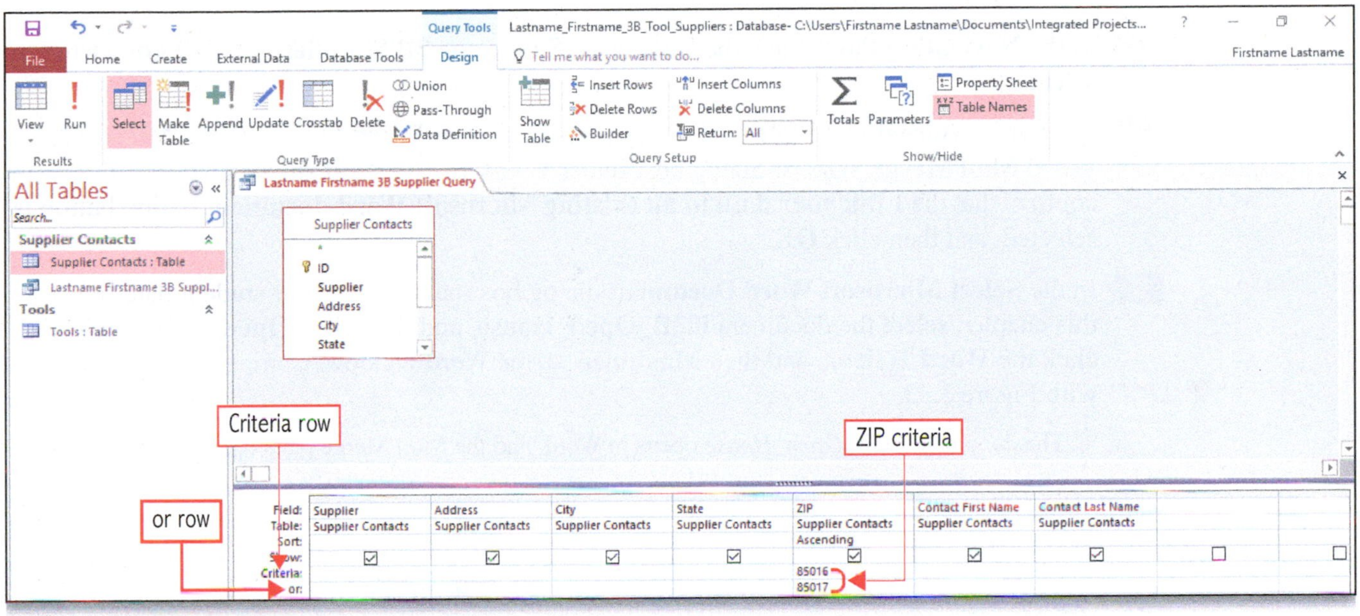

FIGURE 3.32

5 In the **Results group**, click **Run**. Notice that the data is filtered to display only the records with ZIP codes 85016 or 85017.

6 From **Backstage** view, click **Save As**, and then click **Save Object As**. On the right, click the **Save As** button. In the **Save As** dialog box, delete the existing text, and then using your own name, type **Lastname Firstname 3B Suppliers by ZIP Query** and click **OK**.

Access creates a new query based on a copy of your query 3B Tool Supplier Query. It is not necessary to save all queries, but you should save a query if you think you will need the same information again.

7 In **Backstage** view, click the **Print tab**, and then click **Print Preview**. On the **Print Preview tab**, in the **Page Layout group**, click **Landscape**.

8 If you are submitting your files electronically, go to Step 9. If you are printing your files, in the **Print group**, click **Print**, and then in the **Print** dialog box, click **Print**.

9 In the **Close Preview group**, click **Close Print Preview**. Right-click your **Lastname Firstname 3B Suppliers by ZIP Query tab**, and then on the shortcut menu, click **Close**. Resize the Navigation Pane so that all object names are fully displayed.

Access 2016, Windows 10, Microsoft Corporation

The Word Mail Merge Wizard is available in Access. It enables you to set up the mail merge process that uses a table or query in an Access database as the data source for letters, envelopes, and labels. When you are in Access with the source database open, the Export group has a link to the Mail Merge Wizard. You can choose to link the source data to an existing document, or you can choose to create a new document.

Activity 3.19 | Starting Mail Merge in Access

1 In the **Navigation Pane**, click the **Lastname Firstname 3B Suppliers by ZIP Query** to select it.

2 Click the **External Data tab**. In the **Export group**, click **Word Merge**. In the **Microsoft Word Mail Merge Wizard** dialog box, under **What do you want the wizard to do?**, confirm that the **Link your data to an existing Microsoft Word document** option button is selected, and then click **OK**.

3 In the **Select Microsoft Word Document** dialog box, navigate to your student data files for this chapter, select the document **i03B_Open_House**, and then click **Open**. On the taskbar, click the **Word** [w] icon, and then **Maximize** [□] the Word window. Compare your screen with Figure 3.33.

The document *i03B_Open_House* opens in Word, and the Mail Merge pane opens to Step 3 of 6.

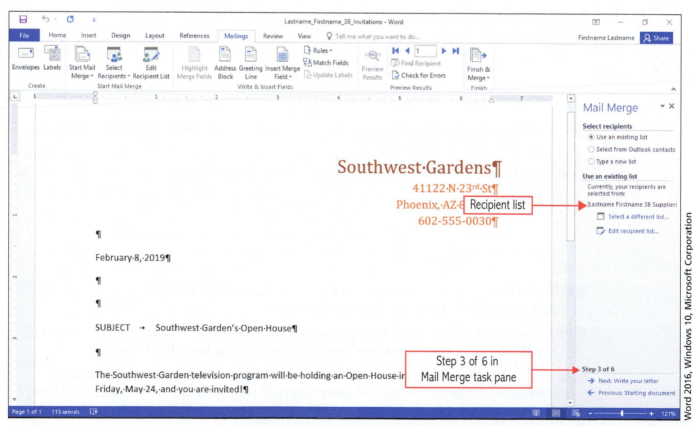

FIGURE 3.33

4 From **Backstage** view, display the **Save As** dialog box, and then save the document in your **Integrated Projects Chapter 3** folder with the file name **Lastname_Firstname_3B_ Invitations** Be sure formatting marks display.

Activity 3.20 | Completing the Mail Merge

1 At the bottom of the **Mail Merge** pane, click **Next: Write your letter**. In the first blank line below the date, click to position the insertion point. In the **Mail Merge** pane, under **Write your letter**, click **Address block**. In the **Insert Address Block** dialog box, under **Specify address elements**, verify that the **Joshua Randall Jr.** format is selected. Click **Match Fields**. Under **Required for Address Block**, click the **First Name arrow**, and then click **Contact First Name**. Click the **Last Name arrow**, and then click **Contact Last Name**. Click the **Company arrow**, click **Supplier**, and then click **OK**. At the bottom of the **Insert Address Block** dialog box, click **OK**.

2 In your document, select the **<<AddressBlock>>** field, being sure to include the paragraph mark. Click the **Layout tab**, and then in the **Paragraph group**, under **Spacing**, use the **down spin box arrow** to set the **After** box to **0 pt**.

3 At the bottom of the **Mail Merge** pane, click **Next: Preview your letters** to display **Step 5 of 6**.

4 At the bottom of the **Mail Merge** pane, click **Next: Complete the merge**. Under **Merge**, click **Edit individual letters**. In the **Merge to New Document** dialog box, verify that the **All** option button is selected, and then click **OK**.

This action creates a new Word document with 16 letters.

5 Save 🖫 the document in your **Integrated Projects Chapter 3** folder with the file name **Lastname_Firstname_3B_Supplier_Invitations** Press Ctrl + Home to move to the beginning of the document. If your instructor directs you to submit your files electronically, go to Step 7.

6 From **Backstage** view, click the **Print tab**. Under Settings, click **Print All Pages**, and then click **Print Current Page**. Click **Print**.

Only the first letter is printed.

7 Near the bottom of the document, double-click to open the footer area. Using **Document Info**, insert the **FileName** field, and then double-click in the document to close the footer area.

8 Display **Backstage** view, and then with the **Info tab** selected, in the lower right corner, click **Show All Properties**. Under **Related People**, be sure your name displays as the **Author**— change it if necessary. Click to the right of **Subject**, and then type your course name and section number. Click to the right of **Tags**, and then type **supplier invitations, merged** Save 🖫 and then **Close** ✕ your **Lastname_Firstname_3B_Supplier_Invitations** Word document.

9 With your **Lastname_Firstname_3B_Invitations** document displayed, display **Backstage** view, and then with the **Info tab** selected, in the lower right corner, click **Show All Properties**. Under **Related People**, be sure your name displays as the **Author**—change it if necessary. Click to the right of **Subject**, and then type your course name and section number. Click to the right of **Tags**, and then type **supplier invitations, merge fields**

10 Save 🖫 and then **Close** ✕ Word. **Close** ✕ Access.

11 Submit your printed or electronic files as directed by your instructor.

END | You have completed Project 3B

END OF CHAPTER

SUMMARY

An Access database is one way for a business to manage its data and be able to quickly retrieve data when it is requested. You can use tables, forms, or queries to modify—update, delete, sort, or filter—data. The data in tables can be exported to a Word document, and it can be formatted as a table or used with the Mail Merge Wizard to complete letters, envelopes, and labels in Word.

KEY TERMS

MATCHING

Match each term in the second column with its correct definition in the first column by writing the letter of the term on the blank line in front of the correct definition.

_____ 1. An organized collection of facts about people, events, things, or ideas related to a particular topic or purpose.

_____ 2. The basic parts of a database that you create to store your data and to work with your data.

_____ 3. All of the categories of data pertaining to one person, place, thing, event, or idea, formatted as a row in a database table.

_____ 4. A single piece of information that is stored in every record and formatted as a column in a database table.

_____ 5. An Access view that displays the detailed structure of a table, query, form, or report, and the view in which some tasks must be performed.

_____ 6. A field that uniquely identifies a record in a table.

_____ 7. The characteristic that defines the kind of data that can be entered into a field, such as numbers, text, or dates.

_____ 8. The action of filling a database table with records.

_____ 9. A database object used to enter data, edit data, or display data from a table or query.

_____ 10. A database object that retrieves specific data from one or more database objects and then, in a single datasheet, displays only the data you specify.

_____ 11. The Access view in which you can make changes to a form or to a report while the object is running—the data from the underlying data source displays.

_____ 12. A feature in Microsoft Office that walks you step by step through a process.

_____ 13. A movable, resizable container for text or graphics.

_____ 14. The process of arranging data in a specific order based on the value in each field.

_____ 15. The conditions in a query that identify the specific records for which you are looking.

A Criteria

B Data type

C Database

D Design view

E Field

F Form

G Layout view

H Objects

I Populate

J Primary key

K Query

L Record

M Sorting

N Text box

O Wizard

MULTIPLE CHOICE

Circle the correct answer.

1. A preformatted database designed for a specific purpose is a:
   A. built-in object   **B.** read only file   **C.** template

2. The Access object that stores data organized in an arrangement of columns and rows, and which is the foundation of an Access database is a:
   A. form   **B.** query   **C.** table

3. The area directly below the ribbon that displays information such as security alerts when there is potentially unsafe, active content in an Office file that you open is the:
   A. Message Bar   **B.** Message pane   **C.** Status bar

4. The area of the Access window that displays and organizes the names of the objects in a database and where you can open objects for use is the:
   A. Object Pane   **B.** Navigation Pane   **C.** Taskbar

5. The Access view that displays data organized in columns and rows similar to an Excel worksheet is:
   A. Datasheet view   **B.** Design view   **C.** Print Preview

6. A term that describes objects and controls that are based on data stored in one or more tables or queries in the database is:
   A. bound   **B.** restricted   **C.** unbound

7. The Access view in which you can view the records in a form but cannot change the layout or design of the form is:
   A. Datasheet view   **B.** Form view   **C.** Draft view

8. A list of variable information, such as names and addresses, that is merged with a main document to create customized form letters, envelopes, or labels is called the:
   A. address block   **B.** data source   **C.** merge fields

9. A portion of the total records available in a table is called a:
   A. subgroup   **B.** subordinate group   **C.** subset

10. The process of displaying only a portion of the data based on matching a specific value to show only the data that meets the criteria you specify is:
    A. filtering   **B.** merging   **C.** sorting

Apply 3A skills from these Objectives:

1 Create an Access Database Using a Template
2 Use an Access Form to Enter and Edit Records
3 Export an Access Table to a Word Document
4 Format a Word Document

Mastering Integration | Project 3C Garden Shows

In the following Mastering Integration project, you will create a list of local garden shows for Southwest Gardens. Your completed files will look similar to Figure 3.34.

PROJECT FILES

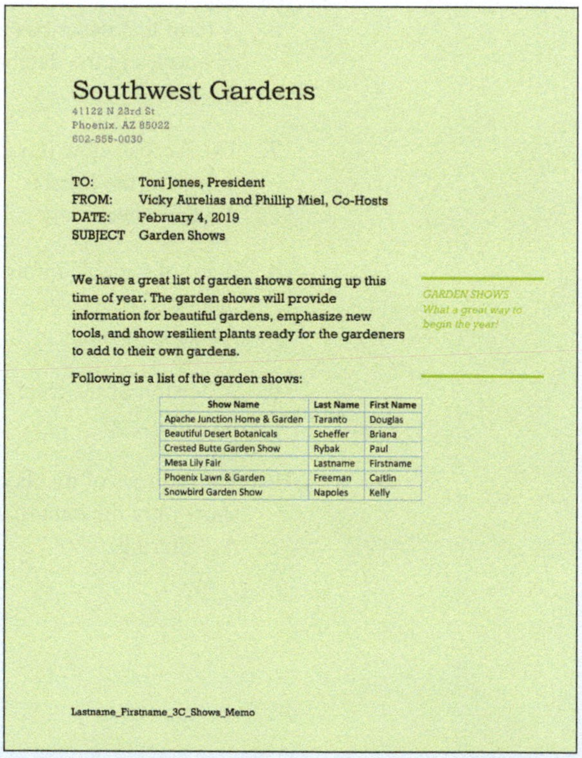

For Project 3C, you will need the following files:

New blank Access database
i03C_Shows_Memo

You will save your files as:

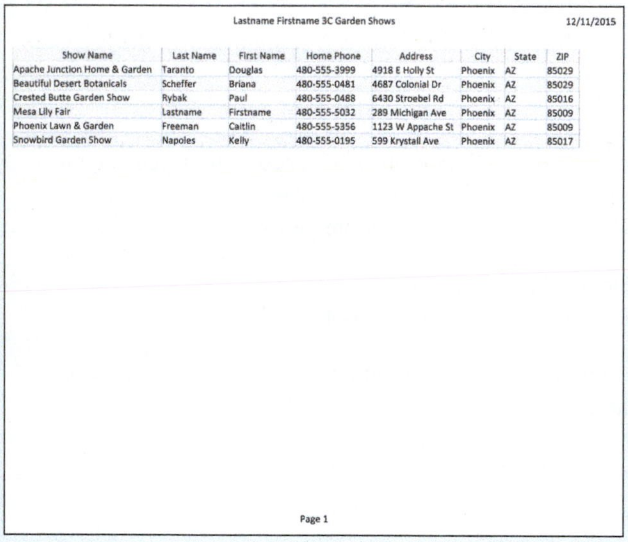

Lastname_Firstname_3C_Garden_Shows
Lastname_Firstnmae_3C_Shows_Memo

PROJECT RESULTS

FIGURE 3.34

(Project 3C Garden Shows continues on the next page)

1 Start Access. Locate the **Sample Template** named **Desktop student database**. **Save** the database in your **Integrated Projects Chapter 3** folder with the file name **Lastname_Firstname_3C_Garden_Shows** If necessary, on the **Message Bar**, click **Enable Content**. **Close** any open objects. If necessary, click **Open** to expand the **Navigation Pane**.

2 In the **Navigation Pane**, **Rename** the **Students** table as **Lastname Firstname 3C Garden Shows Delete** all other objects from the database. If any message boxes display, click **Yes**. Open the **3C Garden Shows** table in **Design** view. Drag down to select all fields beginning with **E-mail Address** and ending with **ID Number**. With all six rows selected, click **Delete Rows**. In a similar manner, delete the **Mobile Phone** field, and then beginning with **Country/Region**, delete the last 11 fields in the table.

3 In the **State/Province** field, delete the text **/Province**. In the **ZIP/Postal Code** field, delete **/Postal Code**. Rename the **ID** field as **Show Name** and change the data type to **Short Text**. Verify the

Show Name field is the **Primary Key**. Display the **Property Sheet** and delete the content next to **Subdatasheet Name**.

4 Click **Save**, and then display the table in Datasheet view. Enter the following garden shows in Table 1, and then apply **Best Fit** to all columns:

5 Create a Form based on the **Lastname Firstname 3C Garden Shows** table. **Save** the form with the name **Lastname Firstname 3C Shows Form** Switch to **Form** view, and add the records in Table 2. In the last record, use your name in the **Last Name** and **First Name** fields.

6 Find the record for **Beautiful Desert Botanicals**, change the **Address** to **4687 Colonial Dr** and then change the **ZIP** to **85029** Find the record for **Gilbert Flower Festival**, and then **Delete** the record. **Close** the form.

7 In the **Lastname Firstname 3C Garden Shows** table, in Datasheet view, on the **Home tab**, in the **Records group**, click **Refresh All**, and then click **Refresh** to display all records. Print the table in **Landscape** orientation, as directed by your instructor.

TABLE 1

Show Name	Last Name	First Name	Home Phone	Address	City	State	ZIP
Phoenix Lawn & Garden	Freeman	Caitlin	480-555-5356	1123 W Apache St	Phoenix	AZ	85009
Apache Junction Home & Garden	Taranto	Douglas	480-555-3999	4918 E Holly St	Phoenix	AZ	85029
Beautiful Desert Botanicals	Scheffer	Briana	480-555-0481	12003 S 35th Ct	Phoenix	AZ	85009
Gilbert Flower Festival	Hevey	Miranda	480-555-6111	7981 Krisdale Dr	Phoenix	AZ	85016

TABLE 2

Show Name	Last Name	First Name	Home Phone	Address	City	State	ZIP
Crested Butte Garden Show	Rybak	Paul	480-555-0488	6430 Stroebel Rd	Phoenix	AZ	85016
Snowbird Garden Show	Napoles	Kelly	480-555-0195	599 Krystall Ave	Phoenix	AZ	85017
Mesa Lily Fair	Last Name	First Name	480-555-5032	289 Michigan Ave	Phoenix	AZ	85009

(Project 3C Garden Shows continues on the next page)

8 **Export** the **Lastname Firstname 3C Garden Shows** table to your **Integrated Projects Chapter 3** folder as an **RTF File**. Save the file with the same name as the table. Do not save the export steps. **Close** the table, saving changes if necessary.

9 Display **Backstage** view, and then click **View and edit database properties**. In the **Properties** dialog box, on the **Summary tab**, in the **Subject** box, type your course name and section number; in the **Author** box, type your first name and last name; and then in the **Keywords** box, type **shows form** Click **OK** to close the dialog box, and **Close** Access.

10 Start Word. Open the file **i03C_Shows_Memo**, and then **Save** the document in your **Integrated Projects Chapter 3** folder as **Lastname_Firstname_3C_Shows_Memo** Insert the file name in the footer. Move to the end of the document, and **Insert** the **Lastname Firstname 3C Garden Shows** RTF file. In the new table, display the columns **Show Name**, **Last Name**, and **First Name**, and then delete any other columns. Adjust the **Cell Size** to **AutoFit to Contents**. Change the **Table Style** to **List Table 3 – Accent 3**, the fourth style in the third row under **List Tables**. **Center** the table between the left and right margins.

11 Select the first paragraph—*Southwest Gardens*—and then change the **Style** to **Title**. Select the second, third, and fourth paragraphs, and then change the **Style** to **Subtitle**. With the paragraphs still selected, click **Line Spacing**, and then click **Remove Space After Paragraph**. Deselect the text, and then **Insert** a **Text Box** with the style **Austin Quote**. In the text box, type **GARDEN SHOWS** Press Enter, and then type **What a great way to begin the year!** Change text wrapping to **Square**. Change the text box **Height** to **1.6"** and the **Width** to **2"**, and then move the text box to the right of the paragraph beginning *We have a great list*. Change the **Page Color** to **Blue, Accent 1, Lighter 60%**, and then apply the theme—**Damask**. Print the document, as directed by your instructor.

12 Display **Backstage** view, click **Properties**, and then click **Show Document Panel**. In the **Author** box, type your first name and last name; in the **Subject** box, type your course name and section number; and then in the **Tags** box, type **shows table Close the Document Information Panel**. **Save** your document, and then **Close** Word.

13 Submit your printed or electronic files as directed by your instructor.

END | You have completed Project 3C

CONTENT-BASED ASSESSMENTS (MASTERY AND TRANSFER OF LEARNING)

Apply 3B skills from these Objectives:

5 Use Mail Merge in Word to Complete Letters Using Access Data
6 Use Mail Merge in Word to Create Envelopes Using Access Data
7 Create and Modify a Query in Access
8 Use Mail Merge in Access

Mastering Integration Project 3D Gardening Basics

In the following Mastering Integration project, you will use the Mail Merge Wizard to create letters and envelopes for local gardening experts. Using a filtered list, you will create additional letters. Your completed files will look similar to Figure 3.35.

PROJECT FILES

For Project 3D, you will need the following files:

New blank Word document
i03D_Gardening_Basics
i03D_Gardening_Experts
i03D_Gardening_Fun

You will save your files as:

New blank Word document
Lastname_Firstname_3D_Gardening_Basics
Lastname_Firstname_3D_Gardening_Experts
Lastname_Firstname_3D_Expert_Letters
Lastname_Firstname_3D_Expert_Envelopes
Lastname_Firstname_3D_Merged_Envelopes
Lastname_Firstname_3D_Gardening_Fun
Lastname_Firstname_3D_Fun_Letters

PROJECT RESULTS

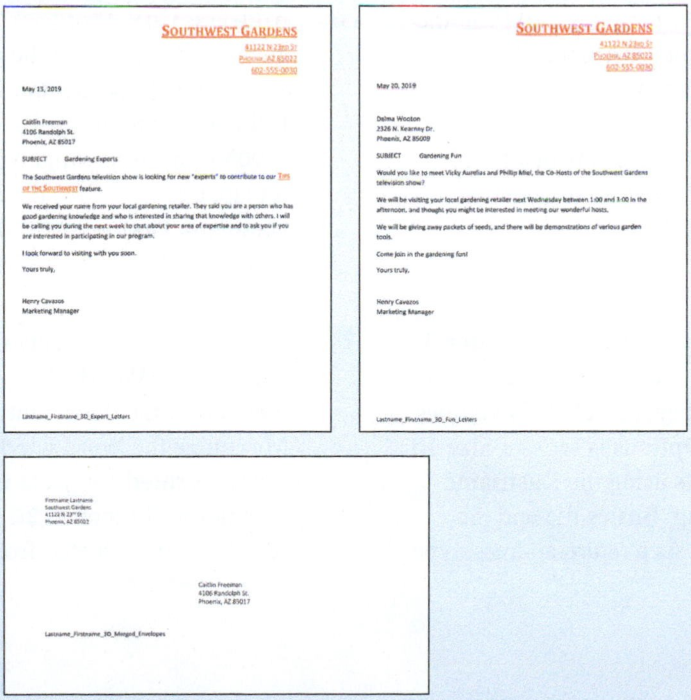
SOUTHWEST GARDENS
41122 N 23RD ST
PHOENIX, AZ 85022
602-555-0030

May 15, 2019

Caitlin Freeman
4106 Randolph St.
Phoenix, AZ 85017

SUBJECT Gardening Experts

The Southwest Gardens television show is looking for new "experts" to contribute to our TIPS OF THE SOUTHWEST feature.

We received your name from your local gardening retailer. They said you are a person who has good gardening knowledge and who is interested in sharing that knowledge with others. I will be calling you during the next week to chat about your area of expertise and to ask you if you are interested in participating in our program.

I look forward to visiting with you soon.

Yours truly,

Henry Cavazos
Marketing Manager

Lastname_Firstname_3D_Expert_Letters

SOUTHWEST GARDENS
41122 N 23RD ST
PHOENIX, AZ 85022
602-555-0030

May 20, 2019

Dalma Wooton
2326 N. Kearney Dr.
Phoenix, AZ 85009

SUBJECT Gardening Fun

Would you like to meet Vicky Aurelias and Phillip Miel, the Co-Hosts of the Southwest Gardens television show?

We will be visiting your local gardening retailer next Wednesday between 1:00 and 3:00 in the afternoon, and thought you might be interested in meeting our wonderful hosts.

We will be giving away packets of seeds, and there will be demonstrations of various garden tools.

Come join in the gardening fun!

Yours truly,

Henry Cavazos
Marketing Manager

Lastname_Firstname_3D_Fun_Letters

Firstname Lastname
Southwest Gardens
41122 N 23rd St
Phoenix, AZ 85022

Caitlin Freeman
4106 Randolph St.
Phoenix, AZ 85017

Lastname_Firstname_3D_Merged_Envelopes

FIGURE 3.35

(Project 3D Gardening Basics continues on the next page)

Mastering Integration Project 3D Gardening Basics (continued)

1 Navigate to the student data files, and locate and open **i03D_Gardening_Basics**. **Copy** the file, and then **Paste** the file in your **Integrated Projects Chapter 3** folder. **Rename** the file with the file name **Lastname_Firstname_3D_Gardening_Basics**

2 Start Word, and open the file **i03D_Gardening_Experts**. **Save** the file in your **Integrated Projects Chapter 3** folder as **Lastname_Firstname_3D_Gardening_Experts** Start the **Step by Step Mail Merge Wizard**. Confirm that you will create letters. **Select Recipients** using the **Lastname_Firstname_3D_Gardening_Basics** file and the **Gardening Experts** table. Insert the **Address Block** in the second blank paragraph below the date. Adjust the **Paragraph Spacing** so there is **0 pt** spacing **Before** and **After**.

3 **Complete the merge**, and merge all letters to a **New Document**. **Save** the new document in your **Integrated Projects Chapter 3** folder as **Lastname_Firstname_3D_Expert_Letters** Insert the file name in the footer. Display the **Document Information Panel**. In the **Author** box, type your first name and last name; in the **Subject** box, type your course name and section number; and then in the **Tags** box, type **expert letters, merged** Print the first letter, as directed by your instructor. **Close** the **Document Information Panel**. **Close** the document. With the file **Lastname_Firstname_3D_Gardening_Experts** displayed, insert the file name in the footer. **Save** your changes, and then from **Backstage** view, click **Close**.

4 Open a new blank Word document. **Save** the document in your **Integrated Projects Chapter 3** folder as **Lastname_Firstname_3D_Experts_Envelopes** Start Mail Merge, and click **Envelopes**. Verify that the **Envelope Options** is set as a **Size 10** envelope. **Select Recipients** using the **Lastname_Firstname_3D_Gardening_Basics** file and the **Gardening Experts** table. As a return address, type

your First Name Last Name and then press [Enter]. Type **Southwest Gardens** and then press [Enter]. Type **41122 N 23rd St** press [Enter], and then type **Phoenix, AZ 85022** Insert the **Address Block**, and then merge all of the envelopes to a **New Document**. **Save** the new document in your **Integrated Projects Chapter 3** folder as **Lastname_Firstname_3D_Merged_Envelopes** Insert the file name in the footer. Display the **Document Information Panel**. In the **Author** box, type your first name and last name; in the **Subject** box, type your course name and section number; and then in the **Tags** box, type **experts envelopes, merged** Print the first envelope, as directed by your instructor. **Save** your changes, and then **Close** the document. In the **Lastname_Firstname_3D_Experts_Envelopes** file, insert the file name in the footer. **Save** your changes, and then **Close** Word.

5 Open the Access file **Lastname_Firstname_3D_Gardening_Basics**. If necessary, on the **Message Bar**, click **Enable Content**. Create a query using the **Simple Query Wizard**. Select the **Gardening Experts** table, and then add the following fields to the **Selected Fields**: **First Name**, **Last Name**, **Address**, **City**, **State**, and **ZIP**. Show a **Detail** query, and then name the query **Lastname Firstname 3D Gardening Experts Query** Set the **Criteria** of the query to only show the **ZIP** code **85009** From **Backstage** view, click the **Save Object As** tab, and then save the revised query as **Lastname Firstname 3D 85009 Experts Query** Resize the Navigation Pane so all object names fully display.

6 With the **85009 Experts Query** selected, export the object using **Word Merge**. From your student data files, select the document **i03D_Gardening_Fun**. **Maximize** the Word window. **Save** the document in the **Integrated Projects Chapter 3** folder as **Lastname_Firstname_3D_Gardening_Fun** Verify the recipients are selected from the **Lastname**

(Project 3D Gardening Basics continues on the next page)

Mastering Integration | **Project 3D Gardening Basics** (continued)

Firstname 3D 85009 Experts Query. Insert the **Address Block** in the second paragraph below the date. Adjust the **Paragraph Spacing** so there is **0 pt** spacing **Before** and **After**. Complete the merge, and then merge all of the letters to a **New Document**.

7 ▶ **Save** the new document in your **Integrated Projects Chapter 3** folder as **Lastname_ Firstname_3D_Fun_Letters** Insert the file name in the footer. Display the **Document Information Panel**. In the **Author** box, type your first name and last name; in the **Subject** box, type your course name and section number; and then in the **Tags** box, type **fun letters, merged** Print the last letter, as directed by your instructor. **Save** your changes, and **Close** the document. In the **Lastname_ Firstname_3D_Gardening_Fun** file, insert the file name in the footer. **Save** your changes, and then **Close** Word. **Close** Access.

8 ▶ Submit your printed or electronic files as directed by your instructor.

◀ **END | You have completed Project 3D**

GO! Solve It   Project 3E Garden Clubs

PROJECT FILES

For Project 3E, you will need the following files:

New blank Word document
i03E_Garden_Clubs
i03E_Club_Information
i03E_Contacts_Letter

You will save your files as:

Lastname_Firstname_3E_Garden_Clubs
Lastname_Firstname_3E_Club_Information
Lastname_Firstname_3E_Contacts_Letter
Lastname_Firstname_3E_Club_Letters
Lastname_Firstname_3E_Club_Envelopes

Southwest Gardens is planning to feature a garden club each week on its show and wants to invite garden clubs to apply. You have been asked to update the contact information for the clubs in a database, modify a form including the contact information, and then create individualized letters and envelopes using mail merge.

Open the **i03E_Garden_Clubs** database, and save it in your **Integrated Projects Chapter 3** folder as **Lastname_Firstname_3E_Garden_Clubs** Create a form based on the Garden Clubs table, and save the form as **Lastname Firstname 3E Clubs Form** Enter the information below, using your First Name and Last Name for the last record. Update the Address Field for the Backyard Gardeners to **9847 Fairmount Ave** and delete the record for Bridlemile Garden Gloves. In the table, apply **Best Fit** to all columns.

Club Name	First Name	Last Name	Address	City	State	ZIP	Phone	E-mail Address
Ocotillo Club	Greta	Myers	14820 S 25th Way	Phoenix	AZ	85029	480-555-0902	Greta@phoenixmail.com
Pots and Planters	First Name	Last Name	4126 W Mercer Ln	Phoenix	AZ	85009	480-555-5032	Firstname@phoenixmail.com

Export the table as an RTF file named **Lastname_Firstname_3E_Clubs_RTF** Open the **i03E_Club_Information** file. Insert the RTF file and delete the **Address, City, State**, and **ZIP** fields. Format the information sheet to display as a one-page document and include a page color, page border, and theme. Save the document as **Lastname_ Firstname_3E_Club_Information**

(Project 3E Garden Clubs continues on the next page)

GO! Solve It | Project 3E Garden Clubs (continued)

Open the **i03E_Contacts_Letter**, and save it as **Lastname_Firstname_3E_Contacts_Letter** Using mail merge, include appropriate merge fields from the Garden Clubs table in the database in the letter. Complete the merge, and then save the merged letters as **Lastname_Firstname_3E_Club_Letters** Create envelopes to be used with the letters, using Southwest Gardens' address as the return address. Save the merged envelopes as **Lastname_Firstname_3E_Club_Envelopes** Insert the file name in the footer for each of the four Word documents. Insert appropriate document properties in all five files. Submit your printed or electronic files as directed by your instructor.

Performance Level

Performance Criteria	Exemplary: You consistently applied the relevant skills.	Proficient: You sometimes, but not always, applied the relevant skills.	Developing: You rarely or never applied the relevant skills.
Create 3E Clubs form and edit data	Form is created, and all data is entered accurately	Form is created and all data is entered, but there are two or fewer errors	Form is not created and/or data is not entered
Export the 3E Clubs table and make modifications	Table is exported accurately, and all modifications are made	Table is exported and modifications are made, but there are two or fewer errors	Table is not exported and/or modifications are not made
Merge the 3E Clubs table with the 3E Contacts Letter	Merge completed accurately	Merge completed with two or fewer errors	Merge not completed
Merge the 3E Clubs table to create envelopes	Merge completed accurately	Merge completed with two or fewer errors	Merge not completed

END | You have completed Project 3E

RUBRIC

The following outcomes-based assessments are open-ended assessments. That is, there is no specific correct result; your result will depend on your approach to the information provided. Make Professional Quality your goal. Use the following scoring rubric to guide you in how to approach the problem and then to evaluate how well your approach solves the problem.

The *criteria*—Software Mastery, Content, Format and Layout, and Process—represent the knowledge and skills you have gained that you can apply to solving the problem. The *levels of performance*—Professional Quality, Approaching Professional Quality, or Needs Quality Improvements—help you and your instructor evaluate your result.

	Your completed project is of Professional Quality if you:	Your completed project is approaching Professional Quality if you:	Your completed project needs Quality Improvements if you:
1-Software Mastery	Choose and apply the most appropriate skills, tools, and features and identify efficient methods to solve the problem.	Choose and apply some appropriate skills, tools, and features, but not in the most efficient manner.	Choose inappropriate skills, tools, or features, or are inefficient in solving the problem.
2-Content	Construct a solution that is clear and well organized, contains content that is accurate, appropriate to the audience and purpose, and is complete. Provide a solution that contains no errors of spelling, grammar, or style.	Construct a solution in which some components are unclear, poorly organized, inconsistent, or incomplete. Misjudge the needs of the audience. Have some errors in spelling, grammar, or style, but the errors do not detract from comprehension.	Construct a solution that is unclear, incomplete, or poorly organized, contains some inaccurate or inappropriate content, and contains many errors of spelling, grammar, or style. Do not solve the problem.
3-Format and Layout	Format and arrange all elements to communicate information and ideas, clarify function, illustrate relationships, and indicate relative importance.	Apply appropriate format and layout features to some elements, but not others. Overuse features, causing minor distraction.	Apply format and layout that does not communicate information or ideas clearly. Do not use format and layout features to clarify function, illustrate relationships, or indicate relative importance. Use available features excessively, causing distraction.
4-Process	Use an organized approach that integrates planning, development, self-assessment, revision, and reflection.	Demonstrate an organized approach in some areas, but not others; or, use an insufficient process of organization throughout.	Do not use an organized approach to solve the problem.

Apply a combination of the 3A and 3B skills.

GO! Think   Project 3F Xeriscape Landscaping

PROJECT FILES

For Project 3F, you will need the following files:

New blank Word document
New blank Access database
i03F_Gardeners_Flyer
i03F_Gardeners_Letter

You will save your files as:

Lastname_Firstname_3F_Xeriscape_Gardeners
Lastname_Firstname_3F_Gardeners_Flyer
Lastname_Firstname_3F_Gardeners_Letter
Lastname_Firstname_3F_Xeriscape_Letters
Lastname_Firstname_3F_Xeriscape_Envelopes

Southwest Gardens is going to begin a new feature on xeriscaping—landscaping with slow-growing, drought-tolerant plants to conserve water and reduce yard trimmings. The show wants to contact local designers who have created xeriscaped garden areas to see how much water they save. You have been asked to enter the contact information for the gardeners in a database, modify a flyer including the contact information, and then create individualized letters and envelopes using mail merge.

Save a new blank Access database as **Lastname_Firstname_3F_Xeriscape_Gardeners** In Access, create a new table that contains the fields below. Save the table as **Lastname Firstname 3F Gardeners** Create a new form based on the table, and then save it as **Lastname Firstname 3F Gardeners Form** Enter the contact information listed below.

First Name	Last Name	Address	City	State	ZIP	Phone
Isaiah	Manzke	4106 Randolph St	Phoenix	AZ	85017	480-555-6111
Andrea	Bramley	7100 N 19th St	Phoenix	AZ	85029	480-555-0488
Vanessa	Mangrove	3622 E Agave Rd	Phoenix	AZ	85016	480-555-3999
Ariel	Rios	6038 E Calle Rosa	Phoenix	AZ	85029	480-555-4774
Anton	Vega	3239 E Weldon Ave	Phoenix	AZ	85029	480-555-3031

Apply Best Fit to the table, and save the changes. Export the **3F Gardeners** table to an RTF document named **Lastname_Firstname__3F_Gardeners** Open the **i03F_Gardeners_Flyer** file. Insert an exported Access table in the flyer, and then delete the ID and Phone columns. Format the flyer to display as a one-page document and include a table style, page color, page border, and theme. Resize table columns so each row displays on one line. Save the flyer as **Lastname_Firstname_3F_Gardeners_Flyer**

(Project 3F Xeriscape Landscaping continues on the next page)

GO! Think   Project 3F Xeriscape Landscaping (continued)

Open the **i03F_Gardeners_Letter** file, and save it as **Lastname_Firstname_3F_Gardeners_Letter** Using mail merge, include appropriate merge fields from the **3F Gardeners** table in the letter. Complete the merge, and then save the merged letters as **Lastname_Firstname_3F_Xeriscape_Letters** Create envelopes to be used with the letters, using Southwest Gardens' address as the return address. Save the merged envelopes as **Lastname_Firstname_3F_Xeriscape_Envelopes** Insert the file name in the footer for each of the four Word documents. Insert appropriate document properties in all five files. Submit your printed or electronic files as directed by your instructor.

END | You have completed Project 3F

Integrating Excel and Access

PROJECT 4A

OUTCOMES
Import Excel data into an Access database and sort or filter in either Excel or Access.

OBJECTIVES

1. Modify an Excel Table
2. Import Excel Data into Access Using the Import Spreadsheet Wizard
3. Sort and Filter Data in an Access Table
4. Create, Modify, and Print an Access Report

PROJECT 4B

OUTCOMES
Create an Access table and query and export Access data into an Excel workbook.

OBJECTIVES

5. Create an Access Table
6. Create an Access Query
7. Export Access Data to Excel

Hellen Sergeyeva/Shutterstock

In This Chapter

In this chapter, you will use the powerful tools of Excel and Access to work with large amounts of data. In Excel, you can analyze and manage your data. In Access, you can track and report your data. Use the import and export features to take advantage of a particular application's features. If you enter a large amount of data into either an Excel workbook or an Access table, it can be difficult to find the results you are seeking. Sorting and filtering data in Excel and Access allows you to view only the desired results.

The projects in this chapter relate to **Midwest HVAC Manufacturer**, one of the country's largest suppliers of heating, ventilation, and air conditioning (HVAC) equipment. The company delivers high-performance climate control parts and systems primarily to wholesale customers. Because of the growing popularity of do-it-yourself projects, the company also has two local retail stores. Two times each year, Midwest HVAC Manufacturer updates its parts catalog, which includes supplies such as fans, motors, heating and cooling coils, filter units, and dehumidification and humidification units. It designs and manufactures all of its own products and has won several engineering and product awards.

HVAC Report

PROJECT ACTIVITIES

In Activities 4.01 through 4.10, you will sort and filter data in an Excel table provided by the retail store to Ray and Noreen Leven, who own a 25-year-old house in Lincoln, Nebraska, that needs a new HVAC unit. You will then import the Excel data into Access, and then sort and filter the data in an Access table. You will create an Access report that lists the HVAC options for the Levens. Your completed files will look similar to Figure 4.1.

PROJECT FILES

For Project 4A, you will need the following files:

New blank Access database
i04A_HVAC_Units
i04A_Midwest_Logo

You will save your files as:

Lastname_Firstname_4A_HVAC_Units
Lastname_Firstname_4A_Levens_HVAC

PROJECT RESULTS

FIGURE 4.1 Project 4A HVAC Report

Objective 1   Modify an Excel Table

Viewing a large amount of data in an Excel workbook can be overwhelming. By using the sort feature, you can organize the data to understand the results more easily. An *Excel table* helps you manage and analyze data. An Excel table is a series of rows and columns that contain related data that is managed independently from the data in other rows and columns in the worksheet.

Activity 4.01 | Sorting Data in an Excel Table

In this activity, you will sort the manufacturer data in an HVAC Units workbook to determine which units provide the highest cooling capacity, and then you will sort the data to determine which units provide the highest heating capacity. Recall that sorting is the process of arranging data in a specific order based on the value in each field.

1 Start Excel. Navigate to the student data files that accompany this chapter, and open the **i04A_HVAC_Units** file. In the location where you are saving your files for this chapter, create a new folder named **Integrated Projects Chapter 4** and then save the file in the folder as **Lastname_Firstname_4A_HVAC_Units**

2 Click the **Insert tab**, and then in the **Text group**, click **Header & Footer**. On the **Design tab**, in the **Navigation group**, click **Go to Footer**. In the **Footer** area, click in the box just above the word *Footer*, and then in the **Header & Footer Elements group**, click **File Name**. Click any cell in the workbook to exit the footer.

3 On the right side of the status bar, click **Normal** ⊞, and then press Ctrl + Home to make cell **A1** the active cell.

4 On the **Insert tab**, in the **Tables group**, click **Table**. In the **Create Table** dialog box, under **Where is the data for your table?**, verify that the range **=$A$1:$I$28** displays, verify that the **My table has headers** check box is selected, and then click **OK**. Compare your screen with Figure 4.2.

The column titles in row 1 form the table headers. Sorting and filtering arrows display in the table's header row.

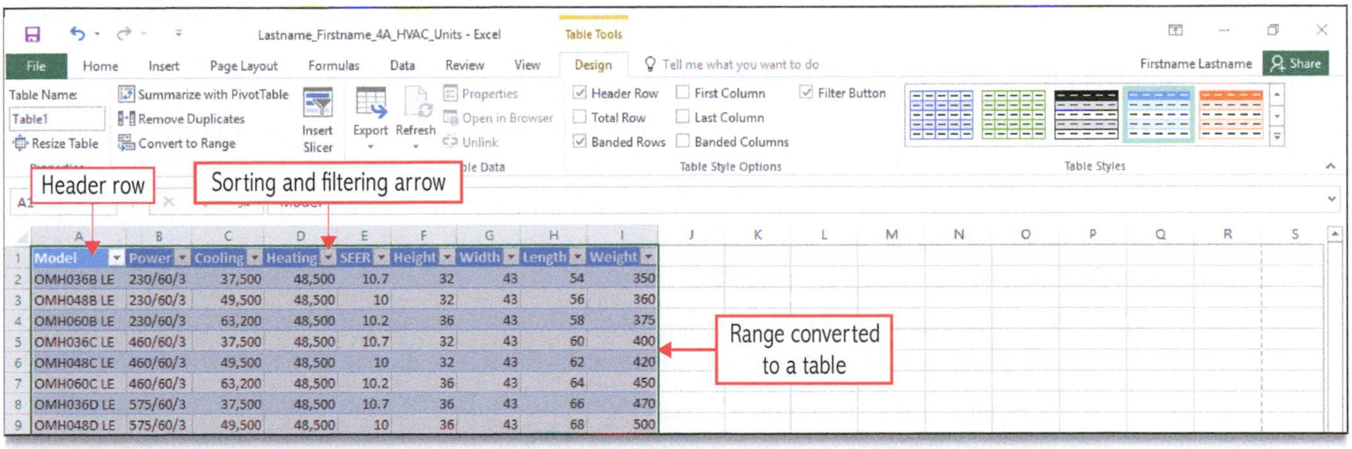

FIGURE 4.2

Excel 2016, Windows 10, Microsoft Corporation

5 In the header row of the table, click the **Cooling arrow**, and then on the menu, click **Sort Largest to Smallest**. Compare your screen with Figure 4.3.

The rows in column C, the Cooling column, are sorted in ***descending order***—text is arranged in reverse alphabetical order (Z to A) or numbers from the highest to the lowest value. ***Ascending order*** arranges text in alphabetical order (A to Z) or numbers from the lowest to the highest value. In cell C1, to the right of the Sort and Filter arrow, notice the small arrow pointing downward indicating that the column is sorted in descending order.

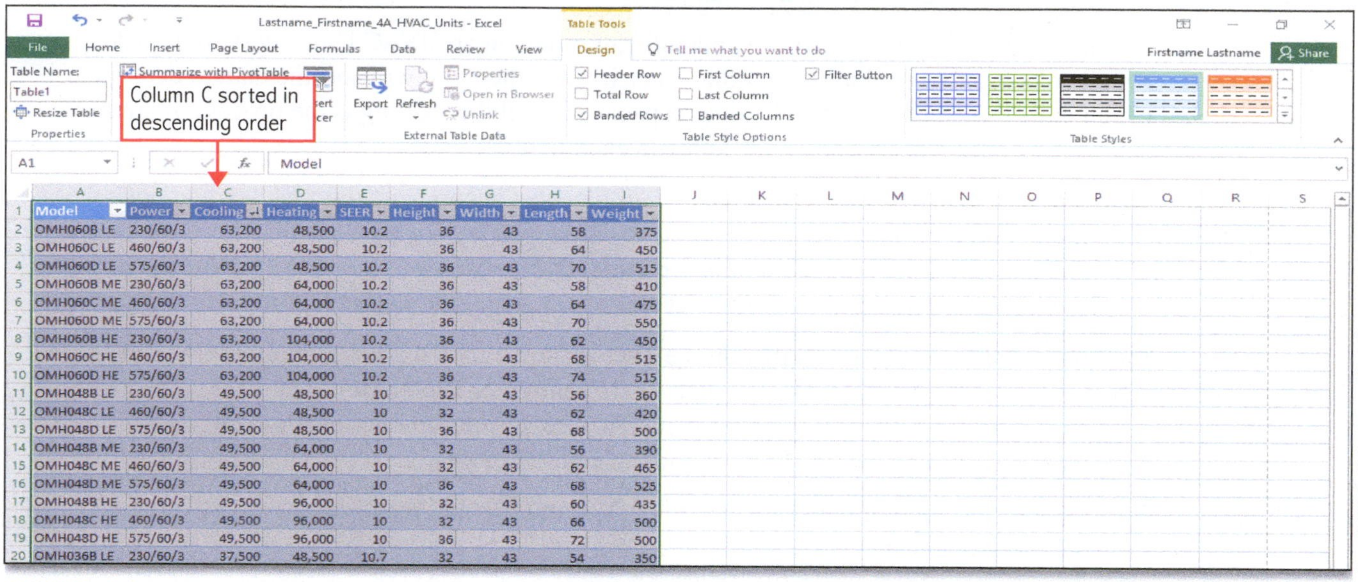

Model	Power	Cooling	Heating	SEER	Height	Width	Length	Weight
OMH060B LE	230/60/3	63,200	48,500	10.2	36	43	58	375
OMH060C LE	460/60/3	63,200	48,500	10.2	36	43	64	450
OMH060D LE	575/60/3	63,200	48,500	10.2	36	43	70	515
OMH060B ME	230/60/3	63,200	64,000	10.2	36	43	58	410
OMH060C ME	460/60/3	63,200	64,000	10.2	36	43	64	475
OMH060D ME	575/60/3	63,200	64,000	10.2	36	43	70	550
OMH060B HE	230/60/3	63,200	104,000	10.2	36	43	62	450
OMH060C HE	460/60/3	63,200	104,000	10.2	36	43	68	515
OMH060D HE	575/60/3	63,200	104,000	10.2	36	43	74	515
OMH048B LE	230/60/3	49,500	48,500	10	32	43	56	360
OMH048C LE	460/60/3	49,500	48,500	10	32	43	62	420
OMH048D LE	575/60/3	49,500	48,500	10	36	43	68	500
OMH048B ME	230/60/3	49,500	64,000	10	32	43	56	390
OMH048C ME	460/60/3	49,500	64,000	10	32	43	62	465
OMH048D ME	575/60/3	49,500	64,000	10	36	43	68	525
OMH048B HE	230/60/3	49,500	96,000	10	32	43	60	435
OMH048C HE	460/60/3	49,500	96,000	10	32	43	66	500
OMH048D HE	575/60/3	49,500	96,000	10	36	43	72	500
OMH036B LE	230/60/3	37,500	48,500	10.7	32	43	54	350

Excel 2016, Windows 10, Microsoft Corporation

FIGURE 4.3

6 Right-click the **Sheet1 tab**, and then on the list, click **Move or Copy**. In the **Move or Copy** dialog box, click **(move to end)**, select the **Create a copy** check box, and then click **OK**.

A copy of Sheet1 is created and automatically named *Sheet1 (2)* to indicate it is a copy. Sheet1 (2) displays and is the active worksheet.

7 On **Sheet1 (2)**, at the top of the **Heating column**–column D–click the **Heating arrow**, and then click **Sort Largest to Smallest**.

To the right of the Heating arrow, notice that the small arrow points downward, indicating the column is sorted in descending order. When you use the Sort and Filter arrow to sort on a different column, the previous sort is turned off. In this case, the arrow pointing downward to the right of the Cooling arrow no longer displays.

8 Right-click the **Sheet1 (2) tab**, and then click **Rename**. With **Sheet1 (2)** selected, type **4A Levens Heating** and then press Enter.

9 Right-click the **Sheet1 tab**, and then click **Rename**. With **Sheet1** selected, type **4A Levens Cooling** and then press Enter. Compare your screen with Figure 4.4.

Notice that the data in the 4A Levens Cooling worksheet remains sorted by the Cooling column. Creating a copy of a worksheet is one way to keep various sort orders available to view at a later time.

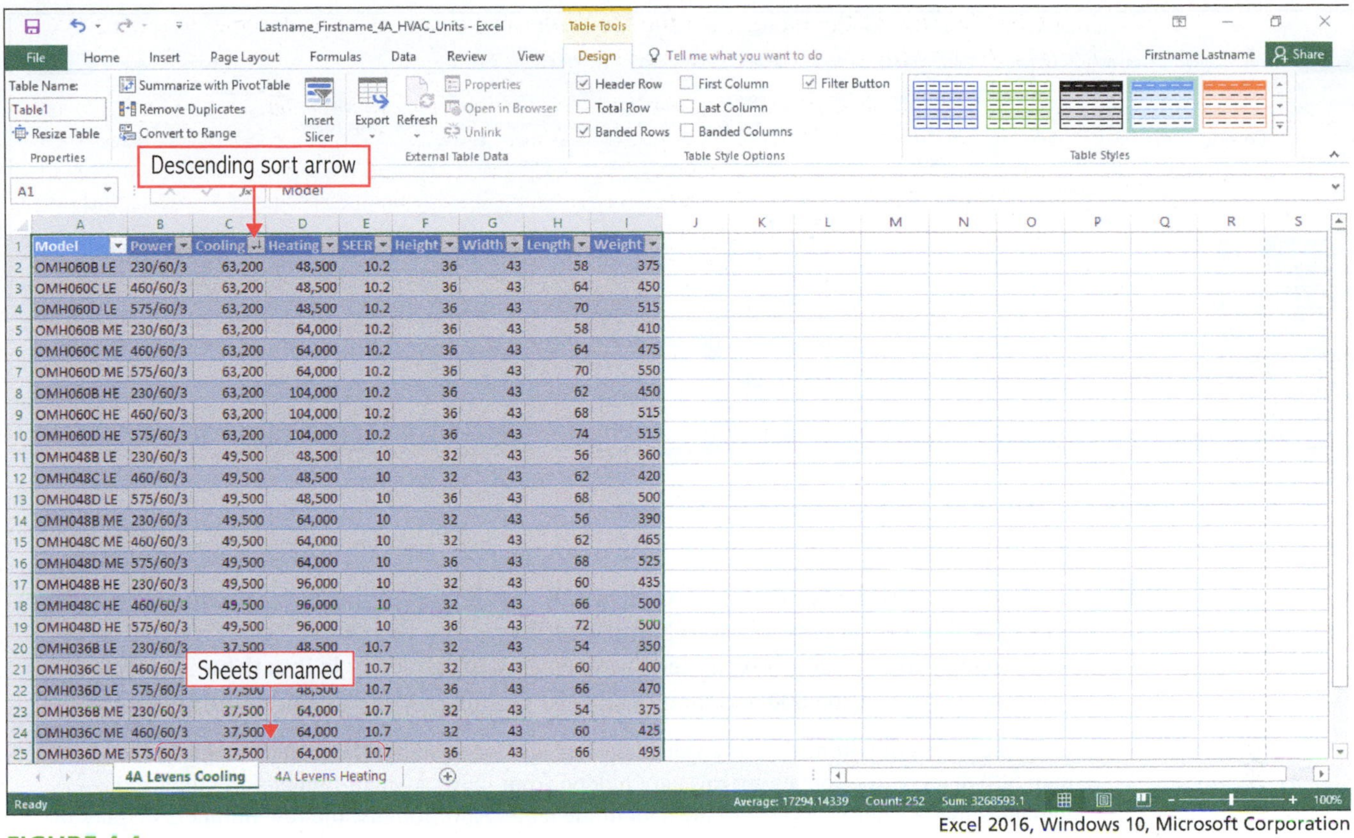

FIGURE 4.4

Excel 2016, Windows 10, Microsoft Corporation

10 ▶ **Save** 🖫 the workbook.

Activity 4.02 | Setting a Custom AutoFilter

Similar to Access tables, when data is sorted, all of the data still displays in the workbook. When you use the *AutoFilter* feature, only a portion of the data (a subset) that meets the criteria you specify is displayed; data that does not meet the criteria is hidden—not deleted. In this case, the retail store wants to see a list of units with gross cooling capacity greater than or equal to 45,000 BTUs (British Thermal Units), and, because it is concerned about shipping costs, the retail store wants to see a list of units that weigh less than 500 pounds.

1 ▶ Click the **4A Levens Heating sheet tab** to make it the active sheet. At the top of the **Cooling column**—column C—click the **Cooling arrow**, point to **Number Filters**, and then click **Greater Than Or Equal To**. In the **Custom AutoFilter** dialog box, under **Show rows where**, verify that **is greater than or equal to** is selected. In the box to the right, type **45000** and then compare your screen with Figure 4.5.

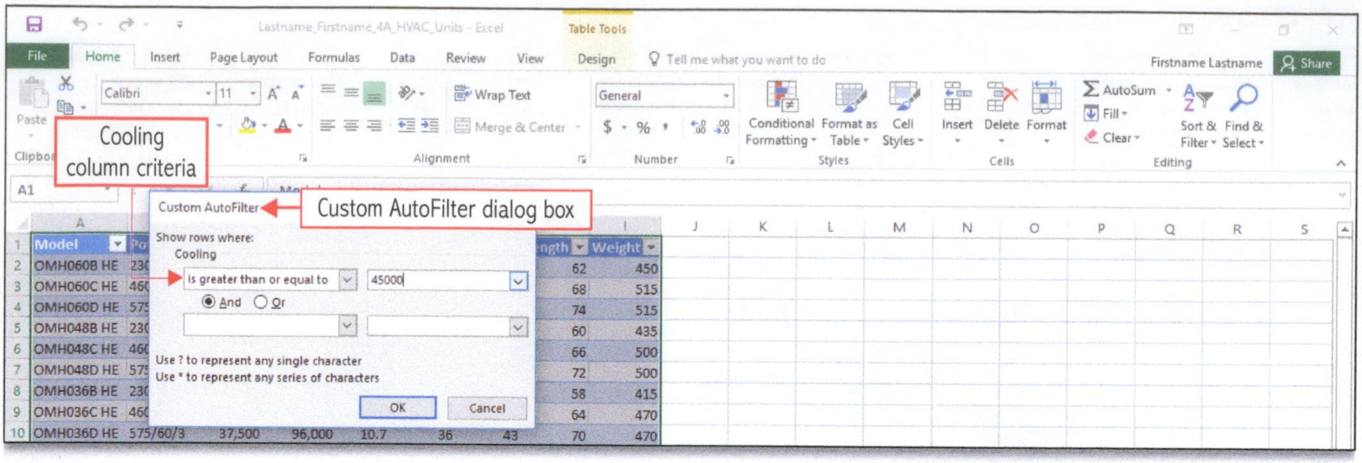

FIGURE 4.5

2 In the **Custom AutoFilter** dialog box, click **OK**. At the top of the **Weight column**—column I—click the **Weight arrow**, point to **Number Filters**, and then click **Less Than**. In the **Custom AutoFilter** dialog box, under **Show rows where**, verify **is less than** is selected. In the box to the right, type **500** and then click **OK**. Compare your screen with Figure 4.6.

Only the rows containing Cooling values greater than or equal to 45000 and Weight values less than 500 display; the remaining rows are hidden from view. A small funnel—the filter icon—indicates that a filter is applied to the data in the table. Additionally, the row numbers display in blue to indicate that some rows are hidden from view. A filter hides entire rows in the worksheet.

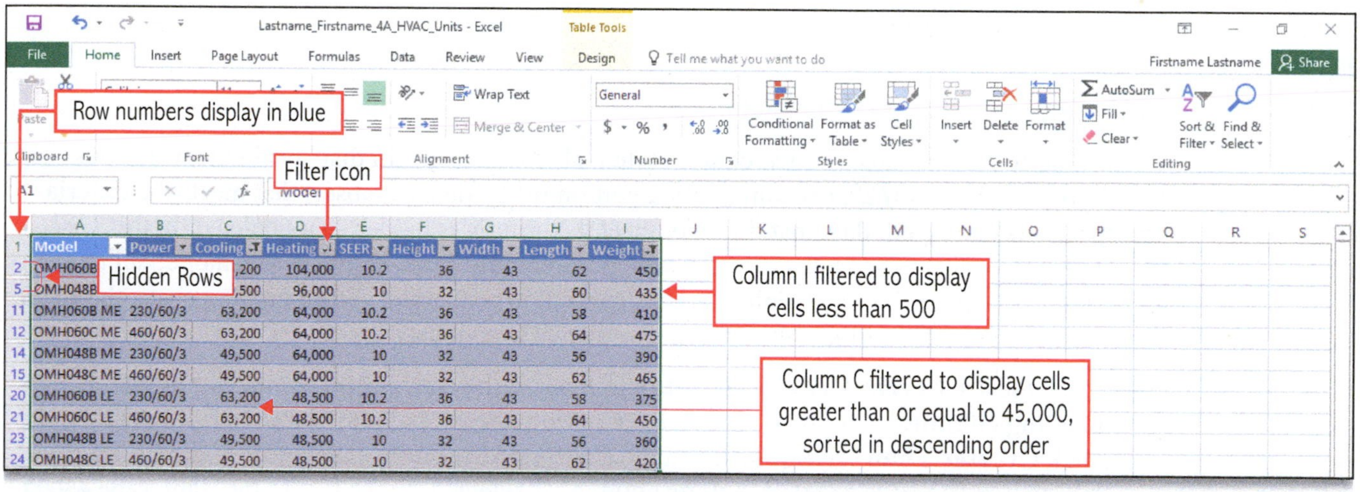

FIGURE 4.6

3 At the top of the **Weight column**—column I—click the **Weight arrow**, and then click **Sort Smallest to Largest**.

To the right of the Weight arrow, a small arrow points upward, indicating the column is sorted in ascending order. The descending arrow in the Heating column no longer displays.

4 **Save** ⊟ the workbook.

Activity 4.03 | Inserting a Calculated Column

One of the advantages of using Excel instead of a calculator is having the application calculate numeric results for you. The cost of shipping the HVAC units to the Levens' region is $1.75 per pound. In this activity, you will use a calculated column to find out how much it costs to ship each unit.

1 Click cell **J1**, type **Shipping Cost** and then press Enter.

> *AutoExpansion* is an Excel table feature in which a new column is automatically included as part of the existing table. In this case, the Shipping Cost column automatically becomes part of the table.

2 Verify that cell **J2** is the active cell. Type the formula **=i2*1.75** and then on the **Formula Bar**, click **Enter** ☑ to accept the entry and keep cell J2 as the active cell. Compare your screen with Figure 4.7.

> A *calculated column* displays in column J. The calculated column uses a single formula that adjusts for each row of a column. The values from the formula display in the cells; and the *underlying formula* displays on the Formula Bar. An underlying formula is the formula entered in a cell and visible only on the Formula Bar. Recall the Formula Bar is an element in the Excel window that displays the value or formula contained in the active cell; you can also enter or edit values or formulas.

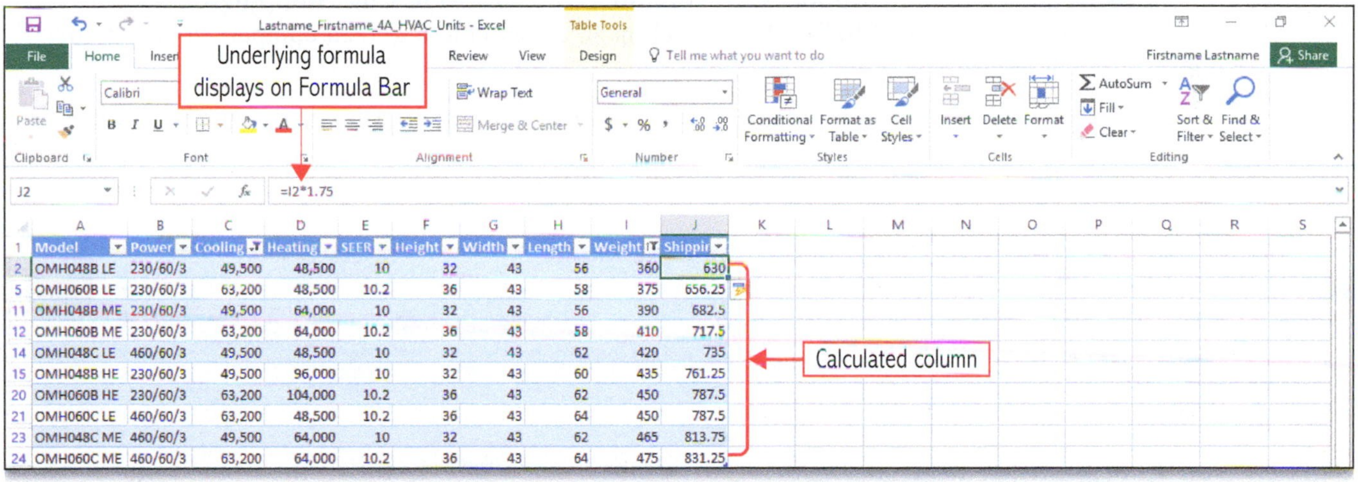

FIGURE 4.7

3 Click the **Formulas tab**, and then in the **Formula Auditing group**, click **Show Formulas**. If necessary, scroll right to view the formulas in column J.

> Recall that the relative cell reference feature will change the cell reference to the correct row, but the number 1.75 remains constant from one row to the next.

4 In the **Formula Auditing group**, click **Show Formulas** to turn off the feature.

🔄 **ANOTHER WAY** To display formulas using a keyboard shortcut, press Ctrl + ～. This is a toggle feature, so Ctrl + ～ will also turn off the feature.

5 Select the range **J2:J24**. Click the **Home tab**, and then in the **Number group**, click **Accounting Number Format** $ ▾. In the **Number group**, click **Decrease Decimal** two times.

6 **Save** 🖫 the workbook.

Activity 4.04 | Applying Conditional Formatting

Analyzing data is simplified by using conditional formatting to highlight cells that meet certain conditions.

1 Verify the cells in **column J** are still selected. On the **Home tab**, in the **Styles group**, click **Conditional Formatting**. Point to **Highlight Cells Rules**, and then click **Less Than**. In the **Less Than** dialog box, type **750** click the **with arrow**, and then click **Yellow Fill with Dark Yellow Text**. Click **OK**, and then click anywhere in the table to deselect the cells in column J.

A ***conditional format*** is a format that changes the appearance of a cell—for example, by adding cell shading or changing font color—based on a condition; if the condition is true, the cell is formatted based on that condition; if the condition is false, the cell is *not* formatted. In this case, the cells in column J that contain a number less than 750 are formatted with yellow fill and dark yellow text.

2 Select **columns A:J**. Point to the line between the column headings A and B to display the [+] pointer, and then double-click.

The widths of columns A through J automatically adjust to the best fit for each column so that all data can be read. Columns will vary in width.

3 At the top of the **Shipping Cost column**—column J—click the **Shipping Cost arrow**, click **Sort Largest to Smallest**. Click in an empty cell, and then compare your screen with Figure 4.8.

The table is no longer sorted by Weight in ascending order; the data is sorted by Shipping Cost in descending order.

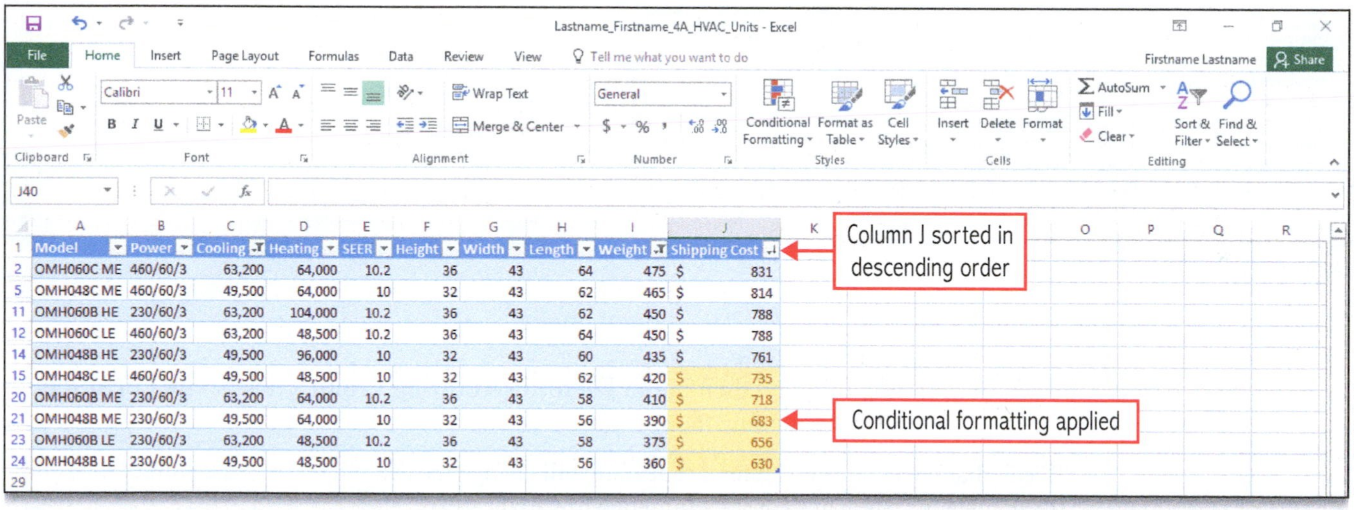

Excel 2016, Windows 10, Microsoft Corporation

FIGURE 4.8

4 On the **Quick Access Toolbar**, click **Undo** [↶].

The Excel table is once again sorted by Weight in ascending order.

5 ▸ Click the **4A Levens Cooling sheet tab** to make it the active sheet. Select cells **A1:A3**. On the **Home tab**, in the **Cells group**, click the **Insert button arrow**, and then click **Insert Sheet Rows**.

Three blank rows are inserted above the selected rows. Because you selected cells in three rows, three new blank rows are inserted.

6 ▸ In cell **A1**, type **Models by Cooling Capacity – Levens** and then on the **Formula Bar**, click **Enter** ✓ to accept the entry and keep cell A1 the active cell.

7 ▸ Select the range **A1:I1**, and then on the **Home tab**, in the **Alignment group**, click **Merge & Center** 🔲▾. In the **Font group**, click **Increase Font Size** Å two times, and then click **Bold** **B**. Click the **Font Color button arrow** A▾, and then in the fifth column, click the first color—**Blue, Accent 1**. Click the **Fill Color button arrow** 🪣▾, and then in the fifth column, select the second color—**Blue, Accent 1, Lighter 80%**.

8 ▸ Select **columns A:I**. Point to the line between any two column headings until the ⊞ pointer displays, and then double-click to adjust the column widths to the best fit. Click in a blank cell, and compare your screen with Figure 4.9.

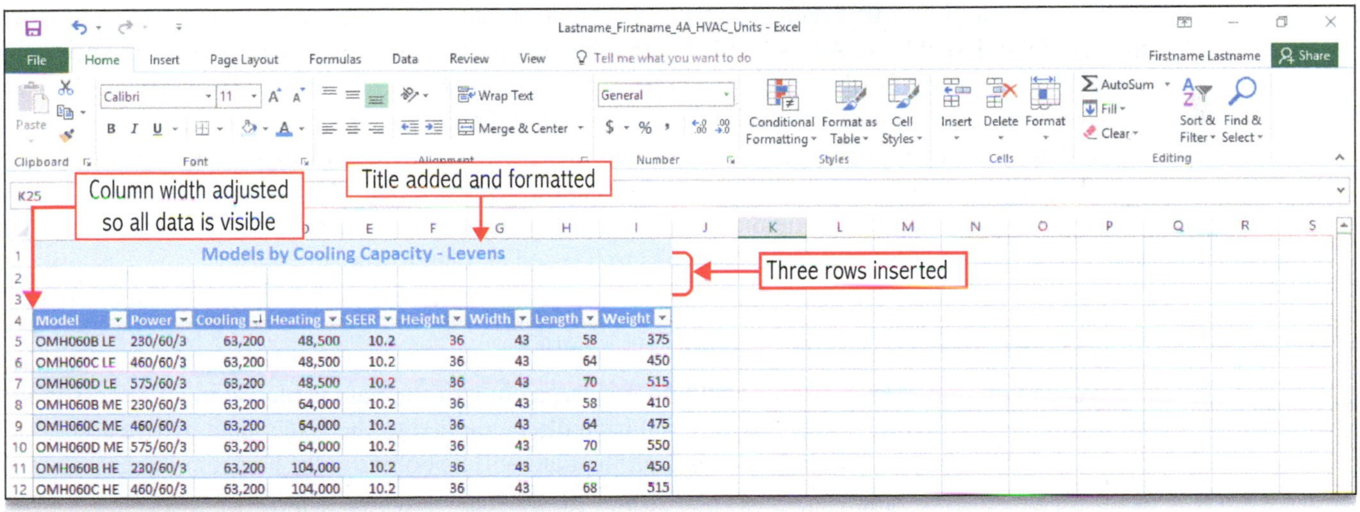

FIGURE 4.9

9 ▸ Select **columns E:H**. Right-click the **Column E** heading, and then on the shortcut menu, click **Hide**. Press Ctrl + Home.

10 ▸ Hold down Shift, and then click the **4A Levens Heating sheet tab**.

Both Excel worksheets are selected.

11 ▸ Click the **Page Layout tab**. In the **Page Setup group**, click **Orientation**, and then click **Landscape**.

Because two worksheets are selected, page formatting is applied to both worksheets at the same time.

12 In the **Page Setup group**, click **Margins**, and then click **Custom Margins**. In the **Page Setup** dialog box, verify that the **Margins tab** is selected. Under **Center on page**, select the **Horizontally** check box, and then click **Print Preview**. Use the navigation area to view your work and to verify that two pages will print.

13 On the left, click the **Info tab**, and in the lower right corner, click **Show All Properties**. Under **Related People**, be sure your name displays as the **Author**—change it if necessary. Click to the right of **Subject**, and then type your course name and section number. Click to the right of **Tags**, and then type **HVAC units, Levens**

14 **Save** 🔲 your workbook, and then print or submit the two worksheets electronically as directed by your instructor. **Close** ⊠ Excel.

Objective 2 | Import Excel Data into Access Using the Import Spreadsheet Wizard

In Access, you can import data from an Excel workbook, which places a copy of the data in an Access table. Importing data is faster and more accurate than retyping the data. You can import the data from Excel to an Access table by copying and pasting the data, by importing an entire worksheet or range of cells, or by linking to an Excel worksheet from an Access database.

The Import Spreadsheet Wizard takes you through the import process step by step. If the Excel data is being imported into a new Access table, the wizard will give you the option of using your Excel column headings as the field names in the Access table. The wizard also allows you to set the data type of each new field and to create a primary key field. If you plan to import Excel data again, you can save the import settings to be used at a later time.

Activity 4.05 | Using the Import Spreadsheet Wizard

When you import data from Excel into Access, a copy of the data is placed in an Access table without altering the Excel data. Even if you have filters applied to the Excel data, where some rows are hidden in your Excel worksheet, all the data will be copied from Excel to Access.

1 Start Access, and then click **Blank desktop database**. In the **Blank desktop database** dialog box, to the right of the **File Name** box, click **Browse** 🟧. In the **File New Database** dialog box, navigate to your **Integrated Projects Chapter 4** folder. In the **File name** box, delete the existing text. Using your own name, type **Lastname_Firstname_4A_Levens HVAC** and then press Enter. In the lower right corner of your screen, click **Create**.

Access creates a new database and opens a table named Table1.

2 Click the **External Data tab**, and then in the **Import & Link group**, click **Excel**. In the **Get External Data – Excel Spreadsheet** dialog box, click **Browse**, and then navigate to your **Integrated Projects Chapter 4** folder. Click your file **Lastname_Firstname_4A_HVAC_Units**, and then click **Open**.

3 Verify that the **Import the source data into a new table in the current database** option button is selected, and then click **OK**. In the **Import Spreadsheet Wizard** dialog box, click the **4A Levens Heating** sheet name, and then compare your screen with Figure 4.10.

You can use the Import Spreadsheet Wizard to import the data from a worksheet or a named range in an Excel workbook.

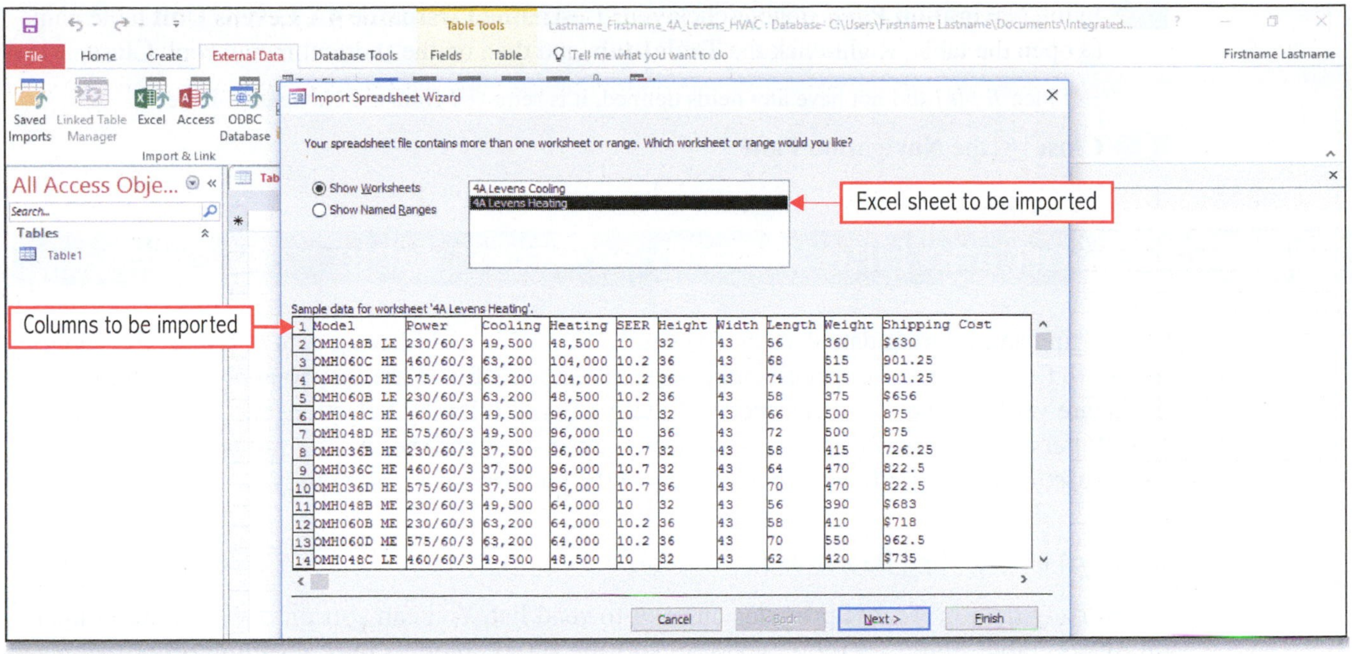

FIGURE 4.10

Access 2016, Windows 10, Microsoft Corporation

4 ▶ Click **Next**. Verify that the **First Row Contains Column Headings** check box is selected, and then click **Next**.

The Import Spreadsheet Wizard enables you to select the data type for each column. Notice that all hidden rows and columns are imported from the Excel worksheet.

5 ▶ Click in the **Shipping Cost column**. Near the top of the dialog box, under **Field Options**, click the **Data Type arrow**, and then click **Currency**. Compare your screen with Figure 4.11.

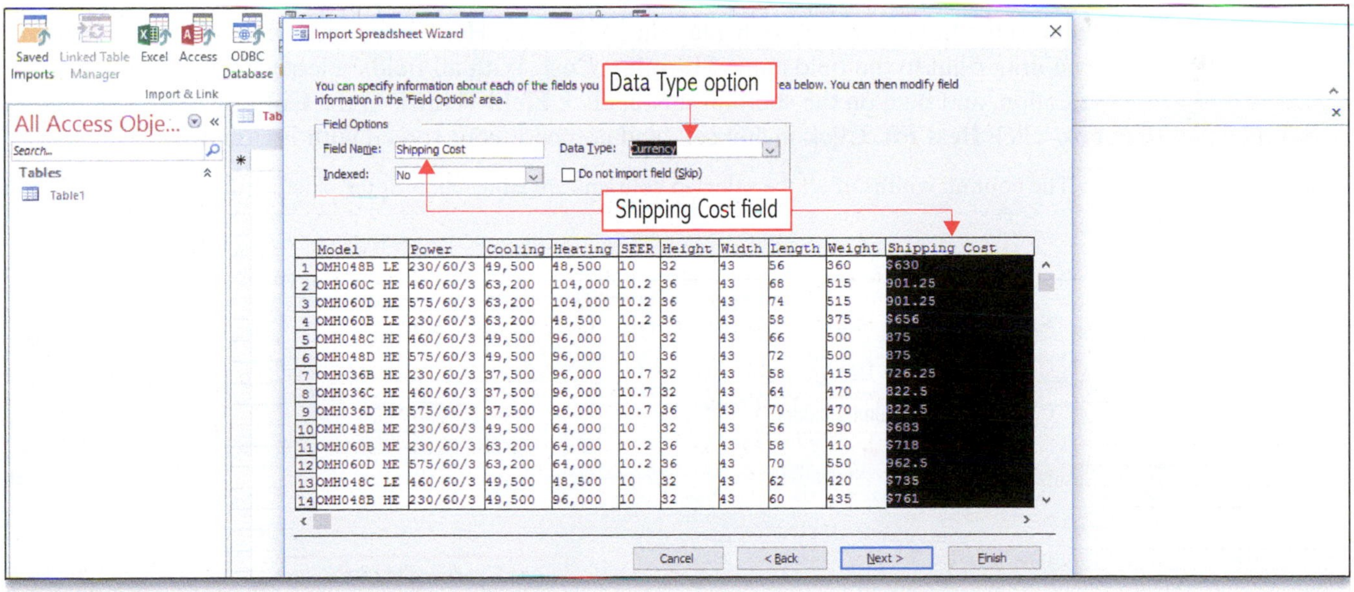

FIGURE 4.11

Access 2016, Windows 10, Microsoft Corporation

6 ▶ Click **Next**. Verify that the **Let Access add primary key** option button is selected, and then click **Next**. Under **Import to Table**, with the existing text selected, using your own name, type **Lastname Firstname 4A Levens Unit** and then click **Finish**. Verify that the **Save import steps** check box is *not* selected, and then click **Close**.

7 In the **Navigation Pane**, double-click your **Lastname Firstname 4A Levens Unit** table name to open the table. Right-click the **Table1 tab**, and then on the shortcut menu, click **Close**.

Since *Table1* did not have any fields defined, it is removed from the Navigation Pane.

8 Close ⟪ the **Navigation Pane**.

Objective 3   Sort and Filter Data in an Access Table

Sorting and filtering data in Access is similar to sorting and filtering data in Excel. You can use a filter to find one or more specific Access records. Access filters are easy to apply and remove. There are various types of filters, such as Filter by Form, Filter by Selection, and Advanced Filter/ Sort. Filters are commonly used to provide a quick answer, and the result is not generally saved for future use; however, if a filter is applied frequently, you can save it as a query.

Activity 4.06 | Sorting Data in an Access Table

Sorting data in Access provides an easy-to-read list. You can sort on one or more fields in an Access table. In this activity, you will sort the HVAC models in descending order by cooling capacity.

1 In the **Lastname Firstname 4A Levens Unit** table, in the **Cooling** field, click the **Cooling arrow**, and then click **Sort Largest to Smallest**.

2 Point to the field name **Height** to display the ⬇ pointer. Hold down the left mouse button, and then drag right to the field name **Length**.

The fields Height through Length are selected.

3 Point to the field name **Height**, right-click, and then on the shortcut menu, click **Hide Fields**.

The fields Height, Width, and Length are hidden from view.

4 Point to the field name **ID** to display the ⬇ pointer. Hold down the left mouse button, and then drag right to the field name **Shipping Cost**. With all fields selected, right-click the selection, and then on the shortcut menu, click **Field Width**. In the **Column Width** dialog box, click **Best Fit**. Click in any cell, and compare your screen with Figure 4.12.

The column widths of all the selected columns are adjusted to fit the existing data.

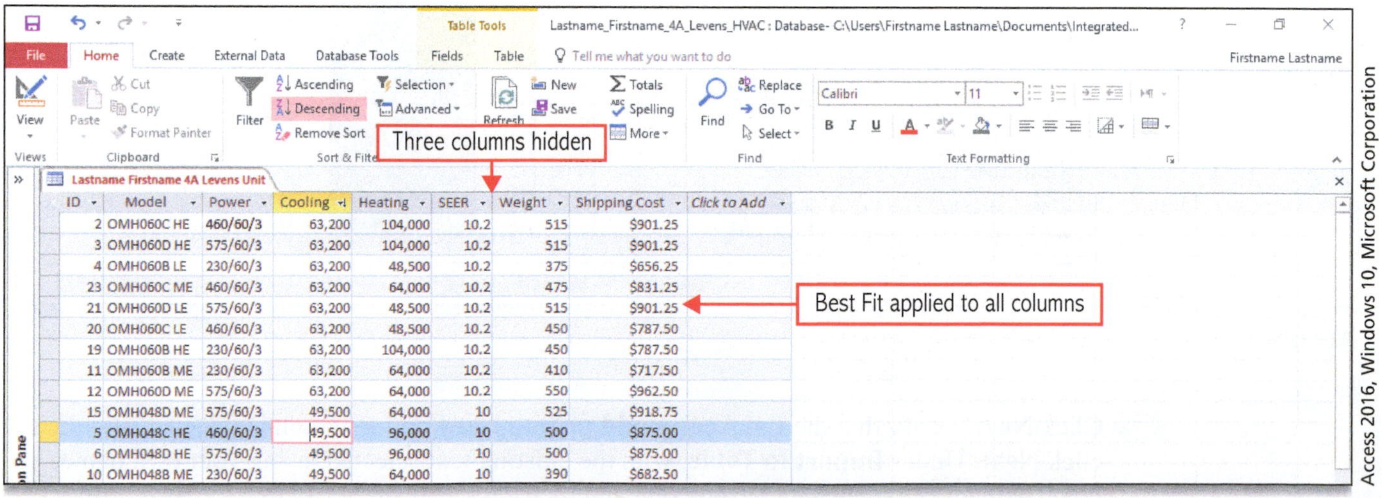

FIGURE 4.12

5 ▸ On the **Quick Access Toolbar**, click **Save** 🔲 to save the changes you have made to the table design.

Activity 4.07 │ Filtering by Selection

By clicking the value that you want to use as the basis for filtering, you can use the filter to find one or more specific Access records. In this activity, you will find the HVAC units that use 460/60/3 power—the type of unit requested by the Levens.

1 ▸ In the **Power** field, click any cell that contains **460/60/3**. Click the **Home tab**. In the **Sort & Filter group**, click **Selection**, and then click **Equals "460/60/3"**. Compare your screen with Figure 4.13.

The Access table is filtered, and the nine records that match the selection are displayed. Notice that the Toggle Filter button is active, and the word *Filtered* displays in the navigation area, indicating that the table is filtered.

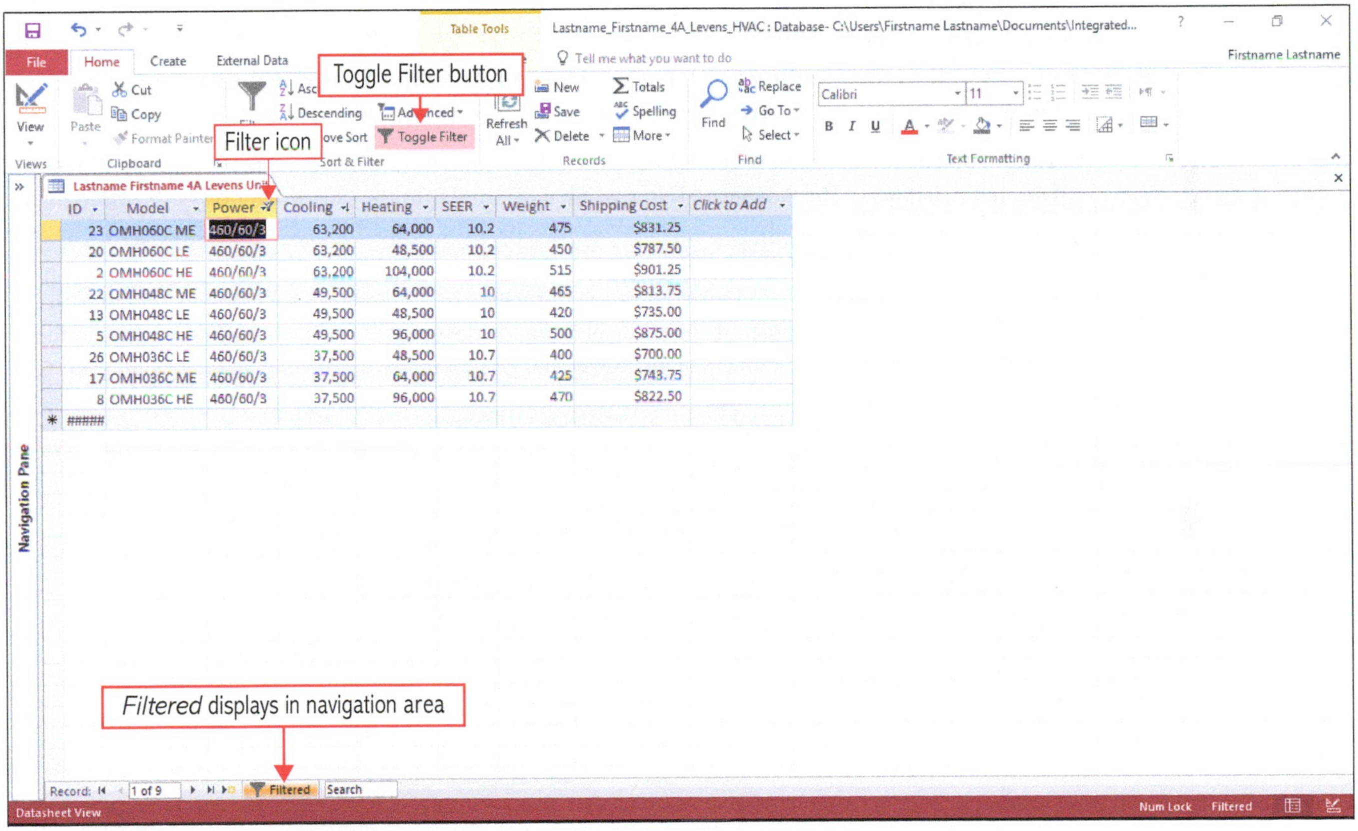

FIGURE 4.13

2 ▸ Right-click the field name **Heating**, and then on the shortcut menu, click **Unhide Fields**. In the **Unhide Columns** dialog box, select the **Height** check box, and then click **Close**.

The Height field displays in the table.

3 ▸ In the **Height** field, click any cell that contains **32**. On the **Home tab**, in the **Sort & Filter group**, click **Selection**, and then click **Less Than or Equal To 32**.

Because the height of the unit must be restricted to a maximum of 32 inches, only units that meet that requirement should display. The table is filtered on both the Power and Height fields—six records display.

4 ▸ **Save** 🔲 your changes to the table design.

Activity 4.08 | Filtering by Advanced Filter/Sort

The Advanced Filter/Sort feature helps you apply a filter that is not a common filter and allows you to save the filter settings as a new query. This type of filtering uses *comparison operators*—symbols that evaluate each field value to determine whether it is the same as (=), greater than (>), less than (<), or in between a range of values as specified by the criteria. In this activity, you will provide the Levens with a list of HVAC units with the highest heating capacity and then the highest cooling capacity.

1 ► On the **Home tab**, in the **Sort & Filter group**, click **Toggle Filter**.

No filters are applied, and all 27 records display in the table. The Width and Length columns remain hidden. The word *Unfiltered* displays in the navigation area, indicating that filters have been created but are not currently applied.

N O T E   Toggle Filter Button

On the Home tab, the Toggle Filter button is used to apply or remove a filter. If no filter has been created, the button is not active—it is not highlighted. After a filter is created, this button becomes active. Because it is a toggle button used to apply and remove filters, the ScreenTip that displays for this button alternates between Apply Filter—when a filter is created but not currently applied—and Remove Filter—when a filter is applied.

---

2 ► Click any cell in the **Cooling** field. On the **Home tab**, in the **Sort & Filter group**, click **Advanced**, and then click **Advanced Filter/Sort**. Compare your screen with Figure 4.14.

The Advanced Filter window and a *field list*—a list of the field names in a table—for the Levens Unit table displays. The Advanced Filter window is similar to the Query window—the *table area* (upper pane) displays the field lists for tables that are used in the filter and the *design grid* (lower pane) displays the design of the filter.

When you started the advanced filter, because your insertion point was in the Cooling field, which was sorted in descending order, this field displays in the design grid and *Descending* displays in the Sort row. The criteria for the filters in the Power and Height fields also display in the design grid.

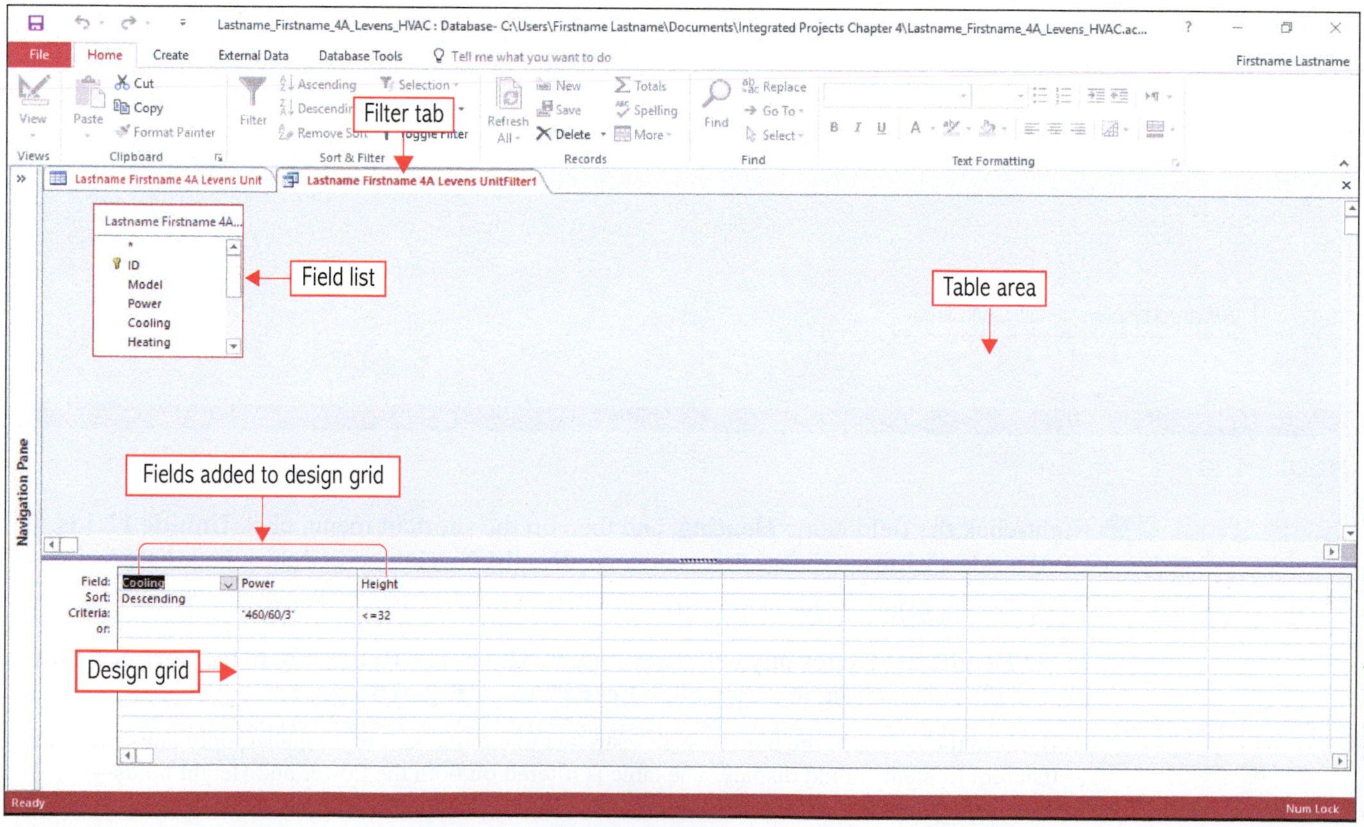

FIGURE 4.14

Access 2016, Windows 10, Microsoft Corporation

> **3** Point to the lower right corner of your **Lastname Firstname 4A Levens Unit** field list to display the [⟷] pointer, and then drag down and to the right to expand the height and width of the field list until all of the field names are visible. Compare your screen with Figure 4.15.

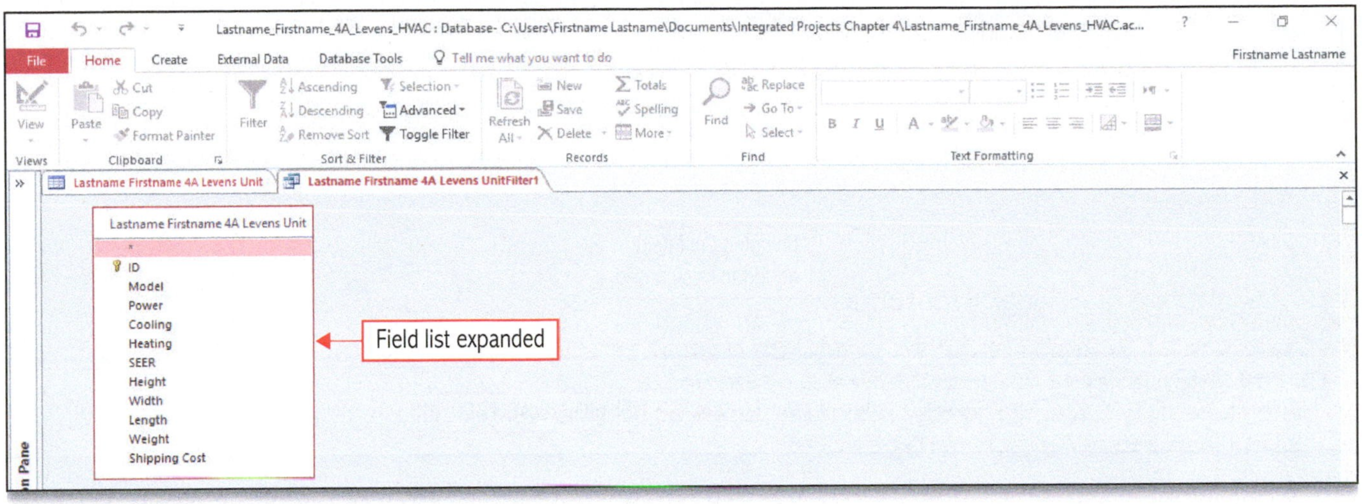

FIGURE 4.15

> **4** In the **Lastname Firstname 4A Levens Unit** field list, double-click the field name **Heating**.

This action adds the Heating field to the design grid.

> **5** In the design grid, in the **Sort** row, click the cell in the **Heating** field, click the **Sort arrow**, and then click **Descending**.

> **6** On the **Home tab**, in the **Sort & Filter group**, click **Toggle Filter** to apply the filter, and then compare your screen with Figure 4.16.

The table displays with the filter applied. Fields that have a Sort designation are sorted from left to right—that is, the sorted field on the left (Cooling) becomes the outermost sort field, and the sorted field on the right (Heating) becomes the innermost sort field.

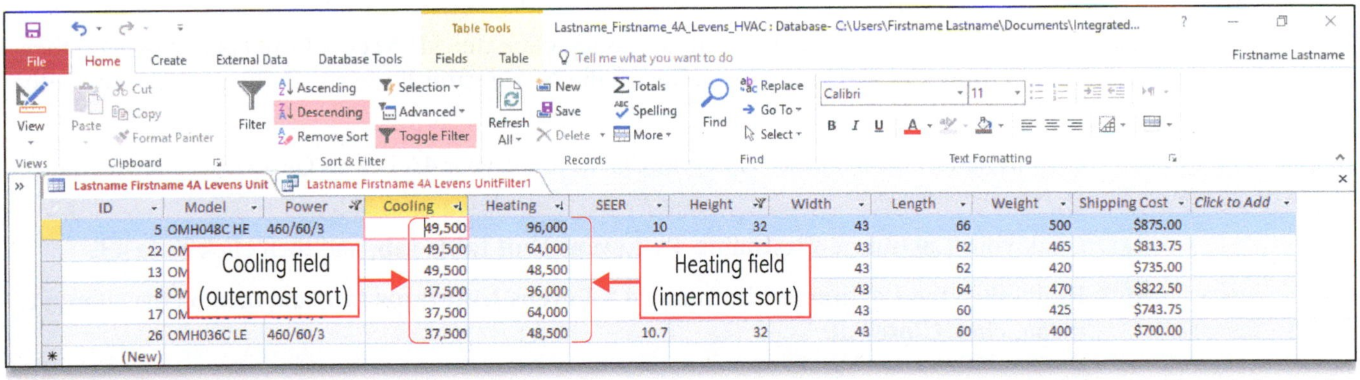

FIGURE 4.16

> **7** Click the **Lastname Firstname 4A Levens UnitFilter1 tab**. In the **Lastname Firstname 4A Levens Unit** field list, scroll as necessary, and then double-click the field name **Shipping Cost**.

Because the Levens are concerned about shipping costs, the Shipping Cost field is added to the design grid.

> **8** In the **Criteria** row, click in the **Shipping Cost** field, type **<650** and then press Enter. Compare your screen with Figure 4.17.

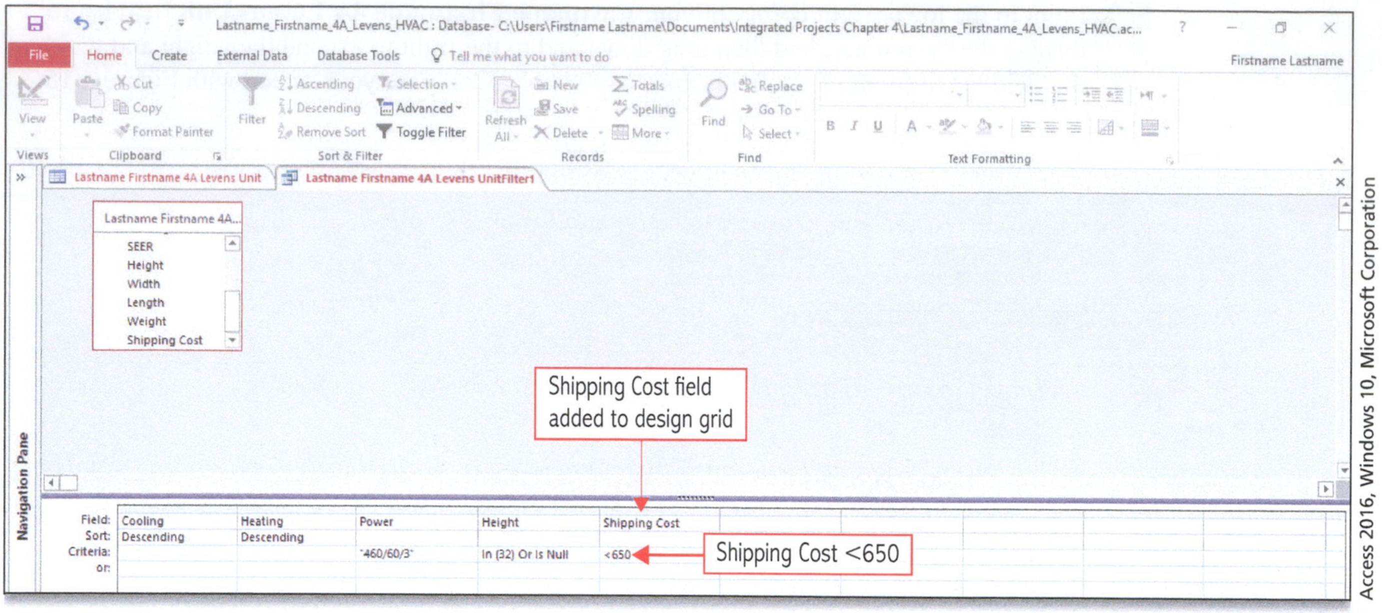

FIGURE 4.17

9 ▶ In the **Sort & Filter group**, click **Toggle Filter**.

The table displays with the filters applied, but no data displays because no data meets all the criteria.

10 ▶ Click the **Lastname Firstname 4A Levens UnitFilter1 tab**. In the **Criteria** row, click in the **Shipping Cost** field. Select **<650**, type **<800** and then click **Toggle Filter**.

The three records that meet the Power criteria of 460/60/3, the Height criteria of 32 or less, and the Shipping Cost criteria of less than $800 display.

11 ▶ Click the **Lastname Firstname 4A Levens UnitFilter1 tab**, and then click **Save** 🖫. In the **Save As Query** dialog box, using your last name, type **Lastname Firstname 4A Levens Query** and then click **OK**.

The Advanced filter is saved as a query.

12 ▶ Open 》 the **Navigation Pane**. If necessary, click the **All Access Objects arrow**, and then click **Tables and Related Views**. Resize the **Navigation Pane** so all object names are fully visible.

Your Lastname Firstname 4A Levens Unit table and your 4A Levens Query display in the Navigation Pane.

13 ▶ Click your **Lastname Firstname 4A Levens Unit table tab**, and then click **Save** 🖫.

14 ▶ Right-click the **Lastname Firstname 4A Levens Unit table tab**, and then on the shortcut menu, click **Close All**.

Objective 4 | Create, Modify, and Print an Access Report

An Access *report* is a database object that summarizes the fields and records from a table (or tables) or from a query in an easy-to-read format suitable for printing. A variety of reports ranging from simple to complex can be created. By thinking about your *record source*—the tables or queries that provide the underlying data for a report—you can create a simple listing of records, or you can group, summarize, or sort the data in a report. To display data in a professional-looking format, consider creating and printing a report rather than printing a table or query.

Activity 4.09 | Creating and Modifying an Access Report

The *Report tool* is an Access feature that creates a report with one mouse click, which displays all of the fields and records from the record source that you select—a quick way to look at the underlying data. You can modify a rough draft of a report in Layout view or Design view. In Layout view, you can see the data while making changes to the report design.

1 In the **Navigation Pane**, double-click your **4A Levens Query**, and then **Close** « the **Navigation Pane**.

2 Click the **Create tab**, and then in the **Reports group**, click **Report**.

> A report based on the query results displays in Layout view. Recall that in Layout view, the report margins and page breaks are visible. If you display a form or report in this view, you can make changes to it.

3 Under **Report Layout Tools**, click the **Page Setup tab**, and then in the **Page Layout group**, click **Landscape**. Scroll to the right, and then compare your screen with Figure 4.18.

> The total of the Shipping Cost field displays. This was inserted by default when Access created the report.

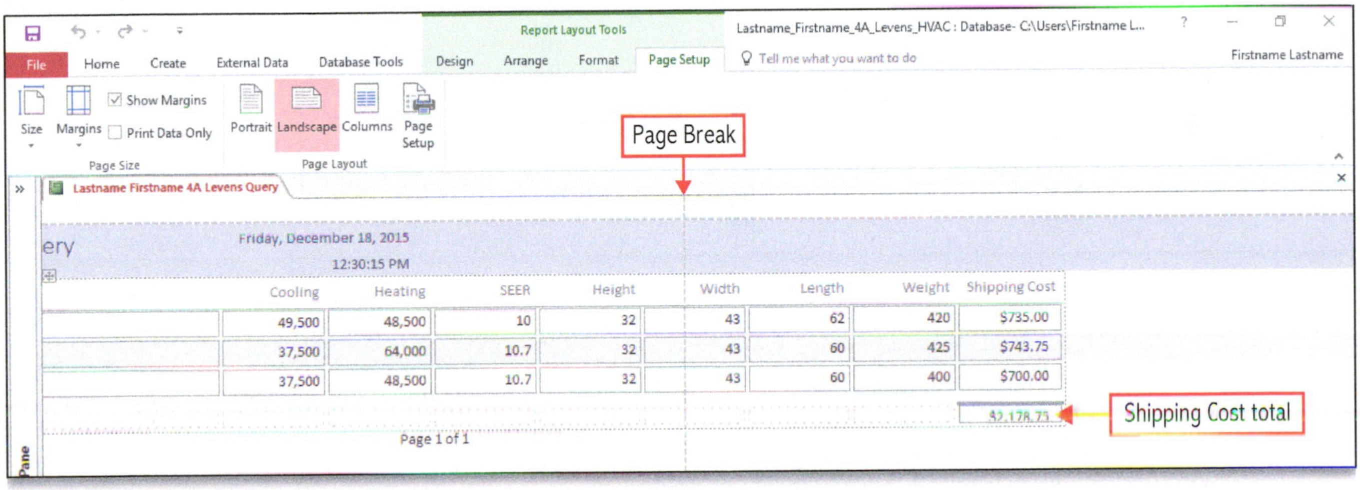

FIGURE 4.18

4 Press Ctrl + Home. Click the field name **ID** to surround it with an orange border and to select the entire column. Right-click the selected field name, and then on the shortcut menu, click **Delete Column** to delete the ID field from the report.

5 Click the field name **SEER**, press and hold Ctrl, and then click the field names **Width** and **Length**. With all three fields selected, right-click any of the selected field names, and then on the shortcut menu, click **Delete Column**.

> The three columns are deleted, and the report is now a one-page document.

6 Click the field name **Shipping Cost**. Under **Report Layout Tools**, click the **Design tab**, and then in the **Grouping & Totals group**, click **Totals**.

> A check mark displays to the left of the Sum option, which means it is selected and the column total displays. In this report, a sum for the Shipping Cost field is of no meaning, because the Levens would never purchase three HVAC models.

7 In the displayed list, click **Sum** to toggle off the column total.

> The Shipping Cost column total no longer displays; however, a horizontal line still displays below the Shipping Cost column.

8 Below the **Shipping Cost** column, click on the horizontal line to display an orange border, and then press Delete.

9 Double-click in the title of the report, and then double-click the word *Query*. Press Backspace two times.

The word *Query* and a space are deleted from the title of the report.

10 At the top right corner of the report, click the **time** to surround it with an orange border, and then press Delete to delete the time from the report.

11 At the top right corner, click the **date** to select it. Point to the lower right corner of the date border until the ↔ pointer displays, and then drag the date to the right until it is right-aligned with the **Shipping Cost** field. Compare your screen with Figure 4.19.

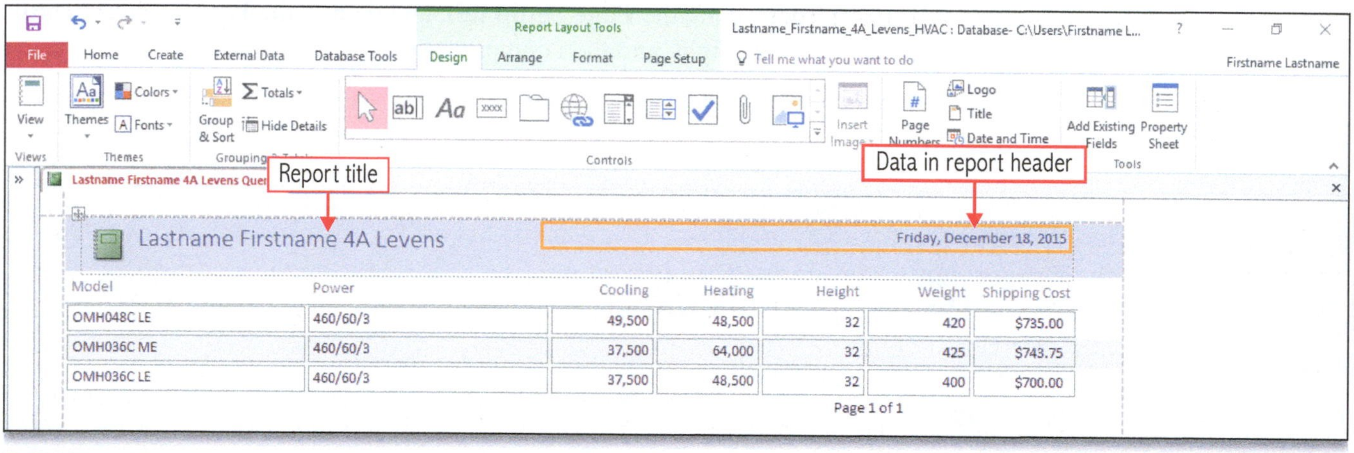

FIGURE 4.19

12 Click **Save** 🖫. In the **Save As** dialog box, using your own name, type **Lastname Firstname 4A Levens Report** and then click **OK**. Right-click your **4A Levens Report tab**, and then on the shortcut menu, click **Close**.

Activity 4.10 | Grouping Data and Printing an Access Report

Information in an Access report is often easier to read and comprehend when it is separated into groups. You can print a report while it is closed or while you have it open in any view. In this activity, you will use the Report Wizard to group your data by the Heating field.

1 **Open** » the **Navigation Pane**, click your **Lastname Firstname 4A Levens Unit** table to select it. Click the **Create tab**, and then in the **Reports group**, click **Report Wizard**.

The *Report Wizard* is an Access feature with which you can create a report by answering a series of questions; Access designs the report based on your answers.

2 In the **Report Wizard** dialog box, under **Tables/Queries**, verify that **Table: Lastname Firstname 4A Levens Unit** is selected.

3 Under **Available Fields**, click **Model** and then click **Add Field** `>` to move the field to the **Selected Fields** list. Double-click the **Cooling** field to the **Selected Fields** list. Use either technique to move the following fields to the **Selected Fields** list in this order: **Heating**, and **Shipping Cost**. Click **Next**.

4 In the **Report Wizard** dialog box, under **Do you want to add any grouping levels?**, double-click the **Heating** field, and then compare your screen with Figure 4.20.

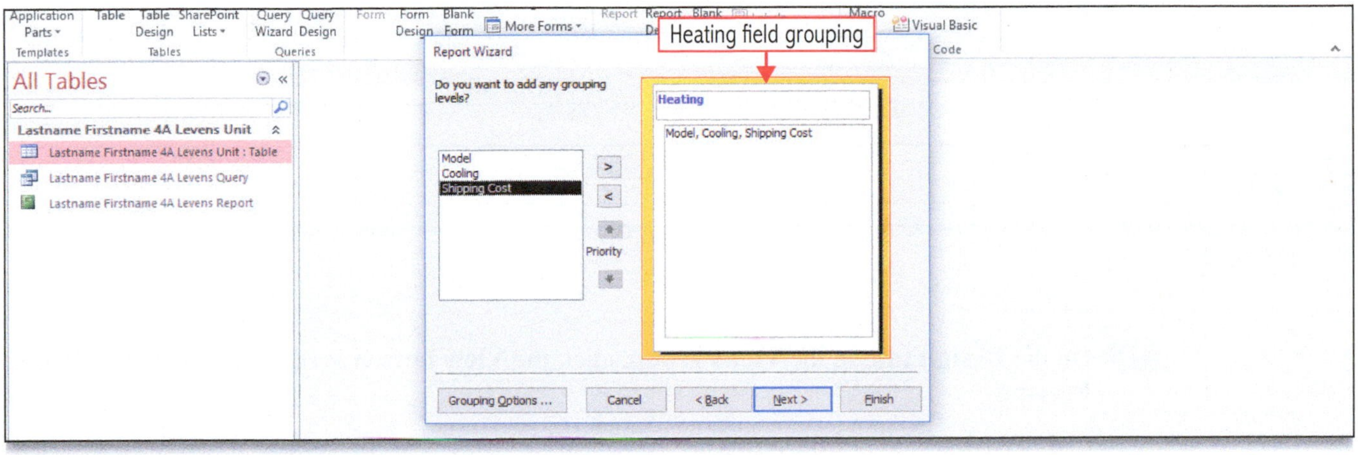

FIGURE 4.20

Access 2016, Windows 10, Microsoft Corporation

5 Click **Next**. Click the **Sort arrow**, and then click **Shipping Cost**. To the right of the **Sort arrow**, click **Ascending** to toggle it to **Descending**, and then click **Next**.

6 Under **Layout**, click the **Block** option button. Under **Orientation**, verify that the **Portrait** option button is selected, and then at the bottom of the dialog box, verify that the **Adjust the field width so all fields fit on a page** check box is selected. Click **Next**.

7 Under **What title do you want for your report?**, using your own name, type **Lastname Firstname 4A Heating** and then click **Finish**.

The 4A Heating report displays in Print Preview. Notice the units are grouped by the Heating field.

8 In the **Close Preview group**, click **Close Print Preview**. **Close** ⊠ the **Field List**. **Close** « the **Navigation Pane**.

9 Under **Report Design Tool**, on the **Design tab**, in the **Header/Footer group**, click **Logo**. In the **Insert Picture** dialog box, navigate to the location of your student data files for this chapter, locate the file **i04A_Midwest_Logo**, and then double-click the file name.

The logo is inserted in the *report header* where information such as logos, titles, and dates is printed at the beginning of a report.

10 With the logo selected, in the **Tools group**, if necessary, click **Property Sheet** to open the **Property Sheet** pane. On the **Property Sheet** pane, on the **All tab**, click **Size Mode**. Click the **Size Mode arrow**, and then click **Stretch**. Click **Width** to select the number, and then type **1.8** Click **Height** to select the number, and then type **0.5** In the **Tools group**, click **Property Sheet** to close the pane. Display the 🔾 pointer, and then drag the logo to the right so the left border is at **approximately 6 inches on the horizontal ruler**. Compare your screen with Figure 4.21.

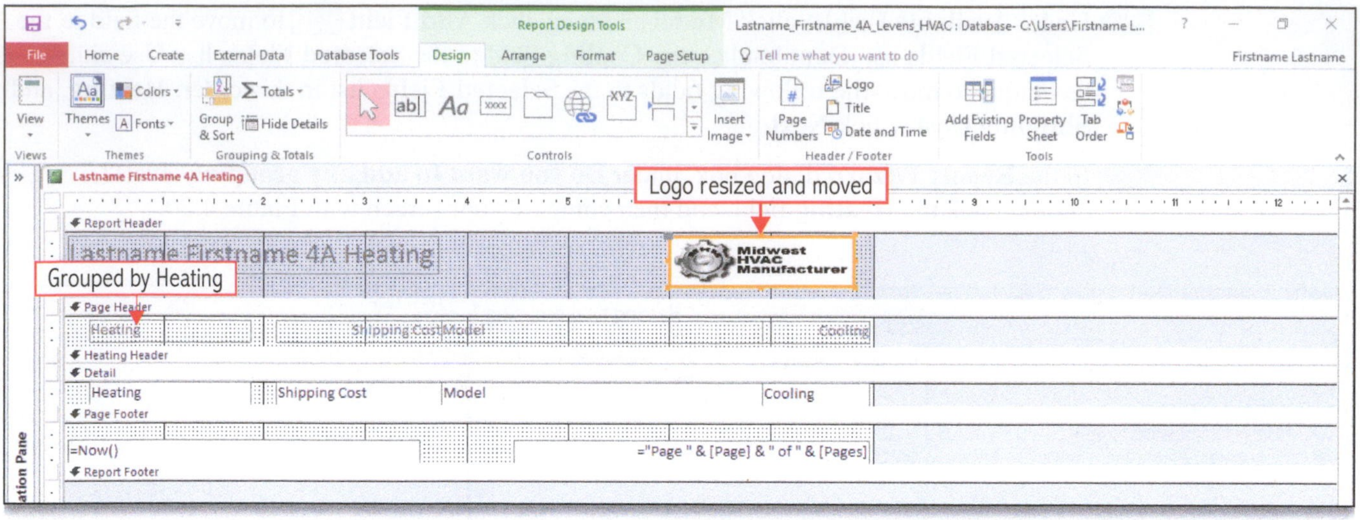

FIGURE 4.21

11 On the **Design tab**, in the **Views group**, click the **View button arrow**, and then click **Print Preview**.

The report displays with the logo in the top right corner.

12 Save ⊟ the report. In the **Close Preview group**, click **Close Print Preview**.

13 Display **Backstage** view, and then on the right, click **View and edit database properties**. In the **Properties** dialog box, on the **Summary tab**, in the **Subject** box, type your course name and section number; in the **Author** box, type your first name and last name; and in the **Keywords** box, type **Levens reports, cooling, heating** and then click **OK**.

14 In the upper left, click the **Back arrow** ⊙, and then click the **Home tab**.

15 If directed by your instructor to print, with the **Lastname Firstname 4A Heating** report displayed, from **Backstage** view, click the **Print tab**, and then click **Print** to print the report. **Open** ⊠ the **Navigation Pane**, double-click the **Lastname Firstname 4A Levens Report**. Using the technique you just practiced, print the **Lastname Firstname 4A Levens Report**.

16 Right-click the **Lastname Firstname 4A Heating report tab**, and then click **Close All**. **Close** ⊠ Access.

17 Submit your printed or electronic files as directed by your instructor.

END | You have completed Project 4A

HVAC Table

PROJECT ACTIVITIES

In Activities 4.11 through 4.18, you will create a new table in an existing Access database and insert records in the table. You will create a one-to-many relationship between tables and create a relationship report. After creating an Access query, you will export the data to Excel. In Excel, you will create a new table style, and then apply the table style and insert subtotals in the table. Your completed files will look similar to Figure 4.22.

PROJECT FILES

For Project 4B, you will need the following files:

New blank Excel workbook
i04B_HVAC_Parts

You will save your files as:

Lastname_Firstname_4B_HVAC_Parts
Lastname_Firstname_4B_HVAC_Models

PROJECT RESULTS

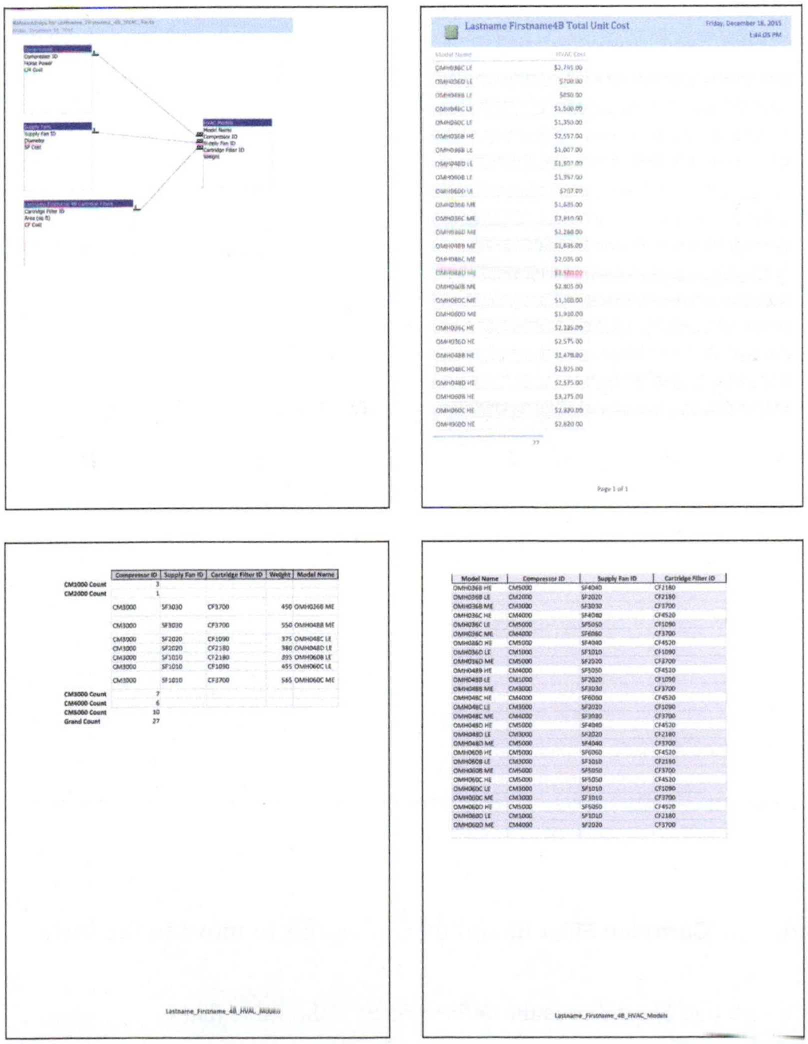

FIGURE 4.22 Project 4B HVAC Table

Objective 5 Create an Access Table

Recall that a table is an Access object that stores your data and is organized in an arrangement of columns and rows. A database may have many tables, with each table containing data about a particular subject. The data in a table can contain many fields with different data types. You can create tables by typing the data in a new blank table or by importing or linking to information stored in a different location.

Activity 4.11 | Creating an Access Table and Entering Data

In this Activity, you will add a table to an existing database.

1 Start Access. Click **Open Other Files**, navigate to the location of your student data files for this chapter, and then open the database **i04B_HVAC_Parts**.

2 If necessary, enable the content. Click the **File tab**, on the left click **Save As**, and then under **File Types**, be sure **Save Database As** is selected. On the right, click **Save As**. In the **Save As** dialog box, navigate to your **Integrated Projects Chapter 4** folder. Using your own name, save the database as **Lastname_Firstname_4B_HVAC_Parts** If necessary, on the Message Bar, click Enable Content.

3 Double-click each of the three table names to open and view the tables. **Close** « the **Navigation Pane**

4 Click the **Create tab**, and then in the **Tables group**, click **Table Design**. Compare your screen with Figure 4.23.

Table1 displays in Design view. Notice there are no entries in the Field Name and Data Type columns.

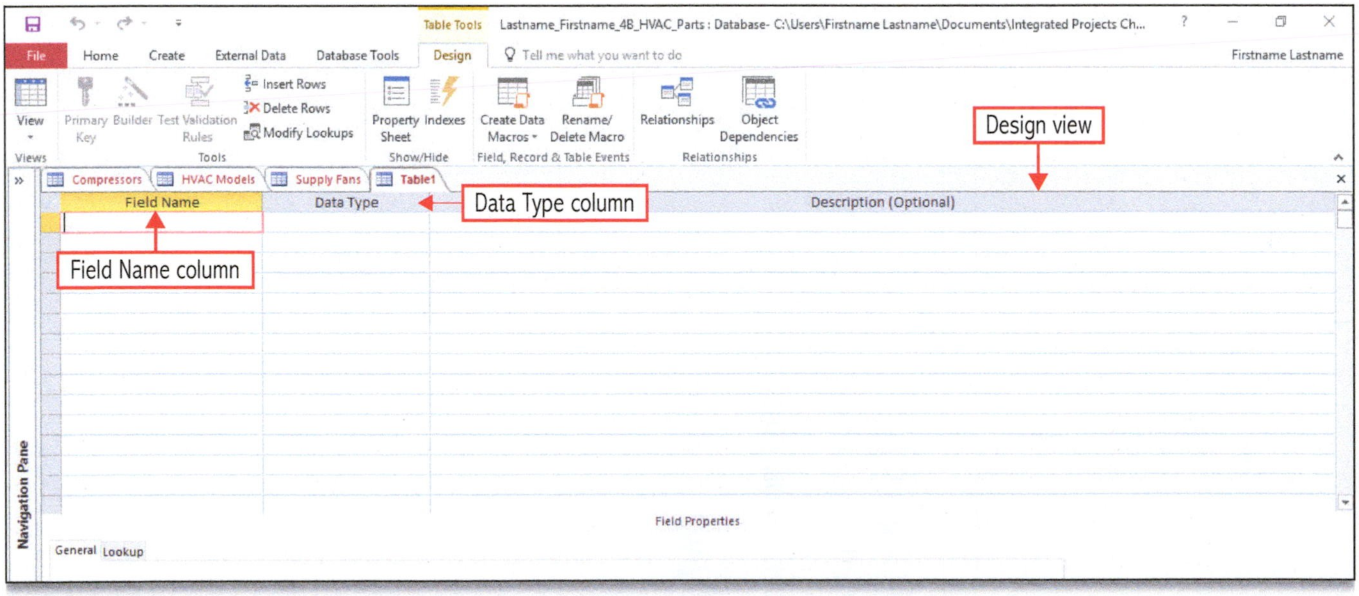

Access 2016, Windows 10, Microsoft Corporation

FIGURE 4.23

5 In the **Field Name column**, type **Cartridge Filter ID** and then press Tab to move to the **Data Type column**.

In the Data Type column, notice that *Short Text* is the ***default value***—the value that is automatically entered in a new record.

6 Press `Tab` two times to move to the next row. In the **Field Name** column, type **Area (sq ft)** and then press `Tab` to move to the **Data Type** column. Click the **Data Type arrow**, and then click **Number**. Press `Tab` two times to move to the next row. Type **CF Cost** and then press `Tab`. In the **Data Type** column, click the **Data Type arrow**, and then click **Currency**.

7 Click the field name **Cartridge Filter ID**. Under **Table Tools**, on the **Design tab**, in the **Tools group**, click **Primary Key**, and then compare your screen with Figure 4.24.

A small key displays in the record selector box of the Cartridge Filter ID field, indicating that this field is the primary key. Recall that a primary key is the field that uniquely identifies a record in a table.

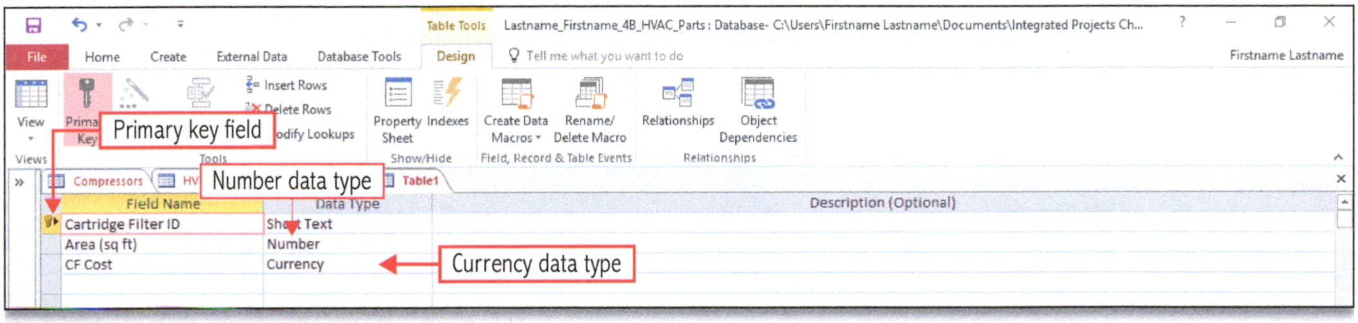

FIGURE 4.24

Access 2016, Windows 10, Microsoft Corporation

8 On the **Design tab**, in the **Views group**, click the top half of the **View** button to switch to Datasheet view. In the message box, click **Yes** to save the table. In the **Save As** dialog box, using your name, type **Lastname Firstname 4B Cartridge Filters** and then click **OK**.

The table design is saved, the table displays in Datasheet view, and the table name displays in the Navigation Pane.

9 Enter the following information in the table:

Cartridge Filter ID	Area (sq ft)	CF Cost
CF1090	20	25
CF2180	24	32
CF3700	40	35
CF4520	50	50

10 Right-click the **Lastname Firstname 4B Cartridge Filters table tab**, and then on the shortcut menu, click **Close All**.

More Knowledge **Good Table Design**

When you create a database, you do not want redundant—duplicate—data because it will increase the possibility of errors and it will take additional time to enter the data multiple times. Because you can use relationships to join—connect—tables, you only need to type data such as a customer name, address, or telephone number one time.

When designing your database tables, divide the information into subject-based tables and consider separating data into its smallest elements. For example, instead of having City, State, and ZIP code as one field, create three separate fields, one for each element. This enables you to sort or filter by any of the three fields.

Activity 4.12 | Creating a One-to-Many Relationship

Access is a *relational database*—a sophisticated type of database that has multiple collections of data within the file that are related to one another. A high-quality database design attempts to remove redundant data. By adding data in one table and creating a *relationship*—an association that you establish between two tables based on common fields—the data only needs to be entered one time but can be referenced by any other related table. In this activity, you will create relationships among the four Access tables.

1 Click the **Database Tools tab**, and then in the **Relationships group**, click **Relationships**. In the **Show Table** dialog box, on the **Tables tab**, click the **Lastname Firstname 4B Cartridge Filters** table name, and then click **Add** to display the table in the Relationships window. Using this technique, add the tables **Compressors**, **HVAC Models**, and **Supply Fans**. **Close** the **Show Table** dialog box, and then compare your screen with Figure 4.25.

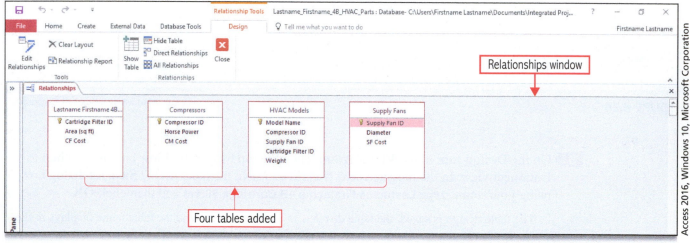

FIGURE 4.25

🔄 **ANOTHER WAY**   Double-click a table name to add it to the Relationships window.

> **NOTE**   Extra Tables in the Relationships Window
>
> In the Relationships window, if you have accidentally added an extra table, right-click the table name, and then on the shortcut menu, click Hide Table.

2 Point to the **HVAC Models** title, hold down the left mouse button, and drag the field list down and to the right side of the Relationships window. Using the same technique, drag the **Supply Fans** field list below the **Compressors** field list, and then drag the **4B Cartridge Filters** field list below the **Supply Fans** field list. Resize the **4B Cartridge Filters** field list so the table name fully displays, if necessary. Compare your screen with Figure 4.26.

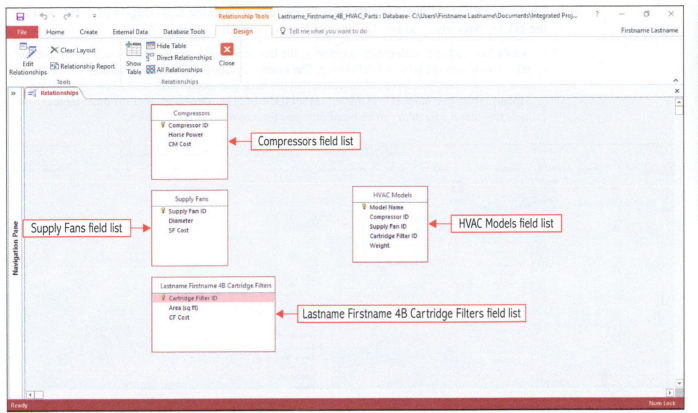

FIGURE 4.26

Access 2016, Windows 10, Microsoft Corporation

3 ▸ In the **Compressors** field list, point to **Compressor ID**, hold down the left mouse button, and then drag to the right to the **HVAC Models** field list until the ⟐ pointer is on top of the **Compressor ID** field name. Release the mouse button.

The Edit Relationships dialog box displays.

4 ▸ In the **Edit Relationships** dialog box, verify that **Compressor ID** displays under both **Table/Query** and **Related Table/Query**. If not, click **Cancel**, and then repeat Step 3. In the **Edit Relationships** dialog box, select the **Enforce Referential Integrity** check box, and then click **Create**.

A *one-to-many relationship* is created. A one-to-many relationship is a relationship between two tables where one record in the first table corresponds to many records in the second table—the most common type of relationship in Access. In this case, the one-to-many relationship is between one compressor and many HVAC models. A *foreign key* is the field that is included in the related table so that it can be joined to the primary key in another table for the purpose of creating a relationship.

Referential integrity is a set of rules that Access uses to ensure that the data between related tables is valid. In this project, it means that records must be added to the Compressors table before matching records can be added to the HVAC Models table.

5 ▸ Using the same technique, create a one-to-many relationship between the **Supply Fan ID** field in the **Supply Fans** field list and the **Supply Fan ID** field in the **HVAC Models** field list. Create a one-to-many relationship between the **Cartridge Filter ID** field in the

Lastname Firstname 4B Cartridge Filters field list and the **Cartridge Filter ID** field in the **HVAC Models** field list. Compare your screen with Figure 4.27.

A *join line*, in the Relationships window, is the line joining two tables that visually indicates the related field and the type of relationship. The infinity symbol ∞ at the right end of the join lines, next to the HVAC Models field, indicates that the data may occur more than once in the HVAC Models table. The number 1 at the left end of the join lines, next to each of the other tables, indicates that a data item can be listed only one time in each of those tables.

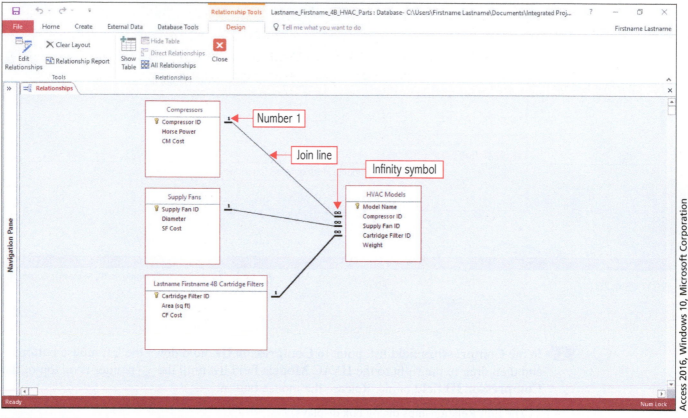

FIGURE 4.27

6 ▸ Under **Relationship Tools**, on the **Design tab**, in the **Tools group**, click **Relationship Report**.

A report showing the relationship between the two tables displays.

ALERT!   **Do you have a two-page report?**

Close the report without saving it. In the Relationships window, drag the HVAC Models field list to the left, closer to the other field lists. Click Relationship Report again, and then verify that you have a one-page report.

---

7 ▸ Click **Save** 🖫. In the **Save As** dialog box, using your own name, type **Lastname Firstname 4B HVAC Relationships** and then click **OK**. If your instructor directs you to submit your files electronically, go to Step 9.

8 ▸ To print the report, in the **Print group**, click **Print**, and then in the **Print** dialog box, click **OK**.

9 ▸ Right-click the **Lastname Firstname 4B HVAC Relationships report tab**, and then click **Close All**.

Activity 4.13 | Adding a Totals Row in an Access Table

A Totals row can be inserted in an Access table. The Totals row uses the functions SUM, AVERAGE, COUNT, MIN, or MAX to quickly summarize the numbers in the column. Gerardo Sanjurjo, the Director of Sales for Midwest HVAC Manufacturer, has asked you to give him the average weight of the HVAC Models.

1 **Open** » the **Navigation Pane**, double-click the **HVAC Models** table name to display the table, and then **Close** « the **Navigation Pane**.

2 On the **Home tab**, in the **Records group**, click **Totals** to add a Total row to the bottom of the table.

3 If necessary, scroll down, and then in the **Total row**, click in the **Weight** field to position the insertion point and display an arrow. Click the **arrow**, and then click **Average**. Compare your screen with Figure 4.28.

The average weight of the HVAC units displays.

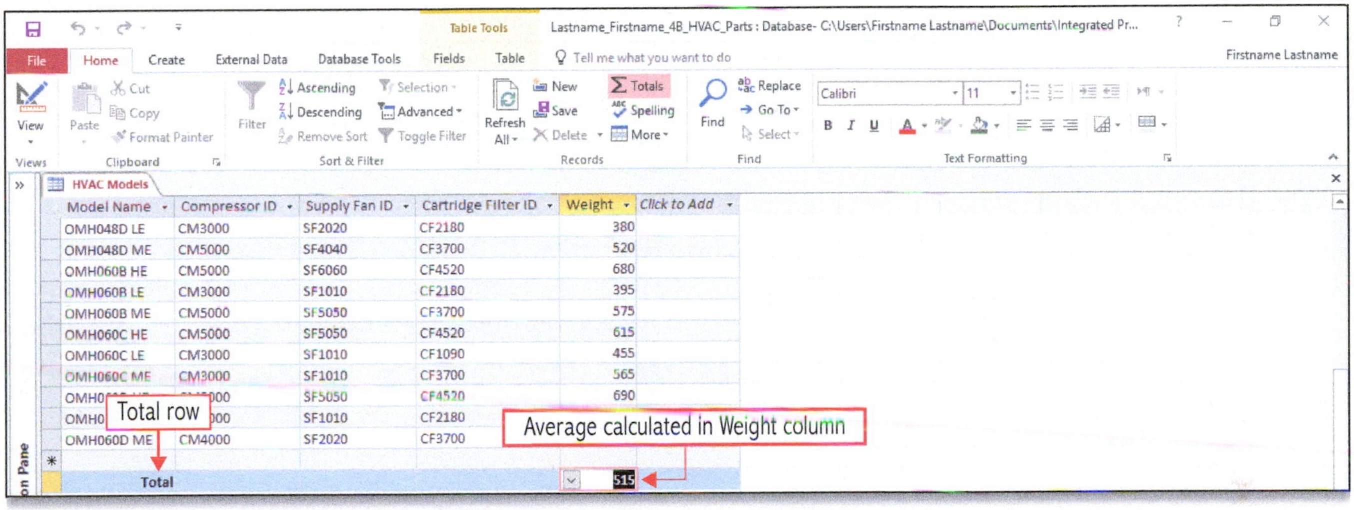

FIGURE 4.28

4 In the **Total row**, click in the **Compressor ID** field, click the **arrow**, and then click **Count**.

Count is the only Total option for a Short Text field. The number of HVAC units (27) displays.

5 **Close** ☒ the table, saving changes.

Objective 6 | Create an Access Query

An *action query* changes the data in the data source or creates a new table. Examples of action queries are an *append query*, which adds a set of records from one or more source tables to one or more destination tables, and an *update query*, which adds or changes data in one or more existing records. Another type of query—a *parameter query*—prompts you to supply the criteria when the query is run. In this project, you will create a select query—a database object that retrieves specific data from one or more tables and then displays the specified data in Datasheet view.

Activity 4.14 | Creating a Select Query

In a relational database, tables are joined by associating common fields. This relationship enables you to include data from more than one table in a query. In this activity, you will create a query that retrieves cost information from three tables.

1 ▶ Click the **Create tab**, and then in the **Queries group**, click **Query Design**. In the **Show Table** dialog box, double-click each of the four table names to add them to the table area of the Query window, and then **Close** the **Show Table** dialog box.

The four field lists with the relationship join lines display.

2 ▶ Point to the lower right corner of the **Compressors** field list until the ⬚ pointer displays, and then drag upward to make the field list smaller. In a similar manner, make the **Supply Fans** and **Lastname Firstname 4B Cartridge Filters** field lists slightly smaller.

3 ▶ Move the **Supply Fans** field list below the **Compressors** field list, and then move the **4B Cartridge Filters** field list below **Supply Fans**. Widen the **Lastname Firstname 4B Cartridge Filters** field list so the table name fully displays, if necessary. Compare your screen with Figure 4.29.

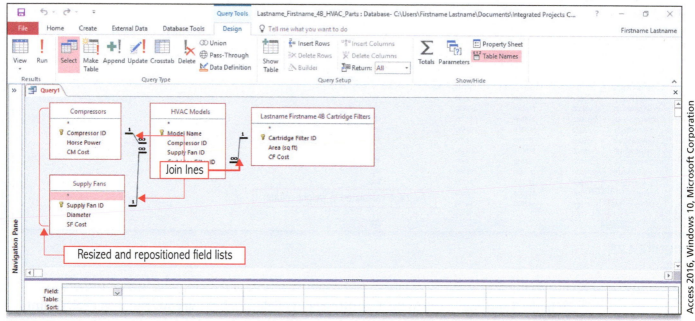

FIGURE 4.29

4 ▶ In the **HVAC Models** field list, double-click **Model Name** to add the field to the grid. In the **Compressors** field list, double-click the **CM Cost** field name. In the **Supply Fans** field list, double-click the **SF Cost** field name, and then in the **Lastname Firstname 4B Cartridge Filters** field list, double-click the **CF Cost** field name.

The fields Model Name, CM Cost, SF Cost, and CF Cost display in the design grid.

5 ▶ Under **Query Tools**, on the **Design tab**, in the **Results group**, click **Run** to display the results of the query.

6 ▶ Click **Save** 🖫. In the **Save As** dialog box, using your own name, type **Lastname Firstname 4B Cost Query** and then click **OK**.

Activity 4.15 | Adding a Calculated Field to a Query

After you run a query, you might return to Design view to make modifications. In this activity, you will modify the query by adding a ***calculated field*** to sum the cost of the different parts to determine the total HVAC unit cost. A calculated field is a field that stores the value of a mathematical operation.

1 On the **Home tab**, in the **Views** group, click the top half of the **View** button to switch to **Design** view. In the **Field** row, right-click in the fifth column—a blank column—and then on the shortcut menu, click **Zoom**.

Although you can type a calculation in the empty Field box in the design grid, the Zoom dialog box gives you more space.

2 In the **Zoom** dialog box, type **HVAC Cost:[CM Cost]+[SF Cost]+[CF Cost]** and then compare your screen with Figure 4.30.

The first element, HVAC Cost, is the new field name. Following the new field name is a colon (:), which separates the new field name from the expression. CM Cost, SF Cost, and CF Cost are each in square brackets, indicating they are existing field names. The plus sign will sum the field contents.

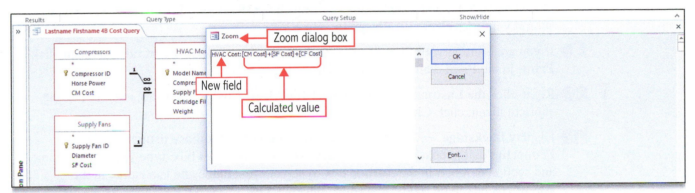

FIGURE 4.30

Access 2016, Windows 10, Microsoft Corporation

3 In the **Zoom** dialog box, click **OK**, and then in the **Results group**, click **Run**. Compare your screen with Figure 4.31.

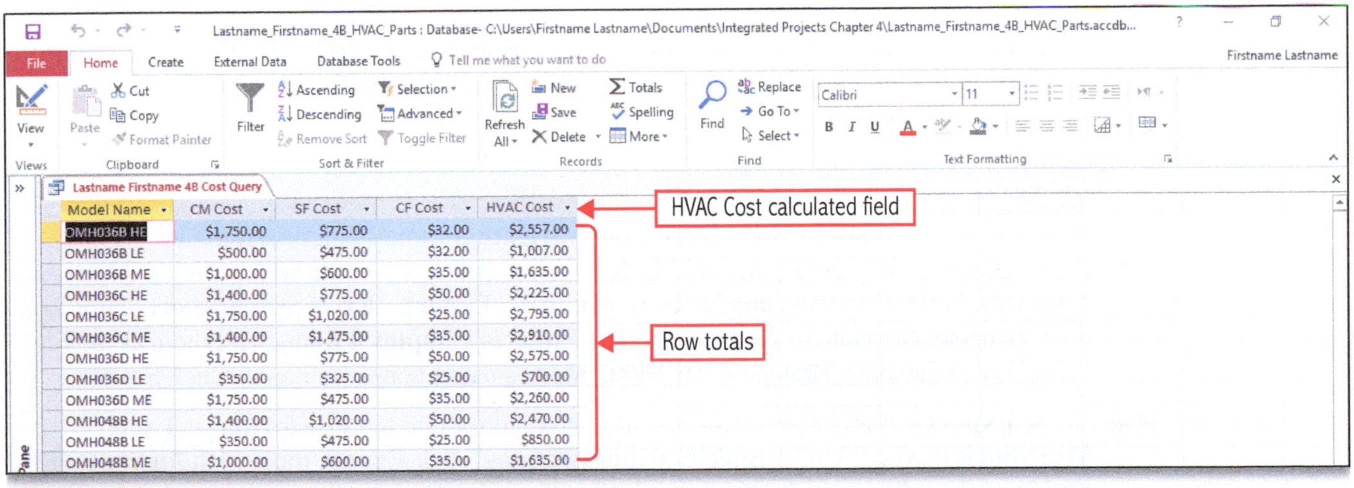

FIGURE 4.31

Access 2016, Windows 10, Microsoft Corporation

ALERT! **Does your screen differ?**

If your calculations in a query do not work, switch to Design view, and then in the Zoom dialog box, correct the expression you typed. Spelling or syntax errors prevent calculated fields from working properly.

4 ▸ Switch to **Design** view. In the **Show** row, in the **CM Cost** field, click the check box to clear it. By using the same technique, clear the check box in the **SF Cost** field and the **CF Cost** field. **Run** the query.

Only the fields Model Name and HVAC Cost display. You do not want to show the individual cost fields in this query.

5 ▸ Display **Backstage** view, click **Save As**, and then click **Save Object As**. On the right, click the **Save As** button, and then in the **Save As** dialog box, using your own name, type **Lastname Firstname 4B Total Unit Cost Query** and then click **OK**.

6 ▸ Click the **Create tab**, and then in the **Reports group**, click **Report**.

A basic report based on the data from the Lastname Firstname 4B Total Unit Cost Query displays.

7 ▸ Double-click the report title, and then double-click the word **Query** and press [Delete]. Select the text **Lastname Firstname 4B Total Unit Cost**. Click the **Home tab**, and then in the **Text Formatting group**, click the **Font Size arrow** [11 ▾] and then click **16**.

8 ▸ Save ⊟ the report. In the **Save As** dialog box, using your own name, type **Lastname Firstname 4B Total Unit Cost Report** and then click **OK**. If your instructor directs you to submit your files electronically, go to Step 10.

9 ▸ If you are printing your files, display **Backstage** view, click the **Print tab**, and then click **Print**. In the **Print** dialog box, click **OK**.

10 ▸ Right-click the **Lastname Firstname 4B Total Unit Cost Report tab**, and then on the shortcut menu, click **Close All**.

11 ▸ Display **Backstage** view, and then click **View and edit database properties**. In the **Properties** dialog box, on the **Summary tab**, in the **Subject** box, type your course name and section number; in the **Author** box, type your first name and last name; in the **Keywords** box, type **HVAC Costs** and then click **OK**. Click **Back** ⊙ to redisplay the database window.

Objective 7 | Export Access Data to Excel

You can export data stored in an Access database to an Excel workbook. When you export the Access data or a database object, a copy of the data is created in the Excel workbook.

Activity 4.16 | Exporting Access Data

1 ▸ **Open** ⊠ the **Navigation Pane**. Resize the **Navigation Pane** so all object names display fully. Click one time on the **HVAC Models** table name to select the table. Click the **External Data tab**. In the **Export group**, click **Excel**. In the **Export – Excel Spreadsheet** dialog box, click **Browse**. Navigate to your **Integrated Projects Chapter 4** folder, and then, as the file name, type **Lastname_Firstname_4B_HVAC_Models** using your own name. Click **Save**.

2 ▸ In the **Export – Excel Spreadsheet** dialog box, verify that the **File format** is **Excel Workbook (*.xlsx)**. Under **Specify export options**, click **Export data with formatting and layout**, and then click **Open the destination file after the export operation is complete**. Click **OK**.

3 ▸ **Maximize** ▫ the Excel window.

4 ▸ Click the **Insert tab**, and then in the **Text group**, click **Header & Footer**. On the **Design tab**, in the **Navigation group**, click **Go to Footer**. In the **Footer** area, click just above the word *Footer*, and then in the **Header & Footer Elements group**, click **File Name**. Click any cell in the workbook to exit the footer.

5 ▶ Near the right side of the status bar, click **Normal** ⊞, and then press Ctrl + Home to make cell **A1** the active cell. Compare your screen with Figure 4.32.

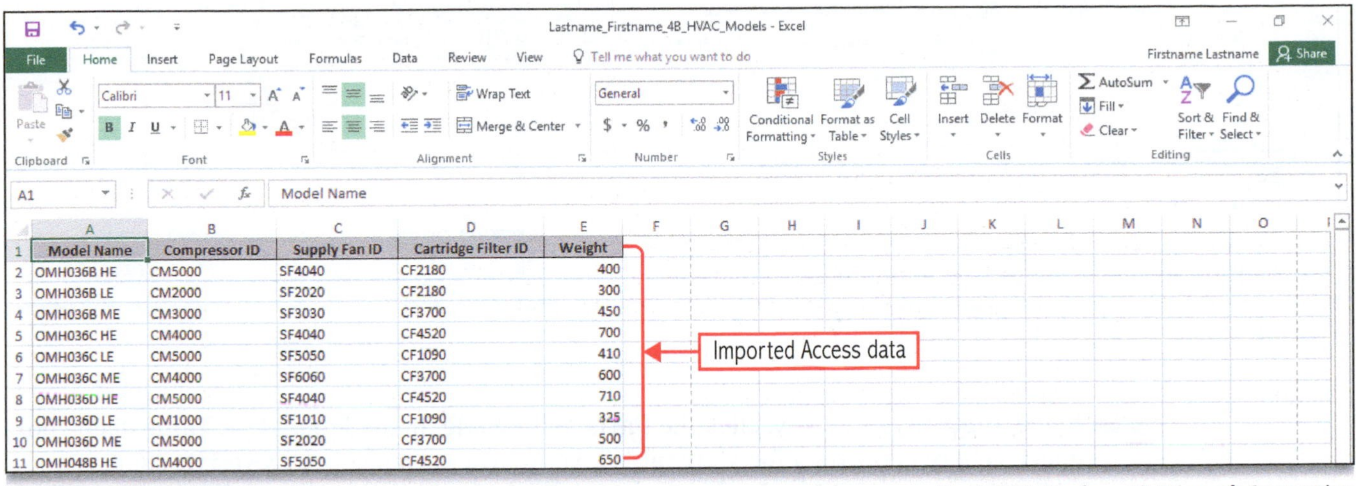

FIGURE 4.32

Excel 2016, Windows 10, Microsoft Corporation

6 ▶ Right-click the column header **A**, and then on the shortcut menu, click **Column Width**. In the **Column Width** dialog box, type **15** and then click **OK**. Select columns **B:D**, and then, using the same technique, change the column width to **20**

7 ▶ Right-click the **HVAC_Models sheet tab**, and then on the shortcut menu, click **Move or Copy**. In the **Move or Copy** dialog box, click **(move to end)**, select the **Create a copy** check box, and then click **OK**.

> A copy of the HVAC_Models sheet is created.

8 ▶ Right-click the **HVAC_Models (2) sheet tab**, and then on the shortcut menu, click **Rename**. With **HVAC_Models (2)** selected, type **4B Parts** and then press Enter. Using the same technique, rename the **HVAC_Models sheet tab** as **4B Subtotals**

9 ▶ Click the **4B Parts sheet tab**. Right-click the column header **E**, and then on the shortcut menu, click **Delete**. Click cell **B29**, and press Delete.

> Column E—Weight—is deleted from the 4B Parts worksheet. The Count in the Compressor ID field is deleted.

10 ▶ **Save** 🖫 the workbook.

Activity 4.17 | Using Table Styles in Excel

Recall that a table style is a predefined set of formatting characteristics, including font, alignment, and cell shading. In this activity, you will create a custom table style.

1 ▶ With the 4B Parts worksheet displayed, press Ctrl + Home. On the **Home tab**, in the **Styles group**, click **Format as Table**. At the bottom of the **Table Styles** gallery, click **New Table Style**.

2 ▶ In the **New Table Style** dialog box, in the **Name** box, type **Parts Table Style**

3 ▶ Under **Table Element**, click **Header Row**, and then click **Format**. On the **Font tab**, under **Font style**, click **Bold Italic**. Click the **Color arrow**, and then in the third column, click the sixth color—**Tan, Background 2, Darker 90%**. Click the **Fill tab**, and then in the eighth column, click the third color (light purple). Click **OK** two times to close the dialog boxes.

4 In the **Styles group**, click **Format as Table**. At the top of the **Table Styles** gallery, under **Custom**, point to the first style, and then compare your screen with Figure 4.33.

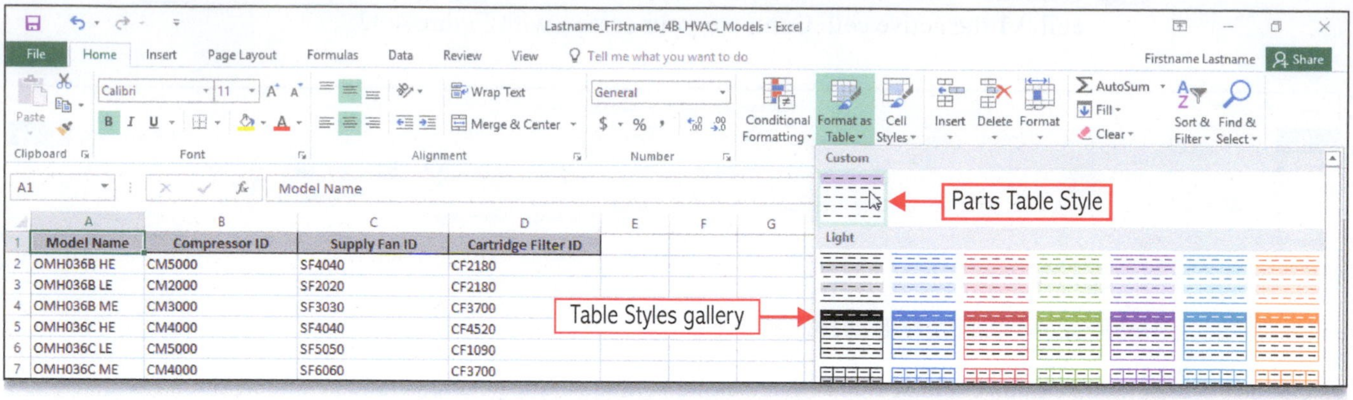

FIGURE 4.33

5 In the **Table Styles** gallery, click the **Parts Table Style**. In the **Format As Table** dialog box, under **Where is the data for your table?**, verify that the range is =$A$1:$D$28; if necessary, select the **My table has headers** check box; and then click **OK**. Under **Table Tools**, on the **Design tab**, in the **Table Styles** group, right-click the **Parts Table Style** and click **Apply (and Clear Formatting)**. Click any cell in the table to deselect the table.

The range is converted to an Excel table, and the Parts Table Style is applied to the table.

6 In the **Table Styles group**, right-click the **Parts Table Style**—the first style—and then on the shortcut menu, click **Modify**. In the **Modify Table Style** dialog box, under **Table Element**, click **Second Row Stripe**. Click the **Stripe Size arrow**, and then click **2**. Click **Format**.

7 In the **Format Cells** dialog box, on the **Fill tab**, in the eighth column, click the second color, and then click **OK** two times to close the dialog boxes. Click in any cell in the table to deselect the table and then compare your screen with Figure 4.34.

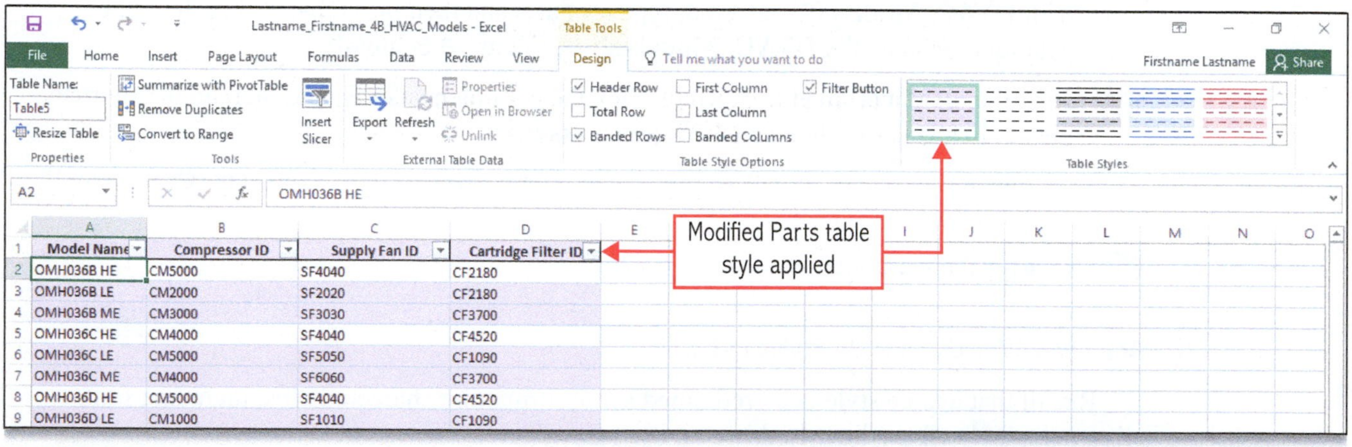

FIGURE 4.34

8 Press [Ctrl] + [Home], and then **Save** 💾 the workbook.

Activity 4.18 | Inserting Subtotals in Excel

In Excel, a list of data can be grouped and summarized in an outline, and then the outline details can be expanded or collapsed. You should sort a column before inserting subtotals. In the following activity, you will count how many Compressor IDs are used by the various HVAC models, and then hide the details of all Compressor IDs except the CM3000.

1 Click the **4B Subtotals sheet tab**. Select the range **A1:A28**, and then point to the right border of the selected range until the ⧉ pointer displays. Compare your screen with Figure 4.35.

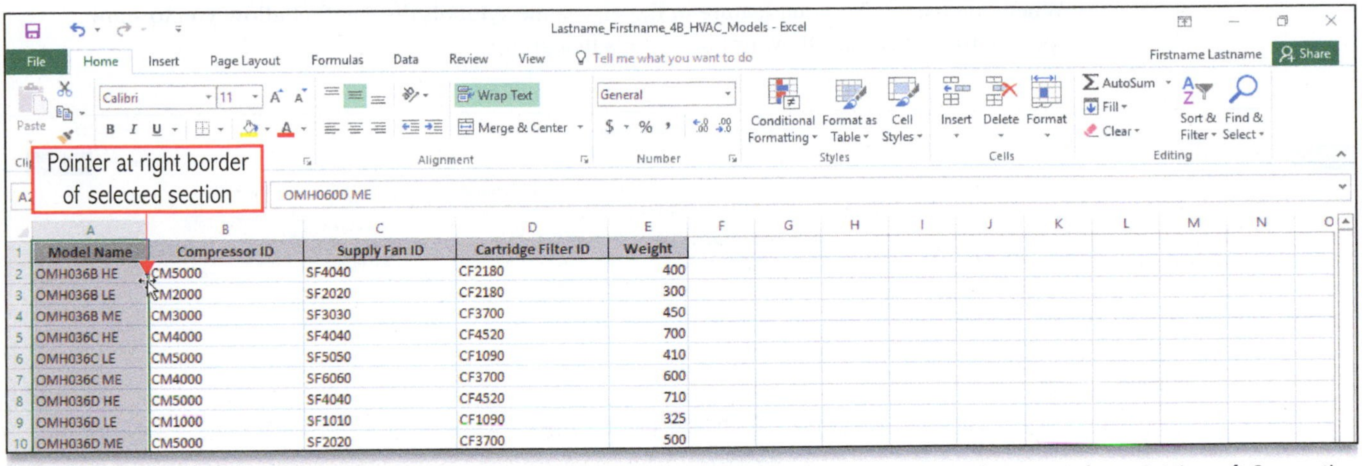

FIGURE 4.35

2 Hold down the left mouse button, drag the selected range to the right to column **F**, and then release the mouse button. The range A1:A28 is moved to cells F1:F28.

3 Right-click the **column heading A**, and then on the shortcut menu, click **Delete**. Point to the right column boundary in column F and double-click to apply Best Fit. Scroll down to display row 29. Right-click the **row heading 29**, and then on the shortcut menu, click **Delete**. Click in any cell.

The blank column A is deleted, and the other columns move to the left.

4 Press Ctrl + Home. On the **Home tab**, in the **Editing group**, click **Sort & Filter**, and then click **Sort A to Z**.

5 Click the **Data tab**, and then in the **Outline group**, click **Subtotal**. In the **Subtotal** dialog box, verify that under **At each change in**, **Compressor ID** displays, and under **Use function**, **Count** displays. Under **Add subtotal to**, select the **Compressor ID** check box to display a check mark, and then clear the **Model Name** check box. Compare your screen with Figure 4.36.

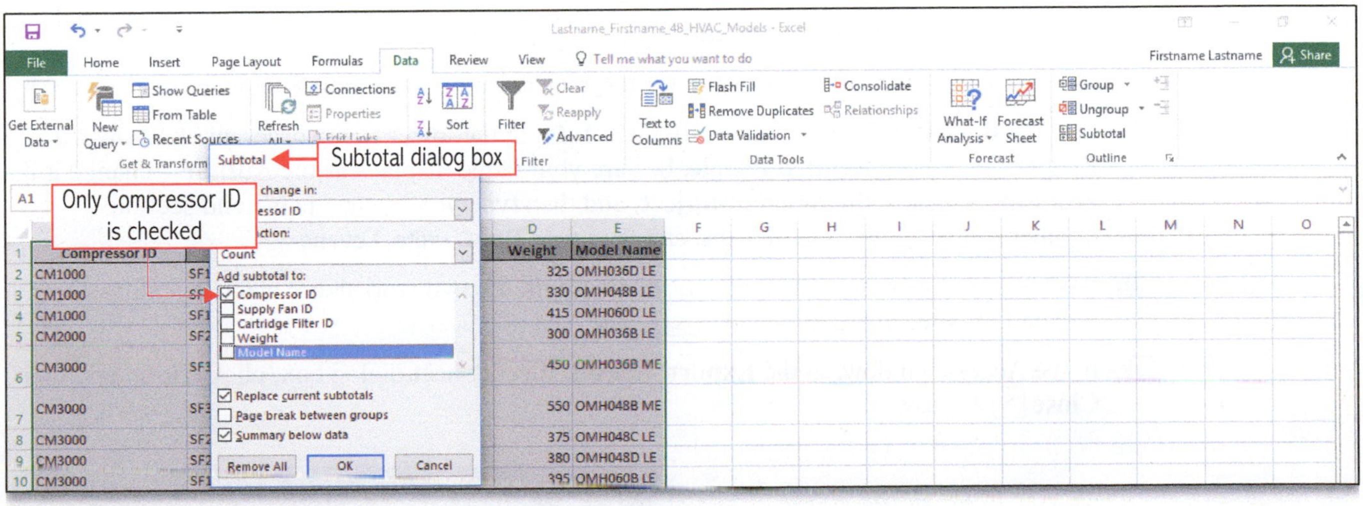

FIGURE 4.36

6 In the **Subtotal** dialog box, click **OK**. Select columns **A:F**. Between the column headings **A** and **B**, point to the column separator until the [+] pointer displays, and then double-click to resize all the columns. Click cell **A1**, and then compare your screen with Figure 4.37.

The widths of columns A through F are adjusted to best fit the data in each column. Data is grouped by Compressor ID and, for each group, a row displays the Count heading and total count. When you use the Subtotal feature in Excel, outline symbols display that allow you to show specific row levels and show or hide details in a group.

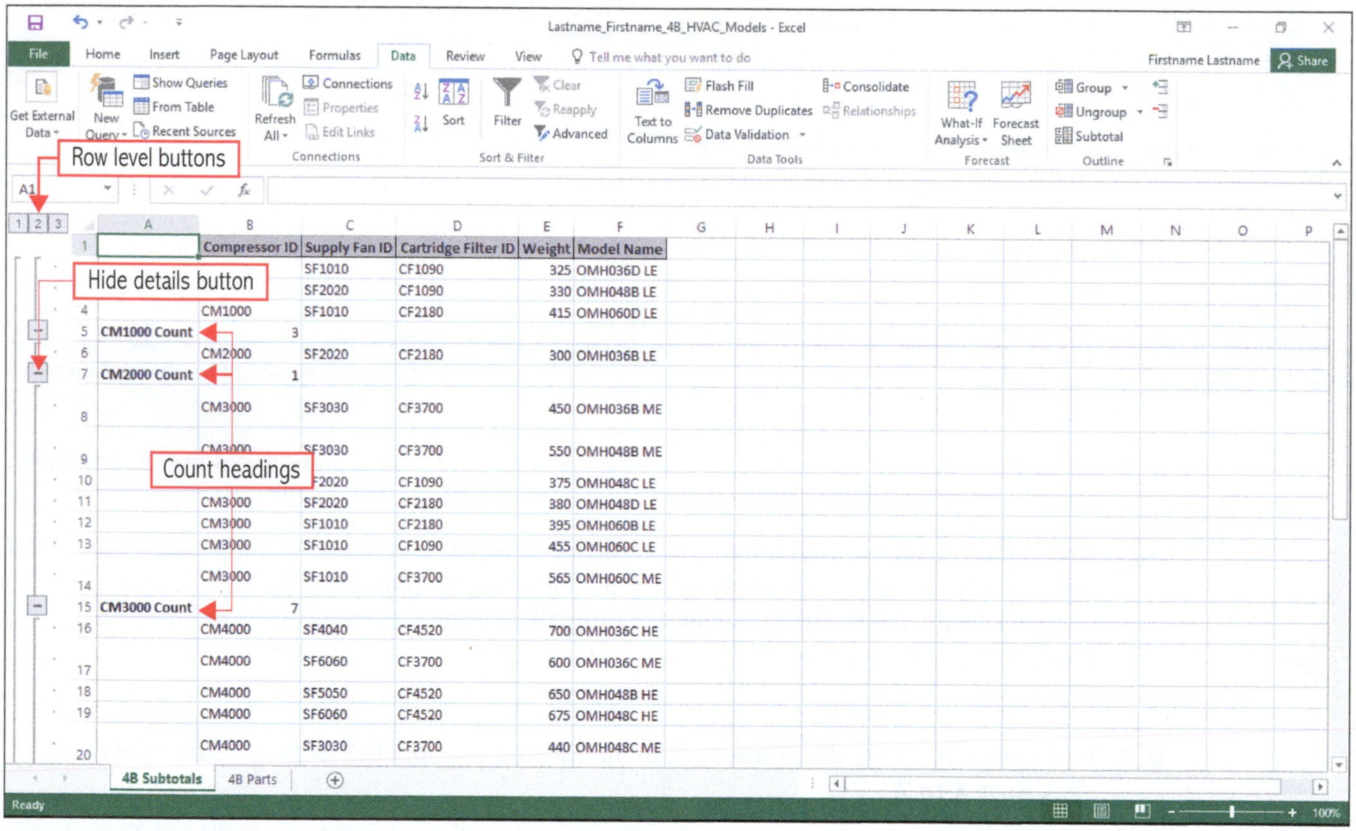

FIGURE 4.37

Excel 2016, Windows 10, Microsoft Corporation

7 At the top left corner of your screen, click the **level** button **2**.

Only the subtotal rows—level 2 rows—display.

8 To the left of row **15**, click **Expand** [⊞].

The details of the CM3000 Compressor ID group are displayed in rows 8 through 14.

9 Display **Backstage** view. On the left, click **Info**, in the lower right corner, click **Show All Properties**. Under **Related People**, be sure your name displays as the **Author**—change it if necessary. Click to the right of **Subject**, and then type your course name and section number. Click to the right of **Tags**, and then type **HVAC units, Levens**

10 **Save** [💾] your workbook, and then print or submit the two worksheets electronically as directed by your instructor. **Close** [×] Excel.

11 In the Access window, in the **Export – Excel Spreadsheet** dialog box, click **Close**, and then **Close** [×] Access.

END | You have completed Project 4B

END OF CHAPTER

SUMMARY

The Excel and Access applications each have advantages when working with large amounts of data. You should work with data in the application that best meets your needs. If you require different results, use the import and export features of Excel and Access to change to a different application. Use the sort and filter features of Excel and Access to display specific data that meets particular criteria.

KEY TERMS

MATCHING

Match each term in the second column with its correct definition in the first column by writing the letter of the term on the blank line in front of the correct definition.

_____ 1. Text is arranged in reverse alphabetical order (Z to A) or numbers from the highest to the lowest value.

_____ 2. Text is arranged in alphabetical order (A to Z) or numbers from the lowest to the highest value.

_____ 3. An Excel table feature in which a new column is automatically included as part of the existing table.

_____ 4. An Excel feature that uses a single formula that adjusts for each row of a column in a data table.

_____ 5. The upper pane of the Advanced Filter window that displays the field lists for tables that are used in the filter.

_____ 6. The lower pane of the Advanced Filter window that displays the design of the filter.

_____ 7. The tables or queries that provide the underlying data for a report.

_____ 8. An Access feature that creates a report with one mouse click, which displays all the fields and records from the record source that you select.

_____ 9. An Access feature with which you can create a report by answering a series of questions; Access designs the report based on your answers.

_____ 10. Information—such as logos, titles, and dates—printed once at the beginning of a report.

_____ 11. The value that is automatically entered in a new record.

_____ 12. An association that you establish between two tables based on common fields.

_____ 13. The field that is included in the related table so the field can be joined with the primary key in another table for the purpose of creating a relationship.

_____ 14. A query that changes the data in the data source or creates a new table.

_____ 15. A query that prompts you to supply the criteria when the query is run.

A Action query

B Ascending order

C AutoExpansion

D Calculated column

E Default value

F Descending order

G Design grid

H Foreign key

I Parameter query

J Record source

K Relationship

L Report header

M Report tool

N Report Wizard

O Table area

MULTIPLE CHOICE

Circle the correct answer.

1. The Excel feature where only a portion of the data (a subset) that meets the criteria you specify is displayed is:
   A. AutoExpansion   B. AutoFill   C. AutoFilter

2. The formula that is entered in a cell and visible only on the Formula Bar is called an:
   A. underlying cell reference   B. underlying formula   C. underlying function

3. A format that changes the appearance of a cell based on a condition—if the condition is true, the cell is formatted based on that condition; if the condition is false, the cell is not formatted—is called a:
   A. conditional format   B. contextual format   C. filtered format

4. Symbols that evaluate each field value to determine whether it is the same as (=), greater than (>), less than (<), or in between a range of values as specified by the criteria are called:
   A. comparison operators   B. logic operators   C. mathematical operators

5. A database object that summarizes the fields and records from a table (or tables) in an easy-to-read format suitable for printing is a:
   A. form   B. query   C. report

6. A relationship between two tables where one record in the first table corresponds to many records in the second table—the most common type of relationship in Access—is:
   A. many-to-one   B. one-to-many   C. one-to-one

7. A set of rules that Access uses to ensure that the data between related tables is valid is called:
   A. conditional integrity   B. referential integrity   C. referential validity

8. In the Relationships window, the line joining two tables that visually indicates the related field and the type of relationship is called a:
   A. join line   B. relationship connector   C. relationship line

9. The name of a query that adds or changes data in one or more existing records is:
   A. append query   B. parameter query   C. update query

10. A field that stores the value of a mathematical expression is called a:
    A. calculated field   B. numeric data type   C. numeric field

Apply 4A skills from these Objectives:

1 Modify an Excel Table
2 Import Excel Data into Access Using the Import Spreadsheet Wizard
3 Sort and Filter Data in an Access Table
4 Create, Modify, and Print an Access Report

Mastering Integration | Project 4C HVAC Installation

In the following Mastering Integration project, you will create a calculated column in Excel to determine the installation cost of HVAC units. In Access you will use the imported worksheet to filter the data and create two reports. Your completed files will look similar to Figure 4.38.

PROJECT FILES

For Project 4C, you will need the following files:

New blank Access database
i04C_HVAC_Installation

You will save your files as:

Lastname_Firstname_4C_HVAC_Installation
Lastname_Firstname_4C_Installation_Cost

PROJECT RESULTS

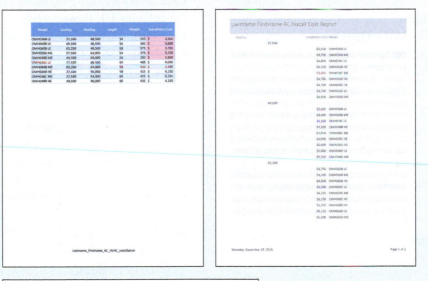

FIGURE 4.38

(Project 4C HVAC Installation continues on the next page)

Mastering Integration | Project 4C HVAC Installation (continued)

1 Start Excel. Open the file **i04C_HVAC_Installlation**. Navigate to your **Integrated Projects Chapter 4** folder, and then save the file with the name **Lastname_Firstname_4C_HVAC_Installation** Insert the file name as a field in the footer. In Normal view, make cell **A1** the active cell.

2 Create a table using the Excel data range **A1:H28**. Change the column width of columns **A:H** to **12** Sort the **Weight column** in **Ascending** order. **Rename** *Sheet1* as **4C Installation Cost**

3 Filter the **Length column** to display numbers **Less Than Or Equal To 60** Click cell **I1**, type **Installation Cost** and then press Enter. In cell **I2**, type the formula **=H2*10** and then on the **Formula Bar**, click **Enter**. Format the numbers in column **I** with the **Accounting Number Format**, and then click **Decrease Decimal** two times. Adjust the width of column **I** to automatically widen to **Best Fit**. To the data in column **I**, apply **Conditional Formatting** to the numbers **less than 4000** to display with **Light Red Fill**.

4 Hide the **Power**, **Height**, and **Width** columns. In the **Page Setup** dialog box, center the page **Horizontally**.

5 Display **All Properties**. Under **Author**, type your first name and last name; to the right of **Subject**, type your course name and section number; and then to the right of **Tags**, type **calculated costs** **Save** your workbook. If directed by your instructor, print the worksheet, and then **Close** Excel.

6 Start Access, and then create a new blank database in your **Integrated Projects Chapter 4** folder with the file name **Lastname_Firstname_4C_Installation_Cost** **Close** the **Table1 tab**. **Import** the Excel file **Lastname_ Firstname_4C_HVAC_Installation**. Let Access add a primary key; name the new Access table **Lastname Firstname 4C Install Cost** Do not save the Import steps. Open the table in Datasheet view.

7 Hide the columns **ID**, **Height**, **Width**, and **Length**, and then adjust the **Field Width** of the remaining

columns to **Best Fit**. Sort the **Heating** field in **Descending** order, and then filter the **Cooling column** to display numbers **Greater Than or Equal To 40,000**

8 Click **Advanced filter**, and then add the field **Power** to the design grid. On the **Criteria row** of the **Power** field, type **=575/60/3** and then click **Toggle Filter**. **Save** the query with the name **Lastname Firstname 4C Power Query** Right-click the **4C Install Cost Filter1 tab**, and then click **Close**. Click **Toggle Filter**, and then click **Save**. **Close** the **4C Install Cost** table.

9 In the **Navigation Pane**, click the **4C Power Query** to select it, and then create a report using the Report tool. Using your first and last name, change the title to **Lastname Firstname 4C Power Report** and then **Delete** the columns **ID**, **Power**, **Height**, **Width**, **Length**, and **Installation Cost**. Change the **Page Layout** to **Landscape**. **Save** the report as **Lastname Firstname 4C Power**, If directed by your instructor, print the report, and then **Close** the report.

10 Using the **Report Wizard**, create a report based on the **Lastname Firstname 4C Install Cost** table. Add the fields **Model**, **Cooling**, and **Installation Cost**. Group by the **Cooling** field, then sort by the **Installation Cost** field in **Ascending** order. Using your first and last name, type the report name **Lastname Firstname 4C Install Cost Report** If directed by your instructor, print the report, and then **Close** the report. Resize the Navigation Pane so all object names fully display.

11 Display **Backstage** view, and then click **View and edit database properties**. On the **Summary** tab, in the **Subject** box, type your course name and section number; in the **Author** box, type your first name and last name; in the **Keywords** box, type **cost query, reports** and then click **OK**. **Close** Access. Submit your printed or electronic files as directed by your instructor.

END | You have completed Project 4C

Apply 4B skills from these Objectives:

5 Create an Access Table

6 Create an Access Query

7 Export Access Data to Excel

Mastering Integration | Project 4D Fan Costs

In the following Mastering Integration project, you will add a table to an existing Access database, create a relationship between tables, and add a calculated field to a query. In Excel, using the exported Access data, you will apply a custom table style. Your completed files will look similar to Figure 4.39.

PROJECT FILES

For Project 4D, you will need the following files:

New blank Excel workbook
i04D_Fan_Types

You will save your files as:

Lastname_Firstname_4D_Fan_Types
Lastname_Firstname_4D_Fan_Costs

PROJECT RESULTS

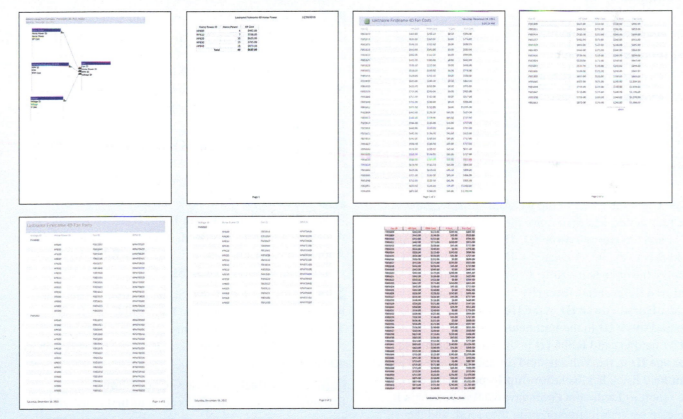

FIGURE 4.39

(Project 4D Fan Costs continues on the next page)

1 Start Access. Open the database **i04D_Fan_Types**. Save the database in your **Integrated Projects Chapter 4** folder as **Lastname_Firstname_4D_Fan_Types** Enable the file content. Create a new table, and then in **Design** view, add the following field names and data types:

Field Name	Data Type
RPM ID	**Short Text**
RPM	**Short Text**
RPM Cost	**Currency**

2 Set the field **RPM ID** as the **Primary Key**. **Save** the table as **Lastname Firstname 4D RPM** display the table in Datasheet view, and then add the following data:

RPM ID	RPM	RPM Cost
RPM70100	**900**	**$123**
RPM70200	**1200**	**$136**
RPM70300	**1800**	**$152**
RPM70400	**3600**	**$171**
RPM70500	**1800/900**	**$230**
RPM70600	**1800/1200**	**$240**

3 **Close** the table. In the **Relationships** window, add the four tables, and then move the **Fan** field list to the right and the **Horse Power ID**, **4D RPM**, and **Voltage** field lists to the left. Resize the **4D RPM** field list to display the table name fully. Create a **Relationship** and **Enforce Referential Integrity** between the following fields: **Horse Power ID** in the **Horse Power** field list and **Horse Power ID** in the **Fan** field list; **RPM ID** in the **RPM** field list and **RPM ID** in the **Fan** field list; and **Voltage ID** in the **Voltage** field list and **Voltage ID** in the **Fan** field list. Click **Relationship Report**; save a copy of the report as **Lastname Firstname 4D Relationships** If directed by your instructor, print the report, and then **Close All** open objects.

4 In the **Navigation Pane**, right-click the **Horse Power** table, and click **Rename**. Using your name, type **Lastname Firstname 4D Horse Power** and press Enter. Open the **4D Horse Power** table, and then insert a **Totals row**. In the **Horse Power** field, in the Totals row,

Sum the data. In the **HP Cost** field, in the **Totals row**, **Average** the data. If directed by your instructor, print the table, and then **Close** the table, saving changes.

5 Create a new query, and then add all four tables to the table area of the **Query** window. Adjust the location and size of the four field lists to display all fields and join lines. In the design grid, add the fields **Fan ID**, **HP Cost**, **RPM Cost**, and **V Cost**. Insert a calculated column with the field name **Fan Cost** that adds the three cost fields. **Run** the query. **Save** the query as **Lastname_Firstname_4D_Fan_Costs** and then **Close** the query.

6 Use the Report tool to create a report based on the **4D_Fan_Costs** query. Save the report as **Lastname Firstname 4D Fan Cost Report** If directed by your instructor, print the report, and then **Close** the report object.

7 Use the **Report Wizard** to create a report based on the **Fan** table. Add **Fan ID**, **Horse Power ID**, **RPM ID**, and **Voltage ID** to the report. Group by **Voltage ID**, and then sort by **Horse Power ID** in **Descending** order. Name the report **Lastname Firstname 4D Fan Parts** If directed by your instructor, print the report, and then **Close** the report.

8 Export the **Lastname_Firstname_4D_Fan_Costs** query to Excel as **Lastname_Firstname_4D_Fan_Costs**, and open it. Insert the file name as a field in the footer.

9 Create a new Table Style named **Fan Table Style**. Format the **Header row** with **Bold**; Font Color **Red, Accent 2**; and Fill Color **Red, Accent 2, Lighter 80%**. Apply and Clear Formatting in the **Fan Table Style** to your data in the range **$A$1:$E$48**.

10 Modify the **Fan Table Style**. Format the **Second Row Stripe**, with Stripe Size **3** and Fill Color **Red, Accent 2, Lighter 80%**. Adjust the column width of columns **A:E** to display all data. **Rename** the sheet tab as **4D Fan Style**

11 Display **Backstage** view. Click **Show All Properties**. Under **Author**, type your first name and last name; to the right of **Subject**, type your course name and section number; and to the right of **Tags**, type **custom table style** Save the workbook. Click the **Page Layout tab**. In the **Scale to Fit** group, click the **Height arrow**, and then click **1 page**. If directed by your instructor, print the worksheet, and then **Close** Excel, saving changes.

(Project 4D Fan Costs continues on the next page)

12 In Access, **Close** the **Export – Excel Spreadsheet** dialog box. Display **Backstage** view. Click **View and edit database properties**. In the **Subject** box, type your course name and section number; in the **Author** box, type your first name and last name; in the **Keywords** box, type **fan costs, calculated** and then click **OK**. **Close** Access. Submit your printed or electronic files as directed by your instructor.

> **END | You have completed Project 4D**

GO! Solve It   Project 4E Cooling Costs

PROJECT FILES

For Project 4E, you will need the following files:

New blank Access database
i04E_HVAC_Cooling

You will save your files as:

Lastname_Firstname_4E_HVAC_Cooling
Lastname_Firstname_4E_Cooling_Costs

Karen Laroque, Associate Director of Sales as Midwest HVAC Manufacturer, has asked you to calculate the cost of running HVAC units in summer and provide a report. From the student data files that accompany this chapter, open the **i04E_HVAC_Cooling** Excel file, and save the file as **Lastname_Firstname_4E_HVAC_Cooling** in your **Integrated Projects Chapter 4** folder. Insert the file name in the footer. In the worksheet, insert an Excel table with a header row. Add a calculated column that calculates the cost of cooling using $0.00124 per Cooling BTU formatted with the Accounting Number Format. Filter the data to display only one Heating BTU number of your choice. Apply Best Fit to all columns. Center the worksheet horizontally on a landscape page.

In Access, create a new database and save it as **Lastname_Firstname_4E_Cooling_Costs** Import your **Lastname_Firstname_4E_HVAC_Cooling** Excel file. In the table, filter the data to show only data for the Cooling BTU greater than 50,000 and the Power unit of your choice. Create a report based on your results. Delete the four measurement fields following the Heating BTU field, and be sure the title fits on one line. Add appropriate document properties to the Access and Excel files. Submit your printed or electronic files as directed by your instructor.

(Project 4D Cooling Costs continues on the next page)

GO! Solve It | **Project 4E Cooling Costs** (continued)

Performance Level

	Exemplary: You consistently applied the relevant skills.	Proficient: You sometimes, but not always, applied the relevant skills.	Developing: You rarely or never applied the relevant skills.
Modify the 4E HVAC Cooling worksheet: insert a table, add a calculated column, and filter data	Worksheet table is created, calculated column is added, and data is filtered accurately	Worksheet table is created, calculated column is added, and data is filtered, but there are two or fewer errors	One or more item was not complete
Import the 4E HVAC Cooling worksheet to Access table, and filter table	Table is imported accurately, and filtering is applied accurately	Table is imported accurately, and filtering is applied, but there are two or fewer errors	Table is not imported and/or filtering is not applied
Create a report based on the 4E HVAC Cooling table	Report is created accurately	Report is created with two or fewer errors	Report is not created

Performance Criteria (left side label)

END | You have completed Project 4E

RUBRIC

The following outcomes-based assessments are open-ended assessments. That is, there is no specific correct result; your result will depend on your approach to the information provided. Make Professional Quality your goal. Use the following scoring rubric to guide you in how to approach the problem and then to evaluate how well your approach solves the problem.

The *criteria*—Software Mastery, Content, Format and Layout, and Process—represent the knowledge and skills you have gained that you can apply to solving the problem. The *levels of performance*—Professional Quality, Approaching Professional Quality, or Needs Quality Improvements—help you and your instructor evaluate your result.

	Your completed project is of Professional Quality if you:	Your completed project is approaching Professional Quality if you:	Your completed project needs Quality Improvements if you:
1-Software Mastery	Choose and apply the most appropriate skills, tools, and features and identify efficient methods to solve the problem.	Choose and apply some appropriate skills, tools, and features, but not in the most efficient manner.	Choose inappropriate skills, tools, or features, or are inefficient in solving the problem.
2-Content	Construct a solution that is clear and well organized, contains content that is accurate, appropriate to the audience and purpose, and is complete. Provide a solution that contains no errors of spelling, grammar, or style.	Construct a solution in which some components are unclear, poorly organized, inconsistent, or incomplete. Misjudge the needs of the audience. Have some errors in spelling, grammar, or style, but the errors do not detract from comprehension.	Construct a solution that is unclear, incomplete, or poorly organized, contains some inaccurate or inappropriate content, and contains many errors of spelling, grammar, or style. Do not solve the problem.
3-Format and Layout	Format and arrange all elements to communicate information and ideas, clarify function, illustrate relationships, and indicate relative importance.	Apply appropriate format and layout features to some elements, but not others. Overuse features, causing minor distraction.	Apply format and layout that does not communicate information or ideas clearly. Do not use format and layout features to clarify function, illustrate relationships, or indicate relative importance. Use available features excessively, causing distraction.
4-Process	Use an organized approach that integrates planning, development, self-assessment, revision, and reflection.	Demonstrate an organized approach in some areas, but not others; or, use an insufficient process of organization throughout.	Do not use an organized approach to solve the problem.

Apply a combination of the 4A and 4B skills.

GO! Think Project 4F Filter Efficiency

PROJECT FILES

For Project 4F, you will need the following files:

New blank Access database
i04F_Filter_Efficiency

You will save your files as:

Lastname_Firstname_4F_Filter_Efficiency
Lastname_Firstname_4F_Filter_Costs

Midwest HVAC Manufacturer offers a number of different filters for its heating and cooling units. Information about the HVAC filters is located in file i04F_Filter_Efficiency. You have been asked to prepare an efficiency report. Open the **i04F_Filter_Efficiency** Excel file, and save it as **Lastname_Firstname_4F_Filter_Efficiency** in your **Integrated Projects Chapter 4** folder. Create an Excel table from the existing data, and then sort the Efficiency column in descending order. Select any size in the Width column, and then create an AutoFilter for that size. Insert a calculated column that calculates the filter cost using $0.10 per square inch (Length*Width*.10). Create a conditional format for the Cost column. Apply a table style to the table, and apply Best Fit to all columns. Insert the file name in the footer.

Create a new database with the file name **Lastname_Firstname_4F_Filter_Costs** Import the Excel file, and then sort the Width column in ascending order. Create a query that displays the filters with an Efficiency of 65% (.65) or higher, and then create a report based on the query. Delete the Date, Time, and Page Number controls, and format the title. Add appropriate document properties to both files. Submit your printed or electronic files as directed by your instructor.

END | You have completed Project 4F

Integrating Excel and PowerPoint

PROJECT 5A

OUTCOMES
Create Excel charts and link them to a PowerPoint presentation.

OBJECTIVES

1. Create and Format Excel Charts
2. Link Excel Charts and Data to a PowerPoint Presentation
3. Apply Slide Transitions, Use the Document Inspector, and Mark as Final

PROJECT 5B

OUTCOMES
Create illustrations and paste PowerPoint objects and slides into an Excel worksheet.

OBJECTIVES

4. Create and Modify Illustrations in PowerPoint
5. Copy a PowerPoint Slide and Object into an Excel Workbook
6. Create Hyperlinks
7. Freeze Rows, Repeat Headings, and Insert Comments in Excel

YanLev/Shutterstock

In This Chapter

In this chapter, you will create charts—graphical representations of numeric data—in an Excel worksheet. Excel provides various types of charts to display the data in a professional and meaningful way. You can modify a chart by formatting a chart title, moving or hiding the legend, or displaying additional chart elements, such as axis titles and data labels. You will also create presentations using PowerPoint's wide range of formatting options including themes, layouts, and styles. You can create high-quality graphics using the SmartArt feature. Finally, you will use the copy-and-paste and hyperlink features to share data between Excel and PowerPoint.

The projects in this chapter relate to **Board Anywhere Surf and Snowboard Shop**, a retail store founded by college classmates Dana Connolly and J. R. Kass. After graduating with business degrees, they combined their business expertise and their favorite sports to open their shop. The store carries top brands of men's and women's apparel, goggles and sunglasses, and boards and gear. The surfboard selection includes both classic boards and the latest high-tech boards. Snowboarding gear can be purchased in packages or customized for the most experienced boarders.

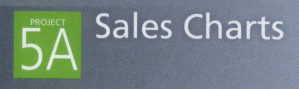
Sales Charts

PROJECT ACTIVITIES

In Activities 5.01 through 5.08, you will use Excel to create a column chart to display the sales data of individual items. Also, you will create a pie chart to compare the monthly sales figures from one year to the next. You will modify a picture in PowerPoint and link the Excel charts to the presentation. Finally, you will change the Excel data and view those changes in PowerPoint. Your completed files will look similar to Figure 5.1.

PROJECT FILES

For Project 5A, you will need the following files:

i05A_Snowboarding_Sales
i05A_Sales_Presentation

You will save your files as:

Lastname_Firstname_5A_Snowboarding_Sales
Lastname_Firstname_5A_Sales_Presentation

PROJECT RESULTS

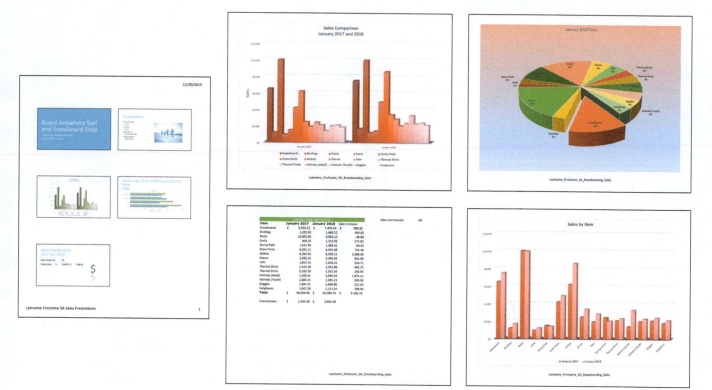

FIGURE 5.1   Project 5A Sales Charts

Objective 1 Create and Format Excel Charts

You can quickly create professional-looking charts in Excel. Various chart types already exist; however, you must determine which chart type will illustrate your data in the best manner. A ***column chart*** is a chart in which the data is arranged in columns. It is useful for showing data changes over a period of time or for illustrating comparisons among items. A ***pie chart*** is a chart that shows the relationship of each part to a whole. Consider using a pie chart when you have only one column or row to plot and each category of data represents part of a total value.

Activity 5.01 | Inserting and Modifying a Column Chart

A column chart is useful to plot Excel data that is arranged in columns or rows. The ***category axis*** is the area along the bottom of a chart that identifies the categories of data; it is also referred to as the ***x-axis***. The ***value axis*** is a numerical scale on the left side of a chart that shows the range of numbers for the data points; it is also referred to as the ***y-axis***.

1. Start Excel. From your student data files, locate and open the file **i05A_Snowboarding_Sales**. In the location where you are saving your files for this chapter, create a new folder named **Integrated Projects Chapter 5** and then using your own name, **Save** the file in the folder as **Lastname_Firstname_5A_Snowboarding_Sales**

2. Click the **Insert tab**, and then in the **Text group**, click **Header & Footer**. Under **Header & Footer Tools**, on the **Design tab**, in the **Navigation group**, click **Go to Footer**. In the **Footer area**, click in the box just above the word *Footer*, and then in the **Header & Footer Elements group**, click **File Name**. Click in any cell in the workbook to exit the footer.

3. Near the right side of the status bar, click **Normal**, and then press Ctrl + Home to make cell **A1** the active cell.

4. Click cell **D2**, type **Sales Increase** and then press Enter. In cell **D3**, type the formula **=c3-b3** and then on the **Formula Bar**, click **Enter**. Point to the fill handle to display the + pointer. Drag down to cell **D18**, and then release the mouse button. Select the range **B3:D3**. On the **Home tab**, in the **Number group**, click **Accounting Number Format** $. Click cell **A1**, and then compare your screen with Figure 5.2.

   Excel copies the formula in cell D3 to cells D4:D18 and displays the values in the cells. The Accounting Number Format has been applied to the range B3:D3.

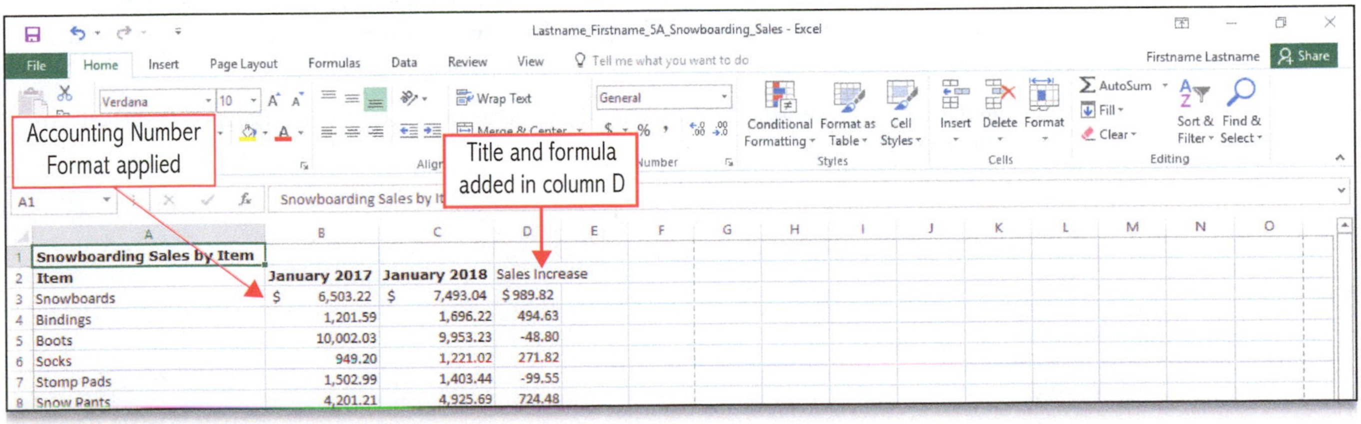

FIGURE 5.2

Excel 2016, Windows 10, Microsoft Corporation

5 Select the range **A1:D1**. On the **Home tab**, in the **Alignment group**, click **Merge & Center**. In the **Styles group**, click **Cell Styles**, and then under **Themed Cell Styles**, click **Accent6**.

6 Select the range **A2:D2**. In the **Alignment group**, click **Center** ▤. In the **Styles group**, click **Cell Styles**, and then under **Themed Cell Styles**, click **20% - Accent6**.

7 Select **columns A:D**. Point to the **column A** header, right-click to display a shortcut menu, and then click **Column Width**. In the **Column Width** dialog box, type **15** and then click **OK**.

8 Select the range **B18:C18**. On the **Home tab**, in the **Editing group**, click **Sum** ∑ AutoSum ▾. Click cell **B3**. In the **Clipboard group**, click **Format Painter** ✷. Select the range **B18:D18**.

> The column totals display in cells B18 and C18, and the Sales Increase displays in cell D18. Recall that you copied a formula from cell D3 to cell D18. After inserting data in cells B18 and C18, the formula in cell D18 provides the Sales Increase result. The range B18:D18 displays using the format copied from cell B3.

9 Select the range **A2:C17**. Click the **Insert tab**. In the **Charts group**, click **Insert Column or Bar Chart** 📊▾, and then under **3-D Column**, click the first style—**3-D Clustered Column**. Under **Chart Tools**, on the **Design tab**, in the **Location group**, click **Move Chart**. In the **Move Chart** dialog box, click the **New sheet** option button, and then on the right, in the **New sheet** box, type **January Sales** and click **OK**.

> A chart is created and moved to a new sheet named January Sales.

10 Under **Chart Tools**, on the **Design tab**, in the **Data group**, click **Switch Row/Column**. In the **Chart Styles group**, click **More** ▾. In the **Chart Styles** gallery, locate and click **Style 11**. In the **Chart Styles group**, click **Change Colors**, and then locate and click **Monochromatic Color 6** (orange). In the **Chart Layouts group**, click **Quick Layout**, and then locate and click **Layout 9**.

> The *Chart Styles gallery* is a group of predesigned *chart styles*—the overall visual look of a chart in terms of its graphic effects, colors, and backgrounds; for example, you can have flat or beveled columns, colors that are solid or transparent, and backgrounds that are dark or light. In the *Chart Layouts gallery*, you can select a predesigned *chart layout*—a combination of chart elements, which can include a title, legend labels for the columns, and the table of charted cells.

11 In the upper right corner of the chart, click **Chart Elements** ➕, point to **Legend**, click the ▶ arrow, and then click **More Options**. In the **Format Legend** pane, under **Legend Position**, click **Bottom**. **Close** ✕ the **Format Legend** task pane, and then compare your screen with Figure 5.3.

> The *legend* is a chart element that identifies the patterns or colors that are assigned to the categories in the chart.

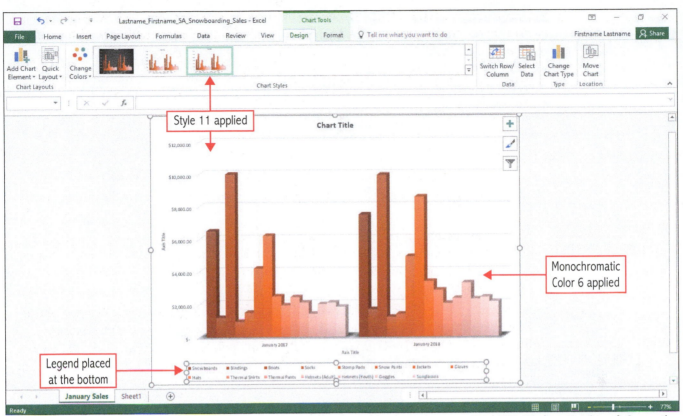

Style 11 applied

Monochromatic Color 6 applied

Legend placed at the bottom

Excel 2016, Windows 10, Microsoft Corporation

FIGURE 5.3

12 In the upper right corner of the chart, click **Chart Elements** ➕ again. Point to **Axes**, click the ▶ **arrow**, and then click **More Options**. Click any number on the vertical axis to select all of the vertical axis labels. In the **Format Axis** pane, below **Axis Options**, scroll down, and then click **Number**. Under **Category**, click the **arrow**, and then click **Currency**. In the **Decimal places** box, select the number **2**, type **0** and press Enter. **Close** ✖ the **Format Axis** task pane.

The values on the vertical axis are formatted as Currency with no decimal places.

13 On the left edge of the chart, click the text *Axis Title*, which is the **Vertical (Value) Axis Title**. At the top of the window, click in the **Formula Bar**, type **Sales** and then press Enter. On the **Home tab**, in the **Font group**, click the **Font Size button arrow** 11 ▾, and then click **14**.

The title *Sales* displays on the vertical axis.

14 At the bottom of the chart, above the legend, click the text *Axis Title*, which is the **Horizontal (Category) Axis Title**. Press Delete to delete the title.

15 Click the text *Chart Title*. Click in the **Formula Bar**, type **Sales Comparison** press Alt + Enter, and then type **January 2017 and 2018** Press Enter to display the new chart title.

The title displays on two lines at the top of the chart. Pressing Alt + Enter enables you to display multiple lines of text in a single cell.

16 Click anywhere in the **Legend** to select it. On the **Home tab**, in the **Font group**, click **Increase Font Size** A᛫ two times, and then click **Bold** B . Compare your screen with Figure 5.4.

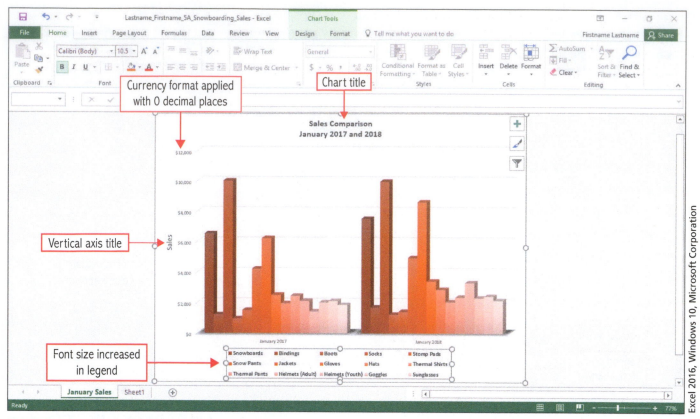

FIGURE 5.4

17 ▶ Right-click the **January Sales sheet tab**, and then on the shortcut menu, click **Move or Copy**. In the **Move or Copy** dialog box, click (**move to end**), select the **Create a copy** check box, and then click **OK**. Right-click the **January Sales (2) sheet tab**, and then on the shortcut menu, click **Rename**. With **January Sales (2)** selected, type **Sales by Item** and then press Enter.

18 ▶ Click in a blank area of the chart. Under **Chart Tools**, click the **Design tab**, and then in the **Data group**, click **Switch Row/Column**. In the **Chart Layouts group**, click **Quick Layout**, and then click **Layout 3**.

The Switch Row/Column button exchanges the row and column data in a chart and changes the legend accordingly. This enables you to display a chart that presents your data in the best manner.

19 ▶ Click the chart title text. Click in the **Formula Bar**, type **Sales by Item** and then press Enter. Compare your screen with Figure 5.5.

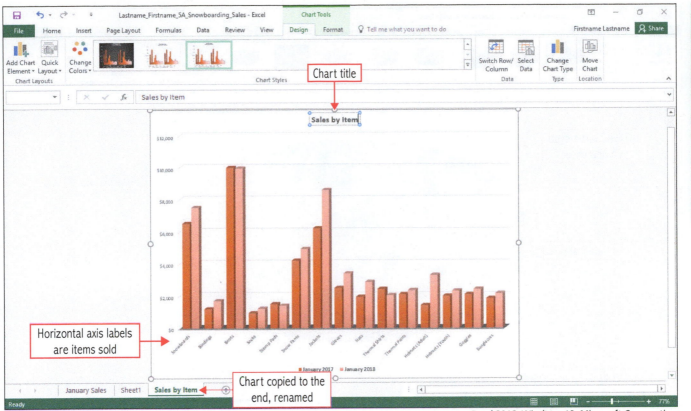

Chart title

Horizontal axis labels are items sold

Chart copied to the end, renamed

Excel 2016, Windows 10, Microsoft Corporation

FIGURE 5.5

20 Right-click the **Sheet1 tab**, and then on the shortcut menu, click **Rename**. With **Sheet1** selected, type **Sales Data** and then press Enter.

21 **Save** 🖫 your workbook.

Activity 5.02 | Inserting and Modifying a Pie Chart

Data that is in one column or one row of an Excel worksheet can be displayed in a pie chart. In a pie chart, the size of each pie slice is equal to its ***data point***—the value that originates in a worksheet cell—compared to the total value of all the slices. The data points display as a percentage of the whole pie. Each pie slice is referred to as a ***data marker***. A data marker is a column, bar, area, dot, pie slice, or other symbol in a chart that represents a single data point.

1 Click the **Sales Data sheet tab**. Select the range **A3:A17**, hold down Ctrl, and then select the range **C3:C17**.

Cells A3:A17 and C3:C17 are selected. Recall that you can hold down Ctrl to select nonadjacent ranges.

2 On the **Insert tab**, in the **Charts group**, click **Insert Pie or Doughnut Chart** 🥧 ▾, and then under **3-D Pie**, click **3-D Pie**. Under **Chart Tools**, on the **Design tab**, in the **Location group**, click **Move Chart**. In the **Move Chart** dialog box, click the **New sheet** option button. In the **New sheet** box, type **January 2018 Sales** and then click **OK**. Compare your screen with Figure 5.6.

The January 2018 ***data series***—the related data points represented by data markers—displays in a pie chart. The data points determine the size of each slice and the legend identifies the pie slices.

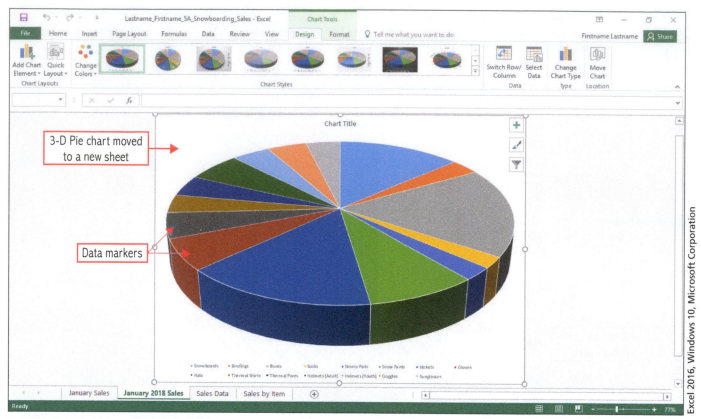

FIGURE 5.6

3 On the **Design tab**, in the **Chart Layouts group**, click **Quick Layout**, and then click **Layout 1**. In the **Chart Styles group,** click **Change Colors**, and under **Colorful**, click **Color 3**.

4 Click the text *Chart Title*, click in the **Formula Bar**, type **January 2018 Sales** and then press Enter.

5 Click one of the data labels on the chart; notice that all the data labels are selected. Click the **Home tab**, and then in the **Font group**, click **Bold** B.

6 Double-click in the white area of the chart to display the **Format Chart Area** pane on the right. If necessary, click **Fill & Line** ◇. Click **Fill**, and then click the **Gradient fill** option button. Click the **Color arrow**, and then in the sixth column, click the fourth color— **Orange, Accent 2, Lighter 40%**. Compare your screen with Figure 5.7.

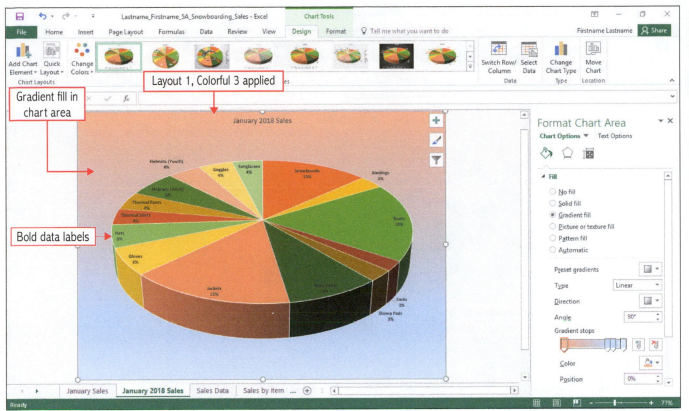

FIGURE 5.7

Excel 2016, Windows 10, Microsoft Corporation

7 ▶ In the **Format Chart Area** task pane, click the **Chart Options arrow**, and then click **Plot Area**. Click **Effects** ⬠, and then click **3-D Rotation**. In the **X Rotation box**, select the existing number and type **145** In the upper right corner of the **Format Chart Area** pane, click **Close** ✕.

The Snowboards data marker is rotated to the bottom right of the pie chart.

8 ▶ Click the chart to select all of the slices, and then click the **Snowboards** slice.

Only the Snowboards data marker—pie slice—is selected.

9 ▶ Point to the **Snowboards** data marker to display the ⬚ pointer. Drag down approximately 0.5 inch, and then release the mouse button. Compare your screen with Figure 5.8.

The Snowboards data marker is pulled out—*exploded*. You can explode one or more slices of a pie chart for emphasis. The entire pie automatically adjusts to a smaller size to fit all the data markers on the chart sheet.

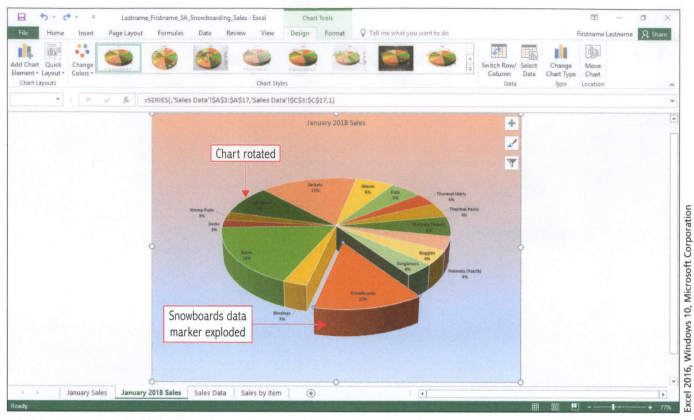

FIGURE 5.8

10 ▸ **Save** 💾 your workbook.

Activity 5.03 │ Inserting an Absolute Cell Reference

In an Excel worksheet, the intersecting column letter and row number form the ***cell reference***—also called the ***cell address***. An Excel formula that includes a cell reference—which may be in a different part of the same worksheet, or in a different worksheet or workbook—uses the data in the cell reference to calculate the value of the formula.

1 ▸ Click the **Sales Data sheet tab**, and then click cell **F1**. Type **Sales Commission** and then press ⎄Tab. In cell **G1**, type **3%** and then on the **Formula Bar**, click **Enter** ✓ to keep cell G1 as the active cell. Point to the line between the **column headings F and G** until the ⊹ pointer displays, and then double-click.

The width of column F automatically adjusts to the best fit—all of the text in cell F1 displays.

2 ▸ Click cell **A20**, type **Commissions** and then press ⎄Tab. In cell **B20**, type **=b18*g1** and then press ⎍F4⎍. On the **Formula Bar**, click **Enter** ✓.

On the Formula Bar, the formula *=B18*$G$1* displays a dollar sign to the left of *G* and to the left of *1*, making it an ***absolute cell reference***. An absolute cell reference refers to cells by their fixed position in a worksheet; an absolute cell reference remains the same when a formula is copied to other cells.

3 ▸ In cell **B20**, drag the fill handle to the right to cell **C20**. Click the **Formulas tab**, and then in the **Formula Auditing group**, click **Show Formulas**. Compare your screen with Figure 5.9.

The formula is copied from cell B20 to cell C20. The reference to cell G1 does not change because it is an absolute cell reference. The reference to cell B18 changes to cell C18 because it is a relative cell reference. Recall that a relative cell reference is the address of a cell based on the relative position of the cell that contains the formula and the cell to which it refers.

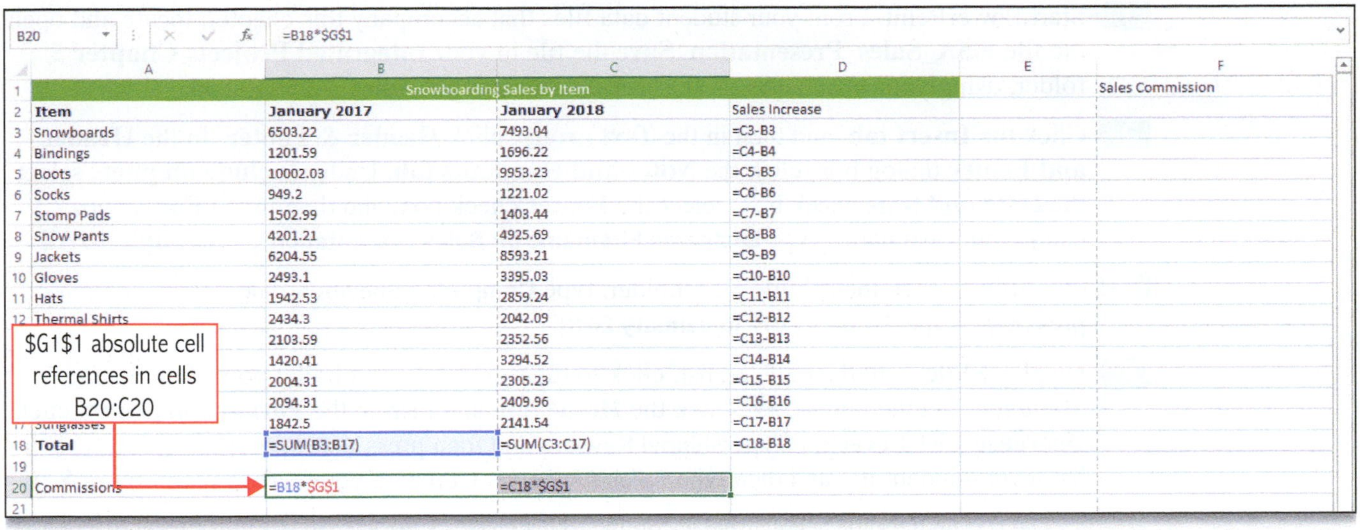

B20 =B18*$G$1

	A	B	C	D	E	F
1	Snowboarding Sales by Item					Sales Commission
2	Item	January 2017	January 2018	Sales Increase		
3	Snowboards	6503.22	7493.04	=C3-B3		
4	Bindings	1201.59	1696.22	=C4-B4		
5	Boots	10002.03	9953.23	=C5-B5		
6	Socks	949.2	1221.02	=C6-B6		
7	Stomp Pads	1502.99	1403.44	=C7-B7		
8	Snow Pants	4201.21	4925.69	=C8-B8		
9	Jackets	6204.55	8593.21	=C9-B9		
10	Gloves	2493.1	3395.03	=C10-B10		
11	Hats	1942.53	2859.24	=C11-B11		
12	Thermal Shirts	2434.3	2042.09	=C12-B12		
13		2103.59	2352.56	=C13-B13		
14		1420.41	3294.52	=C14-B14		
15		2004.31	2305.23	=C15-B15		
16		2094.31	2409.96	=C16-B16		
17	Sunglasses	1842.5	2141.54	=C17-B17		
18	Total	=SUM(B3:B17)	=SUM(C3:C17)	=C18-B18		
19						
20	Commissions	=B18*$G$1	=C18*$G$1			
21						

FIGURE 5.9

Excel 2016, Windows 10, Microsoft Corporation

4 In the **Formula Auditing group**, click **Show Formulas** to turn off the display of formulas.

ANOTHER WAY To toggle the formula view on and off, hold down Ctrl and press `.

5 Click the **Page Layout tab**. In the **Page Setup group**, click **Orientation**, and then click **Landscape**. Right-click the **January Sales sheet tab**, and then on the shortcut menu, click **Select All Sheets**. Click the **Insert tab**, and then in the **Text group**, click **Header & Footer**. In the **Page Setup** dialog box, on the **Header/Footer tab**, click the **Footer arrow**, and then click the file name with your name **Lastname_Firstname_5A_Snowboarding_Sales**. Click **OK**. Right-click the **Sales Data sheet tab**, and then on the shortcut menu, click **Ungroup Sheets**.

6 Display **Backstage** view. On the left, click **Info**, in the lower right corner, click **Show All Properties**. Under **Related People**, be sure your name displays as the **Author**—change it if necessary. Click to the right of **Subject**, and then type your course name and section number. Click to the right of **Tags**, and then type **sales data, charts**

7 **Save** the workbook.

Objective 2 Link Excel Charts and Data to a PowerPoint Presentation

When you want to paste Excel data or a chart in a PowerPoint presentation, the Paste Special feature enables you to create a link—an external reference—from PowerPoint back to the Excel file. This enables you to update the chart or data in Excel and have those changes reflected in the presentation.

Activity 5.04 | Linking Excel Charts to a PowerPoint Presentation

Ali Cardona, the Purchasing Manager at Board Anywhere Surf and Snowboard Shop, is presenting the sales data to the employees. He would like to determine whether the sales of jackets, gloves, hats, and thermal shirts have been sufficient to keep carrying the lines in the retail store. In this Activity, you will complete the PowerPoint presentation Mr. Cardona created by linking Excel charts to specific slides.

1 ▸ Start PowerPoint. From your student data files that accompany this chapter, locate and open the file **i05A_Sales_Presentation**. **Save** the file in your **Integrated Projects Chapter 5** folder, using your own name, as **Lastname_Firstname_5A_Sales_Presentation**

2 ▸ Click the **Insert tab**, and then in the **Text group**, click **Header & Footer**. In the **Header and Footer** dialog box, click the **Notes and Handouts tab**. Under **Include on page**, select the **Date and time** check box, select the **Footer** check box, and then in the **Footer** box, using your own name, type **Lastname Firstname 5A Sales Presentation** Click **Apply to All**.

3 ▸ On **Slide 1**, click the subtitle placeholder, type **Comparing Snowboarding Sales** and then press Enter. Type **January 2017 to January 2018**

4 ▸ Display **Slide 2**. In the bulleted list, click to the right of the last bullet point *Purchasing Manager*, and then press Enter. Click the **Home tab**, and then in the **Paragraph group**, click **Decrease List Level** ⯇. Type **Shinpei Kawano** and then press Enter. Press Tab to decrease the list level—indent it—and then type **Sales Associate** Compare your screen with Figure 5.10.

The text on the slide is organized according to *list levels*. A list level is an outline level in a presentation represented by a bullet symbol and identified in a slide by the indentation and the size of the text.

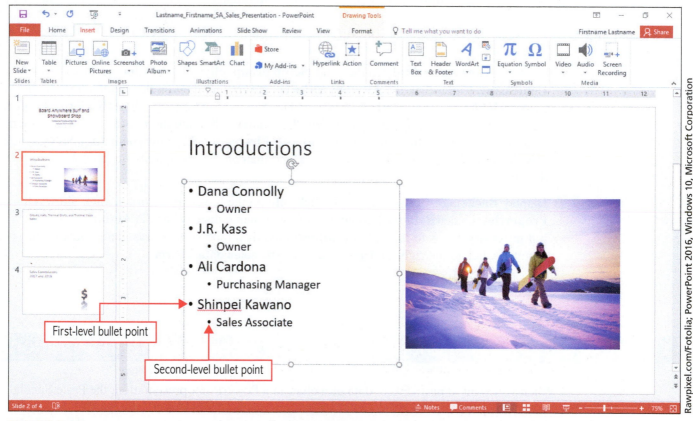

FIGURE 5.10

🔄 **ANOTHER WAY**   To decrease the list level, hold down Shift and press Tab.

5 ▸ On the taskbar, click the **Excel icon** 🟩 to make your **Lastname_Firstname_5A_ Snowboarding_Sales** window active. Click the **January Sales sheet tab**, and then click a blank section of the Chart Area to select the chart. Click the **Home tab**, and then in the **Clipboard group**, click **Copy** 📋.

6 ▷ On the taskbar, click the **PowerPoint icon** to make your **Lastname_Firstname_5A_ Sales_Presentation** window active. If necessary, click Slide 2 to make it the active slide. On the **Home tab**, in the **Slides group**, click the **New Slide button arrow**, and then click **Blank**.

A new blank Slide 3 displays.

7 ▷ On the **Home tab**, in the **Clipboard group**, click the upper portion of the **Paste** button, and then compare your screen with Figure 5.11.

The clustered column chart displays; the chart is linked to the Excel workbook data.

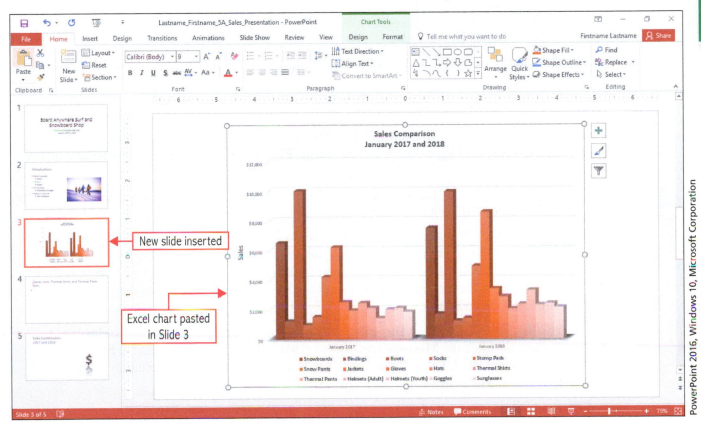

New slide inserted

Excel chart pasted in Slide 3

PowerPoint 2016, Windows 10, Microsoft Corporation

FIGURE 5.11

8 ▷ Display **Slide 4**. In the lower placeholder, click **Insert Chart** . In the **Insert Chart** dialog box, click **Bar**. At the top of the dialog box, locate and click **3D Clustered Bar**. Click **OK**.

A split window named Chart in Microsoft PowerPoint opens and displays sample data.

9 ▷ On the taskbar, click the **Excel icon** , and then click the **Lastname_Firstname_5A_ Snowboarding_Sales** thumbnail to make the window active. Click the **Sales Data sheet tab**. Select the range **A10:C13**. Right-click cell **A10**, and then on the shortcut menu, click **Copy**. On the taskbar, click the **PowerPoint icon** . In the worksheet, click cell **A2,** and then hold down Ctrl and press V.

The data copied from Excel replaces the sample data.

10 ▷ Select cells **B1:C1**. Right-click, click **Format Cells**, and then in the **Format Cells** dialog box, on the **Number tab**, under **Category**, click **Text**. Click **OK**. Click cell **B1**, type **January 2017** and then press Tab. Type **January 2018** and then press Enter.

11 Point to the bottom right corner of cell **D5** to display the ▨ pointer. Drag left to deselect **column D** from the chart data range. Compare your screen with Figure 5.12.

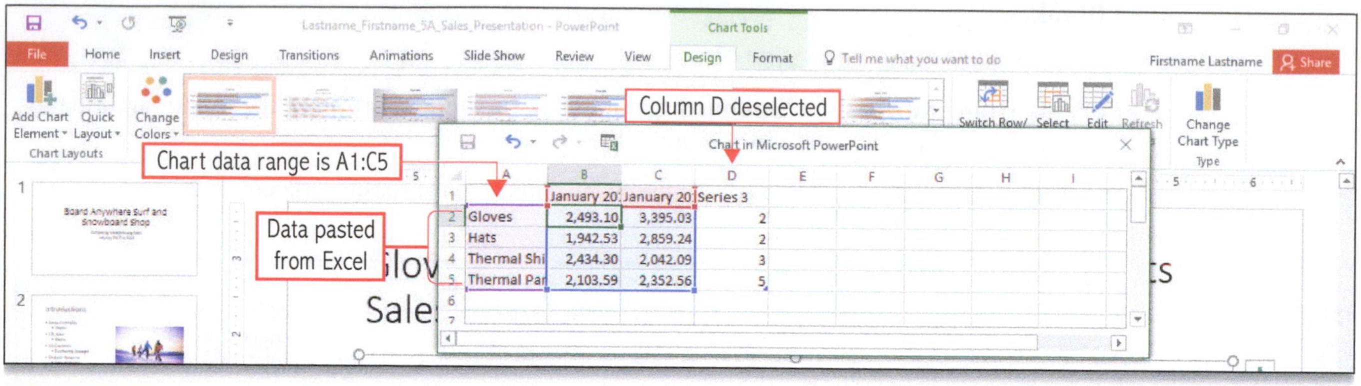

FIGURE 5.12

12 Close ✕ the **Chart in Microsoft PowerPoint** window. On the taskbar, click the **PowerPoint icon** 🅿 to make the **Lastname_Firstname_5A_Sales_Presentation** window active.

Slide 4 displays the bar chart comparing the sales of gloves, hats, thermal shirts, and thermal pants for January 2017 and January 2018.

13 On **Slide 4**, click the **horizontal axis values** to select them, and then click **Chart Elements** ➕. Point to **Axes**, click the **arrow**, and then click **More Options** to display the **Format Axis** pane. Scroll down, if necessary, and click **Number**, and then, under **Category**, click **Currency**. In the **Decimal places** box, delete the number **2**, type **0**, and then **Close** ✕ the **Format Axis** task pane.

14 Display **Slide 1**. Click the **Design tab**, and then in the **Themes group**, click **More** ⬇. Locate and click the **Metropolitan** theme. Click the **Slide Show tab**, in the **Start Slide Show group**, click **From Beginning**, and then view your entire presentation. Notice that by applying the new theme, the colors of your charts have changed.

15 Save 💾 your presentation.

| **More Knowledge** | **Opening a Linked File** |

When you open a file that has a link to an external file, a security notice will automatically display. The notice will inform you that the file contains links and you have the option to update the links. If you trust the source of the file, it is safe to update the links. If you do not know where a file originated, you should cancel the update and investigate where the file was initiated before updating a link.

Activity 5.05 | **Linking Excel Cells to a PowerPoint Presentation**

You can link individual cells in Excel to a PowerPoint presentation. Dana Connolly, one of the owners of Boards Anywhere Surf and Snowboard Shop, wants to increase the sales commission that all of the sales associates earn. In this Activity, you will update the Excel file and verify that the presentation displays the current commission rate.

1 On the taskbar, click the **Excel icon** 🅇 to make your **Lastname_Firstname_5A_Snowboarding_Sales** window active. On the **Sales Data sheet**, select the range **F1:G1**. Right-click the selection, and then on the shortcut menu, click **Copy**. On the taskbar, click the **PowerPoint icon** 🅿 to make your **Lastname_Firstname_5A_Sales_Presentation** window active. Display **Slide 5**. On the **Home tab**, in the **Clipboard group**, click the **Paste**

button arrow, and then click **Paste Special**. In the **Paste Special** dialog box, click the **Paste link** option button, and then under **As**, verify that **Microsoft Excel Worksheet Object** is selected. Click **OK**.

The Excel cells are pasted in Slide 5.

2 With the linked object selected, under **Drawing Tools**, click the **Format tab**, and then in the **Size group**, in the **Shape Height** box, use the up arrow to change the height to **.5**. Drag the linked object so that it is left aligned with the slide title and approximately 0.5 inch below the slide title. Compare your screen with Figure 5.13.

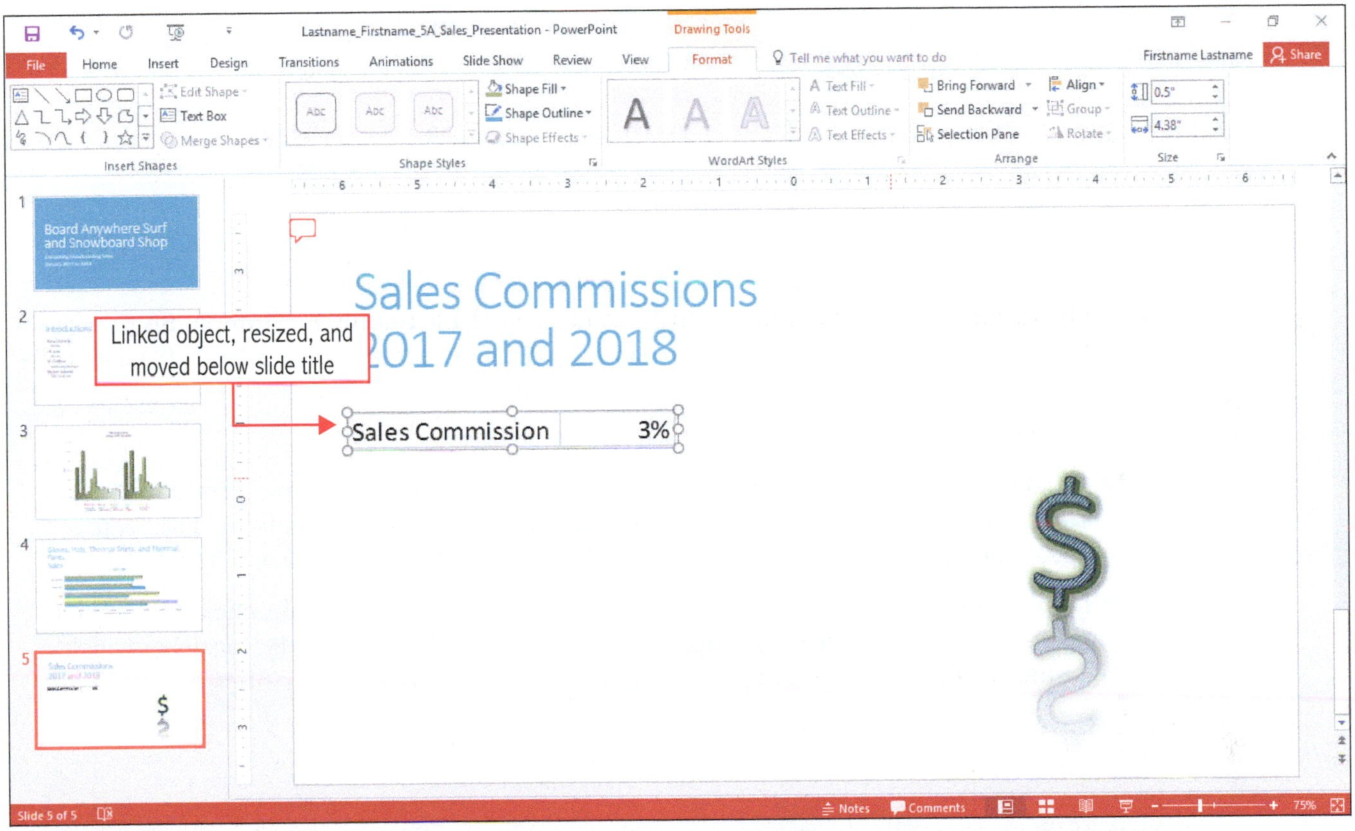

PowerPoint 2016, Windows 10, Microsoft Corporation

FIGURE 5.13

3 On the taskbar, click the **Excel icon** to make your **Lastname_Firstname_5A_Snowboarding_Sales** window active. Press Esc to deselect the range **F1:G1**. Select the range **A20:C20**, right-click the selection, and then on the shortcut menu, click **Copy**.

4 On the taskbar, click the **PowerPoint icon** to make your **Lastname_Firstname_5A_Sales_Presentation** window active. Click the **Home tab**, in the **Clipboard group**, click the **Paste button arrow**, and then click **Paste Special**. In the **Paste Special** dialog box, click the **Paste link** option button. Under **As**, verify that **Microsoft Excel Worksheet Object** is selected, and then click **OK**.

5 With the linked object selected, under **Drawing Tools**, click the **Format tab**, and then in the **Size group**, in the **Shape Height** box, use the up arrow to change the height to **.5**. Drag the linked object under the first linked object so that it displays as shown in Figure 5.14.

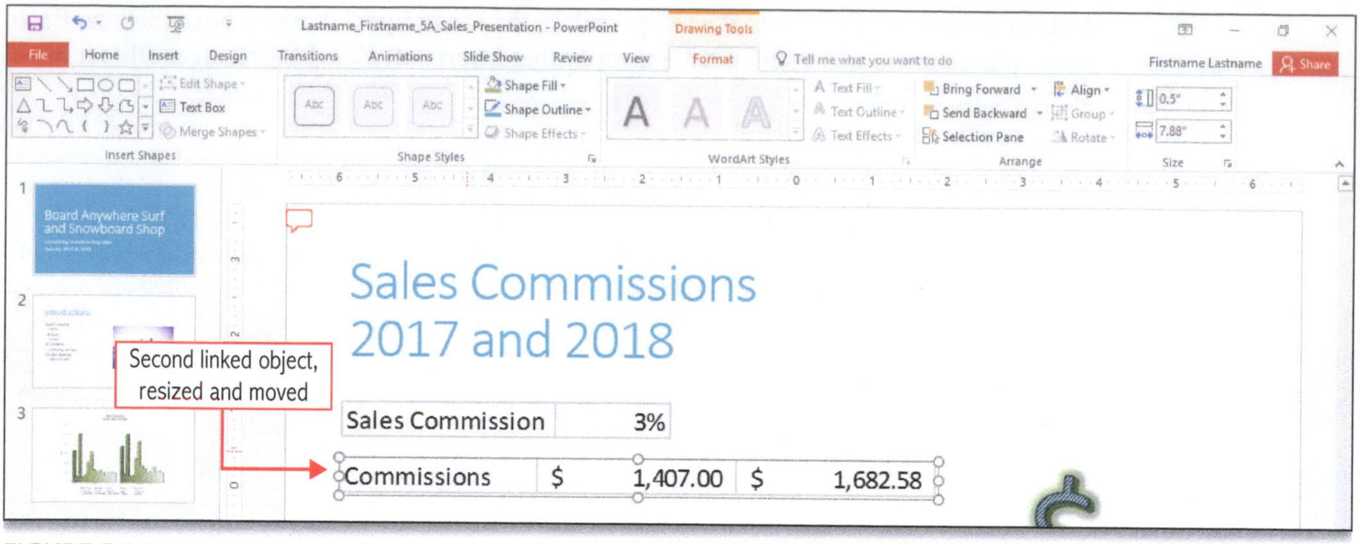

FIGURE 5.14

6 ▶ On the taskbar, click the **Excel icon** [icon] to make your **Lastname_Firstname_5A_ Snowboarding_Sales** window active. Press Esc to deselect the range **A20:C20**. Click cell **G1**, type **5** and then press Enter. **Save** [icon] the workbook.

The commissions in both cells B20 and C20 are updated.

7 ▶ On the taskbar, click the **PowerPoint icon** [icon] to make your **Lastname_Firstname_5A_ Sales_Presentation** window active. Then verify that the Sales Commission has been updated to 5% and the Commissions have been updated to $2,344.99 and $2,804.30.

8 ▶ Display **Slide 2**, and click the picture to select it. Under **Picture Tools**, click the **Format tab**, and then in the **Adjust group**, click **Color**. In the **Recolor** gallery, locate and click **Aqua, Accent color 1 Light**.

9 ▶ **Save** [icon] the presentation.

Objective 3 **Apply Slide Transitions, Use the Document Inspector, and Mark as Final**

PowerPoint has features to ensure that your presentation looks polished and professional. During a presentation, when you move from one slide to the next, the first slide disappears, and the next slide displays. To indicate that the presentation is changing to a new slide, you can add *slide transitions*—the motion effects that occur in Slide Show view when you move from one slide to the next during a presentation.

If you are going to provide an electronic copy of your file to others, use the *Document Inspector* to find and remove hidden data and personal information in a file. Finally, to avoid making inadvertent changes to a finished presentation, use the *Mark as Final* feature, which changes the file to a read-only file—typing and editing commands are turned off.

Activity 5.06 | Inserting Slide Transitions

You can control the speed and type of slide transitions in a presentation.

1 Display **Slide 1**. Click the **Transitions tab**, and then in the **Transition to This Slide group**, click **More**. In the **Transitions** gallery, under **Exciting**, locate the point to the **Ripple** transition. Compare your screen with Figure 5.15.

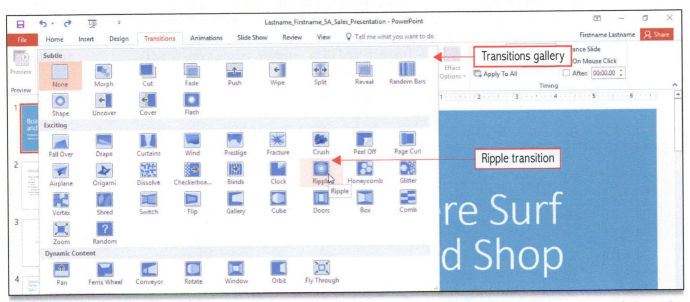

FIGURE 5.15

PowerPoint 2016, Windows 10, Microsoft Corporation

2 In the **Transitions** gallery, under **Exciting**, click **Ripple**. In the **Timing group**, click the **Duration up arrow** to change the time to **01.75**. In the **Timing group**, click **Apply To All**.

> This command applies the transition to all the slides in the presentation. Although you can vary the transitions applied to different slides in a presentation, the result can be distracting to your audience.

3 Click the **Slide Show tab**, in the **Start Slide Show group**, click **From Beginning**, and then view your presentation.

> The presentation is shown with the Ripple transition applied to all slides.

4 Click the **Transitions tab**. In the **Transition to This Slide group**, click **More**, and then under **Subtle**, in the first row, click the third transition—**Fade**. In the **Transition to This Slide group**, click **Effect Options**, and then click **Through Black**. In the **Timing group**, click the **Duration up arrow** to change the time to **02.50**, and then click **Apply To All**.

> The Effect Options vary depending on the transition selected.

5 Click the **Slide Show tab**, in the **Start Slide Show group**, click **From Beginning**, and then view your presentation.

> The presentation is shown with the Fade - Through Black transition applied to all slides.

6 Display **Backstage** view. In the lower right corner, click **Show All Properties**. Under **Related People**, be sure your name displays as the **Author**—change it if necessary. Click to the right of **Subject**, and then type your course name and section number. Click to the right of **Tags**, and then type **sales chart, commission linked**

7 On the left, click **Save** to save and redisplay the presentation.

Activity 5.07 | Running the Document Inspector

Any file you create may contain hidden data and personal information that you may not want to share with others. Hidden data could include comments, revision marks, versions, document properties, or personal information. In this Activity, you will use the Document Inspector to check your file for hidden data.

1 With **Slide 1** the active slide, click the **File tab**, and then on the left, be sure that the **Info tab** is selected. Click **Check for Issues**, and then click **Inspect Document**. In the **Document Inspector** dialog box, verify that all check boxes are selected. If a check box is not selected, click to select it. Click **Inspect**, and then compare your screen with Figure 5.16. Scroll down to review all of the inspection results.

The Document Inspector dialog box displays the inspection results, indicating specific data that was found—including comments and presentation notes.

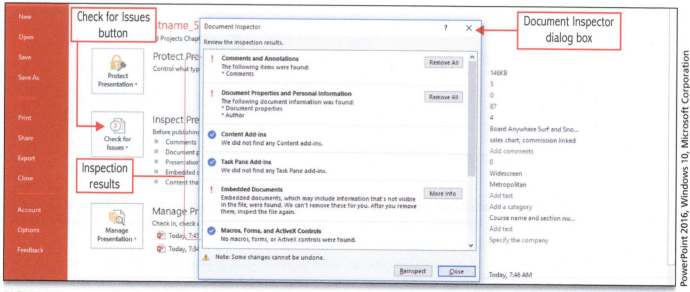

FIGURE 5.16

2 In the **Document Inspector** dialog box, click **Close**, and then **Back** to display the presentation. Click the **Home tab**.

3 Display **Slide 2**, the *Introductions* slide. On the **Status Bar**, click **Notes** to display the note in the Notes pane. Click **Slide 5**, the *Sales Commissions* slide. In the top left corner, click the comment **balloon** to display a comment from Ali Cardona.

A *comment* is a note that can be added from the Review tab and is not generally printed. When you provide an electronic copy of your file to others, you may not want to share the presentation notes and comments.

4 Click the **File tab**, click **Check for Issues**, and then click **Inspect Document**. In the **Document Inspector** dialog box, verify that all check boxes are selected. If a check box is not selected, click to select it. Click **Inspect**. To the right of **Comments and Annotations**, click **Remove All**. Scroll down, and then, to the right of **Presentation Notes**, click **Remove All**.

Although you might want to remove Document Properties and Personal Information, for purposes of this instruction, you will not remove them.

5 Click **Reinspect**. Click **Inspect**, and then verify that no hidden comments or presentation notes were found. **Close** the **Document Inspector** dialog box.

6 ▸ Click **Back**  to redisplay your presentation window. Display **Slide 2**, and then verify that the note has been deleted. Display **Slide 5**, and then verify that the comment has been deleted.

7 ▸ **Save** 🖫 your presentation.

Activity 5.08 | Using Mark as Final

1 ▸ Click the **File tab**, and verify that the **Info tab** is selected. Click **Protect Presentation**, and then click **Mark as Final**. In the message box, click **OK**. In the second message box, read the message, and then click **OK**. Click the **Home tab**, and then compare your screen with Figure 5.17.

The file becomes a read-only file. A Message Bar displays below the ribbon indicating that the presentation is marked as final—thereby preventing the user from making inadvertent changes.

FIGURE 5.17

PowerPoint 2016, Windows 10, Microsoft Corporation

> **NOTE** Marking a Presentation as Final
>
> The Mark as Final feature is not a security feature. Anyone who receives an electronic copy of a file that has been marked as final can remove the Mark as Final status by clicking the Edit Anyway button on the Message Bar. The user can then make changes to the file.

---

2 ▸ If your instructor directs you to submit your files electronically, go to Step 3. To print your presentation, click the **File tab**, and then click the **Print tab**. Under **Settings**, click the **Full Page Slides arrow**, and then under **Handouts**, click **6 Slides Horizontal**. Click **Print**. On the taskbar, click the **Excel icon**. Click the **File tab**, and then click the **Print tab**. Under **Settings**, click the **Print Active Sheets arrow**, and then click **Print Entire Workbook**. Click **Print**. **Close** Excel without saving changes, and then **Close** PowerPoint without saving changes. Go to Step 4.

3 ▸ **Close** PowerPoint without saving changes, and then **Close** Excel without saving changes.

4 ▸ Submit your printed or electronic files as directed by your instructor.

END | You have completed Project 5A

Sessions Presentation

PROJECT ACTIVITIES

In Activities 5.09 through 5.19, you will insert and modify graphics in a PowerPoint presentation. The Board Anywhere Surf and Snowboard Shop sends its most popular surf instructors to the world's best surfing beaches for two-, three-, and four-day training sessions. You will complete the presentation. You will insert and modify SmartArt graphics and online pictures, and then copy some of the presentation objects into an Excel workbook. Finally, you will create hyperlinks in PowerPoint and Excel, modify an Excel workbook, and insert comments. Your completed files will look similar to Figure 5.18.

PROJECT FILES

For Project 5B, you will need the following files:

i05B_Surf_Sessions
i05B_Sessions_Presentation
i05B_Wave

You will save your files as:

Lastname_Firstname_5B_Surf_Sessions
Lastname_Firstname_5B_Sessions_Presentation

PROJECT RESULTS

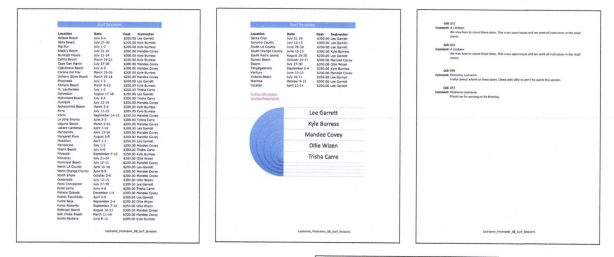

FIGURE 5.18 Project 5B Sessions Presentation

Illustrations and graphics enhance the text in your presentation and help your audience better understand and recall the information. A bulleted list on a slide can be converted into a SmartArt graphic quickly. Adding animation to a PowerPoint object provides additional emphasis. You can change the order of the slides to provide a better presentation.

Activity 5.09 | Inserting and Animating SmartArt Graphics

Recall that a SmartArt graphic is a designer-quality visual representation of your information that you can create by choosing from among many different layouts to communicate your message or ideas effectively. In this Activity, you will modify a PowerPoint presentation started by Shinpei Kawano, a Sales Associate.

1 ▶ Start PowerPoint. From your student data files for this chapter, locate and open the file **i05B_Sessions_Presentation**. **Save** the file in your **Integrated Projects Chapter 5** folder, using your own name, as **Lastname_Firstname_5B_Sessions_Presentation**

2 ▶ Click the **Insert tab**, and then in the **Text group**, click **Header & Footer**. In the **Header and Footer** dialog box, click the **Notes and Handouts tab**. Under **Include on page**, select the **Date and time** check box, and then click the **Fixed** option button. Select the **Footer** check box, and then in the **Footer** box, using your own name, type **Lastname Firstname 5B Sessions Presentation** Click **Apply to All**.

3 ▶ Click the **Design tab**, and then in the **Themes group**, click **More**. Locate and then click the **Droplet** theme. Apply the blue variant. In the **Customize group**, click **Format Background**, and then in the pane on the right, verify that the **Gradient fill** option button is selected. Click the **Color arrow**, and then in the fifth column, click the fifth color—**Blue, Accent 1, Darker 25%**. Click **Apply to All**, and then **Close** the **Format Background** pane. Compare your screen with Figure 5.19.

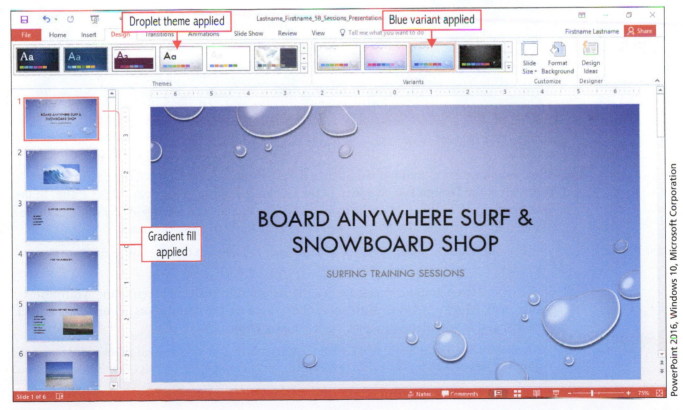

FIGURE 5.19

4 Display **Slide 3**—*Surfing Instructors*. Click the **Home tab**. In the **Slides group**, click **Layout**, and then click **Title and Content**.

5 Click the placeholder containing the names. On the **Home tab**, in the **Paragraph group**, click **Convert to SmartArt Graphic**. In the **SmartArt** gallery, locate and click the **Target List**. Under **SmartArt Tools**, on the **Design tab**, in the **SmartArt Styles group**, click **More** ⬇, and then under **Best Match for Document**, click the fifth style—**Intense Effect**. Click in a blank area of the slide to deselect the SmartArt, and then compare your screen with Figure 5.20.

When you create a SmartArt graphic, the SmartArt Text Pane displays by default; this feature may be toggled off. When you deselect the SmartArt graphic, the SmartArt Text Pane no longer displays.

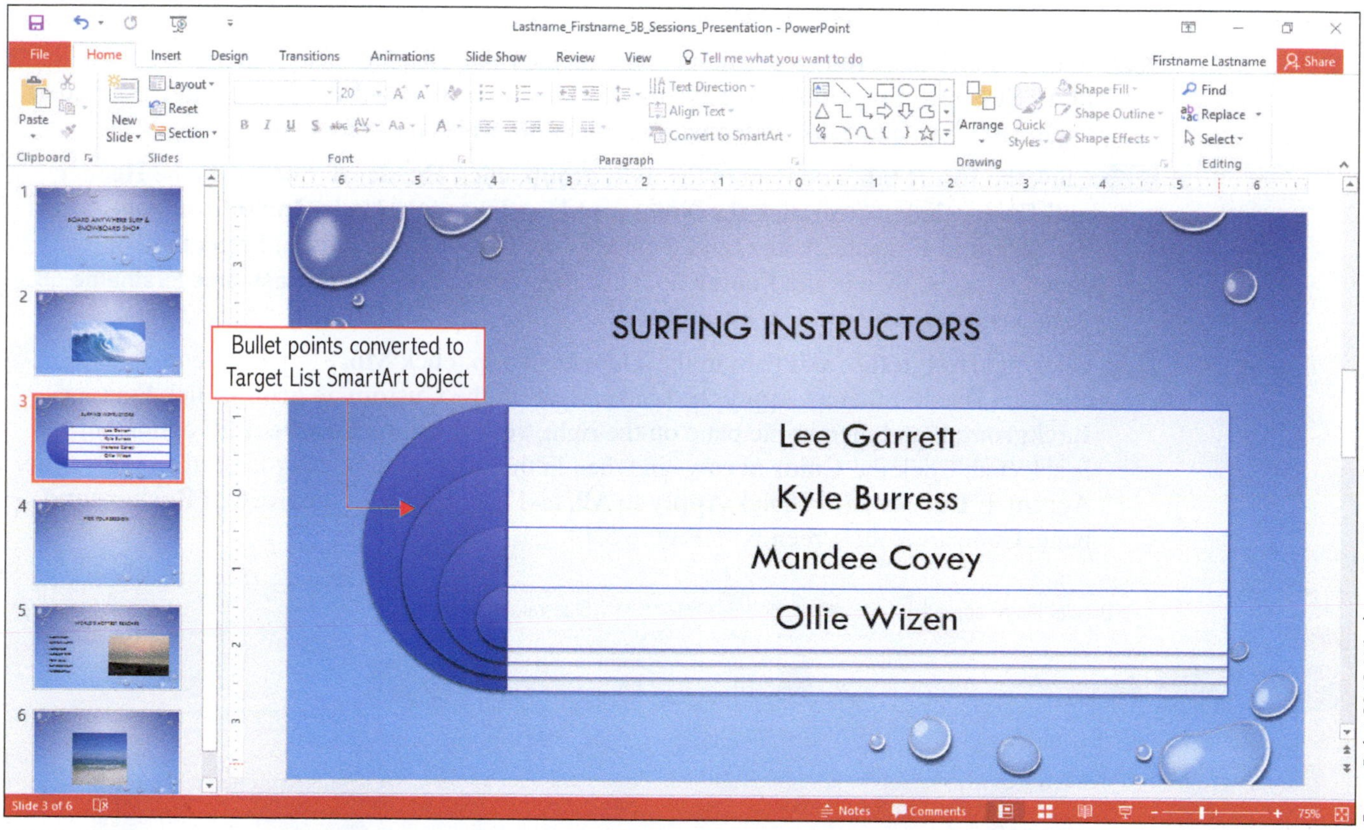

FIGURE 5.20

6 Click the SmartArt graphic. If the SmartArt Text Pane does not display, under **SmartArt Tools**, click the **Design tab**, and then in the **Create Graphic group**, click **Text Pane**. In the **Text Pane**, click to the right of the name *Ollie Wizen*, and then press ⟨Enter⟩. Type **Trisha Carre** and then in the **Create Graphic group**, click **Text Pane** to close the pane.

Recall that in the SmartArt Text Pane you can enter and edit text that displays in the SmartArt graphic.

7 With the SmartArt graphic selected, click the **Animations tab**, and then in the **Animation group**, click **More** ⬇. Under **Entrance**, click **Wipe**. In the **Animation group**, click **Effect Options**, and then under **Sequence**, click **One by One**.

An *animation* effect is added to the graphic. Animation is a visual or sound effect added to an object or text on a slide. The Effect Options will vary depending on the effect applied to the object.

8 Click the **Design tab**—not the SmartArt Tools Design tab—and then in the **Customize group**, click **Format Background**. In the **Format Background** pane, click the **Picture or texture fill** option button, and then under **Insert picture from**, click **File**. Navigate to the location of your student data files, click the file **i05B_Wave**, and then click **Insert**. Compare your screen with Figure 5.21.

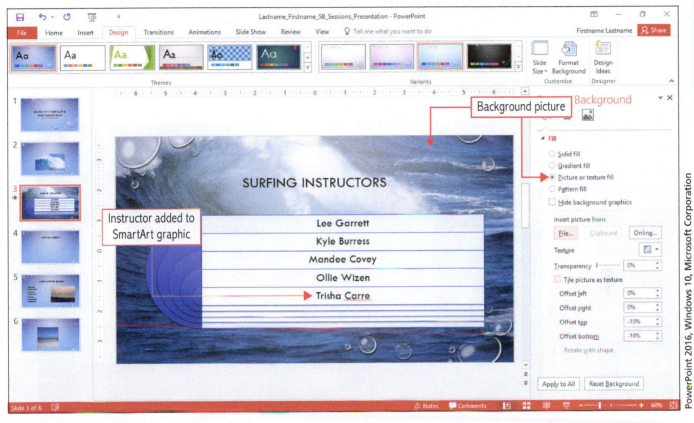

FIGURE 5.21

9 Select the **Hide Background Graphics** check box. **Close** ☒ the **Format Background** pane.

The graphic that was part of the original theme no longer displays at the top of the slide.

> **NOTE**   Formatting Slide Titles
>
> Generally, when designing a presentation, you want to maintain consistency in formats. For example, you should create one slide title format and apply that format to all slide titles in the presentation. Having a variety of slide titles can be distracting to your audience. In this project, however, because you are learning how to apply formatting, you will apply different formats to the various slide titles.

10 Select the slide title text—*Surfing Instructors*. On the mini toolbar, click the **Font Size button arrow** [60 ▾], and then click **72**. With the title selected, under **Drawing Tools**, click the **Format tab**, and then in the **WordArt Styles group**, click **More** [▾]. In the **WordArt Styles** gallery, in the third row, click the fourth style—**Fill - White, Outline - Accent 2, Hard Shadow - Accent 2**. In the **WordArt Styles group**, click **Text Outline**, and then in the third column, click the last color—**Ice Blue, Background 2, Darker 50%**. Click **Text Outline** again, point to **Weight**, and then click **2¼ pt**.

WordArt is a gallery of text styles with which you can create decorative effects, such as shadowed or 3-D text.

11 ▶ With the title still selected, on the **Format tab**, in the **Shape Styles group**, click **Shape Effects**. Point to **3-D Rotation**, and then under **Perspective**, locate and click **Perspective Contrasting Right**. Under **Drawing Tools**, on the **Format tab**, in the **Arrange group**, click the **Bring Forward button arrow**, and then click **Bring to Front**. Deselect the title and then compare your screen with Figure 5.22.

The title displays in front of the SmartArt graphic.

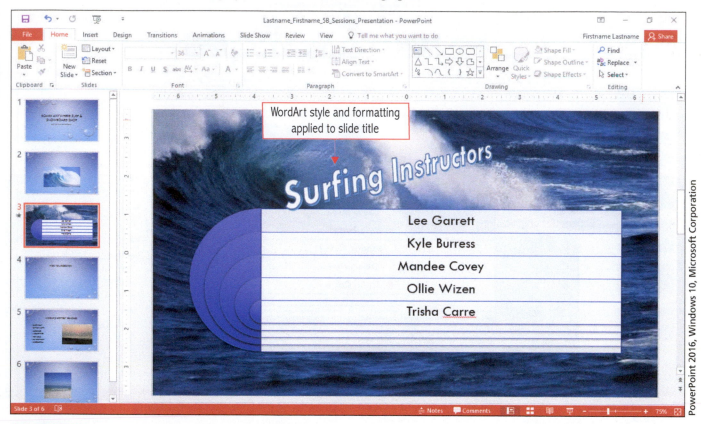

FIGURE 5.22

12 ▶ Display **Slide 5**, and then click the left placeholder. On the **Home tab**, in the **Paragraph group**, click **Convert to SmartArt** 📇. Locate and click **Vertical Block List**. Under **SmartArt Tools**, on the **Design tab**, in the **SmartArt Styles group**, click **More** ⏷, and then under **3-D**, locate and click **Metallic Scene**.

13 ▶ Click the **Animations tab**, and then in the **Animation group**, click **More** ⏷. Under **Entrance**, click **Wipe**. In the **Animation group**, click **Effect Options**, and then under **Sequence**, click **All at Once**.

14 ▶ If necessary, click the SmartArt graphic to select it. Click the **Format tab**, and then in the **Size group**, change the **Width** 🔲 to **9** and then press Enter.

The width of the SmartArt graphic is increased to 9 inches.

15 ▶ Click the picture. Click the **Format tab**, and then in the **Size group**, change the **Shape Width** 🔲 to **9.5** and then press Enter. Under **Picture Tools**, on the **Format tab**, in the **Arrange group**, click **Align** 🔳, and then click **Align Center**. In the **Arrange group**, click **Align** 🔳, and then click **Align Bottom**.

The picture is centered in the middle of the slide but covers the title and the SmartArt graphic.

16 ▶ Under **Picture Tools**, on the **Format tab**, in the **Arrange group**, click the **Send Backward button arrow**, and then click **Send to Back**. Compare your screen with Figure 5.23.

The picture displays in back of the title and SmartArt graphic.

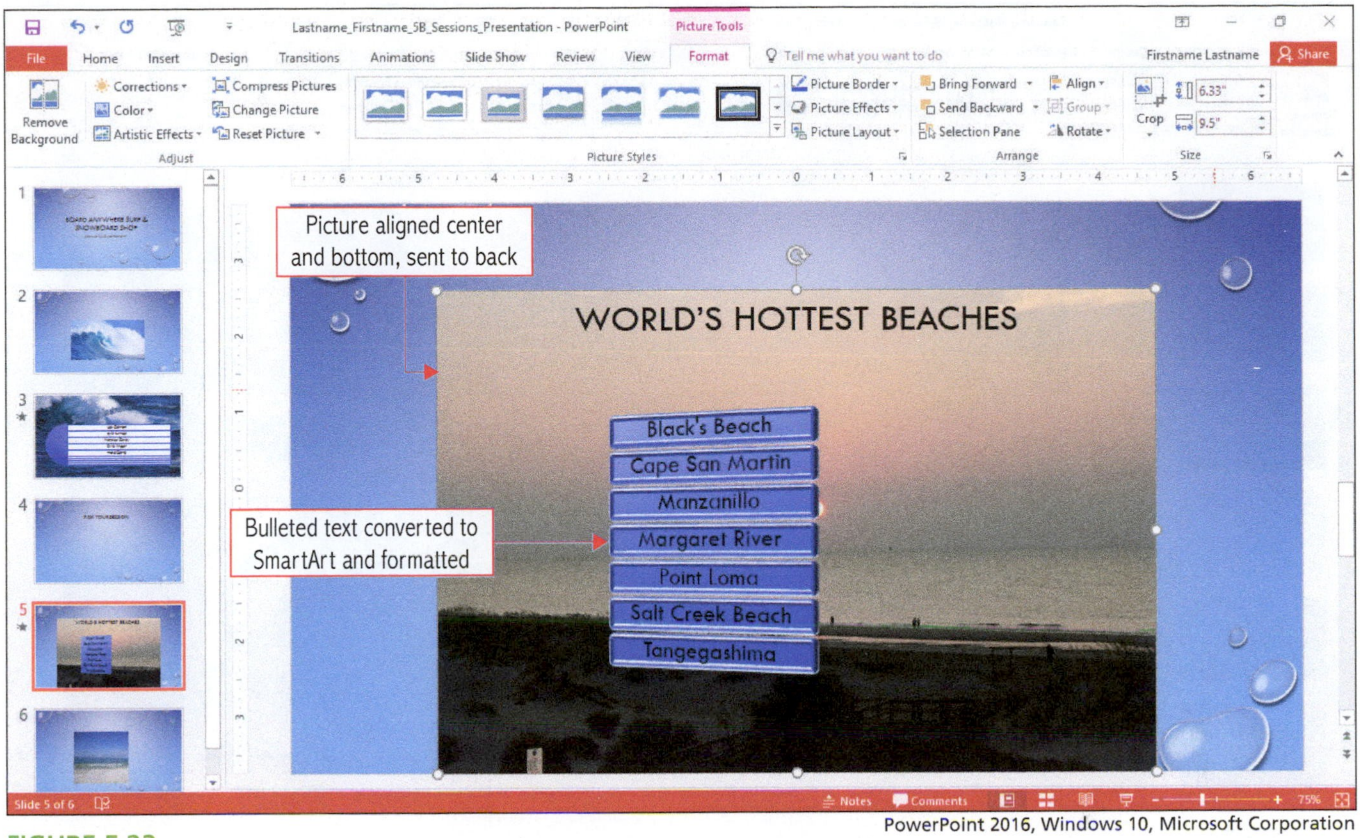

FIGURE 5.23

PowerPoint 2016, Windows 10, Microsoft Corporation

17 **Save** 🖫 the presentation.

Activity 5.10 │ Inserting Online Images

You can make your presentation more interesting and visually appealing by adding media, such as a *clip*—a single media file such as art, sound, animation or a movie.

1 Click **Slide 4**, and then in the right placeholder, click **Online Pictures** 🖼 to open the **Insert Pictures** dialog box. In the **Bing Image Search** box, type **breakers, wave** and then press Enter. Scroll through the search results, click the image displayed in Figure 5.24 or a similar image, and then click **Insert**. Compare your screen with Figure 5.24.

A keyword search returns images that may work for your presentation. Notice the results are licensed under *Creative Commons*. Although you can use these images for assignments, they cannot be used if you are profiting by using the images.

The image is inserted into the right placeholder.

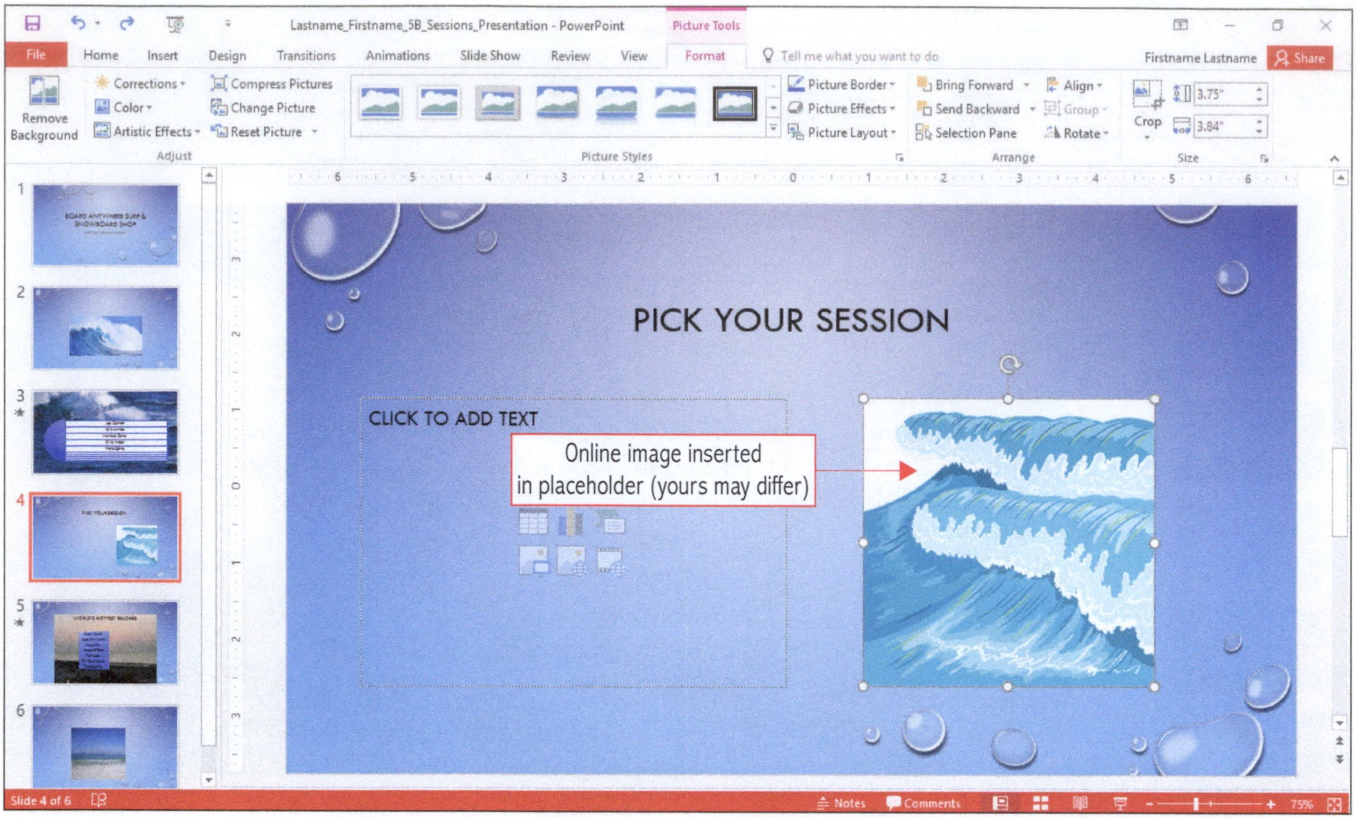

orensila/Fotolia; PowerPoint 2016, Windows 10, Microsoft Corporation

FIGURE 5.24

2 With the image selected, under **Picture Tools**, on the **Format tab**, in the **Size group**, change the **Shape Height** to **4** and then press Enter. In the **Arrange group**, click **Align**, and then click **Align Right**. In the **Arrange group**, click **Align** again, and then click **Align Middle**.

3 In the left placeholder, click **Insert SmartArt Graphic**. In the **Choose a SmartArt Graphic** dialog box, under **List**, locate and click **Vertical Box List**, and then click **OK**. In the SmartArt graphic, click the top box containing the word *Text*, type **2-day** and then click in the middle box. Type **3-day** click in the bottom box, and then type **4-day** Click the outer border of the graphic, and then, under **SmartArt Tools**, on the **Format tab**, change the height of the SmartArt to **4** Drag the SmartArt so that the top of the SmartArt aligns with the top of the image.

4 Click the border of the SmartArt graphic to select the entire graphic. Click the **Animations tab**, and then in the **Animation group**, click **More**. Under **Entrance**, click **Wipe**. In the **Animation group**, click **Effect Options**, and then under **Sequence**, click **All at Once**.

5 Click the **Transitions tab**, and then in the **Transition to This Slide group**, click **Fade**. In the **Transition to This Slide group**, click **Effect Options**, and then click **Through Black**. In the **Timing group**, set the **Duration** to **1.5** and then press Enter. In the **Timing group**, click **Apply To All**.

The Fade - Through Black transition is applied to all slides in the presentation; the transition time between two slides is 1.5 seconds.

6 Click the **Slide Show tab**, and then in the **Start Slide Show group**, click **From Beginning**. View your presentation.

You must click to display the SmartArt graphics because you added animation effects.

7 **Save** your presentation.

Activity 5.11 | Modifying Objects with Effects

You can change the look of an object by adding an effect, such as a reflection or glow.

1 Display **Slide 2**. Click the title placeholder, and then type **You Could Be Here!**

2 Select the title text. Under **Drawing Tools**, click the **Format tab**. In the **WordArt Styles group**, click **Text Effects**, point to **Glow**, and then under **Glow Variations**, in the third row, click the second effect—**Blue, 11 pt glow, Accent color 2**. In the **WordArt Styles group**, click **Text Effects**, point to **Transform**, and then under **Warp**, in the sixth row, click the second effect—**Deflate**. In the **Word Art Styles group**, click **Text Fill**, and then, under **Theme Colors**, click the first color, **White, Background 1**.

3 Click the picture. Under **Picture Tools**, click the **Format tab**, and then in the **Picture Styles group**, click **More**. Locate and click **Bevel Rectangle**. In the **Picture Styles group**, click **Picture Effects**, point to **Shadow**, and then under **Outer**, in the second row, click the second effect—**Offset Center**. Deselect the picture, and then compare your screen with Figure 5.25.

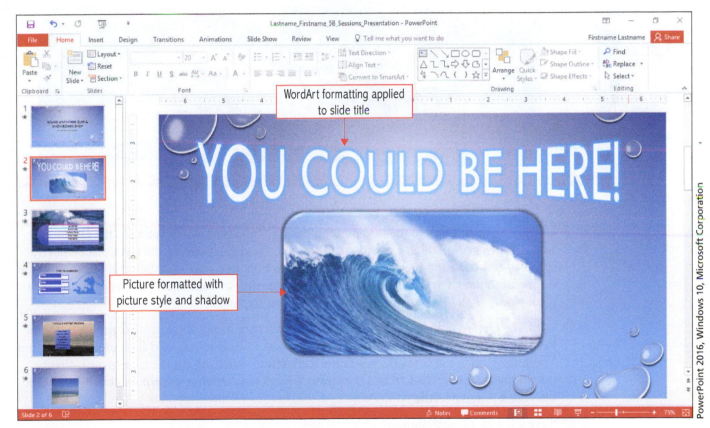

FIGURE 5.25

4 Click **Slide 5**, and then click the outer edge of the picture to select the picture. Under **Picture Tools**, click the **Format tab**. In the **Picture Styles group**, click **Picture Effects**, point to **Soft Edges**, and then click **10 Point**.

5 In the title placeholder, click to the left of *World's Hottest Beaches*, type **Join Us On The** and then press Spacebar. Select the entire title, and then on the mini toolbar, click the **Font Size button arrow**, and click **60**. Under **Drawing Tools**, click the **Format tab**. In the **WordArt Styles group**, click **Text Effects**, point to **Transform**, and then under **Warp**, in the second row, click the first effect—**Chevron Up**. Click **Text Effects** again, point to **Glow**, and then under **Glow Variations**, in the first row, click the first effect—**Blue,**

5 pt glow, Accent color 1. In the **Word Art Styles group**, click **Text Fill**, and then, under **Theme Colors**, click the first color, **White, Background 1**. Click on the slide to deselect the title, and then compare your screen with Figure 5.26.

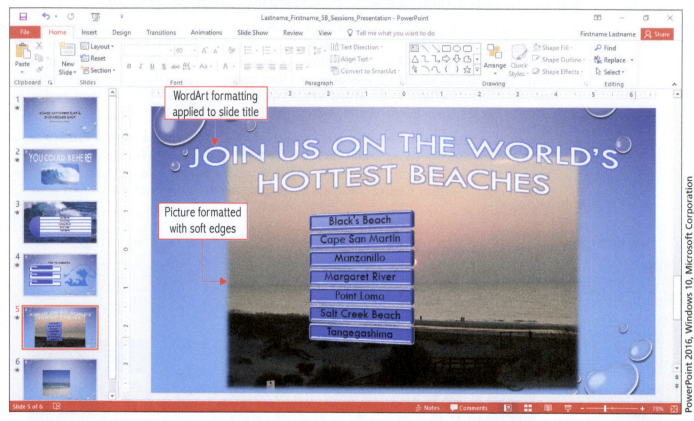

FIGURE 5.26

6 ▶ Display **Slide 6**. Click in the title placeholder, and then type **Contact Us** On the **Home tab**, in the **Slides group**, click **Layout**, and then click **Two Content**. In the right placeholder, type **949-555-0049** and then press Enter. Type **www.boardanywhere.biz** Select all the text in the right placeholder. On the **Home tab**, in the **Paragraph group**, click **Bullets** ☷ ▾, and then click **None**. In the **Paragraph group**, click **Align Right** ▤.

7 ▶ Click the picture in the left placeholder. Under **Picture Tools**, click the **Format tab**. In the **Picture Styles group**, click **Picture Effects**, point to **Reflection**, and then under **Reflection Variations**, click the first effect—**Tight Reflection, touching**. In the **Size group**, change the **Shape Width** ▤ to **4.75** and then press Enter. In the **Arrange group**, click **Align** ▤, and then click **Align Middle**.

8 ▶ **Save** ▣ your presentation.

Activity 5.12 | Using Slide Sorter View

When you are editing your presentation, you can arrange the slides in a different order easily by using the *Slide Sorter View*, which displays *thumbnails* of all of the slides in a presentation. Thumbnails are miniature images of presentation slides.

1 ▶ Click the **View tab**, and then in the **Presentation Views group**, click **Slide Sorter**. Click **Slide 2**, and, holding down the left mouse button, drag it down and to the left of **Slide 6**. Release your mouse button, and compare your screen with Figure 5.27.

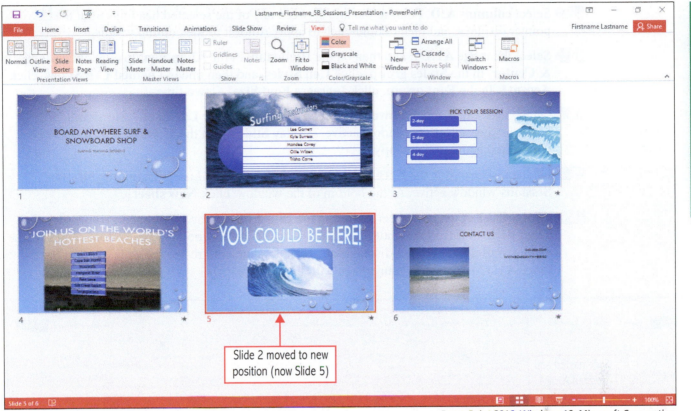

FIGURE 5.27

PowerPoint 2016, Windows 10, Microsoft Corporation

2 ▶ Drag **Slide 2** between **Slide 5** (*You Could Be Here!*) and **Slide 6** (*Contact Us*).

When you rearrange slides, all slides are renumbered based on their new positions.

3 ▶ Drag **Slide 3** to the right of **Slide 1** to make it the second slide in the presentation.

4 ▶ Click the **Slide Show tab**, and then in the **Start Slide Show group**, click **From Beginning**. View your presentation.

5 ▶ Click the **View tab**, and then in the **Presentation Views group**, click **Normal**.

6 ▶ Save 🖫 your presentation.

Objective 5 | Copy a PowerPoint Slide and Object into an Excel Workbook

If you create a SmartArt graphic or shape in PowerPoint, you can copy and then paste it into an Excel workbook. This saves you the time of recreating the object. Additionally, you can copy an entire PowerPoint slide and paste it into an Excel workbook.

Activity 5.13 | Copying and Pasting a PowerPoint Slide

In the following Activity, you will copy the Contact Information slide and paste it into an Excel workbook.

1 ▶ Start Excel. From your student files, open the file **i05B_Surf_Sessions**. Maximize ☐ the Excel window, if necessary. **Save** the file in your **Integrated Projects Chapter 5** folder with the file name **Lastname_Firstname_5B_Surf_Sessions**

2 Select **columns A:D**. Point to the line between any of the selected headings until the ⊞ pointer displays, and then double-click to apply AutoFit to the column widths.

3 Select the range **A1:D1**, and then on the **Home tab**, in the **Alignment group**, click **Merge & Center**. In the **Styles group**, click **Cell Styles**, and then under **Themed Cell Styles**, click **Accent1**. In the **Font group**, click **Increase Font Size** A⁺ two times.

4 On the taskbar, click the **PowerPoint icon** 📘 to make your **Lastname_Firstname_5B_Sessions_Presentation** window active. Display **Slide 6**. On the **Home tab**, in the **Clipboard group**, click **Copy** 📋.

5 On the taskbar, click the **Excel icon** 📗 to make your **Lastname_Firstname_5B_Surf_Sessions** window active. At the bottom of the window, click **New sheet** ⊕.

6 With cell **A1** of the new sheet active, on the **Home tab**, in the **Clipboard group**, click the upper portion of the **Paste** button. With the image selected, point to the bottom center sizing handle until the ⊞ pointer displays, and then drag down to resize the slide to cover the range **A1:J24**. Compare your screen with Figure 5.28.

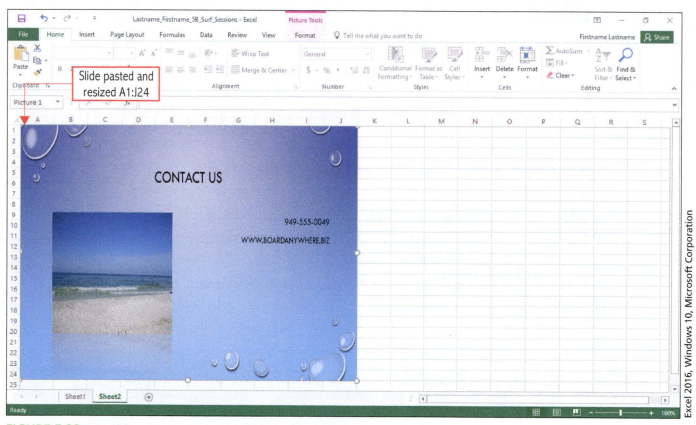

FIGURE 5.28

7 Click the **Page Layout tab**. In the **Page Setup group**, change the **Orientation** to **Landscape**.

8 **Save** 💾 your workbook.

Activity 5.14 | Copying and Pasting an Object

Once you create an object in one Microsoft Office application, you can copy and paste that object into a different application. In this Activity, you will copy a SmartArt graphic in PowerPoint and then paste it into an Excel workbook.

1 ▶ On the taskbar, click the **PowerPoint icon** 🅿️ to make your **Lastname_Firstname_5B_ Sessions_Presentation** window active. Click **Slide 5**—*Surfing Instructors*. Click the SmartArt graphic, and then click the border of the SmartArt graphic.

By clicking the border of an object, you select the entire object, not just a part of the object.

2 ▶ On the **Home tab**, in the **Clipboard group**, click **Copy** 📋.

3 ▶ On the taskbar, click the **Excel icon** 🅧 to make your **Lastname_Firstname_5B_Surf_ Sessions** window active. Click the **Sheet1 sheet tab**. Click cell **A62** to make it the active cell. On the **Home tab**, in the **Clipboard group**, click **Paste**.

The SmartArt graphic is pasted in Sheet1. The top left corner of the graphic is in cell A62.

4 ▶ Under **SmartArt** Tools, on the **Format tab**, in the **Size group**, click **Size**. In the **Shape Height** 📏 box, type **4** and in the **Shape Width** 📏 box, type **5** and then press ⏎. Scroll down to display the entire SmartArt object, and compare your screen with Figure 5.29.

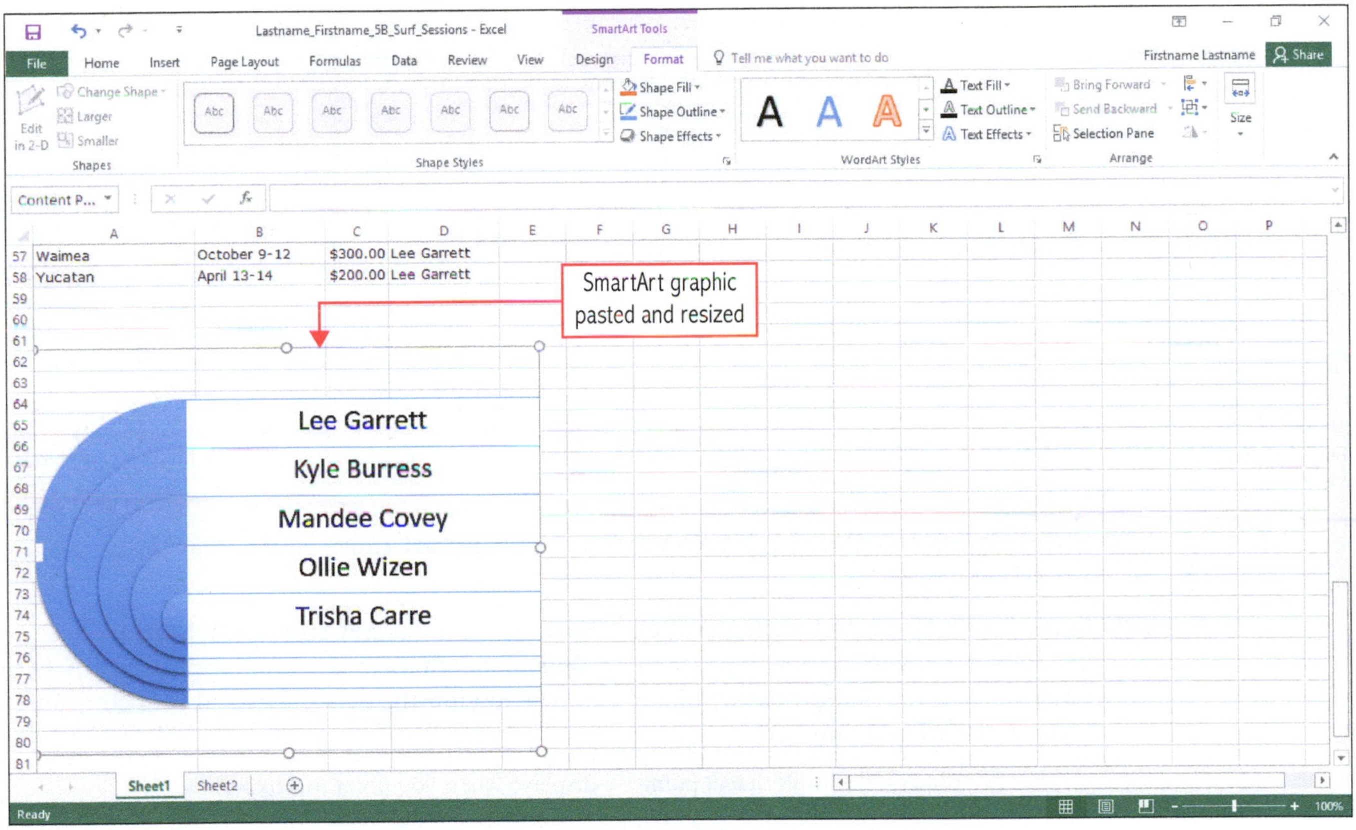

FIGURE 5.29

5 ▶ Right-click the **Sheet1 sheet tab**, and then on the shortcut menu, click **Rename**, type **Session Instructors** and then press ⏎. Right-click the **Sheet2 sheet tab**, and then on the shortcut menu, click **Rename**, type **Contact Info** and then press ⏎.

6 ▶ Save 💾 your workbook.

7 ▶ On the taskbar, click the **PowerPoint icon** 🅿️ to make your **Lastname_Firstname_5B_ Sessions_Presentation** window active. **Save** 💾 the presentation, and then **Close** ✖️ PowerPoint.

Hyperlinks are text, buttons, pictures, or other objects that, when clicked, access other sections of the current file, or another file, or a webpage. A hyperlink gives you immediate access to associated information in another location. The most common type of hyperlink is a *text link*—a link applied to a selected word or phrase. Text links usually display as blue underlined text.

Activity 5.15 | Inserting Hyperlinks in Excel

1 In the **Lastname_Firstname_5B_Surf_Sessions** workbook, click the **Session Instructors sheet tab**, click cell **A60**, type **Contact Information** and then on the **Formula Bar**, click **Enter** ☑.

2 Click the **Insert tab**, and then in the **Links group**, click **Hyperlink**. In the **Insert Hyperlink** dialog box, under **Link to**, click **Place in This Document**, and then compare your screen with Figure 5.30.

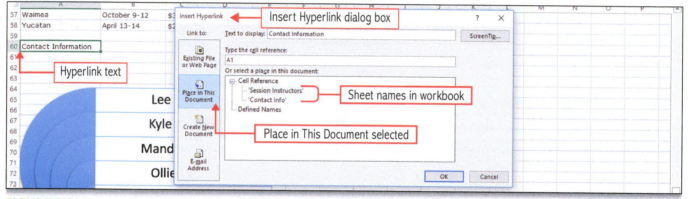

FIGURE 5.30

Excel 2016, Windows 10, Microsoft Corporation

3 Under **Or select a place in this document**, click **'Contact Info'**—the Contact Info worksheet name.

4 In the **Insert Hyperlink** dialog box, click **ScreenTip**. In the **Set Hyperlink ScreenTip** dialog box, click in the box, type **Go to the Contact Information sheet** and then click **OK** two times to close the dialog boxes. Point to cell **A60** to view the ScreenTip, and then compare your screen with Figure 5.31.

The 🖑 pointer—the **Link Select** pointer—displays when you point to a hyperlink.

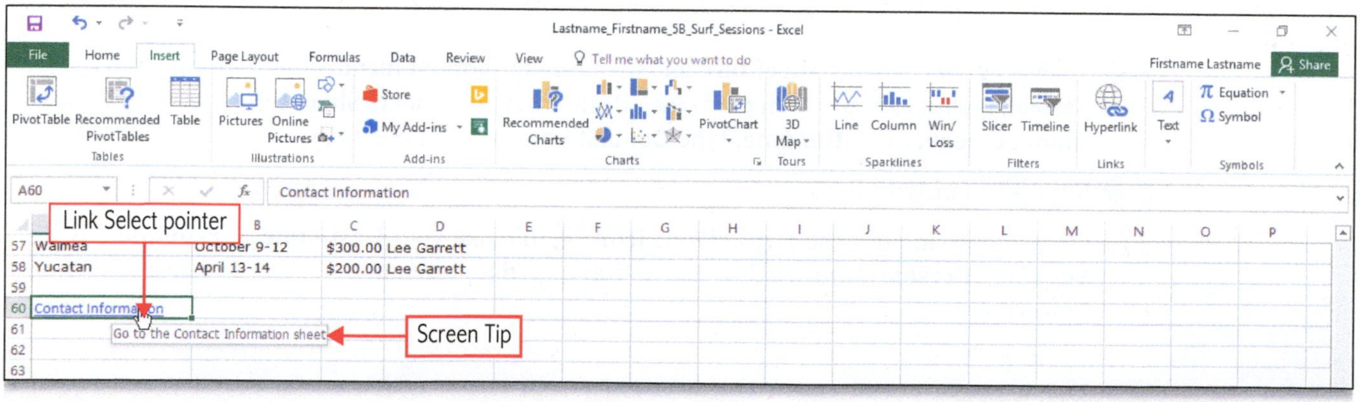

FIGURE 5.31

Excel 2016, Windows 10, Microsoft Corporation

5 ▶ In cell **A60**, click the hyperlink to make the Contact Info sheet the active worksheet.

6 ▶ On the **Contact Info** sheet, click cell **A27**. Type **Instructors** and then on the **Formula Bar**, click **Enter** ☑. On the **Insert tab**, in the **Links group**, click **Hyperlink**. In the **Insert Hyperlink** dialog box, under **Link to**, verify that **Place in This Document** is selected, and then under **Or select a place in this document**, click **'Session Instructors'**. Click **ScreenTip**. In the **Set Hyperlink ScreenTip** dialog box, under **ScreenTip text**, type **Go to the Session Instructors sheet** and then click **OK** two times to close the dialog boxes.

7 ▶ Point to cell **A27** to display the ScreenTip, and then click the hyperlink.

The Session Instructors sheet becomes the active worksheet.

8 ▶ On the **Session Instructors** sheet, click cell **A61**. Type **Sessions Presentation** and then on the **Formula Bar**, click **Enter** ☑.

9 ▶ On the **Insert tab**, in the **Links group**, click **Hyperlink**. In the **Insert Hyperlink** dialog box, under **Link to**, click **Existing File or Web Page**. In the **Look in** box, click the **arrow**, and if necessary, navigate to your **Integrated Projects Chapter 5** folder. Click your PowerPoint file name **Lastname_Firstname_5B_Sessions_Presentation**.

10 ▶ In the **Insert Hyperlink** dialog box, click **ScreenTip**. In the **Set Hyperlink ScreenTip** dialog box, under **ScreenTip text**, type **Go to our Sessions Presentation** and then click **OK** two times to close the dialog boxes. In cell **A61**, click the hyperlink to view the PowerPoint presentation.

ALERT!   **What if my PowerPoint presentation does not display?**

If your presentation does not display, click in cell A61, and then press ⌨Delete. Repeat Steps 8 through 10, being careful to follow all instructions exactly.

---

11 ▶ With your presentation displayed, click the **Slide Show tab**, and then in the **Start Slide Show group**, click **From Beginning**. View the presentation.

Activity 5.16 │ Inserting a Hyperlink from a PowerPoint Slide to an Excel Worksheet

1 ▶ In your PowerPoint presentation, if necessary, to display the rulers, click the View tab, and then in the Show group, select the Ruler check box. Display **Slide 3**. Click the **Insert tab**, and then in the **Illustrations group**, click **Shapes**. Under **Basic Shapes**, in the third row, click the first shape—**Bevel**.

2 ▶ Position the ⊞ pointer at **0 on the vertical ruler** and at **2 1/2 inches to the right of 0 on the horizontal ruler**. Hold down ⌨Shift, and drag down and to the right to draw a square that measures approximately 2 inches. Compare your screen with Figure 5.32.

FIGURE 5.32

PowerPoint 2016, Windows 10, Microsoft Corporation

3 Type **Click here to view session dates**

4 Click on the shape border to select the shape—surround it with a solid line. On the **Insert tab**, in the **Links group**, click **Hyperlink**. In the **Insert Hyperlink** dialog box, under **Link to**, verify that **Existing File or Web Page** is selected. In the Look in box, if necessary, navigate to your **Integrated Projects Chapter 5** folder, and then click the Excel file name **Lastname_Firstname_5B_Surf_Sessions**.

5 In the **Insert Hyperlink** dialog box, click **ScreenTip**. In the **Set Hyperlink ScreenTip** dialog box, under **ScreenTip text**, type **Go to a list of our Surf Sessions** and then click **OK** two times to close the dialog boxes.

6 With the shape still selected, under **Drawing Tools**, click the **Format tab**. If necessary, set the shape height and width to exactly 2″ and then press Enter. In the **Shape Styles group**, click **Shape Fill**, and then, in the fifth row, click the fifth color — **Blue, Accent 1, Darker 25%**. In the **Arrange group**, click **Align** 📭, and then click **Align Middle**.

7 Click the **Slide Show tab**, and then in the **Start Slide Show group**, click **From Current Slide**. In the slide, point to the shape to view the ScreenTip, and then click the shape to view the Excel workbook.

8 On the taskbar, point to the **PowerPoint** 📳 button to display two thumbnails of your presentation window—one in Normal view and the other in Slide Show view. In the **PowerPoint Slide Show** thumbnail, click **Close** ⊠, and then on the taskbar, click the **PowerPoint icon** 📳 to display your presentation in Normal view.

9 On the slide, click the picture to select it. Under **Picture Tools**, click the **Format tab**, and then in the **Adjust group**, click **Color**. Under **Recolor**, locate and click **Blue, Accent color 1 Light**.

After viewing a presentation in Slide Show view, it is typical to make minor adjustments to the slides.

10 Display **Backstage** view. In the lower right corner, click **Show All Properties**. Under **Related People**, be sure your name displays as the **Author**—change it if necessary. Click to the right of **Subject**, and then type your course name and section number. Click to the right of **Tags**, and then type **sessions, hyperlink, Excel**

11 On the left, click **Save** to redisplay the presentation window.

Objective 7 — Freeze Rows, Repeat Headings, and Insert Comments in Excel

A *pane* is a portion of a worksheet bounded by and separated from other portions by vertical and horizontal bars. You can *freeze panes*—a command that enables you to select one or more rows and columns and freeze (lock) them into place; the locked rows and columns become separate panes.

If you are printing a multiple-page worksheet, you can display row or column titles on every page by specifying the rows or columns that you want to repeat. This makes it easier for the reader to identify the information.

Activity 5.17 | Freezing Excel Rows

1 On the taskbar, display your Excel workbook, and then be sure **Session Instructors** is the active sheet.

2 Press Ctrl + Home to make cell **A1** the active cell. Scroll down until **row 40** displays at the top of your Excel window, and notice that all the identifying column titles are out of view.

3 ▸ Press Ctrl + Home, and then in the **row heading area**, click to select **row 4**. On the **View tab**, in the **Window group**, click **Freeze Panes**, and then on the list, click **Freeze Panes**. Click any cell to deselect the row, and then notice that a line displays along the upper border of **row 4**.

By selecting row 4, the rows above—rows 1 through 3—are frozen in place and will not move as you scroll down.

4 ▸ Scroll down to bring **row 40** into view again. Notice that rows 1 through 3 continue to display—they are frozen in place. Compare your screen with Figure 5.33.

Use the Freeze Panes feature when you have long or wide worksheets.

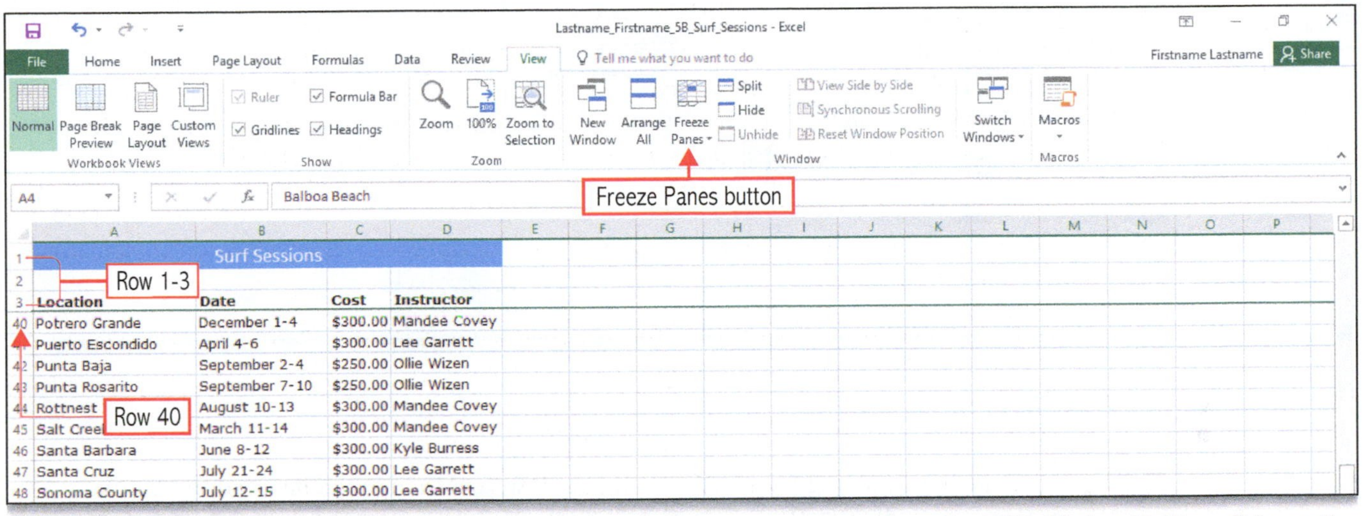

FIGURE 5.33

Excel 2016, Windows 10, Microsoft Corporation

5 ▸ In the **Window group**, click **Freeze Panes**, and then click **Unfreeze Panes** to unlock all rows and columns.

6 ▸ Press Ctrl + Home. **Save** 🖫 your workbook.

More Knowledge **Freeze Columns or Freeze Both Rows and Columns**

You can freeze columns that you want to remain in view on the left of the worksheet. Select the column to the right of the column(s) that you want to remain in view while scrolling to the right, and then click the Freeze Panes command. You can also use the command to freeze both rows and columns; click a *cell* to freeze the rows *above* the cell and the columns to the *left* of the cell.

Activity 5.18 │ Repeating Titles on Multiple Pages

Freezing rows and columns makes it easier to work with a large worksheet on the screen; however, it does not affect the printed pages. To repeat column titles and row titles on every page, you must use the Print Titles command.

1 ▸ Display **Backstage** view, and then click the **Print tab** to display the Print Preview. Below the **Print Preview**, in the navigation bar, click **Next Page** ▸ to display Page 2.

Notice that no column titles display at the top of Page 2.

2 ▸ In the upper left, click ⬅ to redisplay the workbook window. On the **Page Layout tab**, in the **Page Setup group**, click **Print Titles** to display the **Sheet tab** of the **Page Setup** dialog box. Click in the **Rows to repeat at top** box.

3 ▸ In your worksheet, point to the **row 1** header, and then drag down to select **row 1** through **row 3**. Compare your screen with Figure 5.34.

$1:$3 displays in the Rows to repeat at top box, which will display row 1 through row 3 on all the pages of this worksheet.

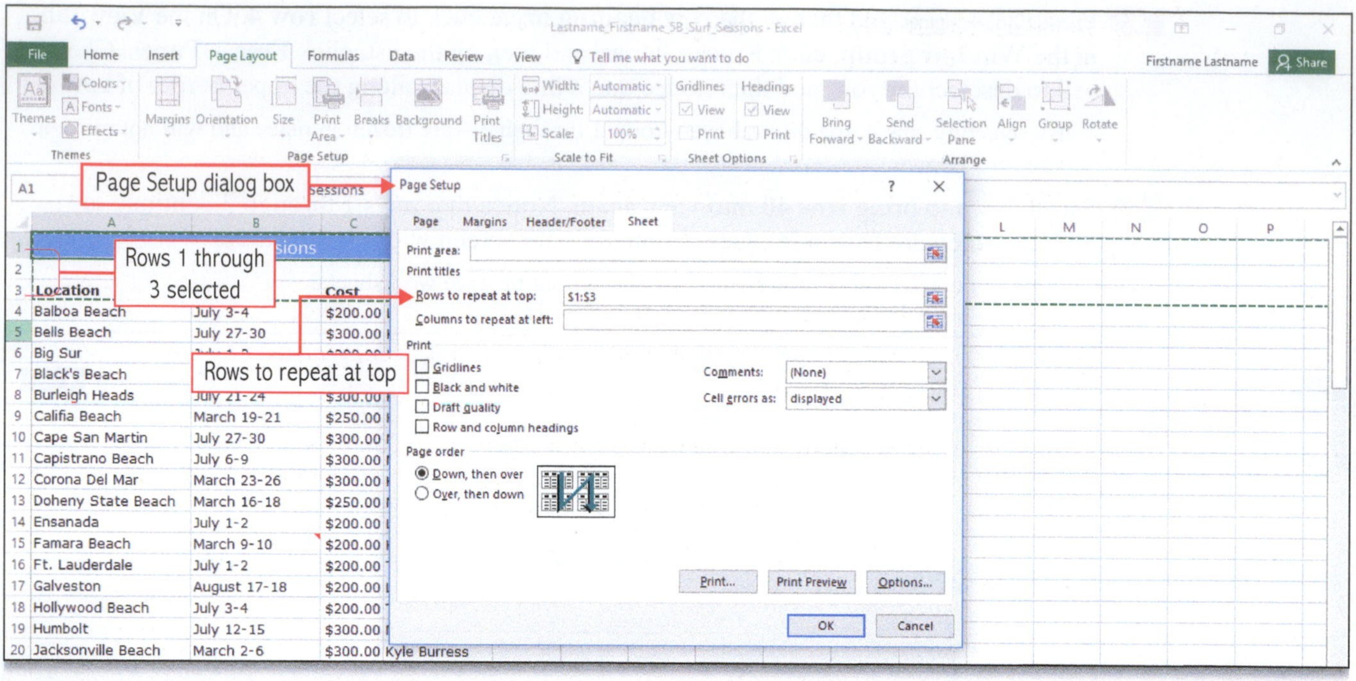

FIGURE 5.34

> **4** In the **Page Setup** dialog box, click **Print Preview**, and then in the navigation bar, click **Next Page** ▶ to display Page 2. Notice that rows 1:3 display at the top of Page 2. Compare your screen with Figure 5.35.

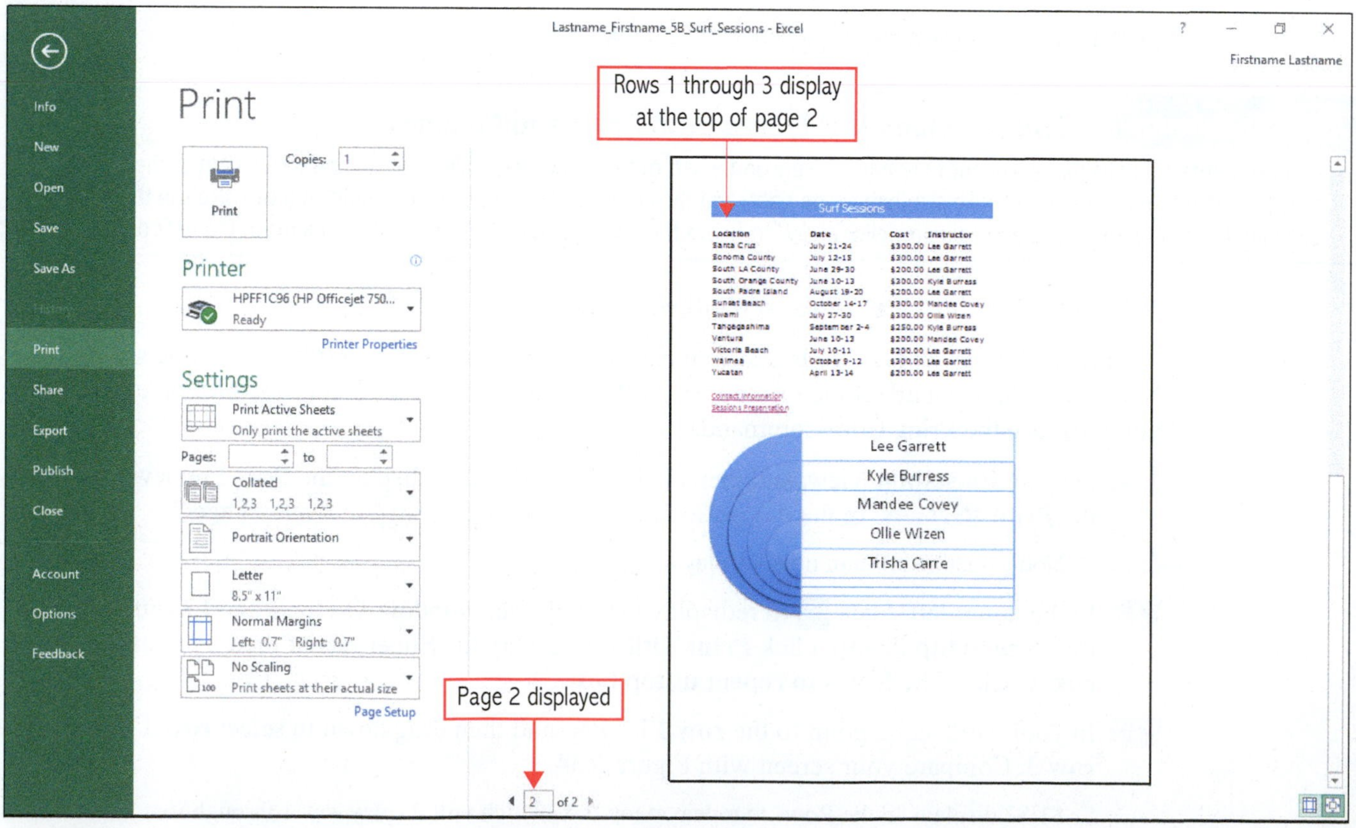

FIGURE 5.35

5 ▶ In the upper left, click ⬅ to redisplay the workbook window. Click the **Home tab**, and then **Save** 🖫 your workbook.

Activity 5.19 | Inserting and Editing Comments

If more than one person is working on a file, you can insert comments to communicate with each other. Recall a comment is a note that can be inserted from the Review tab. You can edit comments and also delete comments when they are no longer needed.

1 ▶ On the **Session Instructors** sheet, click cell **A15**.

2 ▶ With cell **A15** selected, point to cell **B15** to display a comment text box. Compare your screen with Figure 5.36.

In addition to the comment, the name of the person who wrote the comment displays in the comment text box. A red triangle displays in the top right corner of cell B15 to indicate that the cell has a comment attached to it. Notice that cell B24 also has a comment inserted. When you point to a cell containing a red triangle, the attached comment displays.

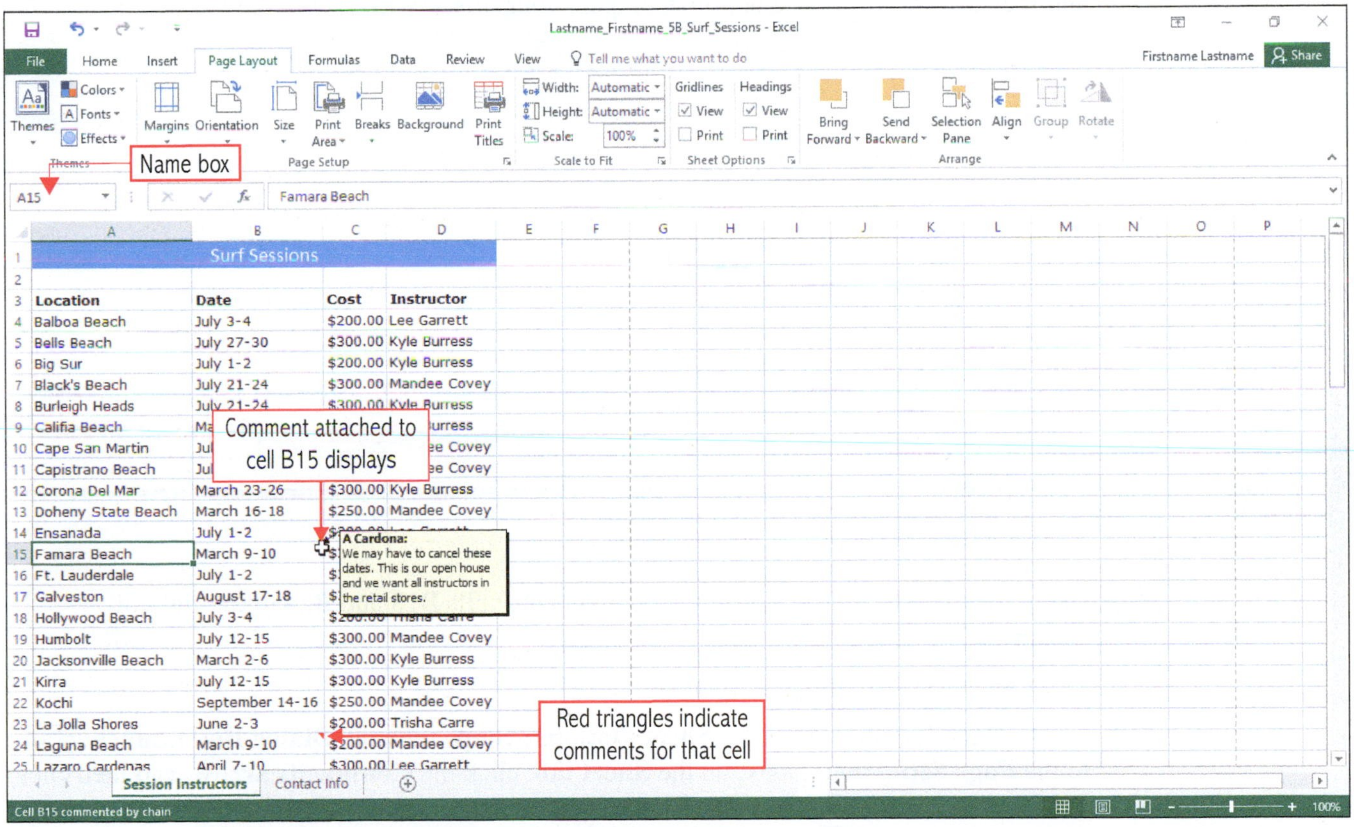

FIGURE 5.36

3 ▶ In the upper right, to the left of the **Formula Bar**, click in the **Name Box**, type **b39** and then press **Enter**. On the **Review tab**, in the **Comments group**, click **New Comment**. In the comment text box, type **Trisha cannot attend on these dates. Check with Kyle to see if he wants this session.**

The **Name Box** is an element of the Excel window that displays the name of the selected cell, table, chart, or object. It is useful to move to a location on the worksheet that is out of view—instead of scrolling.

NOTE Displaying a Name in the Comment Text Box

The User Name automatically displays at the top of the comment text box. The name in your comment text box will vary. If you are using your own computer, your name may display.

4 Click in an empty cell to deselect the comment. Click the **Name Box**, type **d57**, and then press Enter. On the **Review tab**, in the **Comments group**, click **New Comment**. In the comment text box, type **Thank Lee for working on his birthday.**

5 Click cell **B39**, and then on the **Review tab**, in the **Comments group**, click **Edit Comment**. In the comment text box, select *Kyle*, type **Ollie** and then deselect the cell to close the comment. Point to cell **B39** to verify the change.

6 In the **Comments group**, click **Show All Comments**, and notice that the comment covers the data in columns C and D.

7 Click the comment attached to cell **B39**. Point to the comment text box border—not a sizing handle—until the pointer displays. Drag the comment text box to the right of **column D**, and then release the mouse button. Compare your screen with Figure 5.37.

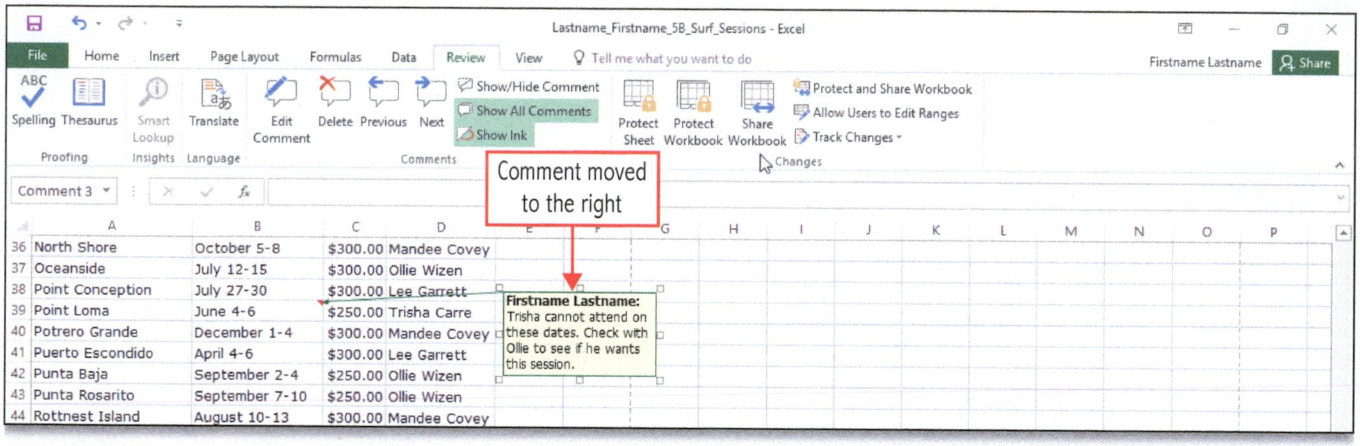

Excel 2016, Windows 10, Microsoft Corporation

FIGURE 5.37

8 Using the same technique, move the comments in cells **B15** and **B24** to the right of **column D**.

All four comments display in columns E and F.

9 On the **Page Layout tab**, in the **Sheet Options group**, click the **Dialog Box Launcher**. In the **Page Setup** dialog box, on the **Sheet tab**, click the **Comments arrow**, and then click **At end of sheet**. Click **Print Preview**, and then below the **Print Preview**, in the navigation bar, click **Next Page** two times.

The comments display on a separate page—Page 3.

10 In the upper left, click to return to the worksheet window. With the **Session Instructors** sheet displayed, hold down Ctrl, and then click the **Contact Info sheet tab**. Click the **Insert tab**, and then in the **Text group**, click **Header & Footer**. On the **Design tab**, in the **Navigation group**, click **Go to Footer**. In the **Footer** area, click just above the word *Footer*, and then in the **Header & Footer Elements group**, click **File Name**. Click in any cell in the workbook to exit the footer. On the right side of the status bar, click **Normal**, and then press Ctrl + Home.

11 Right-click the **Contact Info sheet tab**, and then on the shortcut menu, click **Ungroup Sheets**.

12 Display **Backstage** view. On the left, click **Info**, and then in the lower right corner, click **Show All Properties**. Under **Related People**, be sure your name displays as the **Author**—change it if necessary. Click to the right of **Subject**, and then type your course name and section number. Click to the right of **Tags**, and then type **sessions, hyperlink**

13 Save 💾 your workbook. If your instructor directs you to submit your files electronically, **Close** ⊠ Excel, **Close** ⊠ PowerPoint, and then go to Step 16.

14 To print your workbook, click the **File tab**, and then on the left, click the **Print tab**. Under **Settings**, click the **Print Active Sheets arrow**, and then click **Print Entire Workbook**. Click **Print**, and then **Close** ⊠ Excel.

15 To print your presentation, click the **File tab**, and then click the **Print tab**. Under **Settings**, click the **Full Page Slides arrow**, and then under **Handouts**, click **6 Slides Horizontal**. Click **Print**, and then **Close** ⊠ PowerPoint.

16 Submit your printed or electronic files as directed by your instructor.

END | You have completed Project 5B

END OF CHAPTER

SUMMARY

By using charts in Excel, the data is easier to visualize than simply looking at large data-filled worksheets. In a worksheet, you can freeze rows and columns, repeat headings on multiple printed pages, and insert comments. The copy and paste commands enable you to insert an object in another location or file. In PowerPoint, you can create a professional-looking presentation by adding slide transitions and by inserting and formatting SmartArt graphics, images, and shapes. You can create hyperlinks to access related information within the current file or in another file. Features such as the Document Inspector and Mark as Final help you polish your file before sharing it with others.

KEY TERMS

MATCHING

Match each term in the second column with its correct definition in the first column by writing the letter of the term on the blank line in front of the correct definition.

_____ 1. An Excel chart type that is useful for showing data changes over a period of time or for illustrating comparisons among items.

_____ 2. An Excel chart type that shows the relationship of each part to a whole.

_____ 3. The area along the bottom of a chart that identifies the categories of data.

_____ 4. The numerical scale on the left side of a chart that shows the range of numbers for the data points.

_____ 5. The overall visual look of a chart in terms of its graphic effects, colors, and backgrounds.

_____ 6. The combination of chart elements that can be displayed in a chart such as a title, legend, labels for the columns, and the table of charted cells.

_____ 7. A chart element that identifies the patterns or colors that are assigned to the categories in the chart.

_____ 8. The identification of a specific cell by its intersecting column letter and row number.

_____ 9. The motion effect that occurs in Slide Show view when you move from one slide to the next during a presentation.

_____ 10. A Microsoft Office feature that enables you to find and remove hidden data and personal information in a file.

_____ 11. A Microsoft Office feature that changes the file to a read-only file—typing and editing commands are turned off.

_____ 12. A visual or sound effect that is added to an object or text on a slide.

_____ 13. In PowerPoint, miniature images of presentation slides.

_____ 14. Text, buttons, pictures, or other objects that, when clicked, access other sections of the current file, another file, or a webpage.

_____ 15. An element of the Excel window that displays the name of the selected cell, table, chart, or object.

A Animation

B Cell reference

C Chart layout

D Chart style

E Column chart

F Document Inspector

G Hyperlinks

H Legend

I Mark as Final

J Name Box

K Pie chart

L Slide transition

M Thumbnails

N x-axis

O y-axis

MULTIPLE CHOICE

Circle the correct answer.

1. A numerical scale on the left side of a chart that shows the range of numbers is the:
   A. category axis   **B.** value range   **C.** value axis

2. The value that originates in a worksheet cell and that is represented in a chart by a data marker is a:
   A. data point   **B.** data value   **C.** data series

3. The action of pulling out one or more pie slices from a pie chart for emphasis is:
   A. expanding   **B.** exploding   **C.** extracting

4. The identification of a specific cell by its intersecting column letter and row number is the:
   A. cell address   **B.** data address   **C.** data reference

5. A cell reference that refers to cells by their fixed position in a worksheet is:
   A. a relative cell reference   **B.** a relative data reference   **C.** an absolute cell reference

6. In Excel, a note that you add from the Review tab and is generally not printed is a:
   A. comment   **B.** message   **C.** note

7. Predefined graphics included with Microsoft Office or downloaded from the Internet are called:
   A. SmartArt   **B.** clip art   **C.** WordArt

8. A presentation view that displays thumbnails of all of the slides in a presentation is:
   A. Print Preview   **B.** Slide view   **C.** Slide Sorter view

9. In Excel, a portion of a worksheet bounded by and separated from other portions by vertical and horizontal bars is a:
   A. panel   **B.** pane   **C.** window

10. The command that enables you to select one or more rows and columns and lock them into place is:
    A. Freeze Panes   **B.** Lock Panes   **C.** Split Panes

Mastering Integration | Project 5C Snowboarding Bags

In the following Mastering Integration project, you will create charts in an Excel workbook and copy charts and data from Excel into a PowerPoint presentation. Your completed files will look similar to Figure 5.38.

PROJECT FILES

For Project 5C, you will need the following files:

i05C_Snowboarding_Bags

i05C_Bags_Presentation

You will save your files as:

Lastname_Firstname_5C_Snowboarding_Bags

Lastname_Firstname_5C_Bags_Presentation

PROJECT RESULTS

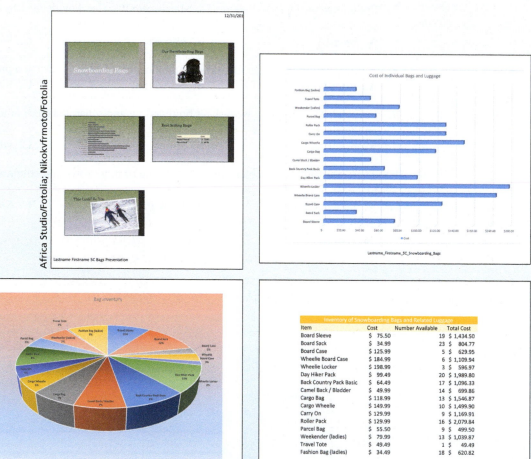

Africa Studio/Fotolia; Nikokvfrmoto/Fotolia

FIGURE 5.38

(Project 5C Snowboarding Bags continues on the next page)

Mastering Integration   Project 5C Snowboarding Bags (continued)

1 Start Excel. Open the Excel file **i05C_Snowboarding_Bags**. **Save** the file in the **Integrated Projects Chapter 5** folder with the file name **Lastname_Firstname_5C_Snowboarding Bags**

2 In cell **D2**, type **Total Cost** In cell **D3**, type the formula **=b3*c3** and then copy the formula down through cell **D18**.

3 Select columns **A:D**, and then adjust the column width automatically to accommodate the widest item in each column. Select cells **A1:D1**. Apply the cell style **Accent4**, and then **Merge & Center** the selected cells. Select cells **A2:D2**, and then apply the cell style **20% - Accent4**.

4 Select cells **A2:B18**. Insert a **3-D Clustered Bar** chart, and then move the chart to a chart sheet, with the sheet name **Cost Chart** Apply the **Quick Layout 2**, right-click the **Legend**, and then click **Delete**. Format the **Vertical (Category) Axis** as **Bold**. Change the **Chart Title** to **Cost of Individual Bags and Luggage**

5 **Rename** the **Sheet1 tab** as **Inventory Cost** Insert the file name as a field in the footer of all worksheets. **Ungroup Sheets**, and then return to Normal view.

6 Select cells **A3:A18** and **C3:C18**, and then insert a **3-D Pie** chart. Move the chart to a chart sheet, with the sheet name **Available Bags** Apply the **Chart Style 6** and the **Quick Layout 1**. Format the **Series 1 Data Labels** as **Bold**. Format the **Chart Area** with **Gradient fill** and the **Color** as **Orange, Accent 2, Lighter 40%**. Insert a **Chart Title** above the chart with the text **Bag Inventory**

7 Click the **Inventory Cost sheet tab**, and then press Ctrl + Home. Display **Backstage** view. Click **Properties**, and then click **Show All Properties**. Under **Author** box, type your first name and last name; in the **Subject** box, type your course name and section number, and then in the **Tags** box, type **inventory, charts** **Save** the workbook.

8 Start PowerPoint. Open the file **i05C_Bags_Presentation**. Save the file in the **Integrated Projects Chapter 5** folder with the file name **Lastname_Firstname_5C_Bags_Presentation**. Insert the file name as

a footer in the **Notes and Handouts tab**, add a **Fixed Date**, and **Apply to All**.

9 Click **Slide 2**, and then insert a new *Slide 3* with the **Blank** layout. **Copy** the **Cost Chart** from the Excel workbook, and then **Paste** it in the new blank **Slide 3**.

10 Insert a new *Slide 4* with the **Title Only** layout. Add the title **Best Selling Bags** In the Excel file **Lastname_Firstname_5C_Snowboarding_Bags**, on the **Inventory Cost** sheet, copy cells **A2:B4**. **Paste Link** the cells into the new **Slide 4** of the presentation. Change the **Height** of the linked object to **1.5** and then **Align** the object in the **Middle** and **Center** of the slide.

11 Click **Slide 1**. Apply the design theme **View**. Change the **Background** to **Gradient**, **Olive Green, Accent 3, Darker 25%**, and then **Apply to All**.

12 In the Excel file **Lastname_Firstname_5C_Snowboarding_Bags**, on the **Inventory Cost** sheet, press Esc, and then change the number in cell **B3** to **75.5** Press Ctrl + Home, **Save** the Excel workbook, and then **Close** Excel. Verify the change has been made on Slide 4 of your presentation.

13 On **Slide 5**, change the **Height** of the picture to **5**. Drag the picture to the top right so the top right corner is at the **5.5 inches to right of the 0 on the horizontal ruler and at 2 inches above 0 on the vertical ruler**. Change the **Picture Style** to **Rotated, White**.

14 Click **Slide 1**. Apply the **Slide Transition** using the **Wipe** transition, change the **Duration** to **1.50**, and then **Apply to All** slides.

15 Display **Backstage** view. Click **Show All Properties**. Under **Author**, type your first name and last name; in the **Subject** box, type your course name and section number, and then in the **Tags** box, type **Excel charts, linked** In **Backstage** view, **Mark as Final**, and then click **OK** two times. **Save** the presentation, and then **Close** PowerPoint.

16 Submit your printed or electronic files as directed by your instructor.

> **END | You have completed Project 5C**

Apply 5B skills from these Objectives:

4 Create and Modify Illustrations in PowerPoint

5 Copy a PowerPoint Slide and Object into an Excel Workbook

6 Create Hyperlinks

7 Freeze Rows, Repeat Headings, and Insert Comments in Excel

In the following Mastering Integration project, you will edit a PowerPoint presentation by applying a theme, inserting SmartArt, modifying graphics, and creating a hyperlink to an Excel workbook. In the workbook, you will paste a PowerPoint object, create titles on multiple pages, and insert comments. Your completed files will look similar to Figure 5.39.

PROJECT FILES

For Project 5D, you will need the following files:

i05D_Tee_Shirts
i05D_Shirt_Presentation

You will save your files as:

Lastname_Firstname_5D_Tee_Shirts
Lastname_Firstname_5D_Shirt_Presentation

PROJECT RESULTS

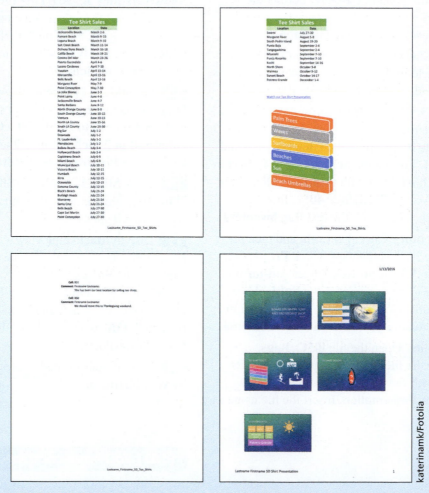

katerinamk/Fotolia

FIGURE 5.39

(Project 5D Tee Shirts continues on the next page)

1 Start PowerPoint. Open the file **i05D_Shirt_Presentation**. **Save** the file in the **Integrated Projects Chapter 5** folder with the file name **Lastname_Firstname_5D_Shirt_Presentation** Add the name of the file on the **Handouts** footer, and then **Apply to All**. Apply the theme **Celestial**, and select the second **Variant**.

2 On **Slide 3**, in the left placeholder, click **Convert to SmartArt Graphic** to insert the graphic **Vertical Bullet List**. Format the object **Width** to **4** and the **Height** to **4** Change the **SmartArt Style** to **Brick Scene** and **Change Colors** to **Colorful – Accent Colors**. Animate the graphic with the **Fade** animation, **All At Once**.

3 Insert a new **Slide 4** with the **Title and Content** layout. In the title placeholder, type **Tee Shirt Designs** In the lower placeholder, click **Online Pictures**. Search for **surfboard waves** and insert an appropriate picture. Change the picture **Height** to **6** and then **Align Center** and **Align Middle**.

4 On **Slide 2**, add the title **Surf's Up!** Select the title, and then apply the **WordArt Style—Fill – White, Text 1, Outline – Background 1, Hard Shadow – Accent 1**. Click **Text Effects**, and then under **Bevel**, apply the **Cool Slant** effect. Change the **Font Size** to **66**. **Center** the title in the placeholder. In the left placeholder, insert the SmartArt graphic **Vertical Box List**. In the graphic, type the names of the beaches **Margaret River**, **Ventura**, and **Kirra** Add the **Slide Transition—Uncover** Apply the **From Right Effect Option**. Change the **Duration** to **1.5** and then **Apply to All**.

5 Start Excel. Open the file **i05D_Tee_Shirts**. **Save** the file in the **Integrated Projects Chapter 5** folder with the file name **Lastname_Firstname_5D_Tee_Shirts** Insert the file name as a field in the footer. Return to Normal view. **Rename** the **Sheet1 tab** as **Shirt Locations**

6 Adjust the column width of **columns A:B** to display all data. Select cells **A1:B1**, and then apply the **Cell**

Style—Accent 6. **Merge & Center** the cells, apply **Bold** format, and then change the **Font Size** to **20**. Select cells **A2:B2**, apply the **Cell Style—40% - Accent6**, apply **Bold** format, and then **Center** the cells.

7 In cell **A62**, type **Watch our Tee Shirt Presentation** and then **Insert** a **Hyperlink** to your file **Lastname_Firstname_5D_Shirt_Presentation**. Add a **ScreenTip** with the text **See our great tee shirt designs.**

8 Make the PowerPoint presentation the active window. On **Slide 5**, click the **Sun** shape, and then insert a hyperlink to the Excel file **Lastname_Firstname_5D_Tee_Shirts**. In the left placeholder, select the SmartArt object. Change the picture **Width** to **5** and apply a **Bevel—Angle**.

9 On **Slide 3**, **Copy** the SmartArt graphic. Make the Excel window active, and then in cell **A66**, **Paste** the SmartArt object. Change the **Height** of the graphic to **4** and the **Width** to **3** Click cell **B31**, and then **Insert** the **Comment This has been our best location for selling tee shirts.** Click cell **B50**, and then **Insert** the **Comment We should move this to Thanksgiving weekend.**

10 Set the comments to print **As displayed on sheet**. Format the **Print Titles** so the **Rows to repeat at top** include row 1 and row 2. Press Ctrl + Home. Display **Backstage** view. Click **Show All Properties**. In the **Author** box, type your first name and last name; in the **Subject** box, type your course name and section number; and then in the **Tags** box, type **hyperlink, comments** Save the workbook, and then **Close** Excel.

11 In your presentation, click **Slide 1**. Display **Backstage** view. Click **Show All Properties**. In the **Author** box, type your first name and last name; in the **Subject** box, type your course name and section number; and then in the **Tags** box, type **Excel hyperlink Save** your presentation, and then **Close** PowerPoint.

12 Submit your printed or electronic files as directed by your instructor.

END | You have completed Project 5D

Apply a combination of the 5A and 5B skills.

GO! Solve It   Project 5E Board Logos

PROJECT FILES

For Project 5E, you will need the following files:

i05E_Board_Logos
i05E_Logos_Presentation

You will save your files as:

Lastname_Firstname_5E_Board_Logos
Lastname_Firstname_5E_Logos_Presentation

J. R. Kass, one of the owners of Board Anywhere Surf and Snowboard Shop, wants to commission an artist to create new board logos for the company. Mr. Kass has created an Excel workbook that lists the artists and their commission prices. He has also narrowed the field down to four logos and placed them in a PowerPoint presentation. He has asked you to complete both files.

Open the file **i05E_Board_Logos**. Adjust the column widths so that all data displays and apply a cell style to the title. Create a chart to display the Last Name and Commission on a new sheet with an applicable name. Format the chart using a chart layout and a chart style. Insert at least two comments on the Artists worksheet. Rename the data sheet with a descriptive name. Insert the file name in the footer of all worksheets. Save the file as **Lastname_Firstname_5E_Board_Logos** Open the file **i05E_Logos_Presentation**. Save the presentation as **Lastname_Firstname_5E_Logos_Presentation** Insert the file name in the handouts footer. In the presentation, apply a design theme. Add titles containing the names of artists to the slides; select any names from the Excel workbook. For each logo, adjust the size or add an effect. Insert a new slide at the end of the presentation, and then Paste link the Excel chart, and resize it as necessary. In both files, add appropriate information to the Properties. Submit your printed or electronic files as directed by your instructor.

Performance Level

Performance Criteria	Exemplary: You consistently applied the relevant skills.	Proficient: You sometimes, but not always, applied the relevant skills.	Developing: You rarely or never applied the relevant skills.
Create and format chart in 5E_Board_Logos worksheet	Chart is created, moved to its own sheet, and formatted accurately	Chart is created, but there are two or fewer errors in placement or formatting	Chart is not created, or it is not moved and formatted
Insert two comments in 5E_Board_Logos_worksheet	Two comments are inserted and placed accurately in the worksheet	Two comments are inserted and placed with two or fewer errors	Comments are not inserted in the worksheet
Format 5E_Logos_Presentation	Formatting is applied to the presentation: Design theme, titles added, images resized or formatted accurately	Table is exported and modifications are made, but there are two or fewer errors	Table is not exported and/or modifications are not made
Insert a new slide in 5E_Logos_Presentation with link to Excel chart	New slide inserted, and Excel chart is linked to the presentation accurately	New slide inserted, and Excel chart is placed with two or fewer errors	New slide is not inserted

END | You have completed Project 5E

OUTCOMES-BASED ASSESSMENTS (CRITICAL THINKING)

RUBRIC

The following outcomes-based assessments are open-ended assessments. That is, there is no specific correct result; your result will depend on your approach to the information provided. Make Professional Quality your goal. Use the following scoring rubric to guide you in how to approach the problem and then to evaluate how well your approach solves the problem.

The *criteria*—Software Mastery, Content, Format and Layout, and Process—represent the knowledge and skills you have gained that you can apply to solving the problem. The *levels of performance*—Professional Quality, Approaching Professional Quality, or Needs Quality Improvements—help you and your instructor evaluate your result.

	Your completed project is of Professional Quality if you:	Your completed project is approaching Professional Quality if you:	Your completed project needs Quality Improvements if you:
1-Software Mastery	Choose and apply the most appropriate skills, tools, and features and identify efficient methods to solve the problem.	Choose and apply some appropriate skills, tools, and features, but not in the most efficient manner.	Choose inappropriate skills, tools, or features, or are inefficient in solving the problem.
2-Content	Construct a solution that is clear and well organized, contains content that is accurate, appropriate to the audience and purpose, and is complete. Provide a solution that contains no errors of spelling, grammar, or style.	Construct a solution in which some components are unclear, poorly organized, inconsistent, or incomplete. Misjudge the needs of the audience. Have some errors in spelling, grammar, or style, but the errors do not detract from comprehension.	Construct a solution that is unclear, incomplete, or poorly organized, contains some inaccurate or inappropriate content, and contains many errors of spelling, grammar, or style. Do not solve the problem.
3-Format and Layout	Format and arrange all elements to communicate information and ideas, clarify function, illustrate relationships, and indicate relative importance.	Apply appropriate format and layout features to some elements, but not others. Overuse features, causing minor distraction.	Apply format and layout that does not communicate information or ideas clearly. Do not use format and layout features to clarify function, illustrate relationships, or indicate relative importance. Use available features excessively, causing distraction.
4-Process	Use an organized approach that integrates planning, development, self-assessment, revision, and reflection.	Demonstrate an organized approach in some areas, but not others; or, use an insufficient process of organization throughout.	Do not use an organized approach to solve the problem.

Apply a combination of the 5A and 5B skills.

GO! Think   Project 5F Protective Gear

PROJECT FILES

For Project 5F, you will need the following files:

i05F_Protective_Gear
i05F_Protective_Presentation

You will save your files as:

Lastname_Firstname_5F_Protective_Gear
Lastname_Firstname_5F_Protective_Presentation

Dana Connolly, one of the owners of Board Anywhere Surf and Snowboard Shop, believes it is important to stress snowboarder safety. He wants his sales associates to emphasize snowboarding protective gear—such as helmets, goggles, and shin guards—that is available in the retail store.

Open the **i05F_Protective_Gear** file, and save it as **Lastname_Firstname_5F_Protective_Gear** In the worksheet, adjust column widths so that all data displays. Apply a style to the titles and set the titles to repeat on all printed pages. Create a chart on a new sheet. Format the chart, using a chart layout and chart style. Rename the sheets containing data. Insert the file name in the footer of all worksheets. Open the file **i05F_Protective_Presentation**, and save the presentation as **Lastname_Firstname_5F_Protective_Presentation** Apply a design theme and variant, and then add appropriate titles to the slides. On Slide 2, convert the bulleted list to a SmartArt object, and apply formatting. Insert a blank slide after Slide 2, and paste the Excel chart as a link. Insert a shape on one of the slides and modify the shape with at least two effects. Insert appropriate text in the shape and create a hyperlink to the Excel workbook. Add a slide transition to all slides. In the Excel worksheet, add a hyperlink to the presentation. In both files, add appropriate information to the properties. Submit your printed or electronic files as directed by your instructor.

END | You have completed Project 5F

Integrating Publisher and Access

PROJECT 6A

OUTCOMES
Build a newsletter in Publisher and insert recipients and data fields from Access.

OBJECTIVES

1. Construct a Newsletter in Publisher
2. Format a Newsletter
3. Use Mail Merge to Insert Names from an Access Table into a Publication
4. Insert Access Data Fields into a Publication

PROJECT 6B

OUTCOMES
Set Access field properties and create a publication using a template.

OBJECTIVES

5. Set Field Properties in an Access Table
6. Create a Publication Using a Publisher Template
7. Modify the Layout of a Publication

btmedia/Shutterstock

In This Chapter

In this chapter, you will create publications using Microsoft Publisher, a business publishing program that helps you create, design, and publish professional-looking promotional and communication materials to be used for print, email, and the Internet. You can customize a publication for mailing by inserting names, addresses, or any field from an Access database. In Access tables, changing field settings enables you to enter the records quickly and more accurately. You can set default values and input masks for individual fields in a table. It is good practice to maintain database records on a regular basis to ensure that the data is current and accurate.

The projects in this chapter relate to **Florida Port Community College**, located in St. Petersburg, Florida—a coastal city near the Florida High Tech Corridor. With 60 percent of Florida's high-tech companies and a third of the state's manufacturing companies located in the St. Petersburg and Tampa Bay areas, the college partners with businesses to play a vital role in providing a skilled workforce. The curriculum covers many areas, including medical technology, computer science, electronics, aviation and aerospace, and simulation and modeling. The college also serves the community through cultural, athletic, and diversity programs and adult basic education.

Student Newsletter

PROJECT ACTIVITIES

In Activities 6.01 through 6.12, you will edit a newsletter for new students attending Florida Port Community College. You will modify the color, font, and text schemes. Additionally, you will insert and format images and other objects. After adding student records to an Access database, you will use mail merge to create a customized newsletter for each recipient. Your completed documents will look similar to Figure 6.1.

PROJECT FILES

For Project 6A, you will need the following files:

i06A_New_Students
i06A_Student_Data
i06A_Beach

You will save your files as:

Lastname_Firstname_6A_New_Students
Lastname_Firstname_6A_Merged_Students
Lastname_Firstname_6A_Student_Data

PROJECT RESULTS

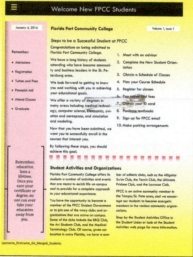
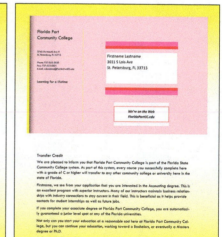

FIGURE 6.1 Student Newsletter

Objective 1 Construct a Newsletter in Publisher

You can use Publisher templates to create various business publications including advertisements, awards, business cards, business forms, calendars, labels, newsletters, and resumes. When documents are used repeatedly, you can save the layout and then simply change the content as required for the new version. Aisha Leinen, the Admissions Director for Florida Port Community College (FPCC), would like to send a newsletter to students who have been admitted to FPCC. Each week, she plans to send the newsletter to those students who have been accepted that week.

Activity 6.01 | Constructing a Newsletter

Ms. Leinen has started the newsletter in Publisher and has asked you to complete it.

1 Start Publisher, and then on the left, click **Open Other Publications**. Under **Open**, click **Browse**, and then navigate to the location of the student data files for this instruction. Open the file **i06A_New_Students**. If necessary, to display the rulers, click the View tab, and then in the Show group, click the Rulers check box.

2 Click the **File tab**, on the left click **Save As**. Under **Save As**, click **Browse**, and then in the **Save As** dialog box, navigate to the location where you are saving your files. Click **New folder**, type **Integrated Projects Chapter 6** and then press Enter two times. In the **File name** box, using your own name, type **Lastname_Firstname_6A_New_Students** and then click **Save**. Take a moment to study the parts of the Publisher screen, as shown in Figure 6.2.

The Pages pane, at the left of your screen, displays thumbnails of the pages in a publication. Page 1 of the publication displays.

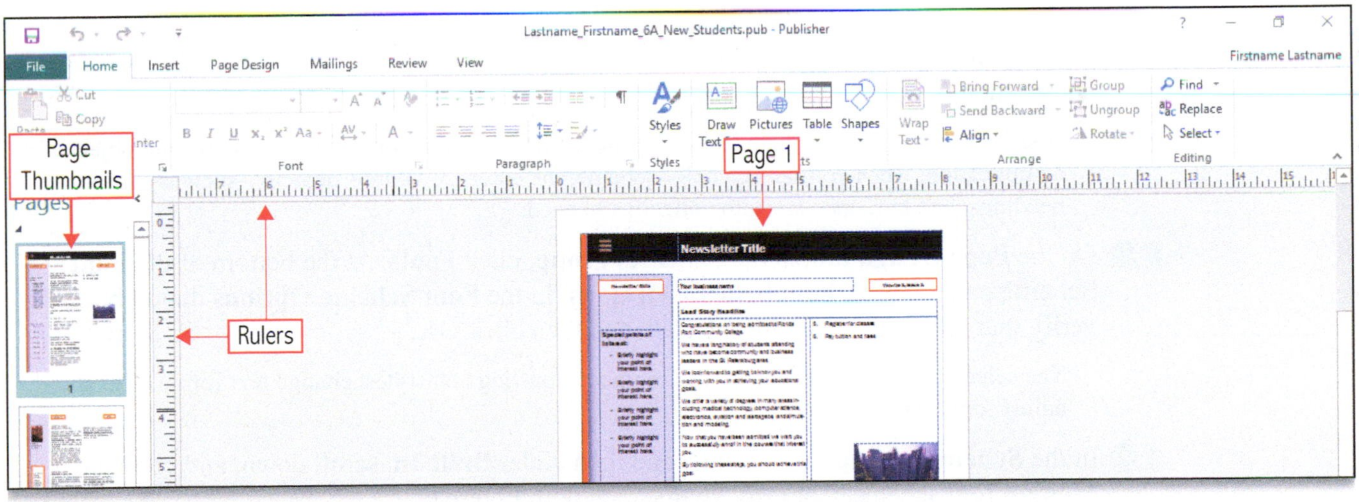

Publisher 2016, Windows 10, Microsoft Corporation

FIGURE 6.2

3 On the **Insert tab**, in the **Header & Footer group**, click **Footer**.

A Footer text box displays on a ***master page***. A master page contains the design and layout elements, including headers and footers, that you want to repeat on multiple pages of your publication. By default, every publication contains a master page. The master page screen displays a pale colored background.

4 In the **Footer** text box, using your own name, type **Lastname Firstname 6A New Students** and then on the **Master Page tab**, in the **Close group**, click **Close Master Page**.

This action will display the footer on all pages of the newsletter.

5 In the **Pages** pane, click **Page 2**. Hold down [Shift], and then click **Page 3**. With both pages selected, right-click the selection, and then on the shortcut menu, click **Delete**. In the message box, click **Yes** to delete the pages.

Pages 2 and 3 are deleted. Page 4 is renumbered as Page 2. The publication now has two pages.

6 In the **Pages** pane, click **Page 1**. At the top of the page, select the text *Newsletter Title*, and then type **Welcome New FPCC Students**

7 At the top left corner of the page, in the text box, select the text *Newsletter Date*. On the **Insert tab**, in the **Text group**, click **Date & Time**. In the **Date and Time** dialog box, under **Available formats**, click the third format, and then click **OK**.

The current date displays in the text box.

8 To the right of the date, select the text *Your business name*, and then type **Florida Port Community College** Click in a blank area of the newsletter to deselect the text box.

9 **Save** 🖫 your newsletter.

Activity 6.02 | Applying a Color Scheme and a Font Scheme

Publisher includes a number of color and font schemes to create a professional-looking publication. You can select an existing scheme, or you can customize the colors and fonts in your publications.

1 Click the **Page Design tab**, and, in the **Schemes group**, click **More** ▼.

2 In the **Color Schemes** gallery, point to a few of the color schemes to view how the colors affect your publication. Scroll down, and then under **Built-In (classic)**, click the **Summer** color scheme.

A *color scheme* is a predefined set of harmonized colors that you can apply to text and objects. In a publication, when you select a color scheme, the colors of various objects—such as text boxes, headings, and borders—are automatically changed.

3 On the **Page Design tab**, in the **Schemes group**, click **Fonts**. At the bottom of the **Font Scheme** gallery, click **Font Scheme Options**. In the **Font Scheme Options** dialog box, verify that all check boxes are selected, and then click **OK**.

The selected check boxes enable you to update existing text styles, change text formatting, and adjust font sizes.

4 In the **Schemes group**, click **Fonts**, and then under **Built-In**, scroll down, and click the **Median** font scheme. Compare your screen with Figure 6.3.

A *font scheme* is a predefined set of fonts that is associated with a publication. Within each font scheme, both a primary font and a secondary font are specified. Generally, a primary font is used for titles and headings, and a secondary font is used for body text. Font schemes make it easy to change all the fonts in a publication to give it a consistent appearance.

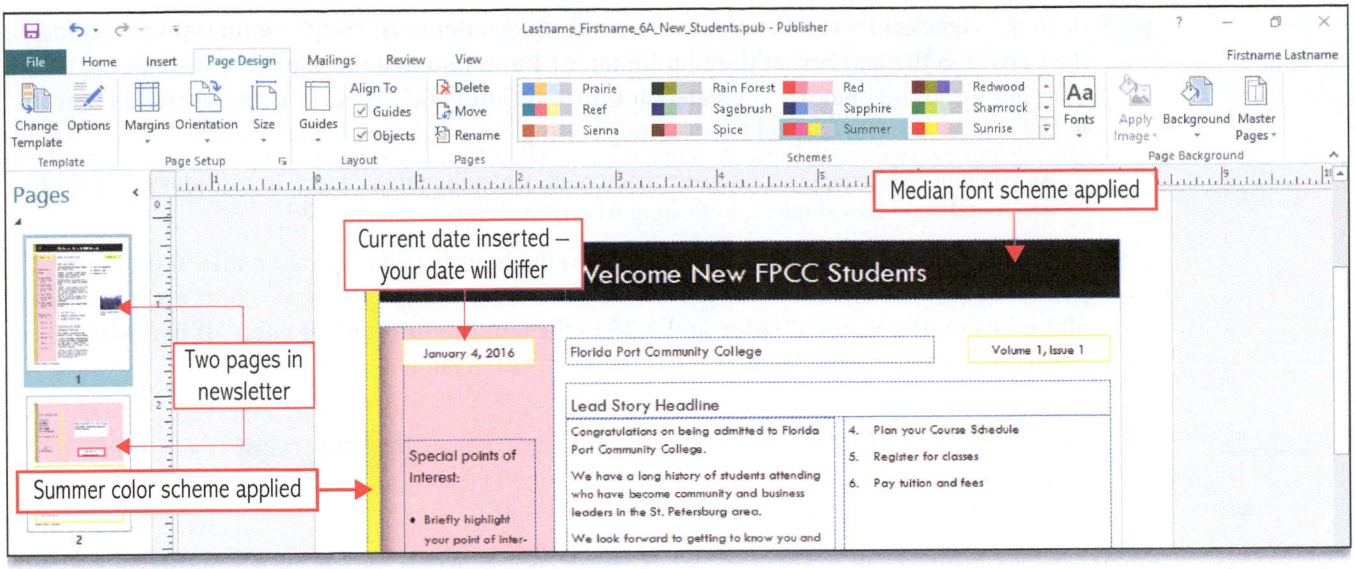

FIGURE 6.3

Publisher 2016, Windows 10, Microsoft Corporation

5 ▸ At the bottom of **Page 1**, select the title *Secondary Story Headline*, and then type **Student Activities and Organizations**

6 ▸ Click in the text box below the revised heading to select the text. Under **Text Box Tools**, click the **Format tab**. In the **Font group**, click the **Font Size button arrow** [10 ▾], and then click **11**. With the placeholder text still selected, type **Florida Port Community College offers its students a number of activities and events that are meant to enrich life on campus and to provide for a complete approach to your educational experience.** Press [Enter].

7 ▸ Type **You have the opportunity to become a member of the FPCC Student Government or to join one of the many clubs and organizations that are active on campus. Some of the clubs include the BBQ Club, the Art Students Club, and the Medical Technology Club. Of course, given our location in sunny Florida, we have a number of athletic clubs, such as the Alligator Swim Club, the Tennis Club, the Ultimate Frisbee Club, and the Lacrosse Club.** Press [Enter].

8 ▸ Type **FPCC is an active community member in the Tampa/St. Pete area, and we encourage our students to become energetic members in the various community organizations.** Press [Enter], and then type **Stop by the Student Activities Office in the Student Union or look at the Student Activities web page for more information.**

9 ▸ **Save** 🖫 your newsletter.

Activity 6.03 | Inserting a Building Block

Building blocks are reusable pieces of content—for example, borders, text boxes, logos, and calendars—that are stored in galleries. In this Activity, you will insert a Page Part—a text box—building block.

1 ▸ At the lower left corner of **Page 1**, click the object *Inside this issue*, and notice sizing handles display to indicate that the entire object is selected. Right-click the object, and then on the shortcut menu, click **Delete Object**.

2 ▸ Click the **Insert tab**, and then in the **Building Blocks group**, click **Page Parts**. In the **Page Parts** gallery, scroll down if necessary, and then under **Pull Quotes**, click the first pull quote—**Brackets**.

3 With the **Brackets** text box selected, point to the border until the 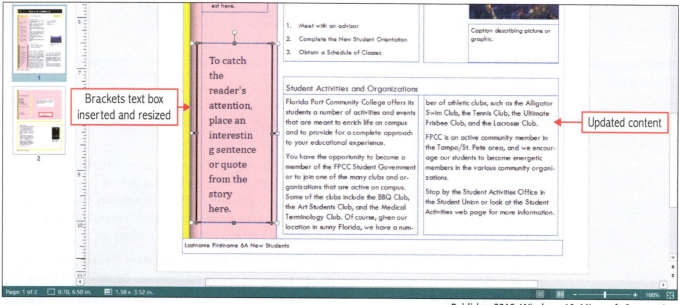 pointer displays, and then position the text box at the bottom left of **Page 1** so that the top left corner of the text box, not the sizing handle, is located at **approximately 6.5 inches on the vertical ruler** and **0.75 inch on the horizontal ruler**. Nudge using the arrow keys as necessary.

As you move an object in a Publisher document, you will notice a black line displays on both the horizontal and vertical rulers, indicating where your object is positioned.

4 With the **Brackets** text box selected, point to the bottom right sizing handle until the pointer displays, and then resize the text box so the bottom right corner is at **approximately 10 inches on the vertical ruler** and **2.25 inches on the horizontal ruler**. If necessary, use the arrow keys to nudge the text box into the position shown in Figure 6.4.

Brackets text box inserted and resized

Updated content

Student Activities and Organizations

1. Meet with an advisor
2. Complete the New Student Orientation
3. Obtain a Schedule of Classes

Caption describing picture or graphic.

To catch the reader's attention, place an interesting sentence or quote from the story here.

Florida Port Community College offers its students a number of activities and events that are meant to enrich life on campus and to provide for a complete approach to your educational experience.

You have the opportunity to become a member of the FPCC Student Government or to join one of the many clubs and organizations that are active on campus. Some of the clubs include the BBQ Club, the Art Students Club, and the Medical Terminology Club. Of course, given our location in sunny Florida, we have a num-

ber of athletic clubs, such as the Alligator Swim Club, the Tennis Club, the Ultimate Frisbee Club, and the Lacrosse Club.

FPCC is an active community member in the Tampa/St. Pete area, and we encourage our students to become energetic members in the various community organizations.

Stop by the Student Activities Office in the Student Union or look at the Student Activities web page for more information.

Lastname Firstname 6A New Students

FIGURE 6.4

Publisher 2016, Windows 10, Microsoft Corporation

5 Click in the text box to select the text. Under **Text Box Tools**, click the **Format tab**, in the **Font group**, click the **Font Size button arrow** 10, and then click **12**. In the **Alignment group**, click **Align Center**.

6 With the text selected, type **Remember, education lasts a lifetime. Once you earn your certificate or degree, no one can ever take your education away from you.**

7 Click outside of the publication to deselect the text box, and then **Save** your newsletter.

Activity 6.04 | Applying a Text Style

You can customize the styles of headings, bullets, or other text in your publication.

1 Scroll up to the top of **Page 1**, and then select the heading *Lead Story Headline*. Under **Text Box Tools**, click the **Format tab**. In the **Font group**, click the **Font Size button arrow** `10 ▾`, and then click **14**. Type **Steps to be a Successful Student at FPCC**

2 In the text box that displays a picture, click the picture to select it and the caption below it. Right-click the picture, and then on the shortcut menu, click **Cut**.

3 In the text box below the heading, click one time in the paragraph that begins *Congratulations on being admitted*. Press `Ctrl` + `A` to select all the text in the text box. Under **Text Box Tools**, on the **Format tab**, in the **Font group**, click the **Font Size button arrow** `10 ▾`, and then click **12**.

4 In the right text box, click to the right of the text *6. Pay tuition and fees*, and then press `Enter`.

This text is recognized by Publisher as a list; the number 7 automatically displays to continue the list.

5 Type **Obtain your student ID card** and then press `Enter`. Type **Purchase textbooks** and then press `Enter`. Type **Sign up for FPCC student email** and then press `Enter`. Type **Make parking arrangements** and then compare your screen with Figure 6.5.

A list of 10 items displays in the text box.

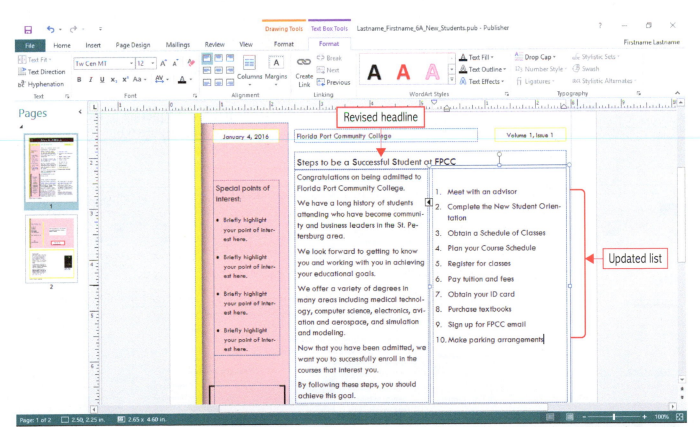

FIGURE 6.5

6 In the lower text box, select the heading *Student Activities and Organizations*. On the **Home tab**, in the **Styles group**, click **Styles**. In the **Styles** gallery, scroll down, and then click **Heading 3**. In the **Font group**, click **Bold** `B`.

7 Scroll up, and then at the top of the page, select the heading *Florida Port Community College*. In the **Styles group**, click **Styles**, scroll down, and then click **Organization Name 2**. In the **Font group**, click the **Font Size button arrow** [10 ▾], and then click **14**. Click **Bold** [B]. Click in a blank area of the page to deselect the text box.

8 **Save** [💾] your newsletter.

You can format a publication in a number of ways. To control the flow of text, you can apply *text wrapping*—which refers to the manner in which text displays around an object, such as a picture. You can format the background of a document by adding a color, a texture, or an image.

Activity 6.05 | Changing Text Wrapping

In this Activity, you will insert an online image and change the way the existing text wraps around the graphic.

1 Click the **Insert tab**. In the **Illustrations group**, click **Online Pictures**. In the **Insert Pictures** dialog box, to the right of **Bing Image Search**, type **Florida beach** and then press [Enter]. Scroll to locate an applicable image.

Online images can be inserted using a Bing search to make your publication more interesting and visually appealing. Notice the search results are licensed under Creative Commons. Although you can use these images for assignments, they cannot be used if you are profiting by using the images.

2 Double-click the image to insert it in your newsletter. Under **Picture Tools**, on the **Format tab**, in the **Size group**, click in the **Shape Width** box [▭]. Type **2.5** and then press [Enter].

3 Point to the picture until the [↖] pointer displays, and then move the picture to the center of the text box in the middle of the page. Compare your screen with Figure 6.6.

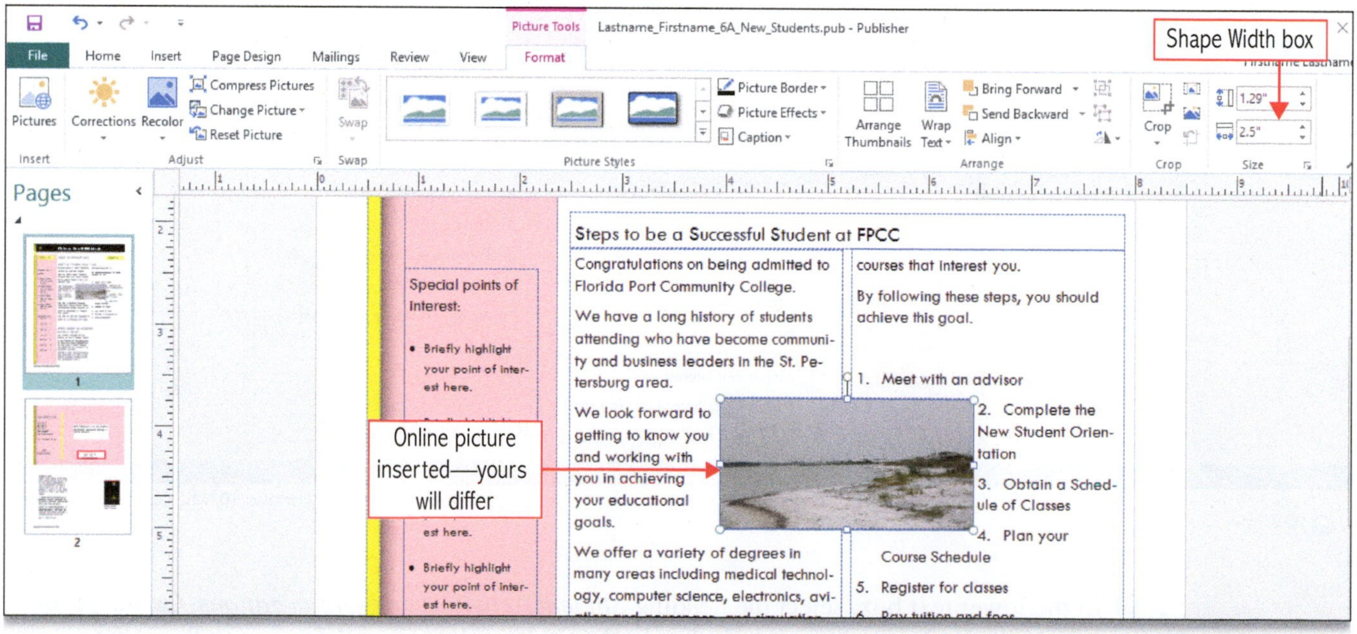

FIGURE 6.6

Publisher 2016, Windows 10, Microsoft Corporation

4 Under **Picture Tools**, on the **Format tab**, in the **Arrange group**, click **Wrap Text**, and then click **Top and Bottom**.

The text stops at the top of the picture's frame and continues below the bottom of the frame.

5 In the **Arrange group**, click **Wrap Text**, click **None**, and then notice that the image displays on top of the text.

6 In the **Arrange group**, click the **Send Backward button arrow**, and then click **Send to Back**.

In this arrangement, the text displays on top of the picture—as if the image is not there. Use the commands in the Arrange group to indicate how images should display in relation to existing text.

7 In the **Adjust group**, click the **Dialog Box Launcher** 🔲. In the **Format Picture** dialog box, on the **Picture tab**, adjust the **Brightness** to **65%** and click **OK.** Click a blank area of your newsletter, and then compare your screen with Figure 6.7.

Increasing the brightness gives the picture a washed-out look.

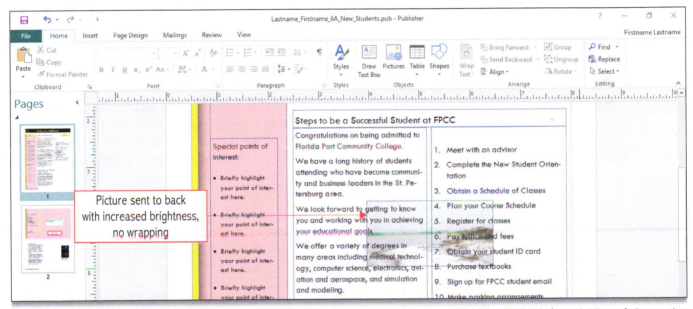

FIGURE 6.7

Publisher 2016, Windows 10, Microsoft Corporation

8 Save 🔲 your newsletter.

Activity 6.06 | Inserting a Design Accent

In this Activity, you will add a design accent building block to your newsletter.

1 Click the **Insert tab**, and then in the **Building Blocks group**, click **Borders & Accents**. In the **Borders & Accents** gallery, under **Bars**, in the first row, point to the second accent— **Awning Stripes**—and click to insert it in your newsletter. Compare your screen with Figure 6.8.

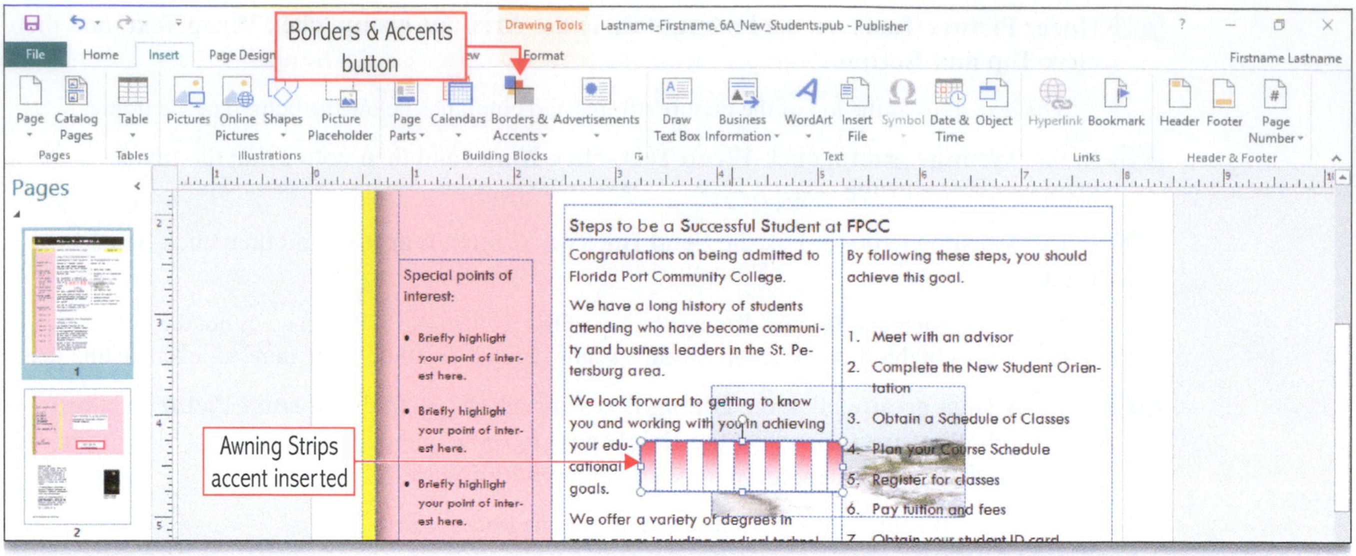

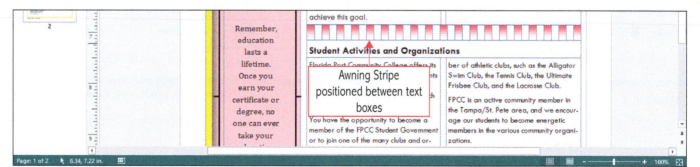

FIGURE 6.8

> **2** With the **Awning Stripes** accent selected, point to the left border until the pointer displays, and then move the object so the top left corner is at **approximately 7 inches on the vertical ruler** and **2.5 inches on the horizontal ruler**.

> **3** Point to the bottom right sizing handle until the pointer displays, and then resize the object so that the Awning Stripes accent is stretched and extends to the right margin. The stripes should fit between the bottom of the text in the first article and the top of the headline of the second article. Use the arrow keys to position the Awning Stripes accent so the bottom border touches the top border of the lower text box. Click a blank section of your newsletter, and then compare your screen with Figure 6.9.

FIGURE 6.9

> **4** In the **Pages** pane, click **Page 2**, and then scroll up to display the top of **Page 2**.

> **5** On the **Insert tab**, in the **Building Blocks group**, click **Borders & Accents**. Under **Emphasis**, click **Stripes**.

6 With the object selected, under **Drawing Tools**, click the **Format tab**; and then in the **Size group**, set the **Shape Height** 🔗 to **2** and then press Enter. Set the **Shape Width** 🖼 to **3** and then press Enter. In the **Arrange group**, click **Send Backward**.

7 Point to the border of the object to display the 🔲 pointer, and then move the object so the stripes display above and below the right text box that contains the text that begins *Type address here*. Compare your screen with Figure 6.10.

> The Stripes object surrounds the address text box.

8 Below the address text box, in the text box beginning with the paragraph *We're on the Web*, select the text example@example.com, type **FloridaPortCC.edu** and then **Save** 💾 your newsletter.

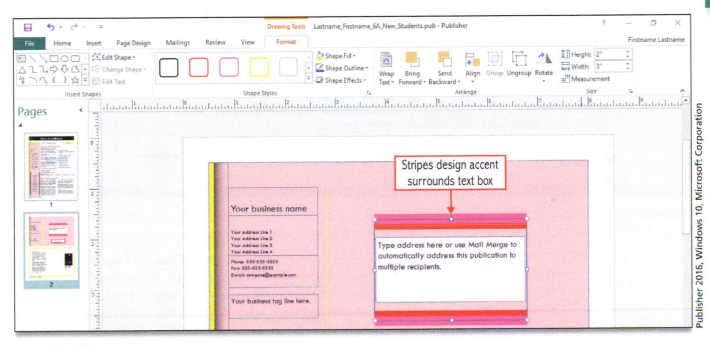

FIGURE 6.10

Activity 6.07 | Formatting the Newsletter Background

1 On the **Pages** pane, click **Page 1**. At the top left corner of the page, click the heading *Special points of interest* to select the heading, and then type **Remember:** Under the new heading, click the first bullet point.

> All of the bullet points are selected.

2 Type the following list, pressing Enter after each list item, *except* for the last item. Compare your screen with Figure 6.11.

Admissions
Registration
Tuition and Fees
Financial Aid
Attend Classes
Graduate

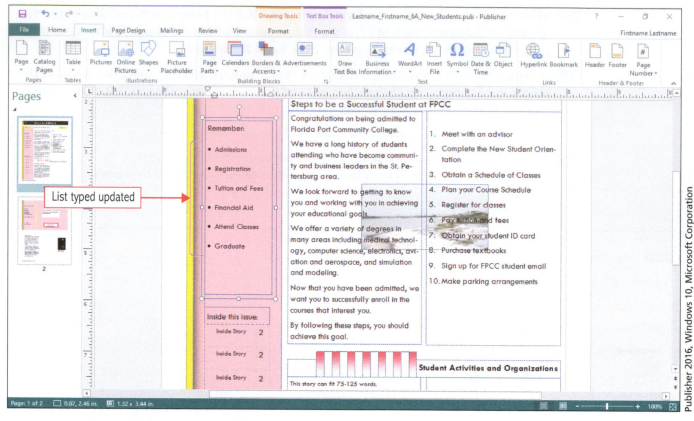

FIGURE 6.11

3 Click in a blank area of the newsletter to deselect the text box. Click the **Page Design tab**, and then in the **Page Background group**, click **Background**. Under **Gradient Background**, in the first row, point to the third background—**Accent 3 Horizontal Gradient**. Right-click the background, and then on the shortcut menu, click **Apply to All Pages**.

> The selected background is applied to both pages of the newsletter.

4 Save your newsletter.

Activity 6.08 | Running the Design Checker

After you have created a publication, it is a good idea to review it. The *Design Checker* is a feature that automatically reviews your publication for a range of design and layout flaws and provides options to fix any identified problems.

1 In the **Pages** pane, click **Page 2**. At the top left corner of the page, select the text *Your business name*, and then type **Florida Port Community College**

2 Below the active text box, in the next text box that begins with the text *Your Address*, select all four lines of text. Click the **Home tab**. In the **Font group**, click the **Font Size button arrow** 10, and then click **11**. Type **2745 Dartmouth Ave N** and then press Enter. Type **St. Petersburg, FL 33713** and then press Enter.

3 Below the active text box, in the next text box, select the phone number and then type **727-555-0030** Select the fax number, and then type **727-555-0031** Select the e-mail address, and then type **admissions@FloridaPortCC.edu**

4 In the next text box, select the text *Your business tag line here.*, and then type **Learning for a lifetime**

5 Click the text box that contains the text *Organization* and the pyramid image. On the **Home tab**, in the **Clipboard group**, click **Cut** ✂ to delete the entire text box—the text and the image—from the publication. Compare your screen with Figure 6.12.

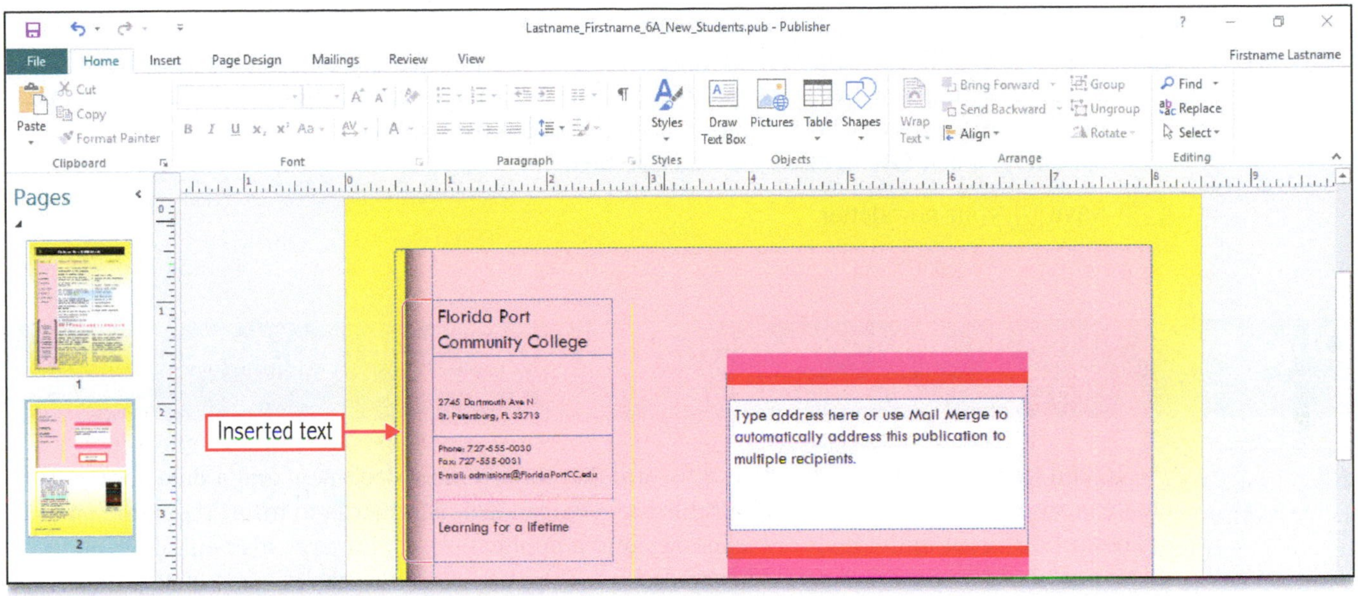

FIGURE 6.12

6 Click the **File tab**, verify the **Info tab** is selected, and then click **Run Design Checker**.

The Design Checker automatically runs and displays the results in the Design Checker pane on the right.

7 At the bottom of the **Design Checker** pane, click **Design Checker Options**. In the **Design Checker Options** dialog box, under **Page Range**, click the **Current page(s)** option button. Click the **Checks tab**. Under **Checks in this category**, scroll down to verify that all the check boxes are selected, and then click **OK**.

The Design Checker runs and displays the results in the Design Checker pane.

8 In the **Design Checker** pane, under **Select an item to fix**, locate the first item—**Text box is empty (Page 2)**.

This text box will be completed in a later Activity.

9 In the **Design Checker** pane, under **Select an item to fix**, click the **Low-resolution picture (Page 2) arrow**, and then click **Go to this Item**.

The picture on Page 2 is selected.

10 In the **Design Checker** pane, under **Select an item to fix**, click the **Low-resolution picture (Page 2) arrow** again, and then click **Explain**.

> The Publisher Help window opens. You will modify this picture in a later Activity.

11 **Close** ⊠ the Publisher Help window. Click in a blank area of the publication to deselect the picture.

12 **Close** ⊠ the **Design Checker** pane.

13 Click the **Review tab**, and then in the **Proofing group**, click **Spelling**.

> Beginning at the current location, Publisher begins checking the spelling of text in your publication.

14 Check the spelling in your newsletter, making any necessary corrections. If a message box displays asking whether you want to check the rest of your publication, click **Yes**. Continue making any necessary corrections, until a message box displays *The spelling check is complete*. Click **OK** to close the message box.

15 **Save** 🖫 your newsletter.

Objective 3 Use Mail Merge to Insert Names from an Access Table into a Publication

Recall that in Word, mail merge is a feature that joins a main document and a data source to create customized letters or labels. In Publisher, you can use mail merge to insert the name and address of different individuals or businesses into a publication. Mail merge also enables you to insert placeholders for other data fields to make each publication unique.

Activity 6.09 | Modifying an Existing Access Database

1 Start Access. On the left, click **Open Other Files**, under *Open*, click **Browse**, and then navigate to the location where your student data files are located. Open the file **i06A_Student_Data**. If necessary, enable the content. Click the **File tab**, click **Save As**, under *File Types* click **Save Database As**, and then under *Save Database As*, click **Save As**. In the **Save As** dialog box, navigate to your **Integrated Projects Chapter 6** folder. In the **File name** box, delete the existing text, and then using your own name, type **Lastname_Firstname_6A_Student_Data** Click **Save**. On the **Message Bar**, click **Enable Content**.

2 Under **Tables**, right-click **Students**, and then on the shortcut menu, click **Rename**. Using your own name, type the new table name **Lastname Firstname 6A Students** and then press Enter. Double-click the new table name **Lastname Firstname 6A Students** to open the table. **Close** ⟪ the **Navigation Pane**.

3 Click the **Create tab**, and then in the **Forms group**, click **Form**. Under **Form Layout Tools**, on the **Design tab**, in the **Views group**, click the upper portion of the **View** button to display the form in Form view.

4 On the **Quick Access Toolbar**, click **Save** 🖫. In the **Save As** dialog box, using your name, type **Lastname Firstname 6A Student Form** and then click **OK**.

5 At the bottom of the form, click **New (blank) record** ▶✹. Add the following records and use your own name for the last record—the First Name and Last Name fields. Compare your screen with Figure 6.13.

Student ID	First Name	Last Name	Address	City	State	ZIP	Phone Number	Degree
20-8699944	**Casey**	**Drees**	**908 Sydney Washer Rd**	**St. Petersburg**	**FL**	**33714**	**727-555-2187**	**Computer Information**
20-7385522	**Clifton**	**Durfey**	**8309 Dahlia Ave**	**Tampa**	**FL**	**33605**	**813-555-0185**	**Computer Information**
20-6682011	**Firstname**	**Lastname**	**3611 S Lois Ave**	**St. Petersburg**	**FL**	**33713**	**727-555-0286**	**Accounting**

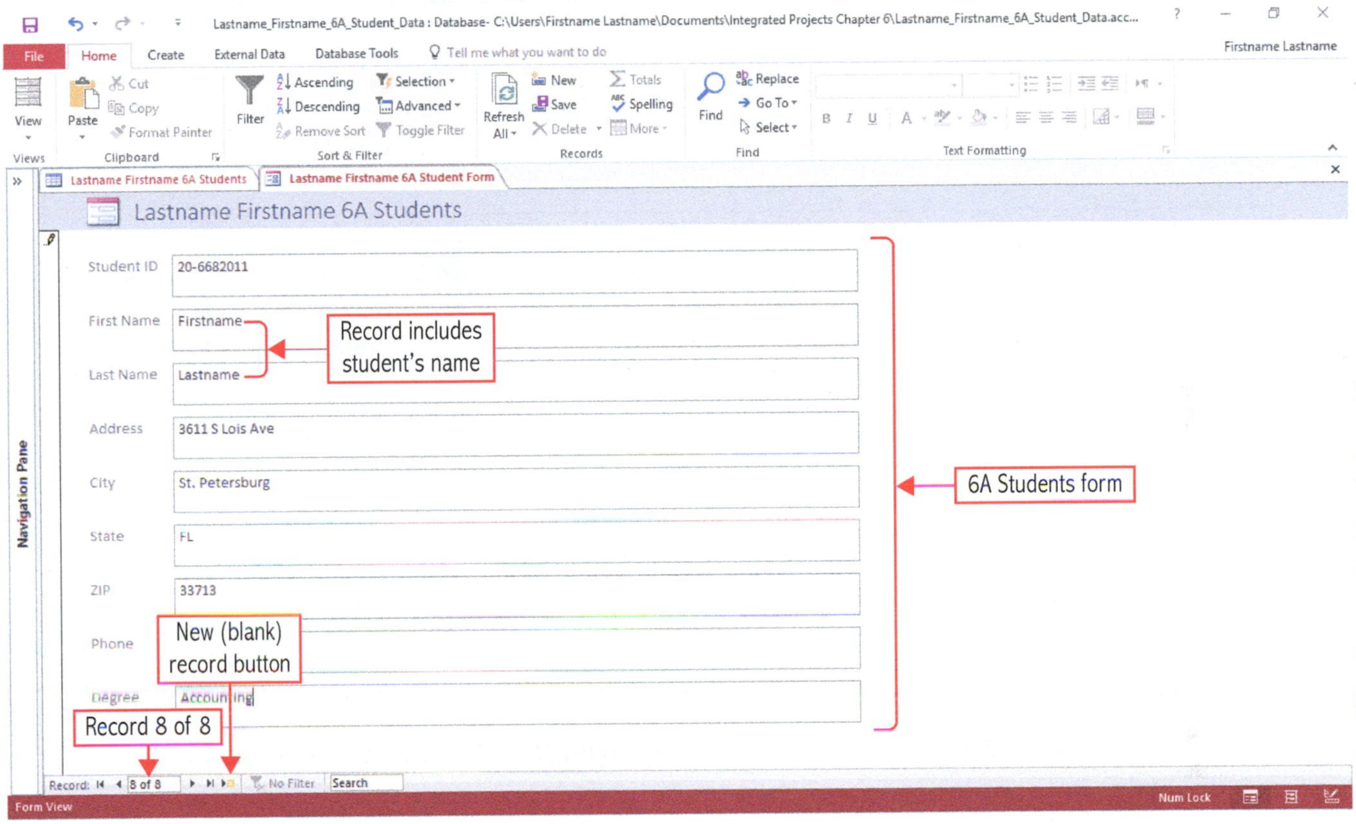

Publisher 2016, Windows 10, Microsoft Corporation

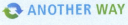

FIGURE 6.13

6 Press Enter to accept the record with your name.

7 At the bottom of the form, in the navigation area, click **Previous Record** to display record 8—the record containing your name. Carefully review the form to make sure you entered all data correctly. Using the same technique, review records 7 and 6.

It is important that your data is entered correctly because you will use the records in a later Activity.

8 Click the **Create tab**, and then in the **Reports group**, click **Report Wizard**. In the **Report Wizard** dialog box, verify that the **6A Students** table is selected. Under **Available Fields**, double-click the fields **First Name**, **Last Name**, **Address**, **City**, **State**, and **ZIP**, and then click **Next** two times.

Since you will not be applying any grouping to the report, you can click Next to bypass that step in the Wizard.

ANOTHER WAY Click the field name, and then click Add Field to move a field from the Available Fields list to the Selected Fields list.

9 ▶ Under **What sort order do you want for your records?**, click the **sort box arrow**, and then click **Last Name**. Click **Next**.

The default sort order is Ascending, or A-Z.

10 ▶ Under **Orientation**, click **Landscape**, and then click **Next**. Under **What title do you want for the report?**, select the existing text, and then using your own name, type **Lastname Firstname 6A Students Report** and then click **Finish**. Compare your screen with Figure 6.14.

The report displays in Print Preview.

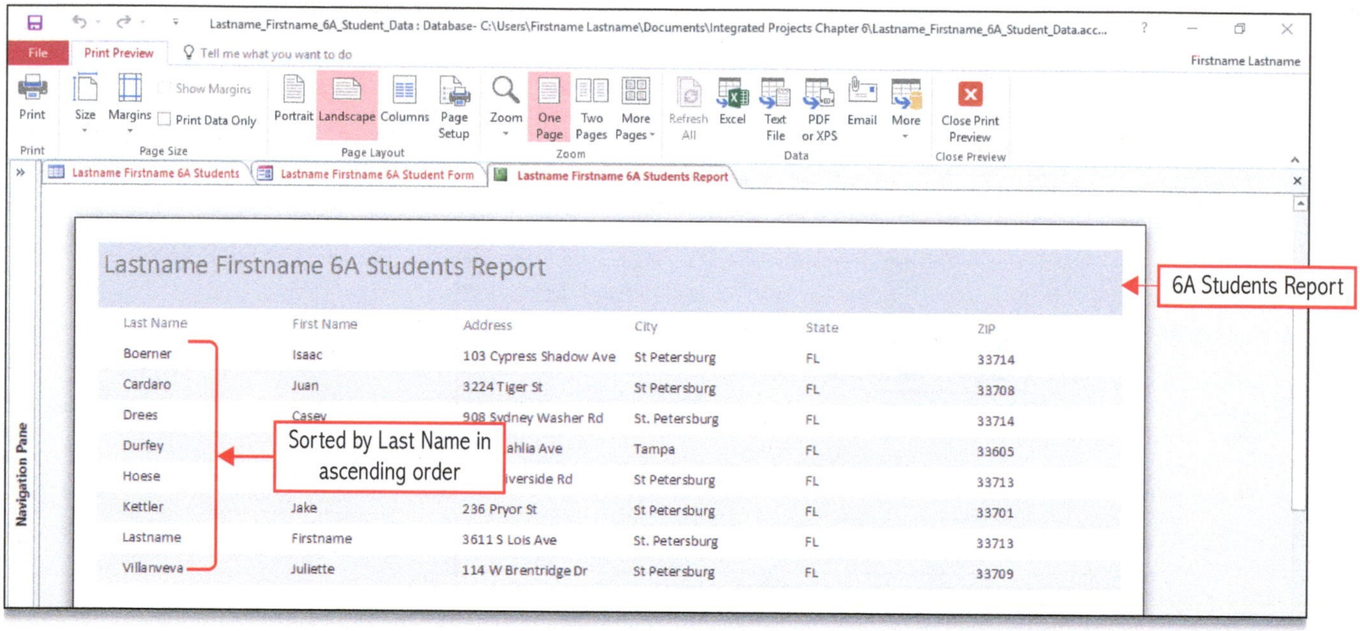

FIGURE 6.14

Publisher 2016, Windows 10, Microsoft Corporation

11 ▶ If your instructor directs you to submit your files electronically, go to Step 13.

12 ▶ To print the report, on the **Print Preview tab**, in the **Print group**, click **Print**, and then click **OK**.

13 ▶ Right-click the **Lastname Firstname 6A Students Report tab**, and then on the shortcut menu, click **Close All**. If a message box displays, click **Yes** to save the changes to the design of the report.

14 ▶ Click the **File tab**, verify the **Info tab** is selected, and then at the right of your screen, click **View and edit database properties**. In the **Properties** dialog box, on the **Summary tab**, in the **Subject** box, type your course name and section number; in the **Author** box, type your first name and last name; and then in the **Keywords** box, type **students, contact info** Click **OK** to close the dialog box.

15 ▶ **Close** ☒ Access.

Activity 6.10 | Importing and Sorting a Recipient List from Access

You can import a recipient list to a new or existing publication. As the data source for the recipient list, you can use an Outlook Contact list, an Excel workbook, a Word table, an Access database, or a text file. In this Activity, you will import a recipient list from an Access database.

1 With your newsletter displayed, if necessary, in the Pages pane, click Page 2. Click the **Mailings tab**. In the **Start group**, click the **Mail Merge button arrow**, and then click **Step-by-Step Mail Merge Wizard**.

The Mail Merge pane displays on the right.

2 In the **Mail Merge** pane, under **Create recipient list**, verify that the **Use an existing list** option button is selected. At the bottom of the task pane, click **Next: Create or connect to a recipient list**.

3 In the **Select Data Source** dialog box, navigate to your **Integrated Projects Chapter 6** folder, select your Access file **Lastname_Firstname_6A_Student_Data**, and then click **Open** to display the **Mail Merge Recipients** dialog box. Compare your screen with Figure 6.15.

The records from the Students table in your database display. The Mail Merge Recipients dialog box contains options for sorting and filtering the records.

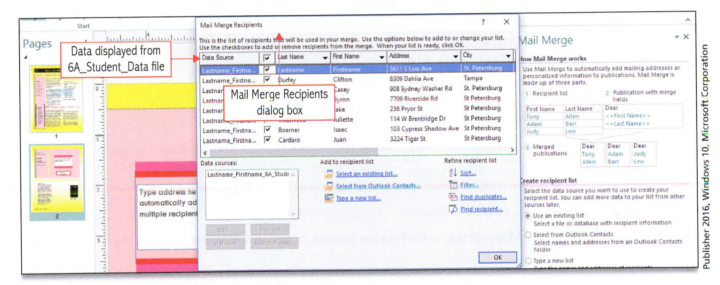

FIGURE 6.15

4 In the **Mail Merge Recipients** dialog box, under **Refine recipient list**, click **Sort**. In the **Filter and Sort** dialog box, click the **Sort by arrow**, scroll down, and then click **Degree**. Verify that the **Ascending** option is selected, and then click **OK**. In the **Mail Merge Recipients** dialog box, scroll right to display the **Degree** field, and then compare your screen with Figure 6.16.

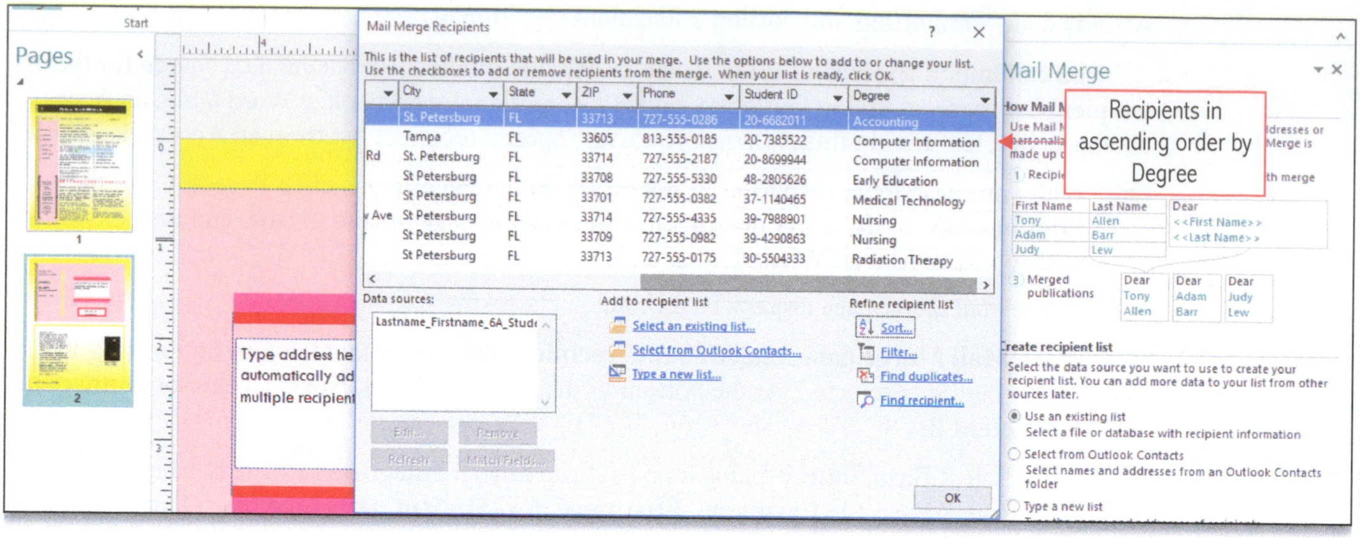

Publisher 2016, Windows 10, Microsoft Corporation

FIGURE 6.16

5 In the **Mail Merge Recipients** dialog box, click **OK**. On **Page 2** of your publication, near the top right, click the text box containing the text that begins *Type address here*. Press Ctrl + A to select the entire paragraph, and then press Delete.

6 In the **Mail Merge** pane, under **More items**, click **Address block**. In the **Insert Address Block** dialog box, under **Specify address elements**, verify that the format **Joshua Randall Jr.** is selected, and then click **OK**.

The Address Block merge field displays in the text box. Recall that when you insert a merge field, the field name is always surrounded by double angle brackets (<< >>).

7 On the **Mailings tab**, in the **Preview Results group**, click **Preview Results** to turn on the feature.

Your name displays in the newsletter. Recall that you sorted the recipients by degree; because your degree program is Accounting, your name displays as the first record.

8 **Save** your newsletter.

9 On the **Mailings tab**, in the **Preview Results group**, click **Preview Results** to turn off the feature.

Objective 4 Insert Access Data Fields into a Publication

In addition to using the mail merge feature to insert the recipient's name and address, you can further personalize documents by inserting data fields. Most people appreciate mailings that include specific information related to their interests. These mailings help to build loyalty between an individual and the organization. To personalize a publication, you must have the information stored in a data source such as Access.

Activity 6.11 | Inserting Data Fields

In this Activity, you will insert the degree program in which each student is enrolled in your newsletter.

1 At the bottom right of your screen, on the Status bar, change the **Zoom level** to **80%**. Scroll to view the bottom left of **Page 2**, and then click the paragraph that begins *We are pleased to inform you*. Press Ctrl + A to select all of the text in the text box. On the **Home tab**, in the **Font group**, click the **Font Size button arrow** [10 ▾], and then click **12**.

In the original publication, a link was created between the left text box and the right text box. When you increased the font size, the excess text that did not fit in the left text box was automatically inserted in the right text box.

2 In the text box, click at the end of the first paragraph, which ends *state of Florida*, and then press Enter. In the **Mail Merge** pane, under **Prepare your publication**, click **First Name**, type a comma, and then press Spacebar.

The First Name merge field is inserted in the newsletter.

3 Type **we see from your application that you are interested in the** and then press Spacebar.

4 In the **Mail Merge** pane, under **Prepare your publication**, scroll down, click **Degree**, and then press Spacebar. Type **degree. This is an excellent program with superior instructors. Many of our instructors maintain business relationships with industry connections to stay current in their field. This is beneficial as it helps to provide contacts for student internships as well as future jobs.** Compare your screen with Figure 6.17.

An *overflow* icon displays near the bottom right corner of the text box. Overflow is text that does not fit within a text box. The text is hidden until it can be linked to flow into a new text box or until the existing text box is resized.

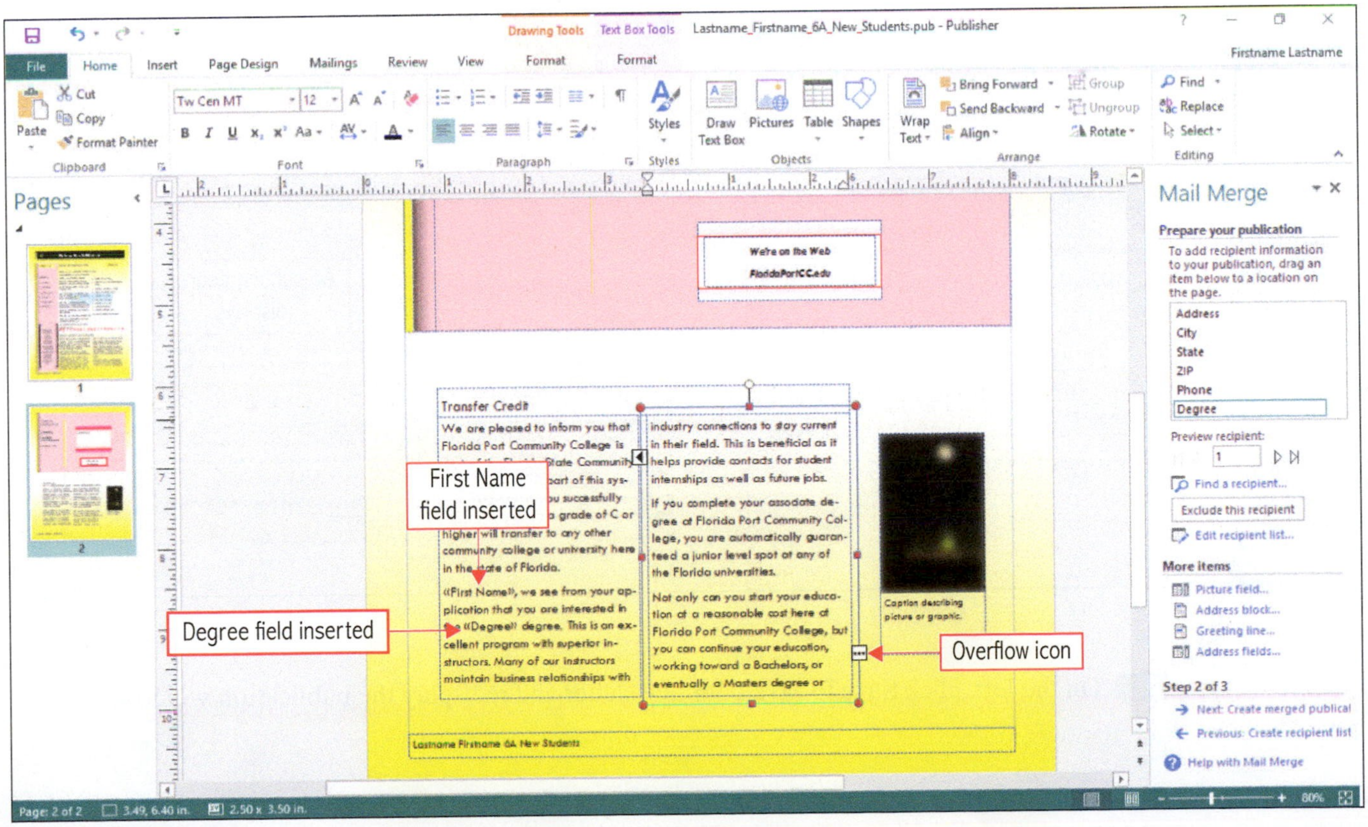

FIGURE 6.17

5 To the right of the text box with overflow, click the picture one time to select it. Right-click the picture, and then on the shortcut menu, click **Delete Object**. Click in the text box with the paragraph that begins *We are pleased*. Under **Text Box Tools**, click the **Format tab**, and then in the **Linking group**, click **Break**. To the right of the existing text, right-click in the empty text box, and then on the shortcut menu, click **Cut**.

Breaking the link causes the overflow text to be attached to the text box on the left. This action enabled you to cut the left text box without deleting any existing text.

6 Right-click the text box at the lower left corner of the page, and then on the shortcut menu, click **Format Text Box**. In the **Format Text Box** dialog box, click the **Size tab**. Under **Size and rotate**, delete the number in the **Width** box, type **6.5** and then click **OK**.

All of the text displays in a single box that displays across the page.

7 In the **Mail Merge** pane, under **Step 2 of 3**, click **Next: Create merged publication**.

8 In the **Mail Merge** pane, under **Create merged publications**, click **Print preview**. Below the **Print Preview**, in the navigation area, if necessary, click Next to display Page 2. At the bottom right corner of the window, change the **Zoom level** to **80%**. Compare your screen with Figure 6.18.

Your name displays in the address block field. In the inserted paragraph, your first name displays in the First Name field and Accounting displays in the Degree field.

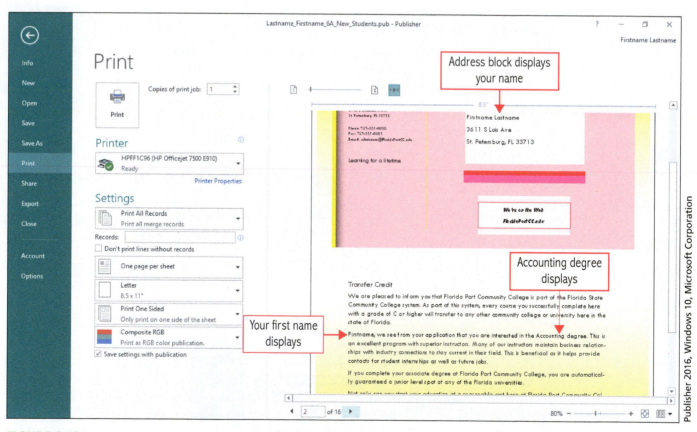

FIGURE 6.18

9 On the left, click **Save** to save your newsletter and redisplay the publication window.

Activity 6.12 | Completing and Printing the Merged Newsletter

When you complete the mail merge, a number of personalized documents are created within the file. You can print one or all of the documents.

1 In the **Mail Merge** pane, under **Create merged publications**, click **Merge to a new publication**.

Eight newsletters—16 pages—are created. After completing the merge, the new publication is no longer connected to the data source.

2 In the merged document, on the **Insert tab**, in the **Header & Footer group**, click **Footer**. In the footer, double-click the word **New**, and then type **Merged** On the **Master Page tab**, in the **Close group**, click **Close Master Page**.

The footer *Lastname Firstname 6A Merged Students* displays on all pages of the publication.

3 In the **Mail Merge** pane, under **Merged publication pages**, click **Save this publication**. Navigate to your **Integrated Projects Chapter 6** folder. In the **File name** box, delete the existing text, and then using your own name, type **Lastname_Firstname_6A_Merged_Students** Click **Save**.

4 **Close** [X] the **Mail Merge** pane. In the **Pages** pane, click **Page 2** of the first newsletter. Scroll to view the top of the page, and then compare your screen with Figure 6.19.

Your name displays in the address text box.

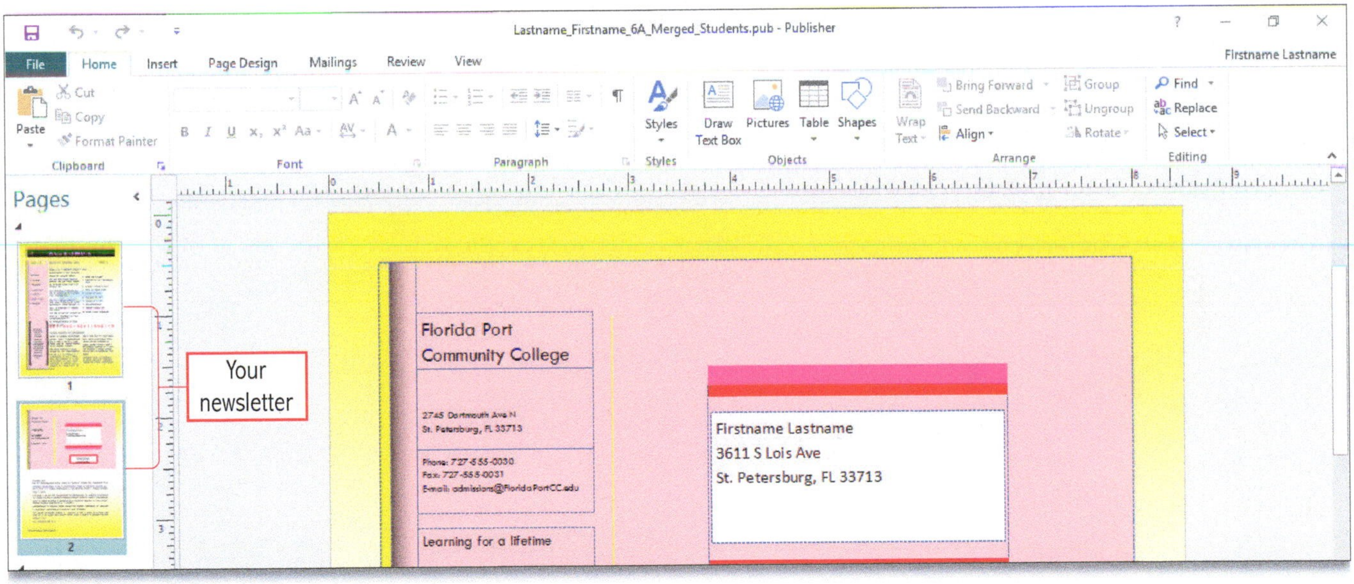

FIGURE 6.19

5 Display **Backstage** view. On the left, click **Info**, on the right, click **Publication Properties**, and then click **Advanced Properties**. In the **Properties** dialog box, on the **Summary tab**, in the **Subject** box, type your course name and section number; in the **Author** box, type your first name and last name; and then in the **Keywords** box, type **student newsletter, merged** Click **OK** to close the dialog box.

6 On the left, click **Save** to save your publication and redisplay the publication window. If your instructor directs you to submit your files electronically, go to Step 8.

7 To print your publication, click the **File tab** and then click **Print**. Under **Settings**, click the **Print All Pages arrow**, and then click **Print Custom Pages**. In the **Pages** box, type **1-2** and then click **Print**.

8 Close ⊠ your **Lastname_Firstname_6A_Merged_Students** publication. With your **Lastname_Firstname_6A_New_Students** publication displayed, **Save** 🖫 the file, and then **Close** ⊠ Publisher.

9 Submit your printed or electronic files as directed by your instructor.

END | You have completed Project 6A

PROJECT
6B Internship Postcard

PROJECT ACTIVITIES

In Activities 6.13 through 6.22, you will add an input mask and a default value to Access data fields. After creating a lookup field and entering data, you will create a report. In Publisher, you will use a template to create a postcard. Finally, using mail merge, you will create postcards for specific recipients. Your completed files will look similar to Figure 6.20.

PROJECT FILES

For Project 6B, you will need the following files:

New blank Publisher publication
New blank Access database
i06B_FPCC_Logo

You will save your files as:

Lastname_Firstname_6B_FPCC_Students
Lastname_Firstname_6B_Technology_Postcard
Lastname_Firstname_6B_Internship_Postcard

PROJECT RESULTS

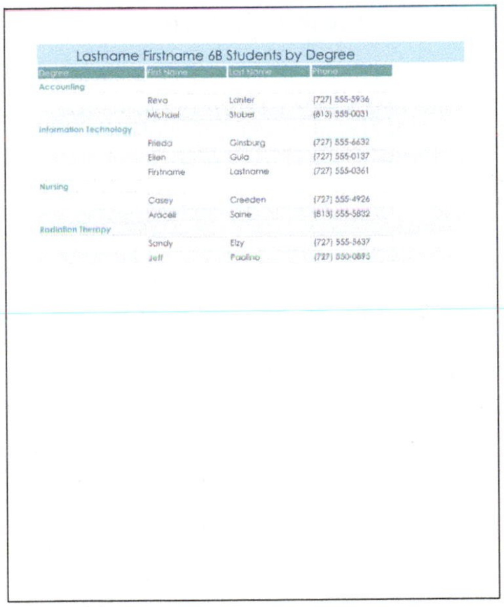

Lastname Firstname 6B Students by Degree

Degree	First Name	Last Name	Phone
Accounting			
	Reva	Lanter	(727) 555-3936
	Michael	Stuber	(813) 555-0031
Information Technology			
	Frieda	Ginsburg	(727) 555-6632
	Ellen	Gula	(727) 555-0137
	Firstname	Lastname	(727) 555-0361
Nursing			
	Casey	Creeden	(727) 555-4926
	Araceli	Saine	(813) 555-5832
Radiation Therapy			
	Sandy	Elzy	(727) 555-5637
	Jeff	Paolino	(727) 550-0895

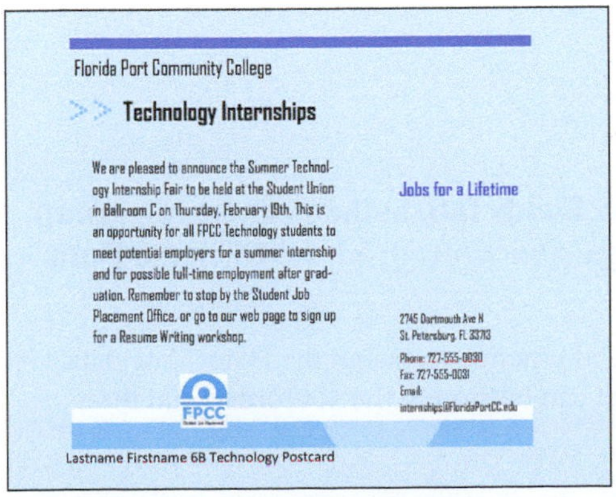

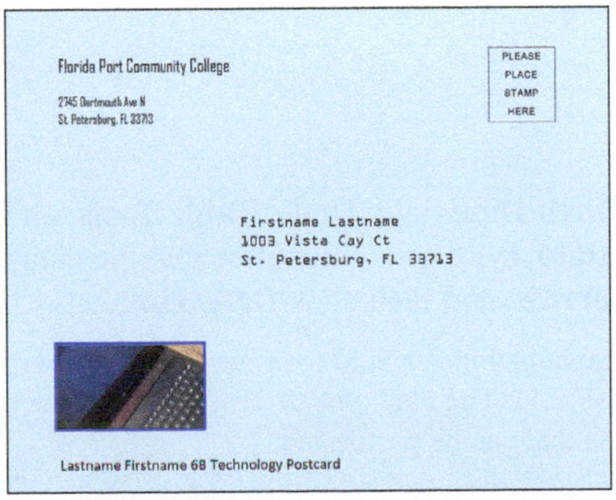

FIGURE 6.20 Internship Postcard

Recall that the structure of an Access table is the underlying design, including field names and data types. When you create an Access database, you can improve your data entry accuracy by setting *field properties*—characteristics of a field that control how the field displays and how data is entered in the field.

Activity 6.13 │ Inserting an Input Mask and a Default Value

You should set field properties before you enter any data in a table. If you change field properties after you have entered records in your table, you might lose some of the data. In this Activity, you will set field properties for the ID, Phone, and State fields of a table.

1 Start Access, and then click **Blank desktop database**. In the **Blank desktop database** dialog box, click **Browse** ▣. In the **File New Database** dialog box, navigate to your **Integrated Projects Chapter 6** folder. In the **File name** box, if necessary, select the existing text, and then using your own name, type **Lastname_Firstname_6B_FPCC_Students** Click **OK**. In the **Blank desktop database** dialog box, click **Create**.

Access creates a new database and opens a table named Table1 in Datasheet view.

2 At the top of the second column, click the text *Click to Add* to display a list of data types.

Recall that a data type is the characteristic that defines the kind of data that can be entered in a field such as numbers, text, or dates.

3 Click **Short Text**, and notice that in the second column, the text *Click to Add* changes to *Field1*, which is selected. Type **First Name** and then press Enter.

The second column displays *First Name* as the field name, and the data type list displays in the third column.

4 In the data type list, click **Short Text**, type **Last Name** and then press Enter. In a similar manner, add each of the following fields to the table, selecting the **Short Text** data type.

Address
City
State
ZIP
Phone
Birth Date
Degree

5 Click the **Birth Date** field. Under **Table Tools**, on the **Fields tab**, in the **Formatting group**, locate the **Data Type** box, and notice that the data type *Short Text* displays. Click the **Data Type box arrow**, and then click **Date/Time**.

When a table includes a field for entering dates, it is good practice to assign the Date/Time data type to the field. The data type determines the value that can be stored, the sort order, and the operations that can be performed.

6 Double-click the **ID** field, type **Student ID** and then press Enter. Under **Table Tools**, on the **Fields tab**, in the **Formatting group**, locate the **Data Type** box, and notice that the data type *AutoNumber* displays. Click the **Data Type box arrow**, and then click **Short Text**.

By default, when creating a new database, Access assigns the AutoNumber data type to the default ID field. Here, because students are assigned Student IDs in a specific format, you must change the data type and use a more descriptive name.

7 Under **Table Tools**, on the **Fields tab**, in the **Views group**, click **View** to switch to Design view. In the **Save As** dialog box, using your name, type **Lastname Firstname 6B All FPCC Students** and then click **OK**.

8 Under **Field Name**, click **Phone**, and then under **Field Properties**, click the **Input Mask** property box.

An ***input mask*** is a set of literal characters and placeholder characters that control what can and cannot be entered in an Access field. Use an input mask whenever you want users to enter data in a specific way.

9 On the right side of the **Input Mask** property box, click **Build** [...]. In the **Input Mask Wizard** dialog box, under **Input Mask**, verify that **Phone Number** is selected, and then click **Finish**. **Save** the table, and then compare your screen with Figure 6.21.

The input mask displays in the Field Properties area. A 0 placeholder indicates a required digit, and a 9 placeholder indicates an optional digit or space. The area code is enclosed in parentheses and a hyphen (-) separates the three-digit prefix from the four-digit number. The exclamation point (!) at the left of the input mask causes the field to be filled in from left to right. The field will display an underscore character (_) for each digit.

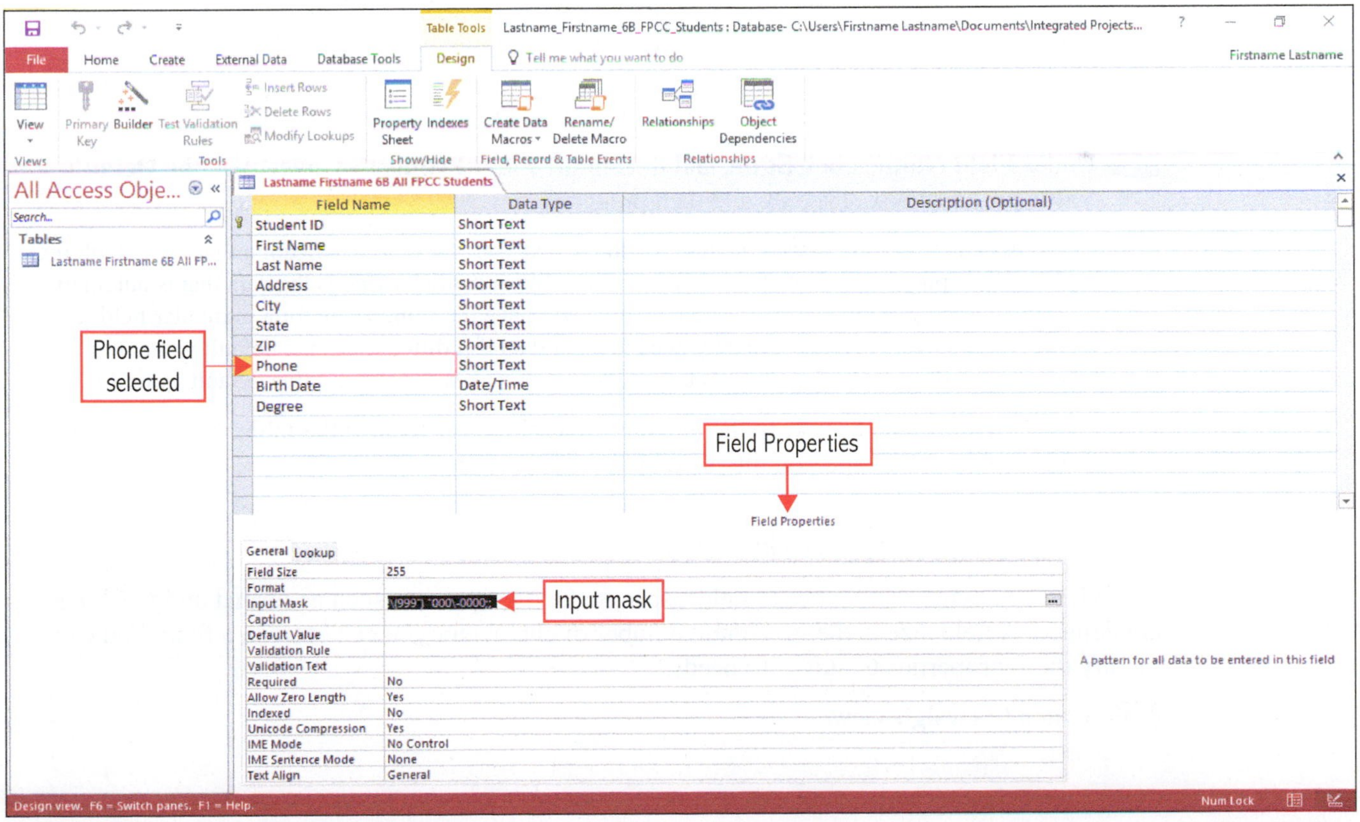

FIGURE 6.21

Access 2016, Windows 10, Microsoft Corporation

10 Under **Field Name**, click **Student ID**, and then under **Field Properties**, click the **Input Mask** property box. Type **12-0000000** and then press Enter. Compare your screen with Figure 6.22.

The input mask for the Student ID field displays. All student ID numbers begin with 12-. By typing 12- in the input mask, you will only need to type the unique seven-digit portion of each student's ID number. An input mask can be a ***validation rule***—limiting or controlling what users can enter in a field. By using validation rules, data entry errors can be reduced.

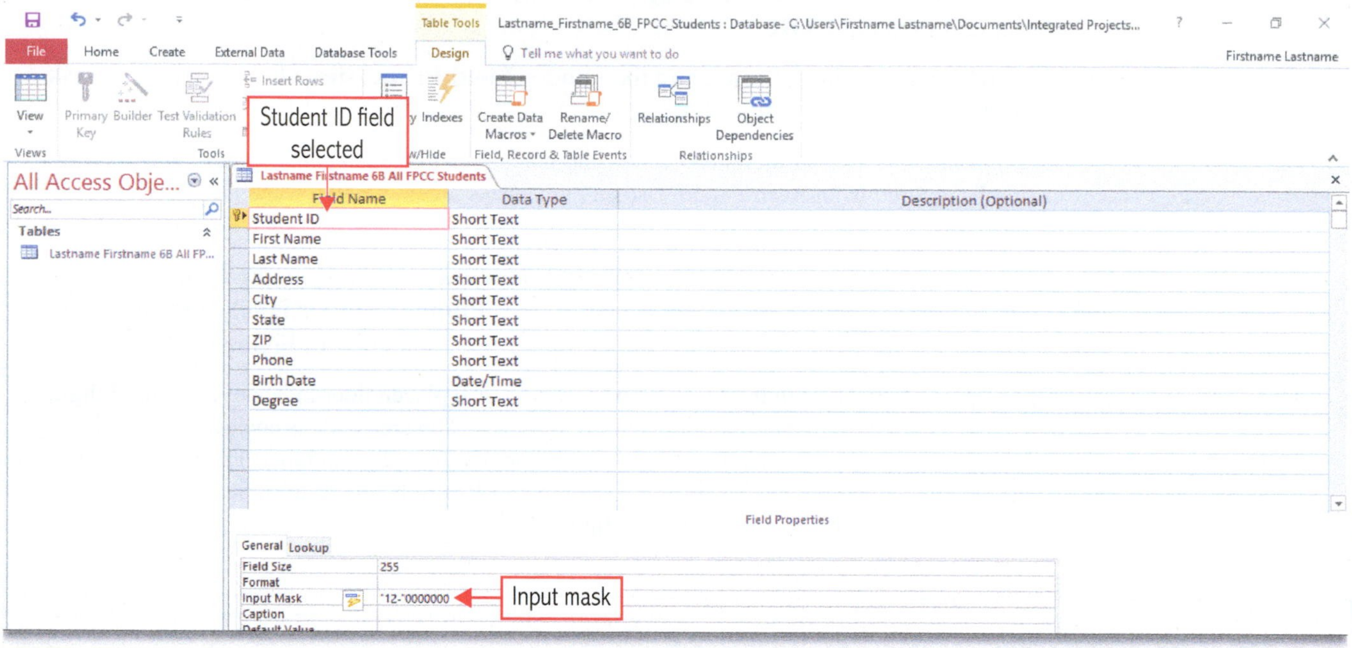

Access 2016, Windows 10, Microsoft Corporation

FIGURE 6.22

11 Under **Field Name**, click **State**, and then in the **Field Properties** area, click the **Default Value** property box. Type **FL** and then press Enter.

Access automatically inserts quotes around the text you just typed, indicating that the default text *FL* will display in the State field. In an Access table, a ***default value*** is the data that is automatically entered in a field. If most of the records will have the same value for a particular field, creating a default value means you only need to enter data if it differs from the default value. In this case, because most of the students live in Florida, it makes sense to use the default value *FL*.

12 Switch to **Datasheet** view. In the message box, click **Yes** to save the table. Notice the State field displays FL as the default value in the new record.

Activity 6.14 | Modifying the Field Properties

When you assign data types to fields, specific field properties, such as format and ***field size***, are defined. A field size is the maximum number of characters you can enter in a field. You can modify these properties to suit your needs.

1 Switch to **Design** view.

2 Under **Field Name**, click **Birth Date**. Under **Field Properties**, click the **Format** property box, and then click the **Format arrow** to display various date and time formats. In the list, click the **Short Date** format, and then compare your screen with Figure 6.23.

The term Short Date displays in the Format property box. When a date is entered, it will display as mm/dd/yyyy. In the Field Properties area, the last item—Show Date Picker—displays the property *For dates*. The **date picker** is a calendar control that is used to select a date. When entering a date in the Birth Date field, the Date Picker icon will display to the right of a cell. Clicking the Date Picker icon displays a calendar and allows the user to select a date quickly.

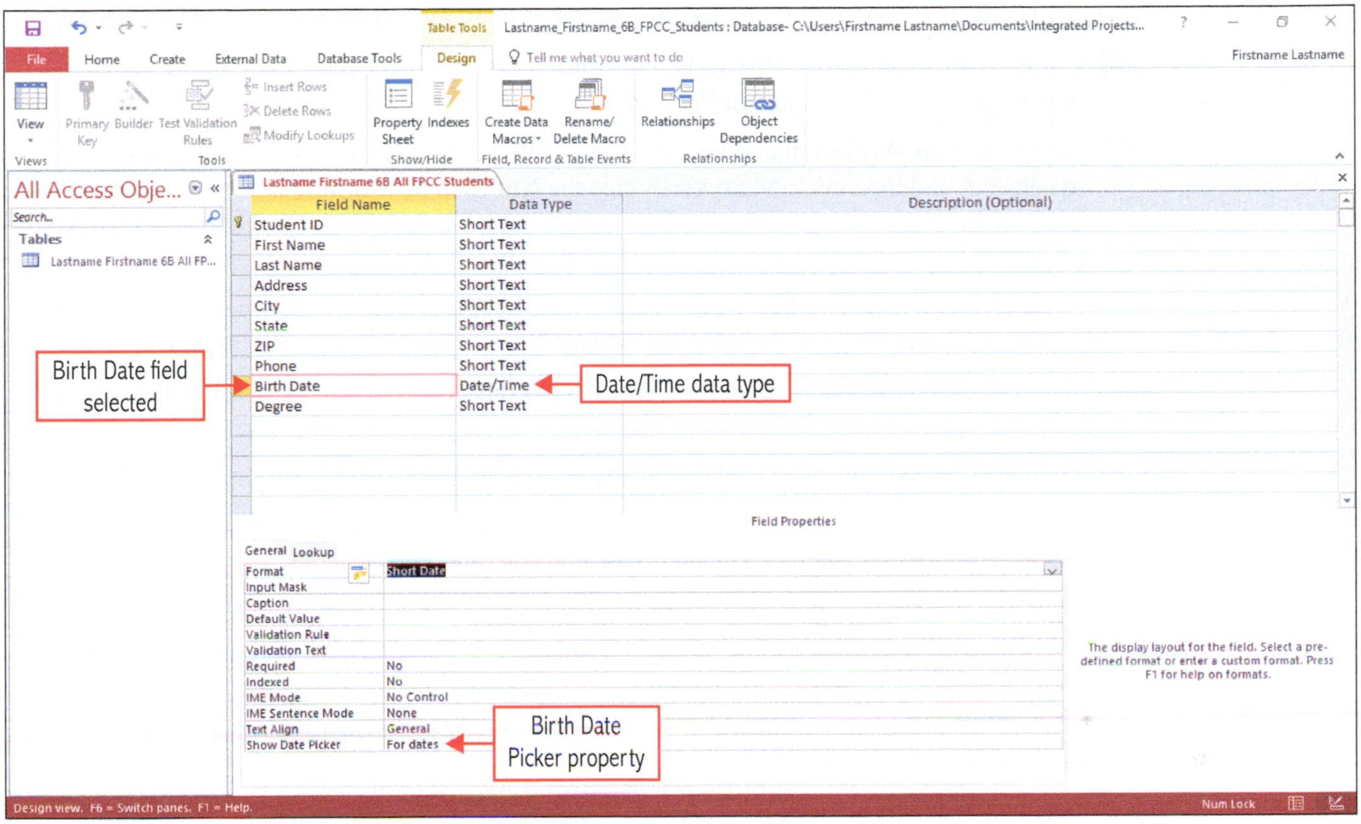

FIGURE 6.23

3 Under **Field Name**, click **First Name**, and then under **Field Properties**, click the **Field Size** property box. Select the number *255*, type **30** and then press Enter.

Recall that field size is the maximum number of characters you can enter in a *Short Text* field. You changed the Firstname field to 30 because you do not expect any student to have a first name longer than 30 characters.

4 Under **Field Name**, click **Last Name**, and then in the **Field Properties** area, click **Field Size**. Select the number *255*, type **30** and then press Enter.

5 Using the same technique, change the field size of the following fields.

Field Name	Student ID	Address	City	State	ZIP	Phone	Degree
Field Size	10	60	50	2	10	10	50

The field size cannot be changed for the Birth Date field because it is a Date/Time data type.

6 Save  the table.

> **More Knowledge** | **Entering Data in a Table**
>
> If you have valid data in a field that contains more characters than allowed by the field size property, switch to Design view, increase the Field Size for the field, switch back to Datasheet view, and then continue entering your data.

Activity 6.15 | Inserting a Lookup Field

The *Lookup Wizard* creates a list box to look up a value in another table, query, or list of values. Most of the students at Florida Port Community College live in either Tampa or St. Petersburg. Using a list box for the City field will minimize the amount of typing when entering the student records.

1 Under **Data Type**, in the **City** field, click the **Short Text** data type, click the **Data Type arrow**, and then click **Lookup Wizard**.

2 In the **Lookup Wizard** dialog box, click the *I will type in the values that I want* option button to select it, and then click **Next**. Verify that the **Number of columns** is **1**, and then press Tab. Type **St. Petersburg** and then press Tab. Type **Tampa** and then click **Finish**. If you mistakenly press Enter, the next dialog box of the wizard displays. If that happens, click the Back button.

> Because many students live in St. Petersburg and Tampa, these cities are added to a list. When entering data, you can choose the city from a list instead of typing the entire name.

3 With the **City** field selected, in the **Field Properties** area, click the **Default Value** property box, and then type **St. Petersburg**

4 Switch to **Datasheet** view. In the message box, click **Yes** to save the table.

> In the City field, the default value St. Petersburg displays. Since most of the students are from St. Petersburg, setting this as the default value will save time when entering student records.

5 Click the first cell under the **City** field, and then click the arrow to display the list of cities. Compare your screen with Figure 6.24.

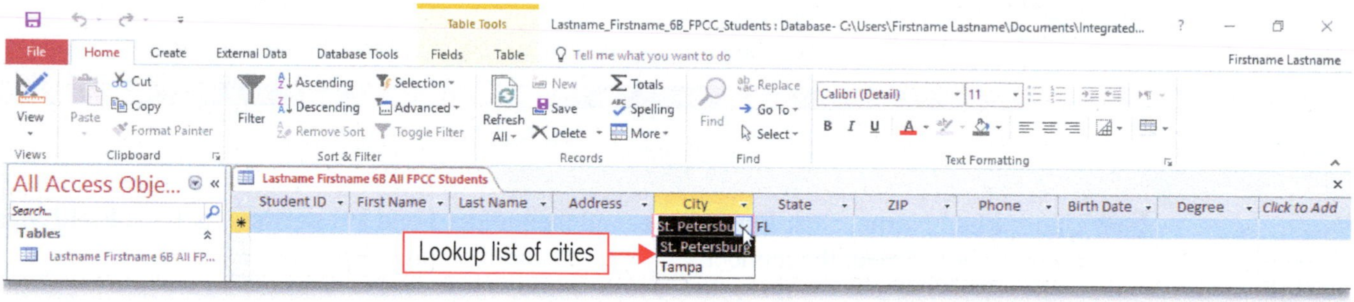

FIGURE 6.24

Access 2016, Windows 10, Microsoft Corporation

6 Close ☒ the **6B All FPCC Students** table.

7 If necessary, in the Navigation Pane, click the **6B All FPCC Students** table to select it. Click the **Create tab**, and then in the **Forms group**, click **Form**.

8 Switch to **Form** view. **Close** ☒ the **Navigation Pane**.

Activity 6.16 | Inputting Data with a Lookup Field

1 In the **Student ID** field, type **5** and then press `Tab`. Compare your screen with Figure 6.25.

A message box displays indicating that the value you entered is not appropriate for the input mask you created. Recall that you are required to enter seven digits in the ID field—one for each zero in the input mask. The input mask automatically displays *12-* to the left of any number you type, in this case 5.

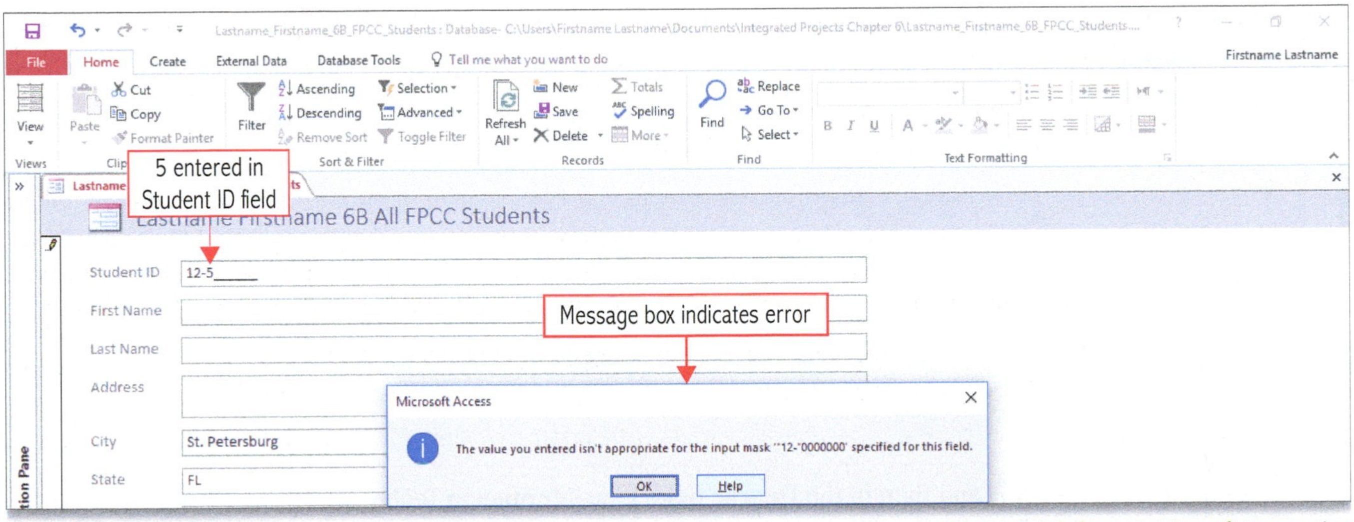

Access 2016, Windows 10, Microsoft Corporation

FIGURE 6.25

2 In the message box, click **OK**. In the **Student ID** field, with the insertion point to the right of *5*, type **223461** and then press `Enter`.

3 In the **First Name** field, type **Frieda** and then press `Tab`. In the **Last Name** field, type **Ginsburg** and then press `Tab`. In the **Address** field, type **9506 N 13th St** and then press `Tab` three times.

Because you used the Lookup Wizard to create a list and set St. Petersburg as the default value, you can skip the City field for a St. Petersburg address when entering the student records by pressing `Enter` or `Tab` to move to the next field. Additionally, because you inserted FL as the default value for the State field, you can skip that field by pressing `Enter` or `Tab` to move to the next field.

4 In the **ZIP** field, type **33714** and then press `Tab`. In the **Phone** field, type **7275556632** and then press `Tab`.

Because you set up the phone input mask, you do not need to type the parentheses, the dash, or any spaces.

5 In the **Birth Date** field, type **5/9/93** and then compare your screen with Figure 6.26.

You could click the Date Picker icon, which displays to the right of the Birth Date field, to select the date; however, you would be navigating through a large number of years. In this case, typing the date is a faster way to input the data.

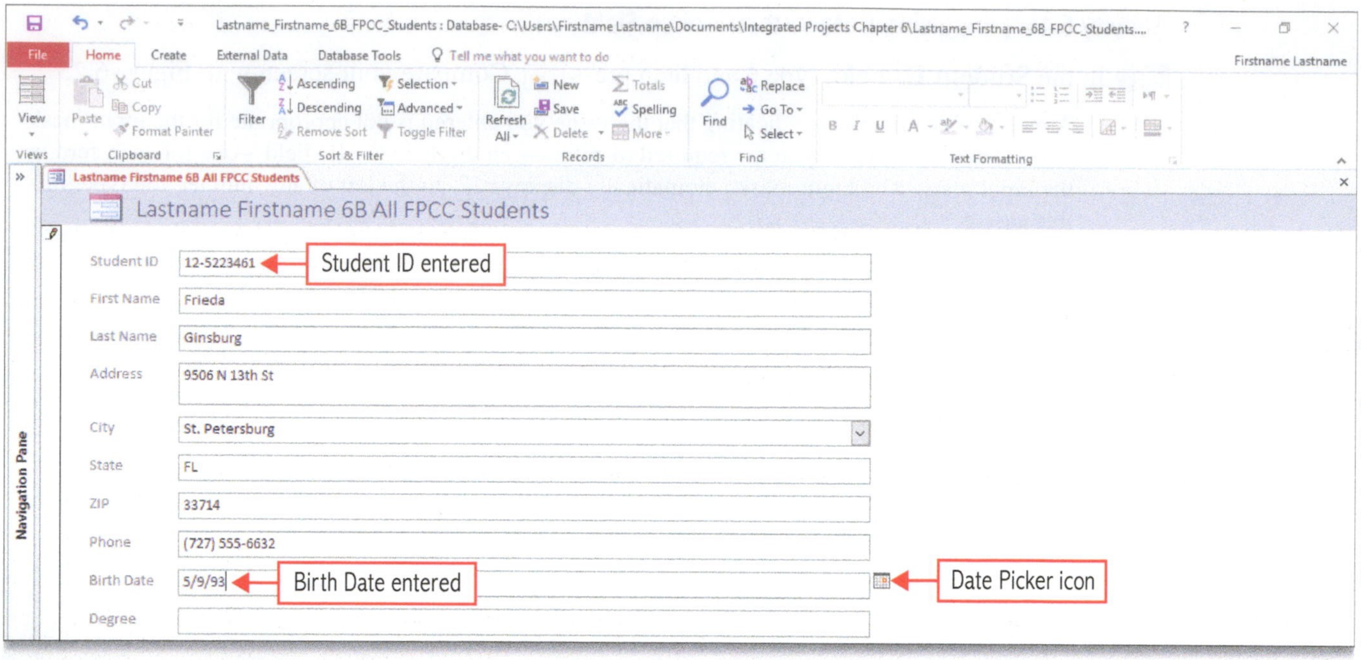

FIGURE 6.26

6 ▶ Press Tab, and then in the **Degree** field, type **Information Technology**

The date is accepted, and Access automatically adjusts the date to 5/9/1993 to match the Short Date format property you set for the Birth Date field.

7 ▶ Press Tab to accept the student record and to move to the next new record.

8 ▶ In the **Student ID** field, type **4881127** and then press Tab. In the **First Name** field, type **Michael** and then press Tab. In the **Last Name** field, type **Stober** and then press Tab. In the **Address** field, type **828 Raysbrook Dr** and then press Tab.

9 ▶ In the **City** field, type the letter **t** and then compare your screen with Figure 6.27.

The city name *tampa* displays in the City field. A list item will display in the field when you type the first letter of an item in the list. You do not need to capitalize the letter—when you move to the next field, the first letter will be capitalized because that is the way the item was entered in your list. This feature makes data entry faster.

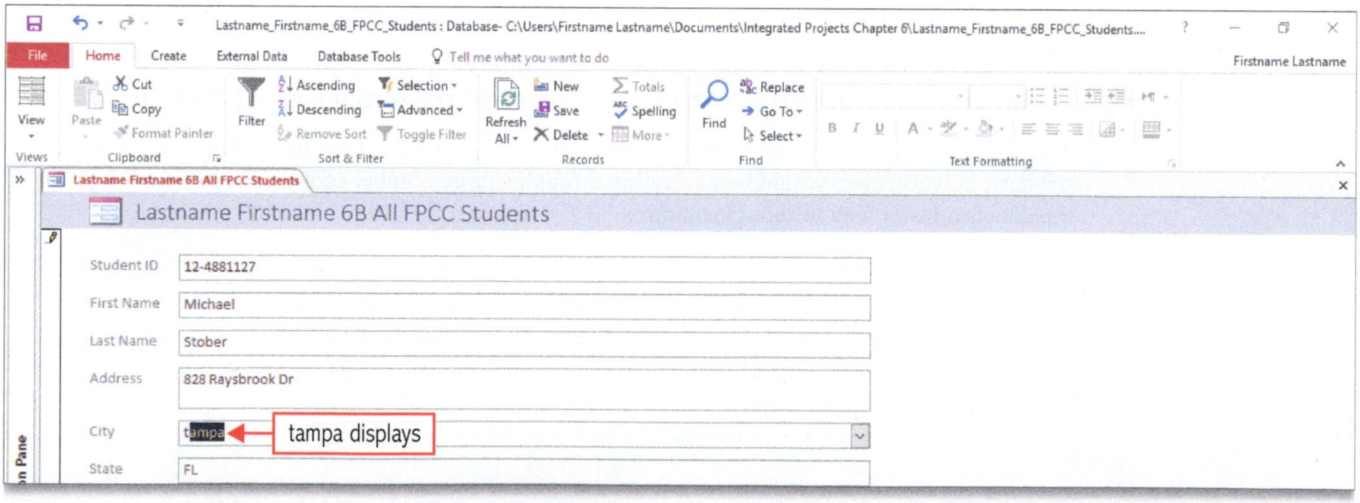

FIGURE 6.27

10 Press Tab two times. In the **ZIP** field, type **33621** and then press Tab. In the **Phone** field, type **8135550031** and then press Tab. In the **Birth Date** field, type **11/26/98** and then press Tab.

11 In the **Degree** field, type **Accounting** and then press Tab to accept the record and move to the next new record.

12 Using the same technique, enter the following student records. For the last student, type your own first name and last name. Press Tab after entering your Degree to accept the record. Note: Because all the students are from Florida, the State field is not listed in the following table; press Tab to skip the State field and accept FL.

Student ID	First Name	Last Name	Address	City	ZIP	Phone	Birth Date	Degree
7820522	Jeff	Paolino	11008 Connacht Way	St. Petersburg	33713	7275550895	5/7/90	Radiation Therapy
4637811	Reva	Lanter	12825 Astonwood Dr	St. Petersburg	33709	7275555936	8/13/97	Accounting
6488259	Casey	Creeden	5502 Terrace Ct	St. Petersburg	33708	7275554926	9/12/91	Nursing
1184755	Ellen	Gula	10200 N Armenia Ave	St. Petersburg	33709	7275550137	4/28/96	Information Technology
1849915	Araceli	Saine	1326 New Bedford Dr	Tampa	33605	8135555832	12/27/80	Nursing
8335796	Sandy	Elzy	1910 S 47th St	St. Petersburg	33708	7275555637	3/28/92	Radiation Therapy
6184273	Firstname	Lastname	1003 Vista Cay Ct	St. Petersburg	33713	7275550361	10/12/96	Information Technology

13 At the bottom of your screen, in the navigation area, click **Previous record** ◄ to check all the data in each of the nine records and correct any data entry errors.

14 Right-click the **6B All FPCC Students form tab**, and then on the shortcut menu, click **Save**. In the **Save As** dialog box, under **Form Name**, using your name, type **Lastname Firstname 6B FPCC Student Form** and then click **OK**.

15 Close ☒ the **6B FPCC Students** form.

Activity 6.17 | Grouping and Sorting Using the Blank Report Tool

The **Blank Report tool** enables you to create a report from scratch by adding the fields you designate in the order you want them to display. This tool provides a quick way to build a report, especially if you are including only a few fields. In this Activity, you will create a report listing the FPCC students—grouped by their degree program and sorted in ascending order by last name.

1 On the **Create tab**, in the **Reports group**, click **Blank Report**.

2 If necessary, on the Design tab, in the Tools group, click **Add Existing Fields** to display the **Field List** pane on the right. In the **Field List** pane, click **Show all tables**, and then click the **plus sign** (+) to the left of **6B All FPCC Students**. In the **Field List** pane, double-click the field **First Name**, and then compare your screen with Figure 6.28.

The Firstname field is added to the report.

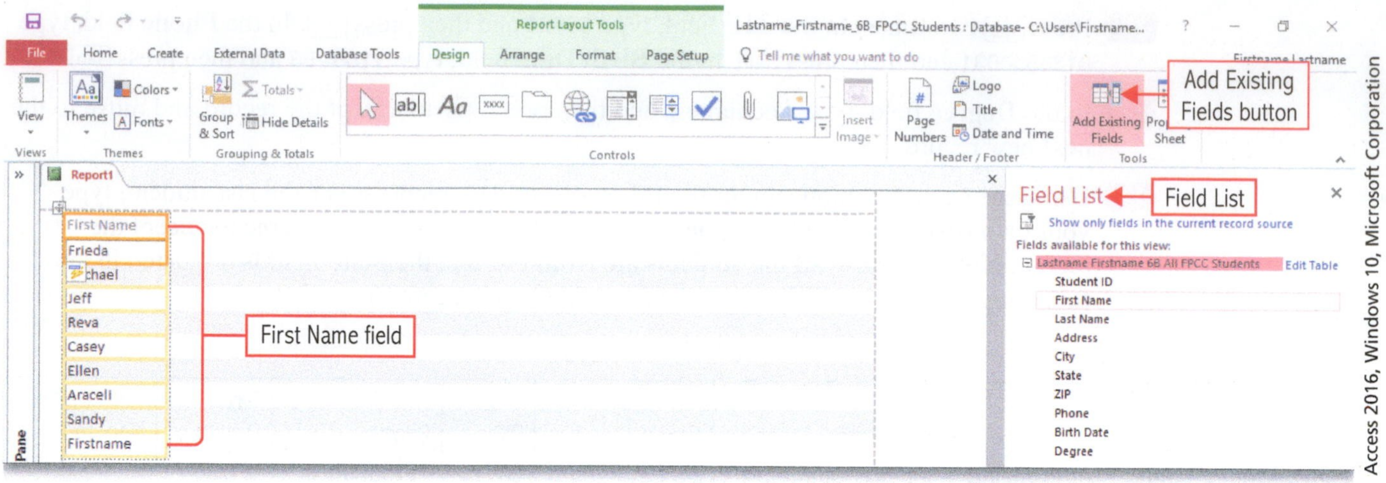

FIGURE 6.28

3 In the **Field List** pane, double-click the fields **Last Name**, **Phone**, and **Degree** to add the fields to the report. **Close** ☒ the **Field List**.

4 Under **Report Layout Tools**, on the **Design tab**, in the **Grouping & Totals group**, click **Group & Sort**. Compare your screen with Figure 6.29.

The Group, Sort, and Total pane displays below the report. The pane contains an *Add a group* button and an *Add a sort* button.

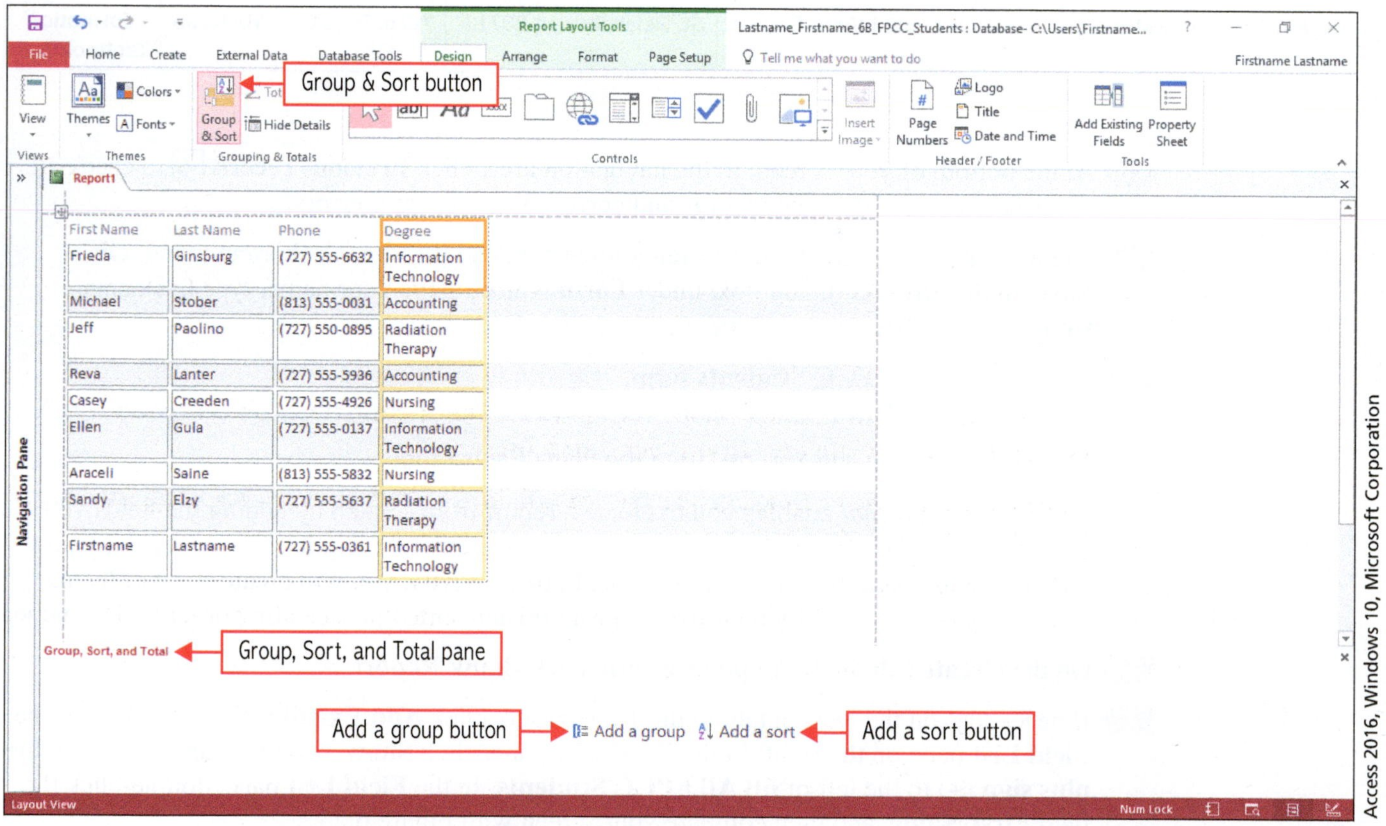

FIGURE 6.29

5 ▶ Click **Add a group**, and then click **Degree**.

The Degree field moves to the left of the report; the students are grouped in ascending order by their degrees. *Grouping* enables you to separate groups of records visually and to display introductory and summary data for each group in a report.

6 ▶ Click **Add a sort**, and then click **Last Name**. Compare your screen with Figure 6.30.

The students are listed by the Degree field, and then within the Degree field, the students are sorted in ascending order by the Last Name field.

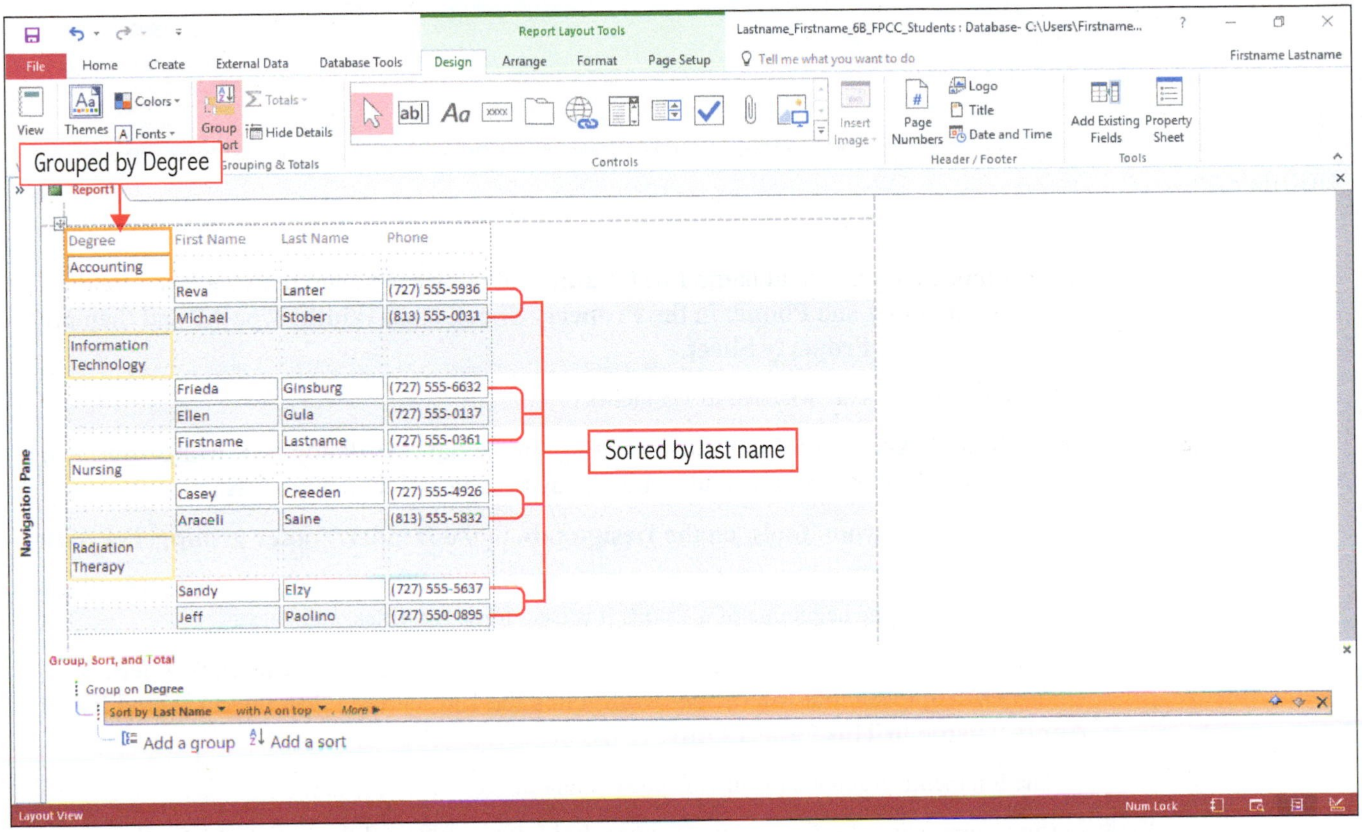

FIGURE 6.30

7 ▶ Under **Report Layout Tools**, on the **Design tab**, in the **Grouping & Totals group**, click **Group & Sort** to close the **Group, Sort, and Total** pane.

8 ▶ Under **Report Layout Tools**, on the **Design tab**, in the **Tools group**, click **Property Sheet** to display the Property Sheet pane.

The *Property Sheet* is a list of characteristics—properties—for fields or controls on a form or report in which you can make precise changes to each property associated with the field or control.

9 ▶ In the report, click the **Degree** field name. In the **Property Sheet** pane, click the **Format tab**. Click **Width** to select the number, type **2** and then press Enter. Compare your screen with Figure 6.31.

The width of the Degree column in the report is increased to 2 inches so each degree is displayed on one line.

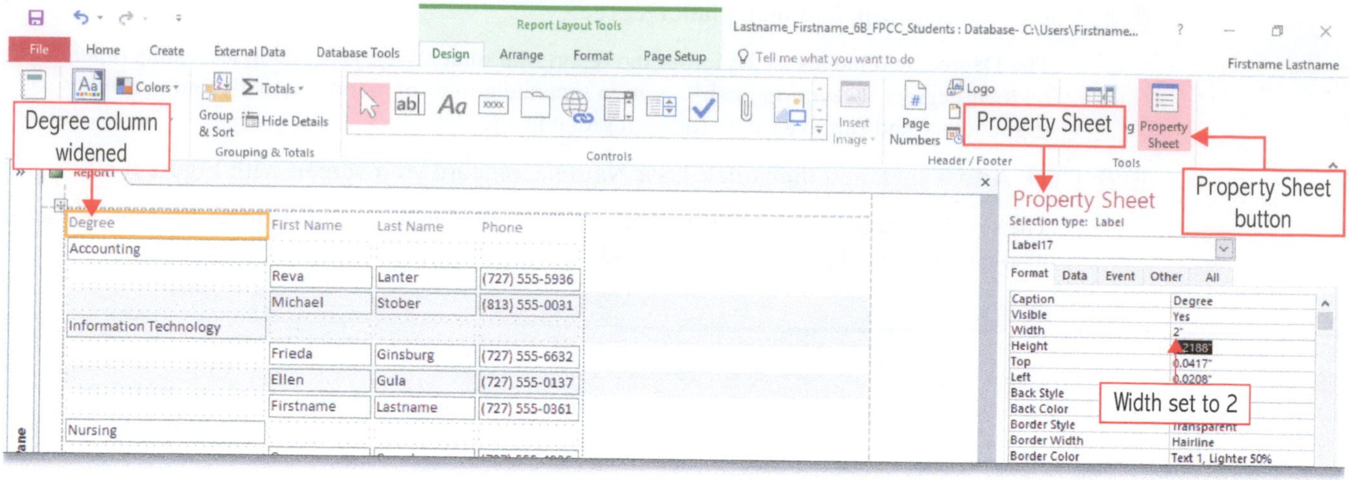

Access 2016, Windows 10, Microsoft Corporation

FIGURE 6.31

10 In the report, click the field name **First Name**, hold down Ctrl, and then click the field names **Last Name** and **Phone**. In the **Property Sheet**, click **Width**, type **1.5** and then press Enter. **Close** ☒ the **Property Sheet**.

All three columns are widened to 1.5 inches.

11 On the **Quick Access Toolbar**, click **Save**. In the **Save As** dialog box, using your own name, type **Lastname Firstname 6B Students by Degree** and then click **OK**.

12 Under **Report Layout Tools**, on the **Design tab**, in the **Header/Footer group**, click **Title**.

The title displays at the top of the page in the ***report header***. The report header is information printed once at the beginning of a report; it is used for logos, titles, and dates.

13 Under **Report Layout Tools**, on the **Design tab**, in the **Themes group**, click **Themes**. Under **Office**, locate the **Ion** theme. Right-click the **Ion** theme. From the displayed list, click **Apply Theme to This Object Only**.

The Ion theme is applied to only the current report.

14 In the report, click the field name **Degree**, hold down Shift, and then click the field name **Phone**—release the mouse button. With all four field names selected, under **Report Layout Tools**, click the **Format tab**. In the **Font group**, click the **Background color button arrow**, and then under **Theme Colors**, in the eighth column, click the first color—**Green, Accent 4**. Click the **Font Color button arrow**, and then under **Theme Colors**, click the first color—**White, Background 1**.

15 In the report, click **Accounting**, hold down Shift, and then click **Radiation Therapy**—release the mouse button. With all four fields selected, in the **Font group**, click the **Font Color button arrow**, and then under **Theme Colors**, in the eighth column, click the first color—**Green, Accent 4**. Apply **Bold** B.

16 Click the **Home tab**. In the **Views group**, click the **View button arrow**, and then click **Print Preview**. Compare your screen with Figure 6.32.

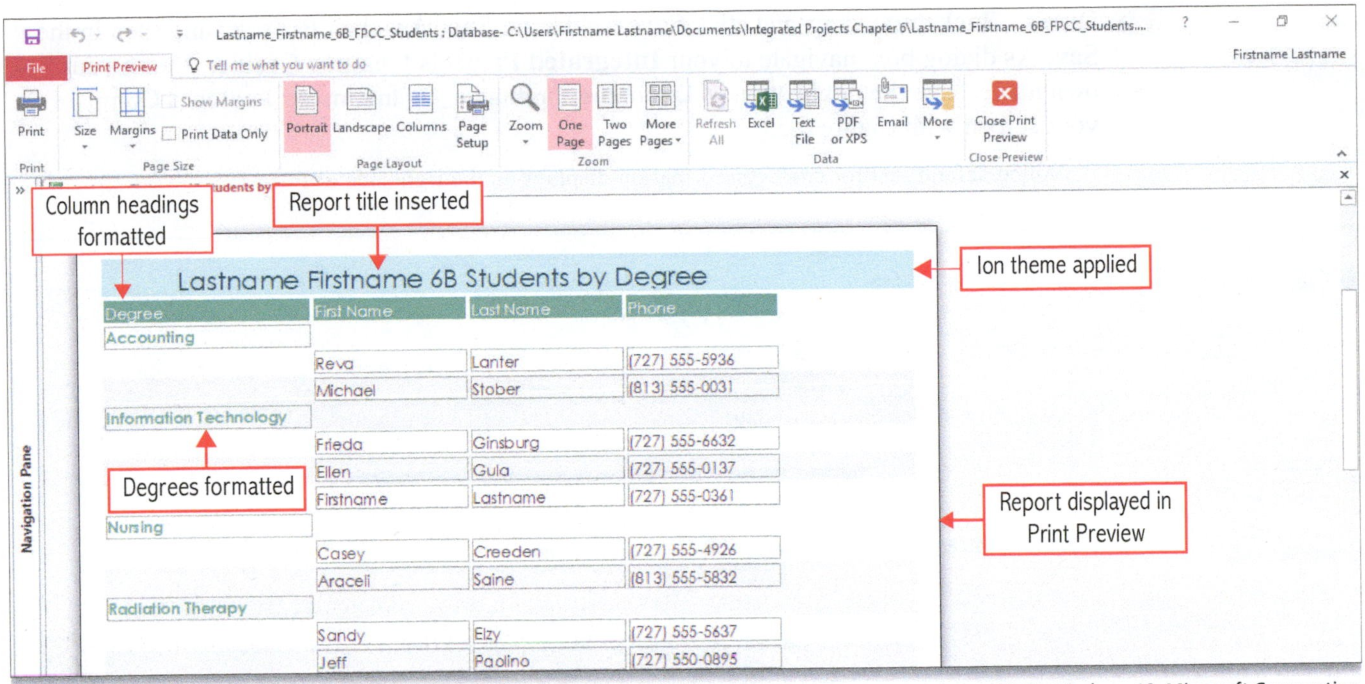

Access 2016, Windows 10, Microsoft Corporation

FIGURE 6.32

17 From **Backstage** view, click **View and edit database properties**. In the **Properties** dialog box, on the **Summary tab**, in the **Subject** box, type your course name and section number; in the **Author** box, type your first name and last name; and then in the **Keywords** box, type **report, phone, degree** Click **OK** to close the dialog box. On the left, click **Save** to return to the database window. If your instructor directs you to submit your files electronically, go to Step 20.

18 To print the report, on the **Print Preview tab**, in the **Print group**, click **Print**, and then click **OK**.

19 **Close** ☒ the **6B Students by Degree report**. If necessary, in the message box, click **Yes** to save the changes to the design of the report. **Close** ☒ Access.

Objective 6 Create a Publication Using a Publisher Template

Use a template to speed the creation of a publication. Recall that a template is a preformatted publication designed for a specific purpose. There are templates to match almost any publication need. You can use a Publisher template installed on your computer, or you can download a template from Microsoft Office Online.

Activity 6.18 | Using a Publication Template

Brad Futral, the Director of the Student Job Placement Office, is conducting a Job Fair for technology students. In this Activity, you have been asked to create a postcard to remind students to attend the Job Fair.

1 Start Publisher, on the right, under **Suggested searches**, click **BUILT-IN**. Scroll down, and click **Postcards**. Under **Built-In Templates**, under **Marketing**, click the **Arrows** postcard. At the right, under **Customize**, click the **Color scheme arrow**, scroll down and then click **Marine**. In the lower right corner, click **Create**.

A new publication based on the Arrows postcard template displays.

2 ▶ Display **Backstage** view, and click **Save As**. Under **Save As**, click **Browse**, and then in the **Save As** dialog box, navigate to your **Integrated Projects Chapter 6** folder. Using your own name, save the publication as **Lastname_Firstname_6B_Internship_Postcard** Compare your screen with Figure 6.33.

Notice default text for contact information displays on the right side of Page 1.

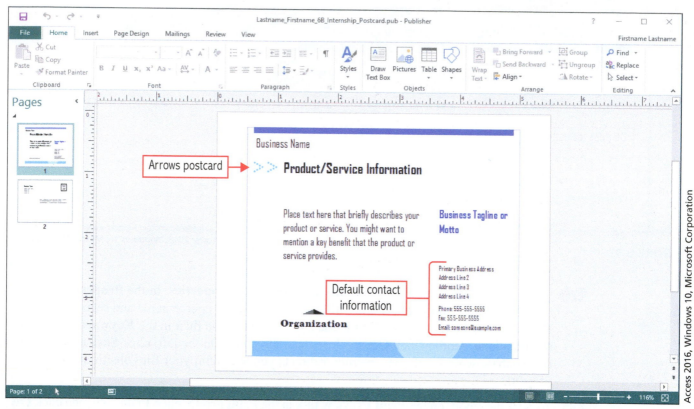

FIGURE 6.33

3 ▶ Click the **Insert tab**, and then in the **Header & Footer group**, click **Footer**. In the **Footer** text box, type **Lastname Firstname 6B Internship Postcard** and then on the **Master Page tab**, in the **Close group**, click **Close Master Page**.

Activity 6.19 | Inserting Business Information

A **business information set** is a customized group of information—including items such as a company name, address, phone number, email address, and logo—that can be used to quickly fill in appropriate areas in a publication.

1 ▶ Click the **Insert tab**. In the **Text group**, click **Business Information**, and then near the bottom of the list, click **Edit Business Information**.

The Create New Business Information Set dialog box displays.

2 ▶ In the **Create New Business Information Set** dialog box, under **Individual name**, select the text, and then type **Brad Futral** Under **Job position or title**, select the text, and then type **Director, Student Job Placement**

3 ▶ Under **Organization name**, select the text, and then type **Florida Port Community College** Under **Address**, select all the text, type **2745 Dartmouth Ave N** and then press **Enter**. Type **St. Petersburg, FL 33713** Under **Phone, fax and email**, select the phone number, and then type **727-555-0030** Select the fax number, and then type **727-555-0031** Select the email address, and then type **internships@FloridaPortCC.edu**

4 Under **Tagline or motto**, select the text *Business Tagline or Motto*, and then type **Jobs for a Lifetime**

5 In the **Business Information set** name box, select the text, type **Futral** and then click **Save**.

6 In the **Business Information** dialog box, click **Update Publication**, and then compare your screen with Figure 6.34.

Notice the college name displays at the top of Page 1, and the new contact information displays at the right.

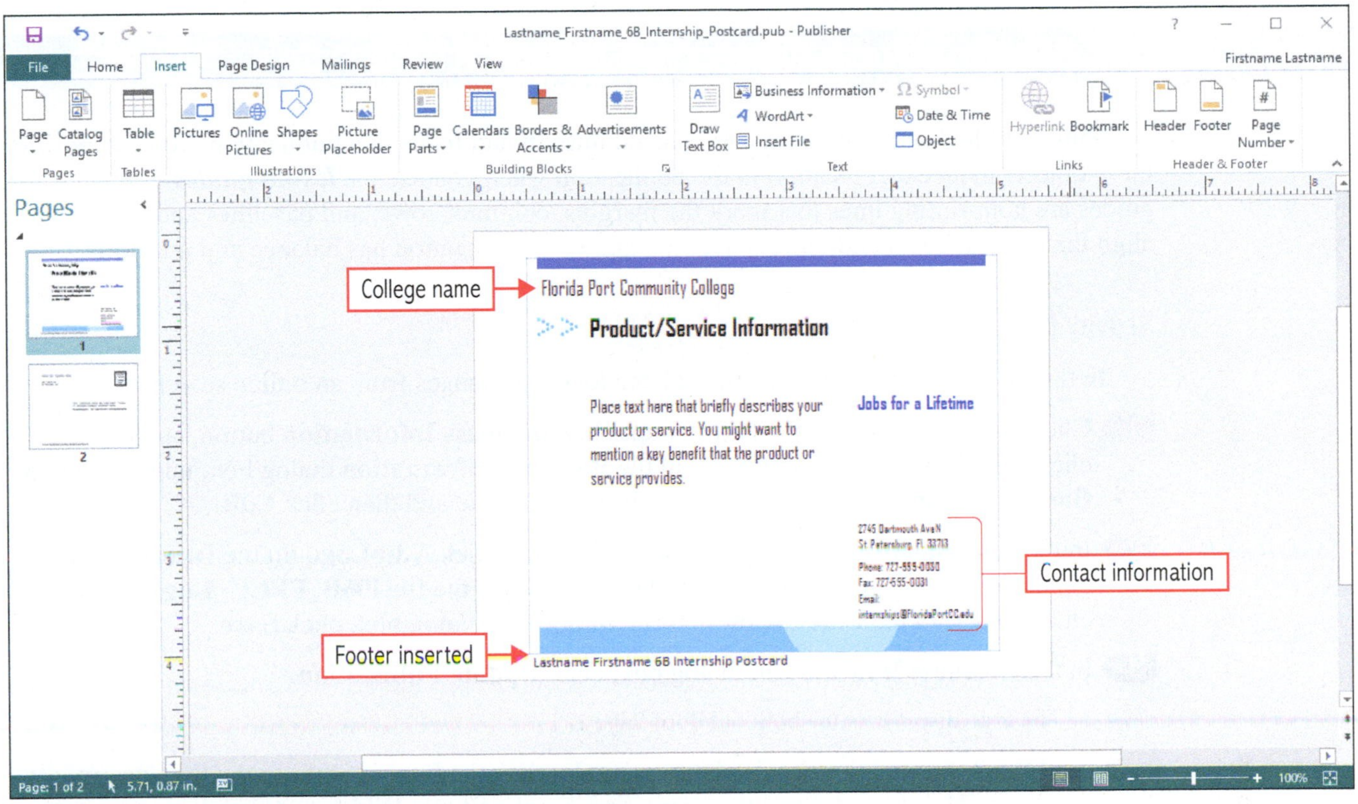

FIGURE 6.34

Access 2016, Windows 10, Microsoft Corporation

7 On **Page 1**, click the heading **Product/Service Information**, and then type **Technology Internships**

8 With the text box selected, under **Drawing Tools**, click the **Format tab**. In the **Size group**, set the **Shape Height** to **0.4** and then press Enter.

9 In the middle of the page, click the text box containing the paragraph that begins *Place text here*. Point to the border to display the pointer, and then drag the text box so the top left corner is located at **approximately 0.75 inch on the horizontal ruler** and **1.25 inches on the vertical ruler**. Under **Drawing Tools**, click the **Format tab**. In the **Size group**, set the **Shape Height** to **1.8** and then press Enter. Click in the text box, and then under **Text Box Tools**, click the **Format tab**. In the **Text group**, click **Text Fit**, and then click **Shrink Text on Overflow**.

The Shrink Text on Overflow feature will automatically change the font size to accommodate the text that is typed in the text box.

10 With the entire paragraph that begins *Place text here* selected, type **We are pleased to announce the Summer Technology Internship Fair to be held at the Student Union in Ballroom C on Thursday, February 19th. This is an opportunity for all FPCC Technology students to meet potential employers for a summer internship and for possible full-time employment after**

graduation. Remember to stop by the Student Job Placement Office, or go to our web page to sign up for a Resume Writing workshop.

Notice that as you type the font size is reduced to allow all the text to display in the text box.

11 ▶ Click the **Review tab**, and then in the **Proofing group**, click **Spelling**. Continue to check the spelling in your publication until a message box displays *The spelling check is complete*, and then click **OK**.

12 ▶ **Save** 🖫 your publication.

Objective 7 │ Modify the Layout of a Publication

Building blocks and other images can add interest and focus to a publication. You can position these objects in an exact location in the publication when you use the *layout guides*. Layout guides are nonprinting lines that mark the margins, columns, rows, and baselines and are used to align the text, pictures, and other objects so that your publication has balance and uniformity.

Activity 6.20 │ Inserting Images

In this Activity, you will insert the college logo and images from an online search.

1 ▶ Click the **Insert tab**. In the **Text group**, click **Business Information** button, and then click **Edit Business Information**. In the **Business Information** dialog box, under **Select a Business Information set**, verify that *Futral* displays, and then click **Edit**.

2 ▶ In the **Edit Business Information Set** dialog box, click **Add Logo**. In the **Insert Picture** dialog box, navigate to your student data files, select the file **i06B_FPCC_Logo**, and then click **Insert**. In the **Edit Business Information Set** dialog box, click **Save**.

3 ▶ In the **Business Information** dialog box, click **Update Publication**.

The logo displays at the bottom left of Page 1.

4 ▶ Click the logo, and then, under **Picture Tools**, click the **Format tab**. In the **Size group**, set the **Shape Height** to **0.5** and then press ⏎. Set the **Shape Width** to **1** and then press ⏎. In the **Arrange group**, click the **Bring Forward button arrow**, and then click **Bring to Front**. Compare your screen with Figure 6.35.

FIGURE 6.35

5 In the **Pages** pane, click **Page 2**. Click the **Insert tab**, and then in the **Illustrations group**, click **Online Pictures**. To the right of **Bing Search**, type **instructors computers** and press Enter. Scroll as necessary to locate an image, and then click and insert the image. Under **Picture Tools**, on the **Format tab**, in the **Size** group, set the **Shape Width** to **2** and then press Enter.

The selected image is inserted in the publication.

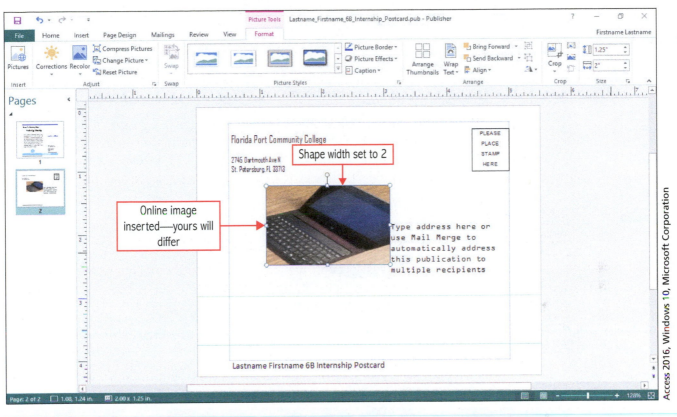

FIGURE 6.36

6 Click in a blank area of the page. Click the **Page Design tab**, and then in the **Page Background group**, click **Background**. In the **Background** gallery, under **Solid Background**, in the second row, right-click the second background—**30% tint of Accent 2**—and then on the shortcut menu, click **Apply to All Pages**.

The background is applied to both pages of the publication.

7 **Save** 🖫 your publication.

Activity 6.21 | Using Layout Guides

Margin guides are nonprinting lines on the top, bottom, left, and right sides of the page that define the page margins. A *ruler guide* is a nonprinting horizontal or vertical line that can be aligned to any position on the ruler.

1 Click the **View tab**, and then in the **Show group**, verify that the **Guides** check box is selected.

2 Point to the horizontal ruler to display the ⬍ pointer. Hold down the left mouse button, drag down to the **3.75 inch mark on the vertical rule**, and then release the mouse button to display the horizontal ruler guide.

3 Using the same technique, position another horizontal guide at the **3 inch mark on the vertical rule**.

4 ▸ Point to the vertical ruler to display the ⊹ pointer. Hold down Shift, and then drag the vertical ruler to the right of the 0 to the **0.5 inch mark on the horizontal ruler** to create a vertical ruler guide. The right edge of the vertical ruler should be touching the 0.5 inch mark. Compare your screen with Figure 6.37. If necessary, drag the picture as shown in the figure.

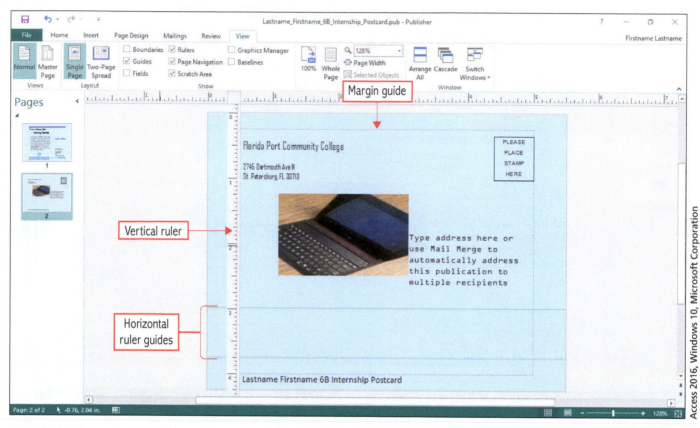

FIGURE 6.37

5 ▸ Point to the picture until the ⊹ pointer displays. Drag the picture down and to the left until the bottom left corner is at **3.75 inches on the vertical ruler** and **0.5 inch on the horizontal ruler**.

The image should be touching both the lower horizontal ruler guide and the vertical ruler.

6 ▸ Click the image to select it, and point to the top right sizing handle until the ⟋ pointer displays. Decrease the size of the image so the top right corner is touching the horizontal guide at **3 inches on the vertical ruler**. Compare your screen with Figure 6.38.

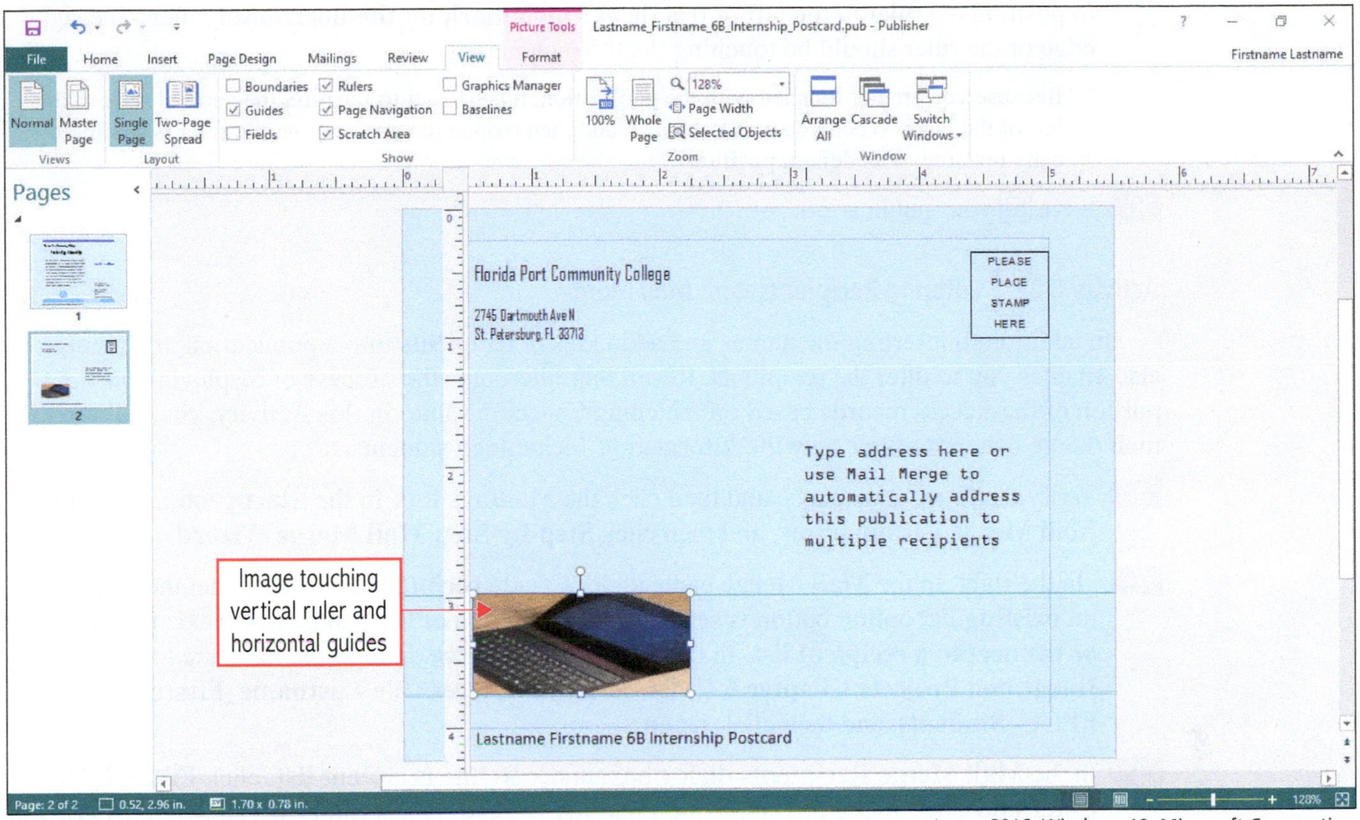

Access 2016, Windows 10, Microsoft Corporation

FIGURE 6.38

7 With the image selected, under **Picture Tools**, click the **Format tab**. In the **Picture Styles group**, click **Picture Border**, and then under **Scheme Colors**, in the second column, click the first color—**Accent 1 (RGB (0, 51, 204))**.

8 In the **Arrange group**, click **Rotate Objects** ⬛, and then click **Flip Horizontal**. Compare your screen with Figure 6.39.

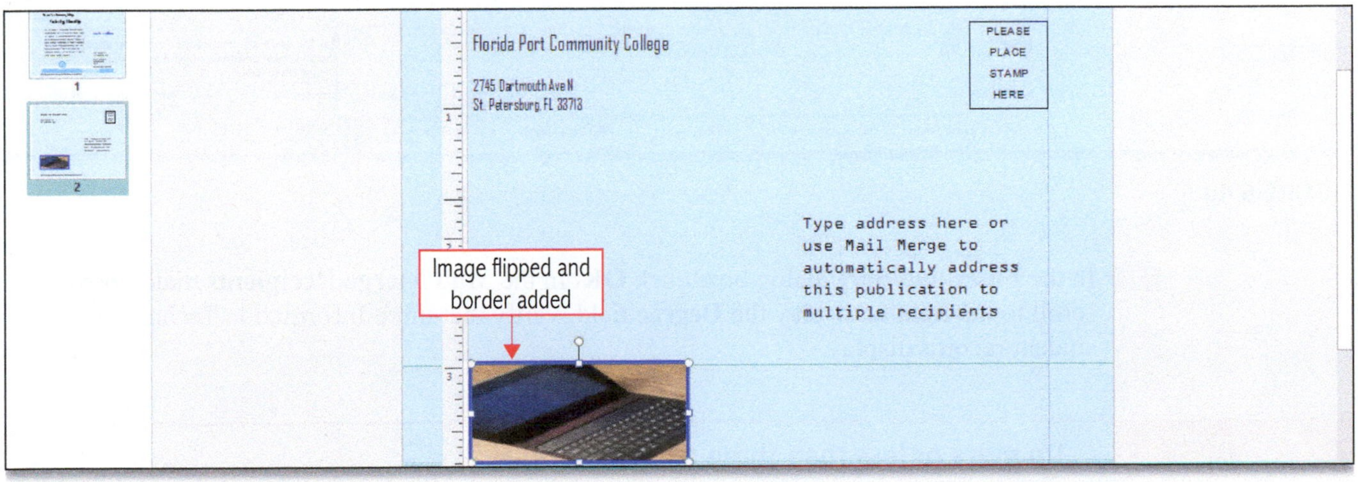

Access 2016, Windows 10, Microsoft Corporation

FIGURE 6.39

9 On **Page 2**, point to the lower horizontal ruler guide, right-click, and then on the shortcut menu, click **Delete Guide**. Using the same technique, delete the other horizontal ruler guide. Point to vertical ruler to display the ⬛ pointer, and then hold down Shift and drag to the left to position the ruler to the left of 0 at the **0.5 inch mark on the horizontal ruler**. The right edge of the ruler should be touching the 0.5 inch mark.

Because you are not finished with the publication, it is helpful to position the vertical ruler to the left of the page. When you exit Publisher, and then reopen the application, the ruler is automatically restored to its default position.

10 ▶ **Save** 🔲 your publication.

Activity 6.22 │ Filtering Recipients with Mail Merge

In addition to inserting the names and addresses of recipients into a publication, mail merge also enables you to filter the recipients. Recall that filtering is the process of displaying only a portion of the Access records based on matching a specific value. In this Activity, you will use the mail merge feature to filter only the Information Technology students.

1 ▶ Verify that **Page 2** displays, and then click the **Mailings tab**. In the **Start group**, click the **Mail Merge button arrow**, and then click **Step-by-Step Mail Merge Wizard**.

2 ▶ On the right, in the **Mail Merge** pane, under **Create recipient list**, verify that the **Use an existing list** option button is selected. At the bottom of the pane, click **Next: Create or connect to a recipient list**. In the **Select Data Source** dialog box, navigate to your **Integrated Projects Chapter 6** folder, select your Access file **Lastname_Firstname_6B_FPCC_Students**, and then click **Open**.

3 ▶ In the **Mail Merge Recipients** dialog box, under **Refine recipient list**, click **Filter**. In the **Filter and Sort** dialog box, click the **Field arrow**, and then scroll down and click **Degree**. Verify that the **Comparison** box contains **Equal to**. Click in the **Compare to** box, type **Information Technology** and then compare your screen with Figure 6.40.

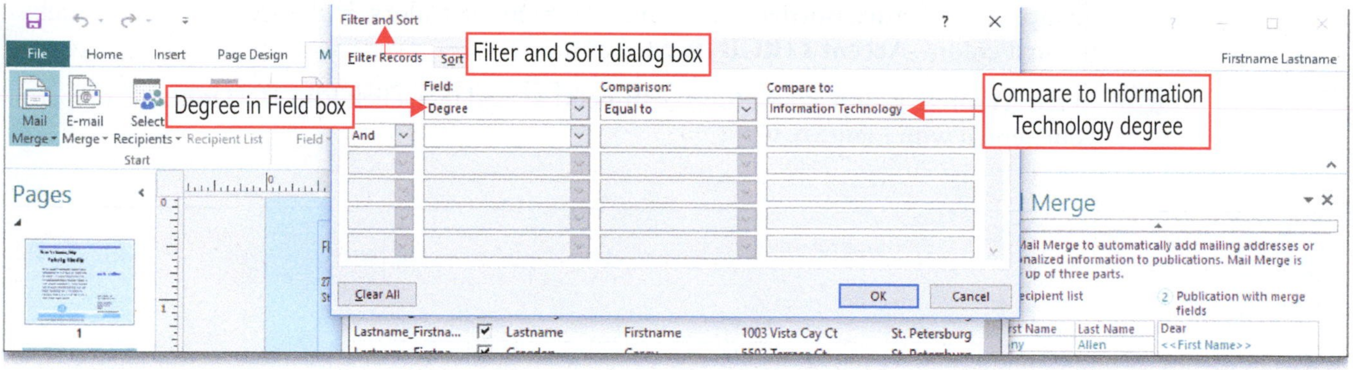

FIGURE 6.40

4 ▶ In the **Filter and Sort** dialog box, click **OK**. In the **Mail Merge Recipients** dialog box, scroll to the right to display the **Degree** field. Verify that three Information Technology student records display.

| **ALERT!** | **Do more or less than three students display?** |

If three students do not display, the data in your Access database is not accurate. Cancel the Mail Merge, open your Access database Lastname_Firstname_6B_FPCC_Students, and correct any incorrect data or misspelled words.

---

5 ▶ In the **Mail Merge Recipients** dialog box, click **OK**. On **Page 2** of your publication, click the text box to select the paragraph that begins *Type address here*.

6 ▶ In the **Mail Merge** pane, under **More items**, click **Address block**. In the **Insert Address Block** dialog box, under **Specify address elements**, verify that the format **Joshua Randall Jr.** is selected, and then click **OK**.

7 ▶ In the **Mail Merge** pane, under **Step 2 of 3**, click **Next: Create merged publication**. In the **Mail Merge** pane, under **Create merged publications**, click **Merge to a new publication**.

Three postcards (six pages) are created as a new Publisher file.

8 ▶ Click the **Insert tab**, and then in the **Header & Footer group**, click **Footer**. In the footer, double-click the word **Internship**, and then type **Technology** On the **Master Page tab**, in the **Close group**, click **Close Master Page**.

9 ▶ In the **Mail Merge** pane, under **Merged publication pages**, click **Save this publication**. Under **Save As**, click **Browse**, and then in the **Save As** dialog box, navigate to your **Integrated Projects Chapter 6** folder. In the **File name** box, delete the existing text, and then using your own name, type **Lastname_Firstname_6B_Technology_Postcard** Click **Save**. **Close** ⊠ the **Mail Merge** pane.

10 ▶ Click the **File tab**, verify the **Info tab** is selected, click **Publication Properties**, and then click **Advanced Properties**. In the **Properties** dialog box, on the **Summary tab**, in the **Subject** box, type your course name and section number; in the **Author** box, type your first name and last name, and then in the **Keywords** box, type **technology postcards, merged** Click **OK** to close the dialog box.

11 ▶ On the left, click **Save** to redisplay the publication window. If your instructor directs you to submit your files electronically, go to Step 13.

12 ▶ To print your document, in the **Pages** pane, click the **Page 2** that contains your name. Hold down ⑤ Shift, and then click the **Page 1** directly above your Page 2. Click the **File tab**, and then click the **Print tab**. Under **Settings**, click the **Print All Pages arrow**, and then click **Print Selection**. Under **Settings**, in the **Copies of each page** box, type 1 Click **Print**.

13 ▶ Display **Backstage** view, and click **Close**, saving changes if necessary. **Close** ⊠ the **Mail Merge** pane. **Save** 🖫 your **Lastname_Firstname_6B_Internship_Postcard** publication, and then **Close** ⊠ Publisher.

14 ▶ Submit your printed or electronic files as directed by your instructor.

END | You have completed Project 6B

END OF CHAPTER

SUMMARY

In Microsoft Publisher, you can create many different types of publications. Use a template—located on your computer or downloaded from the Internet—to begin a publication quickly. You can insert pictures or other images and then format the objects in Publisher. Publisher's Mail Merge Wizard enables you to personalize a publication by inserting a recipient list and other data fields located in an Access database. In Access, you can set field properties to make data entry faster and more accurate.

KEY TERMS

MATCHING

Match each term in the second column with its correct definition in the first column by writing the letter of the term on the blank line in front of the correct definition.

_____ 1. The page that contains the design and layout elements, including headers and footers, that you want to repeat on multiple pages of your publication.

_____ 2. A predefined set of harmonized colors that can be applied to text and objects.

_____ 3. A predefined set of fonts that is associated with a publication, where a primary font and a secondary font are specified.

_____ 4. Reusable pieces of content—for example, borders, text boxes, logos, and calendars—that are stored in galleries.

_____ 5. The manner in which text displays around an object such as a picture.

_____ 6. Characteristics of a field that control how the field displays and how data can be entered in the field.

_____ 7. A set of literal characters and placeholder characters that control what can and cannot be entered in an Access field.

_____ 8. Criteria that limit or control what users can enter in a field.

_____ 9. In Access, the data that is automatically entered in a field.

_____ 10. The maximum number of characters you can enter in a field.

_____ 11. A calendar control that is used to select a date.

_____ 12. An Access feature that creates a list box to look up a value in another table, query, or a list of values.

_____ 13. An Access tool with which you can create a report from scratch by adding the fields you designate in the order you want them to display.

_____ 14. Nonprinting lines that mark the margins, columns, rows, and baselines and are used to align the text, pictures, and other objects so that the publication has balance and uniformity.

_____ 15. Nonprinting lines on the top, bottom, left, and right sides of the page that are used to define the page margins.

A Blank Report tool

B Building blocks

C Color scheme

D Date picker

E Default value

F Field property

G Field size

H Font scheme

I Input mask

J Layout guide

K Lookup Wizard

L Margin guides

M Master page

N Text wrapping

O Validation rule

MULTIPLE CHOICE

Circle the correct answer.

1. A Publisher feature used to insert the name and address of different individuals or businesses into a publication to make each one unique is:
   A. Mail merge   **B.** a business information set   **C.** the Design Checker

2. Predesigned graphic elements—for example, bars and emphasis images—display in the:
   A. Online Picture gallery   **B.** Design Accents gallery   **C.** Shapes gallery

3. A Publisher feature that automatically reviews a publication for a range of design and layout flaws and provides options to fix any identified problems is the:
   A. Design Checker   **B.** Design Troubleshooter   **C.** Design Wizard

4. Text that does not fit within a text box is called:
   A. excess   **B.** overflow   **C.** overspill

5. The characteristic that defines the kind of data that can be entered in a field, such as numbers, text, or dates, is the:
   A. field type   **B.** record type   **C.** data type

6. In a new blank database, Access creates a default ID field with the data type:
   A. AutoNumber   **B.** Number   **C.** Text

7. An Access report feature that allows you to separate groups of records visually and to display introductory and summary data for each group is a report is called:
   A. filtering   **B.** grouping   **C.** sorting

8. A list of characteristics for fields or controls on a form or report in which you can make precise changes to each property associated with a field or control is called a:
   A. Field List   **B.** Property List   **C.** Property Sheet

9. A customized group of information—including items such as a company name, address, phone number, email address, and logo—that can be used to quickly fill in appropriate places in a publication is called a:
   A. business information set group   **B.** personal building block   **C.** user information

10. A nonprinting horizontal or vertical line that can be aligned to any position on the ruler is called a:
    A. column guide   **B.** row guide   **C.** ruler guide

Mastering Integration   Project 6C Registration Flyer

In the following Mastering Integration project, you will complete a flyer for the Florida Port Community College registration department listing the various fees students may be charged. Your completed documents will look similar to Figure 6.41.

PROJECT FILES

For Project 6C, you will need the following files:

i06C_Registration_Flyer
i06C_Student_Fees

You will save your files as:

Lastname_Firstname_6C_Registration_Flyer
Lastname_Firstname_6C_Student_Fees
Lastname_Firstname_6C_Merged_Flyer

Apply **6A** skills from these objectives:

1 Construct a Newsletter in Publisher
2 Format a Newsletter
3 Use Mail Merge to Insert Names from an Access Table into a Publication
4 Insert Access Data Fields into a Publication

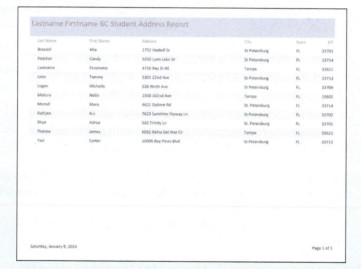

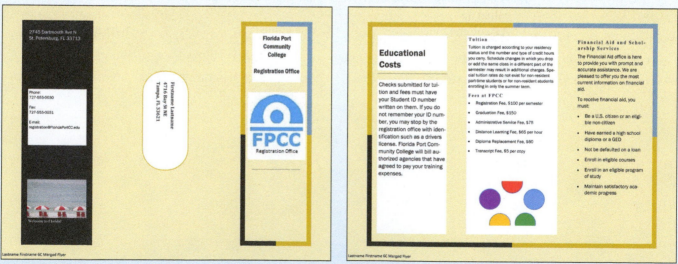

FIGURE 6.41

(Project 6C Registration Flyer continues on the next page)

1 Start Publisher. Locate and open the data file **i06C_ Registration_Flyer**. **Save** the file in the **Integrated Projects Chapter 6** folder as **Lastname_Firstname_6C_ Registration_Flyer** Type the file name in the footer, and then **Close** the footer. Apply the color scheme **Technic**, and then apply the font scheme **Economy**. At the top left of **Page 1**, select the paragraphs that begin *Your Address*, and then change the **Font Size** to **12**. Type **2745 Dartmouth Ave N** press Enter, and then type **St. Petersburg, FL 33713** In the next text box, delete the phone number, and type **727-555-0030** Delete the fax number, and type **727-555-0031** Delete the email address, and type **registration@FloridaPortCC.edu**

2 At the top right of **Page 1**, select the text *Organization name*, type **Florida Port Community College** and then press Enter two times. Type **Registration Office** Select all the text in the text box, apply the style **Title 3**, and then **Center** the text.

3 Click in the middle of **Page 1**. On the **Insert tab**, in the **Building Blocks group**, click **Page Parts**, and then under **Pull Quotes**, click **Portal**.

Position the text box so that the top middle sizing handle is at **approximately 3 inches on the vertical ruler** and **5.5 inches on the horizontal ruler**. In the text box, select the text, change the **Font Size** to **12**, and then click **Italic**.

4 On **Page 2**, select the heading *Main Inside Heading*, and then type **Educational Costs** In the middle text box, select the text *Secondary Heading*, and then type **Tuition** Select the text *Heading*, and then type **Fees at FPCC** Insert an **Online Picture** related to **business person, technology** and then insert an applicable image. Change the text wrapping to **Top and Bottom**, change the **Shape Height** of the image to **1.5** inches, and then position the image in the middle box, so that the top left corner is at **approximately 5.5 inches on the vertical ruler and 4.25 inches on the horizontal ruler**. Select all the text in the right text box, and then change the **Font Size** to **12**.

5 On **the Page Design tab**, in the **Page Background group**, display the **Background** gallery, click the background **30% tint of Accent 2**, and then **Apply to All Pages**. Display **Page 1**, and **Save** the publication.

6 Start Access. Open the file **i06C_Student_Fees**. From **Backstage** view, click **Save As**, and then save the file in the **Integrated Projects Chapter 6** folder as **Lastname_Firstname_6C_Student_Fees** and Enable Content, if necessary. Create a new form based on the **Students** table, and then **Save** the form with the name **Lastname Firstname 6C Student Form** Enter the following records using your name in the last record:

First Name	Last Name	Address	City	State	ZIP	Phone Number	Degree
Mara	Monell	4621 Duhme Rd	St. Petersburg	FL	33714	727-555-5351	Architecture Design
Nello	Mallory	1550 102nd Ave	Tampa	FL	33605	813-555-5832	Criminal Justice
Adrea	Rhyn	503 Trinity Ln	St. Petersburg	FL	33701	727-555-0894	Architecture Design
Firstname	Lastname	4716 Bay St NE	Tampa	FL	33621	813-555-0303	Accounting

(Project 6C Registration Flyer continues on the next page)

Mastering Integration Project 6C Registration Flyer (continued)

7 Create a report using the **Report Wizard**. From the **Students** table, add the fields **First Name**, **Last Name**, **Address**, **City**, **State**, and **ZIP**. **Sort** by the **Last Name** field, use **Landscape** orientation, and title the report **Lastname Firstname 6C Student Address Report** Print the report as directed by your instructor. **Close** all open objects. Display the **Properties** dialog box. In the **Subject** box, type your course name and section number; in the **Author** box, type your first name and last name; and then in the **Keywords** box, type **contact info Close** Access.

8 In your publication, on the **Mailings tab**, open the **Step-by-Step Mail Merge Wizard**. Connect to your Access file **Lastname_Firstname_6C_Student_Fees** as the recipient list. **Sort** the students by the **Last Name** field. On **Page 1** of your publication, click the **Pull Quote** text box that begins *To catch*, and then select all the text. Under **More items**, insert the **Address block**. Click the

border of the text box, and then under **Drawing Tools**, click the **Format tab**. In the **Arrange group**, click the **Rotate button arrow**, and then click **Rotate Right 90°**. **Merge to a new publication**. **Save** the merged publication in your **Integrated Projects Chapter 6** folder as **Lastname_Firstname_6C_Merged_Flyer** Change the footer to display the file name. Print the complete flyer with your name as directed by your instructor.

9 Display the **Properties** dialog box. In the **Subject** box, type your course name and section number; in the **Author** box, type your first name and last name; and then in the **Keywords** box, type **students, merged Save** your changes, and then **Close** the publication.

10 With your **Lastname_Firstname_6C_Registration_Flyer** displayed, click **Save**, and then **Close** Publisher. Submit your printed or electronic files as directed by your instructor.

End | You have completed Project 6C

CONTENT-BASED ASSESSMENTS (MASTERY AND TRANSFER OF LEARNING)

Apply 6B skills from these Objectives:

5 Set Field Properties in an Access Table

6 Create a Publication Using a Publisher Template

7 Modify the Layout of a Publication

Mastering Integration | Project 6D FPCC Clubs

In the following Mastering Integration project, you will create and modify an Access database, create a newsletter from a Publisher template, and then use the mail merge feature to create personalized flyers that will be sent to students interested in the golf club. Your completed files will look similar to Figure 6.42.

PROJECT FILES

For Project 6D, you will need the following files:

New blank Access database
New blank Publisher publication
i06D_Clubs_Logo

You will save your files as:

Lastname_Firstname_6D_FPCC_Clubs
Lastname_Firstname_6D_Campus_Clubs
Lastname_Firstname_6D_Merged_Clubs

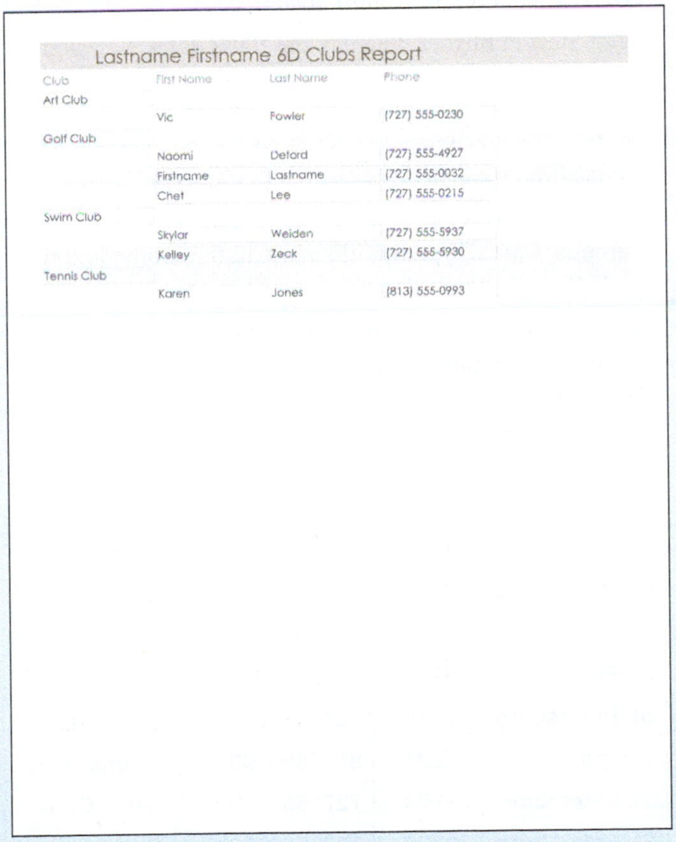

Lastname Firstname 6D Clubs Report

Club	First Name	Last Name	Phone
Art Club			
	Vic	Fowler	(727) 555-0230
Golf Club			
	Naomi	Deford	(727) 555-4927
	Firstname	Lastname	(727) 555-0032
	Chet	Lee	(727) 555-0215
Swim Club			
	Skylar	Weiden	(727) 555-5937
	Kelley	Zeck	(727) 555-5930
Tennis Club			
	Karen	Jones	(813) 555-0993

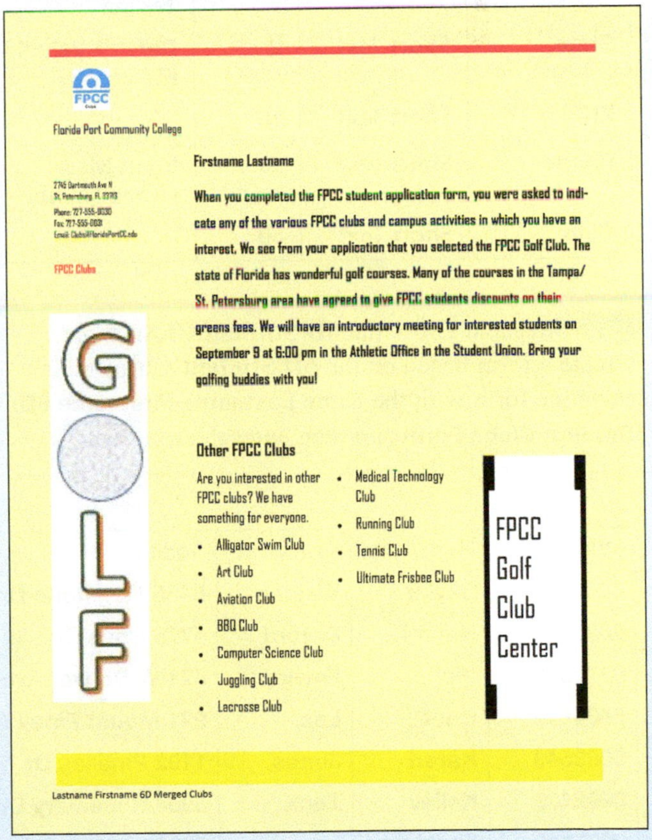

FIGURE 6.42

(Project 6D FPCC Clubs continues on the next page)

1 ▶ Start Access. **Create** a **Blank Database. Save** the database in the **Integrated Projects Chapter 6** folder as **Lastname_Firstname_6D_FPCC_Clubs** In the new **Table1**, **Save** the table as **Lastname Firstname 6D Student Clubs** Insert the following fields, data types, and properties:

Field Name	Data Type	Field Size	Other Properties
Student ID	Short Text	10	Input Mask: 12-0000000
First Name	Short Text	30	
Last Name	Short Text	30	
Address	Short Text	60	
City	Short Text	50	Lookup Wizard: St. Petersburg, Tampa
State	Short Text	2	Default Value: FL
ZIP	Short Text	10	
Phone	Short Text	10	Input Mask: Phone Number
Club	Short Text	50	

2 ▶ **Save** and **Close** the **6D Student Clubs** table. Create a form based on the **6D Student Clubs** table. **Save** the form with the name **Lastname Firstname 6D Student Clubs Form** and then enter the following

student records. In the last record, type your first name and last name.

3 ▶ Use the **Blank Report** tool to create a report. Add the field names **First Name**, **Last Name**, **Phone Number**, and **Club**. **Group** by the **Club** field, and then **Sort** by the **Last Name** field. Display the **Property Sheet** pane, and then change the **Width** of all report columns to **1.5 Save** the report as **Lastname Firstname 6D Clubs Report** and then add the **Title** to the report. Display the **Themes** gallery, and then apply the **Wisp** theme to this object only. As directed by your instructor, **Print** the report. **Close** all open objects.

4 ▶ Display the **Properties** dialog box. In the **Subject** box, type your course name and section number; in the **Author** box, type your first name and last name; and then in the **Keywords** box, type **students, clubs Close** the Properties dialog box, and **Close** Access.

5 ▶ Start Publisher. Display the **BUILT-IN** Newsletter templates; locate and click the **Arrows** design. Apply the **Sunrise** color scheme, and then, under **Options**, change the **Page Size** to **One-page spread. Create** the publication. **Save** the publication in your **Integrated Projects Chapter 6** folder as **Lastname_Firstname_6D_Campus_Clubs** Type the file name in the footer, and then click **Close Master Page**.

6 ▶ Delete **Page 1**, **Page 2**, and **Page 3**. Create a new business information set for Marcus Simmons using the following information. The logo is located in your student data files.

Student ID	First Name	Last Name	Address	City	ZIP	Phone Number	Club
4209863	Skylar	Weiden	8465 Flagstone Dr	St. Petersburg	33714	7275555937	Swim Club
2085626	Naomi	Deford	4776 Cove Cir	St. Petersburg	33708	7275554927	Golf Club
0172079	Vic	Fowler	421 W Denver Ave	St. Petersburg	33713	7275550230	Art Club
5504826	Chet	Lee	221 Mount Piney Ave	St. Petersburg	33713	7275550215	Golf Club
3093543	Karen	Jones	1102 Pinellas Dr	Tampa	33621	8135550993	Tennis Club
0992709	Kelley	Zeck	5904 Rosemary Dr	St. Petersburg	33709	7275555930	Swim Club
0977548	Firstname	Lastname	3526 Iris St	St. Petersburg	33708	7275550032	Golf Club

(Project 6D FPCC Club continues on the next page)

Individual name	**Marcus Simmons**
Job position	**FPCC Athletic Director**
Organization name	**Florida Port Community College**
Address	**2745 Dartmouth Ave N St. Petersburg, FL 33713**
Phone Number	**727-555-0030**
Fax	**727-555-0031**
E-mail	**Clubs@FloridaPortCC.edu**
Tagline	**FPCC Clubs**
Logo	**i06D_Clubs_Logo**

7 **Save** the business data set as **Simmons** and then click **Update Publication**. Insert an **Online Picture** related to **golf, females** and insert an applicable image. Under **Picture Tools**, on the **Format tab**, in the **Arrange group**, click **Wrap Text**, and then click **Tight**. Resize the **Width** to **2**. Move the image so the top left corner is at **approximately 4 inches on the vertical rules** and **0.5 inch on the horizontal ruler**. In the lower right corner of the page, **Cut** the image, and then in the same location, **Cut** the text box.

8 Locate the text box containing the text *We're on the Web*, select the text, then type **FPCC Golf Club Center** in the text box, and then drag the text box to the lower right corner. Adjust the size of the text box so the top edge is at **approximately 6 inches on the vertical ruler** and the lower edge is at **approximately 9.5 inches on the vertical ruler**.

9 Click the heading *Back Page Story Headline*, and then type **Other FPCC Clubs** Select the heading, and then change the **Font Size** to **16**. Click the text box with the paragraph that begins *This story can fit*, and then change the **Font Size** to **14**. Type **Are you interested in other FPCC clubs? We have something for everyone.** Then press Enter. Type the names of the following clubs, pressing Enter after each club name except the last one.

Alligator Swim Club
Art Club
Aviation Club
BBQ Club
Computer Science Club
Juggling Club
Lacrosse Club
Medical Technology Club
Running Club
Tennis Club
Ultimate Frisbee Club

10 Select the club names, and then apply **Small Bullets**. Click in a blank area of the page. Display the **Background** gallery, and then under **Solid Background**, in the second row, click the second background—**30% tint of Accent 2**.

11 Open the **Mail Merge** task pane. Use your file **Lastname_Firstname_6D_FPCC_Clubs** as the recipient list. **Filter** the recipient list to display only students interested in the **Golf Club**. Click the top right text box with the paragraph beginning *This would be*. Resize the text box so the lower border is at **5.5 inches on the vertical ruler**. Change the **Font Size** to **14**. From the **Mail Merge** task pane, insert the **First Name** field, press Spacebar, insert the **Last Name** field, and then press Enter.

12 Type **When you completed the FPCC student application form, you were asked to indicate any of the various FPCC clubs and campus activities in which you have an interest. We see from your application that you selected the FPCC Golf Club. The state of Florida has wonderful golf courses. Many of the courses in the Tampa/St. Petersburg area have agreed to give FPCC students discounts on their greens fees. We will have an introductory meeting for interested students on September 9 at 6:00 pm in the Athletic Office in the Student Union. Bring your golfing buddies with you!** **Save** the publication.

13 Complete the **Merge to a new publication**. Save the publication in your **Integrated Projects Chapter 6** folder as **Lastname_Firstname_6D_Merged_Clubs** In the footer, double-click **Campus**, and then type **Merged** As directed by your instructor, print the newsletter that displays your name.

14 Display the **Properties** dialog box. In the **Subject** box, type your course name and section number; in the **Author** box, type your first name and last name; and then in the **Keywords** box, type **golf, merged Save** your changes, and then **Close** the publication. **Save** the **Lastname_Firstname_6D_Campus_Clubs** publication, and then **Close** Publisher. Submit your printed or electronic files as directed by your instructor.

End | You have completed Project 6D

Apply a combination of the 6A and 6B skills.

GO! Solve It Project 6E Construction Management

PROJECT FILES

For Project 6E, you will need the following files:

New blank Publisher publication
i06E_Construction_Management
i06E_CM_Logo

You will save your files as:

Lastname_Firstname_6E_Construction_Management
Lastname_Firstname_6E_Construction_Conference
Lastname_Firstname_6E_Merged_Conference

In past years, Florida has been hit hard by hurricanes and other bad weather. The construction industry, working with Florida Port Community College, has put a renewed emphasis on training the Construction Management students to build structures that meet current building codes. You have been asked to create a flyer inviting all Construction Management students to attend a conference.

Save the Access file **i06E_Construction_Management** with the file name **Lastname_Firstname_6E_Construction_Management** Create a form named based on the Students table, save it as **Lastname Firstname 6E Student Form** and then add the following student records. Use your first name and last name for the last record.

First Name	Last Name	Address	City	State	ZIP	Phone Number	Degree
Kayla	Crumm	1171 54th Ave	St. Petersburg	FL	33714	727-555-0092	Construction Management
Ryan	Ingerson	2501 W Isabel St	St. Petersburg	FL	33708	727-555-5832	Information Systems
Alyssa	Maden	5304 Cypress St	St. Petersburg	FL	33701	727-555-0362	Construction Management
Firstname	Lastname	2513 Frierson Ave	St. Petersburg	FL	33701	727-555-0186	Construction Management

Create a report using the **Report Wizard** that includes the fields **First Name**, **Last Name**, **Phone Number**, and **Degree**. Group the data by **Degree** and sort the data by **Last Name**. Change the column widths so all data is visible.

Create a new publication based on a Publisher template of your choice. Save the file as **Lastname_Firstname_6E_Construction_Conference** and then insert the file name in the footer.

In a text box, add information about the Construction Management conference to be held on campus on March 3–4. In another text box, list Florida cities that have had damage due to hurricanes. Insert and format appropriate online images. Create a business set for Mr. Fasone using the following information.

(Project 6E Construction Management continues on the next page)

GO! Solve It **Project 6E Construction Management** (continued)

Individual name	**Taylor Fasone**
Job position	**Director, Construction Management Program**
Organization name	**Florida Port Community College**
Address	**2745 Dartmouth Ave N St. Petersburg, FL 33713**
Phone Number	**727-555-0030**
Fax	**727-555-0031**
E-mail	**construction@FloridaPortCC.edu**
Tagline	**Building a better Florida**
Logo	**i06E_CM_Logo**
Business Information set name	**Fasone**

Start mail merge and choose your Access file **Lastname_Firstname_6E_Construction_Management** as the data source. Filter the recipients to show only the Construction Management students. Insert the student's name and mailing address. Save the publication. Complete the merge to a new publication. Save the merged publication as **Lastname_Firstname_6E_Merged_Conference** and then update the footer. Add appropriate document properties to all three files. Submit your printed or electronic files as directed by your instructor.

Performance Level

Performance Criteria		Exemplary: You consistently applied the relevant skills.	Proficient: You sometimes, but not always, applied the relevant skills.	Developing: You rarely or never applied the relevant skills.
	Create 6E Student Form and enter data	Form is created, all records are entered accurately	Form is created and records entered, but there are two or fewer errors	Form is not created or records are not entered
	Create 6E Report	Report is created using the correct fields and formatting	Report is created using the correct fields, with two or fewer errors	Report includes more than two errors or was not created
	Create 6E Construction Conference publication	Publication created to include all content and formatted accurately	Publication created, but there are two or fewer errors in content or formatting	Publication includes more than two errors or was not created
	Create 6E Merged Conference publication	Main document is set up correctly, data file is filtered, merged documents are created accurately	Main document is set up, data file is filtered, merged documents are created, but there are two or fewer errors	Merge is not completed

END | You have completed Project 6E

RUBRIC

The following outcomes-based assessments are open-ended assessments. That is, there is no specific correct result; your result will depend on your approach to the information provided. Make Professional Quality your goal. Use the following scoring rubric to guide you in how to approach the problem and then to evaluate how well your approach solves the problem.

The *criteria*—Software Mastery, Content, Format and Layout, and Process—represent the knowledge and skills you have gained that you can apply to solving the problem. The *levels of performance*—Professional Quality, Approaching Professional Quality, or Needs Quality Improvements—help you and your instructor evaluate your result.

	Your completed project is of Professional Quality if you:	Your completed project is approaching Professional Quality if you:	Your completed project needs Quality Improvements if you:
1-Software Mastery	Choose and apply the most appropriate skills, tools, and features and identify efficient methods to solve the problem.	Choose and apply some appropriate skills, tools, and features, but not in the most efficient manner.	Choose inappropriate skills, tools, or features, or are inefficient in solving the problem.
2-Content	Construct a solution that is clear and well organized, contains content that is accurate, appropriate to the audience and purpose, and is complete. Provide a solution that contains no errors of spelling, grammar, or style.	Construct a solution in which some components are unclear, poorly organized, inconsistent, or incomplete. Misjudge the needs of the audience. Have some errors in spelling, grammar, or style, but the errors do not detract from comprehension.	Construct a solution that is unclear, incomplete, or poorly organized, contains some inaccurate or inappropriate content, and contains many errors of spelling, grammar, or style. Do not solve the problem.
3-Format and Layout	Format and arrange all elements to communicate information and ideas, clarify function, illustrate relationships, and indicate relative importance.	Apply appropriate format and layout features to some elements, but not others. Overuse features, causing minor distraction.	Apply format and layout that does not communicate information or ideas clearly. Do not use format and layout features to clarify function, illustrate relationships, or indicate relative importance. Use available features excessively, causing distraction.
4-Process	Use an organized approach that integrates planning, development, self-assessment, revision, and reflection.	Demonstrate an organized approach in some areas, but not others; or, use an insufficient process of organization throughout.	Do not use an organized approach to solve the problem.

Apply a combination of the 6A and 6B skills.

PROJECT FILES

For Project 6F, you will need the following files:

New blank Publisher publication
i06F_Field_Trip

You will save your files as:

Lastname_Firstname_6F_Field_Trip
Lastname_Firstname_6F_Trip_Info
Lastname_Firstname_6F_Merged_Info

Florida Port Community College offers field trips for its students. You have been asked to create a one-page flyer announcing upcoming trips.

Save the Access file **i06F_Field_Trip** with the file name **Lastname_Firstname_6F_Field_Trip** In the **Students** table, adjust the field size property to a smaller size for all fields. Create a default value for the **State** field. Create a form based on the **Students** table, and then add the following students. Use your first name and last name for the last record.

First Name	Last Name	Address	City	State	ZIP	Phone
Morgan	Woelfel	6232 Oak Cluster Cir	St. Petersburg	FL	33702	727-555-0440
Landon	Heidemann	5621 Samter Ct	St. Petersburg	FL	33702	727-555-0679
Firstname	Lastname	2241 20th St	St. Petersburg	FL	33713	727-555-5346

Create a report with your choice of fields and title. Group the data by one field, and then sort by another field. Use a Publisher template to create a brochure. Add the file name to the footer, and then save the publication with the file name **Lastname_Firstname_6F_Trip_Info** Add information in the various text boxes about the different types of field trips that are available. Add appropriate titles and headings to the text boxes. Insert and format appropriate images. Apply a color scheme and font scheme. Use the mail merge feature to insert the student recipient names and addresses in the publication. Save the file. Complete the merge to a new publication. Save the new merged publication as **Lastname_Firstname_6F_Merged_Info** and then update the footer. Add appropriate document properties to all three files. Submit your printed or electronic files as directed by your instructor.

End | You have completed Project 6F

Integrating Word, Excel, Access, and PowerPoint

7 INTEGRATED PROJECTS 2016

PROJECT 7A

OUTCOMES
Create a Word template, an Excel PivotTable report, and an Excel PivotChart report.

OBJECTIVES

1. Create and Save a Template in Word
2. Insert a Combo Box and an Option Group in an Access Form
3. Create a PivotTable Report and a PivotChart Report in Excel
4. Import Data into a PowerPoint Presentation

PROJECT 7B

OUTCOMES
Insert functions in Excel and insert a cover page and a table of contents in a Word document.

OBJECTIVES

5. Use Excel Functions
6. Create a Report in Word Using Data from Other Applications

nickolya/Fotolia

In This Chapter

In this chapter, you will use Word, Excel, Access, and PowerPoint to take advantage of the way the applications work with one another. By using the most appropriate application to complete the work with the data you have, you can create graphics or input data in one application and then export the data to another application without having to take the time to recreate the graphic or retype the data. It is important to identify the most suitable software to produce the desired solutions and to best utilize the features in the various applications.

The projects in this chapter relate to **Select National Properties Group**, a diversified real estate company that develops, builds, manages, and acquires a wide variety of properties nationwide. Among the company's portfolio of properties are shopping malls, mixed-use town center developments, high-rise office buildings, office parks, industrial buildings and warehouses, multi-family housing developments, educational facilities, and hospitals. Residential developments are mainly located in and around the company's hometown, Chicago; commercial and public buildings in the portfolio are located nationwide. The company is well respected for its focus on quality and commitment to the environment and economic development of the areas where it operates.

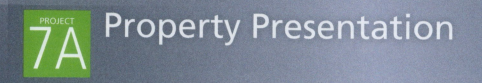

Property Presentation

PROJECT ACTIVITIES

In Activities 7.01 through 7.16, you will use Word, Access, Excel, and PowerPoint to create a variety of files to share information with customers and employees regarding the property portfolio of Select National Properties Group. Your completed files will look similar to Figure 7.1.

PROJECT FILES

For Project 7A, you will need the following files:

New blank Word document
New blank Excel workbook
i07A_Property_Data
i07A_Property_Presentation

You will save your files as:

Lastname_Firstname_7A_Leasing_Fax
Lastname_Firstname_7A_Midtown_Developers
Lastname_Firstname_7A_Property_Data
Lastname_Firstname_7A_Property_PivotTable
Lastname_Firstname_7A_Property_Presentation

PROJECT RESULTS

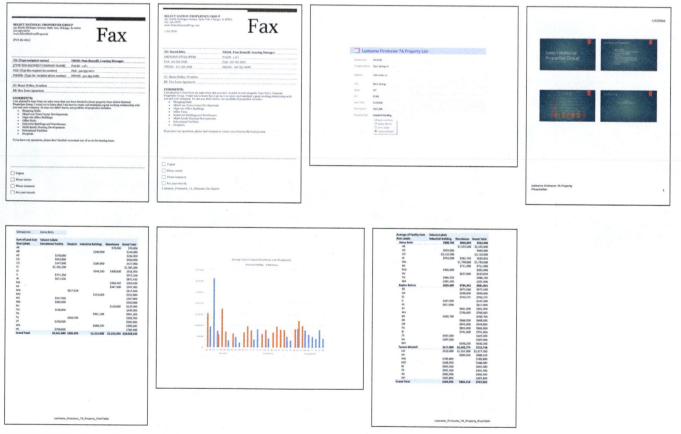

FIGURE 7.1 Property Presentation

In previous chapters, you have used templates in Access, PowerPoint, and Publisher; templates are also available for Word. A Word template determines the basic structure for a document and contains document settings such as fonts, page layout, and styles. You can create a customized template so that you do not have to recreate the basic document every time it is needed.

Activity 7.01 | Creating a Fax Template

Pam Stancill, the leasing manager, would like to send a fax to all new leasing customers to let them know that their business is appreciated and that he is available to assist them. In this Activity, you will create a template that he can reuse for each new customer.

1   **Start** Word. In **Backstage** view, click **New**. Click in the search box, and type **Fax** Scroll down, locate, and then click **Fax (Urban Theme)**. Verify that *Fax (Urban Theme)*—not *Mail Merge Fax (Urban Theme)*—is selected.

2   Click **Create**. If necessary, scroll to the top of the page, and compare your screen with Figure 7.2.

A new document based on the Urban Fax template is created. To the right of FROM, the user name displays—your name will differ.

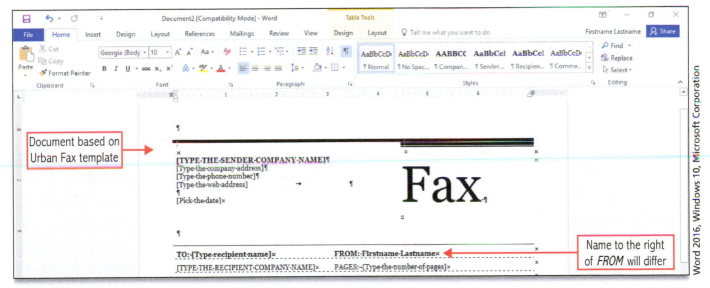

FIGURE 7.2

3   On the **Quick Access Toolbar**, click **Save** 🖫. Under *Save As*, click **Browse**. In the **Save As** dialog box, change **Save As type** to **Word Template**. Notice that the location is the Templates folder on your computer.

4   In the **Save As** dialog box, navigate to the location where you are saving your files, click **New folder**, type **Integrated Projects Chapter 7** and then press [Enter] two times. In the **File name** box, delete the existing text, type **Lastname_Firstname_7A_Leasing_Fax** and then press [Enter]. If a message box displays to upgrade to the newest file format, click OK.

Activity 7.02 | Changing Data in a Template

You can customize an installed template to better serve your needs. In this Activity, you will modify the ***content controls*** to add the company name and company information. A content control is an area in a template indicated by placeholder text that can be used to add text, pictures, dates, or lists.

1 ▷ At the top of the page, locate and click the content control *TYPE THE SENDER COMPANY NAME*, type **Select National Properties Group** and then press ⟨Tab⟩ to select the content control *Type the company address*. Type **321 North Michigan Avenue, Suite 700, Chicago, IL 60601** and then press ⟨Tab⟩. With the content control *Type the phone number* selected, type **312-555-0070** and then press ⟨Tab⟩. With the content control *Type the web address* selected, type **www.SelectNationalProp.com**

> The template defines the font format of the content controls. In this case, the first content control displays the company name in all uppercase letters.

2 ▷ To the right of **FROM**, click the content control, on the left side of the content control, click the content control tab, and the press ⟨Delete⟩. Type **Pam Stancill, Leasing Manager**

> Text typed in the Author content control will display in the Author box of the Document Information panel. For purposes of this instruction, because you will be entering different information in the Author box, it is necessary to delete the content control and simply type the text.

NOTE | Displaying the User Name

The FROM content control can automatically display the user name from the computer at which you are working.

---

3 ▷ To the right of **PAGES**, click the content control *Type the number of pages*, and then type **1 of 1**

4 ▷ Below the **PAGES** heading, to the right of **FAX**, click the content control *Type the sender fax number*, and then type **312-555-0071** Below the text you just typed, to the right of **PHONE**, click the content control *Type the sender phone number*, and then type **312-555-0080**

5 ▷ To the right of **CC**, select the content control *Type text*, and then type **Shaun Walker, President**

6 ▷ To the right of **RE**, select the content control *Type text*, and then type **New Lease Agreement** Compare your screen with Figure 7.3.

> The data you are entering in the template will remain the same for all customers. You are not entering recipient data because those content controls will change for each recipient.

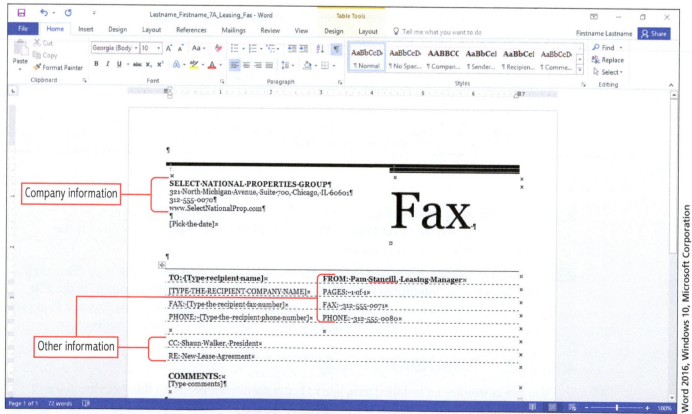

FIGURE 7.3

7 Below **Comments**, click the content control *Type comments*, and then type **I am pleased to hear from my sales team that you have decided to lease property from the Select National Properties Group. I want you to know that I am here to create and maintain a good working relationship with you and your company. In case you didn't know, our portfolio of properties includes:** and then press Enter.

8 On the **Home tab**, in the **Paragraph group**, click **Bullets** . Type each of the following property types, pressing Enter after each type.

Shopping Malls

Mixed-use Town Center Developments

High-rise Office Buildings

Office Parks

Industrial Buildings and Warehouses

Multi-family Housing Developments

Educational Facilities

Hospitals

9 On the **Home tab**, in the **Paragraph group**, click **Bullets** to turn it off. Type **If you have any questions, please don't hesitate to contact any of us on the leasing team.**

10 On the **Home tab**, in the **Paragraph group**, click **Line and Paragraph Spacing** , and then click **Add Space Before Paragraph**. Compare your screen with Figure 7.4.

Paragraph spacing of 12 pt is inserted above the paragraph.

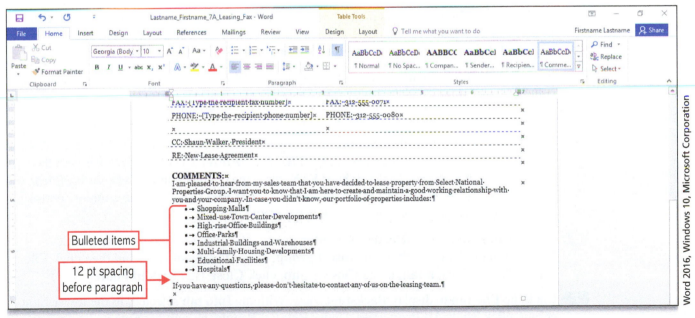

FIGURE 7.4

11 Click the **Review tab**, and then in the **Proofing group**, click **Spelling & Grammar**. Check the spelling of the document, correct any misspelled words, and verify that you spelled the names correctly.

12 Click the **File tab** to display **Backstage** view. With the **Info tab** selected, in the lower right corner, click **Show All Properties**. Under **Related People**, be sure your name displays as the **Author**—change it if necessary. Click to the right of **Subject**, and then type your course name and section number. Click to the right of **Tags**, and then type **fax, midtown** If you are instructed to submit your files electronically, go to Step 14.

13 To print your document, in **Backstage** view, click the **Print tab**, and then click **Print**.

14 Save 🖫 your document, and then Close ☒ Word.

Activity 7.03 | Creating a New Document from a Template

1 On the taskbar, click **File Explorer** 🗀. Navigate to the **Integrated Projects Chapter 7** folder, and then locate the file **Lastname_Firstname_7A_Leasing_Fax**. To the left of the file name, notice that the icon has a blue stripe at the top, indicating that the file is a Word template, not a Word document. Compare your screen with Figure 7.5.

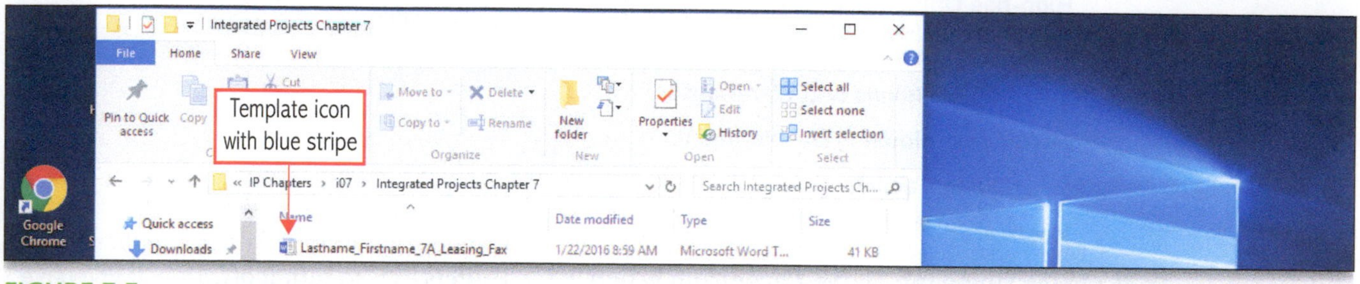

FIGURE 7.5   Word 2016, Windows 10, Microsoft Corporation

2 Double-click the **Lastname_Firstname_7A_Leasing_Fax** file name to start Word and to open a new document based on the template.

In the title bar, notice that the document name is Document1. If you have other documents open, the number in the document name may vary.

3 Click Save 🖫. In the Save As dialog box, navigate to the **Integrated Projects Chapter 7** folder, and then save the document as **Lastname_Firstname_7A_Midtown_Developers** If you are asked if you want to save changes to the template file, click **No.**

4 Near the top of the document, click the content control *Pick the date*. Click the content control arrow, and then click **Today**.

The current date displays in the content control.

5 To the right of **TO**, click the content control *Type recipient name*, and then type **David Riley** Below **TO,** click the content control *TYPE THE RECIPIENT COMPANY NAME*, and then type **Midtown Developers** To the right of **FAX**, click the content control *Type the recipient fax number*, and then type **312-555-5939** To the right of **PHONE**, click the content control *Type the recipient phone number*, and then type **312-555-5949**

6 On the **Insert tab**, in the **Header & Footer group**, click **Footer**, and then click **Edit Footer**. On the **Design tab**, in the **Insert group**, click **Document Info**, and then click **File Name**. On the **Design tab**, in the **Close group**, click **Close Header and Footer**.

7 Click the **File tab** to display **Backstage** view. With the **Info tab** selected, in the lower right corner, click **Show All Properties**. Under **Related People**, be sure your name displays as the **Author**—change it if necessary. Click to the right of **Subject**, and then type your course name and section number. Click to the right of **Tags**, and then type **fax, midterm** If you are instructed to submit your files electronically, go to Step 9.

8 To print your document, in **Backstage** view, click the **Print tab**, and then click **Print**.

9 Save 🖫 your document, and then **Close** ☒ Word. **Close** ☒ File Explorer.

Objective 2 | Insert a Combo Box and an Option Group in an Access Form

In an Access form, a *form control* is an object that displays data, performs an action, and enables you to view and work with information. Form controls include text boxes, labels, check boxes, and subform controls.

Activity 7.04 | Adding a Combo Box to an Access Form

Recall that a form is a database object that you can use to enter, edit, or display data from a table or query. A *combo box* is a form control that combines a drop-down list with a text box, providing a more compact way to present a list of choices. A combo box enables you to select a value from a list or to enter a value that is not listed.

1 Start Access, in the lower left, click **Open Other Files**, click **Browse**, and then navigate to your student data files. Open the database **i07A_Property_Data**. In **Backstage** view, click **Save As**, click **Save Database As**, and then on the right, click the **Save As** button. In the **Save As** dialog box, navigate to your **Integrated Projects Chapter 7** folder, and then using your own name, save the database as **Lastname_Firstname_7A_Property_Data**

2 On the **Message Bar**, click **Enable Content**.

3 In the **Navigation Pane**, click the **Property List** table name one time to select it. Click the **Create tab**, and then in the **Forms group**, click **Form**. Switch to **Design** view. **Close** [«] the **Navigation Pane**.

4 In the form, under **Detail**, click the ninth label control—**Property Type**—which is the control on the left in the first column. Hold down [Ctrl] and then click the **Property Type** text box control on the right, the **Salesperson ID** label control, and the **Salesperson ID** textbox control. With all four controls selected, press [Delete].

All four controls are deleted from the form. A *label control* is a control on a form or report that contains descriptive information, typically a field name. A *text box control* is bound control on a form or report that displays the data from the underlying table or query.

5 Under **Form Design Tools**, on the **Design tab**, in the **Controls group**, click **More** [�], and verify **Use Control Wizards** [⬙] is active (framed).

6 In the **Controls** gallery, click **Combo Box** [▦]. At the bottom of the form, move the pointer below the **Facility Cost** text box control, and then click one time. Compare your screen with Figure 7.6.

The combo box control, including a corresponding label control (dotted box on the left), is inserted on the form and the Combo Box Wizard dialog box displays. A *combo box control* is a control on a form or report that displays a list from the underlying table or query.

ALERT! **Does the Combo Box Wizard not display?**

If the Combo Box Wizard dialog box does not display, on the Quick Access Toolbar, click the Undo button. Repeat Steps 5 and 6, being careful to click only one time to insert the combo box control; double-clicking will insert the control but cause the Combo Box Wizard not to display.

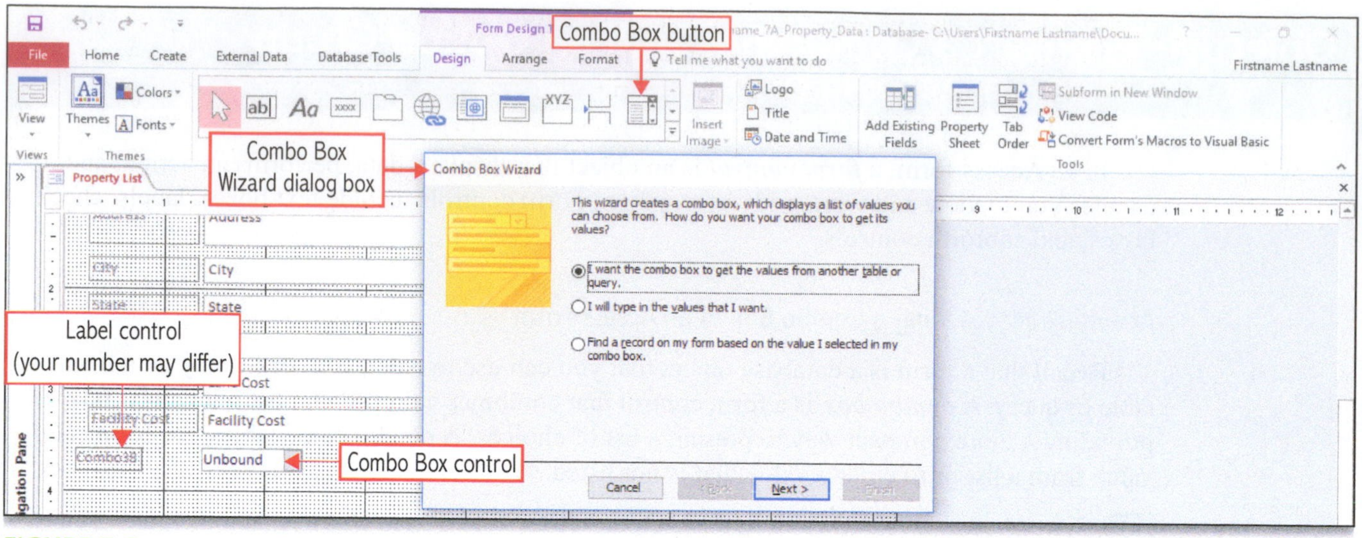

Access 2016, Windows 10, Microsoft Corporation

FIGURE 7.6

7 In the **Combo Box Wizard** dialog box, click the **I will type in the values that I want** option button, and then click **Next**. Verify that the **Number of columns** is **1**, and then press Tab. Type the following list of property types, pressing Tab after each property type except the last list item.

Educational Facility

High-rise Office Building

Hospital

Industrial Building

Mixed-use Town Center Development

Multi-family Housing Development

Office Park

Shopping Mall

Warehouse

NOTE Moving Back in a Wizard

If you accidentally press Enter instead of Tab, the next screen of the wizard will display. To return to the list, click the Back button.

8 Click **Next**. Click the **Store that value in this field** option button, and then click the **arrow**. In the field list, click **Property Type**, and then click **Next**. Under *What label would you like for your combo box?*, type **Property Type** and then click **Finish**.

When data is entered in the form, the selected combo box list item will be stored in the Property Type field.

9 Switch to **Form** view. With *Record 1* displayed, at the bottom of the form, click the **Property Type arrow**, and notice that all entries do not fully display. Press Esc to close the **Property Type** combo box list.

10 ▶ Switch to **Design** view. Click the **Property Type** label control (on the left), point to the upper left corner to display the [icon] pointer, and then drag to the right slightly to left-align the control with those above it. Click the **Property Type** combo box control, point to the right middle sizing handle to display the [icon] pointer, and then drag to the right to **4 inches on the horizontal ruler**. Point to the left middle sizing handle to display the [icon] pointer, and drag to the left until the text box control aligns the control with those above it. Compare your screen with Figure 7.7.

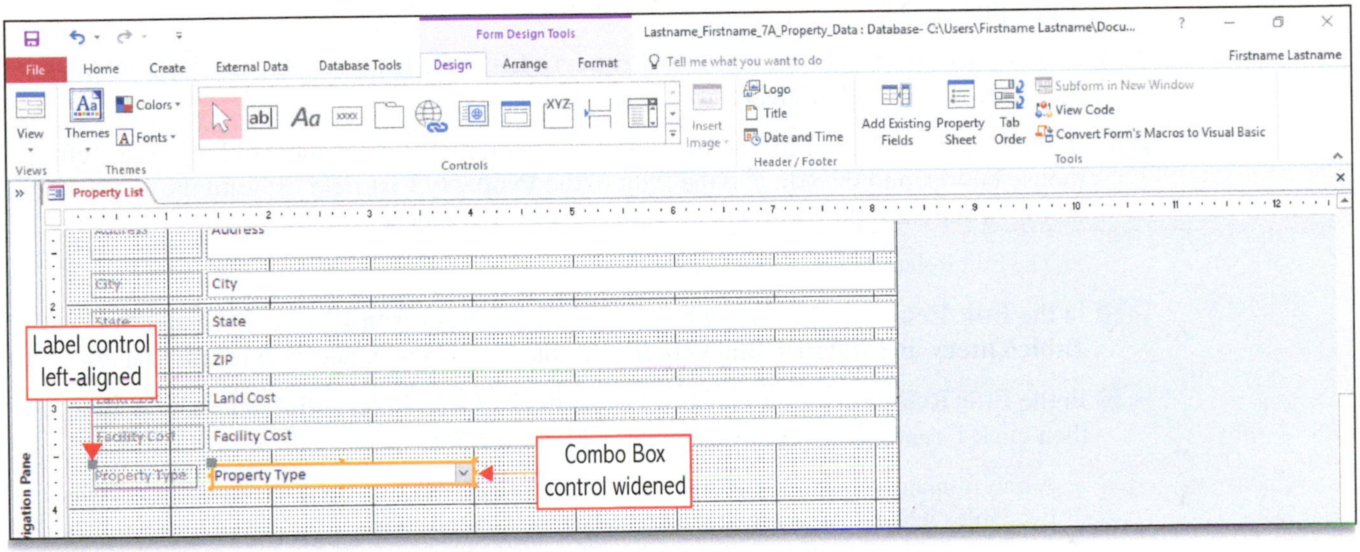

FIGURE 7.7

11 ▶ In the **Form Header** section, click the text *Property List* which is the **Title** text box control, and then click to the left of the text *Property List* to position the insertion point. Using your own name, type **Lastname Firstname 7A** and then press [Spacebar]. Click in a blank area of the form to deselect the control.

12 ▶ Switch to **Form** view. Click the **Property Type arrow**, and notice that all property types are fully displayed. Press [Esc] to close the **Property Type** combo box list.

13 ▶ On the **Quick Access Toolbar**, click **Save** [icon]. In the **Save As** dialog box, using your own name, type **Lastname Firstname 7A Property List Form** and then click **OK**. Close the form.

Activity 7.05 | Adding a Relationship

Recall that a relationship is an association that is established between two tables using common fields. You will create a relationship between the Salesperson ID field in the Property List table and the Salespeople table.

1 ▶ Open [»] the **Navigation Pane**. Double-click the **Salespeople** table name to open the table in Datasheet view.

The Salespeople table displays showing two fields—the *Salesperson ID* field and the *Salesperson* field.

2 ▶ In the **Navigation Pane**, double-click the **Property List** table name to open the table. Scroll to the right to view the **Salesperson ID** field.

The Salesperson ID is a number that identifies each salesperson. The name of each salesperson does not display in the Property List table.

3 Right-click the **Property List** table tab, and then on the shortcut menu, click **Close All**. Close ⟨«⟩ the **Navigation Pane**.

4 Click the **Database Tools tab**, and then in the **Relationships group**, click **Relationships**. If the *Show Table* dialog box does not display, on the Design tab, in the Relationships group, click the Show Table button.

5 In the **Show Table** dialog box, on the **Tables tab**, click the **Salespeople** table name, and then click **Add**. Click the **Property List** table name, and then click **Add**. **Close** the **Show Table** dialog box.

6 Point to the lower right corner of the **Property List** field list to display the ⟨⟩ pointer, and then drag down until all fields are displayed.

7 In the **Salespeople** field list, point to the **Salesperson ID** field name, hold down the left mouse button, and then drag to the right to the **Property List** field list until the ⟨⟩ pointer is on top of the **Salesperson ID** field name. Release the mouse button.

The Edit Relationships dialog box displays.

8 In the **Edit Relationships** dialog box, verify that **Salesperson ID** displays under both **Table/Query** and **Related Table/Query**. If not, click **Cancel**, and then repeat Step 7.

9 In the **Edit Relationships** dialog box, select the **Enforce Referential Integrity** option, and then click **Create**. Compare your screen with Figure 7.8.

A one-to-many relationship is created. A one-to-many relationship is a relationship between two tables where one record in the first table corresponds to many records in the second table. In this case, the Salesperson ID can only appear one time in the Salespeople table, but it can appear many times in the Property List table. One salesperson can be assigned to work with many properties.

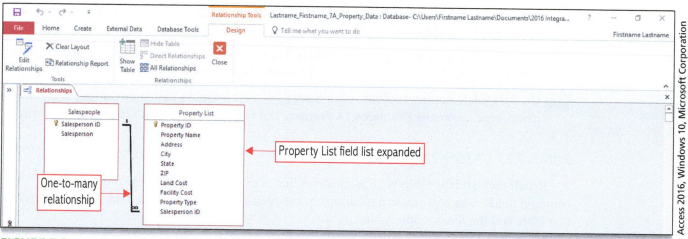

FIGURE 7.8

10 Save ⟨⟩ the relationship. Under **Relationship Tools**, on the **Design tab**, in the **Relationship**s group, click **Close**.

Activity 7.06 | Adding an Option Group to an Access Form

An *option group* is an object on a form or report that displays a limited set of alternatives where only one option can be selected at a time. An option group consists of a group frame and a set of check boxes, toggle buttons, or option buttons. When an option button is selected, a number is stored in the Access table. The value of an option group can only be a number, it cannot be text.

1 Open ⟩⟩ the **Navigation Pane.** Double-click the **Salespeople** table to open it. To the left of *Salesperson ID 1*—Kaylee Behrns—click **Expand** ⊞. Compare your screen with Figure 7.9.

> All of the 31 properties for which Kaylee Behrns is responsible display. This is the result of creating a relationship between the Property List table and the Salespeople table. In this table, each salesperson has a unique ID number.

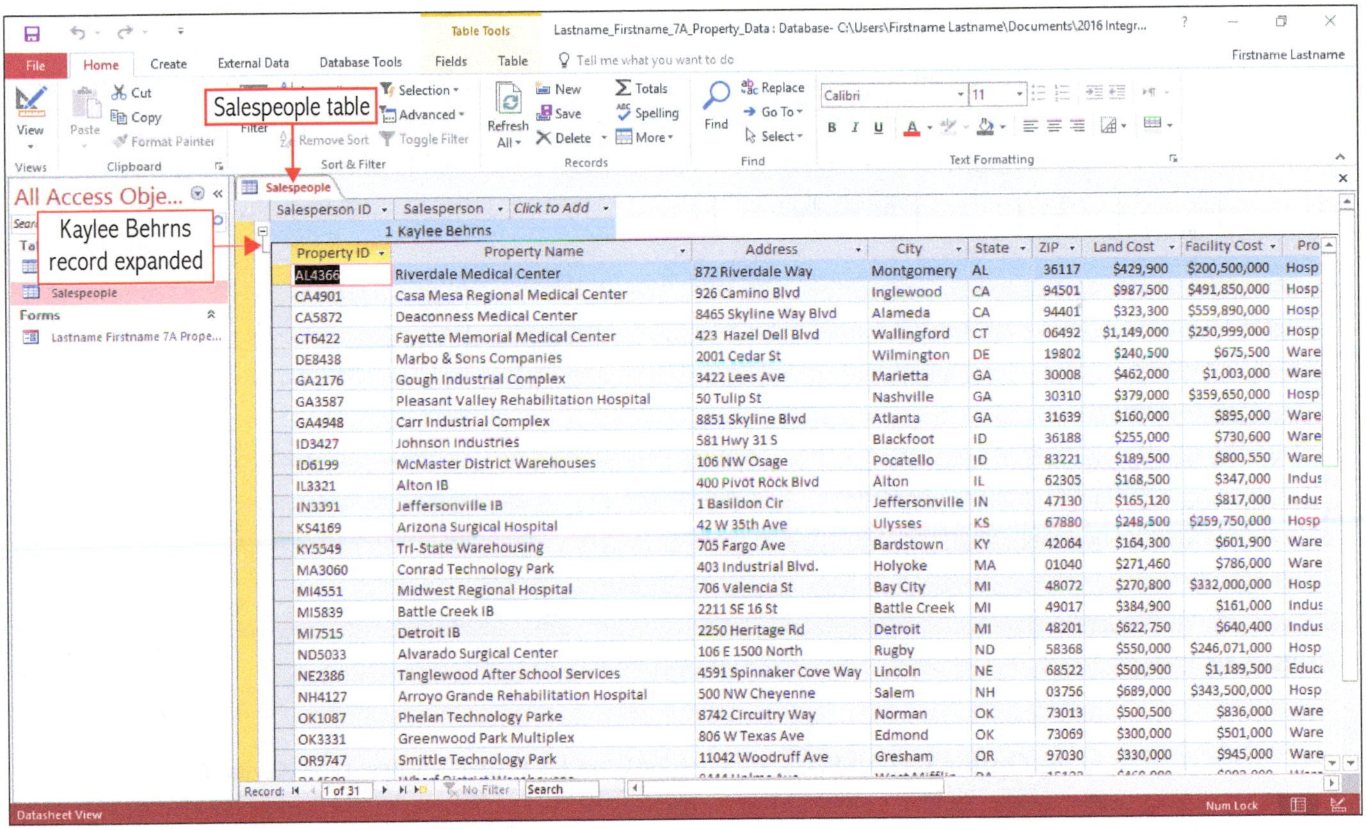

FIGURE 7.9

2 In the **Navigation Pane**, double-click the **Property List** table. Scroll to the right until the **Salesperson ID** field is displayed.

> Because of the one-to-many relationship in this table, the Salesperson ID can be entered many times instead of only one time in the Salesperson table.

3 Right-click the **Property List table tab**, and then on the shortcut menu, click **Close All**.

4 In the **Navigation Pane**, right-click the **Lastname Firstname Property List Form** name. On the shortcut menu, click **Design View**. **Close** « the Navigation Pane.

5 Under **Form Design Tools**, on the **Design tab**, in the **Controls group**, click **More** ▾, and then verify that **Use Control Wizards** is active. Locate and click the **Option Group** button. At the bottom of the form, point below the **Property Type** text box control (white), and then click one time. Compare your screen with Figure 7.10.

The Option Group Wizard dialog box displays.

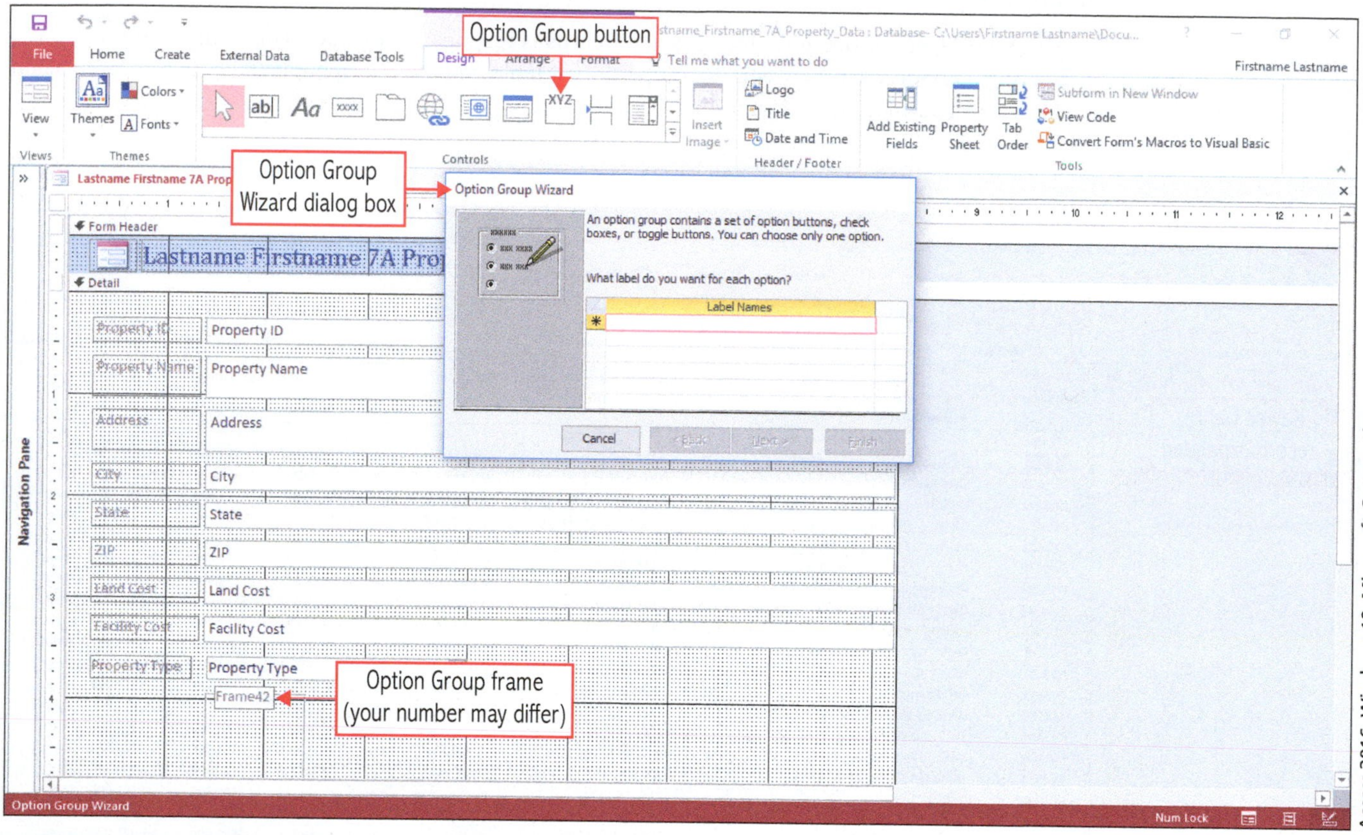

Access 2016, Windows 10, Microsoft Corporation

FIGURE 7.10

6 In the **Option Group Wizard** dialog box, under **Label Names**, type **Kaylee Behrns** and then press Tab. Type **Jenna Betts** and press Tab, then type **Tyrone Mitchell** and click **Next**.

7 Under **Do you want one option to be the default choice?**, click the **No, I don't want a default** option button, and then click **Next**.

8 Under **What value do you want to assign to each option?**, verify the value for Kaylee is *1*, Jenna is *2*, and Tyrone is *3*, and then click **Next**.

Recall that the value of an option group must be a number, not text. In this form, when an option button is selected for a salesperson, the number 1, 2, or 3 will be stored in the Property List table, and then because of the relationship between the two tables, the name of the salesperson can be queried.

9 Under **What do you want to do with the value of a selected option?**, click the **Store the value in this field** option button. Click the **arrow**, and then click the **Salesperson ID** field name. Click **Next**.

10 Under **What type of controls do you want in the option group?**, verify that **Option buttons** is selected. Under **What style would you like to use?**, click the **Shadowed** option button, and then click **Next**.

11 Under **What caption do you want for the option group?**, type **Salesperson Name** and then click **Finish**.

12 Click the border of the **Salesperson Name option group** control. With the entire control selected, not an individual name box, point to the border to display the pointer. Drag the option group control so that the control is left-aligned with the **Property Type** combo box control, and the Salesperson Name caption displays below the Property Type combo box control. Compare your screen with Figure 7.11.

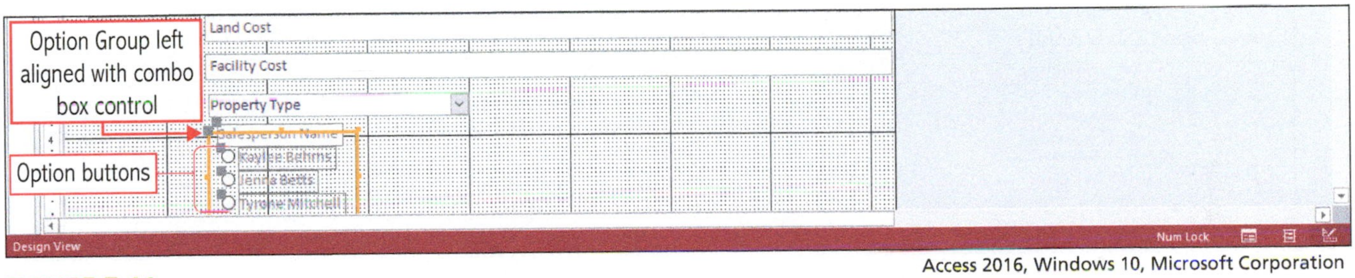

Access 2016, Windows 10, Microsoft Corporation

FIGURE 7.11

13 **Save** the changes to the form.

Activity 7.07 | Entering Data Using a Combo Box and an Option Group

1 Switch to **Form** view. At the bottom of the form, click **New (blank) record**. Add the following record:

Property ID	**WY2709**
Property Name	**Rock Springs IB**
Address	**100 Linden Ln**
City	**Rock Springs**
State	**WY**
ZIP	**82901**
Land Cost	**150000**
Facility Cost	**407800**

2 In the **Property Type** combo box control, click the **arrow**, and then click **Industrial Building**. In the **Salesperson Name** option group, click the **Tyrone Mitchell** option button, and then compare your screen with Figure 7.12.

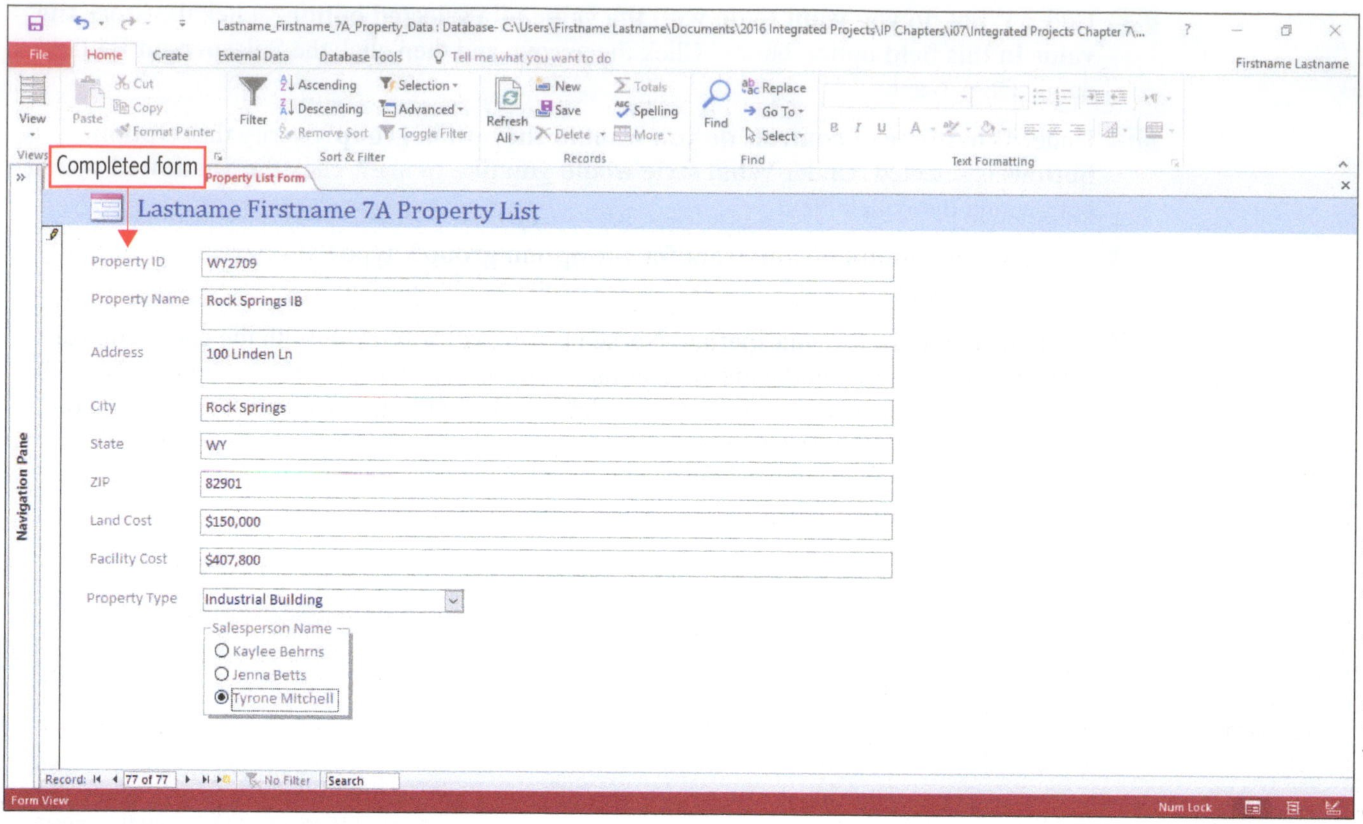

FIGURE 7.12

3 ▶ Press Enter to display a new blank record. Using the same technique, add the following records. Take your time to enter the data accurately.

Property ID	Property Name	Address	City	State	ZIP	Land Cost	Facility Cost	Property Type	Salesperson
WV7101	Woodland Daycare Center	320 Green St	Frankford	WV	24938	250600	450100	Educational Facility	Kaylee Behrns
IA3624	Broaddus Warehouse	145 Tudor Dr	Waterloo	IA	50112	140500	215400	Warehouse	Jenna Betts
MI5189	Kite Subsystems Co	8692 Technology Blvd	Berkeley	MI	48708	290100	980550	Warehouse	Tyrone Mitchell

4 ▶ Verify that you have 80 records. Close the form. If you are instructed to submit your files electronically, go to Activity 7.08.

5 ▶ Open the **7A Property List form**. To print one record, in **Backstage** view, click the **Print tab**, and then click **Print Preview**. On the **Print Preview tab**, in the **Page Layout group**, click the **Landscape** button. On the **Print Preview tab**, in the **Close Preview group**, click the **Close Print Preview** button. Below the form, in the navigation area, click **Last record** ▶. With Property ID **WY2709** displayed, in **Backstage** view, click the **Print tab**, and then click the **Print** button. In the **Print** dialog box, under **Print Range**, click the **Selected Record(s)** option button. Click **OK** to close the dialog box.

6 ▶ Close the form.

304 **Integrated Projects 2016** | Chapter 7: INTEGRATING WORD, EXCEL, ACCESS, AND POWERPOINT

Activity 7.08 | Creating an Access Query

In the previous Activity, when you entered the property records and selected the Salesperson option button, a number was stored in the Salesperson ID field in the Property List table. In order to see which salesperson is responsible for each property, you will create a query that includes fields from both tables in the database.

1 On the **Create tab**, in the **Queries group**, click **Query Wizard**. In the **New Query** dialog box, verify that **Simple Query Wizard** is selected, and then click **OK**.

2 Under **Tables/Queries**, verify that **Table: Property List** displays. Under **Available Fields**, double-click the field names **Property Name**, **Address**, **City**, **State**, **ZIP**, **Land Cost**, **Facility Cost**, and **Property Type**.

3 Under **Tables/Queries**, click the **arrow**, and then click the **Salespeople** table name. Under **Available Fields**, double-click the field name **Salesperson**. Compare your screen with Figure 7.13.

The selected field names from both tables display under Selected Fields.

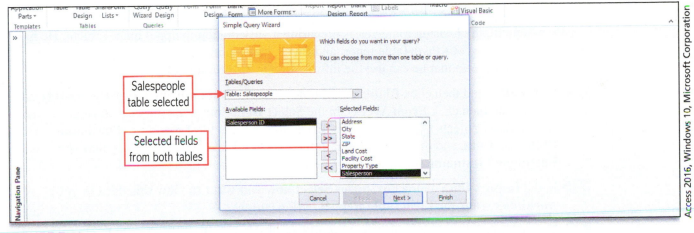

FIGURE 7.13

4 Click **Next** two times.

5 Under *What title do you want for your query?*, using your own name, type **Lastname Firstname 7A Property List Query** and then click **Finish**.

6 Scroll to the right, if necessary, and notice the names of the salespeople display in the Salesperson field.

The names of the salespeople come from the Salesperson field in the Salespeople table. All of the other fields come from the Property List table. Because the tables are related, you can display any field from either table in a query.

7 In **Backstage** view, on the right, click **View and edit database properties**. In the **Properties** dialog box, on the **Summary tab**, in the **Subject** box, type your course name and section number; in the **Author** box, type your first name and last name; and then in the **Keywords** box, type **form controls, query** Click **OK** to close the dialog box. On the left, click **Save** to redisplay the database window.

8 Right-click your **Property List Query tab**, and then on the shortcut menu, click **Close**. **Close** ☒ Access.

Although Access is generally the best application to use for storing data, you can import the data into Excel to manipulate it using features such as the *PivotTable report* and the *PivotChart report*.

A PivotTable is an interactive, cross-tabulated Excel report that summarizes and analyzes data. In a PivotTable, you can *pivot*—move a row to a column or a column to a row—to see different views and summaries of the source data. You can display the details for areas of interest or calculate the different summaries such as averages. Use a PivotTable when you want to analyze related totals or compare several facts about each value, especially when you have a long list of figures to sum.

A PivotChart is a graphical representation of the data in a PivotTable. The advantage of creating a PivotChart instead of a standard Excel chart is that you can pivot the data displayed in the PivotChart just as you can in a PivotTable.

Activity 7.09 | Importing Access Data into Excel

Pam Stancill, the Leasing Manager, is preparing a presentation to upper management. He has asked you to use Excel's PivotTable report and PivotChart report features to analyze the data in the Access database so that he can use the information in his presentation.

1 ▶ Start Excel, and then click **Blank workbook**. Click the **Data tab**, click **Get External Data group**, and then click **From Access**. In the **Select Data Source** dialog box, navigate to your **Integrated Projects Chapter 7** folder. Click your Access file **Lastname_Firstname_7A_Property_Data**, and then click **Open**. In the **Select Table** dialog box, verify that your **Lastname Firstname Property List Query** is selected, and then click **OK**.

2 ▶ In the **Import Data** dialog box, under **Select how you want to view this data in your workbook**, click the **PivotTable Report** option button.

3 ▶ Under *Where do you want to put the data?*, verify that the **Existing worksheet** option button is selected and that **=$A$1** displays in the box. Click **OK**. Compare your screen with Figure 7.14.

The *PivotTable Field List*, on the right side of your screen, enables you to move fields to different areas in the PivotTable or PivotChart. The *Field Section*—the upper portion of the pane—contains the available field names you can add to the *Area Section*. The Area Section—the lower portion of the pane—contains four quadrants where field names are placed to determine how the report will display. The graphic at the left of your screen is replaced with the PivotTable as you select fields in the pane.

ALERT!   **Does your PivotTable Fieldkey List layout differ?**

If the PivotTable report has been used previously on your computer, the arrangement of the Field Section and the Area Section of the PivotTable Field List may display in a different layout. To change to the layout shown in this instruction, near the top of the pane, to the right of Choose fields to add to report, click the Tools arrow, and then click Fields Section and Area Section Stacked.

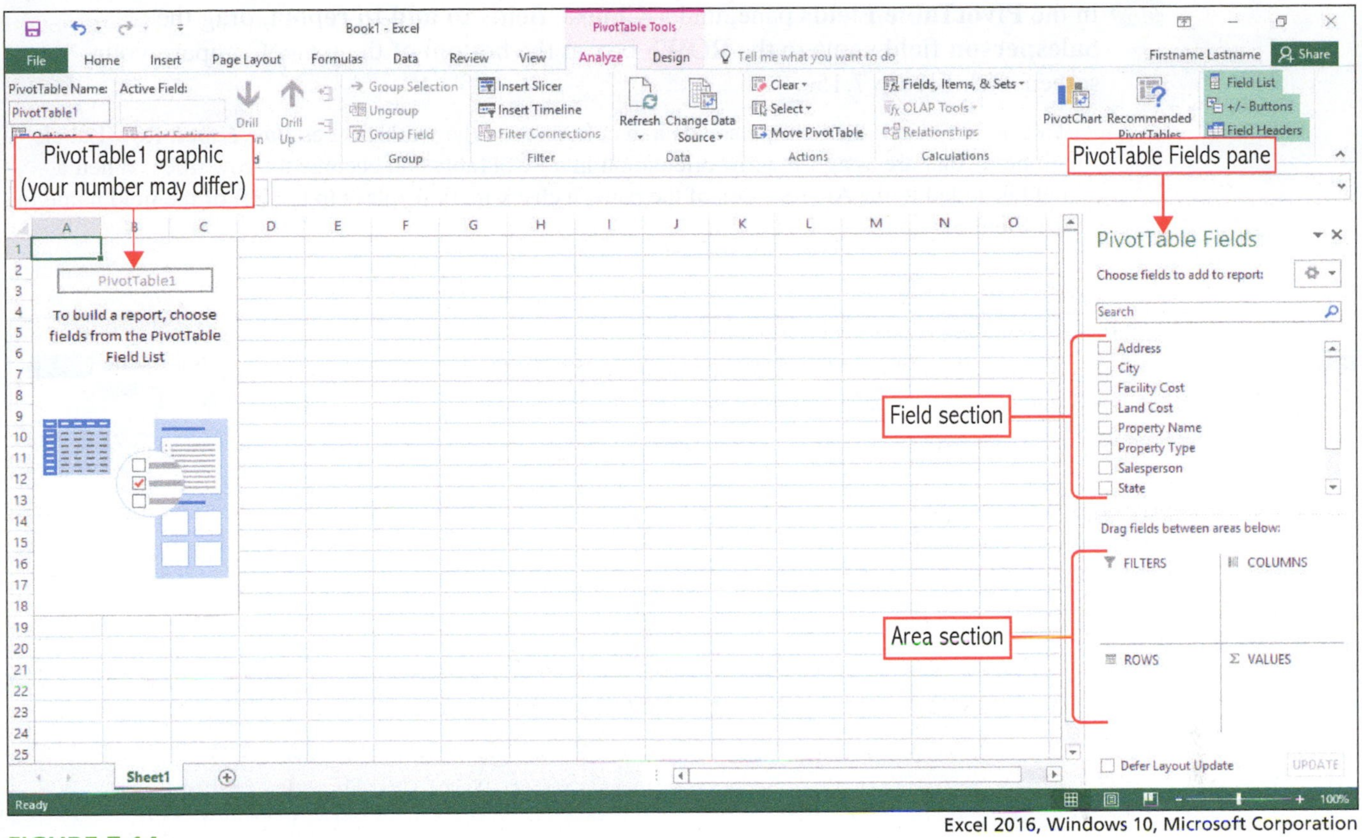

FIGURE 7.14

Excel 2016, Windows 10, Microsoft Corporation

4 ▶ On the **Quick Access Toolbar**, click **Save** 🖫. On the left, click **Save As**, and then click **Browse**. In the **Save As** dialog box, navigate to your **Integrated Projects Chapter 7** folder, and then using your own name, save the file as **Lastname_Firstname_7A_Property_PivotTable**

NOTE | Addressing a Security Warning

When you import Access data into Excel, you are linking the two files. If you close and then reopen your linked Excel file, a Security Warning may display alerting you that the file is linked. Click the Enable Content button, and then click OK.

Activity 7.10 | Creating a PivotTable

To create a PivotTable, you will add the fields from the PivotTable Fields pane. Within the PivotTable, you can display the level of detail, create calculations, and sort or filter the data.

1 In the **PivotTable Fields** pane, under **Choose fields to add to report**, drag the **Salesperson** field name to the **ROWS** box at the bottom of the pane. Compare your screen with Figure 7.15.

This action places the Salesperson data in column A of the worksheet as *Row Label*. Row Labels are fields that are assigned a row orientation in a PivotTable and become the row titles. When a field is added to the Area Section of the pane, a check mark displays to the left of the field name in the Field Section.

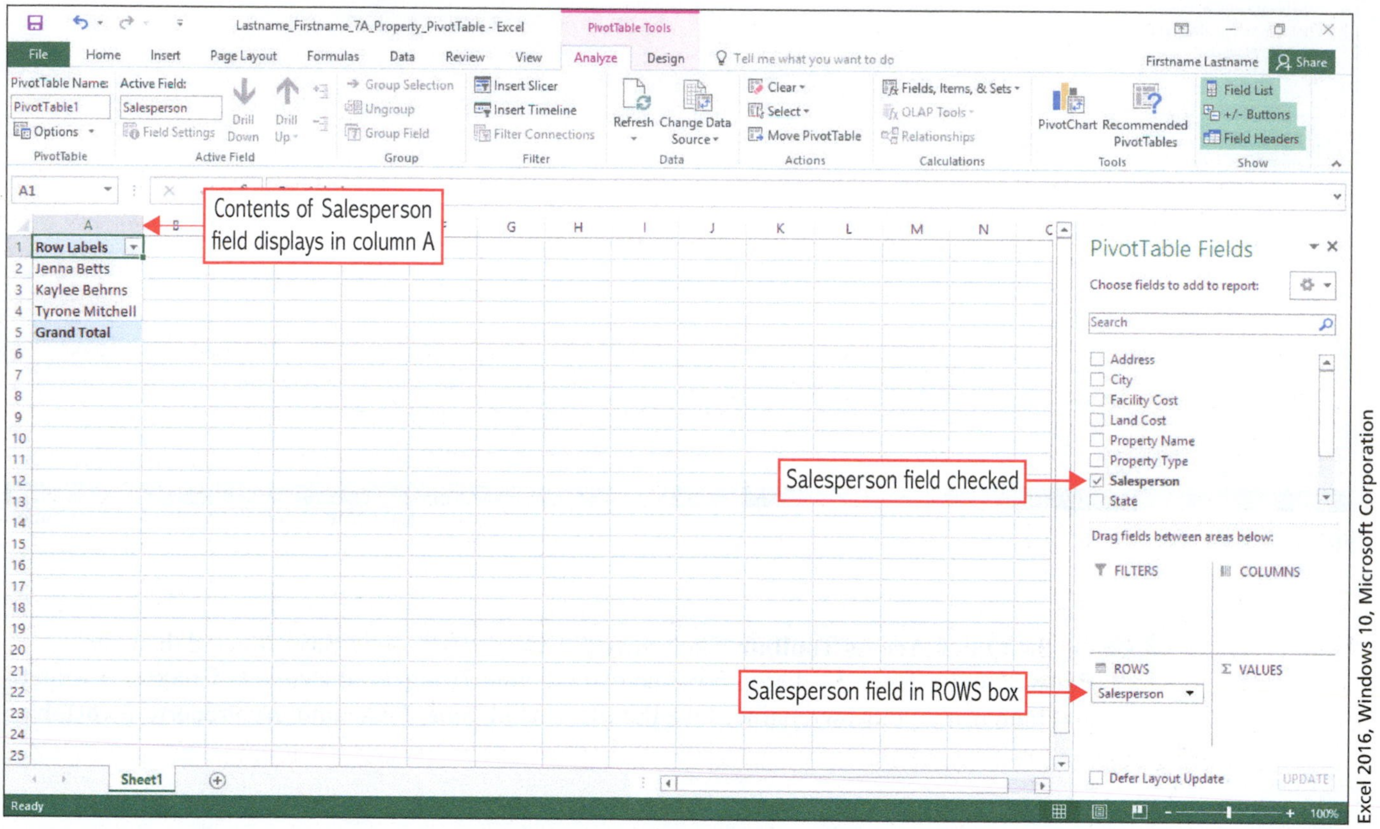

FIGURE 7.15

2 In the **PivotTable Fields** pane, drag the **Property Type** field to the **COLUMNS** box at the bottom of the pane.

Column Labels are fields that are assigned a column orientation in a PivotTable and become the column titles.

3 In the **PivotTable Fields** pane, drag the **Land Cost** field down to the **VALUES** box. Compare your screen with Figure 7.16.

The *Values area* contains the cells in a PivotTable that summarize quantitative data. The default is to sum the figures, but you can display the values in a variety of other ways, such as the average, maximum, or minimum.

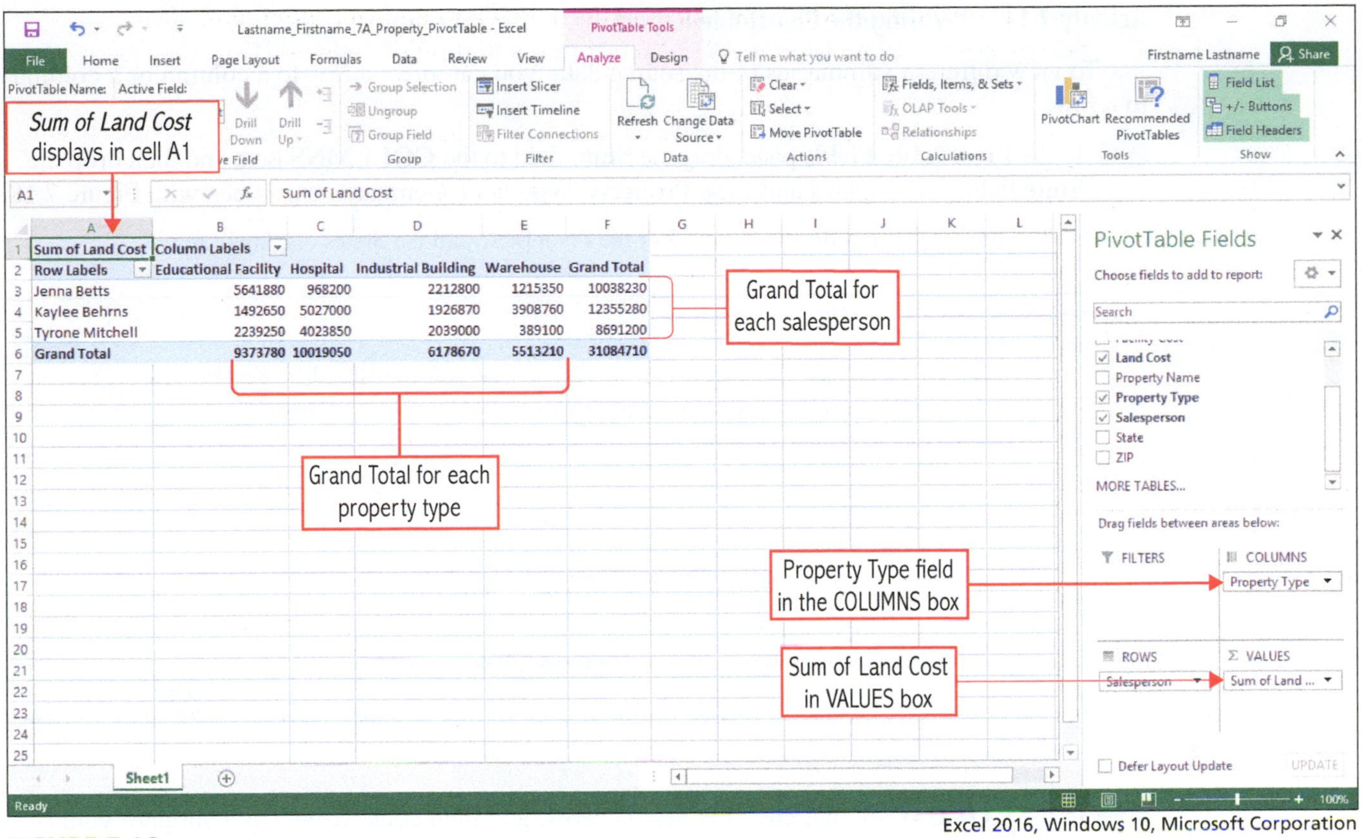

FIGURE 7.16

Excel 2016, Windows 10, Microsoft Corporation

4 ▶ Under **PivotTable Tools**, on the **Analyze tab**, in the **Active Field group**, click **Field Settings**. In the **Value Field Settings** dialog box, at the bottom left, click **Number Format**. In the **Format Cells** dialog box, under **Category**, click **Currency**. Click the **Decimal places down arrow** two times to display **0**. Verify that the **Symbol** is **$** and then click **OK**. In the **Value Field Settings** dialog box, click **OK**, and then compare your screen with Figure 7.17.

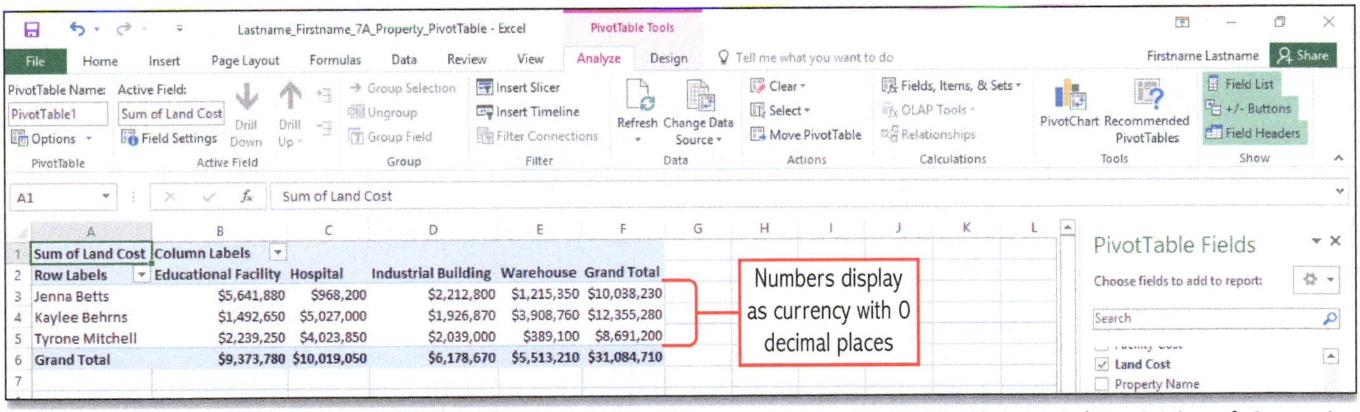

FIGURE 7.17

Excel 2016, Windows 10, Microsoft Corporation

5 ▶ Click cell **A10**.

The PivotTable Fields pane and the PivotTable contextual tabs no longer display because the PivotTable is not selected.

6 ▶ Click cell **A1** to select the PivotTable and to display the PivotTable Fields pane.

7 ▶ **Save** 🖫 your workbook.

Activity 7.11 | Pivoting the PivotTable Report

To view different summaries of the source data, you can pivot a row to a column or a column to a row.

1 In the **PivotTable Fields** pane, drag the **State** field to the **COLUMNS** box, and then drop the **State** field so it displays under the **Property Type** field. Compare your screen with Figure 7.18.

The Property Types display in row 2 of the PivotTable and the States display in row 3.

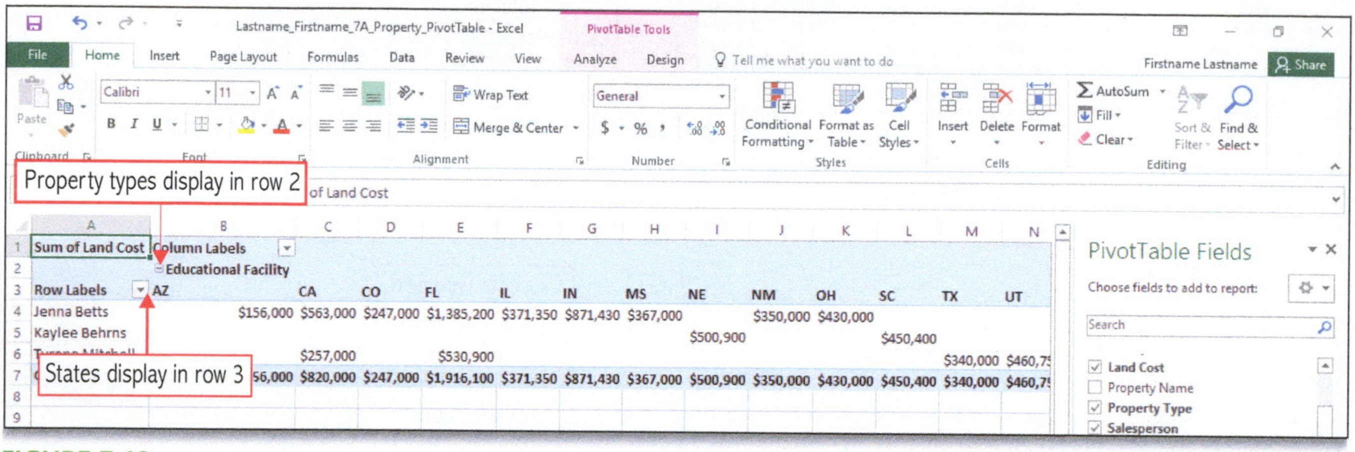

FIGURE 7.18

2 In the **COLUMNS** box, click the **State arrow**, and then click **Move Up**. Compare your screen with Figure 7.19.

In the PivotTable, the States display in row 2, and the Property Types display in row 3.

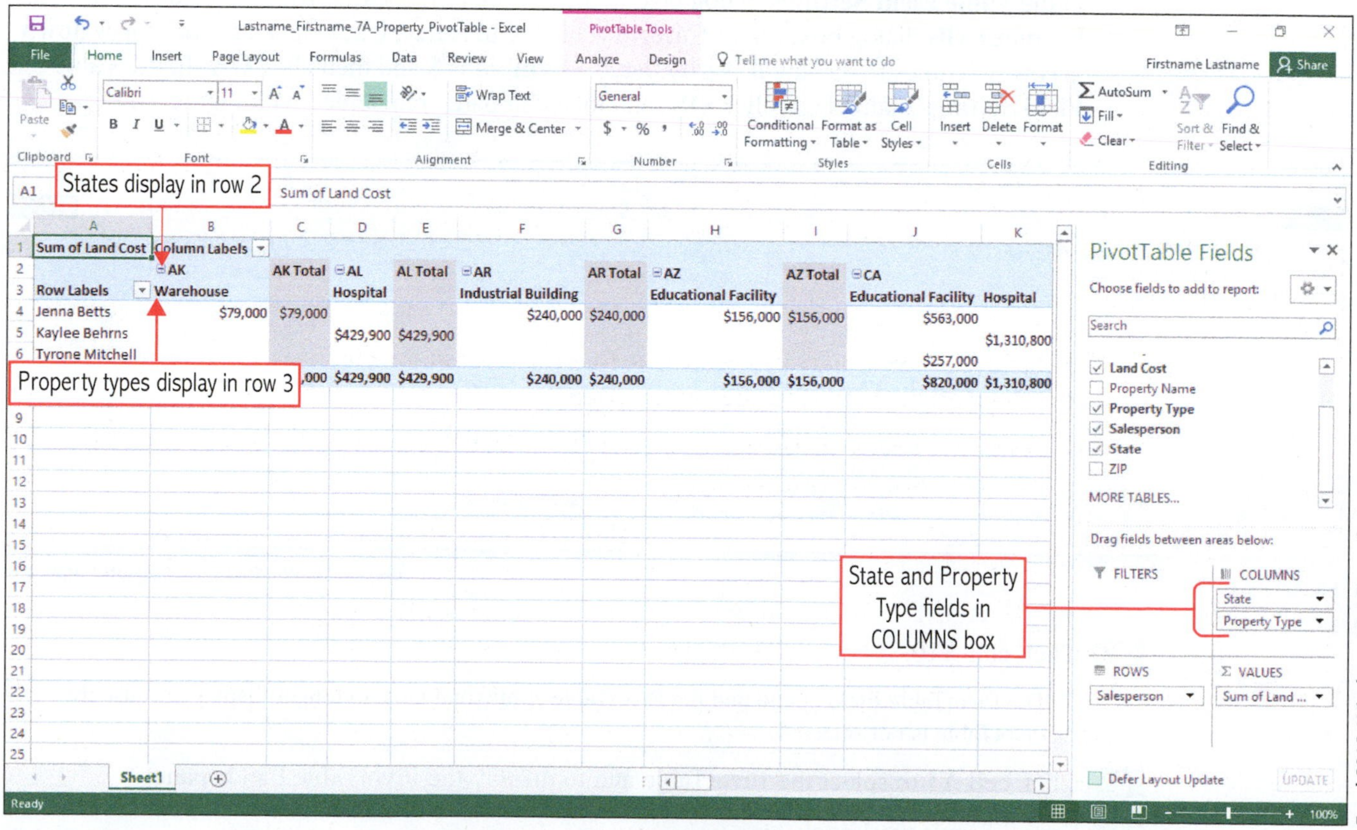

FIGURE 7.19

3 In **Backstage** view, click the **Print tab**. At the bottom of the **Print Preview**, in the navigation area, click the **Next Page** button ▶ to view the pages.

There are 15 pages in the report. One reason to use a PivotTable is that you can present the data in a concise manner. As currently formatted, this report does not meet that requirement.

4 Click the **Home tab** to display the worksheet. In the **COLUMNS** box, click the **State arrow**, and then click **Move to Row Labels**. In the **ROWS** box, if necessary, drag the State field so that it displays below the Salesperson field. Compare your screen with Figure 7.20.

In the PivotTable, the State field is pivoted—changed from a column label to a row label. In the Row Labels box, the State field displays below the Salesperson field.

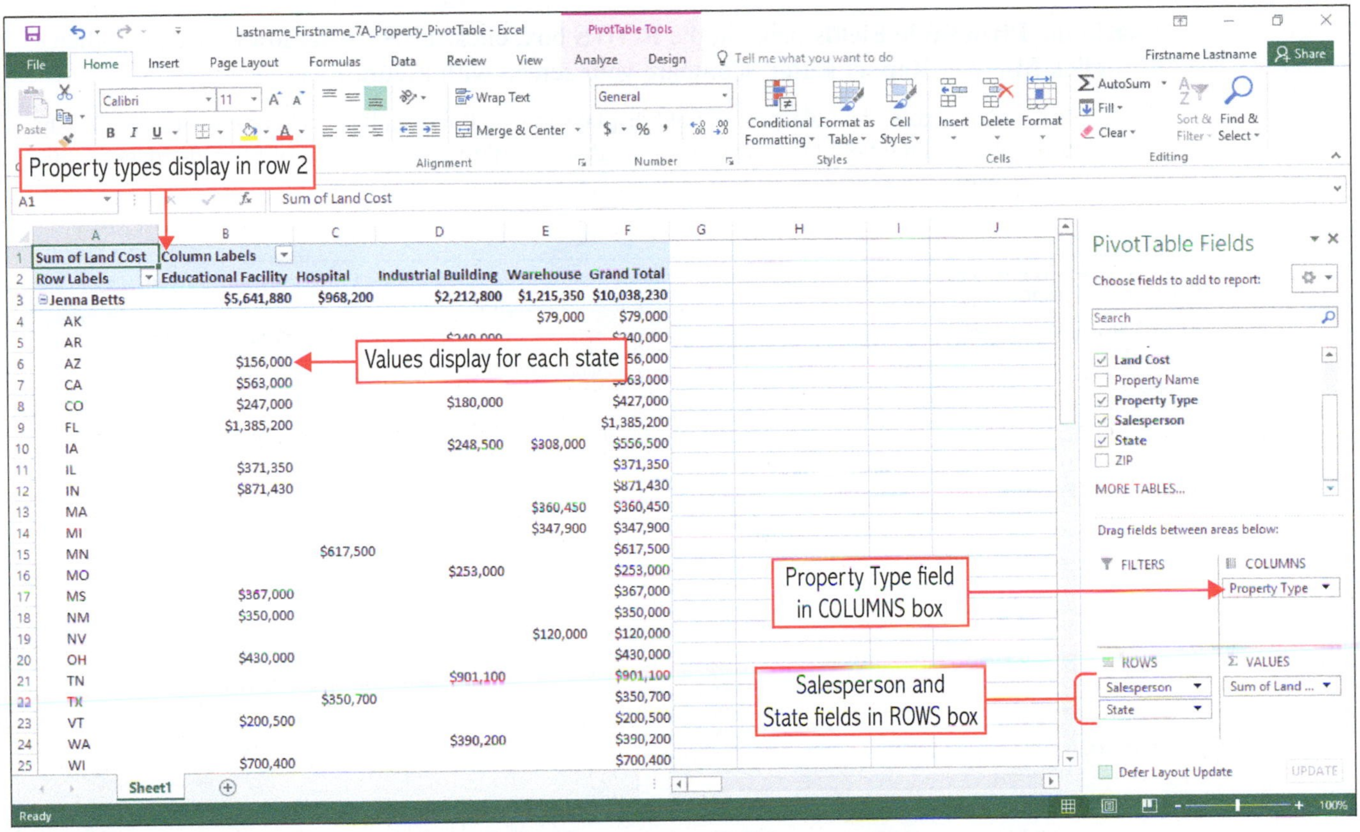

FIGURE 7.20

5 In **Backstage** view, click the **Print tab**. Below the **Print Preview**, in the navigation area, click **Next Page** ▶ to view the second page.

There are two pages in the report. By pivoting the fields, the same data is presented in a more concise manner—a two-page report instead of a 15-page report.

6 Click the **Home tab**. In cell **A3**, to the left of the name *Jenna Betts*, click **Collapse** −. Scroll down, and then in cell **A28**, to the left of the name *Tyrone Mitchell*, click **Collapse** −.

Only the details for the salesperson Kaylee Behrns display. The details are hidden for Jenna Betts and for Tyrone Mitchell, but the totals for these two salespeople display.

7 Right-click the **Sheet1 sheet tab**, and then on the shortcut menu, click **Rename**. Type **Behrns Detail** and then press Enter.

8 Press Ctrl + Home. **Save** 🖫 the workbook.

Activity 7.12 | Filtering the PivotTable Report

Recall that filtering is the process of displaying only a subset of data. In this Activity, you will use the ***Report Filter*** area to display the information for only one salesperson at a time. The Report Filter is the area on a PivotTable that is used to restrict the data that displays.

1 Right-click the **Behrns Detail sheet tab**, and then on the shortcut menu, click **Move or Copy**. In the **Move or Copy** dialog box, click **(move to end)**, and then select the **Create a copy** check box. Click **OK**.

A new Behrns Detail (2) sheet is created and selected. You would normally use the same worksheet to filter data in various ways. For purposes of this instruction, however, you are creating copies of worksheets and applying filters.

2 In the **PivotTable Fields** pane, in the **ROWS** box, click the **Salesperson arrow**, and then click **Move to Report Filter**. Compare your screen with Figure 7.21.

In the PivotTable, the Salesperson field displays in row 1 above all the other fields. In cell B1, the term *(All)* and the field filter arrow indicate that the Salesperson field is not filtered—data for all salespersons displays.

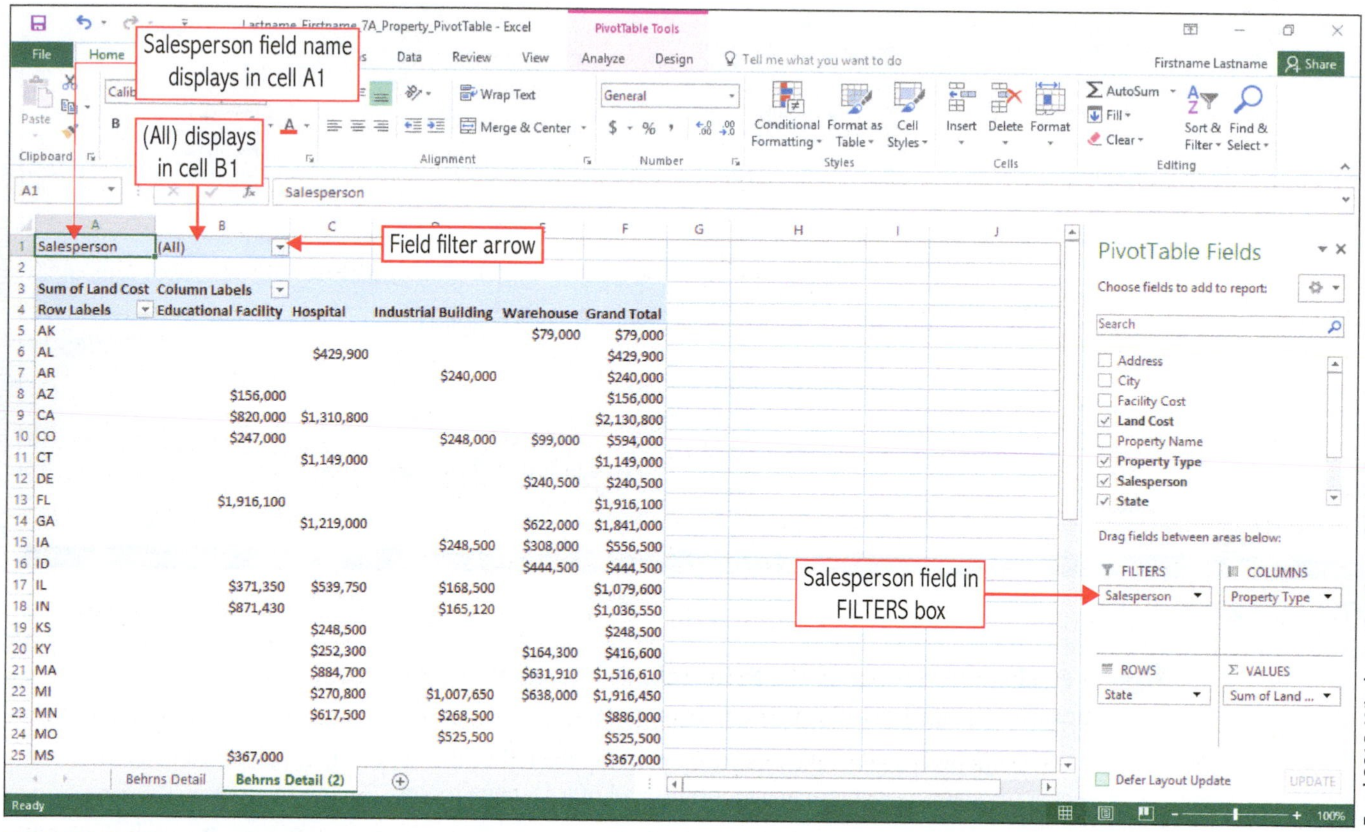

FIGURE 7.21

Excel 2016, Windows 10, Microsoft Corporation

3 In cell **B1**, click the **Salesperson filter arrow** [▾], click **Tyrone Mitchell**, and then click **OK**. Compare your screen with Figure 7.22.

Only the data for Tyrone Mitchell displays. The totals do not display for the other salespeople. The filter icon in cell B1 informs the reader that a filter is applied to the PivotTable.

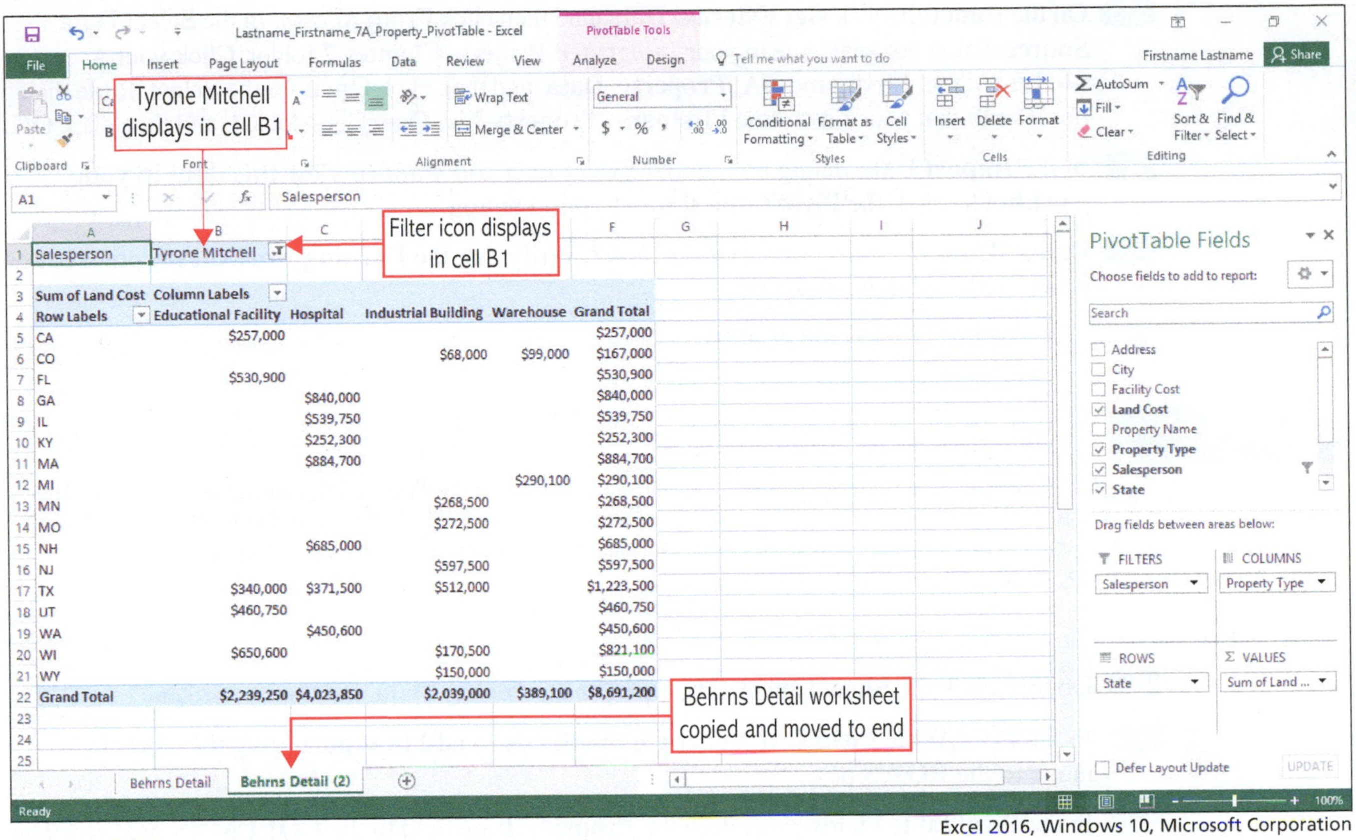

Excel 2016, Windows 10, Microsoft Corporation

FIGURE 7.22

4 ▸ Right-click the **Behrns Detail (2) sheet tab**, and then on the shortcut menu, click **Rename**. Type **Mitchell Detail** and then press Enter.

🔄 **ANOTHER WAY**   Double-click the sheet tab to select the sheet name, type the new sheet name, and then press Enter.

5 ▸ Right-click the **Mitchell Detail sheet tab**, and then on the shortcut menu, click **Move or Copy**. In the **Move or Copy** dialog box, click (**move to end**), and then select the **Create a copy** check box. Click **OK**.

A new Mitchell Detail (2) sheet is created and selected.

6 ▸ In cell **B1**, click the **Salesperson filter arrow** ▾ click **Jenna Betts**, and then click **OK**.

Only the data for Jenna Betts displays.

7 ▸ Right-click the **Mitchell Detail (2) sheet tab**, and then on the shortcut menu, click **Rename**. Type **Betts Detail** and then press Enter.

8 ▸ Save 💾 the workbook.

Activity 7.13 │ Using a Drill-Down Indicator

One of the features of a PivotTable is the **drill-down indicator**—a feature that shows the detailed records of a PivotTable total. Pam Stancill has asked you to create a new PivotTable report to display the Facility Cost by Property Type and by State, and then use the drill-down indicator to show the detailed records for the state of Illinois. To determine in which state the company has the most investments in hospitals, you will sort the PivotTable by hospitals and then display the detailed records for the state of California.

1 ▸ At the bottom of the worksheet window, click **New Sheet** ⊕ to create a fourth worksheet in the workbook.

2 On the **Data tab**, click **Get External Data**, and then click **From Access**. In the **Select Data Source** dialog box, navigate to your **Integrated Projects Chapter 7** folder. Click your Access file **Lastname_Firstname_7A_Property_Data**, and then click **Open**. In the **Select Table** dialog box, verify that your **Lastname Firstname Property List Query** is selected, and then click **OK**.

3 In the **Import Data** dialog box, under **Select how you want to view this data in your workbook**, click the **PivotTable Report** option button.

4 Under *Where do you want to put the data?*, verify that the **Existing worksheet** option button is selected, and then click **OK**.

A new PivotTable report displays.

> **NOTE** Creating a New PivotTable Report
>
> Every time you create a new PivotTable report, Excel will automatically number the report—PivotTable1, PivotTable2, and so on. Your PivotTable names may vary depending on how many reports you have created. In real-world practice, you can pivot the same PivotTable to present the data in various ways. Here, so that you can submit variations of your work to your instructor, you will import the Access data again to create another PivotTable report.

5 Double-click the **Sheet4 sheet tab**, type **Facility Cost by State** and then press Enter.

6 In the **PivotTable Field List**, under **Choose fields to add to report**, drag the **State** field name to the **ROWS** box.

7 In the **PivotTable Fields** pane, drag the **Property Type** field to the **COLUMNS** box, and then drag the **Facility Cost** field to the **VALUES** box. Compare your screen with Figure 7.23.

The States are listed in column A and the Property Types display in row 2.

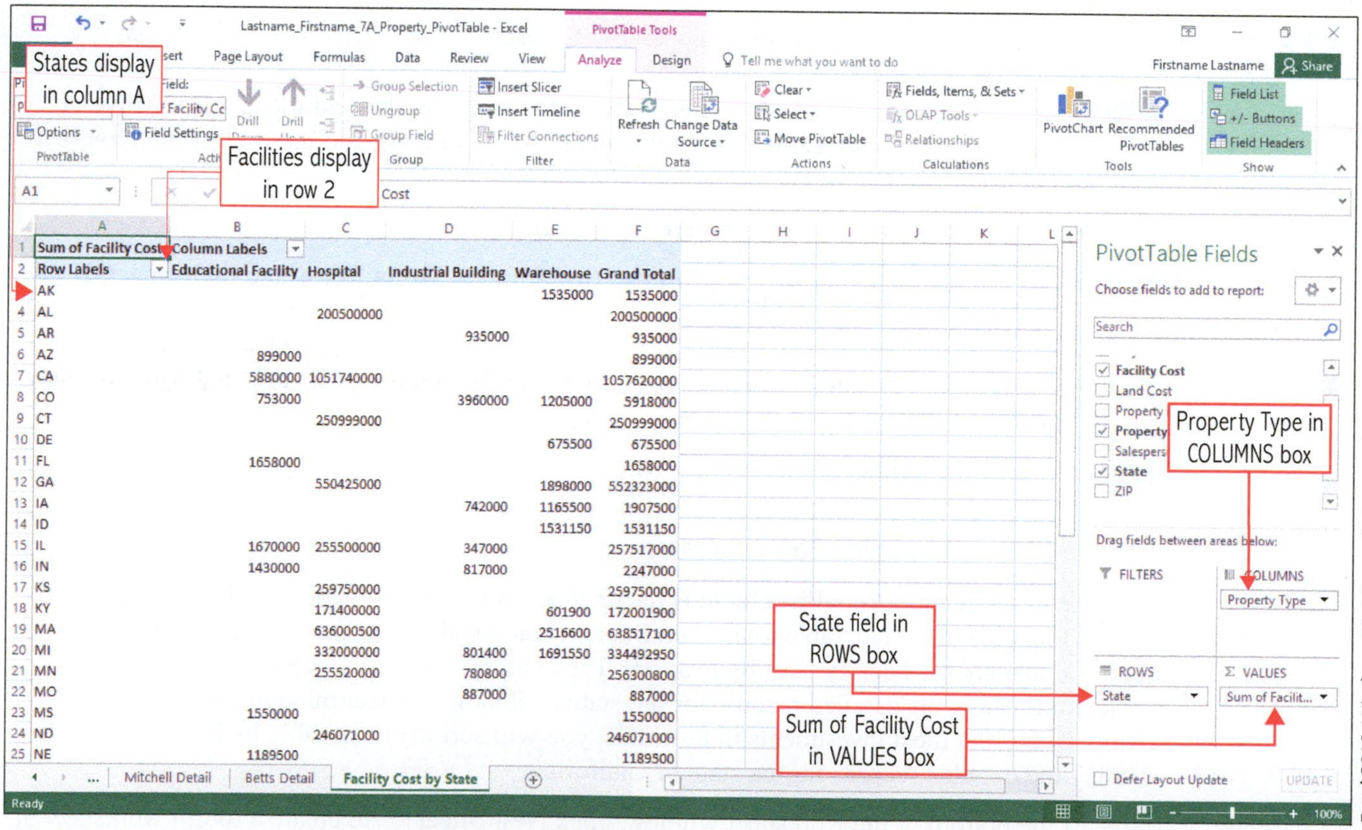

Excel 2016, Windows 10, Microsoft Corporation

FIGURE 7.23

8 Under **PivotTable Tools**, on the **Analyze tab**, in the **Active Field group**, click the **Field Settings** button. In the **Value Field Settings** dialog box, at the bottom left, click **Number Format**. In the **Format Cells** dialog box, under **Category**, click **Currency**. Click the **Decimal places** down arrow two times to display **0**. Verify that the **Symbol** is **$**, and then click **OK**. In the **Value Field Settings** dialog box, click **OK**.

The numbers in the PivotTable are formatted as currency with 0 decimal places.

9 Click cell **F15**. Verify that cell F15 represents the Grand Total for the state of Illinois (IL).

ALERT!   **Is your Grand Total different?**

If the Grand Total for the state of Illinois does not display in cell F15, return to Activity 7.7, Step 3, and verify that you entered the Access data accurately.

---

10 Double-click cell **F15**, and then click cell **A6** to deselect the table. Compare your screen with Figure 7.24.

A new Sheet5 is created, and the detailed records of the Illinois properties are displayed. Your sheet number may differ.

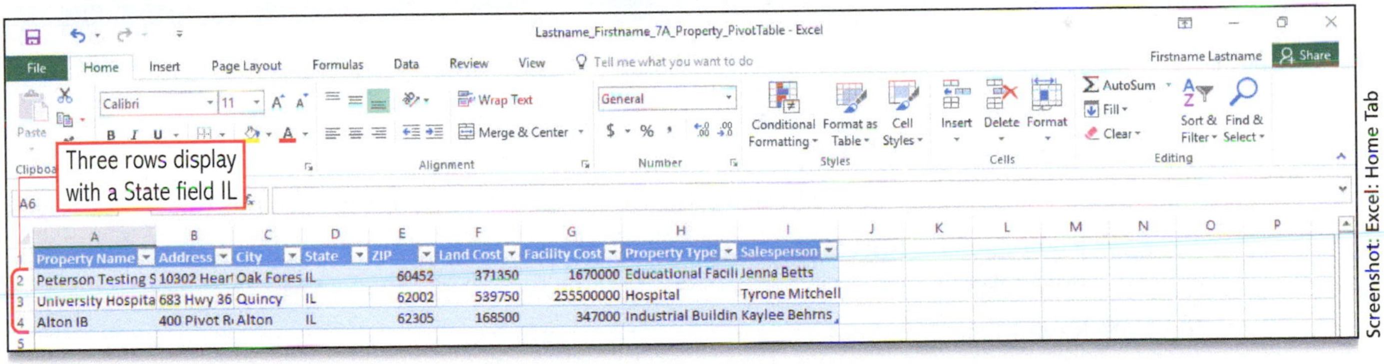

FIGURE 7.24

11 Rename the new sheet **IL Detail**.

12 Click the **Facility Cost by State sheet tab**. Click any cell in **column C**—the Hospital property type field. On the **Home tab**, in the **Editing group**, click **Sort & Filter**, and then click **Sort Largest to Smallest**. Compare your screen with Figure 7.25.

Column C is sorted in descending order.

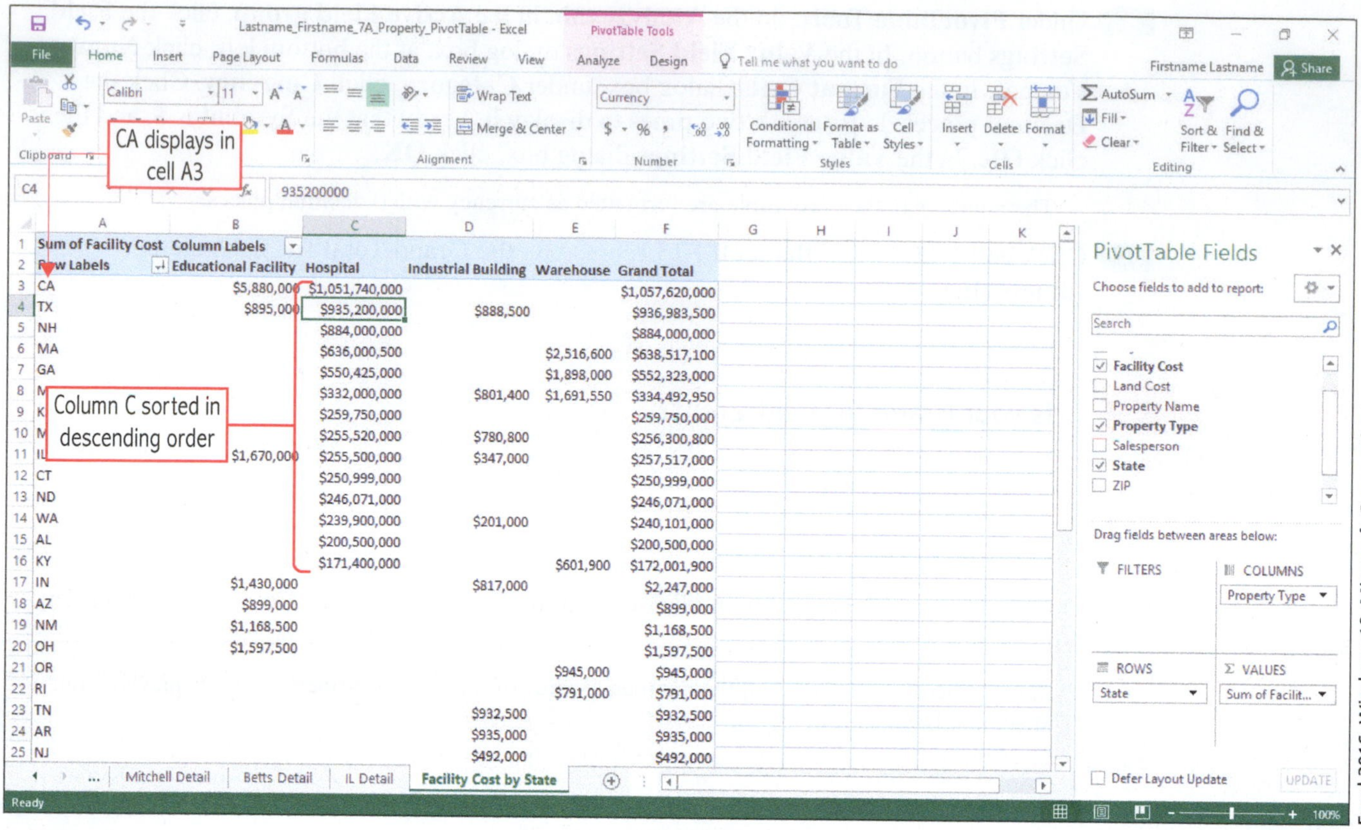

Excel 2016, Windows 10, Microsoft Corporation

FIGURE 7.25

13 Double-click cell **C3**.

A new Sheet6 is created, and the detailed records of the hospitals in California (CA) are displayed.

14 Right-click the **Sheet6 sheet tab**, and then from the shortcut menu, click **Rename**. Type **CA Hospitals** and then press Enter.

15 **Save** the workbook.

Activity 7.14 | Creating and Modifying a PivotChart Report

A PivotChart is based on a PivotTable, and the two are interactive. If you change the way the data displays on the PivotChart, it changes the display of the same data on the related PivotTable. Morgan Bannon-Navarre, the Select National Properties Group CFO, has asked you to create a PivotChart showing the average cost of investments the company has for industrial buildings and warehouses.

1 Click the **Facility Cost by State sheet tab**. Under **PivotTable Tools**, click the **Analyze tab**, and then in the **Tools group**, click **PivotChart**. In the **Insert Chart** dialog box, on the left, verify that **Column** is selected, and then in the row of charts at the top, click the fourth style—**3-D Clustered Column**. Compare your screen with Figure 7.26.

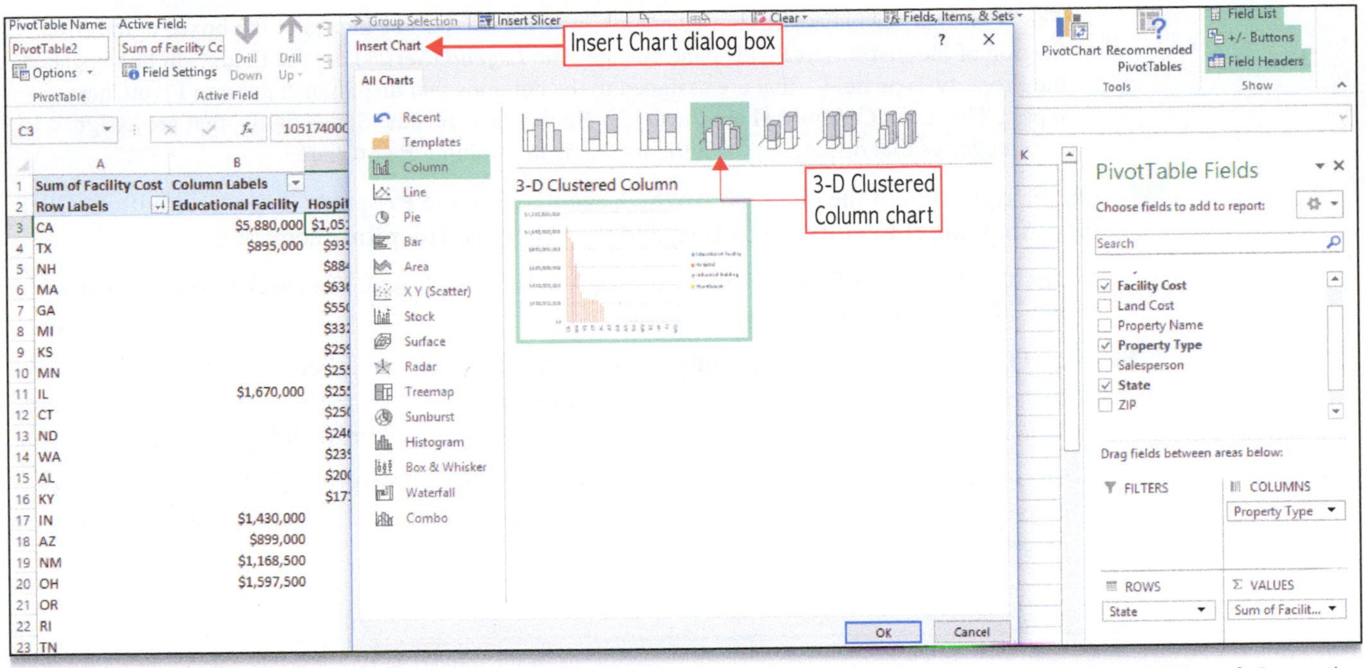

FIGURE 7.26

Excel 2016, Windows 10, Microsoft Corporation

2 ▶ In the **Insert Chart** dialog box, click **OK**.

A chart and the field buttons Sum of Facility Cost, State, and Property Type display.

3 ▶ Under **PivotChart Tools**, click the **Design tab**, and then in the **Location group**, click **Move Chart**. In the **Move Chart** dialog box, click the **New sheet** option button, in the **New sheet** box, type **Average Cost Chart** and then click **OK**. Compare your screen with Figure 7.27.

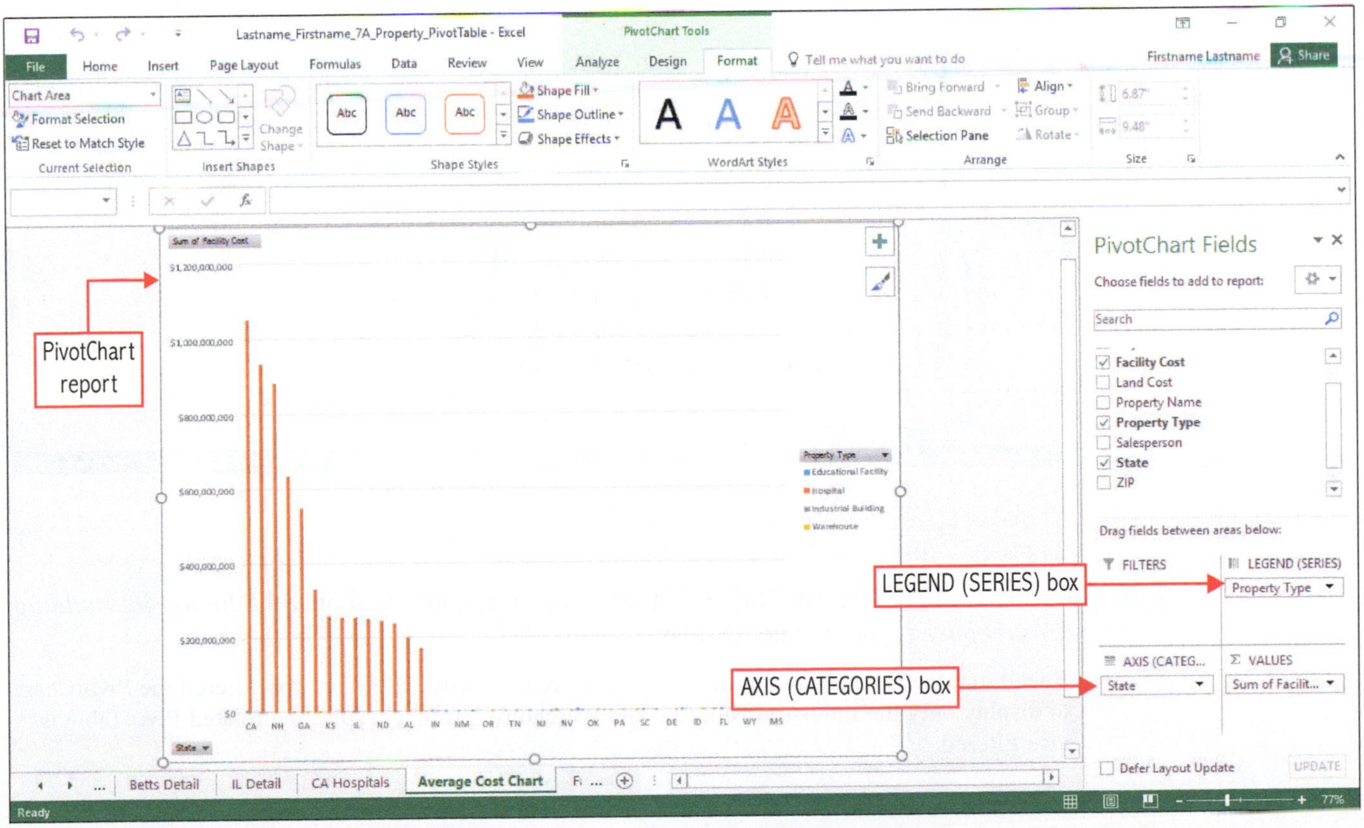

FIGURE 7.27

Excel 2016, Windows 10, Microsoft Corporation

The PivotChart displays on a new Average Cost Chart sheet. The names of the boxes in the Area Section of the PivotChart Fields pane change. The *Legend (Series)* are the fields—in this instance the Property Type field—that are assigned to the columns that display in a column PivotChart report. The *Axis (Categories)* are the fields—in this instance, the States field—that are assigned to the categories that display on the horizontal axis in a column PivotChart.

4 ▶ On the right side of the chart, above the **Legend**, click the **Property Type** field button. Click the **Educational Facility** check box, and then click the **Hospital** check box.

The check boxes for Educational Facility and Hospital are cleared. The check boxes for Industrial Building and Warehouse are selected.

5 ▶ Click **OK**. Under **PivotChart Tools**, click the **Analyze tab**, and then in the **Show/Hide group**, click **Field List**. Then, in the **Show/Hide group**, click the lower portion of the **Field Buttons** button; on the list, click **Hide All**. Compare your screen with Figure 7.28.

The PivotChart is filtered to display facility costs for only the Industrial Building and Warehouse property types. The PivotChart Fields pane and the PivotChart Field Buttons are toggled off and no longer display.

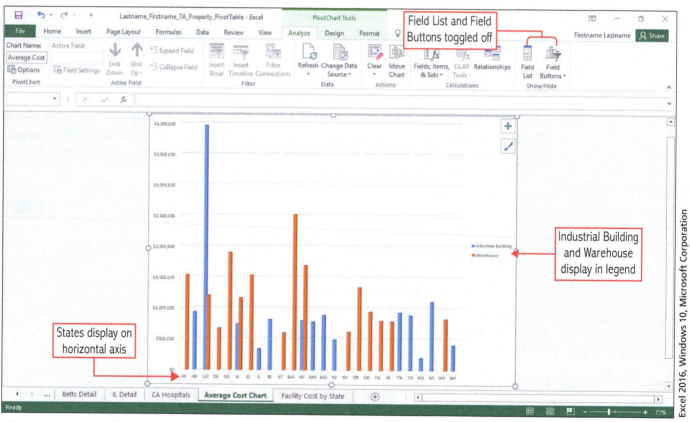

FIGURE 7.28

6 ▶ Click the **Facility Cost by State sheet tab**. In **row 2**, notice that only the *Industrial Building* and *Warehouse* property types display.

Recall that the PivotChart and the PivotTable are interactive. Because you filtered the PivotChart to display only the Industrial Building and Warehouse property types, the related PivotTable is also filtered.

7 Scroll down to view **row 29**, and then notice the **Grand Total** values. Click anywhere in the table. Under **PivotTable Tools**, click the **Analyze tab**, and then in the **Active Field group**, click **Field Settings**. In the **Value Field Settings** dialog box, under **Summarize value field by**, click **Average**, and then click **OK**. Notice that the **Grand Totals** are lower numbers because they are averages and not totals. Scroll up to view cell **A1**, and notice that the heading is changed to *Average of Facility Cost*. Compare your screen with Figure 7.29.

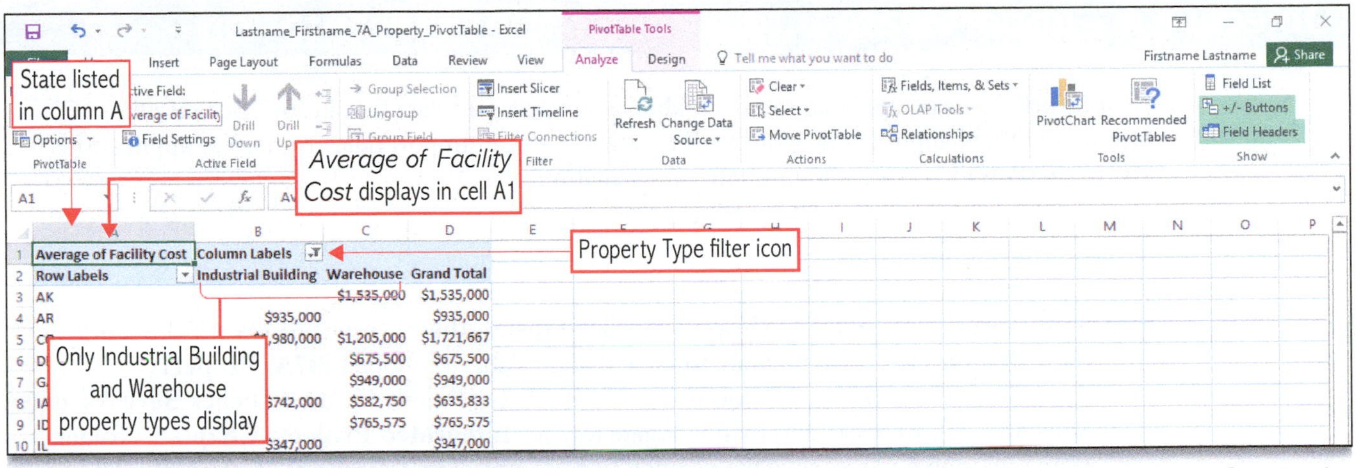

FIGURE 7.29

8 Under **PivotTable Tools**, on the **Analyze tab**, in the **Show group**, click **Field List** to display the **PivotTable Fields** pane, and then drag the **Salesperson** field name down to the **ROWS** box. Move the **Salesperson** field above the **State** field name.

The fields are pivoted to display the Average of Facility Cost for each salesperson.

9 Click the **Average Cost Chart sheet tab**.

The PivotChart reflects the changes made in the PivotTable. Columns are grouped by the name of the salesperson. Within each group, the states display in alphabetical order.

10 **Close** ☒ the **PivotChart Fields** pane.

11 Under **PivotChart Tools**, click the **Design tab**. In the **Chart Layouts group**, click **Add Chart Element**. Click **Chart Title**, and then click **Above Chart**. Type **Average Cost of Industrial Buildings and Warehouses** and then press Enter.

12 On the right side of the chart, click **Chart Elements** ➕, point to **Legend**, click the arrow, and then click **Top**. In the chart, click the **Legend** to select it. On the **Home tab**, in the **Font group**, click **Increase Font Size** A˄ two times. In the **Font group**, click **Bold** B.

13 Right-click the **Mitchell Detail** sheet, and then on the shortcut menu, click **Select All Sheets**. On the **Insert tab**, in the **Text group**, click **Header & Footer**. On the **Design tab**, in the **Navigation group**, click **Go to Footer**. In the **Footer** area, click the box just above the word *Footer*, and then in the **Header & Footer Elements group**, click **File Name**. Click any cell in the worksheet to exit the footer.

14 On the right side of the status bar, click **Normal** ▦, and then press Ctrl + Home to make cell **A1** the active cell. Right-click any sheet tab, and then on the shortcut menu, click **Ungroup Sheets**.

15 Click the **File tab** to display **Backstage** view. On the left, click **Info**, in the lower right corner, click **Show All Properties**. Under **Related People**, be sure your name displays as the **Author**—change it if necessary. Click to the right of **Subject**, and then type your course name and section number. Click to the right of **Tags**, and then type **costs, PivotTable, PivotChart**

16 On the left, click **Save** to save your workbook and redisplay the workbook window.

Objective 4   Import Data into a PowerPoint Presentation

PowerPoint is an application that enables you to present data to a group. Because the Microsoft Office applications work well together, you can import data from other applications into PowerPoint to create a high-quality presentation.

Activity 7.15 │ Copying Data into a PowerPoint Presentation

1 Start PowerPoint, and at the lower left, click **Open Other Presentations**. Click **Computer**, click **Browse**, and then navigate to your student data files. Open **i07A_Property_ Presentation**. Click the **File tab** to display **Backstage** view. On the left click **Save As**, under *Save As*, click **Browse**, and then navigate to your **Integrated Projects Chapter 7** folder. Using your own name, save the presentation as **Lastname_Firstname_7A_Property_ Presentation** If necessary, to display the rulers, on the View tab, in the Show group, select the Ruler check box.

2 Click the **Insert tab**, and then in the **Text group**, click **Header & Footer**. In the **Header and Footer** dialog box, on the **Notes and Handouts tab**, select the **Footer** check box. As the footer, using your own name, type **Lastname Firstname 7A Property Presentation** and then click **Apply to All**.

3 Start Word. Navigate to your **Integrated Projects Chapter 7** folder, and then open your document **7A_Midtown_Developers**. Under **Comments**, select the list of eight property types. On the **Home tab**, in the **Clipboard group**, click **Copy** 📋.

4 On the taskbar, click the **PowerPoint** button to redisplay your **Lastname_Firstname_7A_ Property_Presentation**. Click **Slide 2**. Click the **Home tab**, and then in the **Clipboard group**, click the upper portion of the **Paste** button. With the placeholder border selected, point to the middle left sizing handle to display the ⟷ pointer, and then drag to the left to approximately **4 inches left of 0 on the horizontal ruler**. Delete any bullets and extra spaces that copied from the original text.

The eight property types from the Word document are pasted in Slide 2.

5 Click anywhere in the placeholder, and then press [Ctrl] + [A] to select all the text in the placeholder. On the **Home tab**, in the **Font group**, click the **Font Size button arrow** [60 ▾], and then click **24**. In the **Paragraph group**, click **Bullets** [≣ ▾], and then click **Filled Round Bullets**. If necessary, drag the text box up slightly. Click in a blank area of the slide and then compare your screen with Figure 7.30.

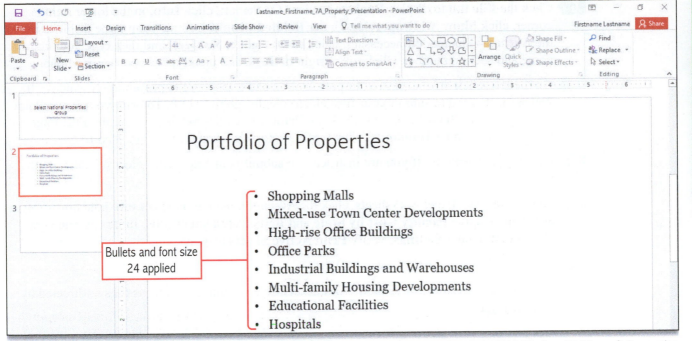

FIGURE 7.30

PowePoint 2016, Windows 10, Microsoft Corporation

6 ▶ On the taskbar, display your **Excel** workbook. Click the **Average Cost Chart sheet tab**. Click in a blank area of the chart, and then verify that the entire chart is selected. On the **Home tab**, in the **Clipboard group**, click **Copy** 🗐.

7 ▶ On the taskbar, redisplay your **PowerPoint** presentation, and then display **Slide 3**. On the **Home tab**, in the **Clipboard group**, click the upper portion of the **Paste** button.

The Excel PivotChart report Average Cost of Industrial Buildings and Warehouses displays on Slide 3.

Activity 7.16 │ Modifying the PowerPoint Presentation

1 ▶ On the **Home tab**, in the **Slides group**, click the **New Slide button arrow**, and then click **Title and Content**. On the new slide, **Slide 4**, click the **Title** placeholder, and then type **Contact Us**

2 ▶ Click the bottom placeholder, type **312-555-0070** and then press Enter. Type **www. SelectNationalProp.com** and then press Ctrl + A. On the **Home tab**, in the **Paragraph group**, click **Bullets** 📋▾ to remove the bullets. In the **Paragraph group**, click **Center** ☰.

3 ▶ Click **Slide 1**. On the **Design tab**, in the **Themes group**, click **More** ▾. In the **Themes** gallery, under **Office**, locate and click the **Ion** theme.

4 ▶ Click the **Transitions tab**, and then in the **Transition to This Slide group**, click the **Fade** transition. In the **Timing group**, click **Apply To All**.

5 ▶ Click the **Slide Show tab**. In the **Start Slide Show group**, click **From Beginning**, and then view your presentation, clicking the mouse to advance through the slides. When the black slide displays, click the mouse one more time to display the presentation in Normal view.

6 Click the **File tab** to display **Backstage** view. On the left, click **Info**, in the lower right corner, click **Show All Properties**. Under **Related People**, be sure your name displays as the **Author**—change it if necessary. Click to the right of **Subject**, and then type your course name and section number. Click to the right of **Tags**, and then type **properties, portfolio**

7 On the left, click **Save** to save your presentation and redisplay the presentation window. If you are instructed to submit your files electronically, go to Step 8. To print your PowerPoint presentation, in **Backstage** view, click the **Print tab**. Under **Settings**, click the **Full Page Slides arrow**, under **Handouts**, click **6 Slides Horizontal**, and then click **Print**.

8 **Close** ☒ PowerPoint. If you are instructed to submit your Excel files electronically, go to Step 10.

9 To print selected Excel worksheets, click the **Average Cost Chart sheet tab**, hold down Ctrl, and then click the **Facility Cost by State** and **Betts Detail sheet tabs**. In **Backstage** view, click **Print**. Under **Settings**, verify **Print Active Sheets** displays, and then click **Print**.

10 **Close** ☒ Excel, and then **Close** ☒ Word.

11 Submit your electronic or printed Word, Excel, PowerPoint, and Access files as directed by your instructor.

> **END | You have completed Project 7A**

Retail Report

PROJECT ACTIVITIES

In Activities 7.17 through 7.22, you will import data from Access into Excel, and then use Excel functions to help determine loan information. Morgan Bannon-Navarre, the Select National Properties Group CFO, is considering the purchase of several retail stores and has asked you to analyze the data. Your completed files will look similar to Figure 7.31.

PROJECT FILES

For Project 7B, you will need the following files:

New blank Excel worksheet
i07B_Retail_Stores
i07B_Retail_Report

You will save your files as:

Lastname_Firstname_7B_Store_Payments
Lastname_Firstname_7B_Retail_Report

PROJECT RESULTS

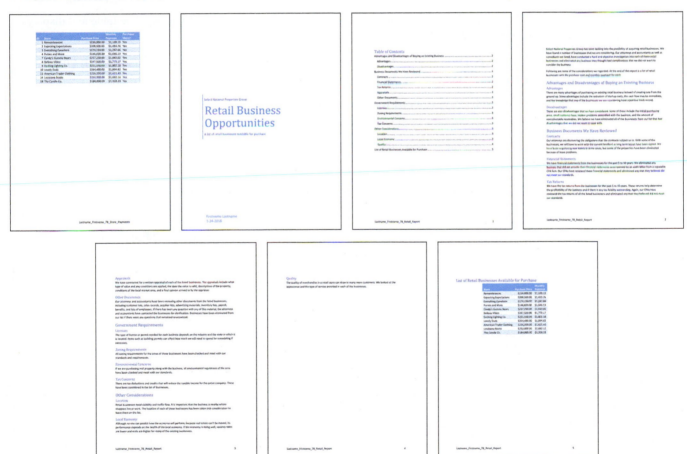

FIGURE 7.31 Retail Report

Objective 5 Use Excel Functions

A ***function*** is a predefined formula—a formula that Excel has already built for you—that performs calculations by using specific values—***arguments***—in a particular order. An argument is any value that the function uses to perform operations or calculations. Common arguments used with functions include numbers, text, cell references, and names.

Activity 7.17 | Inserting the PMT Function

Morgan Bannon-Navarre, the company CFO, is considering the purchase of several retail stores. He has created a list of stores and their purchase prices in an Access database and needs to decide if the company should purchase any of these properties. To purchase any stores, he knows the company would borrow the money for 20 years at an annual interest rate of 6 percent. Excel's ***PMT function*** calculates the payment for a loan based on constant payments and a constant interest rate. In the following Activity, you will import the retail store data into Excel, and then use the PMT function to calculate the monthly payment for each store.

1. Start Excel, and then open a **Blank workbook**. Click the **Data tab**, click **Get External Data**, and then click **From Access**. In the **Select Data Source** dialog box, navigate to the location of your student data files, and then open the Access database **i07B_Retail_Stores**.

   Because there is only one table in the database, Excel automatically selects the table and displays the Import Data dialog box.

2. In the **Import Data** dialog box, under **Select how you want to view this data in your workbook**, verify that the **Table** option button is selected.

3. Under **Where do you want to put the data?**, verify that the **Existing worksheet** option button is selected, and then click **OK**. Compare your screen with Figure 7.32.

   The data from the Access table—the ID, Store and Purchase Price fields—displays as a table in the worksheet.

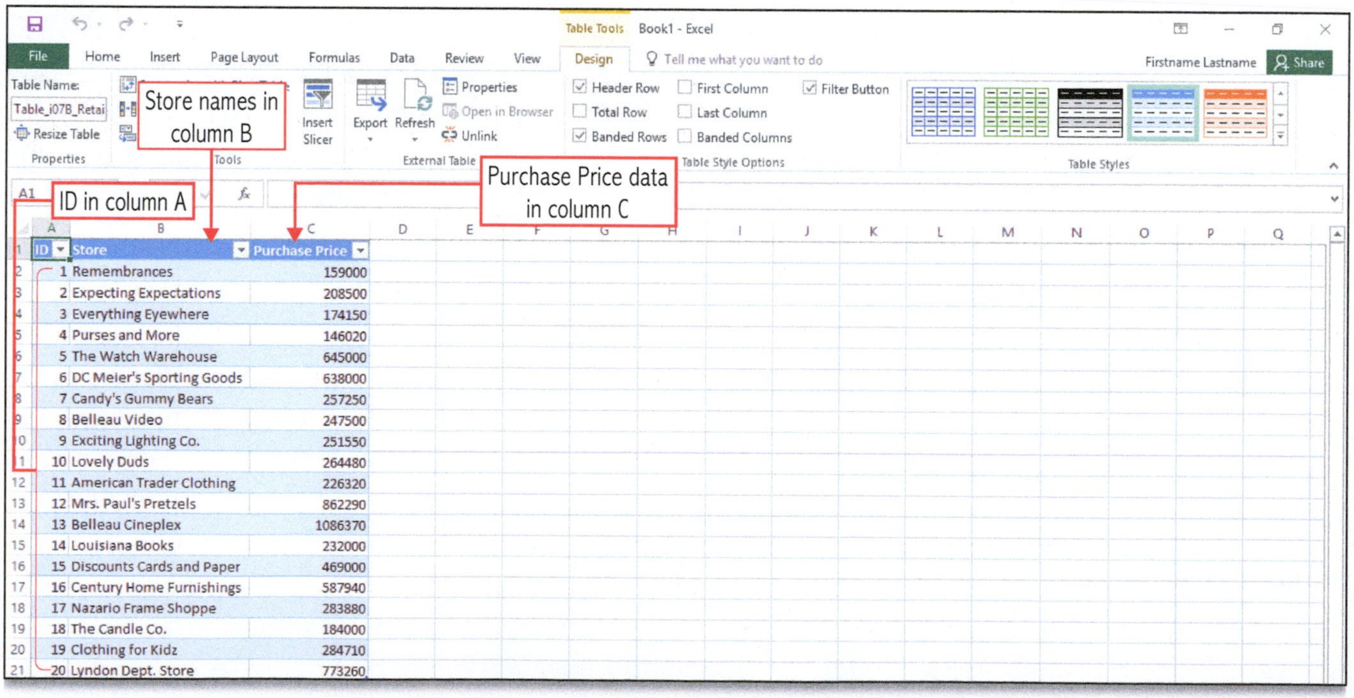

FIGURE 7.32

4 On the Quick Access Toolbar, click **Save** 🖫. Under *Save As*, click **Browse**, and then in the **Save As** dialog box, navigate to your **Integrated Projects Chapter 7** folder, and then using your own name, save the file as **Lastname_Firstname_7B_Store_Payments**

5 Click cell **D1**. Type **Monthly** and then hold down Alt and press Enter. Type **Payment** and then press Enter.

> Pressing Alt + Enter causes the heading *Monthly Payment* to display on two lines in cell D1. The heading format from the table is automatically applied to the new Monthly Payment column title.

6 Verify that cell **D2** is the active cell. Click the **Formulas tab**, and then in the **Function Library group**, click **Financial**. Scroll down the list, and then click **PMT** to display the **Function Arguments** dialog box. If necessary, move the Function Arguments dialog box so that the data in columns A:C is visible.

> **NOTE**   Function Arguments
>
> The Function Arguments dialog box separates the different arguments of the function so that you can input the arguments one by one. As you click each argument box, an explanation of the argument displays at the bottom of the dialog box. Argument names that display in bold are required for the function. Argument names that are not bold are optional. When you complete the arguments and click OK, the structure of the function will automatically be entered in the active cell.

7 In the **Function Arguments** dialog box, in the **Rate** argument box, type **6%/12** and then press Tab.

> The monthly interest rate of 0.005 displays to the right of the Rate argument box. The 6% interest rate is an annual interest rate, but you want to calculate a monthly payment. In order to determine a monthly interest rate, you must divide the annual rate by 12—the number of months in a year.

8 In the **Nper** argument box, type **20*12** and then press Tab.

> The number *240* displays to the right of the Nper argument box. The loan is for 20 years, but you want the PMT function to calculate a monthly payment. To determine how many months you will be paying back the loan, you need to multiply the number of years by 12—the number of months in one year.

9 Verify that the insertion point is in the **Pv** argument box, and then click cell **C2**. Compare your screen with Figure 7.33.

> *159000* displays to the right of the Pv argument box. This is the present value of how much money the company would need to borrow to purchase the Remembrances store. Because the PMT function will be copied to the remaining cells in column D, you use a cell reference instead of typing the actual dollar amount. Below the Type argument box, -1139.125383—the amount of the monthly payment—displays.

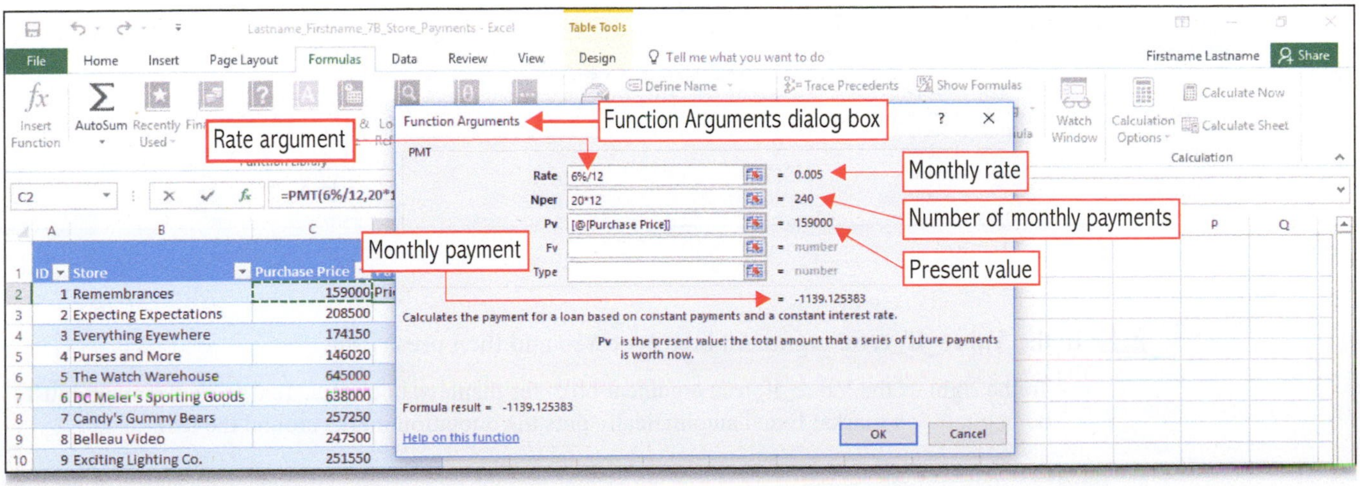

FIGURE 7.33

10 ▸ Delete all of the text in the **Pv** argument box. Type a minus sign (–), and then click cell **C2**.

Notice *-159000* displays to the right of the Pv argument box. In order to display the monthly payment amount as a positive number, in the Pv argument box, it is necessary to type the minus sign before clicking cell C2.

11 ▸ In the **Function Arguments** dialog box, click **OK**.

The monthly payment for each row displays in column D. Recall that in an Excel table, a calculated column uses a single formula that adjusts for each row of the column.

12 ▸ Save 🖫 your workbook.

Activity 7.18 | Inserting the IF Function

The *IF function* uses a logical test to check whether a condition is met, and then returns one value if true and another value if false. Morgan Bannon-Navarre has decided that the company will purchase a store if the monthly payment is less than $2000.

1 ▸ Click cell **E1**. Type **Purchase** and then hold down [Alt] and press [Enter] Type **Store?** and then press [Enter].

The heading *Purchase Store?* displays on two lines in cell E1.

2 ▸ Verify cell **E2** is the active cell. Click the **Formulas tab**, and then in the **Function Library group**, click **Logical**. On the list click **IF**.

3 ▸ In the **Function Arguments** dialog box, in the **Logical_test** box, type **d2<2000** and then press [Tab]. Compare your screen with Figure 7.34.

The logical test is the condition that you are determining is TRUE or FALSE. In this instance, you want to determine if the monthly payment in cell D2 is less than 2000. TRUE automatically displays to the right of the Logical_test argument box because the value in cell D2 is less than 2000. Because the IF function will be copied to the remaining cells in column E, you are using a cell reference.

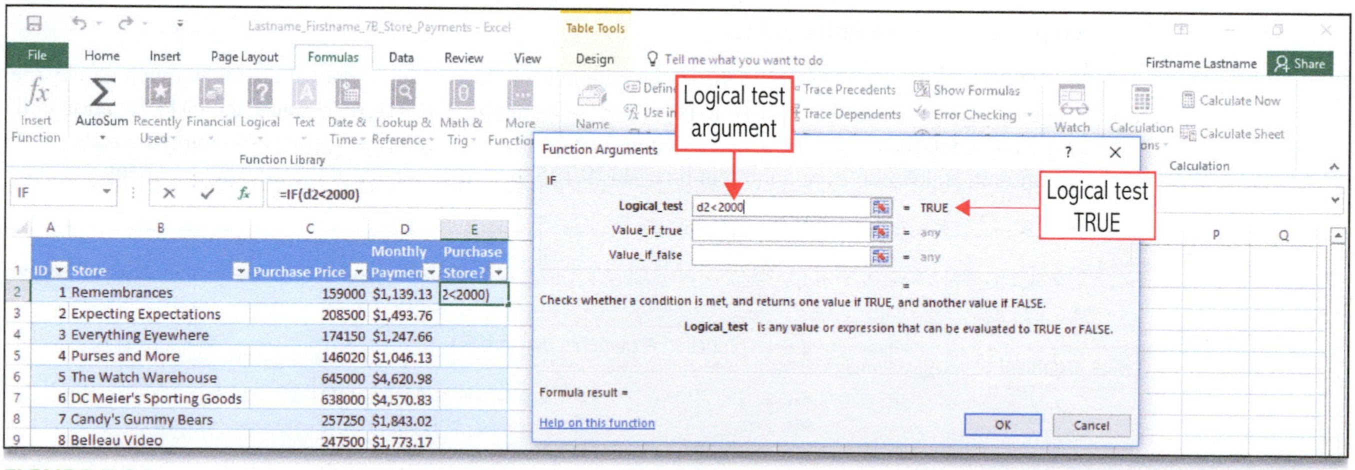

FIGURE 7.34

4 ▸ In the **Value_if_true** argument box, type **Yes** and then press [Tab].

To the right of the Value_if_true argument box, Yes displays in quotes. Text in an argument must be in quotation marks; Excel automatically puts the quotation marks around the text.

5 In the **Value_if_false** argument box, type **No** and then click **OK**.

The result of the IF statement for each row displays in column E.

6 At the top of the **Purchase Store?** column—column E—click the **AutoFilter arrow**. Select the **No** check box to clear it, and then click **OK**. Compare your screen with Figure 7.35.

Only the rows with Yes in column E display. The AutoFilter icon displays in cell E1 to indicate that the column is filtered.

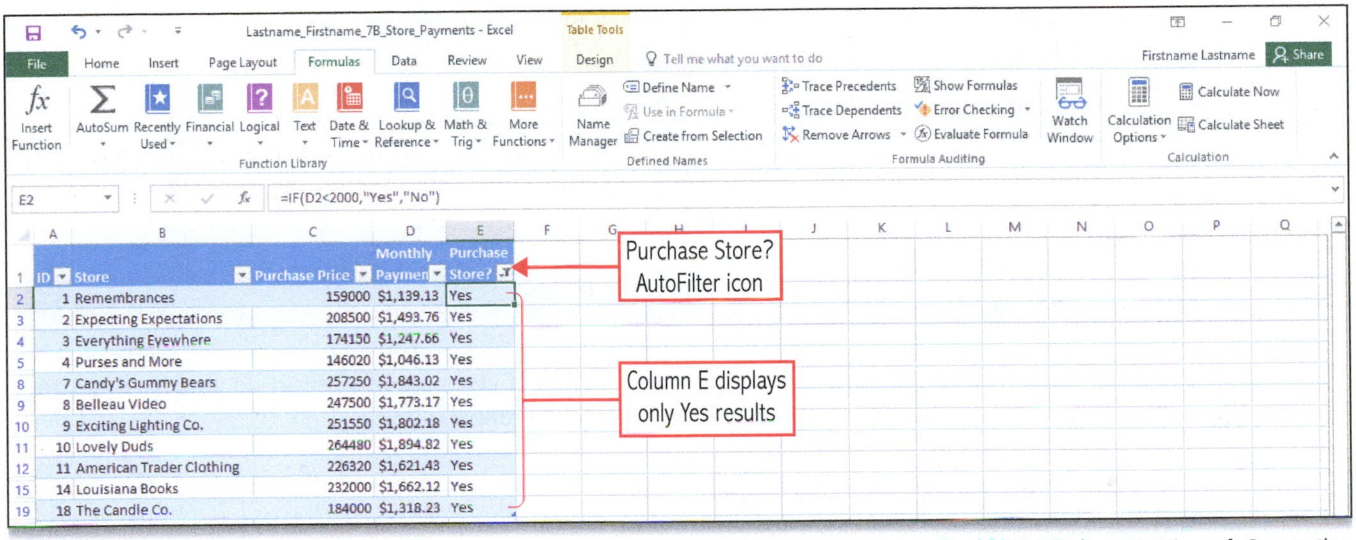

FIGURE 7.35

Excel 2016, Windows 10, Microsoft Corporation

7 Select **column C**. On the **Home tab**, in the **Number group**, click the **Number Format button arrow** [General], and then click **Currency**. Select **columns A:E**. Point to the line between the headings A and B until the [+] pointer displays, and then double-click to AutoFit the columns.

8 Right-click the **Sheet1 sheet tab**, and then on the shortcut menu, click **Rename**. Type **Retail Stores** and then press [Enter].

9 Click the **Insert tab**, and then in the **Text group**, click **Header & Footer**. On the **Design tab**, in the **Navigation group**, click **Go to Footer**. In the **Footer** area, click the box just above the word *Footer*, and then in the **Header & Footer Elements group**, click **File Name**. Click any cell in the worksheet to exit the footer.

10 On the right side of the status bar, click the **Normal** button [⊞], and then press [Ctrl] + [Home] to make cell **A1** the active cell.

11 Click the **File tab** to display **Backstage** view. On the left, click **Info**, in the lower right corner, click **Show All Properties**. Under **Related People**, be sure your name displays as the **Author**—change it if necessary. Click to the right of **Subject**, and then type your course name and section number. Click to the right of **Tags**, and then type **PMT, IF functions**

12 On the left, click **Save** to save your workbook and redisplay the workbook window.

13 To print your workbook, display **Backstage** view, and then click the **Print tab**. Under **Settings**, verify **Print Active Sheets** is selected, and then click the **Print** button. Leave the workbook open.

Using Comparison Operators

You can compare two values using a variety of comparison operators.

COMPARISON OPERATOR	MEANING
=	Equal to
>	Greater than
<	Less than
>=	Greater than or equal to
<=	Less than or equal to
<>	Not equal to

Objective 6 | Create a Report in Word Using Data from Other Applications

In Word, you can include a cover page and a table of contents in a report document. Importing data from other applications enables you to complete a report quickly.

Activity 7.19 | Inserting a Cover Page

A *cover page* is the first page of a complex document that provides introductory information. Word contains a gallery of predesigned cover pages with content controls that enable the user to fill in information, such as the title, author, and date.

1 Start Word. From the student data files that accompany this chapter, open the **i07B_Retail_Report** document. Save the document your **Integrated Projects Chapter 7** folder as **Lastname_Firstname_7B_Retail_Report** If necessary, display formatting marks.

2 On the **Insert tab**, in the **Header & Footer group**, click the **Footer** button, and then click **Edit Footer**. Under **Header & Footer Tools**, on the **Design tab**, in the **Insert group**, click the **Document Info** button, and then click **File Name**. Press Tab two times. On the **Design tab**, in the **Header & Footer group**, click the **Page Number** button, click **Current Position**, and then under **Simple**, click **Plain Number**.

In the footer, the file name is left-aligned and the page number—1—is right-aligned. When you use the Page Number feature, Word automatically numbers all pages of the document.

3 Double-click in the document to close the footer. On the **Insert tab**, in the **Pages group**, click the **Cover Page** button. In the **Cover Page** gallery, scroll down, and then click **Sideline**. Compare your screen with Figure 7.36.

A cover page, which includes content controls, is inserted at the beginning of the document. Because it is a cover page, Word does not assign it a page number. Depending on your computer settings, content controls may automatically display a company name or user name.

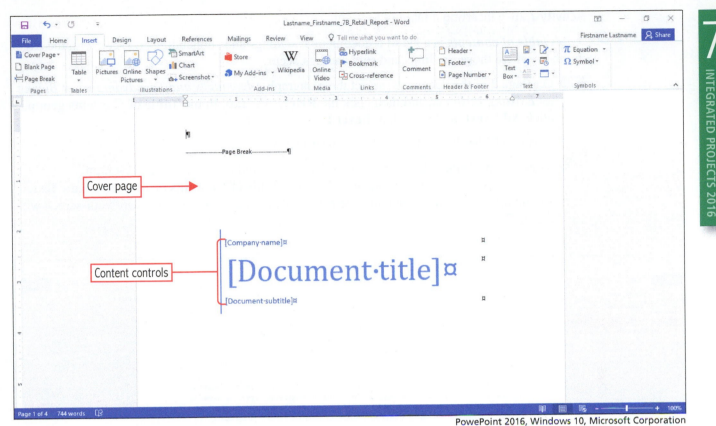

PowePoint 2016, Windows 10, Microsoft Corporation

FIGURE 7.36

4 Click the **Company name content control**, with the text selected, type **Select National Properties Group** and then press Tab to select the text in the Document Title content control.

5 With the text in the **Document title content control** selected, type **Retail Business Opportunities** and then press Tab to select the Document subtitle content control.

6 In the **Document subtitle content control**, with the text selected, click the tab **Subtitle**, and then press Delete to delete the content control. Type **A list of retail businesses available for purchase**

Text typed in the Subtitle content control will display in the Subject box of the Document Information panel. For purposes of this instruction, because you will be entering different information in the Subject box, it is necessary to delete the content control and simply type the text.

7 At the bottom of the page, in the text box, select the first line of text. In the **Author content control**, using your name type **Firstname Lastname** and then press Tab to select the Date content control.

The name you type will automatically display in the Document Information panel in the Author box.

8 Click the **Date content control arrow**, and then click **Today**.

9 **Save** 🖫 your document.

Activity 7.20 | Inserting a Table of Contents

A *table of contents* is a list of a document's headings and subheadings marked with the page numbers where those headings and subheadings occur.

1. On **Page 2** of the document, select the paragraph *Advantages and Disadvantages of Buying an Existing Business*, and then click the **References tab**. In the **Table of Contents group**, click **Add Text**, and then click **Level 1**.

   A Level 1 heading style is applied to the paragraph.

2. Select the paragraph *Advantages*. Hold down Ctrl, and then select the paragraph *Disadvantages*. On the **References tab**, in the **Table of Contents group**, click **Add Text**, and then click **Level 2**. Click to deselect the paragraphs, and then compare your screen with Figure 7.37.

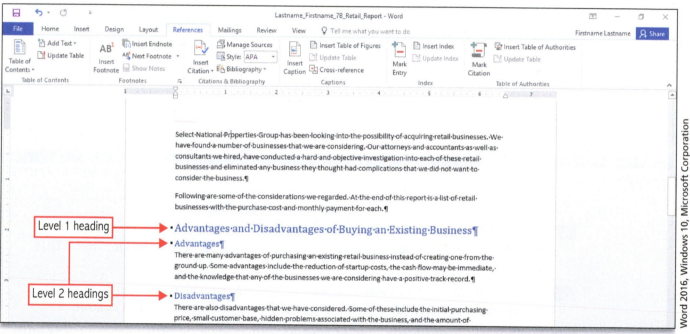

FIGURE 7.37

3. Scroll down, and then select the paragraph *Business Documents We Have Reviewed*. On the **References tab**, in the **Table of Contents group**, **Add Text**, and then click **Level 1**.

4. Select the paragraph *Contracts*. Hold down Ctrl, and then select the paragraphs *Financial Statements*, *Tax Returns*, *Appraisals*, and *Other Documents*. Apply **Level 2**.

5. Using the technique you just practiced, format the paragraphs *Government Requirements* and *Other Considerations* as **Level 1** text. Format the paragraphs *Licenses*, *Zoning Requirements*, *Environmental Concerns*, *Tax Concerns*, *Location*, *Local Economy*, and *Quality* as **Level 2** text.

6. At the top of **Page 2**, click to the left of the paragraph beginning *Select National Properties Group* to position the insertion point. Click the **Insert tab**, and then in the **Pages group**, click **Blank Page**.

   A new blank page is inserted as Page 2 of the document.

7 At the top of the blank **Page 2**, click to the left of the paragraph mark to position the insertion point, and then click the **References tab**. In the **Table of Contents group**, click **Table of Contents**, and then click **Automatic Table 2**. If necessary, scroll up to view the table of contents, and then compare your screen with Figure 7.38.

The table of contents is inserted with all Level 1 and Level 2 paragraph headings displaying on the left and the corresponding page numbers (based on the page number in the footer) displaying on the right.

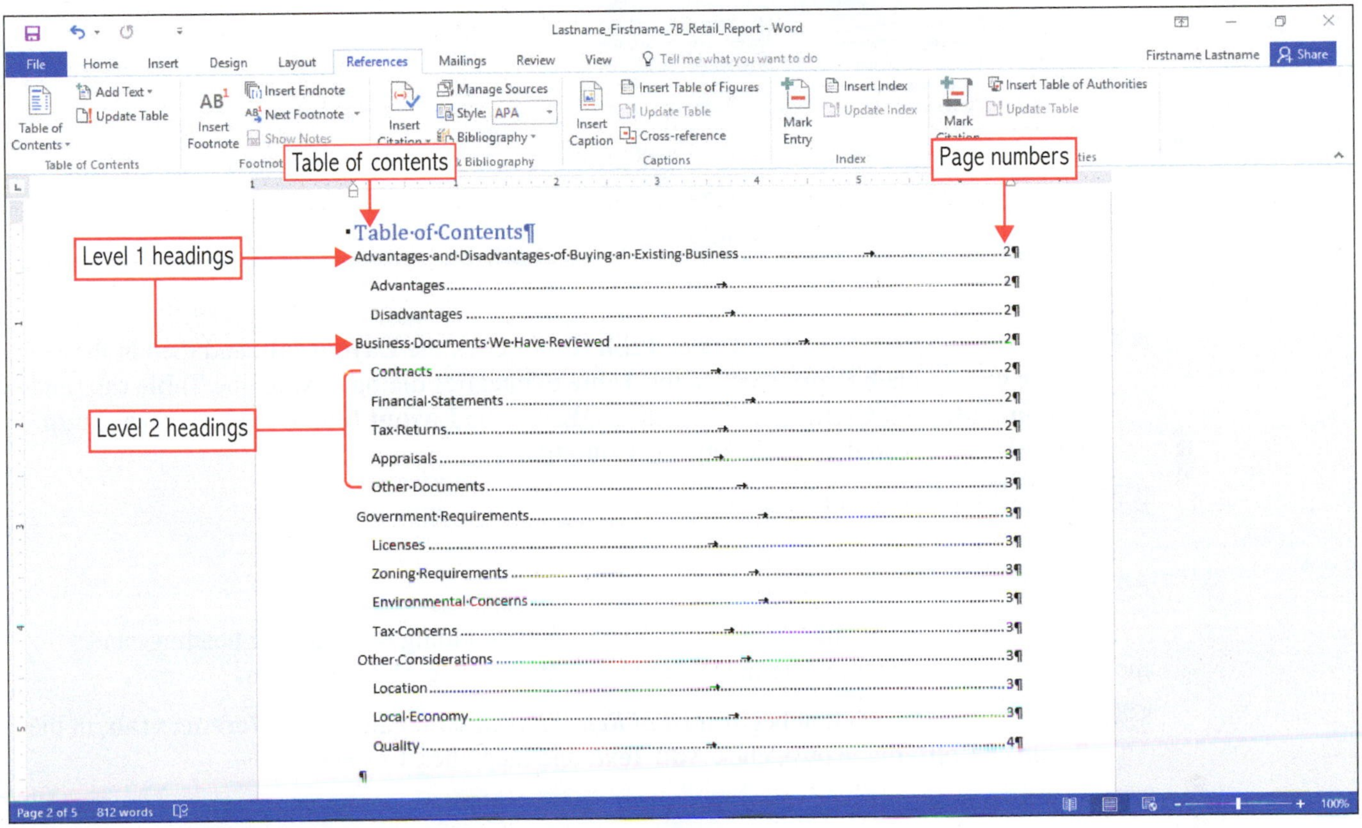

Word 2016, Windows 10, Microsoft Corporation

FIGURE 7.38

8 **Save** your document.

Activity 7.21 | Inserting Data from Other Applications

1 Press Ctrl + End to move to the end of the document.

2 Click the **Insert tab**, and then in the **Pages group**, click **Blank Page**.

A new blank page—Page 6—is added at the end of the document.

3 Type **List of Retail Businesses Available for Purchase** and then press Enter.

4 On the taskbar, click the **Excel** button to display your Excel file. Select the range **B1:D19**, right-click anywhere over the selection, and then click **Copy**.

5 On the taskbar, click the **Word** button to display your Word file.

6 Click the **Home tab**, and then in the **Clipboard group**, click the upper portion of the **Paste** button to insert the Excel data in the document. Compare your screen with Figure 7.39.

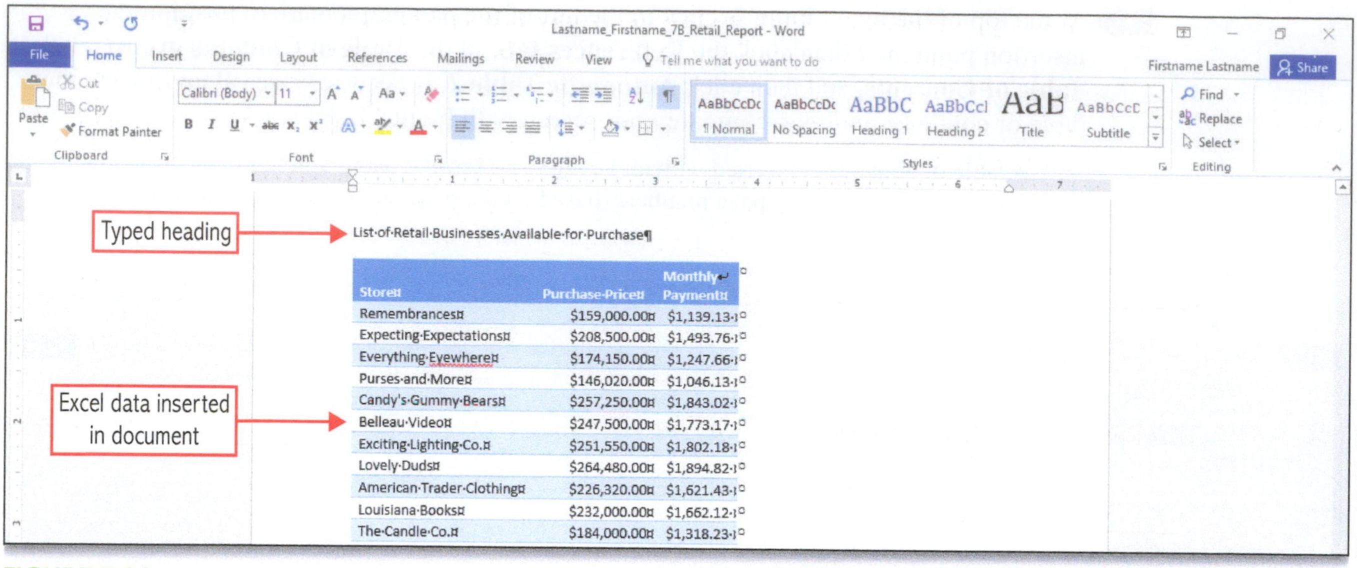

FIGURE 7.39

7 Click in any cell in the table. Under **Table Tools**, click the **Layout tab**, and then in the **Table group**, click **Properties**. In the **Table Properties** dialog box, on the **Table tab**, under **Alignment**, click **Center**, and then click **OK**. On the **Layout tab**, in the **Cell Size group**, click **AutoFit**, and then click **AutoFit Contents**.

8 **Save** the document.

Activity 7.22 | Updating the Table of Contents

Whenever you make changes in a document, such as adding or removing headings and modifying text, you must update the table of contents to reflect those changes.

1 Select the paragraph that begins *List of Retail Businesses*. Click the **References tab**, in the **Table of Contents group**, click **Add Text**, and then click **Level 1**.

2 On the **References tab**, in the **Table of Contents group**, click **Update Table**.

3 In the **Update Table of Contents** dialog box, click the **Update entire table** option button, and then click **OK**. Scroll up to view the table of contents, and then compare your screen with Figure 7.40.

The paragraph that begins List of Retail Business is added to the table of contents. The page number 5 represents the page number that displays in the footer on the last page of the document.

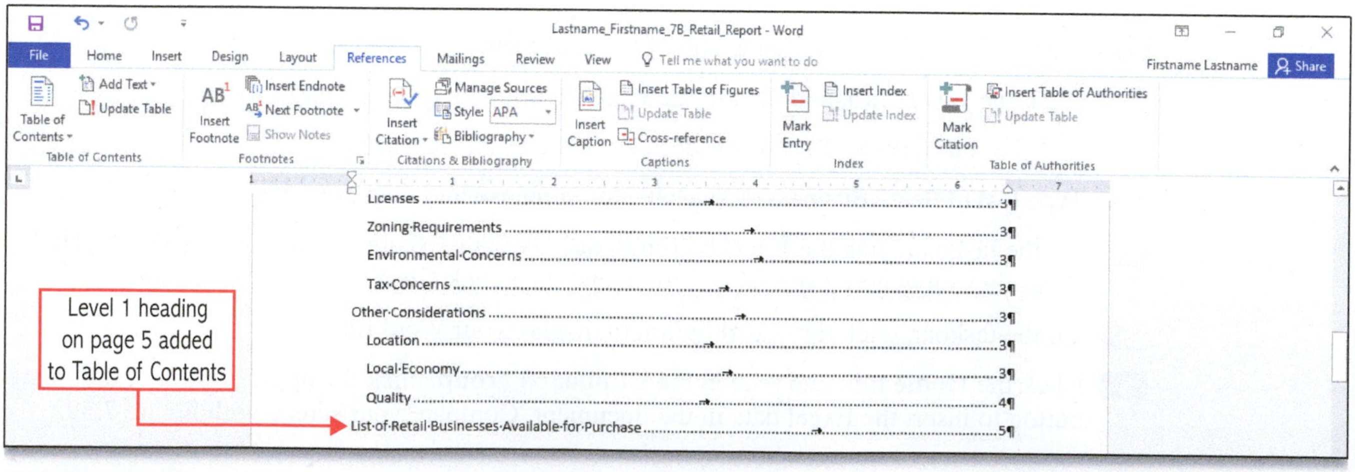

FIGURE 7.40

4 Press Ctrl + Home. Click the **File tab** to display **Backstage** view. On the left, click **Info**, in the lower right corner, click **Show All Properties**. Under **Related People**, be sure your name displays as the **Author**—change it if necessary. Click to the right of **Subject**, and then type your course name and section number. Click to the right of **Tags**, and then type **cover page, TOC**

5 On the left, click **Save** to save your document and redisplay the Word window. If you are instructed to submit your files electronically, go to Step 7.

6 To print your document, display **Backstage** view, click the **Print tab**, and then click **Print**.

7 **Close** ☒ Word, and then **Close** ☒ Excel. If a message box displays asking if you want to save changes, click **Yes**.

8 Submit your printed or electronic files as directed by your instructor.

END | You have completed Project 7B

END OF CHAPTER

SUMMARY

It is a common task to work with Access data in an Excel workbook in order to take advantage of the data analysis and charting features, the flexibility in data arrangement and layout, and the many features that are not available in Access. The main advantage of importing and exporting data between applications is that you can work with the best features of each of the applications—Word, Excel, Access, and PowerPoint—without retyping or recreating the data; this can save time and improve accuracy.

KEY TERMS

MATCHING

Match each term in the second column with its correct definition in the first column by writing the letter of the term on the blank line in front of the correct definition.

_____ 1. In an Access form, an object that displays data, performs actions, and lets the user view and work with information.

_____ 2. A form control that combines a drop-down list with a text box, providing a more compact way to present a list of choices.

_____ 3. A control on a form or report that contains descriptive information, typically a field name.

_____ 4. A bound control on a form or report that displays the data from the underlying table or query.

_____ 5. An object on a form or report that displays a limited set of alternatives where only one option can be selected at a time.

_____ 6. A graphical representation of the data in a PivotTable.

_____ 7. A location in the PivotTable Fields pane containing the available field names that you can add to the Area Section.

_____ 8. The location in the PivotTable Fields pane that contains four quadrants where field names are placed to determine how the report will display.

_____ 9. Fields that are assigned a column orientation in a PivotTable and become the column titles.

_____ 10. The cells in a PivotTable report that summarize quantitative data.

_____ 11. The area on a PivotTable that is used to restrict the data that displays.

_____ 12. The fields that are assigned to the columns that display in a column PivotChart report.

_____ 13. The fields that are assigned to the categories that display on the horizontal axis in a column PivotChart report.

_____ 14. The first page of a complex document that provides introductory information.

_____ 15. A list of a document's headings and subheadings, marked with the page numbers where those headings and subheadings occur.

A Area Section

B Axis (Categories)

C Column labels

D Combo box control

E Cover page

F Field Section

G Form control

H Label control

I Legend (Series)

J Option group

K PivotChart report

L Report Filter

M Table of contents

N Text box control

O Values area

MULTIPLE CHOICE

Circle the correct answer.

1. In a template, an area indicated by placeholder text that can be used to add text, pictures, dates, or lists is called a:
   A. content control
   B. form control
   C. report control

2. An interactive, cross-tabulated Excel report that summarizes and analyzes data is called a:
   A. Pivot report
   B. PivotChart report
   C. PivotTable report

3. An Excel feature that enables you to move fields to different areas in the PivotTable or PivotChart report is the:
   A. PivotTable dialog box
   B. PivotTable Fields pane
   C. Excel Field List

4. Fields that are assigned a row orientation in a PivotTable report and become the row titles are called:
   A. cell labels
   B. field labels
   C. row labels

5. A PivotTable feature that shows the detailed records of a PivotTable total is the:
   A. Drill-down indicator
   B. Field Expander
   C. Total Filter

6. Any value that an Excel function uses to perform operations or calculations is called the:
   A. argument
   B. operator
   C. variable

7. An Excel function that calculates the payment for a loan based on constant payments and a constant interest rate is the:
   A. NPV function
   B. PMT function
   C. RATE function

8. An Excel function that uses a logical test to check whether a condition is met, and then returns one value if true, and another value if false is the:
   A. FALSE function
   B. IF function
   C. TRUE function

9. In a predesigned cover page, text typed in the Subtitle content control will automatically display in the Document Information Panel in the:
   A. Author box
   B. Subject box
   C. Title box

10. When changes are made to a document, such as adding or removing headings and modifying text, you should reflect those changes by updating the:
    A. cover page
    B. document properties
    C. table of contents

Mastering Integration   Project 7C Texas Facilities

Apply 7A skills from these Objectives:

1 Create and Save a Template in Word

2 Insert a Combo Box and an Option Group in an Access Form

3 Create a PivotTable Report and a PivotChart Report in Excel

4 Import Data into a PowerPoint Presentation

In the following Mastering Integration project, you will create and modify an Access form. You will export the facility records to Excel, where you will create a PivotTable report and a PivotChart report. You will import the PivotChart into a PowerPoint presentation. Your completed files will look similar to Figure 7.41.

PROJECT FILES

For Project 7C, you will need the following files:

New blank Excel workbook
i07C_Texas_Facilities
i07C_Facilities_Presentation

You will save your files as:

Lastname_Firstname_7C_Texas_Facilities
Lastname_Firstname_7C_Facilities_PivotTable
Lastname_Firstname_7C_Facilities_Presentation

PROJECT RESULTS

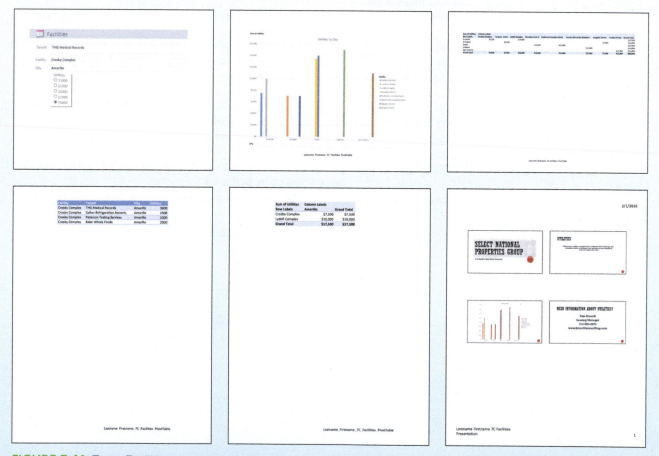

FIGURE 7.41 Texas Facilities

(Project 7C Texas Facilities continues on the next page)

1 ▶ Start Access. Navigate to your data files, and then open the database **i07C_Texas_Facilities**. In **Backstage** view, click the **Save Database As tab**, and then save the file in your **Integrated Projects Chapter 7** folder as **Lastname_Firstname_7C_Texas_Facilities** On the **Message Bar**, click **Enable Content**.

2 ▶ Create a form based on the **Facilities** table. In **Design View**, delete the **Facility**, **City**, and **Utilities** form controls. Under the **Tenant** form control, insert a **Combo Box**. In the **Combo Box Wizard** dialog box, click the **I will type in the values that I want** option button, and then click **Next**. Type the following list of facilities, and then store the value in the **Facility** field, and label the combo box **Facility:**

Crosby Complex
Lantana Center
Lydell Complex
Meridian Park IV
Parkwood Complex South
Rancho Bernardo Multiplex
Spyglass Center
Traders Pointe

3 ▶ Below the *Facility* combo box control, insert a **Combo Box**. In the **Combo Box Wizard** dialog box, click the **I will type in the values that I want** option button, and then click **Next**. Type the following list of cities, and then store the value in the **City** field and label the combo box **City:**

Amarillo
Arlington
Dallas
Lubbock
San Antonio

4 ▶ Below the *City* combo box control, insert an **Option Group**. Type the following Label Names.

$1000
$1500
$2000
$2500
$3000

5 ▶ Do not set a default choice. Type the following list of values next to each Label Name.

Label	Values
$1000	**1000**
$1500	**1500**
$2000	**2000**
$2500	**2500**
$3000	**3000**

6 ▶ Store the value in the **Utilities** field, use **option buttons**, apply the **Raised** style, and then in the option group caption, type **Utilities:** If necessary move the form controls on the form to line up with the other form controls. Resize the form controls so all data can be read. **Save** the form as **Lastname Firstname 7C Facilities Form** Add the following records.

Tenant	Facility	City	Utilities
THG Medical Records	**Crosby Complex**	**Amarillo**	**$3000**
Broaddus Technologies	**Lydell Complex**	**Amarillo**	**$2500**

7 ▶ Display **Backstage** view, click View and edit database properties. In the **Subject** box, type your course name and section number, in the **Author** box, type your firstname and lastname, and then in the **Keywords** box, type **form controls** Close the **Properties** dialog box. If directed by your instructor, print the form for THG Medical Records **Close All** objects, and then **Close** Access.

8 ▶ **Start** Excel. **Import** the table in the Access file **Lastname_Firstname_7C_Texas_Facilities** as a **PivotTable Report**. **Save** the Excel file in the **Integrated Projects Chapter 7** folder as **Lastname_Firstname_7C_Facilities_PivotTable** Add the **Facility** field name to the **ROWS** box. Add the **City** field to the **COLUMNS** box. Add the **Utilities** field to the **VALUES** box. Format the **Values Field Settings** to **Currency** with **0 decimal places**. Rename **Sheet1** as **Utilities** Create a **Copy** of the **Utilities** sheet, and then rename the new sheet **Amarillo Utilities** Filter the **City** field to display only *Amarillo*. Double-click cell

(Project 7C Texas Facilities continues on the next page)

C3—the grand total for the Crosby Complex. Rename the new sheet **Crosby Complex** and then widen the columns so that all data displays.

9 On the **Utilities** sheet, create a **Clustered Column PivotChart** report based on the PivotTable. Move the chart to a new sheet named **Utilities Chart** Pivot the chart so the **City** field is in the **Axis Fields** box and the **Facility** field is in the **Legend Fields** box. Above the chart, insert a **Chart Title** with the text **Utilities by City**. Insert the file name in the footer of all worksheets. **Ungroup** the worksheets, and then return to **Normal** view. **Close** the PivotTable Fields pane and the PivotChart Fields pane. Show all properties. Next to **Author**, type your firstname and lastname, next to **Subject** box, type your course name and section number, and then next to **Keywords** box, type **Crosby, PivotChart Save** your changes.

10 **Start** PowerPoint, and then open the data file **i07C_Facilities_Presentation. Save** the file in the **Integrated Projects Chapter 7** folder as **Lastname_Firstname_7C_Facilities_Presentation** In the handouts, insert the footer **Lastname Firstname 7C Facilities**

Presentation and then **Apply to All**. Apply the design theme **Wood Type** to all slides. In the Excel file, on the **Utilities Chart** worksheet, **Copy** the **Utilities by City** PivotChart to a new blank **Slide 3** of the presentation. Insert a new **Slide 4** with the layout **Title and Content**. Add the title **Need Information About Utilities?** In the lower placeholder, type the following information.

Pam Stancill
Leasing Manager
312-555-0070
www.SelectNationalProp.com

11 In the lower placeholder, toggle off the bullet points, **Center** the paragraphs, and then change the **Font Size** to **36**. Display **Backstage** view, and click **Show All Properties**. In the **Author** box, type your first name and last name, in the **Subject** box, type your course name and section number, and then in the **Tags** box, type **PivotChart Save** the presentation. **Close** PowerPoint, and then **Close** Excel. Submit your printed or electronic files as directed by your instructor.

END | You have completed Project 7C

CONTENT-BASED ASSESSMENTS (MASTERY AND TRANSFER OF LEARNING)

Apply 7B skills from these Objectives:

5 Use Excel Functions

6 Create a Report in Word Using Data from Other Applications

Mastering Integration Project 7D Office Parks

In the following Mastering Integration project, you will import a list of office parks into Excel. You will use the SUM, PMT, and IF functions, and then import the data into a Word report. The report will be made available to customers of the Select National Properties Group. Your completed files will look similar to Figure 7.42.

PROJECT FILES

For Project 7D, you will need the following files:

New blank Excel workbook
i07D_Office_Parks
i07D_Parks_Report

You will save your files as:

Lastname_Firstname_7D_Parks_Data
Lastname_Firstname_7D_Parks_Report

PROJECT RESULTS

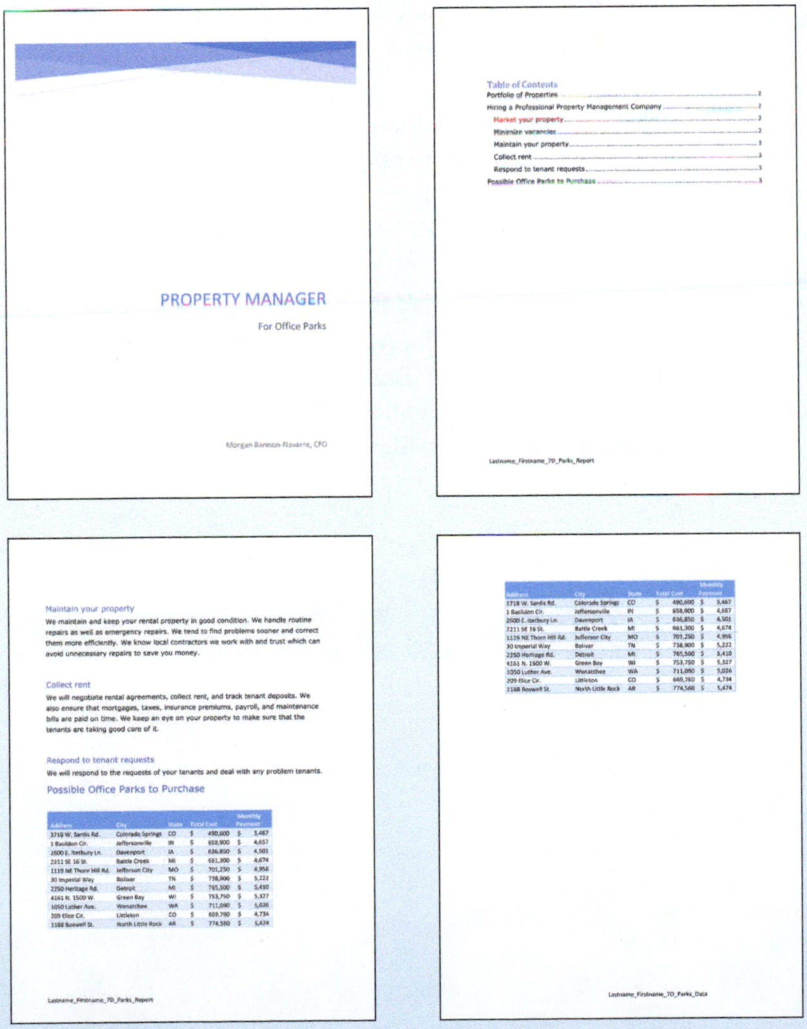

FIGURE 7.42 Office Parks

(Project 7D Office Parks continues on the next page)

1 Start Excel. Import the data from the Access file **i07D_Office_Parks** into an Excel table. **Save** the Excel file in the **Integrated Projects Chapter 7** folder as **Lastname_Firstname_7D_Parks_Data**

2 In cell **G1**, type **Total Cost** In cell **G2**, insert the **SUM** function to add cells **E2:F2**. In cell **H1**, type **Monthly Payment** so that it displays on two lines. In cell **H2**, insert the **PMT** function to calculate the monthly payment. The rate is 7%, the loan is for 25 years, and the present value is the Total Cost. (Your result should display as a positive number). In cell **I1** type **Purchase?** In cell **I2**, insert the **If** function. If the Monthly Payment is less than $5500, *Yes* should display, otherwise, *No* should display. Filter **column I** to only display the cells that contain *Yes*.

3 Format **columns E:H** using **Accounting Number Format** with **0** decimals. Adjust the width of the columns to display all data. Hide **columns D:F** and **column I**. **Rename** Sheet1 as **Office Parks** and then insert the file name in the footer as a field. Return to **Normal** view, and then **Save** the workbook.

4 **Start** Word, and then open the file **i07D_Parks_Report**. **Save** the file in the **Integrated Projects Chapter 7** folder as **Lastname_Firstname_7D_Parks_Report** Insert the file name in the footer. Insert the **Facet** cover page. Type the following information in the content controls.

Document title	**Property Manager**
Document subtitle	**For Office Parks**
Date	**Today**
Company	**Select National Properties Group**

5 Delete the **Abstract** content and the **Email** content control. Delete the **Author** content control, and then type **Morgan Bannon-Navarre, CFO** In the report, format the following paragraphs as **Level 1**: *Portfolio of Properties* and *Hiring a Professional Property Management Company*. Format the following paragraphs as **Level 2**: *Market your property*, *Minimize vacancies*, *Maintain your property*, *Collect rent*, and *Respond to tenant requests*. Insert a blank Page 2.

On the new blank **Page 2**, insert a **Table of Contents** with the **Automatic Table 2** style. Move to the end of the document, type **Possible Office Parks to Purchase** and then press Enter two times.

6 From the Excel file **Lastname_Firstname_7D_Office_Parks**, copy cells **A1:H19**. **Paste** the cells at the end of the Word report. Format the table to AutoFit Contents. Select the paragraph **Possible Office Parks to Purchase**, change the **Font** to **Verdana**, and then format the paragraph as **Level 1**. **Update** the table of contents. Press Ctrl + Home.

7 In your Word document, display **Backstage** view, and click **Show All Properties**. In the **Author** box, type your first name and last name, and then in the **Tags** box, type **cover page, TOC Save** your changes, and then **Close** Word.

8 In Excel, display **Backstage** view, and click **Show All Properties**. In the **Author** box, type your firstname and lastname, In the **Tags** box, type **PMT, IF functions Save** your changes, and then **Close** Excel. Submit your printed or electronic files as directed by your instructor.

END | You have completed Project 7D

Apply a combination of the 7A and 7B skills.

GO! Solve It **Project 7E Educational Facilities**

PROJECT FILES

For Project 7E, you will need the following files:

New blank Excel workbook
i07E_Facilities_Data
i07E_Educational_Report

You will save your files as:

Lastname_Firstname_7E_Educational_Facilities
Lastname_Firstname_7E_Educational_Report

The Select National Properties Group is considering selling some of its educational facilities. The facilities have been tracked in an Access database. Shaun Walker, the President of the company, has asked you to prepare a report. Import the Access data in the file **i07E_Facilities_Data** as a table into Excel. Using the PMT function, calculate the monthly payments the company could expect. The company would charge an 8% rate over 10 years. The result should be a positive number. Mr. Walker also asked you to calculate an extra processing fee for monthly loan payments using the IF function. If a monthly loan payment is less than $6000, the company would charge a processing fee of $150; otherwise, there would be no processing fee. Filter the rows to display only those facilities where there is a $0 processing fee. Hide all of the address fields and the processing fee column. Save the Excel file as **Lastname_Firstname_7E_Educational_Facilities**

Open the Word document **i07E_Educational_Report**, and then save the file as **Lastname_Firstname_7E_Educational_Report** Add a cover page of your choice, and then complete the content controls on the cover page. In the report, format headings as Level 1 or Level 2, and then insert a table of contents on a new page. In the worksheet, hide all of the address fields and the processing fee column, and then paste the Excel data into the Word document. Add an appropriate heading formatted as Level 1, and then update the table of contents. In each file, insert the file name as a field in the footer, and then add appropriate document properties. Submit your printed or electronic files as directed by your instructor.

(Project 7E Educational Facilities continues on the next page)

Project 7E Educational Facilities (continued)

Performance Level

Performance Criteria	Exemplary: You consistently applied the relevant skills.	Proficient: You sometimes, but not always, applied the relevant skills.	Developing: You rarely or never applied the relevant skills.
Import data into 7E Educational Facilities workbook, insert PMT and IF functions, and filter data	Worksheet table is crated, functions are inserted, and data is filtered accurately	Worksheet table is created, functions are inserted, and data is filtered, but there are two or fewer errors	One or more items was not complete
Insert cover page and table of contents in 7E Educational Report	Cover page and table of contents are both created, table of contents is updated with new content	Cover page and table of contents are both created, but there are two or fewer errors	One or more items was not complete
Copy and paste Excel data into 7E Educational Report	Excel data is pasted into the Word report, Level 1 title is added	Excel data is pasted into the Word report with two or fewer errors	Excel data is not pasted into Word report

END | You have completed Project 7E

RUBRIC

The following outcomes-based assessments are open-ended assessments. That is, there is no specific correct result; your result will depend on your approach to the information provided. Make Professional Quality your goal. Use the following scoring rubric to guide you in how to approach the problem and then to evaluate how well your approach solves the problem.

The *criteria*—Software Mastery, Content, Format and Layout, and Process—represent the knowledge and skills you have gained that you can apply to solving the problem. The *levels of performance*—Professional Quality, Approaching Professional Quality, or Needs Quality Improvements—help you and your instructor evaluate your result.

	Your completed project is of Professional Quality if you:	Your completed project is approaching Professional Quality if you:	Your completed project needs Quality Improvements if you:
1-Software Mastery	Choose and apply the most appropriate skills, tools, and features and identify efficient methods to solve the problem.	Choose and apply some appropriate skills, tools, and features, but not in the most efficient manner.	Choose inappropriate skills, tools, or features, or are inefficient in solving the problem.
2-Content	Construct a solution that is clear and well organized, contains content that is accurate, appropriate to the audience and purpose, and is complete. Provide a solution that contains no errors of spelling, grammar, or style.	Construct a solution in which some components are unclear, poorly organized, inconsistent, or incomplete. Misjudge the needs of the audience. Have some errors in spelling, grammar, or style, but the errors do not detract from comprehension.	Construct a solution that is unclear, incomplete, or poorly organized, contains some inaccurate or inappropriate content, and contains many errors of spelling, grammar, or style. Do not solve the problem.
3-Format and Layout	Format and arrange all elements to communicate information and ideas, clarify function, illustrate relationships, and indicate relative importance.	Apply appropriate format and layout features to some elements, but not others. Overuse features, causing minor distraction.	Apply format and layout that does not communicate information or ideas clearly. Do not use format and layout features to clarify function, illustrate relationships, or indicate relative importance. Use available features excessively, causing distraction.
4-Process	Use an organized approach that integrates planning, development, self-assessment, revision, and reflection.	Demonstrate an organized approach in some areas, but not others; or, use an insufficient process of organization throughout.	Do not use an organized approach to solve the problem.

GO! Think | Project 7F Office Tenants

PROJECT FILES

For Project 7F, you will need the following files:

New blank Word document
New blank Excel workbook
i07F_Office_Tenants
i07F_Tenants_Presentation

You will save your files as:

Lastname_Firstname_7F_Tenants_Template
Lastname_Firstname_7F_Tenant_Jones
Lastname_Firstname_7F_Tenants_Data
Lastname_Firstname_7F_Tenants_Presentation

Pam Stancill, the Leasing Manager, would like to send each new tenant a letter explaining the various expenses they will incur. Ms. Stancill has been tracking the tenant expenses in an Access database.

In Word, select a Letter template. Create a letter from Ms. Stancill. Include the company name and address: 321 North Michigan Avenue, Suite 700, Chicago, IL 60601. Complete the template by typing appropriate text explaining anticipated expenses. Include a list of expenses that the tenant will pay—such as taxes, insurance, telephone, water, electricity, gas, management fees, and maintenance fees. Include a sentence telling the tenant to contact her with any questions. Ms. Stancill's phone number is 312-555-0070. Save the template as **Lastname_Firstname_7F_Tenants_Template** Open a new document, based on the template, and then send the letter to Clay Jones, 4334 North Orange Blvd, Grant, Florida 32949. Save the letter as **Lastname_Firstname_7F_Tenant_Jones** In both documents, insert the file name in the footer, add appropriate document properties, and save your changes.

Import the data from the Access database **i07F_Office_Tenants** into an Excel workbook as an PivotTable report. Save the workbook as **Lastname_Firstname_7F_Tenants_PivotTable** Add the **Office Tenant** field name to the **ROWS** box. Add the **Square Footage** field to the **COLUMNS** box. Add the **Taxes** field to the **VALUES** box. Format the **Values Field Settings** appropriately. Filter the data so only buildings with at least 2000 square feet display. Rename **Sheet1**. Create a **Clustered Column PivotChart** report based on the PivotTable. Move the chart to a new sheet. Format the chart, including a Chart Title. Insert the file name as a field in the footer. Add appropriate document properties. Open the PowerPoint presentation **i07F_Tenants_Presentation**. Add a new slide, and then insert the list of expenses from your Word document. Move and resize the list as need and add a slide title. Add a new slide, and then insert the tax chart. Apply a design theme, and then insert the file name as a footer on the Handouts. Add appropriate document properties, and save your changes. Submit your printed or electronic files as directed by your instructor.

END | You have completed Project 7F

OUTCOMES

In this capstone case you will:

Create a form and enter records in an Access database, export the data into an Excel workbook, copy Excel data into a Word document, and use Mail Merge to generate letters and envelopes.

Adamantine Jewelry

Adamantine Jewelry is based in Milan, Italy, one of the world's leading centers for fashion and design. The company's designers take inspiration from nature, cultural artifacts, and antiquities to produce affordable, fashionable jewelry that is sold through major retailers in the United States. With a 40-year history, the company is well respected among its retail customers and has expanded to online and television retailers in recent years. In addition to women's bracelets, rings, and earrings, the company also produces sport and fashion watches for men and women.

Apply a combination of the Chapters 1–7 skills.

GO! Solve It — Capstone Case 1 Jewelry Sale

PROJECT FILES

For Capstone Case 1, you will need the following files:

New blank Excel workbook
i01cc_Jewelry_Customers
i01cc_Sale_Invitation

You will save your files as:

Lastname_Firstname_1cc_Jewelry_Customers
Lastname_Firstname_1cc_Jewelry_Discount
Lastname_Firstname_1cc_Phoenix_Invitations
Lastname_Firstname_1cc_Phoenix_Envelopes

Jennifer Bernard, the Adamantine Jewelry U.S. sales director, has been planning a sale with the manager of the Phoenix retail store. If the sale goes well at the Phoenix store, she would like to use the same promotion at the other Adamantine Jewelry store locations.

Ms. Bernard maintains an Access database **i01cc_Jewelry_Customers** that lists customer information and has written a letter in the **i01cc_Sales_Invitation** document. Navigate to the location where you are saving your files, and create a new folder named **Integrated Projects Capstone Cases** Open the file **i01cc_Jewelry_Customers**, and save the database in your **Integrated Projects Capstone Cases** folder, using your own name, with the file name **Lastname_Firstname_1cc_Jewelry_Customers**

In the Jewelry Customers table, add a Short Text field named **Jewelry Preference** after the ZIP field. Create a form based on the Jewelry Customers table. Add a combo box to the form that lists the following types of jewelry: Bracelets, Earrings, Fashion Watches, Necklaces, Rings, and Sport Watches. Store the value in the Jewelry Preference field, and then label the combo box **Preference** Using the form, add a jewelry preference to all customer records, using each jewelry type at least one time. Add the following records, using your first name and last name for the last record. Save the form as **Lastname Firstname 1cc Jewelry Customers Form**

First Name	Last Name	Address	City	State	ZIP	Jewelry Preference
Allison	**Plasek**	**33 Herman Ave**	**Concord**	**MA**	**01742**	**Rings**
Firstname	**Lastname**	**4126 Mercer Ln**	**Phoenix**	**AZ**	**85009**	**Necklaces**

Create an Access report that contains all the fields from the Jewelry Customers table. Group the report by the **Jewelry Preferences** field, and then sort the data by the **City** field. Using your own name, title the report **Lastname Firstname 1cc Jewelry Preferences Report**

Open a new blank Excel workbook. Import the **Jewelry Types** Access table as an Excel table. In column C, add the title **Discount** and then insert an IF function by typing the following directly into the Formula Bar: **=IF([Cost]>15000,[Cost]*0.2,0)** to calculate a 20% discount on jewelry that costs greater than $15,000. Format columns B and C using the **Currency** format and **zero** decimal places. Filter the table to display only the jewelry that displays **a discount amount other than zero** in column C. Save the Excel workbook in your **Integrated Projects Capstone Cases** folder, using your own name, as **Lastname_Firstname_1cc_Jewelry_Discount**

(Capstone Case 1 Jewelry Sale continues on the next page)

GO! Solve It Capstone Case 1 Jewelry Sale (continued)

Open the **i01cc_Sales_Invitation** Word document, and save as **Lastname_Firstname_1cc_Sales_Invitation**. Insert the current date below the company phone number. Format the four lines that comprise the company name, address and phone number by centering the four lines and apply bold. Apply a theme to the document. Insert a text box that includes the statement **What a perfect time to shop for a Mother's Day gift!** Position the text box so your document has a professional appearance. In the Excel workbook, copy the filtered data and paste it at the end of the Word document. Center the table in the document.

To merge the letter with the Access Jewelry Customer list, begin the Mail Merge Wizard. In Step 3, in the Mail Merge Recipients dialog box, under Refine recipient list, click Filter, as the Field select City from the drop-down arrow, and make it equal to **Phoenix**. Sort by **Last Name**. In Step 4 of the Wizard, insert the **Address Block** two lines below the date. In the letter, click to place your insertion point at the end of the paragraph that begins *We see from your*, click More items, and in the Insert Merge Field dialog box, insert the merge field **Jewelry Preferences**, and then type a period. Preview the document and make any necessary changes. Complete the merge, and then save the new document to your **Integrated Projects Capstone Cases** folder, using your own name, as **Lastname_Firstname_1cc_Phoenix_Invitations** Use mail merge to create envelopes for the Phoenix customers. In the return address, type your name, and then use the Adamantine Jewelry address from the top of the letter. Save the merged envelopes as **Lastname_Firstname_1cc_Phoenix_Envelopes**

In all of your files, insert the file name as a field in the footer, and insert appropriate document properties. Submit all files as directed by your instructor.

Performance Level

Performance Element	Exemplary: You consistently applied the relevant skills.	Proficient: You sometimes, but not always, applied the relevant skills.	Developing: You rarely or never applied the relevant skills.
Add a combo box to a form	A combo box is added to the form and displays appropriately	A combo box is added to the form but does not display appropriately	A combo box is not added to the form
Create a report	The report is created, and all data displays appropriately	The report is created, but either the data is not grouped or it is not sorted	The report is not created
Insert the IF function and apply a filter	The IF function is inserted, and the data is filtered correctly	The IF function is inserted, but the data is not filtered correctly	The IF function is not inserted
Insert and position a text box	The text box is inserted and positioned appropriately	The text box is inserted but is not positioned appropriately	The text box is not inserted
Filter an Access data source	The data source is filtered using the correct field and value	The data source is filtered but does not use the correct field or does not use the correct value	The data source is not filtered
Insert text and merge fields in a letter and in an envelope	Text and merge fields are inserted appropriately	At least one item is not inserted appropriately	No items are inserted appropriately

END | You have completed Capstone Case 1

Integrating Word, Excel, and PowerPoint

OUTCOMES

In this capstone case you will:

Create an outline in Word, create an Excel chart, create a PowerPoint presentation that includes data imported from a Word document, and link an Excel chart to the presentation.

Skyline Bakery & Café

Skyline Bakery & Café is a chain of casual dining restaurants and bakeries based in Boston. Each restaurant has its own in-house bakery, which produces a wide variety of high-quality specialty breads, breakfast sweets, and desserts. Breads and sweets are sold by counter service along with coffee drinks, gourmet teas, fresh juices, and sodas. The full-service restaurant area features a menu of sandwiches, salads, soups, and light entrees. Fresh, high-quality ingredients and a professional and courteous staff are the hallmarks of every Skyline Bakery & Café.

Apply a combination of the Chapters 1–7 skills.

GO! Solve It **Capstone Case 2 Specialty Coffees**

PROJECT FILES

For Capstone Case 2, you will need the following files:

New blank PowerPoint presentation
i02cc_Coffee_Types
i02cc_Coffee_Sales

You will save your files as:

Lastname_Firstname_2cc_Coffee_Types
Lastname_Firstname_2cc_Coffee_Sales
Lastname_Firstname_2cc_Coffee_Presentation

Nancy Goldman, chief baker at Skyline Bakery & Café, has been researching the possibility of adding specialty coffees to the restaurant menu. She has listed different coffees in a Word document and projected annual sales in an Excel workbook. Ms. Goldman's contact information is 37 Newbury Street, Boston, MA 02116, 617-555-0037, www.skylinebakery.biz

If you have not done so already, navigate to the location where you are saving your files and create a new folder named **Integrated Projects Capstone Cases** Open the Word file **i02cc_Coffee_Types**. Save the document in your **Integrated Projects Capstone Cases** folder, using your own name, as **Lastname_Firstname_2cc_Coffee_Types** Insert the file name in the footer. In Outline view, promote to Level 1 the headings Coffees, Coffee Definitions, and the names of each of the different types of coffee. Demote to Level 2 each of the paragraphs located after each of the Level 1 headings. Move the headings and related subheadings—Espresso Con Panna, Espresso Granita, and Espresso Romano—so they display after Espresso. Add appropriate document properties.

Open the Excel file **i02cc_Coffee_Sales**. Save the workbook in your **Integrated Projects Capstone Cases** folder, using your own name, as **Lastname_Firstname_2cc_Coffee_Sales** Insert the SUM function in row 14 and in column F and apply appropriate number formats to all numbers. Add an appropriate row title and column title in cells A14 and F3. Merge and center the title and subtitle, and apply a cell style. Apply a cell style to the headings in the range A4:A14 and the range B3:F3. Insert a column chart that shows all coffee types and quarters. The chart should display on a new sheet named **Projected Sales Chart** Change the chart style and add an appropriate title. Rename the Sheet 1 tab as **Projected Coffee Sales** All worksheets should have a professional appearance. Insert the file name in the footer of all worksheets and add appropriate document properties.

In a new blank PowerPoint presentation, import the Word outline to create the slides. Save the presentation in your **Integrated Projects Capstone** Cases folder, using your own name, as **Lastname_Firstname_2cc_Coffee_Presentation** On Slide 1, add the title **Skyline Bakery & Café** and subtitle **New Specialty Coffees** On a new slide following the last slide of the presentation, link the chart from the Excel workbook. Following the chart slide, on a new slide, insert the contact information for Nancy Goldman. Insert a picture that displays a female chef. Insert at least two more appropriate pictures or clip art images on other slides in the presentation and adjust them to create a pleasing effect. Add a design theme and variant if appropriate, and apply a transition to all slides. Apply a WordArt style to all slide titles except on the first slide. Insert the date and the file name in the footer so that the footer displays on all notes and handouts. Add appropriate document properties.

(Capstone Case 2 Specialty Coffees continues on the next page)

GO! Solve It | **Capstone Case 2 Specialty Coffees** (continued)

Submit all files as directed by your instructor.

Performance Level

Performance Element

	Exemplary: You consistently applied the relevant skills.	Proficient: You sometimes, but not always, applied the relevant skills.	Developing: You rarely or never applied the relevant skills.
Apply outline levels	Paragraphs are assigned appropriate levels	At least one paragraph is not assigned an appropriate level	No levels are assigned to paragraphs
Insert the SUM function	The SUM function is inserted, and all values display correctly	The SUM function is inserted, but not all values display correctly	The SUM function is not inserted
Apply cell styles	All title and heading cells have cell styles applied	At least one title or heading cell does not have a cell style applied	No title or heading cells have cell styles applied
Create a column chart	The chart is created and displays appropriately	The chart is not a column chart or does not have a chart style applied	The chart is not created
Create a presentation from an outline	The information displays appropriately on all slides	Not all information displays, or at least one slide is not created	The presentation is not created
Insert and format objects	All objects are inserted and formatted appropriately	At least one object is not inserted, or it is not formatted appropriately	No objects are inserted in the presentation

END | You have completed Capstone Case 2

Integrating Access, PowerPoint, and Publisher

OUTCOMES

In this capstone case you will:

Set Access field properties, create a PowerPoint presentation using a template, create a publication using a template, and use Mail Merge to generate postcards.

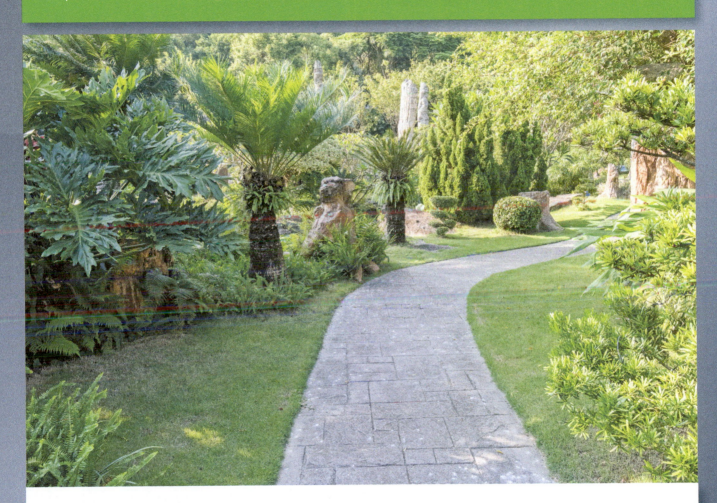

Southwest Gardens

The southwest style of gardening is popular in many areas of the country, not just in the yards and gardens of Arizona and New Mexico. The stylish simplicity and use of indigenous, hardy plants that are traditional in the southwest United States make for beautiful, environmentally friendly gardens in any part of the country. Produced by Media Southwest Productions, the television show *Southwest Gardens* is broadcast nationwide. The show and its website provide tips and tricks for beautiful gardens and highlight new tools and techniques. The show's hosts present tours of public and private gardens that showcase the Southwest style.

PROJECT FILES

For Capstone Case 3, you will need the following files:

New blank Publisher publication
New blank PowerPoint presentation
i03cc_Cooks_Data
i03cc_Tang_Logo

You will save your files as:

Lastname_Firstname_3cc_Cooks_Data
Lastname_Firstname_3cc_Cooks_Presentation
Lastname_Firstname_3cc_Cooks_Postcard
Lastname_Firstname_3cc_Merged_Postcard

David Tang, marketing manager for Southwest Gardens, wants to add a cooking segment to the television broadcast. He has created an Access database that lists cooks who are interested in demonstrating their recipes. He has asked you to create a PowerPoint presentation that he can use to help persuade the show's co-hosts, Vicky Aurelias and Phillip Miel, as well as the show's executives, that the cooking segment is a good idea. Because Mr. Tang is confident that the cooking segment will be approved, he has also asked you to create a postcard in Publisher that can be mailed to each of the cooks. David Tang's business information is 41122 N 23rd St., Phoenix, AZ 85022, 602-555-0030, www.southwestgardens.tv

If necessary, navigate to the location where you are saving your files and create a new folder **Integrated Projects Capstone Cases** Open the file **i03cc_Cooks_Data**. Save the file in your **Integrated Projects Capstone Cases** folder, using your own name as **Lastname_Firstname_3cc_Cooks_Data** Edit the table design by adding a default value to a field. Create a form based on the Cooks table, and then enter the following data—the City field is **Phoenix** and the State field is **AZ** for all five records. Use your own name in the last record.

First Name	Last Name	Address	Zip	Phone	Recipe
Miranda	Hevey	2409 Voltaire Ave	85016	480-555-0185	Spicy Roasted Red Pepper Dip
Anita	Delgado	8343 Tonto Ln	85208	480-555-5332	Spinach, Avocado, and Papaya Salad
Firstname	Lastname	2103 Sapium Way	85208	480-555-2081	Green Chile Stew

Save the form as **Lastname Firstname 3cc Cooks Form** Add appropriate database properties.

Start PowerPoint and save the presentation to your **Integrated Projects Capstone Cases** folder as **Lastname_Firstname_3cc_Cooks_Presentation** using your own name. Apply a design template and a variant. Create an appropriate title slide. On one slide create a SmartArt graphic that includes a list of fresh fruits that might be used in recipes. On another slide, create a SmartArt graphic that includes a list of fresh vegetables. Insert a slide mentioning that Toni Jones is president of Media Southwest Productions. On the same slide, insert a note reminding the speaker to thank Toni Jones for attending and to introduce the two summer interns, Karen Galvin and Henry Cavazos, who have

(Capstone Case 3 Cooking Show continues on the next page)

been working with the cooks. Add at least two additional slides with text that could help persuade the audience to support Mr. Tang's idea. Insert additional text and at least two images to create a professional appearance. Insert the file name in a footer to display on all notes and handout pages. Add appropriate document properties.

Open a Publisher postcard template for a mailing to be sent to cooks participating in the cooking segment. Save the publication in your **Integrated Projects Capstone Cases** folder, using your own name, as **Lastname_Firstname_3cc_Cooks_Postcard** Create a business information set for Mr. Tang. Add a tag line and the logo i03cc_Tang_Logo from your student files. In a text box, thank the cook for participating and mention that Mr. Tang is looking forward to tasting the recipe. Copy one of the SmartArt graphics listing fresh fruit and vegetables from your PowerPoint presentation, and then paste it in the publication. Apply a color scheme and a font scheme, and add a design accent. Modify the publication to create a professional appearance. Use mail merge and the Access database to insert the Recipe field in the paragraph you typed. Add the address block at the appropriate place in the publication. Filter the data to include only cooks with the ZIP field 85208. Save your changes, and then complete the merge. Save the new merged publication, using your own name, as **Lastname_Firstname_3cc_Merged_Postcard** Insert the file name in the footer, and add appropriate document properties.

Submit all files as directed by your instructor.

Performance Level

Performance Element	Exemplary: You consistently applied the relevant skills.	Proficient: You sometimes, but not always, applied the relevant skills.	Developing: You rarely or never applied the relevant skills.
Add default value	A default value and an input mask are added appropriately	Either a default value or an input mask is not added appropriately	Neither a default value nor an input mask is added appropriately
Create SmartArt graphics	Two SmartArt graphics are created and display appropriate information	One SmartArt graphic is not created or does not display appropriate information	No SmartArt graphics are created
Insert a note on a slide	The note is inserted on the appropriate slide and does not contain spelling or grammar errors	The note is not inserted on the appropriate slide, or the note contains spelling or grammar errors	The note is not inserted
Create and format a postcard	The postcard contains appropriate text and objects and is formatted to create a professional appearance	Some text is inappropriate, at least one object is missing, or the formatting does not create a professional appearance	The postcard is not created
Insert merge fields from a filtered data source	The merge fields are inserted, and the data source is filtered using the correct field	Not all merge fields are inserted, or the data source is not filtered using the correct field	No merge fields are inserted, and the data source is not filtered

END | You have completed Capstone Case 3

OUTCOMES

In this capstone case you will:

Import Excel data into an Access database, create an Access report, create PivotTable and PivotChart reports, use Mail Merge to generate letters and envelopes, and create a PowerPoint presentation that includes a linked PivotChart.

Midwest HVAC

Manufacturer

Midwest HVAC Manufacturer is one of the country's largest suppliers of heating, ventilation, and air conditioning (HVAC) equipment. The company delivers high-performance climate control parts and systems primarily to wholesale customers. Because of the growing popularity of do-it-yourself projects, they also have two local retail stores. Two times each year, Midwest HVAC Manufacturer updates its parts catalog, which includes supplies such as fans, motors, heating and cooling coils, filter units, and dehumidification and humidification units. It designs and manufactures all of its own products and has won several engineering and product awards.

Apply a combination of the Chapters 1–7 skills.

GO! Solve It | **Capstone Case 4 Advertising Letter**

PROJECT FILES

For Capstone Case 4, you will need the following files:

New blank Access database
i04cc_HVAC_Customers
i04cc_HVAC_Savings
i04cc_Advertising_Letter
i04cc_Maintenance_Presentation

You will save your files as:

Lastname_Firstname_4cc_HVAC_Customers
Lastname_Firstname_4cc_HVAC_Savings
Lastname_Firstname_4cc_Advertising_Letter
Lastname_Firstname_4cc_Merged_Letters
Lastname_Firstname_4cc_Merged_Envelopes
Lastname_Firstname_4cc_Maintenance_Presentation

Lecia Beecroft, Marketing Director at Midwest HVAC Manufacturer, is planning to send an advertising letter to current customers in an effort to increase the number of customers who participate in the company's preventive maintenance program. She would also like to make a presentation available to interested customers. Ms. Beecroft's contact information is Marketing Manager, 4437 Harney St., Omaha, NE 68179, 402-555-0707.

If necessary, navigate to the location where you are saving your files, and then create a new folder named **Integrated Projects Capstone Cases** Open a blank Access database, and save it in your **Integrated Projects Capstone Cases** folder as **Lastname_Firstname_4cc_HVAC_Customers** Import the data from the Excel workbook i04cc_HVAC_Customers. Be sure the ZIP field imports as Short Text. Create a form based on the 4cc HVAC Customers table, and then enter the following records. The State field for all records is **AZ** Enter your name in the last record.

First Name	Last Name	Address	City	Zip	Phone	Model
Nathaniel	**Plasek**	**1847 S 28th St**	**Chandler**	**85226**	**480-555-2778**	**OMH044B HE**
Sidney	**Paolino**	**3002 W 49th Way**	**Mesa**	**85208**	**480-555-3113**	**OMH048C LE**
Firstname	**Lastname**	**488 Carol Way**	**Phoenix**	**85009**	**480-555-8827**	**OMH070B LE**

Save the form as **Lastname Firstname HVAC Customer Form** Create a report that groups the data by the Model field and sorts the data by the Last Name field. Do not include the ID, address, city, state, and ZIP fields in the report. Make any necessary changes to the layout to create a professional appearance. Save the report as **Lastname Firstname HVAC Customer Report** Add appropriate database properties.

Open the **i04cc_HVAC_Savings** file. Save the file in your **Integrated Projects Capstone Cases** folder as **Lastname_Firstname_4cc_HVAC_Savings** Create a PivotTable report that displays the Power field as a COLUMN, the Height field as a ROW, and the Weight field as the VALUE. Rename the worksheet **Height** Create similar PivotTable reports for the Width and Length fields, and rename the worksheets appropriately. From the HVAC Units worksheet, create a PivotChart that reflects the savings from the maintenance program based on the Power and Heating BTU fields. Move the chart to

(Capstone Case 4 Advertising Letter continues on the next page)

GO! Solve It   Capstone Case 4 Advertising Letter (continued)

a new sheet, and make any design changes to give the chart a professional appearance. Adjust the layout of all worksheet pages to print on one page. For all worksheets, insert the file name in the footer, and then add appropriate document properties.

Open the **i04cc_Advertising_Letter** file. Save the document in your **Integrated Projects Capstone Cases** folder, using your own name, as **Lastname_Firstname_4cc_Advertising_Letter** Format the company address so it displays as a letterhead. Format the document using Word features—such as themes, page colors, and page borders—to create a letter with a professional appearance. Below the company address, insert the current date. Use mail merge and your Access database to insert the address block, and adjust paragraph spacing. Apply a filter for those customers who have purchased the OMH070B LE model. Complete the merge. Save the new document as **Lastname_Firstname_4cc_Merged_Letters** Insert the file name in the footer, and add appropriate document properties. Create envelopes for the OMH070B LE customers only. Use your name in the return address and the Midwest HVAC Manufacturer company address. Save the merged envelopes in the **Integrated Projects Capstone Cases** folder as **Lastname_Firstname_4cc_Merged_Envelopes** Insert appropriate document properties.

Open the **i04cc_Maintenance_Presentation** file. Save the file in your Integrated Projects Capstone Cases folder as **Lastname_Firstname_4cc_Maintenance_Presentation** Insert the file name to display in the footer on all notes and handout pages. In a new slide at the end of the presentation, link the Excel PivotChart report. In a new final slide, add the contact information for Lecia Beecroft. Adjust any slide elements to create a professional appearance. Add a design theme with variant if appropriate, and apply a transition to all slides. Add appropriate document properties.

Submit all files as directed by your instructor.

Performance Level

Performance Element	Exemplary: You consistently applied the relevant skills.	Proficient: You sometimes, but not always, applied the relevant skills.	Developing: You rarely or never applied the relevant skills.
Import Excel data to an Access database	All data is imported to an Access table and displays appropriately	Some data is not imported to the Access table, or the data does not display appropriately	No data is imported to the Access table
Create a report	The report is created, and all data is grouped and sorted appropriately	The report is created, but either the data is not grouped or it is not sorted	The report is not created
Create PivotTable and PivotChart reports	All PivotTable and PivotChart reports are created and display appropriately	At least one PivotTable or PivotChart report is not created or does not display appropriately	No PivotTable or PivotChart reports are created
Filter the data source for mail merge (Access table)	The table is filtered using the correct field and value	The table is filtered but does not use the correct field or does not use the correct value	The table is not filtered
Insert text and merge fields in a letter and in an envelope	Text and merge fields are inserted appropriately	At least one item is not inserted appropriately	No merge fields are inserted
Link a PivotChart report in a slide	A PivotChart report is linked in a slide and displays appropriately	A PivotChart report is linked in a slide but does not display appropriately	A PivotChart report is not linked in a slide

END | You have completed Capstone Case 4

Integrating Word, Excel, and PowerPoint

OUTCOMES

In this capstone case you will:

Create and filter an Excel table, create a SmartArt graphic, and create a PowerPoint presentation that includes pasted objects.

Board Anywhere Surf and Snowboard Shop

College classmates Dana Connolly and J. R. Kass grew up in the sun of Orange County, California, but they also spent time in the mountain snow. After graduating with business degrees, they combined their business expertise and their favorite sports to open Board Anywhere Surf and Snowboard Shop. The store carries top brands of men's and women's apparel, goggles and sunglasses, and boards and gear. The surfboard selection includes both classic and the latest high-tech boards. Snowboarding gear can be purchased in packages or customized for the most experienced boarders. Connolly and Kass are proud to count many of Southern California's extreme sports games participants among their customers.

GO! Solve It Capstone Case 5 Helicopter Jumps

PROJECT FILES

For Capstone Case 5, you will need the following files:

i05cc_Jumps_Presentation
i05cc_Jump_Dates
i05cc_Jump_Flyer

You will save your files as:

Lastname_Firstname_5cc_Jump_Dates
Lastname_Firstname_5cc_Jump_Flyer
Lastname_Firstname_5cc_Jumps_Presentation

Dana Connolly and J. R. Kass, the owners of Board Anywhere Surf and Snowboard Shop, are adding adventure traveling to their offerings—specifically helicopter jumps for snowboarders. They have started a flyer in Word that will be printed and available at the local ski resorts. An Excel workbook contains the dates and costs for the helicopter jumps. The owners also plan to run a PowerPoint presentation in their retail store.

If necessary, navigate to the location where you are saving your files, and create a new folder named **Integrated Projects Capstone Cases** Start Excel, and open the **i05cc_Jump_Dates** file. Save the workbook in your **Integrated Projects Capstone Cases** folder as **Lastname_Firstname_5cc_Jump_Dates** Copy the Instructors worksheet to a new worksheet. In the new worksheet, create an Excel table and apply a table style. Filter the table to display only data related to instructor Sarah Begren sorted by date. Rename the worksheet as **Begren** On the Instructors worksheet, insert a new row 1, and then type the company name spread across two lines. Merge and center the text so it displays above all the columns containing data. The headings in row 1 and row 2 should display on all pages when the worksheet is printed. Sort the list by date. For the date title, insert a comment that mentions that more dates may be added. Format the worksheet using cell styles. Adjust column widths and wrap text as necessary to create a professional appearance. Insert the file name in the footer on all worksheets, and then add appropriate document properties.

Start Word, and open the **i05cc_Jump_Flyer** file. Save the file in your **Integrated Projects Capstone Cases** folder as **Lastname_Firstname_5cc_Jump_Flyer** and then insert the file name in the footer. Insert a SmartArt graphic listing the five instructors. Paste the Excel table displaying the dates for Sarah Begren into the Word document. Format the document using Word features—such as text effects, font styles, themes, and page borders—to create a flyer with a professional appearance. Adjust any text, spacing, margins, or objects so the document displays on one page. Add appropriate document properties.

Open the PowerPoint presentation **i05cc_Jumps_Presentation**. Save the file in your **Integrated Projects Capstone Cases** folder as **Lastname_Firstname_5cc_Jumps_Presentation** Insert the file name in the footer on all pages of the notes and handouts. Add text to each slide to answer the question in the title. On the slide at the end of the presentation, insert the reservation information **949-555-0049** and **www.boardanywhere.biz** Insert a new slide at the end of the presentation, and then paste the SmartArt graphic from the Word document. Insert a picture on at least three slides. Add a design theme and apply

(Capstone Case 5 Helicopter Jumps continues on the next page)

GO! Solve It   Capstone Case 5 Helicopter Jumps (continued)

a transition to all slides. Make any adjustments so the presentation has a professional appearance. Add appropriate document properties.

Submit all files as directed by your instructor.

Performance Level

Performance Element	Exemplary: You consistently applied the relevant skills.	Proficient: You sometimes, but not always, applied the relevant skills.	Developing: You rarely or never applied the relevant skills.
Create and filter an Excel table	The table is created and filtered correctly	The table is created but is not filtered correctly	The table is not created
Insert a comment	A comment is inserted in the correct cell	A comment is inserted but is not in the correct cell	A comment is not inserted
Create a SmartArt graphic	A SmartArt graphic is created, and all names display	A SmartArt graphic is created, but at least one name does not display	A SmartArt graphic is not created
Format a document	The document is formatted appropriately and displays on one page	The document is not formatted appropriately or does not display on one page	The document is not formatted appropriately
Add text and objects to a presentation	Appropriate text is added and is free from spelling and grammar errors	Some text is inappropriate or contains at least one spelling or grammar error	Text is not inserted
Format a presentation	A design theme and transition are applied to all slides	A design theme or a transition is not applied to all slides	A design theme and a transition are not applied

END | You have completed Capstone Case 5

Integrating Word, Excel, Access, and PowerPoint

OUTCOMES

In this capstone case you will:

Create a PivotTable, import Excel data into an Access database, group and sort data to create an Access report, and paste a PivotTable in a Word document and in a PowerPoint presentation.

Florida Port Community College

Florida Port Community College is located in St. Petersburg, Florida, a coastal port city located near the Florida High-Tech Corridor. With 60 percent of Florida's high-tech companies and a third of the state's manufacturing companies located in the St. Petersburg and Tampa Bay areas, the college partners with businesses to play a vital role in providing a skilled workforce. The curriculum covers many areas, including medical technology, computer science, electronics, aviation and aerospace, and simulation and modeling. The college also serves the community through cultural, athletics, and diversity programs and adult basic education.

CONTENT-BASED ASSESSMENTS (CRITICAL THINKING)

Apply a combination of the Chapters 1–7 skills.

GO! Solve It | Capstone Case 6 FPCC Graduation

PROJECT FILES

For Capstone Case 6, you will need the following files:

New blank Access database
i06cc_Graduation_Report
i06cc_Graduating_Students
i06cc_Graduation_Presentation

You will save your files as:

Lastname_Firstname_6cc_Graduation_Report
Lastname_Firstname_6cc_Graduating_Students
Lastname_Firstname_6cc_Students_Data
Lastname_Firstname_6cc_Graduation_Presentation

Leyla Barwari, vice president of Academic Affairs at Florida Port Community College, wants to provide information for graduating students. Students who have graduation questions can contact the Advisement and Counseling Office at 727-555-0030 or visit the website FloridaPortCC.edu Ms. Barwari would like to provide a report to students who are close to earning a degree and need information regarding graduation. She has created a list of graduating students in an Excel worksheet but thinks it would be easier to maintain the list in an Access database. She would also like a PowerPoint presentation that will run in the Student Union.

If necessary, navigate to the location where you are saving your files, and then create a new folder named **Integrated Projects Capstone Cases** Start Word, and open the file **i06cc_Graduation_Report**. Save the document in your **Integrated Projects Capstone Cases** folder, using your own name, as **Lastname_Firstname_6cc_Graduation_Report** and then insert the file name in the footer. Following the paragraph referring to the deans, insert a table, and enter the following data:

Dean	College Department
Henry Krasnow	Adult Education
Caitlin Freeman	Aviation & Aerospace
Richard Plasek	Business & Information Technology
Mary George	Humanities
Ella Hall	Mathematics

Resize the table to fit the contents, apply a table style and center the table on the page. Insert a cover page, and include a picture or graphic on the cover page. Format headings, and then create a table of contents on a blank page.

Start Excel, and open the file **i06cc_Graduating_Students**. Save the workbook in your **Integrated Projects Capstone Cases** folder as **Lastname_Firstname_6cc_Graduating_Students** Create a PivotTable report on a new worksheet that shows the total fees due from the students for each college department. Rename the worksheet with an appropriate name, and scale width of the worksheet to fit one page. Insert the file name in the footer on all worksheets. Add appropriate document properties.

Open a new blank Access database, and then save the database in your **Integrated Projects Capstone Cases** folder as **Lastname_Firstname_6cc_Student_Data** From Excel,

(Capstone Case 6 FPCC Graduation continues on the next page)

import the Graduating Students worksheet. Create an Access report listing the fields **First Name**, **Last Name**, **College Department**, and **Fees Due**. Group the report by **College Department**, and sort by **Last Name**. Title the report **Lastname Firstname 6cc Student Fees** Create a query that displays the fields **First Name**, **Last Name**, **Address**, **City**, **State**, and **ZIP** and displays only the Humanities students. Save the query as **Lastname Firstname 6cc Humanities Students Query** Create a report based on the query, sort the report by Last Name, and then save the report as **Lastname Firstname 6cc Humanities Students** Add appropriate database properties.

Start PowerPoint, and open the file **i06cc_Graduation_Presentation**. Save the presentation to your **Integrated Projects Capstone Cases** folder **as Lastname_Firstname_6cc_Graduation_Presentation** Insert the file name in the footer to display on all notes and handout pages. Insert appropriate pictures on at least three slides. Format the graphics by adding effects—for example, reflections or glows. Insert a new blank slide and paste the PivotTable report from Excel, and then modify the column headings. Paste the Word table listing the college deans in a new slide. At the end of the presentation, insert a slide listing the contact information for students who have graduation questions. Apply a design theme to all slides, and then add appropriate document properties.

In your Word document, in the body text, above the Graduate with Honors heading, type the heading **Fees Due by College Department** Under the heading, paste the PivotTable report from Excel, and then modify the column headings. Format the document to create a professional appearance using features such as themes, page colors, page borders, or page layouts. Update the table of contents.

Submit all files as directed by your instructor.

Performance Level

Performance Element	Exemplary: You consistently applied the relevant skills.	Proficient: You sometimes, but not always, applied the relevant skills.	Developing: You rarely or never applied the relevant skills.
Insert a cover page and table of contents	The cover page and table of contents are inserted appropriately	Either the cover page or the table of contents is not inserted appropriately	Neither the cover page nor the table of contents is inserted
Create a PivotTable report	The PivotTable report is created and displays the correct data	The PivotTable report is created, but not all data displays correctly	The PivotTable report is not created
Create an Access report from a table	The report is created, and all data is grouped and sorted correctly	The report is created, but either the data is not grouped or the data is not sorted	The report is not created
Create a report from a query	The report is created and displays only the filtered data	The report is created, but the data is not filtered appropriately	The report is not created
Insert objects in a presentation	All objects are inserted and display appropriately	At least one item is not inserted or does not display appropriately	No items are inserted
Insert a Word table and a PivotTable report	The Word table and a PivotTable report are inserted correctly	The Word table or the PivotTable report is not inserted correctly	The Word table and the PivotTable report are not inserted

END | You have completed Capstone Case 6

Integrating Word, Excel, Access, and PowerPoint

OUTCOMES

In this capstone case you will:

Insert a function in Excel, create and filter an Excel table, create queries and reports in Access, export an Access table to a Word document, and link Excel data to a Word document and a PowerPoint presentation.

Select National Properties Group

Select National Properties Group is a diversified real estate company that develops, builds, manages, and acquires a wide variety of properties nationwide. Among the company's portfolio of properties are shopping malls, mixed-use town center developments, high-rise office buildings, office parks, industrial buildings and warehouses, multi-family housing developments, educational facilities, and hospitals. Residential developments are mainly located in and around the company's hometown, Chicago; commercial and public buildings in the portfolio are located nationwide. The company is well respected for its focus on quality and commitment to the environment and economic development of the areas where it operates.

Apply a combination of the Chapters 1–7 skills.

GO! Solve It | **Capstone Case 7 Sale Properties**

PROJECT FILES

For Capstone Case 7, you will need the following files:

New blank Access database
New blank PowerPoint presentation
i07cc_Killgorn_Letter
i07cc_Sale_Properties

You will save your files as:

Lastname_Firstname_7cc_Sale_Properties
Lastname_Firstname_7cc_SNPG_Properties
Lastname_Firstname_7cc_Killgorn_Letter
Lastname_Firstname_7cc_Sales_Presentation

Tate Plasek, Sales Manager, has an Excel workbook listing properties for sale. If a property is sold, Select National Properties Group will finance the property loan for 30 years at 7.5% interest. If the monthly payment of a property is greater than $300,000, the company will give the buyer a 1% discount of the selling price. Lisa Killgorn is interested in purchasing the Harvest Properties Warehouse, one of the company's properties. She lives at 2231 University Drive, Tempe, AZ 85280.

If necessary, navigate to the location where you are saving your files, and create a new folder named **Integrated Projects Capstone Cases** Open the file **i07cc_Sale_Properties**, and then save the workbook in your **Integrated Projects Capstone Cases** folder, using your own name, as **LastnameFirstname_7cc_Sale_Properties** Copy the Properties worksheet to a new worksheet, and then rename the worksheet as **Payments** In the Payments worksheet, convert the data to a table. In column G, insert a calculated column using the PMT function to calculate the monthly payment for each of the properties. In column H, insert a calculated column using the IF function to determine the amount of the discount if property qualifies for it. Determine the totals for columns F:H. Apply conditional formatting to cells with a selling price between $40,000,000 and $70,000,000. Copy the Payments worksheet to a new worksheet, and then rename the new worksheet as **Harvest Properties** Filter the table to display only the data for the Harvest Properties Warehouse. Insert the file name in the footer so that it displays on all worksheets. Add appropriate document properties.

Create a blank Access database, and then save it in your **Integrated Projects Capstone Cases** folder as **Lastname_Firstname_7cc_SNPG_Properties** Import the data from the Properties worksheet. Create a query that displays all fields, except the ID field, for properties located in Florida and Georgia. Save the query as **Lastname Firstname 7cc FL GA Query** Export the query result as an RTF file to your **Integrated Projects Capstone Cases** folder. Create another query that displays all fields, except the ID field, for all properties with selling prices less than $1,000,000. Save the query as **Lastname Firstname 7cc Price Query** For each query, create and format a report. Save each report with the name as the query, substituting the word **Report** for Query. Add appropriate database properties.

Create a PowerPoint presentation using a template of your choice; the presentation will be shown to prospective buyers attending a sales conference. Save the presentation

(Capstone Case 7 Sale Properties continues on the next page)

GO! Solve It Capstone Case 7 Sale Properties (continued)

to your **Integrated Projects Capstone Cases** folder as **Lastname_Firstname_7cc_Sales_Presentation** Insert the file name in the footer to display on all pages of the notes and handouts. Modify the slides to help persuade buyers to purchase property from Select National Properties Group. On one slide, inform the audience that the company sells many properties. On the same slide, link the cell from the Excel Payments worksheet that displays the total selling price. On a new slide, insert a SmartArt graphic that lists some of the different types of properties that the company develops and manages. At the end of the presentation, insert a slide that contains the contact information for Mr. Plasek. Insert additional text, pictures, and clip art to enhance the presentation. Format any text or other objects to create a professional appearance. Add appropriate document properties.

Open the file **i07cc_Killgore_Letter**, and then save the document in your **Integrated Projects Capstone Cases** folder as **Lastname_Firstname_7cc_Killgorn_Letter** Insert the file name in the footer. Format the letterhead for Mr. Tate Plasek. Insert the current date, and then insert Lisa Killgorn's name and address and a proper salutation. Following the first paragraph, copy the SmartArt graphic from your presentation to the letter, changing text wrapping and resizing as necessary. Following the second paragraph, from Excel, on the Harvest Properties worksheet, link cells F1:G38 (first and second row) to the Word document. Under the third paragraph, insert the RTF file listing the Florida and Georgia properties. Format the document to create a professional appearance. Add appropriate document properties.

Submit all files as directed by your instructor.

Performance Level

Performance Element	Exemplary: You consistently applied the relevant skills.	Proficient: You sometimes, but not always, applied the relevant skills.	Developing: You rarely or never applied the relevant skills.
Insert PMT and IF functions	The PMT and IF functions are inserted, and the correct values display	The PMT function or IF function is not inserted, or all values do not display correctly	The PMT function and the IF function are not inserted
Create two reports from queries	The reports are created and display the correct data	One report is not created, or some data in either report does not display correctly	Neither report is created
Insert text and objects in a letter	All text and objects are inserted appropriately	At least one item is not inserted appropriately	No items are inserted appropriately
Create a SmartArt graphic	The SmartArt graphic is created and displays the correct information	The SmartArt graphic is created, but not all information is correct	The SmartArt graphic is not created
Insert text and objects in a presentation	All text and objects are inserted appropriately	All text and objects are inserted appropriately	No items are inserted appropriately

END | You have completed Capstone Case 7

Glossary

Absolute cell reference A cell reference that refers to cells by their fixed position in a worksheet; an absolute cell reference remains the same when a formula is copied to other cells.

Accounting Number Format The Excel number format that applies a thousand comma separator where appropriate, inserts a fixed US dollar sign aligned at the left edge of the cell, applies two decimal places, and leaves a small amount of space at the right edge of the cell to accommodate a parenthesis for negative numbers.

Action query A query that changes the data in the data source or creates a new table.

Animation A visual or sound effect that is added to an object or text on a slide.

Append query A query that adds a set of records from one or more source tables to one or more destination tables.

Area Section The location in the PivotTable Field List task pane that contains four quadrants where field names are placed to determine how the report will display.

Argument Any value that an Excel function uses to perform operations or calculations.

Ascending order Text is arranged in alphabetical order (A to Z) or numbers from the lowest to the highest value.

Auto Fill An Excel feature that extends values into adjacent cells based on the values of selected cells.

AutoExpansion An Excel table feature in which a new column is automatically included as part of the existing table.

AutoFilter An Excel feature where only a portion of the data (a subset) that meets the criteria you specify is displayed; the data that does not meet the criteria is hidden—not deleted.

AutoFit A Word feature that adjusts the width of the columns in a table to fit the cell content of the widest cell in each column.

AutoNumber An Access data type that describes a unique sequential or random number assigned by Access as each record is entered and that is useful for data that has no distinct field that can be considered unique.

AutoSum Another name for the SUM function.

Axis Fields (Categories) The fields that are assigned to the categories that display on the horizontal axis in a column PivotChart report.

Black slide A slide that displays at the end of a PowerPoint presentation indicating that the slide show is over.

Blank Report tool An Access tool with which you can create a report from scratch by adding the fields you designate in the order you want them to display.

Bound A term that describes objects and controls that are based on data stored in one or more tables or queries in the database.

Building blocks Reusable pieces of content—for example, borders, text boxes, logos, and calendars—that are stored in galleries.

Business information set A customized group of information—including items such as a company name, address, phone number, email address, and logo—that can be used to quickly fill in appropriate places in a publication.

Calculated column An Excel feature that uses a single formula that adjusts for each row of a column in a data table.

Calculated field A field that stores the value of a mathematical expression.

Category axis The area along the bottom of a chart that identifies the categories of data; also referred to as the x-axis.

Cell A small box formed by the intersection of a column and a row.

Cell address Another name for *cell reference*.

Cell reference The identification of a specific cell by its intersecting column letter and row number.

Character spacing An Office feature that allows you to increase or decrease the space between characters.

Chart layout The combination of chart elements that can be displayed in a chart such as a title, legend, labels for the columns, and the table of charted cells.

Chart Layouts gallery A group of predesigned chart layouts that you can apply to an Excel chart.

Chart sheet A workbook sheet that contains only a chart and is useful when you want to view a chart separately from the worksheet data.

Chart style The overall visual look of a chart in terms of its graphic effects, colors, and backgrounds; for example, you can have flat or beveled columns, colors that are solid or transparent, and backgrounds that are dark or light.

Chart Styles gallery A group of predefined chart styles that you can apply to an Excel chart.

Clip A single media file such as art, sound, animation, or a movie.

Color scheme A predefined set of harmonized colors that can be applied to text and objects.

Column chart A chart in which the data is arranged in columns. It is useful for showing data changes over a period of time or for illustrating comparisons among items.

Column Labels Fields that are assigned a column orientation in a PivotTable report and become the column headings.

Combo box control A form control that combines a drop-down list with a text box, providing a more compact way to present a list of choices.

Comma Style The Excel number format that inserts thousand comma separators where appropriate, applies two decimal places, and leaves a small amount of space at the right edge of the cell to accommodate a parenthesis for negative numbers.

Comment A note that can be added from the Review tab and is generally not printed.

Comparison operators Symbols that evaluate each field value to determine if it is the same (=), greater than (>), less than (<), or in between a range of values as specified by the criteria.

Conditional format A format that changes the appearance of a cell—for example, by adding cell shading or changing font color—based on a condition; if the condition is true, the cell is formatted based on that condition, if the condition is false, the cell is *not* formatted.

Content control In a template, an area indicated by placeholder text that can be used to add text, pictures, dates, or lists.

Contextual tabs Tabs that are added to the ribbon when a specific object, such as a table, is selected and that contain commands relevant to the selected object.

Cover page The first page of a complex document that provides introductory information.

Criteria The conditions in a query that identify the specific records for which you are looking.

Data marker A column, bar, area, dot, pie slice, or other symbol in a chart that represents a single data point.

Data point The value that originates in a worksheet cell and that is represented in a chart by a data marker.

Data series The related data points represented by data markers.

Data source A list of variable information, such as names and addresses, that is merged with a main document to create customized form letters, envelopes, or labels.

Data type The characteristic that defines the kind of data that can be entered into a field, such as numbers, text, or dates.

Database An organized collection of facts about people, events, things, or ideas related to a particular topic or purpose.

Datasheet view The Access view that displays data organized in columns and rows similar to an Excel worksheet.

Date picker A calendar control that is used to select a date.

Decimal tab stop A tab stop in which the text aligns with the decimal point at the tab stop location.

Default value The value that is automatically entered in a new record.

Default value (property) In Access, the data that is automatically entered in a field.

Descending order Text is arranged in reverse alphabetical order (Z to A) or numbers from the highest to the lowest value.

Design Checker A Publisher feature that automatically reviews a publication for a range of design and layout flaws and provides options to fix any identified problems.

Design grid The lower pane of the Advanced Filter window that displays the design of the filter.

Design view An Access view that displays the detailed structure of a table, query, form, or report and the view in which some tasks must be performed.

Destination file The file where the linked data or object is inserted.

Document Inspector A Microsoft Office feature that enables you to find and remove hidden data and personal information in a file.

Drill-down indicator A PivotTable feature that shows the detailed records of a PivotTable total.

Embedded chart A chart that displays as an object within a worksheet.

Excel table A series of rows and columns that contains related data that is managed independently from the data in other rows and columns of the worksheet.

Explode The action of pulling out one or more pie slices from a pie chart for emphasis.

Field A placeholder that displays preset content, such as the current date, the file name, a page number, or other stored information.

Field (Access) A single piece of information that is stored in every record and formatted as a column in a database table.

Field list A list of the field names in a table.

Field property Characteristics of a field that control how the field displays and how data can be entered in the field.

Field Section A location in the PivotTable Field List task pane containing the available field names that you can add to the Area Section.

Field size The maximum number of characters you can enter in a field.

Fill handle A small black square located in the lower right corner of a selected cell.

Filtering The process of displaying only a portion of the data based on matching a specific value to show only the data that meets the criteria you specify.

Font scheme A predefined set of fonts that is associated with a publication, where a primary font and a secondary font are specified.

Foreign key The field that is included in the related table so the field can be joined with the primary key in another table for the purpose of creating a relationship.

Form A database object used to enter data, edit data, or display data from a table or query.

Form control In an Access form, an object that displays data, performs actions, and lets the user view and work with information.

Form view The Access view in which you can view the records, but you cannot change the layout or design of the form.

Formula A mathematical expression that contains functions, operators, constants, and properties, and returns a value to a cell.

Formula Bar An element in the Excel window that displays the value or formula contained in the active cell and permits you to enter or edit the values or formulas.

Freeze Panes A command that enables you to select one or more rows and columns and freeze (lock) them into place; the locked rows and columns become separate panes.

Function A predefined formula that performs calculations by using specific values in a particular order.

Gallery An Office feature that displays a list of potential results instead of just the command name.

Grouping An Access report feature that enables you to separate groups of records visually and to display introductory and summary data for each group in a report.

Hyperlinks Text, buttons, pictures, or other objects that, when clicked, access other sections of the current file, another file, or a webpage.

IF function An Excel function that uses a logical test to check whether a condition is met, and then returns one value if true and another value if false.

Input mask A set of literal characters and placeholder characters that control what can and cannot be entered in an Access field.

Join line In the Relationships window, the line joining two tables that visually indicates the related field and the type of relationship.

Label control A control on a form or report that contains descriptive information, typically a field name.

Layout guides Nonprinting lines that mark the margins, columns, rows, and baselines and are used to align the text, pictures, and other objects so that the publication has balance and uniformity.

Layout view The Access view in which you can make changes to a form or to a report while the object is running. The data from the underlying data source displays.

Legend A chart element that identifies patterns or colors that are assigned to the categories in the chart.

Legend Fields (Series) The fields that are assigned to the columns that display in a column PivotChart report.

Linking The process of inserting information from a source file into a destination file, while maintaining the connection between the two files.

List levels A list level is an outline level in a presentation represented by a bullet symbol and identified in a slide by the indentation and the size of the text.

Live Preview A technology that shows the result of applying an editing or formatting change as the pointer is moved over the results presented in the gallery.

Lookup Wizard An Access feature that creates a list box to look up a value in another table, a query, or a list of values.

Mail merge A Microsoft Word feature that joins a main document and a data source to create customized letters, envelopes, or labels.

Main document In a mail merge, the document that contains the text or formatting that remains constant.

Margin guides Nonprinting lines on the top, bottom, left, and right sides of the page that are used to define the page margins.

Mark as Final A Microsoft Office feature that changes the file to a read-only file—typing and editing commands are turned off.

Master page The page that contains the design and layout elements, including headers and footers, that you want to repeat on multiple pages of your publication.

Merge & Center A command that joins selected cells into one large cell and then centers the contents in the new cell.

Message Bar The area directly below the ribbon that displays information such as security alerts when there is potentially unsafe, active content in an Office document that you open.

Mini toolbar A small toolbar containing frequently used formatting commands that displays as a result of selecting text or objects.

Minus outline symbol A formatting mark that indicates there are no subordinate heading or body text paragraphs.

Name Box An element of the Excel window that displays the name of the selected cell, table, chart, or object.

Navigation Pane The area of the Access window that displays and organizes the names of the objects in a database; from here, you can open objects for use.

Normal view The primary editing view in PowerPoint where you write and design your presentation.

Normal view (Excel) A screen view that maximizes the number of cells visible on your screen and keeps the column letters and row numbers close to the columns and rows.

Notes Page view A view where you can work with notes in a full page format.

Notes pane A PowerPoint element that displays below the Slide pane and allows you to type notes regarding the active slide.

Objects The basic parts of a database that you create to store your data and to work with your data; for example, tables, forms, queries, and reports.

One-to-many relationship A relationship between two tables where one record in the first table corresponds to many records in the second table—the most common type of relationship in Access.

Option group An object on a form or report that displays a limited set of alternatives where only one option can be selected at a time.

Outline symbol A small gray circle that identifies heading and body text paragraphs in an outline.

Outline view A document view that shows headings and subheadings, which can be expanded or collapsed.

Overflow Text that does not fit within a text box.

Page Layout view (Excel) A screen view in which you can use the rulers to measure the width and height of data, set margins for printing, hide or display the numbered row heading and lettered column heading, and change the page orientation.

Pane In Excel, a portion of a worksheet bounded by and separated from other portions by vertical and horizontal bars.

Parameter query A query that prompts you to supply the criteria when the query is run.

Pie chart A chart that shows the relationship of each part to a whole.

Pivot The action of moving a row to a column or a column to a row in an Excel PivotTable or PivotChart.

PivotChart report A graphical representation of the data in a PivotTable.

PivotTable Field List An Excel feature that enables you to move fields to different areas in the PivotTable or PivotChart report.

PivotTable report An interactive, cross-tabulated Excel report that summarizes and analyzes data.

Placeholder A slide element that reserves a portion of a slide and serves as a container for text, graphics, and other slide elements.

Plus outline symbol A formatting mark that indicates there are subordinate heading or body text paragraphs.

PMT function An Excel function that calculates the payment for a loan based on constant payments and a constant interest rate.

Populate The action of filling a database table with records.

Primary key A field that uniquely identifies a record in a table.

Print Layout view A view of a document that looks like a sheet of paper and displays margins, headers, footers, and graphics.

Print Preview A view of a document that displays information exactly as it will print based on the options that are selected.

Property Sheet A list of characteristics—properties—for fields or controls on a form or report in which you can make precise changes to each property associated with the field or control.

Query A database object that retrieves specific data from one or more database objects—either tables or other queries—and then, in a single datasheet, displays only the data you specify.

Quick Tables A selection of preformatted tables.

Record All of the categories of data pertaining to one person, place, thing, event, or idea, and which is formatted as a row in a database table.

Record source The tables or queries that provide the underlying data for a report.

Referential integrity A set of rules that Access uses to ensure that the data between related tables is valid.

Relational database A sophisticated type of database that has multiple collections of data within the file that are related to one another.

Relationship An association that you establish between two tables based on common fields.

Relative cell reference The address of a cell based on the relative position of the cell that contains the formula and the cell referred to.

Report A database object that summarizes the fields and records from a table (or tables) or from a query in an easy-to-read format suitable for printing.

Report Filter The area on a PivotTable that is used to restrict the data that displays.

Report header Information—such as logos, titles, and dates—printed once at the beginning of a report.

Report tool An Access feature that creates a report with one mouse click, which displays all the fields and records from the record source that you select.

Report Wizard An Access feature with which you can create a report by answering a series of questions; Access designs the report based on your answers.

Rich Text Format (RTF) A universal document format that can be read by nearly all word processing programs and that retains most text and paragraph formatting.

Row Labels Fields that are assigned a row orientation in a PivotTable report and become the row headings.

Ruler guide A nonprinting horizontal or vertical line that can be aligned to any position on the ruler.

Run The process in which Access searches the records in the table(s) included in a query design, finds the records that match the specified criteria, and then displays those records in a datasheet.

Select query A type of Access query that retrieves (selects) data from one or more tables or queries, displaying the selected data in a datasheet.

Shortcut menu A context-sensitive menu that displays commands and options relevant to the selected object.

Sizing handles The small squares or circles that display on each corner and in the middle of each side of a chart or graphic.

Slide pane A PowerPoint screen element that displays a large image of the active slide.

Slide Show view A view where the slides fill the computer screen, which enables you to view the presentation the way your audience will see it.

Slide Sorter view A presentation view that displays thumbnails of all of the slides in a presentation.

Slide transitions The motion effects that occur in Slide Show view when you move from one slide to the next during a presentation.

Slides/Outline pane A PowerPoint screen element that displays either the presentation outline (Outline tab) or all of the slides in the form of thumbnails (Slides tab).

SmartArt A designer-quality representation of your information that you can create by choosing from the many different layouts to effectively communicate your message or ideas.

Sorting The process of arranging data in a specific order based on the value in each field.

Source file The file where the data or object is created.

Speaker's notes Notes that are printed for the speaker to refer to as a presentation is being delivered.

Status bar A horizontal bar at the bottom of the presentation window that displays the current slide number, number of slides in a presentation, the applied theme, View buttons, Zoom slider, and Fit slide to current window button.

Subset A portion of the total records available in a table.

SUM function A predefined formula that adds all the numbers in a selected range of cells.

Tab order An Access setting that refers to the order in which the fields are selected when the Tab key is pressed when using a form.

Tab stop A specific location on a line of text, marked on the Word ruler, to which you can move the insertion point by pressing the Tab key, and which is used to align and indent text.

Table A format for information that organizes and presents text and data in columns and rows.

Table (Access) The object that is the foundation of an Access database.

Table area The upper pane of the Advanced Filter window that displays the field lists for tables that are used in the filter.

Table of contents A list of a document's headings and subheadings marked with the page numbers where those headings and subheadings occur.

Table Style A predefined set of formatting characteristics, including font, alignment, and cell shading.

Template A preformatted database designed for a specific purpose.

Text box A movable, resizable container for text or graphics.

Text box control A bound control on a form or report that displays the data from the underlying table or query.

Text link A hyperlink applied to a selected word or phrase.

Text Pane A SmartArt element where text that displays in the graphic can be entered and edited.

Text wrapping The manner in which text displays around an object, such as a picture.

Theme A predefined set of colors, fonts, lines, and fill effects that are professionally designed.

Thumbnails In PowerPoint, miniature images of presentation slides.

Underlying formula The formula that is entered in a cell and visible only on the Formula Bar.

Update query A query that adds or changes data in one or more existing records.

Validation rule Criteria that limit or control what users can enter in a field.

Value axis A numerical scale on the left side of a chart that shows the range of numbers for the data points; also referred to as the y-axis.

Values area The cells in a PivotTable report that summarize quantitative data.

View buttons A set of commands that control the look of the presentation window.

Wizard A feature in Microsoft Office that walks you step by step through a process.

WordArt A gallery of text styles with which you can create decorative effects, such as shadowed or 3-D text.

X-axis Another name for the category (horizontal) *axis*.

Y-axis Another name for the value (vertical) *axis*.

Zooming The action of increasing or decreasing the viewing area on the screen.

Index

O

P

defined, 13
Excel workbook, 13–15
presentation, 64
speaker's notes, 65–66
Word document, 15–16
printing
Access reports, 158–160
Access tables, 105–107
envelopes, 121–122
Excel workbooks, 13–15
letters, 119
newsletters, 255–256
presentations, 63–64
slide handouts, 64
speaker's notes, 64–65
Word documents, 15–16
promoting Outline levels, 50–51
Proofing group, 25, 78, 84, 248, 272, 295
Proofing tab, 25
Property Sheet, 159, 267–268
publications
data fields, 252–256
Design Checker, 246–248
layout, 272–277
Mail Merge and, 248–252
Publisher, 235
templates, 237, 269–272, 278
Publisher. *See also* **integration; newsletters; postcards; publications**
defined, 235
uses, 235, 278
Pv argument box, 325–326

Q

queries (Access)
action, 167
append, 167
calculated field in, 169–170
creating, 168–170
criteria, 125, 167
defined, 101, 122
forms, 101, 305
parameter, 167
running, 124
select, 122–124, 168
Simple Query Wizard, 122–123, 305
sorting/filtering data in, 124–125
types, 167
update, 167
Query Wizard, 122, 305
Quick Access Toolbar, 6, 8, 100, 102, 119, 148, 153, 248, 268, 293, 297, 299, 307, 325
Quick Tables, 19–20, 22

R

Rate argument box, 325
recipient lists, 251–252, 276–277
records
Access tables, 99
added to tables, 100–101
defined, 99

forms
deleting, 104–105
editing, 104
entering, 101–103
New (blank) record button, 102, 248–249, 303
subset of, 122
record source, 156–157
referential integrity, 165, 300
reflections, 213, 214, 362
relational databases, 164, 168. *See also* **databases**
relationships
Access forms, 299–300
defined, 164, 299
one-to-many, 164–166, 299–300
Relationships window, 164–166
relative cell reference, 11, 27, 147, 196
replacing pictures, in presentations, 75–78
Report Filter, 312–313
reports (Access), 158–160. *See also* **PivotChart reports;**
PivotTable reports
Blank Report tool, 265–269
creating, 157–158
grouping data, 158–160
header, 159, 268
printing, 158–160
Report tool, 157
Report Wizard, 158–159, 249
two-page, 141, 259
reports (Word), 328–333
cover page, 328–329
data, from other applications, 331–332
table of contents, 330–333
Review tab, 25, 78, 84, 204, 223–224, 227, 248, 272, 295
Rich Text Format (RTF)
Access tables exported to, 107–108
defined, 79, 108
presentations as Outline/RTF file, 79–80
rows. *See also* **Excel workbooks; Excel worksheets; tables**
freezing, 220–221
headings, on multiple workbook pages, 221–223
Rows & Columns group, 21, 22, 109
Word tables, inserting/deleting, 20–22
Row Labels, 308, 312–315, 319
RTF. *See* **Rich Text Format (RTF)**
.rtf extension, 109
rulers
guides, 273–276
Word, 3, 9, 49
rules, validation, 260
running queries, 124

S

Sample Templates, 97, 293
saving
Excel workbooks, 8–9
presentations as Outline/RTF files, 79–80
Save As dialog box, 6–7
Word documents, 6–8
secondary font, 238